P9-APL-864

A History of
LATIN AMERICA
to 1825

THE BLACKWELL HISTORY OF THE WORLD

General Editor: **R.I. Moore**

*The Origins of Human Society
Peter Bogucki

*A History of India
Burton Stein

A History of South-East Asia
Anthony Reid

A History of China
Morris Rossabi

*A History of Japan
Conrad Totman

*A History of Australia, New Zealand and the Pacific
Donald Denoon, Philippa Mein-Smith & Marivic Wyndham

A History of the Eastern Mediterranean
Nicholas Doumanis

The Western Mediterranean and the World
Teofilo F Ruiz

A History of Western Europe
Robin Briggs

A History of Central and Northern Europe
Robert Frost

*A History of Russia, Central Asia and Mongolia: Volume I
David Christian

A History of Russia, Central Asia and Mongolia: Volume II
David Christian

A History of the Ancient Americas
Fred Spier

*A History of Latin America
Third edition: A History of Latin America to 1825
Peter Bakewell

Foundations of the Modern World
R.I. Moore

The Early Modern World
Sanjay Subrahmanyam

*The Birth of the Modern World
C. A. Bayly

The Crisis of the Modern World
C. A. Bayly

* Denotes title published

A History of
LATIN AMERICA
to 1825

Third Edition

Peter Bakewell

in collaboration with Jacqueline Holler

A John Wiley & Sons, Ltd., Publication

This Third edition first published 2010
© 2010 Peter Bakewell and Jacqueline Holler

Edition history:
A History of Latin American; c.1450 to the Present, 2nd edition; Peter Bakewell; June 2003; Wiley-Blackwell
A History of Latin America; Peter Bakewell; July 1997; Wiley-Blackwell

Blackwell Publishing was acquired by John Wiley & Sons in February 2007. Blackwell's publishing program has been merged with Wiley's global Scientific, Technical, and Medical business to form Wiley-Blackwell.

Registered Office
John Wiley & Sons Ltd, The Atrium, Southern Gate, Chichester, West Sussex, PO19 8SQ, United Kingdom

Editorial Offices
350 Main Street, Malden, MA 02148-5020, USA
9600 Garsington Road, Oxford, OX4 2DQ, UK
The Atrium, Southern Gate, Chichester, West Sussex, PO19 8SQ, UK

For details of our global editorial offices, for customer services, and for information about how to apply for permission to reuse the copyright material in this book please see our website at www.wiley.com/wiley-blackwell.

The right of Peter Bakewell and Jacqueline Holler to be identified as the author of this work has been asserted in accordance with the Copyright, Designs and Patents Act 1988.

All rights reserved. No part of this publication may be reproduced, stored in a retrieval system, or transmitted, in any form or by any means, electronic, mechanical, photocopying, recording or otherwise, except as permitted by the UK Copyright, Designs and Patents Act 1988, without the prior permission of the publisher.

Wiley also publishes its books in a variety of electronic formats. Some content that appears in print may not be available in electronic books.

Designations used by companies to distinguish their products are often claimed as trademarks. All brand names and product names used in this book are trade names, service marks, trademarks or registered trademarks of their respective owners. The publisher is not associated with any product or vendor mentioned in this book. This publication is designed to provide accurate and authoritative information in regard to the subject matter covered. It is sold on the understanding that the publisher is not engaged in rendering professional services. If professional advice or other expert assistance is required, the services of a competent professional should be sought.

Library of Congress Cataloging-in-Publication Data

Bakewell, P. J. (Peter John), 1943–
  A history of Latin America to 1825 / by Peter Bakewell ; in collaboration with Jacqueline Holler. – 3rd ed.
    p. cm. – (The Blackwell history of the world)
  Previous ed.: A history of Latin America : c. 1450 to the present. 2004.
  Includes bibliographical references and index.
  ISBN 978-1-4051-8368-0 (pbk. : alk. paper) 1. Latin America–History. I. Holler, Jacqueline Zuzann, 1964– II. Bakewell, P. J. (Peter John), 1943– History of Latin America. III. Title.
  F1410.B175 2010
  980–dc22

                                        2009037492

A catalogue record for this book is available from the British Library.

Set in 10/12.5pt Plantin by SPi Publisher Services, Pondicherry, India
Printed in Singapore

01   2010

ABOUT THE COVER IMAGE

We see here what was undoubtedly the most famous hill anywhere in the Spanish empire: the Cerro Rico, or "Rich Hill," of Potosí high up in the eastern Andes of what is now Bolivia. The source of the Cerro's fame, and also of the envy that it inspired in Spain's enemies, was the enormous amount of silver ore that it contained. Between 1545, when Spaniards first found ores here, and the 1650s, about half of the immense amount of silver that Spanish America produced came from Potosí. Many mine openings can be seen below the peak of the Cerro. Herds of llamas carry ore down to refineries where the silver is extracted. By the late 1500s (probably the time of this picture) Potosí had almost a hundred refineries. It was an industrial city. A typical refinery is in the foreground. Ore is finely crushed by a stamp-mill, and is then combined with mercury in the tanks at the bottom left. The silver in the resulting silver–mercury amalgam can then be isolated by heating, which removes the mercury by evaporation. The refinery is operated by skilled native workers, probably wage laborers. Forced native workers did most of the actual mining.

For Max and Nicholas
par nobile fratrum

CONTENTS

List of Illustrations	x
List of Maps	xiii
Photo Essay	xiv
Series Editor's Preface	xv
Preface to the Third Edition	xviii
Conventions Used in the Text	xix
Maps	xx
PART I BASES	1
1 Lands and Climates	5
2 American Peoples	22
Ancient Peoples	26
Formative Peoples	30
Classic Peoples	35
Aztecs and Incas	47
Less Known Cultures	61
3 Iberia and Africa	68
PART II APPROACHES	93
4 Columbus and Others	97
5 Experiment in the Caribbean	109
6 Military Conquest	126
PART III DOMINATION	141
7 Administration: The Power of Paper	145
8 Church: Friars, Bishops, and the State	171

9 Society: Old Orders Changed   195
10 Economy: Ships and Silver   225

Photo Essay   259

PART IV MATURE COLONIES   275

11 The Seventeenth Century: A Slacker Grip   281
Challenges to Spain   281
Production, Taxes, and Trade in America   297
Indians in the Heartlands: Making their own Space   307
Indians on the Peripheries   316
Africans   322
Women   328
Arts, Formal and Popular   338
Varieties of *Mestizaje*   346

12 Eighteenth-Century Spanish America:
Reformed or Deformed?   349
People, Production, and Commerce   351
Bourbon Revisions of Rules and Principles   364
Society: Change and Protest   374
Creole Self-Awareness: Rejection and Reception of Europe   386
The Eighteenth-Century Balance   395

PART V PORTUGAL IN AMERICA   397

13 Colonial Brazil: Slaves, Sugar, and Gold   401
Explorers, Interlopers, and Settlers   401
Indians and Jesuits   406
Sugar   410
People and Government   415
Outsiders: The Dutch, and Others, in Brazil   419
Movement Inland: Slavers, Prospectors, and Stockmen   424
Seventeenth-Century Society   430
The Indians and Father Vieira   433
Government and Economy in the Seventeenth Century   436
The Age of Gold   444
Pombal and Reform   451
Products of Mind and Sensibility   455

PART VI INDEPENDENCE AND BEYOND   463

14 Independence   465
15 Epilogue   495

Glossary 505

Notes 510

Bibliography 536

Index 563

Chronologies for each part appear after the part-title page.

LIST OF ILLUSTRATIONS

1.1   The Bolivian *altiplano* (*c.* 4,000 meters) near La Paz, looking
      east to the peaks of the Cordillera Real of the Andes   11
1.2   An Andean volcano: Misti (*c.* 5,800 meters) in southern Peru,
      with the town of Arequipa in the foreground   11
1.3   The Cerro Rico (Rich Hill) of Potosí (Bolivia), seen from
      a square in an Indian quarter of the town   12
1.4   Sucre, capital of Bolivia until the end of the nineteenth
      century, and before that, as La Plata, seat of the *Audiencia*
      of Charcas   12
1.5   An Andean *hacienda*: Cayara, in a high valley near
      Potosí (Bolivia)   13
1.6   Interior ranges of the Sierra Madre Occidental, Mexico:
      the valley of the Bolaños river (state of Jalisco)   13
1.7   The volcano Popocatépetl seen from the roofs of Puebla,
      in central Mexico   14
2.1   Seated hunchback holding a mirror, a ceramic figurine
      from Las Bocas (Puebla, Mexico) in the Olmec style dating
      from 1000 to 500 BC   23
2.2   Maya "eccentric" flint, probably from the Late Classic period
      (eighth and ninth centuries AD) and the Petén (northern
      Guatemala or southern Belize)   23
2.3   Aztec rattlesnake, carved from basalt, with day-signs
      incised into it   24
2.4   Impersonator of Xipe Totec, "our lord with the flayed skin,"
      a powerful Aztec fertility god   24
2.5   Ceramic stirrup-spout vessel with a scroll ornament,
      from the north coast of Peru, but in the Chavín style   25
2.6   Part of the lower wall of Sacsahuaman, just outside
      Cuzco in Peru   25

2.7	*Quipu*: an example of the device made of knotted, colored strings used in the Andes to record information	26
11.1	*The Annunciation*, by Cristóbal de Villalpando (Mexico, c. 1650–1714)	282
11.2	*Archangel with a Matchlock Gun, Salamiel Paxdei* ("peace of God")	282
11.3	*Archangel Michael Triumphant*, a seventeenth-century polychromed mahogany sculpture	283
11.4	*Our Lady of Pomata*. A painting of the miracle-working statue of the Virgin of the Rosary at Pomata, a small town on the west shore of Lake Titicaca in Peru	283
11.5	St. Augustine defeating heresy, represented by Martin Luther	284
11.6	Biblical prophets in front of the church of Bom Jesus de Matozinhos, at Congonhas do Campo, Brazil, sculptured in soapstone (1800–5)	284
11.7	View of the Plaza Mayor of Mexico City, 1797, by José Joaquín Fabregat	285
11.8	An early example of the invasion of north European taste: Mexican-made chairs (1750–1800) in the "Mexican Chippendale" style	285
11.9	An eighteenth-century Peruvian table, of cedar	286
11.10	The Metropolitan Cathedral of Mexico City	339
11.11	The Capilla de los Reyes (Chapel of the Kings), 1718–37, in the Cathedral of Mexico City	339
11.12	The facade of the cathedral of Zacatecas, in mid-northern Mexico, c.1750	340
11.13	San Francisco, at Acatepec in central Mexico, c. 1730	340
11.14	The Santuario de la Virgen (Sanctuary of the Virgin), at Ocotlán (near Tlaxcala in central Mexico), c. 1745	341
11.15	The central portal of the church of San Lorenzo, Potosí (Bolivia), 1728–44	341
11.16	The mission church of Yaguarón, near Asunción (Paraguay), 1761–84	342
11.17	Yaguarón, interior view	342
11.18	Chapel of the Third Order of St. Francis at São João del Rei, Brazil, by O Aleijadinho, 1774	343
12.1	Santiago Matamoros (St. James the Greater in the guise of Moor killer)	387
12.2	Don Antonio de Mendoza, first viceroy of New Spain (1535–49)	387
12.3	Don Francisco de Toledo, fifth viceroy of Peru (1569–81)	388
12.4	St. Rose of Lima, canonized in 1671, the first American-born saint	388
12.5	Sor Juana Inés de la Cruz, scholar and greatest of colonial Mexican poets	389
12.6	Equestrian statue of Charles IV	389

12.7	Simón Bolívar (1783–1830) late in his career	390
12.8	José de San Martín (1778–1850), with his staff	390
13.1	Indigenous and alien still at odds: Bolivian Indians versus donkey	459
13.2	Young llamas in Bolivia	459
13.3	A modern example of the three-roller mill for crushing sugar cane, in Santa Cruz (eastern Bolivia)	460
13.4	*Casta* painting: *De Mulato y Española, Morisco* ("From Mulatto and Spanish Woman, Morisco"), by Francisco Clapera, *c.* 1785	460
13.5	*Casta* painting. *De Español e India nace Mestiza* ("From Spaniard and Indian Woman is Born a Mestiza"), by Francisco Clapera, *c.* 1785	461
13.6	A Dominican friar with an Indian weaving woman in the central Andes	461

LIST OF MAPS

1   South America in the mid seventeenth century: mountains,
    rivers, large towns, and *audiencia* districts   xx
2   Middle America in the mid seventeenth century: mountains,
    large towns, and *audiencia* districts   xxi
3   Major movements of conquest and settlement
    in Spanish America (general directions rather than precise routes,
    are shown)   xxii
4   Colonial Mexico: principal towns and regions   xxiii
5   North-west South America, showing current national boundaries   xxiv
6   Colonial Brazil   xxv

PHOTO ESSAY

1	View of the Peruvian *montaña* from Machu Picchu	261
2	Terracing at Pisac in the Vilcanota valley, Peru	263
3	Pyramid of the Sun at Teotihuacán, Mexico	265
4	The North Acropolis at Tikal, Guatemala	267
5	Franciscan church at Tepeaca, Mexico	269
6	Detail of the main portal of the monastic church of San Francisco, Lima	271
7	Antonio José de Sucre Alcalá, 1795–1830: bronze statue, Plaza Mayor, Sucre, Bolivia	273

SERIES EDITOR'S PREFACE

THERE is nothing new about the attempt to understand history as a whole. To know how humanity began and how it has come to its present condition, to grasp its relation to nature and its place in the cosmos, is one of the oldest and most universal of human needs, expressed in the religious and philosophical systems of every civilization. Only in the last few decades, however, has it begun to appear both necessary and possible to meet that need by means of a rational and systematic appraisal of attainable knowledge. History claimed its independence as an autonomous field of scholarship, with its own subject matter and its own rules and methods, and not just a branch of literature, rhetoric, law, philosophy, or religion, in the second half of the nineteenth century. World History began to do so in only the closing decades of the twentieth. Its emergence was delayed on the one hand by simple ignorance – because the history of enormous stretches of space and time had been known not at all, or so patchily and superficially as not to be worth revisiting – and on the other by the lack of an acceptable basis upon which to organize and present what knowledge there was.

Both obstacles are now being rapidly overcome. There is almost no part of the world, or period of its history, that is not the subject of vigorous and sophisticated investigation by archaeologists and historians. It is truer than ever before that knowledge is growing and perspectives changing and multiplying more quickly than it is possible to assimilate and record them in synthetic form. Nevertheless, the attempt to grasp the human past as a whole can, and must, be made. A world which faces a common future of headlong and potentially catastrophic transformation needs its common history. At the same time, since we have ceased to believe, as the pioneers of "scientific" history did a century ago, that a complete or definitive account is ultimately attainable by the mere accumulation of information, we are free to offer the best we can manage at the moment. And since we no longer suppose that it is our business as historians to detect or proclaim "The End of History" in the fruition of any grand design, human or divine, there is no single path to trace, or golden key to turn. There is also a growing wealth of ways in which world history can be written. The oldest and simplest view, that world history is best understood as the history of contacts between peoples previously isolated from one another, from which (some think) all change arises, is now seen to be capable of application since the earliest times. An influential alternative focusses upon the tendency of economic exchanges to create selfsufficient but ever expanding "worlds" which sustain successive systems of power and culture. Another seeks to understand the differences between societies and cultures, and therefore the particular character of each, by comparing the ways in which they have developed their values, social relationships, and structures of power.

The Blackwell History of the World does not seek to embody any of these approaches, but to support them all, as it will use them all, by providing a modern, comprehensive, and accessible account of the entire human past. Its plan is that of a barrel, in which the indispensable narratives of very long term regional development are bound together by global surveys of the interaction between regions, and the great transformations which they have experienced in common, or visited upon one another. Each volume, of course, reflects the idiosyncrasies of its sources and its subjects, as well as the judgment and experience of its author. In combination some two dozen volumes will offer a framework in which the history of every part of the world can be viewed and most aspects of human activity can be compared, at different times and in different cultures. A frame imparts perspective; comparison implies respect for difference. That is the beginning of what the past has to offer to the future.

The history of Middle and South America is by no means easy to fit into a framework of world history. To an even greater extent than other histories it is dominated, at least in the imagination of outsiders, by a few spectacular images – the exotic splendor of the Aztec and Inca civilizations, and the fabulous wealth their destruction promised to the first European arrivals; the devastation of native populations by conquest and disease, and their replacement by African slaves; the miseries of plantation economies, the heady triumphs of early revolution and the failure of the nations born of them – especially by inevitable comparison with their North American counterparts – to establish stable and powerful political and economic structures in its wake. But if generalizations are easy the reality that lies behind them is bewilderingly complicated. A geography of extremes was uncongenial to communication, and its North/South axis made cultural transmission and adaptation much harder and slower than in Eurasia, where migrants from East to West had to cope with correspondingly more gradual changes in climate and conditions. An ecology in itself both various and fragile was devastated and remodeled by conquest and its consequences. Geography and ecology presented every imaginable combination of circumstance and environment to their human inhabitants, themselves infinitely variable in their cultural and ethnic inheritances. The dazzling civilizations encountered by the *conquistadores* had developed quite recently, for the Neolithic revolution had come late to the Americas, most of whose inhabitants retained much less developed lifestyles. The European colonists brought with them contrasting cultural and political inheritances, and constructed highly differentiated economies, which they supplied with labor on a vast scale from Africa, but also in the nineteenth century from India and China. Even without the conflicting pressures from the world beyond it is hardly remarkable that societies composed of such various ingredients have experienced such extremes of wealth and poverty, in their cultural and political as well as in their economic history. To the historian, whose most difficult task is always to strike the proper balance between the general and the particular, they pose a peculiarly unnerving challenge. Peter Bakewell has responded to it with an account of formidable composure and reassuring clarity.

R. I. Moore

PREFACE TO THE THIRD EDITION

THE two earlier editions of this history of Latin America carried the story into the twentieth century. This new edition ends with the achievement of political independence by almost all the countries in the years 1810–1825. Discussion of native American peoples before the European explorations, conquests, and settlements has been expanded. A section has been added on those aspects of African history that bear on the slave trade to the Americas, and there is now fuller treatment of Africans and their descendants in Spanish America. Above all, the previous inadequacy of the discussion of the history of women and gender in colonial Iberoamerica has been remedied by Jacqueline Holler, for whose expert additions I am most grateful. Dr. Holler also suggested needed improvements to various passages on other aspects of social history.

I would like to restate here my gratitude to friends and colleagues who helped me with the colonial parts of the first and second editions – Michael Conniff, Brooke Larson, Donna Pierce, Laurel Seth, the late Mary Elizabeth Smith, Susan Socolow, Karen Stolley, Sharon Strocchia, and William Taylor. In preparing this new edition I have benefited greatly from the knowledge and advice of Dennis Cordell, Alan Covey, Adam Herring, David Meltzer, Frank Proctor III, Susan Ramírez, Ben Vinson, and David Weber. The gaps that remain in this telling of Latin America's pre-colonial and colonial history, along with misunderstandings and mistakes that readers will surely find, are of my own doing.

I am grateful also to the members of the Wiley-Blackwell editorial staff with whom I have consulted while working on this new version of the book: Tessa Harvey, Peter Coveney, and Deirdre Ilkson and Galen Smith, his assistants. They have been generous with advice, patience, and encouragement.

Finally, my thanks to my family for putting up with my bouts of author's distraction, impatience, and ill humor; and particularly to Susan not only for that, but for her guidance on the history of art, for reading various parts of this and the earlier versions, and for her perceptive and always helpful comments.

Peter Bakewell
Dallas, August 2008

Conventions Used in the Text

References to the *Recopilación de Leyes de los Reinos de las Indias* are given in the order book, title, law. Thus *Recopilación*, 1.2.3 means book 1, title 2, law 3.

"Peso," in the context of the colonial centuries, means the Spanish *peso de a ocho*, or "piece of eight" (see Glossary). Amounts given originally in some other denomination have been converted to pesos of this sort.

"Indian" is widely used to mean the people resident in the Americas before the arrival of Europeans, and the descendants of those same people. The term is of course inaccurate; Columbus was the perpetrator of the misidentification. But other possibilities ("Amerinds," "Native Americans," "indigenes," and so on) seem awkward or ugly.

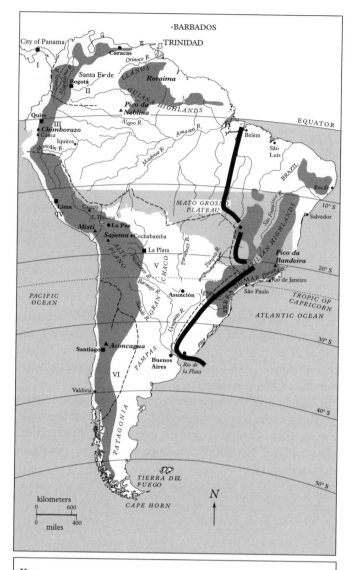

MAP 1   South America in the mid seventeenth century: mountains, rivers, large towns, and *audiencia* districts

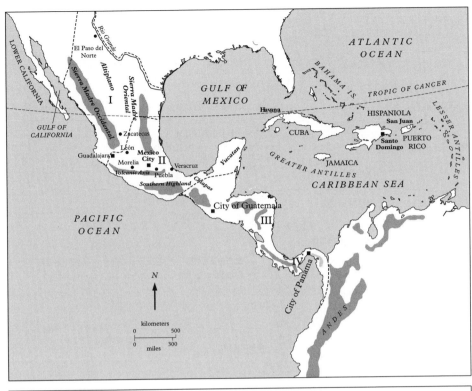

Key

■ *audiencia* capitals　　•　other major towns　　---- *audiencia* boundaries

I　*audiencia* of New Galicia (or Guadalajara)　　II　*audiencia* of New Spain (or Mexico)

III　*audiencia* of Guatemala　　IV　*audiencia* of Panama

MAP 2　Middle America in the mid seventeenth century: mountains, large towns, and *audiencia* districts

Santa Fe

ATLANTIC OCEAN

(1550–1600)

Zacatecas

1529–30

1546

1519

CUBA

HISPANIOLA

PUERTO RICO

Tenochtitlan

1523

JAMAICA

1511

1509

1508

1515–23

1509

Panama City

1536–7

1530–2

1536–8

Santa Fe de
Bogotá

Quito

1534

Cajamarca

1533

Cuzco

PACIFIC OCEAN

1540–1

Asunción

1537

1580

N

Santiago

Buenos
Aires

kilometers

0   500   1000

0   200 400 600

miles

MAP 3   Major movements of conquest and settlement in Spanish America (general directions rather than precise routes, are shown)

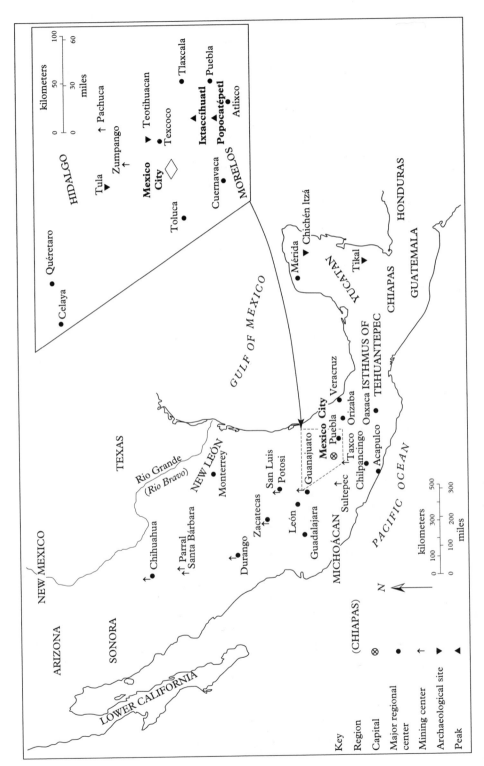

MAP 4   Colonial Mexico: principal towns and regions

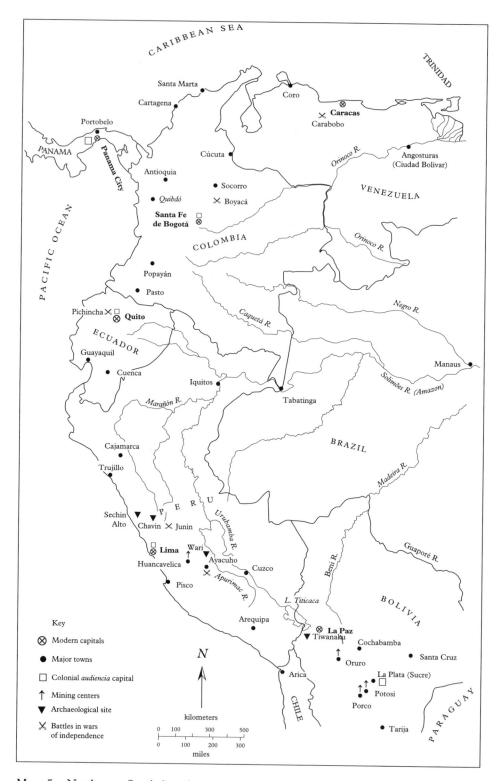

Key

- ⊗ Modern capitals
- ● Major towns
- ☐ Colonial *audiencia* capital
- ↑ Mining centers
- ▼ Archaeological site
- ✕ Battles in wars of independence

N

kilometers

| 0 | 100 | 300 | 500 |

| 0 | 100 | 200 | 300 |

miles

MAP 5   North-west South America, showing current national boundaries

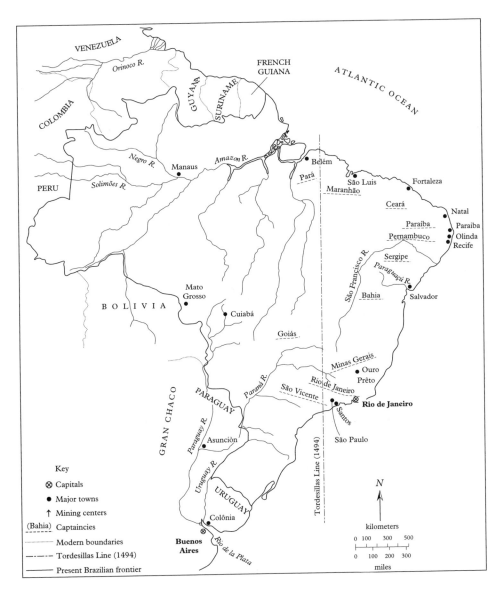

VENEZUELA

Orinoco R.

COLOMBIA

GUYANA

SURINAME

FRENCH
GUIANA

ATLANTIC OCEAN

Negro R.

Amazon R.

Manaus •

PERU

Solimões R.

• Belém

Pará

São Luis

Fortaleza

Maranhão

Ceará

Natal

Paraíba

Paraiba

Pernambuco

Olinda
Recife

Sergipe

Paraguaçú R.

São Francisco R.

Mato
Grosso •

BOLIVIA

• Cuiabá

Bahia

Salvador

Goiás

Minas Gerais

• Ouro
Prêto

Rio de Janeiro

São Vicente

⊗ Rio de Janeiro

GRAN CHACO

PARAGUAY

Paraná R.

Santos

Paraguay R.

Asunciòn •

São Paulo

N

Uruguay R.

URUGUAY

Tordesillas Line (1494)

• Colônia

Buenos
Aires ⊗

Rio de la Plata

kilometers

0   100   300   500

0   100   200   300

miles

Key

⊗ Capitals

• Major towns

↑ Mining centers

(Bahia) Captaincies

········ Modern boundaries

—·—· Tordesillas Line (1494)

—— Present Brazilian frontier

MAP 6   Colonial Brazil

PART I

BASES

CHRONOLOGY

12,500 BP (before present) Most recent date accepted for the first arrival in the Americas of people from Asia. Arrivals may have occurred up to 20,000 years earlier

*c.*10,000 BP Earliest date for first plant cultivation in the Americas (Guitarrero cave, Peru)

9,000–6,800 BP Time range for first cultivation of maize

*c.*4,000 BP End of "Archaic" phase of human development in the Americas

*c.*4,000 BP to *c.*AD 0 "Formative" or "Pre-Classic" phase of human development in the Americas

*c.*3,800 BP First appearance of Olmec culture, at San Lorenzo (southern Mexico)

*c.*3,000 BP First human occupation of the Chavín site in the Peruvian Andes

*c.*200 BC–*c.*AD 650 Rise, florescence, and fall of Teotihuacán

*c.*200 BC–*c.*AD 900 Rise, florescence, and fall of the Classic Maya

*c.*100 BC–*c.*AD 100 Start of Classic period in Middle America (corresponding to "Early Intermediate" to "Middle Horizon" in the central Andes)

*c.*100 BC–AD 1000 Rise, florescence, and fall of Tiwanaku

AD 711 Moorish incursion into Spain begins

*c.*AD 900–late 1400s Rise, florescence, and fall of Chimú culture in northern Peru

*c.*AD 900–early 1500s Post-Classic period of native cultures (Middle America) corresponding to "Late Intermediate" to "Late Horizon" periods in central Andes

*c.*AD 1000 Norsemen reach North America

1200s Moors expelled from Portugal. Moors in Spain restricted to the Emirate of Granada

Late 1200s Catalan voyages to north-west Africa, and possibly a Genoese visit to the Canaries

1320–50 Tenochtitlan-Tlatelolco, the Aztec capital, begins to rise

1393 Castilian exploration of Canaries

*c.*1400 Start of Inca imperial expansion

early 1400s First caravels built in Iberia

1415 Portuguese capture of Ceuta in North Africa

1420s Portuguese settle Madeira

late 1420s Formation of the Triple Alliance, the basis of Aztec expansion

1427 Definitive discovery of the Azores by the Portuguese

1444 Portuguese reach Cape Verde, westernmost point of Africa

1460s Substantial settlement of Azores by Portugal

1469 Marriage of Isabella of Castile and Ferdinand of Aragon

1479 Treaty of Alcáçovas: Castile's rights to the Canaries, and Portugal's to the Azores, Cape Verdes, and Madeira, mutually accepted

1487 Dedication of the Great Temple in Tenochtitlan

1488 Bartolomeu Dias rounds southern Africa, for Portugal

1492 Spanish conquest of Granada; expulsion of Jews from Spain; Columbus's first voyage to America

1494 Treaty of Tordesillas: Castile and Portugal partition exploration and exploitation of the world (Portugal, east of *c.*50°W; Castile, west of that meridian)

1504 Death of Isabella

FURTHER READING FOR PART I

The basic work on Latin American geography is still Preston James, *Latin America*. Harold Blakemore and Clifford T. Smith (eds), *Latin America: Geographical Perspectives*, provides essays on regions by specialists; see also Robert B. Kent, *Latin America: Regions and People*.

The first volume of Leslie Bethell (ed.), *The Cambridge History of Latin America*, has chapters on native cultures before the arrival of Europeans. See also *The Cambridge History of the Native Peoples of the Americas*, volume 2: *Mesoamerica*, edited by Richard E. W. Adams and Murdo MacLeod, and volume 3: *South America*, edited by Frank Salomon and Stuart B. Schwartz, and, more briefly, Alvin M. Josephy, Jr., *America in 1492*, and Karen Olsen Bruhns, *Ancient South America*. Of the many works available on the Aztecs, the most engaging is Inga Clendinnen, *Aztecs: An Interpretation*. A more recent general account is Michael E. Smith, *The Aztecs*. On the Incas, see María Rostworowski de Diez Canseco, *History of the Inca Realm*, Terence D'Altroy, *The Incas*, and Michael E. Moseley, *The Incas and their Ancestors: The Archaeology of Peru*. The sixteenth-century view of the Incas provided by Garcilaso de la Vega, *Royal Commentaries of the Incas*, remains fascinating. Aspects of Inca and Aztec culture are compared by Geoffrey W. Conrad and Arthur A. Demarest in *Religion and Empire*.

Generally for exploration, see John. H. Parry, *The Age of Reconnaissance* and *The Discovery of the Sea*. For Portuguese explorations, Bailey W. Diffie and George D. Winius, *Foundations of the Portuguese Empire, 1415–1580*, and A. H. de Oliveira Marques, *History of Portugal*. For Portugal and Spain, Charles Verlinden, *The Beginnings of Modern Colonization*. For Spain, Felipe Fernández-Armesto, *Ferdinand and Isabella*; Peggy K. Liss, *Isabel the Queen*; David A. Boruchoff (ed.), *Isabel la Católica, Queen of Castile: Critical Essays*; and J. H. Elliott, *Imperial Spain, 1469–1716*. For Africa, John Thornton, *Africa and Africans in the Making of the Atlantic World, 1400–1800*.

[1] *LANDS AND CLIMATES*

BROADLY considered, Latin America's geography is not friendly to human occupation, or favorable to people's activities. The struggle to live and thrive on the land has produced over the past 5,000 years or more some astonishingly ingenious human adaptations. But even today, with an unprecedented arsenal of technology at their disposal, people are far from overcoming the challenges posed by geography. Mountains still present a forbidding barrier to movement, transport, and economic development; rivers are, with the exception of the Amazon and the Paraná-Paraguay in South America, less easily navigated than the map might suggest, and mostly lead to places where rather few people want to go; in various countries excessive rainfall or, at the other extreme, aridity, seriously reduce the area available for growing food.

Enough variety can doubtless be found in most large regions of the world for the label "land of contrasts" to be aptly applied to them. But Middle America (Mexico and the seven small nations of Central America) and South America can surely lay a peculiarly strong claim to the title. In them, variations of terrain, climate, vegetation, and resources are often packed together very closely. From the fully tropical, warm, and wet city of Veracruz on the Gulf coast of Mexico it is only 120 kilometers to the permanent snows crowning the Pico de Orizaba (a volcano which, at 5,747 meters, is the highest peak in Mexico). An even more striking shift takes place in north-eastern Colombia, where the Sierra Nevada de Santa Marta rises to snowy heights exceeding 5,500 meters within 50 kilometers of the luxuriantly vegetated Caribbean coast. Rapid changes also happen without any vertical movement. Particularly remarkable is the transition from wet tropical forest to sand desert, with a small intervening zone of savanna and scrub, that takes place over about 400 kilometers of the southern Ecuadorian and north Peruvian coasts. Many other examples of swift change exist. Among the obvious are the passage from high, cool semi-desert around the Bolivian capital of La Paz, over the snows of the eastern Cordillera Real of the Andes, and down into the humid, semi-tropical valleys called the *yungas* in the interior slopes of the mountains; or the rapid shift in

Paraguay from the fertile, watered lands lying east of the Paraguay river to the thorny scrub of the Gran Chaco west of it; or the move from the cool, deciduous rainforests of southern Chile eastward over the Andes to the chill aridity of Patagonia, in the rain shadow of the mountains.

PHYSICAL GEOGRAPHY

As some of the examples just given suggest, the physical form of the land is a powerful influence on climate, land use, and living conditions in much of Middle and South America. The structure can be imagined simply as a mountainous spine (the western Sierra in Mexico, the Central American ranges, and the Andes in South America) running down the western side of the entire area; and, east of this spine, a trunk consisting of lesser ranges and massifs, plains, and, in the Caribbean, large and small islands. But, for a sense of the influence of geography on Latin America's history, a closer view of the landforms is needed.

MIDDLE AMERICA AND THE CARIBBEAN

Broadly speaking, the geology and surface formations of North America continue down into northern and central Mexico.[1] The largest feature here is the *altiplano* (high plain), which has an altitude of some 1,200 meters at the border with the United States at the Rio Grande. From there it rises gradually southward to reach about 2,400 meters in central Mexico. The plain is flanked on each side by mountains. The Sierra Madre Occidental, to the west, has peaks in excess of 3,000 meters.[2] The eastern range, the Sierra Madre Oriental, is generally a little lower. The Sierras do not reach the coasts. Low plains run from their feet to the sea.

The *altiplano* and its flanking ranges are abruptly cut off, at about 20°N, by Mexico's most imposing physical feature. This is a line of volcanoes (the "volcanic axis"), running from the Pacific to the Gulf shore. Some of the volcanoes still bear their Nahuatl names. Particularly renowned are Popocatépetl (Smoking Mountain, 5,452 meters) and Ixtaccíhuatl (White Lady, 5,273 meters) which overlook from the south-east the broad valley in which Mexico City lies. It is said that on exceptionally smog-free days their snow-covered peaks, once one of the glories of the capital's site, can still be seen from the city. Some of the volcanoes along the axis continue to be active. And in 1943 their number grew when emerging lava split open the earth 300 kilometers west of Mexico City in the state of Michoacán, and a new cone, named Paricutín, began to rise.

South of the volcanic axis lies a large area of old crystalline rock. Although the maximum heights here barely exceed 3,300 meters, long and heavy erosion has made these Southern Highlands one of the most rugged sections of Mexico's surface. To the east of the Highlands lies a region geologically very different from them and from the rest of Mexico: the Yucatán peninsula, which is a large, almost flat, area of limestone projecting northward into the Caribbean.

Because limestone is porous, Yucatan, especially in its northern half, has few surface streams. Water flows in underground channels, and can be reached only where the roofs of underground caverns have collapsed, leaving sink-holes, known locally as *cenotes*.[3] Yucatan provides the largest area of lowland plain in Mexico, but it is less useful than might be supposed because of the lack of accessible water and the poor quality of soil that weathered limestone typically yields. More fertile is the Gulf coast lowland further north in eastern Mexico, which is a continuation of the coastal plain of Texas in the southern United States. Its greatest width, near the border in the north, is some 200 kilometers. By contrast the coastal shelf in western Mexico is rarely more than 100 kilometers wide, and on the southern coast far less than that.

South of Mexico, the Pacific coast ranges in five of the Central American countries – Guatemala, El Salvador, Nicaragua, Costa Rica, and Panama – continue the mountainous western spine of the Americas to the Andes in northern South America. A second link between Middle and South America exists in the islands of the Greater and Lesser Antilles. The first consist of Cuba, Jamaica, Hispaniola (the island now divided between Haiti and the Dominican Republic), and Puerto Rico; the second comprise the many small islands of the Windward and Leeward Islands. The geological structure producing the Lesser Antilles meets the spur of the Andes that extends east-wards from Colombia to form the coastal ranges of Venezuela.[4] In both Central America and the Lesser Antilles occasionally active volcanoes are to be found.

SOUTH AMERICA

The Andes

Thus the westward and eastward rims of the Caribbean converge in the north-ern Andes. These great mountains then run southwards for almost 8,000 kilo-meters to Tierra del Fuego at the tip of South America, forming the longest continuous series of ranges on the face of the earth. The Andes are not a single chain but many, more or less closely connected. Added to this structural diver-sity is variety in formation. Over most of their length, the Andean ranges are the product of folding and faulting of the earth's surface. But in three regions – southern Colombia and Ecuador, central and southern Peru together with the border zone of Bolivia and Chile, and south-central Chile (with nearby areas of western Argentina) – volcanic activity has added other peaks to the land-scape. The highest mountain anywhere in the Andes (and in the Americas), Aconcagua (6,959 meters) in western Argentina, is volcanic. So are many of the highest summits in Ecuador (for example, Cotopaxi at 5,897 meters, and Chimborazo at 6,267); in southern Peru (Misti at 5,822 meters); and in north-western Bolivia (Sajama at 6,520 meters). Many volcanoes are still active, though eruptions may come only at long and unpredictable intervals. The effects of the volcanoes' eruptions generally extend far from the peaks themselves, leaving lava-covered plateaux and thick layers of ash and tuff, often deeply incised by erosion.[5]

Though enormously long, the Andes are narrow, rarely exceeding 350 kilometers in width except in the center of their course, in Bolivia, where the distance across the ranges grows to almost 700 kilometers. Their narrowness is small consolation, however, to anyone trying to cross them; extreme ruggedness and steep slopes make for slow and difficult progress. East–west passes below 3,000 meters are very few (in contrast with passes across the western ranges of North America, which are rarely higher than 2,000 meters). The deep valleys, generally running parallel with the coast, that separate ranges often make east–west movement a still more daunting challenge of multiple climbs and descents. The problem is particularly severe in Colombia, where the Andes split into three distinct cordilleras, with the valleys of the Cauca and Magdalena rivers between them. Less forbidding, but still challenging, is the physical structure of southern Peru and the entire highland zone of Bolivia. Here the traveler to the interior faces first a high coastal range, then a wide plateau (called *altiplano*, like the plateau of northern Mexico), and finally an inland Cordillera Real ("Royal Range") that is as high as the first range, and drops only gradually through chaotically broken terrain towards the central lowlands of South America.

Though rocks and faulting from many geological periods are found in the Andes, the main uplifting and folding that produced the present mountains took place in very recent geological time, between 4 and 15 million years ago.[6] Those same disturbances were accompanied by the volcanic activity that created, for example, the western range of southern Peru and Bolivia. One reason for the great height and brokenness of the Andes is precisely that, in geological terms, they are young. Erosion has not yet greatly worn them down or softened their outlines. Where volcanoes are active, in fact, peaks are still being built up. This is so not only in parts of the Andes, but also in Central America and, to a lesser degree, in Mexico.

The reason for the commonness of volcanoes is that the mountainous western spine of Middle and South America is part of the geologically unstable "ring of fire" around the Pacific. And the existence of that ring results from the fact that the Pacific shores generally mark the lines of meeting of great tectonic plates in the earth's crust. Where the edges of these plates come together, and move against each other, volcanoes, and also earthquakes, are most likely to occur. The western Mexican and Central American coasts mark the boundary between the Cocos plate, offshore, and the North American and Caribbean plates. Almost the entire western coast of South America corresponds with the meeting of the Nazca plate, underlying the Pacific, and the South American plate – a large slab of the earth's crust that forms not only the land mass of South America, but also the seabed eastwards to the mid-Atlantic ridge in the South Atlantic.[7]

Lesser highlands of South America

In contrast with the Andes, the rest of South America is geologically ancient, and, thanks to its distance from grinding and jolting tectonic joints, seismically stable. Again, when set against the Andes, roughly three-quarters of the rest of the continent can be described as a series of plains that are quite smooth and low (under 500 meters). Only two large highland areas rise above the general levels: the Guiana Highlands, almost all of which lie in southern Venezuela, and the Brazilian Highlands, which are inland from the Atlantic in central and southern Brazil. But neither matches the Andes in extent or as a problematic physical feature. The maximum altitudes in these two areas give a sense of the difference: 3,014 meters at the Pico de Neblina at the extreme south of the Guiana Highlands, 1,000 kilometers south of Caracas on the Venezuelan–Brazilian border; and 2,890 meters at the Pico da Bandeira at the eastern edge of the Brazilian Highlands, 300 kilometers or so north-east of Rio de Janeiro. The Brazilian Highlands were a hindrance to inward movement from the settled coast of Brazil in colonial times, though far from an insurmountable barrier. Today they are well populated in many areas, partly because over large areas rain has decomposed their old underlying crystalline rock into good, deep soil. The Guiana Highlands, by contrast, are so remote from other large human occupation in northern South America that they are barely inhabited to this day.

South American plains

More than a half of South America's lowland plain lies in the inland area drained by the Amazon and its tributary rivers. At the western boundary of Brazil with Bolivia, Peru, Ecuador, and Colombia, the Amazon basin extends some 1,400 kilometers north to south; but it narrows eastwards, so that as the great river nears its multiple mouths, it flows through a gap of barely 250 kilometers between the Guiana and Brazilian Highlands. The total area of the Amazon basin (including the Andean and other highland areas where the rivers originate, as well as the plains over which they flow) has been estimated as 6,133,000 square kilometers. It is remarkable how far west the Amazonian drainage area stretches: the headwaters of the Marañón, a major tributary, rise in the Peruvian Andes only 115 kilometers from the Pacific. The Amazon basin's flatness is also impressive. At Iquitos in Peru, 2,700 kilometers west of the river's mouths, the land is only 200 meters above sea level. Modern ocean-going ships drawing up to 4.25 meters can reach Iquitos from the Atlantic. Few of the Amazon's tributaries, however, can be used by ships far from the main stream, because of falls or rapids where they cross formations of crystalline rock. Many of the tributaries are, nonetheless, enormous rivers by standards elsewhere in the world. They contribute to the Amazon's being by far the largest river, in volume, anywhere on earth. Its flow as it enters the Atlantic amounts to about 11 percent of all the water draining from the earth's continents into the oceans.

Amazonia, as the Amazon basin is known, is also the earth's largest area of rainforest. The constant moisture that much of it receives from year-round rain, together with tropical warmth, encourages the growth of tall, closely spaced, trees. The forest itself, until the advent of powerful modern machinery, constituted a strong barrier to travel. In colonial times it was barely settled by Spaniards and Portuguese. Another large disincentive to settlement was the generally low fertility of the forest soils; the constant heavy rains leach soluble minerals out of them, so that when trees are cleared, the ground will normally yield good crops for only a year or two.

North of Amazonia, beyond the Guiana Highlands, lies another lowland region: the plains, or *llanos*, of the Orinoco basin. The Orinoco river rises on the south-west slopes of the Highlands, and wraps around them northward before flowing east through Venezuela to enter the sea through a delta facing the island of Trinidad. The *llanos*, a savanna of mixed grassland and trees, are a plain almost 1,000 kilometers long by 325 kilometers from north to south; but, despite these impressive dimensions, they are of a lesser order of size than the Amazon lowlands.

The third lowland area of the interior, however, is far more Amazonian in scale, and, considered as a scene of human and economic activity over the past several centuries, outranks Amazonia in importance. This is the basin drained by the rivers – the Paraguay, Paraná, and Uruguay are the main streams – that join to form the Río de la Plata (a name that properly belongs only to the estuary through which the three rivers' combined waters enter the South Atlantic). The basin includes the Chaco of western Paraguay and north-western Argentina, and also the fertile lowland plains, known as *pampas*, of southern Uruguay and central Argentina. In colonial times these grassy plains became home to vast numbers of wild cattle and horses. More recently, raising of grains has been added to their function as the richest large pasture lands in South America. Some 400 kilometers south of Buenos Aires the *pampas* come to an end as the land rises into Patagonia, the dry and cold southern third of Argentina.

In addition to its interior lowlands, South America has a perimeter of coastal plains, though these are extensive only in the few places where major rivers, such as the Orinoco, Amazon, and those of the Río de la Plata system, cut through ranges and massifs to reach the sea. There are regions in which the plain disappears altogether. This happens, for example, in the southern quarter of Chile, where mountains run down into the sea, forming an archipelago of hundreds of islands. Elsewhere, some of the more or less narrow coastal plains have had notable historical parts to play. One of these is the thin strip of coastal Peru between the Andes and the Pacific, in some places only a few hundred meters wide, though with deeper valleys running back into the Andean foothills. In those valleys some of the most sophisticated cultures of pre-Columbian Peru developed. Today many of Peru's major towns stand in the same places. On the other side of South America, the Atlantic-facing coastal plain of Brazil, with a maximum width of 170 kilometers, offered in colonial times conditions so favorable for living and farming that it was from the start the heartland of Portuguese America. Once the plain's light tropical forest was cleared, its well-watered soils proved ideal for producing sugar from cane, making the colony Europe's prime, and rich, supplier of that previously rare sweetener.

ILLUSTRATION 1.1 The Bolivian *altiplano* (*c*.4,000 meters) near La Paz, looking east to the peaks of the Cordillera Real of the Andes. Cloud indicates moisture rising westward from the Amazon basin.

ILLUSTRATION 1.2 An Andean volcano: Misti (*c*.5,800 meters) in southern Peru, with the town of Arequipa in the foreground. Owing to the aridity of this region, snow is visible only at the tip of the volcano. Arequipa receives water from streams.

ILLUSTRATION 1.3 The Cerro Rico (Rich Hill) of Potosí (Bolivia), seen from a square in an Indian quarter of the town. Tailings from centuries of mining are heaped on the upper slopes of the Cerro.

ILLUSTRATION 1.4 Sucre, capital of Bolivia until the end of the nineteenth century, and before that, as La Plata, seat of the *audiencia* of Charcas. The town retains much of its colonial air and form, not least in its straight streets and division into rectangular blocks.

ILLUSTRATION 1.5   An Andean *hacienda*: Cayara, in a high valley near Potosí (Bolivia). Note the terracing, now abandoned, on the surrounding slopes. Spanish farm buildings have been on this site since the 1560s.

ILLUSTRATION 1.6   Interior ranges of the Sierra Madre Occidental, Mexico: the valley of the Bolaños river (state of Jalisco).

ILLUSTRATION 1.7 The volcano Popocatépetl seen from the roofs of Puebla, in central Mexico. The volcano is covered in cloud, not smoke.

ENVIRONMENTS

FAVORABLE ZONES

The east coast of Brazil is, in fact, a rare example in Latin America of a low, tropical area that is generally comfortable for human habitation. It is so because of the temperature-moderating effect of the sea and of the winds that blow over it on to the land.

Much of the rest of tropical Latin America, however, is hot and humid to a degree that makes for disagreeable living conditions. And "tropical Latin America" is, in fact, *most* of Latin America. The northern tropic line (the Tropic of Cancer) passes across Mexico some 450 kilometers north of Mexico City, and the southern line (the Tropic of Capricorn) crosses South America at a latitude just south of Rio de Janeiro. Thus roughly half of Mexico, all of Central America, all the Latin American islands of the Caribbean, and two-thirds of South America lie in the tropics.

What above all else provides relief from heat and humidity in substantial parts of that enormous area is height. The mountain ranges and high plateaux that have so often been barriers to movement and development at least offer reductions in temperature. Air temperatures in the earth's lower atmosphere fall on average by about 6.5° Celsius per 1,000-meter rise in altitude. Thus a quite short journey from a tropical coast or forest up into nearby mountains can produce a change from sweltering heat to pleasant warmth.

Highland central Mexico provides an excellent and important example of that sort of shift in temperature. There, Mexico City, at a height of 2,250 meters, has an average temperature of 12.2° in January, and 16.1° in July. (As in all tropical areas, the change in temperature between winter and summer is quite small.) It is far cooler than places on the same latitude on either the Pacific or the Gulf coast of Mexico. A large area that surrounds the city enjoys the same advantage. Mexico is, in fact, blessed with a central strip of high land, limited to the south by the volcanic axis, and extending into the *altiplano* perhaps 300 kilometers north of that line of peaks, that has long offered marvelously benign conditions for human living. In this zone many of the high cultures of pre-Spanish Mexico developed and thrived: Teotihuacán, the first of the mature, "classic," cultures of central Mexico, *c*.AD 0–750; after that, the Toltecs; the Tarascans, to the west in Michoacán; and the Aztecs, the last major culture before the Europeans came. And, in this same favored zone, many of the major towns of modern Mexico lie: from east to west, Puebla, Mexico City, Toluca, Querétaro, Morelia, León, and Guadalajara, to name only the largest.

It is not just moderate temperatures that make highland central Mexico so agreeable for living. Isolation from the sea by coastal escarpments and ranges protects the region from excessive rain; but the barriers of distance and altitude are not so great as to keep out all moisture-bearing air, so that enough rain for successful farming usually falls in the summer months. Add to these benevolent climatic conditions a remarkable fertility of soil, owed first to long-weathered deposits of volcanic ash (contributing minerals), and second to the presence of large areas of now dry lake beds (contributing organic matter), and it is easy to see why this geographical center of Mexico has always been the demographic and cultural center also.

That fertile heartland of Mexico is by far the largest area in tropical Latin America in which the temperature-moderating effect of height produces agreeable living conditions for human beings. But there are many other smaller such areas. The mountain ranges of Central America, for example, have high valleys that are attractively cool relative to nearby coasts and plains. Outside Mexico, however, it is in the northern and central Andes that high places have been most important in favoring growth of population and economic activity.

In the north of South America, for example, are the high basins of the eastern range, or Cordillera Oriental, of Colombia. In one of these is the colonial and present capital of the country, Bogotá, at an altitude of 2,640 meters, and with an average year-round temperature of 14.5° C (a figure that varies, owing to the city's low latitude, only 1° C between the coldest and warmest months). Taking advantage of the farming potential of these basins, the Chibcha culture, the most advanced in the northern Andes, developed in them in pre-conquest times. The Spaniards brought in cattle, and added their own familiar wheat and barley to maize, the staple native grain.[8]

Further south, in Ecuador, the ten basins lying between the two parallel cordilleras that form the Andes were similarly the home of sedentary, agricultural peoples before the Europeans arrived. They continue to support much of the country's peasant population today. The basin partly occupied by Quito, the national capital, is the most heavily settled now. The city, lying only 35 kilometers or so south of the equator, perches on the basin's eastern rim at 2,850 meters. At that altitude wheat, barley, and potatoes grow well. Down below, on the valley floor at about 2,300 meters, maize and pasture-grasses for cattle flourish. The second most populous Andean basin in Ecuador is the southern valley of Cuenca, where, at some 2,500 meters, maize and dairy cattle again thrive.[9] In both cases altitude makes middle-latitude farming possible almost on the equator.

South of Ecuador in the Andes many of the mountain valleys and basins are so high that the cooling effect of altitude becomes more of a problem than a blessing. In these places (still within the tropics, it should be remembered) humans have had to make use of specifically local conditions in order to thrive. The outstanding example is the land surrounding Lake Titicaca, part of which lies in Peru and part in Bolivia. The lake's surface is at slightly above 3,800 meters. Its maximum depth is 280 meters. It is 180 kilometers long and averages some 50 kilometers in width. Titicaca is by far the largest body of water at extreme altitude in the world. Its great volume has a moderating effect on the climate of the immediate surroundings, reducing the chill of great height and so benefiting agriculture. This is one reason for the region's long having been a focus of dense and culturally advanced settlement in the central Andes.

Much smaller areas in the heights of the Peruvian Andes have also been home to dense and sophisticated populations. In them people have over the centuries learned to take advantage of very specific geographical conditions: small areas of fertile alluvial soil laid down in valley bottoms by rivers, and protected from cold winds by the steep slopes of the mountains; or slopes oriented northward (here in the southern hemisphere) to the sun, and covered with terracing to maximize the warmed cultivable area. Such areas are said to have "microclimates," and there are great numbers of them in highland Peru. None has had more historical significance than the valley of Cuzco, in the center-south of the Peruvian Andes. This narrow depression of barely 30 square kilometers, but in which height, latitude, aspect, water, and soil combine favorably for living and farming, became the heart of the Inca empire, the largest and most finely organized of all American native states. The valley, some 3,400 meters above sea level, had been occupied for many centuries before the Incas entered it as a small, migrant tribe about 1200 AD. They set their home community, Cuzco, at the head of the valley. From the 1430s the town grew rapidly in size and splendor, concurrently with an exterior expansion of Inca power up and down the Andes that by 1520 had carried the tribe's and the city's political authority as far away as present northern Ecuador in one direction, and central Chile in the other.

As the Incas began to extend their rule, they took in other similar valleys close to Cuzco, such as those of Yucay and Ollantaytambo. The inhabitants of these valleys had long grown food on their alluvial floors and on irrigated terracing built into the nearby mountainsides. But a particularly interesting part of the history of the southern sierra in Peru, the highest part of the central Andes, is the use made by the Incas and their predecessors of cultivable areas at a variety of other heights. The ranges of the southern sierra indeed offer the widest choice of local environments to be found in the Andes – the most extensive and complex "altitudinal zonation," as it has been called.[10] The highland communities took advantage of this to set up small "colonies" at different heights, using each small area so settled to grow particular foods. So, for example, at the height and latitude of the Cuzco valley, potatoes and other root crops could be grown. But maize, beans, and squash did better in lower, warmer places. And coca and fruits were best grown lower still. Conversely, above the level of Cuzco and other communities sited in high valleys, llamas and alpacas could be grazed on rough grasses.[11] *Puna* is the name given in Peru to the shallow slopes and occasional high plains between the mountains at altitudes running up from roughly 4,000 meters to the snowline at 5,000.[12] This zone has been termed "high-altitude tundra."[13] It has a natural vegetation of *ichu*, a grass so coarse that only the native Andean camelids (llamas and their relatives) have the digestive apparatus needed to benefit from it.

The Incas are the best-known practitioners of the technique of ecological colonization, and used it also for political purposes. So, for example, in the late fifteenth century they sent *mitimaes* (a Quechua term for colonists) from the imperial center to the valleys around Cochabamba in the eastern ranges of what are now the Bolivian Andes. There, at 2,500 meters, maize grew well, and the Cochabamba valleys became one the main granaries of the Inca state.[14] At the same time, however, the colonists served the political purposes of the empire: they contributed to the spread of the "state" language, Quechua; they acted as models in behavior and farming practices for the conquered local people; and they were a constant reminder of Inca power.

The latitude of Cochabamba (the center of present-day Bolivia) is roughly the southern limit of vertical colonization by pre-conquest communities. This is in large part because, with increasing latitude southwards, there is general cooling even at low altitude; hence the range of useful micro-environments at different heights diminishes. An additional difficulty is that in southern Bolivia, northern Chile, and north-western Argentina, the extreme aridity of the coastal plateau reaches far up into the mountains. Almost the only moisture to be found is in the snowcaps of the highest volcanic peaks. In these conditions of high, cold desert, human habitation is hard pressed, although it has long been present to some small, if primitive, degree in the southern *altiplano* of Bolivia, for example. And a little further south, on the *puna* of the Argentine–Chilean border, under the volcanic summits, a pre-Inca Atacaman culture once existed.[15] In slightly less arid conditions a little to the east, where some moisture from the Atlantic penetrates, the Humahuaca and Diaguita (or Calchaquí) farming cultures, again both pre-Inca, flourished in the high basins of north-western and north-central Argentina respectively.[16]

West-coast South America

More or less extreme dryness also affects almost half of the west coast – from northern Peru to central Chile – of South America. The contrast with regions further north (the coasts of Colombia and Ecuador) and further south (lower Chile) is striking. Both of these are remarkably wet. The first receives in places more than 5 meters of rain annually from onshore winds that have absorbed moisture from the warm tropical seas over which they have passed; the second is almost as wet, as a result of fierce high-latitude storms. But over a rapid transition of only 4° of latitude from southern Ecuador to northern Peru, rainfall declines abruptly. And there begins an arid coastal plain that continues southward for 3,200 kilometers, to a point a little short of Santiago, the capital of Chile.[17] In northern Chile this zone is known as the Atacama desert, in parts of which rains never falls.

What accounts for this dryness is a combination of high atmospheric pressure offshore and cold ocean water. From the south Pacific high-pressure cell, which is centered year-round some 1,600 kilometers off the coast of northern Chile, a little below the Tropic of Capricorn, cool and stable air moves towards the land. As it does so, it crosses two distinct cold currents. The first is the Peru Oceanic Current (until recently known as the Humboldt Current), flowing up from the south; and the second, closer to the shore, is the yet cooler Peruvian Coastal Current, also moving north, and the product of the upwelling of cold bottom-water to the surface. The already cool air from the high-pressure cell is further chilled as it flows over these two currents towards the coastline, and arrives there as a dense, dank, meteorologically inactive mass. An almost permanent temperature inversion exists, indeed, along the coast, preventing vertical development of rain-producing clouds. Cloud, though, is certainly abundant in the winter months (June to October) along the Peruvian shore, presenting a puzzling, almost contradictory, spectacle: lowering, heavy masses of water vapor sliding onshore over a sand desert. A downpour constantly seems imminent, but hardly ever comes. Frequently during the winter, though, a thick, wet mist known as *garúa* covers parts of the coast; it is mainly this heavy, dismal drizzle that produces Lima's average annual precipitation of 41 mm.

In summer the sun is strong enough to dissolve the cloud cover, and the weather turns warm, though still humid. But the temperature inversion generally stays in place, preventing warm air from rising and developing into rainclouds. The only circumstance in which this atmospheric stability breaks down (and this shows the immense influence on the coastal climate of the chilly waters offshore) arises when the cold upwelling weakens, and warmer water moves down from the north. Then instability in the air mass above the coast becomes possible, clouds form, and heavy, sometimes torrential, rains fall. The result can be disastrous, since the coastal land, being adapted to aridity, has no protection against the power of cloudbursts and heavy masses of surface water. Floods and erosion are the outcome. These changes in offshore flows and onshore rain are the phenomenon known in Peru as El Niño (The Child), since they often happen around Christmas, in midsummer. El Niño affects, however, only the northern half of the Peruvian coast. Further south the changes in currents that lead to warming of the sea do not happen.

Given that the Peruvian coast is (apart from the occasional downpours of El Niño) without rain, it is remarkable that many of the highest cultures of ancient Peru developed there, and that to this day many of the country's largest towns are found along it. What makes flourishing human settlement possible on this coast is the presence of small rivers dropping down from the Andes. Where these streams cross the desert plain to the sea, vegetation naturally springs up along them in isolated patches of greenery. About forty such "oases" exist up and down the coast. They are larger in the north, where the plain is at its widest, and the rivers bigger and more constant in flow than in the center and south. For thousands of years past humans have maximized the benefit of the westward downflow of water from the Andes through irrigation. The crops grown with the help of this skilful channeling of water sustained such major coastal Peruvian cultures as Paracas (*c.*800–200 BC), Nazca (*c.*100 BC–AD 600), Moche (*c.*0–AD 750), and the immediately pre-Inca, and extensive, kingdom of Chimor (*c.*AD 1050–1500). The towns that the Spaniards built in these coastal oases in colonial times have developed into major current Peruvian centers such as (from north to south) Lambayeque, Trujillo, Lima, and Ica.

LATIN AMERICA OUTSIDE THE TROPICS

In the minority of Latin America that is outside the tropics (the northern half of Mexico and the southern third of South America) modern examples of ingenious human adaptations to adverse living conditions can also be found. In parts of the semi-desert *altiplano* of northern Mexico, for instance, are small areas of intensive farming, made possible by irrigation. In the far south of Argentina, deep into chilly Patagonia, Welsh immigrants in the nineteenth century found it possible to raise sheep and grain in the river valleys of Chubut province. In the twentieth century the farming continued, and population grew also in response to oil and gas discoveries in the south of the province.[18]

But outside the tropics most of the population clusters in the temperate, fertile, more welcoming areas. These are strikingly few, and not large in comparison with the total area. Even to the north and south of the tropic lines the terrain and climates of Latin America pose great difficulties. Northern Mexico is mostly arid; where it is not, it is mountainous. A large part of northern Argentina falls within the hot scrub and thorn forest of the Gran Chaco. Much of southern Argentina consists of high, dry, cold Patagonia. Across the Andes from Patagonia, southern Chile is rugged, cool (to cold), and wet.

The sole truly large area hospitable to humans and farming in non-tropical Latin America is, then, the vast grassy plain that starts in southernmost Brazil and continues into Uruguay and central Argentina as the Pampas. In the nineteenth century the cattle (and, in some areas, sheep) raised on these plains were the source of great economic growth and prosperity, with accompanying human settlement. But in colonial times, with the exception of southern Brazil, where ranchers raised cattle for sale, the plains were barely settled. Countless numbers of wild cattle on the *pampas* provided food and hides for hunting and gathering native people; but very few others lived on the grasslands of Argentina and Uruguay before the nineteenth century.

By contrast, the directly westwards across the Andes in central Chile lay a far smaller, but still substantial, non-tropical area that drew and held a colonial population from the 1540s onward. At about 30° south the overwhelming aridity of the Atacama begins to shade off into a region with a Mediterranean climate of mild, wet winters and dry, sunny summers. This zone, "Middle Chile," extending southwards for some 700 kilometers, is the country's heart-land.[19] And, lying behind the coastal ranges, is the heart of the heartland, the Central Valley, containing Santiago, the capital founded in 1541, and other large towns. From the sixteenth century on, colonial Spaniards were drawn to Middle Chile by its highly favorable conditions for living and agriculture. The region had a particular allure in its suitability for growing wheat and grapes, and so providing the white bread and the wine at the centre of the Spanish diet.

Middle Chile is, however, the only sizeable area on the west coast of South America that is truly favorable to living and farming – and it is a narrow, though long, strip. Almost everywhere else is dense forest or sand desert, too hot or too cold, too wet or too dry. The tendency to geographical extremes is all too typical of Latin America. In the late 1960s, 71 percent of the total area of Middle and South America (just over 20 million square kilometers) was ranked as non-agricultural – that is, not under annual or perennial crops, or used as permanent pasture. Forest, desert, and mountain made up most of this non-agricultural area. In the USA the corresponding figure was 57 percent. It is possible, of course, that some of the unfarmed land might have been unused because of lack of demand for its potential products. And some of it has certainly been brought into production since then, particularly through the clear-ing of rainforests in Amazonia. Nonetheless, the fact that almost three-quarters of Middle and South America's surface was not cultivated in the mid twentieth century, by which time demand for farm products from growing populations was mounting, certainly reflects in part how hard it was, and is, to bring land into production. The sources of the difficulty were as they had always been: unfriendly climate (especially aridity); poor soils (typical of both excessively dry and excessively wet areas); and problems of access (caused above all by mountain barriers). Throughout the history and pre-history of Middle and South America, these conditions have worked powerfully to influence people's decisions about where to live. The result has been that certain atypically favored regions have long held, and continue to hold, the bulk of the populations: the transverse strip of central Mexico immediately north of the volcanoes; the eastern coast of Brazil; the high basins of the Andes from Colombia to Bolivia; the central valley of Mediterranean Chile. True, in some apparently unpromis-ing regions human ingenuity managed to overcome Nature's lack of charity, so that striking concentrations of population, as well as impressive culture, appeared. The Yucatan of the Maya is one such example; though even the Maya declined in the ninth and tenth centuries AD after several hundred years of remarkable florescence – in part, it would seem, because the poverty of their limestone land at last wore them down. A more enduring instance is that of the oases in Peru's coastal desert. They have produced and sustained some of the most highly cultured and densest populations in South America as far back as can be seen; and they still are the sites of Peru's largest and most modern towns. Still, these are exceptions that test the rule. Generally speaking, in comparison with most other great land masses on the globe, Middle and South America give meager provision of territory offering comfortable living and easy conduct of productive activities. Great wealth and ease can be had; but, as the Spanish and Portuguese found, only with a struggle. The native cultures that it was part of that struggle to overcome could have told them as much.

[2] *AMERICAN PEOPLES*

WHEN, three decades or so after Columbus's first voyage, the Spaniards began to penetrate the American mainlands, and to make contact with the great native cultures, they were impressed by what they found. These were a very different rank of people from the islanders of the Caribbean. Of the Aztec capital, Tenochtitlan, Hernán Cortés wrote to the Emperor Charles V in 1520 "I will say ... that these people live almost like those in Spain, and in as much harmony and order as there, and considering that they are barbarous and so far from the knowledge of God and cut off from all civilized nations, it is truly remarkable to see what they have achieved in all things."[1] Thirteen years later, the conquerors of Peru were equally struck by the Inca capital, Cuzco, telling the emperor, "This city is the greatest and finest ever seen in this country or anywhere in the Indies. We can assure your Majesty that it is so beautiful and has such fine buildings that it would be remarkable even in Spain."[2]

By the time these reports were sent in, the conquering Spaniards already knew that these two cities were the hearts of great empires, though they still did not realize the full extent of the Aztecs' and Incas' reach. The Aztecs dominated most of Mexico south of Tenochtitlan, with an influence extending into what is now Guatemala, and a considerable area north-east of Tenochtitlan extending down to the Gulf coast. The total area was not far short of Spain's. Inca control had a much longer span, running some 4,000 kilometers from present northern Ecuador to central Chile (a far greater distance than any dimension of Charles's Holy Roman Empire), though it was largely confined to the Andean highlands. Despite its narrowness, nonetheless, Tawantinsuyu (the "four parts together"), as the Incas called their domain, was the largest native American empire ever assembled, and has been reckoned the largest ever created in the world with Bronze Age technology.[3]

ILLUSTRATION 2.1 Seated hunchback holding a mirror: a ceramic figurine from Las Bocas (Puebla, Mexico) in the Olmec style, and dating from 1000 to 500 BC. Ancient Mexicans polished types of iron ore (e.g. magnetite) to make mirrors. Dallas Museum of Art.

ILLUSTRATION 2.2 Maya "eccentric" flint, probably from the Late Classic period (eighth and ninth centuries AD) and the Petén (northern Guatemala or southern Belize). The object shows the high skill of the Maya in working difficult materials. It represents a crocodile with young maize gods emerging from its back (perhaps symbolizing the earth and sprouting maize plants). Dallas Museum of Art.

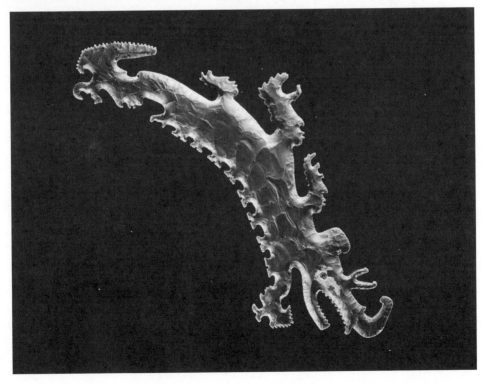

ILLUSTRATION 2.3 Aztec rattlesnake, carved from basalt, with day-signs incised into it. Snakes were the animals most often represented by Aztec sculptors, being elusive, but dangerous, creatures, and connected to the powerful god Quetzalcóatl. Central Mexico, AD 1200–1521. Dallas Museum of Art.

ILLUSTRATION 2.4 Impersonator of Xipe Totec, "our lord with the flayed skin," a powerful Aztec fertility god. In the worship of this god, a victim was sacrificed by excision of the heart; the skin was removed and then put on by a priest or another impersonator of the deity. In this example, the wound in the victim's chest from the sacrificial cut can be seen. Volcanic stone, shell, and paint; central Mexico, AD 1350–1521. Dallas Museum of Art.

ILLUSTRATION 2.5 Ceramic stirrup-spout vessel with a scroll ornament, from the north coast of Peru, but in the Chavín style. Dallas Museum of Art.

ILLUSTRATION 2.6 Part of the lower wall of Sacsahuaman, just outside Cuzco in Peru. This vast construction, perhaps the most impressive example of massive Inca stonework (with some blocks weighing over 100 tons), is now believed to have been created by Pachacutec as a temple more splendid than all others. Archaeologists long thought that Sacsahuaman had been a fortress; the zig-zag triple walls would certainly suggest that purpose. Spaniards from Cuzco took refuge in it in 1536 during an Inca attempt to expel the conquistadores.

ILLUSTRATION 2.7 *Quipu*: an example of the device made of knotted, colored strings used in the Andes to record information. Inca, cotton, AD 1476–1534. Dallas Museum of Art.

ANCIENT PEOPLES

Because the Aztecs and the Incas were the highest cultures in Middle and South America that the Spanish found, and because the Spanish consequently reported on them in such admiring detail, it is often forgotten that there was a long native history that preceded them. Exactly how long this history was is still much debated. But almost all serious archaeologists agree, at least, that the ancestors of the people encountered by the Spaniards in the Americas had originally come from Asia. Most of them crossed into Alaska from the eastern-most tip of what is now Russia at times when the sea bed there was dry as a result of the world-wide lowering of sea levels during the most recent ice ages. (Much water was locked into ice around the poles, and into ice sheets covering land much more distant from the poles than where ice is now found.) At the very latest, people of Asian origin were in the Americas by about 12,500 years before the present (BP). And strong indications exist that they had arrived millennia before that, perhaps reaching even southern South America as long ago as 33,000 BP. Abundant archaeological remains at a site in the south of Chile called Monte Verde are evidence for that distant date. Since at that time the sea had not yet retreated from the strait between eastern Russia and Alaska, those people probably made their way south by boat. Others after them may have moved down the west coasts of the Americas in the same way.[4]

AGRICULTURE

For thousands of years – many thousands if the more distant arrival dates are valid – those early Americans lived by hunting wild creatures, including fish where available, and gathering wild fruits and seeds. The people of Monte Verde, for instance, occasionally killed mastodons (elephant-like animals, now extinct), though their more usual meat diet consisted of guanacos (the wild original form of the llama) and a variety of smaller game. They hunted with spears and bolas (a device consisting of a number of cords tied together, to the other ends of which round stones are attached – the whole thing to be thrown so that it entangles the legs of the animal being hunted, bringing it down). They also ate wild potatoes, along with other tubers, various seeds, nuts, fruits, and berries.[5]

The Monte Verde people were unusual among hunters and gatherers in making durable wooden buildings, in which they lived and possibly carried out various rites. Most hunters and gatherers were more nomadic, moving in groups from season to season as plants ripened in one place or another, or as animal populations shifted, like the humans, in search of seasonal foods. What brought this mainly wandering lifestyle to an end, although only very slowly, was the coming of plant cultivation – the beginning of farming. This has sometimes been termed a "revolution," and indeed it did, like any revolution worth the name, turn a way of life upside down; but it took several thousand years to do so, as food from farmed plants very gradually replaced what was collected in the wild.

The oldest remains of what are obviously cultivated plants in the Americas have been found at an archaeological site in Peru, the Guitarrero cave high up in the Andes in the mid north of the country. They date from almost 10,000 BP. Oddly enough, at first sight, the remains are not of cultivated food, but of plants grown to yield fibers. These were used to make rough clothes, mats, and bags. The Guitarrero site also contains, however, many remains of cultivated foods, including tubers, local fruits, beans, and chile.

Elsewhere in the Andes other plants were domesticated, and turned into crops. Among them were avocado, coca, quinoa (a fine, nutritious grain still eaten in the high mountains), and, most significant of all for the history of not just the Americas, but the world, the potato. Another root crop, still an essential food in tropical areas around the globe, that was probably domesticated in South America was cassava (also called manioc, and yuca). The most likely area for its first cultivation is south-western Amazonia, which may also be the place of first domestication of peanuts. Far to the north, in Middle America, yet another native plant that has become a world staple was brought into cultivation. This was maize. Archaeologists have made long and intense efforts to discover where and when maize began to be transformed from a wild grass into the plant that today bears great cobs of corn. A very early form of maize may have existed in Panama around 9,000 BP; but a plant closer to modern maize seems to be most strongly associated with southern Mexico, beginning about 6,800 BP. Over the succeeding millennia, people in the lands that are now called Mexico and Central America also began growing tomatoes, various sorts of squash, beans, and chile, cacao (the bean from which chocolate is made), amaranth, and vanilla (to name only the most common plants) from wild species that were native to those places. They also domesticated cotton, as did people in South America; but in Middle America cotton was particularly important because of the lack there of wool-bearing animals comparable to the llamas, alpacas, and vicuñas of the Andes. Not having wool, the Middle Americans relied on cotton for clothing, along with rough cloth woven from the agave fiber for outer protection.[6]

Broadly speaking, as people began to domesticate wild plants – that is, began to practice agriculture – they became less nomadic. Preparing the ground, sowing seeds, weeding, and finally harvesting, required that farmers stay in one place for several months of the year. That is not to say that all members of a group had to stay; some would still travel, to hunt and gather. But over the many thousands of years during which the agricultural "revolution" developed, gradually a smaller proportion of the group would do so. Thus the rise of farming is associated with the rise of sedentism, or, more concretely, with the appearance of hamlets and villages. (Not that these were always associated with farming: the hunters and gatherers of Monte Verde, for instance, had groups of permanent dwellings.)

Such enormous importance is attached to domestication of plants and animals, and to subsequent farming, for the development of human societies all over the world, that it is easy to assume that living conditions were always better for farmers than for hunters and gatherers. But that is not necessarily so. Where conditions for farming were poor – soils infertile, land arid or too wet, frosts frequent and unpredictable – subsistence from cultivation could be very hard and uncertain work. At least some hunters and gatherers, in some times and places, were better fed than some farmers.

Nonetheless, in general it is doubtless true that farming, and the sedentism that accompanied it, provided living conditions that allowed human activities to expand and advance. With developing agriculture came growing population in farming areas. A result of this was often that the agricultural zone had to grow, sometimes expanding onto less favorable land than had at first been cultivated. Irrigation might become necessary to bring new land into use. It is also easy to imagine that adjacent farming groups, as they grew in numbers, might come into conflict over land, and that this might lead to the appearance of warriors in the communities. Since defense of farming land would be an important task, it is possible that warriors began to acquire high status in their small societies. Thus farming is linked to the appearance of differences in social status. Indeed there is evidence of the appearance of social ranking in early farming villages. In such villages on the Peruvian coast, for example, archaeologists interpret the obvious differences in the sizes of houses (as indicated by their remaining foundations) as showing the presence of social ranks, or hierarchy.[7]

Priests, in addition to warriors, are also likely to have become more important, and more respected, as farming appeared and progressed. This was because success in farming depended to a large degree on natural conditions being benevolent: not too much heat or cold, enough rain (but no hail), absence of frosts during the growing season, absence of destructive storms, presence of enough water in rivers and streams for irrigation (where it was used), and so on. As had long been the case, people's belief was that these conditions were divinely controlled by gods of rain and storms, of wind, of mountains, of rivers and lakes – of almost everything in nature, indeed. It was the priests' business to know about these divinities and to influence them in humans' favor as far as possible through worship, prayer, and sacrifice. Hence the priesthood became central to the prosperity, or in hard times just the survival, of farming peoples.

Yet another task of priests that also contributed to their rising status was keeping track of time, particularly the passage of the seasons. It must always have been important for hunting and gathering peoples to be aware of seasons, so that they would know when wild animals would be present, and ripe fruit and seeds available, in this or that place. But for farming more precise and reliable tracking of the seasons was a central need, because, for example, seeds should not be planted until the danger of frost had passed, or until rain would soon come. Signs of these times could be read from the local environment itself; but time could be followed far more precisely by observing the movements of sun, moon, and planets in the sky. These heavenly bodies were also considered as deities; thus it was natural that priests should become the timekeepers of their communities. And as knowledge of how to read celestial movements developed over the centuries, an interest in astronomy for its own sake clearly appeared among some native people.

Probably less highly ranked in society than warriors and priests, but still placed above farm laborers, were the makers of craft objects. These people's numbers grew as agriculture expanded and provided ever more time for occupations not directly concerned with finding food and shelter. As time passed, American natives became impressively skilled weavers, pottery makers, and carvers of wood and stone. These various crafts emerged originally from practical needs – for clothing, bags, storage containers, and simple tools. But over many hundreds of generations the skills became more sophisticated, and regionally specialized in accordance with local needs and the availability of raw materials. Thus the peoples of the river valleys on the Peruvian coast, using the simplest of tools, discovered how to spin the cotton they grew and the wool they brought down from the Andes into thread of a fineness rarely equaled now. Mexicans may have done the same with their cotton; but, with the greater humidity of Mexico, very few ancient textiles have survived there to be seen today. Everywhere ceramics tended to become finer, and more elaborate in shape and decoration. Much of the decoration on pots (and woven into textiles also) had symbolic meaning, showing the social or political status of the user, or holding religious significance. But, as with priests' growing interest in astronomy for its own sake, it is likely that some craftsmen and women also became what would now be called artists – people deeply, perhaps primarily, concerned with the aesthetic nature of their products.

Thus the slow rise of agriculture had results that went far beyond just improved reliability of the food supply. It encouraged people to live in fixed settlements – hamlets, villages, and towns in which little by little over thousands of years specialized occupations came into existence, and with them a widening of social and political rank.

FORMATIVE PEOPLES

Archaeologists have given various names to the periods of the ancient past in Middle and South America, and some of the names differ, even for the same period, according to place. But a widely applied term for the 5,000 or so years of the agricultural "revolution" is "Archaic." The Archaic age is generally considered to have drawn to a close soon after 4,000 BP. For roughly the next 2,000 years, what might be called the "cutting-edge" cultures of Middle and South America moved forward through what is often termed the "Formative" or "Pre-Classic" era. (An immediate caution is needed here, however: to speak of the "end" of the Archaic time, or of any other of these archaeological periods, does not mean that it ended everywhere at a particular time. In only some areas did the movement to a more complex and varied way of life take place; in many others, people's behaviors and living circumstances did not change for centuries, or only very little.)

SOUTH AMERICA

The changes distinguishing the formative centuries are not so much qualitative as quantitative – except that at some point, as in any such process, quantitative change grows so large as to become qualitative. In early formative times, then, traits already visible in the late Archaic era became more obvious: larger settlements, greater specialization of occupations, finer and more varied artisanry, clearer rankings in society. One region in which impressive physical signs of these things survive from the early formative time is the north coast of Peru. There, in many of the river valleys crossing the narrow coastal desert, can be seen vast earthen mounds that once served as platforms carrying temples, and whose beginnings date from around 3,800 BP. One example is Sechín Alto, in a branch of the Casma river valley. A great platform, 250 by 300 meters, and still 40 meters high today, it forms the base of a U-shaped compound measuring 1,100 meters long by 250 wide. Around this compound were ranged smaller temple-bearing platforms. The peoples in dozens of the river valleys of northern and central Peru built similar compounds – U-shaped and very large – in those centuries of the formative age.[8] Clearly the multitude of temples crowning the platforms would have required the attention of many priests; supporting the priestly class would have been the work of many commoners; great numbers of laborers were needed to build, maintain, and constantly enlarge the platforms and the structures on them. All this activity reflects long-assembled experience of farming in these arid valleys. The initial soil, except where the rivers had deposited mud and silt, had been mostly sand. The inhabitants had learned to irrigate it with water flowing down from the Andes and channeled, through ever longer and more complex systems of canals, to cultivated fields. The coastal peoples of Peru were, of course, unusually favored in having abundant protein readily at hand, in the form of the fish that thrived in the cold offshore waters. Among their deities, for that reason, were sea gods. But fish had to be caught, in nets that had to be woven from cotton, which had to be grown. The existence of these communities of the Peruvian coast speaks of accumulated experience, specialization of labor, and organization of society (itself difficult to imagine without the presence of a political and administrative structure) that together offer a contrast with the little villages of Archaic times.

In Peru, from the beginning of human presence down to modern times, two streams of cultural development have existed, one on the coast, the other in the mountains. Generally these have been separate streams, but with frequent links through trade, migration of people, and a variety of artistic, architectural, religious and even political influences. So it was in formative times. The U-shape of the coastal ceremonial centers was copied by people across the northern Peruvian mountains; the imitation suggests strongly that the religious beliefs of the coast also spread into the highlands, though certainly with modifications.

The best known of the formative sites in the northern highlands is Chavín de Huantar, a ceremonial center built at nearly 3,180 meters in the valley of the river Mosna, one of hundreds of tributaries of the Amazon on the inland side of the Andes in Peru. Fifteen kilometers to the west are the snowy peaks of the Cordillera Blanca, the highest mountain chain of Peru and the highest tropical chain in the world. The inhabitants of Chavín, unlike those of the coast, suffered no lack of water; seasonal summer moisture boiling/streaming up from the Amazon basin provided plenty of rain.

The first, small, occupation of the Chavín site may go back to around 3,000 BP, but the culture flourished between 2,800 and 2,200 BP. The population was small, reaching its possible maximum of 2,000 to 3,000 in the final two centuries of Chavín's prominence. And prominent it certainly was, in the sense of extending its religious and perhaps economic influence over much of Peru. At the center of its ascendancy stood a particular deity, a creature with a human body and feline face, with eyebrows and hair represented (in typically Chavín style) as snakes. The image of this were-feline (the cat element probably representing the jaguar, the most powerful land creature known to the mountain people) was carved on a 4.5 meter shaft of stone, long referred to by archaeologist as the Lanzón, or "Great Lance." The statue stood in a narrow shaft built into the U-shaped "Old Temple" of Chavín; this was a large platform, made partly of stone, that had within it many narrow passageways and small rooms. These housed other images incised into stone slabs, one of which adds feline traits to a fish – perhaps a linking of coastal and local divine elements. The Lanzón looked out, down a closed passageway, to the east, the direction of the rainforest and the rising sun. It was placed in such a way that a hidden attendant's voice might appear to come from it, which suggests that it may have served as an oracle – a speaking, prophesying divinity.[9]

In its final two centuries Chavín seems to have exported its religion over much of Peru, at least to judge by the appearance of typical motifs of Chavín art in places from the far north to the center-south of both the highlands and coast of Peru. One example is the ceramic container with a semi-circular hollow handle from which projects a spout. "Stirrup-spout" jars of this basic design, but with thousands of local variations in shape and decoration, became the typical vessels for holding and carrying liquids among later Peruvian native people.[10] Another example is the depiction of god-figures bearing an elaborate staff in each hand. Such "staff gods" appear, for instance, painted on large cotton tapestries found in a tomb on the dry Paracas peninsula, 220 kilometers south of Lima, and indeed re-emerge in far later cultures. Exactly how Chavín instilled its beliefs in people over such vast areas remains something of a mystery. It may have sent out missionaries, or encouraged pilgrims to come the great central shrine of the Lanzón – pilgrims who, moreover, brought tributes of woven tapestries and painted or dyed cloth; and of obsidian (a volcanic glass) and objects of beaten gold from the distant southern mountains.

For a long time students of Peru's deep human past saw Chavín as the founding culture of native civilization. Its role in spreading religious beliefs and motifs, and in stimulating technical and aesthetic changes in Peruvians' working of textiles, stone, ceramics, and gold, is still considered central. Nonetheless, its achievements did not arise miraculously out of nothing. Chavín, along with other lesser cultural centers of its time, is now seen, at least in part, as the successor to great and previously under-appreciated earlier cultures, such as that of Sechín Alto on the desert coast.

MIDDLE AMERICA

In Mexico, the culture most like that of Chavín in being considered foundational was that of the Olmecs; although, again like Chavín, it now seems that the Olmecs were less completely new and innovative in their time than previously thought. The term "mother culture" (for the high civilization of pre-Spanish Mexico) long applied to the Olmecs is still valid; but archaeologists are less sure than before that what was once regarded as "early Olmec" might not truly be "pre-Olmec."

The Olmecs' original and central territory was certainly not the most hospitable that Mexico had to offer. It was the hot, humid, tropical lowland at the southernmost limit of the Gulf of Mexico, just where the shoreline runs east–west before turning north up the west side of the Yucatan peninsula. The earliest site carries the Spanish name San Lorenzo. What its inhabitants called it is unknown; it is not even clear what language they used. San Lorenzo was at its height between 3,800 and 3,200 BP, and was succeeded by another place, La Venta. Several other Olmec sites existed at one time or another within a dozen or two kilometers of San Lorenzo.

Like the people of Chavín, the Olmecs are mainly identified today by the style of the artistic objects that they produced. The extensive spread of their influence over southern and central Mexico is traced in the same way. Given the heat and humidity of their area, most of what remains from the Olmecs is in durable materials: pottery and stone. Most of these surviving objects probably had a religious or political meaning, although "art for art's sake" very probably became a growing concern as time passed.

The fundamental motif of Olmec art is a blend of human and feline traits. In this the Olmecs resembled the Chavín people. Both had a depth of fearful respect for the jaguar that made the animal seem partly divine to them. But specific to the Olmecs is the portrayal of the blended figure as a baby, or as an androgynous creature with baby-like qualities: the body chubby and smooth, with a rather long, fat face, particularly wide and heavy in the jaw. The Olmecs also worshiped other fierce, deified animals that were familiar to them, or so their carved representations of caymans, eagles, and sharks – or of fantastical blends of these creatures – indicate. Intricately carved figurines made of local basalt, or, if smaller, jade or serpentine (a green stone), have been found not only in the Olmec heartland, but far away in central and western Mexico. In fact, not only these sculptures with religious meaning, but also more practically useful objects such as pottery bowls and bottles, clearly of the Olmecs' making, and occasionally mural paintings in Olmec style, have been found in places ranging from the Valley of Mexico (in which modern Mexico City stands) to sites further south in the present states of Morelos and Oaxaca, to the south-western state of Guerrero. Olmec jade carvings, indeed, have been found outside Mexico, in the present countries of Guatemala, El Salvador, and Costa Rica. The implication is that their religious ideas and economic impact spread far beyond their home area on the Gulf coast, although whether these influences went along with any political or military domination is impossible to say.

What are undoubtedly the best known of Olmec sculptures did not travel, and could not have done so. These are the great stone heads, the largest almost 3 meters high, of which 10 have been unearthed at San Lorenzo. The stone for these massive pieces of sculpture is a basalt found in mountains 80 kilometers away. It was most likely towed to San Lorenzo on rafts floating on rivers and the sea, and then dragged up the slope of the plateau, by simple human numbers, on rollers. The assumption is that the great heads were representations of powerful rulers. In their square, well-fleshed faces, African features have sometimes been seen; but a more likely reading is the familiar Olmec blend of human and feline.

Again like the cultures of the north Peruvian coast of the same centuries, the Olmecs were builders on a large scale – an enormous scale, indeed, given that they lacked metal tools and had no carts or wheelbarrows with which to move earth. The San Lorenzo site consists of a natural plateau, about 1.2 kilometers from north to south, that was in places artificially raised by at least 7 meters with earth hauled up from the surrounding plain. After excavating (in addition to the great heads) large basalt blocks that are thought to be thrones, and many smaller sculptures of human beings, cat-based creatures, birds, and a multitude of combinations of these elements, archaeologists now believe that Olmec rulers, their authority drawn from supernatural sources, lived on the top of the plateau. On its slopes, which were terraced, were the wattle-and-daub huts of commoners. These people were mostly occupied in growing maize on nearby higher ground, safe from the flooding that took place in the rainy season. Some of them must also have been the masons and sculptors of basalt and jade responsible for the prolific stonework of the plateau.

About 3,200 BP San Lorenzo's population and activities went into decline. As with so many ancient American sites, it is impossible to say for sure why this happened. Perhaps it had to do with a shift in the course of the nearby river, the Coatzacoalcos, which complicated the flow of goods to and from the plateau. In any case, San Lorenzo was then succeeded as the prime Olmec site by La Venta, built on a island amidst marshes some 80 kilometers to the north-east. Here the Olmecs created a type of structure that was to become common in many later sites of other cultures: a great stepped pyramid, in this case 34 meters high and made of clay. Whether this pyramid supported a temple, or whether the top simply served as a place of worship closer to the gods, is unknown. The site also possesses several other raised platforms and mounds. Among them have been found various monuments cut from basalt, including four more enormous heads and stelae, or stone posts. On one of those are carved scenes showing baby were-jaguars, with clearly religious meaning.

The holders of political and religious power who lived at La Venta would have required the support of many thousands of farmers and other commoners. Food was most likely grown on the levees of the many rivers that flowed nearby through the marshes. In fact, this particular area is likely to have been a zone of intensive farming for thousands of years before La Venta appeared. The site flourished for between 800 and 900 years, apparently being intentionally destroyed between 2,300 and 2,400 BP, although by whom and why are unanswered questions.

In addition to monumental architecture, great ceremonial centers surrounded by the dwellings of supporting commoners, exceptional sculpture of stone and jade on both the grand and minute scale, and the wide social ranking observable at San Lorenzo and La Venta, the Olmecs left much else for later Mexicans to take up and develop. For instance, at San Lorenzo exist the remains of a court for playing the ball game typical of Middle American cultures. It is plainly impossible to say whether this was the first of all such courts; and even if it were, games with balls are likely to have been played earlier without courts. But from San Lorenzo on, the ball court became a standard feature of ceremonial sites. The result of the game, played by two teams of a few men, had prophetic meaning – indicating, for example, which of two spiritual forces was more powerful at that particular time. At a site called El Manatí, only a few kilometers from San Lorenzo, archaeologists found in 1988 seven ancient rubber balls, preserved by the fresh water of the local springs. The find was unique; no other examples of balls, made from the natural latex of southern Mexican trees for use in the ball game, have survived.

Then again, at a late Olmec site named Tres Zapotes that flourished after La Venta, small but unmistakable traces have appeared of mental accomplishments that were to be central to the succeeding high cultures of Mexico. On a stela discovered there in 1939 appears a date, written (that is, carved) in the symbols that became standard among later cultures: a dot signifying "one" and a bar meaning "five." The date has been read as September 3, 32 BC, which means that the stela was put up extremely late in Olmec times, indeed in a period of cultural transition in southern Mexico from Olmec to Maya. But archaeologists regard Tres Zapotes as an Olmec, rather than Mayan, place. Just as significant as this appearance of numerical symbols is that fact that the date is written in what is called the "Long Count" – a system of measuring time created by Middle Americans that had as its starting date August 13, 3114 BC. The appearance of the Long Count date on this stela suggests that the Olmec invented this sort of calendar. They may also have begun creating the hieroglyphic type of writing that the Maya, above all others, developed into an expressive and complex system in later centuries.[11]

CLASSIC PEOPLES

The formative cultures, of which Chavín is the chief example in the central Andes, and the Olmec in Middle America, laid down many firm bases – religious, artistic, intellectual, economic, social, political – which later peoples could develop into still greater accomplishments. There was no sudden leap forward, of course; change and advance came gradually, as they always had. But if a date can be applied to this new shift, it would be an approximate one of 100 BC to AD 100. The leading cultures between then and about AD 1000 are termed "Classic" in Middle America, and (a little confusingly) "Early Intermediate" (running into "middle horizon") in the central Andes.

SOUTH AMERICA

In that part of the Andes, and in fact in the whole of South America, the longest lasting of those cultures had its center at Tiwanaku (or Tiahuanaco), a site about 15 kilometers from the southern tip of Lake Titicaca. The place is in what is now Bolivia, and modern Bolivians regard Tiwanaku with great pride as evidence of the high accomplishments of their country's ancient people. Much of the stonework of Tiwanaku has decayed or been removed. But enough remains to show that there was a large ceremonial center, dominated by a masonry platform, the Akapana, about 200 meters in length and width, and 15 meters high. Around it were other platforms, buildings, courtyards, stairways, and – a particularly notable feature of the site – many monumental gateways, some cut out from huge single pieces of stone. Into these were typically carved images of pairs of beings, of which the biggest is the so-called "Gateway God" on the largest portal, who carries in each hand a vertical staff. Archaeologists think it likely that he is a revival of the staff god of Chavín. The ceremonial center of Tiwanaku was, then, a place for religion, and also, very probably, the home of the rulers of the community and of the far larger area that it came to dominate. Around the center to a distance of 10 kilometers have been found traces of residential compounds and houses, equipped with large drains for water and sewage. Remains of pottery, bone, metal, stone, and tools in the very large area surrounding the ceremonial center leave no doubt that in Tiwanaku were concentrated many craftsmen and artists.[12] And some of the houses were evidently the homes of the people who tended to the needs of priests and governing lords.

One of those needs was obviously food; and Tiwanaku made strikingly innovative use of the level land around the southern end of the great lake for farming. At the culture's full development, from perhaps AD 500 to 900, 100,000 hectares of this land were intensively farmed. The natural cold at this great height (almost 4,000 meters) was moderated by Titicaca's enormous volume of water; the warming promoted plant growth. Because the land was almost flat, Tiwanaku had no need to imitate the many other Andean cultures that constructed terraces on mountainsides to create more farming land. But it did develop an equally impressive technique of ridging fields. In these soil was gathered up into long, raised strips, reaching 15 by 200 meters in width and length. Separating the strips were water-filled ditches. The deliberation with which the strips were raised, some having a foundation of large and small rock, suggests that state supervision went into the creation of ridged fields. In the soil forming the top of the strips, crops – doubtless potatoes and other tubers above all – were planted. The farming method yielded two crops a year, in part because, in addition to the general warming provided by the lake, the water in the ditches retained heat that was released at night, stimulating growth or, at least, minimizing frost damage. To ensure the presence of water for that purpose and, of course, to provide moisture for the plants' roots, the Tiwanaku farmers – they could almost be called "agricultural engineers" – channeled rivers and streams to the proper places. And where water was excessive, they used canals to remove it. All in all there are striking resemblances between Tiwanaku's ridged fields and the *chinampa* farming used in the Valley of Mexico by the Aztecs and their predecessors. Both made for intensive use of limited land and produced high yields of crops. (*Chinampas* are described in the account given of the Aztecs later in this chapter.)

Besides being remarkable farmers, the Tiwanakans were keen long-distance traders. The shores of Lake Titicaca are prime llama-raising terrain; great herds of these animals carried goods to and from Tiwanaku. The exchange was probably above all one of craft goods from Tiwanaku (cloth, wooden carvings, beakers, and other clay items) for foods grown at lower altitudes. It is clear, in fact, that Tiwanaku, as it moved to its full development from AD 500, set up colonies lower down the mountains. One area in which excavations have revealed such colonization in some detail is the valley of the Moquegua river, between Titicaca and the Pacific coast. Here, using canals to irrigate flatlands, farmers grew maize, tubers, beans, peanuts, squash, pumpkin, and fruits, some for their own consumption and some, archaeologists assume, to be carried to Tiwanaku, 300 kilometers away.

Just as the Olmecs had exerted a powerful economic, religious, artistic, and possibly political influence over much of central and southern Mexico and northern Central America, Tiwanaku dominated, in the same ways, what has been called the "southern, highland pole of Andean civilization."[13] The two cultures are also similar in two other ways. First, both were very long-lived – the Olmecs at least 800 years, and Tiwanaku 1,000 years; second, no definitive reason exists for the decline and disappearance of either of them. But decline they did, just like every other dominant culture before and after them in the Americas, and, indeed, elsewhere in the world.

For part of the long period in which Tiwanaku exercised its deep cultural and economic influence over southern Peru, much of highland Bolivia, and northern parts of Chile, another highland culture left its mark on much of the rest of Andean Peru. This was Wari (or Huari), 700 kilometers north-west of Tiwanaku, close to the modern Peruvian city of Ayacucho at a height of 2,800 meters. Here, roughly between AD 500 and 750, flourished a ceremonial center and town of 10,000 to 35,000 people, a place made distinctive by the great stone walls that separated its patio-like rectangular living areas, some of which consisted of multi-story, inward-facing galleries. Lying as it did among steep mountains, Wari depended on the terracing of slopes for its food supply, drawing irrigation water through canals from sources high above it. Its craftsmen turned gold, silver, copper, lapis lazuli, spondylus shells, and other materials imported from distant origins into fine jewelry, and also produced distinctive ceramics and points for spears and arrows. Wari created a subsidiary ceremonial center in Tiwanaku's terrain in the Moquegua valley, on the top of a steep, free-standing peak named Cerro Baúl. More impressive still, however, were the many daughter centers it established in most of the great highland basins of the Andes, from near Cuzco (the later Inca capital) in the south, 1,000 kilometers northwards to the vicinity of Cajamarca in the far north of present Peru.[14] These seem to have been cultural outposts of Wari rather than bases for military domination and colonization (although a case can be made for some of them having been centers of Wari government[15]). From them, however, Wari clearly introduced its methods of highland terracing and irrigation to areas in which these had previously been less developed.[16]

Wari's direct influence was almost entirely limited to the mountains of central and northern Peru. A culture now much better known than Wari, largely because of the enormous number of appealing ceramic pieces that survive from it, dominated the northern third of Peru's coast during the centuries of Wari's highland prominence (although starting much earlier). This was the Moche (or Mochica) culture, which flourished between roughly 0 and AD 750. The Moche people's main urban center was in the river valley of the same name, some 450 kilometers up the coast from Lima. There, built on the slopes of a white hill (Cerro Blanco) stood two vast ceremonial platforms, the Huaca de la Luna ("Holy Place of the Moon") and the Huaca del Sol ("Holy Place of the Sun"), which was the largest solid structure made of adobe bricks ever erected in the Andes. The 500 meters separating the two were filled with splendid buildings and houses, the latter arranged in compounds. The Huaca del

Sol, the highest part of which reached 40 meters, is thought to have been both a governing palace and a burial place for deceased rulers. The Huaca de la Luna, by contrast, was a site for religious ceremonies, which included the sacrifice of captured warriors – or so archaeologists' excavation of the remains of male bodies showing signs of violent death strongly suggests.

In some of the site's urban compounds, craftsmen worked. From the compounds came much of the characteristic Moche ceramic work that can still be seen in abundance in museums today. Moche potters particularly focused on producing stirrup-spout jars, many of which, it is thought, were intended for use as libation vessels – that is, containers from which liquids could be poured during religious ceremonies. The range of shapes and designs of these jars was enormous, and included human heads or bodies, a variety of animals, and human and animal forms combined into images of evidently divine beings. Particularly admired still are the "portrait heads" – stirrup jars bearing molded faces that seem to be depictions of actual people. The supposition is that these were images of high-ranking men in Moche society. But commoners were also often the subject matter of stirrup jars, with the molded clay showing them in a multitude of activities: hunting, being tended to by healers when ill, giving birth, playing flutes, to name only a few.[17] Highly unusual among American native cultures is the Moche potters' explicit depiction of sexual acts, between humans and between humans and animals. The purpose of these images is still undecided, although, as is the usual assumption when ancient objects displaying sexuality are found, archaeologists suggest some link with fertility.

The Moche decorated some of their jars with remarkably fine painted lines, creating images that rival, in their vivid precision, the decorations on Classical Greek ceramic vessels. There are scenes of religious ceremonies, hunting and fishing, food-gathering, groups of warriors dashing along in what is termed "ritual running," and much else. These images convey a most lively sense of action and motion. Frequent among them are war-related scenes: warriors engaged in one-to-one conflict, or the presentation of captives, stripped naked, to rulers of the triumphant faction before being sacrificed. It seems quite clear from such depictions that the Moche were a combative culture. The scenes of individual combat, however, and the absence of pictures of warriors fighting in groups or attacking places, also suggest that the aim of fighting was more likely the taking of victims for ritual sacrifice than the capture of towns or territory.[18] This may mean – though it is far from conclusive proof – that the Moche were not a militarily aggressive or expansive culture. On the other hand, the presence of Moche-style archaeological remains and artifacts in the river valleys of the northern third (almost 600 kilometers) of the present Peruvian coast shows that, like Wari, the Moche's cultural, and probably religious, influence was extensive. Political control is a much more open question. The likelihood is that, close to the home territory in the Moche river valley, direct governmental authority existed. Further away to the north, the Moche may have exercised some political control through pre-existing local authorities who adopted Moche beliefs and ways of life.[19]

Many other central Andean cultures from before AD 1000 deserve mention. Whether dwellers of mountain valleys or of the fertile oases created by rivers in the coastal desert, the Andean peoples left evidence of their remarkable beliefs, customs, and achievements in the form of terracing, irrigation works, buildings, sculpture, exquisite textiles and jewelry, and ceramics whose forms, decorations, and craftsmanship still astonish. The sampling presented in the preceding pages gives only a brief impression of their accomplishments.

MIDDLE AMERICA

Extraordinary as the central Andeans were in the first millennium AD, their contemporaries in Middle America were no less so in ways both similar and different. Two great cultures particularly stand out: Teotihuacán, which had its center in a north-eastern branch of the great Valley of Mexico; and the Maya, who occupied much of the Yucatan peninsula and smaller areas immediately south of it in what are now Honduras and Guatemala.

Teotihuacán

The people of Teotihuacán left abundant archaeological evidence of their lives and multiple talents, but what stands out above all is their city itself. For the first time in the Americas, native people created an urban space that time travelers from the present would instantly recognize as a city. First, there was the impressive scale of the place – 20 square kilometers of built-up area, divided into rectangular blocks by a grid of streets. This great concentration of people had begun to agglomerate from earlier farming villages around 200 BC, and reached its maximum number of 125,000 to 200,000 by the early 300s AD.

Second, the city possessed a monumental central axis, running roughly north and south, and consisting of a wide avenue more than 2 kilometers long. At the north end of this avenue ("Avenue of the Dead," as it is now commonly called) stands a massive, shallow-sloped pyramid, thought to have served as the base of a temple dedicated to worship of the moon. About 1 kilometer to the south, on the east side of the avenue, is a still larger, similarly shaped, pyramid, once bearing a temple for the worship of the sun. A further kilometer southward lies a square quadrangle, each side measuring 400 meters. Within this structure, now named the Ciudadela ("citadel" in Spanish), are found a pyramid and temple dedicated to the cult of the feathered serpent – a powerful and complex Mexican god of Classic and later times, known to the Aztecs as Quetzalcóatl (literally "Quetzalbirdsnake"). Into the walled space surrounding that pyramid it is estimated that 60,000 spectators of religious acts could have fitted. On each side of the great avenue, particularly at the north end, can still be seen smaller pyramids on which the temples of lesser gods once stood; and the residential compounds of powerful lords were also ranged along that central aorta of the city.

Third, visitors from the present would be struck by the obvious planning of Teotihuacán's design. If the city began with the running together of older settlements, early in its growth surveyors and planners clearly took its expansion in hand, laying out the central avenue and another major street that crosses it at right-angles near the Ciudadela, and then decreeing that each of the resulting four quarters of the city develop on a grid pattern. The differences in size and decoration of the walled compounds that made up the grid, and of the rooms that each compound contained, suggest strongly that there was a wide range of social and economic status among the dwellers of the city. The largest compounds – those, for instance, along the Avenue of the Dead – were adorned with splendid painted murals, mostly showing religious figures and symbols.

Fourth, modern visitors might well regard Teotihuacán as something like an industrial center. The city is thought to have gained control of a rich source of green obsidian at Pachuca, about 60 kilometers to the north-east. Certainly there were a hundred or more workshops in Teotihuacán where specialized craftsmen worked this obsidian into sharp blades, points for darts and spears, and even miniature human figures – a remarkable display of skill, given the difficulty of shaping such a hard and brittle material. Teotihuacán exported its obsidian manufactures over much of southern and central Mexico. It also supported many able potters, stone carvers, and weavers. The spirit of much of Teotihuacán's surviving artwork is – if compared with the naturalistic vividness of the Moche, or the elegance of the Classic Maya – tends to the simple and serious. The seriousness, if not the simplicity, may reflect the spirit of the city and its culture.

Fifth, the sum of much of the preceding – the monumentality, the sheer size of the urban area and its population, its physical organization, and evidence of large-scale production and of trade – would remind visitors from a great metropolis of the present that cities are concentrations of power. In contrast to most modern cities, Teotihuacán's power clearly rested on religion first and foremost, but it had economic reinforcement and very probably political projection. There is little doubt that Teotihuacán had a profound influence over the course of people's lives in much of central Mexico during most of the first six centuries AD,[20] although, as always with ancient cultures from which no written records survive, the boundary between influence and control cannot be defined. The appearance of Teotihuacán-made vases in the tombs of nobles in much of Mexico, and of clearly Teotihuacán designs in even Mayan images, suggests at least that holders of power respected the city and its culture and may also have drawn authority from an association with it. Perhaps, like the Moche in the far north of Peru, Teotihuacán influenced the course of distant affairs by controlling local rulers. A particularly suggestive possibility of this exists at Kaminaljuyú, a place on the fringes of modern Guatemala City that has been described as "a miniature copy of Teotihuacán." The tombs of Maya nobles there contain both copies of Teotihuacán objects and actual imports of ceramics and of mirrors made of glassy iron ore from its workshops.[21]

The Maya

Contact between Teotihuacán and the Maya far to the south is undisputed. It was largely a one-way affair, with goods, possibly travelers, and certainly an impression of power and sophistication moving from Teotihuacán far and wide into the great area of Maya culture in northern central America and the Yucatan peninsula. On the carved stone images of leaders that remain in many Maya centers appear motifs from Teotihuacán, indicating that these locally powerful men revered the great city and culture of central Mexico, and wished to declare, and permanently record, their connection with it.[22]

The Maya, nonetheless, possessed and developed a culture of their own – or a set of linked cultures – that has come down to the present more brilliantly than even Teotihuacán's. In part, that is because instead of creating one great city the Maya built hundreds of urban places of varying size – religious, governmental, and residential centers – over a distance, south to north, of 800 kilometers, from the mountains of Guatemala's Pacific coast to the far tip of the great low plain of the Yucatecan peninsula. New discoveries of Maya sites are still being made, and many of those already found have not been investigated, or only partly so. Most of the discoveries reveal new aspects, abilities, and accomplishments of the ancient Maya, so that modern awareness of their culture is constantly refreshed. That awareness is also reinforced by the continuing existence of some 7.5 million speakers of Maya languages in the lands occupied by their ancient ancestors. The current Maya live simpler and poorer lives than at least the elites – the large elites – of the old societies, though not perhaps than the common people of old. But direct lines between present and past exist in religious ideas and means of everyday living.

The "Classic" period of the Maya, the time of their highest achievements, is generally defined as running from around AD 250 to the late 800s. But Maya traits can be seen emerging many centuries earlier, and recent discoveries of sophisticated Maya places, such as El Mirador and San Bartolo in the Petén region in the extreme north of present Guatemala, where architecture and wall paintings of Classic scale and skill have emerged, make some think that the beginning of the Classic era could well be moved back by three or more centuries to the 200s BC.

One of the many remarkable features of the Maya's high culture is that they extended it successfully from the fertile and well-watered lands of Guatemala onto the dry, barren terrain of the Yucatan peninsula. The limestone of Yucatan gave them the double problem of a poor, thin, alkaline soil and lack of surface water. How they managed to grow enough of their staple food, maize, in such conditions has not yet been fully understood. Clearly their skill in using slash and burn methods to create briefly fertile clearings in the scrubby Yucatecan forest was well advanced. In some areas they built up raised fields for intensive farming. Hunting of deer, the pig-like peccary, and howler monkeys, all abundant in the forest, contributed to the diet, as probably also did fruits grown in plots around the common people's wood and thatch houses. But, all that considered, it is still clear that the Maya of the low-lying Yucatan peninsula had to strive to produce the basic food they needed to create and sustain their splendid culture.

Problematic for farming as limestone was (and is), it is in that stone that much of ancient Maya culture has been preserved. First, they used it for building.

Like some other stones that are soft before being quarried, limestone hardens with exposure to the elements. Those qualities made it easy to extract, shape, and carve (though Maya masons had only tools made of some harder stone), and then surprisingly durable. Further, the Maya converted limestone to lime by roasting it in kilns, and then, by mixing the lime with more or less finely crushed limestone and water, produced both mortar in which to set blocks of building stone, and cement which, when poured with chunks of limestone, yielded a concrete from which strong and durable cores of walls could be formed.[23] The exteriors of buildings were often given a smooth finish of fine mortar, or covered with thin sheets – a veneer – of limestone attached with mortar. Perhaps it was the use of mortar and the workability of limestone that also led the Maya to discover – and they were the only American natives to do so – how to make arches. The Maya arch was not a "true" arch, made from wedge-shaped stones, but rather a corbelled structure. In this, flat stones were laid horizontally on top of each other. Each successive stone projected closer to the center line of the space that the arch was to enclose, until at the top a single stone was laid to complete the frame. Each horizontal stone was anchored back into the surrounding wall. Clearly a corbelled arch can bear less weight than a true arch; but using it enabled the Maya to frame doorways with stone, and, more distinctively still, to build stone vaults by joining a series of arches together. The resulting corbelled vaults were certainly narrow, but they served to construct entire, multi-roomed, buildings. Since these were made solely of stone, mortar, and cement, they have survived to the present far more intact than the wood-roofed buildings standard among American native people (even among the Inca, those other great American workers of stone).

Using limestone and mortar the Classic Maya created the host of urban centers that survive in generally good condition to fascinate both modern archaeologists and tourists. These places typically consisted of ensembles of raised platforms, stairways linking them, rectangular vaulted buildings, and steep-sided pyramids bearing vaulted temples, which were often decorated with elaborate "roof-combs" carved from stone. In the vaulted buildings lived kings, lords, and priests, and in them also kings held court. The common people had wood and thatch huts, sometimes ranged around small plazas. Where, as in the southern extreme of Yucatan and in northern Guatemala, there was risk of seasonal flooding, huts would be built on low earth platforms. Streets were absent, and the dominant arrangement of the commoners' housing was scattering around the monumental centers. Maya urban places generally grew by slow accretion, not by planning.

Also typically to be found in the ceremonial centers were groups of limestone posts, now usually termed stelae, ranging in height from a few feet up to 6 meters or more. Most stelae were covered in dense carving, showing (in relief) human figures, and around them row upon row of intricate symbols, or glyphs. It was long evident that the glyphs were some sort of writing, but until about 1960 the subject of the writing was uncertain, and very few of the symbols had been read. Then it became clear that the writing on stelae related the history of the figures shown in relief. Great advances were made during the final third of the twentieth century in deciphering the symbols. As a result, for many Classical Maya sites there is now a record of successive rulers and of the salient events – particularly the wars and the battles – of their reigns. The reading of Maya glyphs – in itself truly one of the triumphs of archaeology in the past hundred years – has contributed greatly to correcting a pervasive earlier misunderstanding of Classic Maya times. The people of that culture were not, as had often been thought, tranquil lovers of peace. Quite to the contrary – and this is confirmed by scenes of warfare shown in mural paintings and on various ceramic objects – they were no less belligerent than any other Classic or Pre-Classic American natives. The generally small states governed from the many ceremonial centers were in constant conflict with each other. Urban places were seized and sacked, their rulers captured and executed, and their people enslaved.

That the warlike aspect of Maya culture was so long in becoming clear is the result, in good part, of the complexity of the writing in which events were recorded. The system combined logograms – drawings that showed, with varying degrees of literalness and symbolism, actual objects – with signs denoting syllables in Maya speech (that is, particular sounds). So, for instance, the name of the great seventh-century ruler of the city-state of Palenque, Pakal, could be written as a drawing of a hand-shield, since the Maya word for such a shield was *pakal*. (To the uninitiated, however, it is not at all obvious that this drawing shows such a shield.) Or the name could be written as three signs denoting the sounds *pa*, *ka*, and *la* – with it being understood that the final *a* was not sounded. Or a combination of the logogram and the sound signs might be used.[24] It is not hard to see why a script made up of such unpredictable symbols took so long to decipher. Worth noting in particular is that the use of syllabic signs means that Maya writing was becoming phonetic – that is, moving towards a spelling system consisting of symbols indicating sound alone such as is common in the writing of modern languages. That, along with its sophisticated capacity to record and convey information, made it the most advanced writing system of any developed by American native people. The Aztecs, for instance – a later culture – used a simpler sort of script consisting mostly of rather literal pictures of the objects being recorded.

The Maya similarly surpassed other American natives in their skill with arithmetic, which they used largely to record the passage of time in complex calendars, and to keep track of the movements of the sun, moon, and planets for religious purposes. They were able to predict the positions of these heavenly bodies, for any particular day, for thousands of years into the future, and knew where they had been thousands of years in the past. Their calculations made use of the concept of zero, which they may have created themselves, or learned from the Olmec before them.

What may, however, most deeply impress visitors to ancient Maya sites or to museums in which Maya ceramics and sculpture are on display, is the distinctive aesthetic of Classic Maya work and art. It is like none other in the ancient Americas, and many find it superior to all others. Above all, Classic Maya painters, potters, and sculptors developed and displayed an amazing facility with line, producing images of the greatest elegance.[25] The fluidity of Maya line may remind the modern viewer of the celebration of line in art nouveau. On vases, pieces of shell or polished jade, stelae, building facades, and doubtless the bark-paper pages of thousands of books that have long since disappeared, Maya artists and writers created images recording history, myth, and religion that rarely fail to fascinate as much for their innate aesthetic quality as for the information or message they convey. A king, shown in relief on limestone, in Classic pose – arms and legs crossed, with elaborate headdress of long, sweeping feathers set on a high, curved head that is turned in profile, and body tautly inclined to one side over some inferior official or slave – is one such common, captivating image. There are endless other examples.

Kings, stela-making, high craft and art, elaborate ritual of ruling and religion, monumental building – all came to an end in the ninth century AD, or did so at least everywhere except the northern third of Yucatan. The explanations for this collapse of the Classic Maya are a little firmer than those of the decline of earlier high cultures in Middle and South America. There is good physical evidence, for instance, of droughts in much of the Maya area between AD 800 and 1050. And there are strong signs, in the form of previously undiscovered remains of numerous commoners' huts, that the Maya population had grown larger than archaeologists long thought. Just how these conditions interacted to cause decline is still, however, undecided. The broad supposition is that overpopulation led to soil depletion and excessive felling of trees (for fuel and building) – with the latter probably bringing erosion of slopes and declining rainfall. As the land became ever less able to support its population (this incapacity being worsened by the droughts), warfare between city-states, and even between social classes within the states, intensified. There are indeed, in the 800s AD, many signs of attack and destruction, in the form of wrecked buildings and defaced stelae in the monumental centers. Whatever the precise course of events, there is no doubt that, with one exception, the ninth century AD brought to an end almost 1,000 years of splendid and distinctive Maya accomplishment.

THE POST-CLASSIC

Middle America

The exception was the north of Yucatan. There a site surviving from Classic times, Chichén Itza, flourished as a Post-Classic center until the early 1200s AD, with its now much-admired pyramid (known as El Castillo), the largest ball court in Middle America, and many other monumental buildings. Chichén Itza stimulates much debate among archaeologists because its religious symbolism, architecture, and many artifacts found in and around it show a deep influence of the contemporaneous Toltec culture of central Mexico. The debate is over the direction of the influence – whether Mayans went to central Mexico and brought back Toltec traits, or whether the Toltec, often considered to be an aggressive and expansive culture, invaded Yucatan and imposed their customs and designs on the northern Yucatec Maya. The latter is perhaps more likely. The extent of Chichén Itza's own influence is also debated; some believe that it dominated much of Yucatan, far exceeding in its political reach anything achieved by even the greatest of the Classical centers.[26] It certainly controlled at least the north of the peninsula. Nevertheless, it too came to an end, for reasons still uncertain, around AD 1200. Some sixty years later, however, another center arose in the far north of Yucatan – Mayapan, created by a people called the Itza whose origins were in the south of the peninsula. Mayapan became a sizeable town of some 12,000 people spread over 6.5 square kilometers, and ringed by a defensive wall, though lacking any of the architectural splendor of Chichén Itza. But like Chichén Itza it came to dominate much of Yucatan, living on the tribute of peoples that it had overcome. Internal dissension brought Mayapan down in the mid fifteenth century.

With the passing of Mayapan's domain, Yucatan reverted to the political conditions of the Classic era: smaller states, now sixteen in number, in constant tension and conflict. There was not, however, any recovery of the high culture of Classic times. Most of the remaining Maya were village-dwellers. They lived still from the slash-and-burn farming that had provided the subsistence base for the Classic places, and venerated still the old gods, if with now far simpler ceremony. But, for them, the great monumental centers of the Classic era became, with their lengthening abandonment, places of mystery and wonder. It was a Maya culture in that reduced state that the Spanish first encountered in the early 1500s.[27]

The change from Classic to Post-Classic culture exemplified by the rise of Chichén Itza in Yucatan also took place in other parts of Middle and South America (where, for the central Andes, archaeologists use the term "Late Intermediate" instead of "Post-Classic"). The clearest distinction made between Classic and Post-Classic was for a long time one of peace and war: it seemed that Middle and South American natives between, very roughly, 0 and AD 1000 lived with minimal conflict, and those after that date in constant military struggle. Now – and the Maya are a typical case – that contrast no longer seems as clear. Conflict existed within, and between, Classic cultures. Nonetheless, in Post-Classic (or Late Intermediate) times, a more plainly martial ethos does seem to have pervaded many cultures. Warriors gained higher social rank. More towns (like Mayapan) had defensive works around them. Human sacrifice may have become more common in civic and religious ceremonies. And, with as always some exceptions, many would say that the quality and variety of art work, in all mediums, fell – or at least became plainer, less inventive. Of the Post-Classic art of central Mexico an expert observer has said: "It was the kind of strong, static art produced by artisans guided by Spartan, not Athenian, ideals."[28]

In Mexico one notable Post-Classic culture (though rather late-flourishing, after AD 1200) was that of the Mixtec, people of the mountains of the north and west of the present state of Oaxaca. By the mid 1300s they were expanding into the Valley of Oaxaca, one of the largest fertile areas in the whole of the Southern Highlands. In doing so, they overran and occupied sites previously held by the Zapotecs, for many centuries past the masters of the valley. One of those places was Monte Albán, now among the most visited archaeological sites in Mexico, and a city that had existed from Pre-Classic times. But, unlike the Zapotec, the Mixtec did not build impressive cities. And like the post-Mayapan Maya, they lived in small, politically distinct kingdoms.

In central Mexico, by contrast, what was to become the most imposing society of Post-Classic times, before the Aztecs, was already taking shape in Late Classic times. This was the culture of the Toltec. Its center was the city of Tula (or Tollan), set on a hilltop site some 75 kilometers north of Mexico City. At its full extent, reached probably by AD 1000, Tula had an area of 16 square kilometers, and a population of 30,000 to 40,000. Its ceremonial center contained three pyramids, though of no great height or mass, two ball courts, and, most distinctively, a palace with a roof supported by scores of stone columns. Although Toltec stonework and sculpture were crude, angular, and static when set against Maya work, Tula had many able potters and many expert workers of obsidian – who drew their raw material from the same source near Pachuca thought to have been used centuries earlier by Teotihuacán.

For the history of Tula two sources exist. On the one hand is modern archaeology; on the other, a mass of myth, preserved by the Aztecs and related by them to sixteenth-century Spaniards committed to recording the native past. For the Aztecs, Tula was a place of great, inspiring, and mysterious accomplishments, an example to be imitated and a culture with which they were anxious to claim whatever link they could devise. It is partly because of the awe felt by the Aztecs for Tula that the Toltecs have often been supposed a mighty political force in central Mexico in their time, perhaps the rulers of much of that whole region. But archaeological evidence for a Toltec empire has not – or not yet – been found.

One possibly potent myth descending from Tula told of a rivalry in the city in the late 900s AD that resulted in the expulsion of the priest-ruler Topiltzin, a devotee of the feathered serpent god, Quetzalcóatl. Having retreated to the Gulf coast, Topiltzin then departed eastward on a raft of interlaced snakes – but not before declaring that he would return in due course to reclaim his rightful domain. Some 500 years later, it is possible that the Aztecs saw a connection between the arrival of the Spaniards and the promised reappearance of Topiltzin – and that their will to resist the conquistadores may thus have been weakened. But that is only a possibility, and more unlikely than probable.

Whatever the true extent of Toltec power, it was not enough to withstand the effects of drought, internal factions, and quite probably attack by nomads migrating southward from the *altiplano* in the mid or late 1100s AD. The city center was burned and its buildings wrecked. Lighter occupation of the site continued for centuries; but, as with the Maya, the splendor was gone.

South America

The culture most comparable to that of the Toltec in South America after AD 1000 was that of the Chimú, on the north coast of Peru. In this case, however, there is no doubt about political control over a wide area – a Chimú empire, indeed, with a capital city named Chan Chan in the same river valley as had been earlier occupied by the Moche. The beginnings of Chan Chan go back to the late 800s AD, not long after the subsidence of Moche culture. But the full growth of the city came only with the beginning of the imperial expansion, around AD 1350. Over the following century, the Chimú people subjugated to a greater or lesser degree the river valleys of the Peruvian coast over a distance of 1,000 kilometers, from the present frontier between Peru and Ecuador in the north down almost to where Lima stands today. Their empire thus included two-thirds of the irrigated land of coastal Peru, and probably two-thirds of the coastal population. It was, as far as can be told, the second largest native state ever created in South America, outdone only by the empire of its eventual conquerors, the Incas.

Chan Chan, the Chimú capital, was an imposing city at its height in the fourteenth and fifteenth centuries. It lay close to the Pacific shore in the Moche valley, and consisted, at its heart, of ten great rectangular enclosures – some of them 500 meters on their long sides – containing the palaces of the successive supreme rulers of the empire. Within the adobe walls of the compounds also stood subsidiary buildings, cane huts for retainers, and platforms, with many interior chambers, that served as opulent tombs of rulers. Outside the imperial city center were smaller compounds holding the residences of lesser nobles, and a mass of houses for commoners. The population of Chan Chan, at its peak, reached at least 35,000, and possibly many more. Like all the cultures of the Peruvian coast before it, Chan Chan and the other towns of the empire up and down the coast existed precariously close to the limits of their water supply. In the capital itself, water for domestic use was drawn from wells; but increasingly dry conditions from AD 1100 onwards meant that wells had to be dug ever deeper. Excess of water could also occasionally cause even more urgent problems. In precisely the year 1100, in fact, an episode of El Niño brought deluges that wrecked the irrigation system of the Moche valley above Chan Chan. At evidently immense effort the system was rebuilt in an attempt to maintain the supply of food to the city from the valley. But with increasing drought the Moche river no longer carried down from the Andes enough water for that purpose. Consequently the Chimú began using force to seize land in adjacent valleys. In their home valley and in others the Chimú became great masters of irrigation, even going so far as to attempt cutting a canal, over 80 kilometers long, from the Chicama river, to the north, to the Moche valley. This monumental piece of engineering seems to have been unsuccessful, possibly because of seismic movement of the terrain that it crossed. A final measure of the dependence of Chan Chan and its empire on water is clearly visible in their fall: by one account, at least, a weapon that the Inca used to take the city was simply to threaten cutting off its water higher up the Moche valley.[29]

AZTECS AND INCAS

With such Post-Classic cultures as the Chimú, Toltec, and Mixtec there is a sense of arriving at the end of many millennia of native development in Middle and South America – possibly 300 centuries in which the original migrants from Asia adapted to the American lands, and then, in the final 25 centuries, matured into a series of identifiable cultures that, wave-like, lifted and fell with passing time. To posit the Tula, the Mixtec, and the Chimú as end-points is not to overlook the fact that the Aztec and Inca were also Post-Classic cultures that rose and thrived after AD 1000, and indeed were in many respects the most remarkable of all native peoples anywhere in the Americas after that date. But the Inca and Aztec, unlike all that had come before them, were seen by the Spaniards; and the Spaniards wrote volume upon volume of fact and commentary about the native Americans they encountered, conquered, and then observed. Thus there is a feeling of transition about the Inca and Aztec, and the other less imposing native peoples overrun by the Spanish from 1492 onwards. They both belong to the first stage of the historical, European record of Spanish America and stand clearly as the final stage of the autonomous native past. That is not to say that much does not remain mysterious and poorly comprehended about the Inca and Aztec; but they are far clearer to us than their predecessors in such significant respects as the size of their empires, the nature of their rule and religion, and the organization of their societies and economies.

When the Spaniards first made contact with the Aztecs and Incas, they did not know that these two great states were quite new features on the American landscape. By remarkable coincidence, they had both essentially come into being – burst onto the scene, indeed – 100–150 years before the European invaders appeared. And in both cases, their eruption brought to an end a long period in which the centers of Mexico and of the Andean highlands were filled with small, jostling, polities (political units) – towns and cities, with their immediately surrounding areas. (The Chimú in Peru, while certainly centralizers like the Aztecs and Incas, were a coastal culture.) These small units combined the residues from the collapse of earlier, centralizing states (in Mexico the Toltec and more distantly Teotihuacán, and in the Andes Tiwanaku and Wari) with new migrant people.

Mexica-Aztecs

The story of the reassembling of power into large states is, for both the Incas and the Aztecs, long, and clearer in its later stages than in its beginnings. In the Aztec case, it seems that the origin of the citizens of what finally became the imperial capital, Tenochtitlan, was a small tribe, calling itself the Mexica, that drifted into the Valley of Mexico in the mid to late thirteenth century.[30] This band was possibly the last to arrive in the valley of many similar migrant groups that had originated in the north and west of Mexico, and had then been drawn southward by the benign climate, the fertility, and perhaps the sophistication of the central area. Several of these groups believed that they had first come into being in a place, probably mythical, called Aztlan. That belief led to the later use of the general name "Aztec" for the descendants of the migrants who lived in the Valley of Mexico, although they did not call themselves that.[31]

The Mexica – a small sub-group of the Aztecs – were crude in comparison with the peoples of the existing valley towns, being gatherers rather than growers, nomads rather than dwellers. The valley was already full. No obvious niche awaited the Mexica. They survived for several decades as mercenary fighters in the constant conflicts among the city-states. Then they finally found refuge on what, according to their own history, were unoccupied swampy islands in the largest lake, Texcoco, on the valley floor (though archaeologists have unearthed pre-Mexica remains on the island sites).[32] There, somewhere between 1320 and 1350, they began to build what was for many years a twin town, Tenochtitlan-Tlatelolco.

Until well into the next century, the Mexica survived, indeed thrived, as fighting vassals, and then junior allies, of one of the leading forces in the valley's power struggles: the Tepaneca, whose chief town was Azcapotzalco, on the shore of the lake, 8 kilometers or so north-west of Tenochtitlan. As the Mexica fought successfully for the Tepaneca, their society was gradually militarized. Warriors acquired an ever greater central power, tending to push aside the authority and practices of the *calpullin* (a Nahuatl term for traditional social groups, perhaps originally bound by ties of kin, whose members generally lived on and cultivated a common piece of land). The new, war-sanctioned supreme leaders, the *tlatoque* (singular, *tlatoani*: "he who speaks"), and an emergent nobility below them, the *pipiltin*, gained lands for themselves as reward for their efforts in the Tepaneca expansion.[33] This, by the early 1400s, had passed beyond the valley's limits to the north and west, and had begun to take on an imperial tone.[34]

Finally the Mexica grew to possess such military strength, expertise, and confidence that they resolved to turn on their Tepaneca masters. A crisis of succession in Azcapotzalco in the late 1420s gave the opportunity. The Mexica joined forces with Texcoco, a leading city on the east side of the valley that had long been in conflict with the Tepaneca; and to this basic union they added a smaller nearby town, Tlacopan, to form a famous "Triple Alliance." In 1428 this combination defeated the Tepaneca, and took over their lands. These, added to the territories of Texcoco, were the kernel from which sprang the rampant growth of the Aztec empire. The empire is known as "Aztec" rather than "Mexica" because, although the Mexica were the most vigorous military group in the alliance, imperial expansion was the work of all three partners, and soon also of other towns and cities in the valley that the alliance forced into its domain.

Until its final decades in the early 1500s, authority in the Triple Alliance was shared between Texcoco and Tenochtitlan. Texcoco was indeed the senior partner in age and sophistication.[35] But the fiery energy that drove the developing imperial machine was Tenochtitlan's. And this energy was not only material and military, but, perhaps more tellingly, ideological.

For all the small polities of the valley in the pre-imperial time, the model of cultured civilization remained the Toltecs; or, at least, the Toltecs as increasingly idealizing memory portrayed them. Ruling dynasties in the city states proudly proclaimed whatever genealogical links with the Toltecs they could muster.[36] Newcomers sought to create such connections. The Mexica, in the traditional account, did so in around 1372 by requesting from Culhuacan, a city-state south of Tenochtitlan in the valley whose rulers had strong Toltec links, a prince to lead them. The man in question, Acamapichtli, may have been the son of a Mexica father and a princess of Culhuacan.[37] In any case, he is seen as the first *tlatoani* of the Mexica. As such he was the initiator of a dynasty of supreme leaders whose Toltec ancestry gave them, and the Mexica under them, a sense of not only belonging in the valley, but of holding a legitimate right to wield power to which the old *calpulli*-based government could not lay claim.

As Mexica power and self-esteem grew, so also did the status of their particular tribal god Huitzilopochtli ("Southern Hummingbird"). This figure, possibly the deification of some distant Mexica hero, was unique to them, and remained a minor god in the fourteenth century. The Mexica, indeed, as part of their assimilation of valley culture, took up the cults of the great enduring divinities of central Mexico: Quetzalcóatl (Plumed Serpent), Tlaloc (god of rain and storms), Tezcatlipoca (Smoking Mirror), and a multitude of only slightly lesser figures. But, as the Aztec empire gained in power after 1428, so too did Huitzilopochtli rapidly rise in public estimation to the level of the old great gods. It was in the reign of Moctezuma I (1440–68) that the first large temple of Huitzilopochtli was built. And the great pyramid that was dedicated, after several amplifications, in the center of Tenochtitlan in 1487 bore two shrines, one for the worship of Tlaloc, and the other, for that of Huitzilopochtli.[38] As Aztec military and political successes multiplied, so did the Mexicas', and others', sense of the god's power. The exaltation of Huitzilopochtli that then seemed due led, so it appeared, to still further imperial gains, and so on in a mutually reinforcing process. Further, Mexica history was quite consciously and purposely reinvented early on in the imperial expansion – during, in fact, the reign of Itzcoatl (1428–40), the *tlatoani* who had led the revolt against the Tepaneca – to promote Huitzilopochtli to the highest rank in the pantheon, as one of the four sons of the creator gods.[39] Another purpose of this rewriting, or, more precisely, repainting of the Mexicas' past (the old picture histories were destroyed) was to establish as "fact" their Toltec heritage; and indeed generally to glorify their heritage in the eyes of their neighbors in the valley.[40]

The propaganda may not have easily undone those neighbors' scorn of the Mexica as crude upstarts. But they all soon found themselves with the choice of bending either to that message or to the reality of Mexica force. For in Itzcoatl's years most of the valley towns were overcome by the Triple Alliance, led by Mexica warriors, and more or less willingly incorporated into the expansive effort of the nascent empire. Moctezuma I, Itzcoatl's successor, then sent imperial forces outside the valley, as did the four subsequent *tlatoque* – Axayacatl (1469–81), Tizoc (1481–6), Ahuitzotl (1486–1502), and Moctezuma II (1502–20) – down to the time of the Spanish conquest. Each new ruler, having been chosen by high councils for his promise as warrior and leader, was expected to prove his worth by making new conquests. These led to the broadening of the imperial bounds by 1519 on the scale already suggested. By the time the Spaniards came, only a few pockets of resistance held out against Aztec pressure in central and southern Mexico.

Exactly what it was that drove the Aztecs of the Valley of Mexico to expand so fast and so far is a matter of vigorous debate among archaeologists and ethnohistorians. One persistent sort of explanation is demographic. It is possible that the growth of Aztec dominance coincided with the rising phase of a slow population cycle that had characterized central Mexico for many centuries past.[41] By this argument, simple need for food in the valley drove its inhabitants to conquer outside it, and to force their new subjects to provide tribute in kind and in labor. The rapid population growth of the city of Tenochtitlan-Tlatelolco itself probably created a particularly urgent demand for tributes of food and other supplies. This would have been an especially strong stimulus for expansion, since Tenochtitlan was the city of the Mexica themselves, the warrior heart of the Aztec body.

The demographic explanation of expansion is, however, open to objections of imprecision, circularity, and over-generality. Who can say what the precise increase of demand for food was in the valley between, say, 1350 and 1500, or if it was necessary for the Aztecs to overrun such a large area in order to meet it? To critics with such doubts, a stronger, but still materialist, line of explanation is that all levels of Aztec society clearly benefited from expansion. Supreme rulers – the *tlatoque* – were confirmed in power by conquests. The nobility – an almost wholly warrior class – gained wealth in land and tribute. Some of this wealth was passed on as patronage to subordinates, and so served to create political support. Influential middle groups in society, such as the priests and administrators whose ranks multiplied as the empire grew, were supported by booty taken in war and by the inflow of tribute that followed it. Social, as well as economic, gain went to the successful warrior. And in late Aztec times, in an ever more rigidly stratified society, martial prowess became the only practicable means of social ascent for the mass of people. Thus warfare and conquest, once embarked on, acquired a momentum of their own because many, or nearly all, saw chances for gain and glory in them.[42]

There is a danger, though, in advancing these pragmatic explanations for expansion. The risk is of making the Aztecs seem rational, twenty-first-century people, responsive to calculations of profit and loss. In reality, their mental world was anything but rational (in the modern sense), and it may well be that a highly distinctive set of ideas about how the universe functioned, an ideology grounded in religion, was the deepest source of their imperial drive. Huitzilopochtli, the minor tribal god of the Mexica elevated in the fifteenth century to the highest heavenly circles, was central in this scheme of things. The Mexica, and the other members of their alliance, did not simply feel the nationalistic urge to spread his cult that might have been expected. Rather, conquest and empire became essential to the proper worship of Huitzilopochtli; and without that proper worship, the belief was that the universe would cease to function.

One part of the exaltation of Huitzilopochtli was his close association with the warrior sun, Tonatiuh (as well as with the ancient, powerful, whimsical force of Tezcatlipoca, one of whose guises was as the young sun of spring and summer).[43] The passage of the sun across the sky was not seen as part of the perpetual natural order, but, in true Aztec fashion, as a constant battle. The battle, in this case, was against the stars' resistance. To keep up the fight, the sun (Huitzilopochtli-Tonatiuh) required to be fed with life itself, an essence to be found only in human blood. Hence, in practical terms, the working of the cosmos demanded continual offerings of blood, obtained by ritual killing.

The Aztecs, indeed, in acting out these beliefs, became perhaps the leading practitioners of human sacrifice of all time. Possibly the greatest of all Aztec ritual slaughters took place at the dedication of the great pyramid of Huitzilopochtli and Tlaloc, in the center of Tenochtitlan, in 1487. On that occasion as many as 20,000 victims may have rendered their life spirit to the gods.[44] Most of these, and most victims at any time, were captives taken in war. Only war could yield the needed supply of sacrificial blood. Thus conquest became part and parcel of the working of the Aztec universe. It is true that ritual battles, the famous "flowery wars" of Aztec Mexico, were staged among the three components of the Alliance, and between the Alliance and a few nearby polities, with the aim of yielding particularly valuable captives for subsequent offerings to the deities.[45] But in general, areas already overwhelmed could not be expected to continue supplying victims, except in the common enough case of rebellion, when military punishment would yield its crop. Territorial extension of combat, therefore, was inevitable.

It was convenient, of course, that expansion also produced tribute needed to sustain the valley's dense population: foodstuffs, cotton cloth in immense amounts, cacao beans, gold dust, and not least feathers – feathers of tropical birds, especially those of the quetzal from the south. Pursuit of these, according to Mexica merchants, seems almost to be have been in itself a reason for conquest, so highly were they valued for picture-making, their shimmering colors seeming to be "Shadows of the Sacred Ones" themselves.[46] Then again, the violence accompanying conquest, and the marching of armies across the land en route to the expanding frontier, had a usefully intimidating effect on previously subjugated polities. So did the constant cutting and plucking out of captives' hearts and the cascading of their blood down the temple stairways in Tenochtitlan. Provincial leaders were often brought in to witness these sights. War, religion, politics, and economics thus intertwined to reinforce both one another and also what became, after 1428, Aztec triumphal expansionism. Some of those who study the Aztecs suspect an element of design in this combination, seeing in it particularly the hand of Tlacaelel, a nephew of Itzcoatl, and a Machiavellian ideologue and kingmaker active almost to the end of the fifteenth century.[47] But it is hard to judge the role of design against that of circumstance in the creation of the Aztec "system."

Rational design seems in a sense, too, at odds with the Aztec mentality. These were an intensely religious people, or, better, a people who were intensely aware of inhabiting a world crowded with bustling, fickle, often malevolent spirits. The great god Tezcatlipoca was archetypical: "Smoking Mirror" was his name, and the fleetingness of vapors and of reflections in polished obsidian his protean nature. He was the creative force that gave children, but also a power that rejoiced to bring random, senseless destruction among humans.[48] In general, the sacred forces, large and small, that crowded in on everyday life were threatening; only constant appeasement through many minor rituals would keep them at bay. The guard must never be let down. The fierce Aztec prohibition of drunkenness, except on proper celebratory occasions, was aimed not so much at maintaining decorous public order as at denying hazardous spiritual forces an open doorway into human affairs.[49]

It took the Spanish invaders decades to reach even a simple understanding of the complexity of Aztec inner life. When they first entered the Valley of Mexico late in 1519, it was the physical, outward splendor of the scene that struck, indeed overwhelmed, them. The conqueror Bernal Díaz del Castillo later recalled that "when we saw all those cities and villages build in the water, and other great towns on dry land ... we were astounded. These great towns and *cues* [pyramids] and buildings rising from the water, all made of stone, seemed like an enchanted vision from the tale of Amadís."[50] The greatest of the towns was the island city of the Mexica themselves, with its twin centers of Tenochtitlan, and, 2 kilometers northwards near the upper shore of the island, Tlatelolco. The inhabited part of the island measured some 4 kilometers north and south and 2.5 kilometers east and west. By the time of the Spaniards' arrival those 10 or so square kilometers held a population of 200,000 or even 300,000 people.[51] Skirting the urbanized area, mostly on the south and west sides, were several square kilometers of *chinampas* – the artificial farming plots consisting of mud dredged up from the lake floor and held in place by submerged fencing of woven reeds. Fertile mud combined with constantly available water filtering in from the lake itself to produce remarkable yields of maize and other crops on *chinampas*. The technique had been long used in the Valley of Mexico, and was one that the Mexica had learned and applied to their island refuge. It provided the added advantage, in fact, of enlarging the island.

The city was clearly planned on a grid pattern, very probably in imitation of Teotihuacán (only 50 kilometers to the north-east), for whose immense ruins the Mexica had the deepest respect. The gridlines consisted of both streets and canals, oriented almost exactly in the cardinal directions. These directions were full of religious meaning for the Aztecs and other Middle Americans; the east–west axis, for instance, marked the movement of the sun day by day. The design of the entire city thus symbolized supernatural forces. Along most of the streets were citizens' dwellings. The canals running parallel to the streets in both cardinal directions made for simple delivery throughout the built area of food and other supplies, brought in by canoe from sources all round the lakes in the valley. They also allowed easy removal of waste, again by canoe.

The city had two great central spaces. One was a large market place in Tlatelolco, in the north of the island. There not only local goods were exchanged, but also imported items, such as clothing, jewelry, feathers, and rare stones, brought in by the *pochteca* – the often wealthy and high-status long-distance merchants among the Mexica, some of whom served also as information gatherers for the rulers of Tenochtitlan. They ranged far from the valley, sometimes indeed beyond the bounds of the Aztec empire. The second great space lay close the center of the island. It was a square enclosed by the *coatepantli* ("snake wall"), each side of which measured some 500 meters. This was above all a religious precinct, and thus the ideological heart of the Aztec state. In it were a ball court, a school for priests, a rack on which the heads of sacrificed victims were displayed – but above all monumental pyramids supporting temples of the major gods. Quetzalcóatl, Tezcatlipoca, and Xipe Totec (the flayed-skin god, symbol of renewal and thus of spring) had their shrines there. Towering over all else was the great pyramid carrying the twin temples dedicated to the worship of Tlaloc, god of rain and storms, and Huitzilopochtli, the Mexicas' own deity, their source of power, and their protector. It was on the steps and ledges of this pyramid that some of fiercest fighting took place when the Spanish found themselves trapped in Tenochtitlan in the early summer of 1520. Cortés had earlier placed an image of the Virgin Mary on the top of the pyramid as an assertion of Christianity and a challenge to Mexica belief. Now he and a few followers fought their way, against fierce opposition, to the top to destroy the temples and the sculpted figures of the gods inside them by fire. His success in doing so, as he reported to the Spanish king, "so much damaged [the Mexicas'] confidence that they began to weaken greatly on all sides."[52] But however shrewd Cortés's realization of the symbolic value to the Mexica of those temples, and however brave his feat in destroying them, the people of Tenochtitlan were not fatally dispirited. Within days they had driven the Spaniards, with great losses, from the island-city. Indeed, as the Spanish evangelizing priests who followed close on the conquerors' heels quickly discovered, often to their dismay, it took more than the destruction of temples and idols to uproot Mexican Indians' spirituality. Beliefs were deeply embedded in the minds of natives, and in the landscapes in which they lived their daily lives. Even more than for Christians, religion was not something that stopped at the church, or temple, door. Divine forces were a constant and ubiquitous presence.

INCAS

The Inca world, too, was one of encircling spirituality, but the edgy, high-strung quality that tints our image of the Aztecs was absent from it. Certainly the Andean mountain world was full of holy places and holy objects, as it still is: the Quechua word *huaca*, denoting sacredness of site or thing, is still often heard today, and the little roadside shrine or *apachita*, consisting of nothing more than a pile of stones, is a frequent feature of highland journeys. But in religion, as in much else, the Incas seem sober, measured, and subdued when placed beside the Aztecs, almost as if the greater physical height of their lands had cooled their psyches as much as it had the air that they breathed and in which their crops grew.

There was nothing subdued, however, about the rate with which the Inca state expanded in the century and a half before the European invasion. Its growth began in the late 1300s, perhaps two centuries after the Incas' arrival in the Cuzco valley of the southern Peruvian Andes, an event generally placed *c*.AD 1200.[53] They were one among many small ethnic groups taking advantage of the favorable microclimates provided by the high valleys. As with the Mexica, their place of origin is an open question. One of their own creation myths linked them to Lake Titicaca (some 300 kilometers south-east of Cuzco). But that is perhaps more indicative of a desire to connect themselves with Tiwanaku, the greatest of earlier polities in the southern sierra, than it is of their real origin.

The early Incas and their neighbors shared a social organization whose features still persist strongly in the central Andes. Communities were small, no more than villages close to farming and grazing land. The basic unit of society, apart from the family, was the *ayllu*, which seems fundamentally to have been a clan, a group of people descended from some common ancestor. An *ayllu* might extend to more than one village, though its members were required to marry within the group. *Ayllus* in the later, imperial period were governed by hereditary *kurakas*, though it is not clear when such positions became hereditary. *Ayllus* held land around their communities, which members could use as they needed it, to grow food and to pasture llamas and alpacas.[54]

Deeply ingrained into the communal life of these clans was the notion of mutual aid and responsibility, of a reciprocity that was an economic obligation, but even more a moral one.[55] People were expected to lend their labor to cultivate neighbors' land, and expected that neighbors would return the help in due course. All capable people collaborated to support the incapable – orphans, widows, the sick – with food and housing. They also collaborated to produce food offerings to local deities. Early leaders could perhaps call on the labor of *ayllu* members for their own, and communal, purposes. *Kurakas* of imperial times and later certainly did so, and they in turn had a responsibility to reward their subjects in various ways. But what services the early leaders could legitimately expect is unclear, as is much else in the pre-expansionary history of the Incas.

One thing is obvious enough, though: these many small highland polities were in competition for land and water. The Incas certainly took part, and very successfully, in these contests. In some cases they gained access to land and water through marriage alliances with neighboring groups; in others they used force, or the threat of it, to impose themselves. In the 1300s their successes increased, so that by the end of the century they dominated the region around Cuzco to a distance of perhaps 80 kilometers. The valley of Cuzco was by then full of villages and towns, set among irrigated maize fields and occupied by tens of thousands of people. Cuzco, the city, already equipped with large religious and governmental buildings, dominated the other settlements as the Inca capital.[56]

After 1400 the Incas began pushing beyond the Cuzco area, beginning a rapid military and political expansion that made them the rulers of much of western South America by the time the Spaniards appeared there in the 1520s. The start of this truly explosive growth has long been attributed to a single nobleman, Yupanqui, a son of the supreme Inca ruler Viracocha. His heroic success in defending Cuzco against the assault of a neighboring people, the Chanca, is traditionally seen as the initial surge of the energy that powered the empire's growth. The Chanca attack was long thought to have happened in 1438. Now, however, archaeological research puts it at least fifty years earlier. Some of the places that Yupanqui was thought to have conquered after the Chanca invasion are now found to have been under Inca control before it. And instead of the divine aid that, by the traditional account, enabled Yupanqui to defeat the Chanca, already existing, and powerful, Inca armies were most likely the key to his success.[57]

Despite these corrections to the previous semi-mythical story, Yupanqui existed and was clearly the first leader in the great imperial expansion. His military successes established him as the supreme ruler in Cuzco, the Sapa Inca ("Sole Inca"), as the emperors were known. Soon after his victory over the Chanca he changed his name to Pachacutec (or Pachacuti), meaning "cataclysm" or "remaker of the world." In doing so, he may have been imitating leaders of Wari who had also used that name, with possibly the broad aim of legitimizing Inca sovereignty by linking it, if only symbolically, to the power of that ancient place.[58]

If recent research has changed the date of the Chancas' defeat, so have the dates of Pachacutec's reign, and those of his successors, become less certain than was previously thought. Following Spanish chronicles, historians believed that he was in power until 1471; but that date is now far from sure. And if, as is now proposed, he was active before 1400, his reign (and life) would have been extraordinarily long if he ruled to 1471. A possibility exists that, as has happened elsewhere in the world, incoming Inca rulers adopted the name of their immediate predecessor. It is therefore conceivable, though only as speculation, that more than one man named Pachacutec may have ruled in Cuzco for a substantial part of the fifteenth century.[59]

Assuming, however, that there was in fact a single Pachacutec, and likewise only one of each of his successors, the Inca empire had only three rulers, including him, between his ascent to power and the arrival of the Spaniards. Although the dates of their reigns are now uncertain, there is absolutely no doubt that they oversaw a vast extension of Inca rule. Under Pachacutec the great central core of the empire came into being, consisting of the Andean highlands from current southern Bolivia, northward through the entire Peruvian Andes, and on into the southern highlands of present Ecuador. The large and rich polities of the Colla and Lupaqa peoples on the western shores of Lake Titicaca, in which Viracocha (Pachacutec's father) may have earlier shown a predatory interest, were among the notable groups now overcome.

But it was Pachacutec's successor, Tupac (or Topa) Yupanqui, who ruled during the greatest extension of Inca dominion. First, in the closing years of Pachacutec's reign, and then in his own reign during the final decades of the 1400s, he brought in a vast area of mountain and coast south from Titicaca, embracing much of the north-west of current Argentina, and extending down to the Río Maule in central Chile. He then widened the Inca realm, pushing its boundary eastward, down into the interior foothills of the Andes towards

Amazonia. The frontier also moved northward in his time, up into the highlands of what is now central Ecuador. The end result was a domain that extended 3,500 kilometers from north to south. One mighty blow struck by the Incas during this expansion was the capture on the northern coast of the Chimú kingdom, the largest political unit in Peru in the period between Tiahuanacu and the Incas. In overcoming it, the Incas removed their only possible challenger in power and status.

Final, but small, additions were made to Inca territory by the next Sapa Inca, Huayna Capac. Under him the Incas pushed a little further north in the Ecuadorian highland, possibly indeed a little way into present Colombia, and also a little farther inland in what is now eastern Bolivia. Huayna Capac was the last Inca ruler to live out his reign before the Spaniards appeared; he died in the mid 1520s. The slowing of expansion in his time may have been the outcome of natural restraints on imperial growth. The Incas were a highland people, unsuited both physiologically and psychologically to life at low altitudes. It is true that the desert coast was less difficult for them than the humid forests of the interior, their intrusions into which tended to end badly. But growth was finally possible only north and south, in the highlands. By c.1500 it had perhaps gone as far, some 1,800 kilometers above Cuzco and 2,500 kilometers below it, as the available means of administrative and political control allowed.[60]

As the empire expanded in the 1400s, Cuzco itself developed in line with its growing role as a power center. Pachacutec was long thought to have been the prime mover of this development. But, again, his influence is less clear than before, especially because the city is now known to have been quite large and splendid before his time. But there is no doubt that it grew in size and architectural grandeur in the 1400s. Much use was made of the finest Inca masonry, a good deal of which remains today for the visitor to see. The stones, often huge, were cut so exactly that they would fit and hold together without any mortar. So solid was the fit, in fact, that these drystone walls have survived severe earthquakes. Clay models were made of the proposed layout of the city, existing buildings destroyed where necessary, and the ceremonial center expanded. The chief structure of that center was the temple of the Sun, Coricancha – the "Court of Gold" – so called on account of its gold statues and the partial covering of its stone and adobe walls with sheets of beaten gold.[61] This construction was the visible expression of what became increasingly a state and imperial cult of the Sun (Inti in Quechua), which was conceived of as one aspect of a many-faceted sky god. Inti also came to be seen as the founder of the Inca dynasty: emperors drew legitimacy not merely from martial prowess, not merely from divine support, but from divinity itself.[62] Coricancha was also the point on which converged forty-one imaginary lines, or *ceques*, that led to significant points of spiritual or practical value around the city (shrines, for example, or the sites of springs). The appearance not just of the city, but also of its surroundings, became more magnificent as the 1400s progressed. The sides of the Cuzco valley were extensively terraced and irrigated, some of them becoming estates belonging to Inca nobles. The green of

57

cultivation on the slopes and the valley floor created what has been called a "park-like landscape" to surround the imperial capital.[63]

Of the many remarkable features of the Inca empire, the most striking is the speed of its growth. An explanation of this starts with natural conditions. The Andes are immensely rugged; but the difficulties of north–south movement are far smaller than those of moving east and west, since the mountain valleys run roughly parallel to the coast. The famous roads of the Inca, partly inherited from earlier times and partly their own creation, took advantage of these natural valley routes.[64] The roads were narrow, but unobstructed: they were closed to all but those traveling on the state's business. Along a total of 30,000–50,000 kilometers of road moved *chasquis* – relay runners bearing information and orders – and also, when called for, armies.

Imperial growth, though, was not so much a matter of outright conquest by armies as might be imagined. Rather, it seems to have been achieved by combining traditional practices of Andean reciprocity, now expanded to an imperial scale, with intimidation. It is likely that the Incas' defeat of the Chanca, and the boost to their existing power given by that victory, put them in a strong position to use the mechanisms of reciprocity, with underlying threat, to draw weaker groups into alliance with Cuzco. Inca leaders offered *kurakas* – lesser local leaders – gifts of valued items and grand public ceremonies of eating and drinking, in return for tribute and acknowledgment of dominance. Most local leaders in the central Andes, it seems, succumbed to this combination of blandishment and lightly veiled menace.[65] Inca expansion became, in consequence, a rapid and inexpensive affair. The greater the number of polities incorporated in this way, the heavier the pressure the Incas could apply to the next ethnic group they approached. From time to time, of course, they had to fight. But other methods would be tried first. A part of Tupac Yupanqui's successful strategy against the Chimú domain, for example, was reportedly to threaten the water supply crucial to that desert polity's existence.

Warfare may have become the prime means of enlarging the empire only when the Inca reached cultural areas lacking the ingrained reciprocal practices of the central Andes. This may have been another reason for the empire's limits settling where they did, in central Chile and southern Colombia. The people of these areas did not use systems of reciprocity, and so were not conditioned to succumb to Inca gifts. Certainly it was in these distant frontier zones that the Inca found the fiercest resistance. Huayna Capac spent many years in combat in the north, for a very small gain of territory.[66]

If the means of Inca expansion are fairly clear, the springs of it are harder to define. Initially, success against the Chanca may have created momentum of growth; and taking control of new areas may have become a constant necessity, to obtain goods for redistribution among already subservient local leaders. Then again, Inca individuals had an interest in imperial growth, since it yielded rewards for nobles in the form of land, animals, clothing, and other goods. Moreover, distinction in combat could mean advance in the governing hierarchy for nobles, and social and status gains also for commoners, who might become provincial *kurakas* on the strength of it.[67] The inevitable growth of the apparatus of state and religion also made expansion a temptation, if not a necessity, especially once a certain luxurious splendor became the rule in Cuzco. Part of the tributary labor demanded of newly incorporated regions went to support bureaucracy and elaborate religious cult.

In another sense also, religion spurred expansion. While the Incas had no tutelary god comparable to the Mexicas' Huitzilopochtli, in their imperial period their rulers were keenly conscious of their descent from Inti, the Sun. That sense of their divine origins gave them both confidence in undertaking conquests and the notion that anyone who failed to acknowledge Inca superiority was inviting attack and subjugation.[68] And, naturally enough, success in conquest and expansion only confirmed the Incas' sense that they had divine support.

As the empire expanded, the Inca applied to it an enveloping set of controls. These emanated from Cuzco, the supreme political and religious center (though in late times Tumipampa, in the south of present Ecuador, became a second imperial capital and a center of political and military power).[69] Through Cuzco passed the imaginary lines that divided the empire into its four parts: Chinchasuyu, the north-western quarter, embracing Ecuador and much of northern Peru; Antisuyu, the north-east; Cuntisuyu, the south-west; and Collasuyu, the south-eastern and largest section, comprising the Titicaca basin, highland Bolivia, and northern Argentina and northern Chile. Together these made up Tawantinsuyu, the "four parts together."[70]

The Sapa Inca, quasi-divine supreme ruler, normally resided in Cuzco, though he might, as the case of Huayna Capac shows, go off on long campaigns. Each quarter was governed by a lord (*apo* in Quechua), also usually based in the capital. These governors were generally close relatives of the emperor, members of one of the royal *panaka*s (clans descending from earlier supreme rulers). Below them came a long chain of officials, in strict hierarchy, chief among them the *toqricoq*, who were men from Cuzco, though not necessarily *panaka* members, sent to supervise affairs from various provincial capitals. Under them stood the *kurakas*, normally the hereditary lords of subjugated polities, and the highest-ranking locals in the system. Then followed further ranks of local supervisors, in charge of decimal units of households, from 10,000 down to 10 (though the numbers were not always exact). Outside this fixed hierarchy were census takers, who each year did a new count of imperial subjects so as to determine proper tribute levels, and inspectors, who surveyed and reported on the activities of other administrators.[71]

Tribute collection was a major purpose of the imperial enterprise. Tribute was not set directly in goods, but in labor obligations that produced goods. One type of labor tax was the *mit'a*, signifying a required period of service in the imperial armies, in public works of some sort (making roads or public buildings, for example), or in immediate attendance on the Sapa Inca or other high officers of state. Clearly the *mit'a* removed men temporarily, perhaps for quite long periods, from their homes. The other type of labor demand did not; it obliged local populations to work in farming or tending animals in or near their own communities. In each newly incorporated polity, Inca administrators divided productive land into three, not necessarily equal, parts: one each for support of the local population itself, of the state (including the *panakas* of Cuzco), and of the religious establishment. The labor of the community in question was then applied to each type of land, and the produce (typically potatoes, maize, quinoa, and llamas) distributed accordingly. Some of the food gathered might be placed in local, Inca-built, storehouses as sustenance for passing armies, a reserve against future famines, or simply to provide for people (widows, the elderly, and the sick) who could not feed themselves.

People subjected to these demands for labor were obviously likely to put up some resistance. To minimize it, and indeed generally to promote an acquiescent peace as far as possible, the Inca applied a number of precautionary measures across their expanding domain. One such was to resettle a quarter to a third of newly taken groups in other areas, so as to break up possible nodes of resistance. These forced migrants were called *mitimaes*, or *mitmaqkuna*. The same word was applied to trusted subjects who were shifted as colonists out to the periphery, there to act as models of good behavior, or perhaps to improve the working of promising farmlands, or to staff a resident frontier garrison.

Another technique of control was to break up potentially dangerous political structures. Generally, existing lineages of *kurakas* were left in place – if, as often happened, they had submitted to the Incas' typical combination of wooing and menace. Then they would be used as the agents of indirect rule. But where fighting had been needed, and the potential enemy remained strong, local leaders were killed, and the existing political unit fractured into smaller pieces. This was done to the large Chimú kingdom, for instance. In such cases, new local leaders would be assigned, and attached to Cuzco with the standard bonds of reciprocity. A further means of keeping *kurakas* in line was to remove their sons and heirs to Cuzco, for education in Quechua and in Inca practices. The children thus became both hostages and trainees for regional administrative offices. The most sacred *huacas* of subjugated peoples were also removed to Cuzco, with their own attendant priests, as another sort of hostage. (Gathering up the most revered idols of subject peoples in this way, however, was also a means by which the Inca concentrated Andean spiritual force in their own hands.) In a reverse process the Inca, as might be expected, had temples built in newly taken regions for the installation of their sun cult.[72]

Despite these, and other, stratagems of control, the empire was far from being as peaceful and orderly as has sometimes been thought. Internal revolts against Inca taxation and rule flared up continually, particularly in the more distant reaches of Tawantinsuyu, which, being the most recently incorporated, were the least well indoctrinated and least detached from their pre-imperial orientations and loyalties. Quito (the Ecuadorian provinces), for example, was a constant thorn in the Inca flesh. But even more central regions could be troublesome. The Aymara-speaking groups around Lake Titicaca, for instance, prosperous and powerful before the Incas' ascent, were both hard to conquer and hard to keep down. Pachacutec allegedly had to assault them three times, and they rebelled again in the time of Tupac Yupanqui.[73]

Nor were disturbances limited to the provinces, whether far or near. Rivalries in the governing nobility in Cuzco were endemic. Sapa Incas sometimes grew wary of military leaders whose successes in the field seemed to make them resistant to orders from the center. Conflict was particularly likely over the succession to the Sapa Inca-ship itself. The Andean tradition, which the Incas followed, was that leadership should go to the most able candidate (meaning, in the imperial Inca case, the man of greatest military promise). This opened the way for all sorts of intrigue and in-fighting, even if the range of contenders was limited to the previous Sapa Inca's sons, since he generally had many children by a variety of wives. The conflict could extend to multiple murders of rival male siblings. The best-known case of a succession struggle is precisely the competition between two sons of Huayna Capac, Huascar and Atahualpa, in the late 1520s. This was a particularly long and fierce fight, and a tragedy for the Incas, since it fatally weakened their state just as the Spanish arrived on the South American scene.

Nonetheless, the Inca realm was definitely a state, and the most remarkable political and administrative body produced by the Americas up to its time. The Aztec polity in Middle America was the closest comparable entity, but fell far short of the Inca creation in size and in economic and governmental organization. And nothing else that the Spaniards encountered came close even to Aztec sophistication.

LESS KNOWN CULTURES

SOUTH AMERICA

The largest political systems in South America outside Inca lands, at the time the Europeans arrived, were those of what is now northern Colombia: the Tairona, between the Sierra Nevada de Santa Marta and the coast, the Cenu, a little to the south-west, and the Chibcha (or Muisca), south-east again in the high valleys of the eastern cordillera of the Andes. All three were, by Inca imperial standards, tiny polities, with territories in the range of 10,000–25,000 square kilometers. They were, though, in the same size range as the Inca community before its imperial growth began c.1400, and after then are perhaps most readily comparable in territory and authority to the rich peoples, such as the Lupaqa, who lived autonomously around Lake Titicaca before the Incas overwhelmed them. Like these, the Chibcha and their neighbors were ethnic groups. But despite a feeling of shared origin among the members of each group, considerable social stratification had arisen in them. Hereditary elites provided warrior leaders, administrators of justice, and ruling chiefs whose power came in part from their contact with gods. These societies had a firm economic base in intensive, sometimes irrigated, agriculture, supplemented by hunting and by fishing in the large rivers of northern Colombia. They produced a variety of goods of high skill and art. The Chibcha mined and worked the emeralds found in their territory. The Tairona excelled in elaborating the shells they took from their Caribbean beaches. Chibcha, Tairona, and Cenu all produced excellent cotton textiles, as well as fine work in the gold in which Colombia abounds, and in a gold–copper alloy termed *tumbaga*.[74] This metalwork naturally impressed the Spanish. The first expedition to reach Chibcha territory, in 1536, reported excitedly back to Charles V on the "Bogotá" – a high-ranking, but not supreme, chief ruling from a town of that name. The Spaniards apparently mistook him for the Zipa, one of the two paramount chiefs in the Chibcha territory (the other being the Zaque),[75] writing "This Bogotá is the principal lord of this land, with many other nobles and chiefs subject to him. He is a personage of great wealth, because the natives say he has a house of gold and many rich emerald mines. His vassals honor him exceedingly; in truth, the Indians of this kingdom are very subjugated by their lords. He has conquered and tyrannized over much of the land."[76] Here, aside from the emphasis on wealth, there is a clear attempt by conquerors of smaller native groups to exaggerate the political accomplishments of their victims. It was important that they should seem as nearly like those of the Inca and Aztec as possible. The Zipa was certainly no Sapa Inca in embryo. But the Chibcha were locally powerful, which was one of the reasons for the Spaniards' naming their own colonial capital, Santa Fe de Bogotá, after a major town in the Zipa's domains. And that town grew in due course to be the national capital of Colombia.

Apart from the Chibcha, Tairona, and Cenu, the Colombian territory held, of course, many other chiefdoms, less developed than these in governmental practices, social complexity, and technical and artistic achievement. And the rest of what was to become Spanish South America (outside the Inca range) was peopled by a still greater variety of ethnic and cultural groups, ranging from moderately sophisticated village dwellers to the more elemental hunters and gatherers of, for example, the *pampas*.

One set of village dwellers with whom the Spanish came to have close contact were the Guaraní, who lived in parts of present eastern Paraguay, north-central Argentina, and southern Brazil. The total Guaraní population by 1500 may have been around 1.5 million.[77] Their villages consisted of a few large communal houses, in each of which lived a kin group comprising perhaps dozens of families. The head of the principal group was also the village leader, though his authority was mainly confined to relations with other villages. Internally, the Guaraní villages were run through agreement among heads of houses and elders. The Guaraní were members of the very large Tupían language group that extended far up into Amazonia and eastwards to the coast of present Brazil. They were farmers, growing, above all, maize and manioc. Women did the agricultural work and much else, including the making of pottery, baskets, hammocks, and maize beer. Men hunted and fished, providing supplements of protein to the basically vegetarian diet.

Fishers and farmers also were the Mapuche, on the western side of the mountains in the central zones of Chile. These people divided into three subgroups: the Picunche in the north, the Araucanians in the centre, and the Huilliche to the south of them. The name Araucanian has often been used for all three divisions. They were all tough and hardy people, resistant to both the Inca and the Spaniards after them. The Inca, indeed, called the Picunche "wild wolves" on account of their unwillingness to serve the state, and the crudeness, in the Inca view, of their agriculture[78] – even though the Picunche used irrigation ditches on the Inca pattern in their dry, middle-northern zone of Chile. Further south the Araucanians in the central valley of Chile found enough moisture to support rotation farming of maize, beans, and other crops. They bred llamas. Fishing in the Pacific supported coastal dwellers.

South of the small-group cultures, such as the Guaraní and Mapuche, that combined farming and animal-raising with hunting, fishing, and perhaps some gathering, lay the vast lands of the true hunter-gatherers: the people of the *pampas* and Patagonia, east of the Andes, and, over the mountains, those of the forests and islands of the west coast. The Tehuelche on the eastern plains and plateaux hunted the *guanaco* (the wild relative of the llama, alpaca, and vicuña), and the rhea (the wingless, ostrich-like bird native to the region). They lived in tent villages, each village jealously guarding its hunting ground. West of the mountains in southern Chile, and in Tierra del Fuego, dwelt a large number of different groups, speaking a variety of languages and dialects, generally on the move, but each with a recognized fishing territory. Collectively these peoples have been called "sea nomads." They depended on the mobility provided by hollowed-log canoes for their food supply of fish, seabirds, and shellfish. Of all the peoples of what was to become Spanish South America, these perhaps were the most egalitarian in social and political ranking, with respected elders guiding the affairs of extended families.[79]

Brazilian peoples

In the parts of South America that fell from 1500 onwards to Portugal, the range of native cultures, in social, political, and cultural organization, was far narrower than what the Spaniards were to find. Nowhere in the future territory of Brazil was there anything to match even the polities of northern Colombia, let alone organization on the Incaic scale.

Of the many dozens of tribes in the territory of the future Brazil, possibly the most advanced were the Potiguar, inhabitants of the easternmost section of the north coast. They were skilled in farming, hunting, and fishing. They were also powerful warriors, capable, according to Portuguese reports of the late sixteenth century, of putting 20,000 men into the field. With such forces they blocked Portuguese colonizing movement towards the Amazon.[80] The Potiguar were one of many tribes belonging to the Tupí-speaking group of people who inhabited the Brazilian coast. The name Tupinambá was applied in colonial times to many of the tribes living on the east coast. In the far south of Brazil were the Guaraní, whose culture area ran eastwards from Paraguay to the coast. The Guaraní language was a variant of Tupí, and there was little difference, either, between their lifestyle and that of the coast dwellers. The village consisting of several large houses, for instance, was standard from Paraguay to the north coast. Tupí villages had chiefs, and occasionally paramount chiefs could be found, commanding respect in several villages. But chiefs were mainly war leaders; the running of the villages was done by councils made up of the elders of the extended families inhabiting the great houses. Fierce warfare between neighboring Tupí tribes was common, though in this the Guaraní were something of an exception, being conspicuously docile (at least in the face of European colonization). The purpose of fighting may have been in part control of land for farming. But at least as important a motive was the capture of warriors for ritual killing and cannibalism. All the Tupí speakers lived by a combination of hunting, fishing, and farming. Their staple food was manioc, supplemented by peanuts. They also raised cotton. Farming was the work of women; men reserved themselves for hunting and warfare.

There is uncertainty still about the precise number and names of the coastal Tupí groups, but they are much better known and understood than the pre-contact peoples of the interior of Brazil. At least for the Tupí, early European explorers and settlers (Portuguese and others – notably the German Hans Staden) left first-hand descriptions. But by the time Europeans penetrated inland beyond the Tupí areas, mainly in the seventeenth century and later, many interior tribes had disappeared, either dissolved by flight or destroyed by disease.

One way to describe the peoples of the interior, though only with broad brushstrokes, is by the language they used. The Brazilian highlands, for example, from the north coast down to the tributaries of the Paraguay river, were peopled by the Gê speakers, possibly the first humans in Brazilian territory. These, partly because the soils of the interior are less fertile than those of the coastal plain, were poorer farmers than the Tupí, and consequently more dependent on hunting and gathering. They were valiant warriors, who strongly resisted Portuguese westward movement in the seventeenth and eighteenth centuries.

Further west still, in the forests of Amazonia, Arawak speakers predominated. The standard view of these people was for a long time that they were poor and unsophisticated farmers of slash-and-burn plots, limited to that sort of existence by the infertility of forest soils, and that they were therefore condemned to at least a semi-mobile life, as villages had to be close to the cultivated plots of the moment. But gradually archaeology has revealed a more complex and impressive human presence in Amazonia. Large areas in the flood plains beside rivers, and on top of the bluffs overlooking the flood plains, were intensively cultivated for so long that the typically poor soil of the rainforest was permanently altered, often for the better. Permanent villages developed in some regions, with broad, straight roads linking them. This improvement of the soil, with accompanying settlement, seems to have happened even in areas between the many rivers of the Amazon basin, but is mostly found along rivers, particularly in areas where terrain rises close to the banks. Those areas lie around the edges of Amazonia, since the vast center of it is plain of astonishing flatness. One such region is the Llanos ("Plains") de Mojos, now in northeastern Bolivia, and an area through which flow multiple rivers feeding into the Mamoré, a large tributary of the Amazon. Here many large, man-made mounds and even small artificial hills have been identified, built to provide burial places and dry space during floods, together with numerous roads, canals, and raised fields. In the past forty years or so such research as this has slowly given confirmation to sixteenth-century reports by Spanish explorers of Amazonia that the river banks were in places densely populated. It has also contradicted the previously accepted backward projection into the past of the lifestyles of twentieth-century native survivors that anthropologists had observed. That projection led to the belief that slash-and-burn farming, with resulting thin and scattered populations, had always predominated in Amazonia. Now it seems that agriculture was, before the 1500s, more advanced, settlements more substantial and stable, and the total population in the 5–6 million range.[81] That population was devastated by, above all, unfamiliar diseases after the Europeans arrived in South America, and never recovered in either size or accomplishment.

A third large language group – living along the streams flowing into the lower Amazon from the north, along the upper Orinoco, and in the present Guianas and their highlands – was that of the Carib speakers. They were often in conflict with their Arawak neighbors, and apparently indeed pushing south and east against them in late pre-contact times.

THE CARIBBEAN

Arawak speakers, including the Caribs, provide a human and cultural link between South and North America. "Carib" (caribe in Spanish) may have been a European version of "Galibi," the name of people in what are now French Guiana and Surinam whom the Caribs considered their ancestors, as they may well have been. "Carib" lives on in "Caribbean," the name of the sea in which lie the small islands – the Lesser Antilles – that the Caribs inhabited. Anthropologists and historians long thought that the Caribs were a quite distinct people from the Tainos, who lived further north and west, in the Greater Antilles. Then it seemed that the two were more similar than different. But now, once again, the contrasts are emphasized. The two groups spoke different versions of Arawak. The Tainos feared the Caribs, definitely the more warlike of the two cultures, as raiders and potential invaders. The Tainos' political units were larger and more complex, their arts and crafts more sophisticated, and their gods more numerous. Early European accounts of the Tainos do not mention cannibalism among them, but it was the Tainos themselves who told Columbus that the Caribs ate human flesh – using the word cannibal (deriving from Carib) to describe that behavior. The degree, or even existence, of cannibalism among the Caribs is uncertain, although, given that it was quite common in the lowlands of South America, they would not have been exceptional in that respect.[82]

A stronger tie than cannibalism, however – indeed a completely certain tie – between northern South America and the Lesser and Greater Antilles was language. At the time of Columbus's arrival in 1492, almost all the people of the large and small islands of the Caribbean spoke some variation of Arawak.

For that reason, the inhabitants of the Greater Antilles, especially, have often loosely been called "Arawaks." Their name for themselves, however, was Taino, meaning "noble" or "prudent."[83] This high self-regard reflected their relatively complex political and social behavior. By the late fifteenth century they had organized themselves into chiefdoms, the domains of *caciques* (headmen) – a term which the Spaniards picked up and carried to the mainland, applying it everywhere to Indian leaders of all levels of importance. Some *caciques* had authority in dozens of settlements, spread out over hundreds of square kilometers.[84] Territorially speaking, Taino chiefdoms took the basic form of the land bordering a river along its course from a mountain valley to the sea. This arrangement gave access to water, to a variety of land for cultivation, and to the shore and its resources. Fish, shellfish, and turtles figured largely in the diet. Like their distant Amazonian linguistic relatives, the Taino raised turtles, and fish also, in artificial ponds. Water- and land-birds were another source of protein. For carbohydrates, they farmed a variety of root crops: manioc (or cassava), sweet potatoes, peanuts, and others. They grew cotton and tobacco. Slash and burn was the method of farming in some areas. But for growing manioc, the staple of the Taino diet, the simple technique of planting in mounds of earth yielded bountiful returns for little effort.

Taino society in the Greater Antilles was clearly stratified, with chiefs receiving gifts from the newly harvested crops, and enjoying a monopoly of certain foods, among them iguanas (a local delicacy, though the Spaniards were never so persuaded). Chiefs' authority rested typically on such accomplishments as success in war, and possession of a large, seagoing dugout canoe. Their earthly successes were seen as the expression of divine force working in them. They and their relatives lived in separate villages, consisting of large dwellings that housed several related families. Commoners typically inhabited different groups of houses near fields or rivers. Palm thatch was the standard building material. A feature of Taino society that it had in common with the Middle American mainland to the west was the playing of the ball game (here called *batey*), sometimes, it is thought, to give expression to rivalries between chiefs, and hence, as on the mainland, to those between divine powers as well.

AND, FINALLY, FULL CIRCLE TO MEXICO

At the time of the Spanish invasion, *c.*1520, chiefdoms were also to be found in large parts of Mexico, most of them outside Aztec control. One such area, already described, was the Yucatan peninsula, where the descendants of the Classic and Post-Classic Maya polities lived on in quite small and simple polities. Further west, in southern Mexico proper, the Mixtec of that same time were grouped in small towns and kingdoms, some of which were, in the decades before the arrival of the Spanish in Mexico, under strong Aztec influence. But farther west still, and northwards, mainly in what is now the state of Michoacán, the Spanish found another major native culture, that of the Tarascans (or Purépecha), that had resisted Aztec attacks with success. This was a polity larger than anything else in Mexico except for the Aztec empire itself. The capital of the Tarascan domains was Tzintzuntzan, a town on the shore of Lake Pátzcuaro in Michoacán. The Tarascans were the most adept metal workers in Mexico, skilled miners, smelters, and beaters of the copper in which their area abounded.

North of central Mexico, as the land grew dryer and less productive towards the *altiplano*, cultural levels were simpler, and political units smaller. Many minor native groups occupied this fringe zone. Over some of them the Aztecs managed to establish control (especially north-eastwards from the center). But the people of the *altiplano* itself, again many different groups, remained outside the Aztec domain. The Aztecs, in fact, had little reason to try to bring them into it. For almost all the northern peoples were hunter-gatherers, subsisting on the small animals and edible cactus leaves and fruit that the high plateau provided. The cost and effort of subduing them would have been far greater than the value of any tribute they could have sent to Tenochtitlan. The Nahuatl speakers of the center called these people generically the Chichimeca, "of the lineage of the dog." But since the only dogs in pre-conquest Mexico were small creatures esteemed for their edible qualities, the name seems less likely to have been contemptuous than simply a totemic description.[85] In the second half of the sixteenth century the Spaniards came to know and respect the Chichimecas' mettle. Unlike the high cultures of central Mexico, the Spanish found great economic attraction in the north in the form of abundant silver ore. The various nomadic tribes resented the ensuing invasion of their hunting and gathering grounds. The confrontation lasted forty years or more, and cost the Spanish more men and money than the defeat of the Aztecs.

Native Mexico, then, was more than the Aztecs, and South America was more than the Incas. In some respects, indeed, these two best-known cultures of Middle and South America reached lesser peaks of accomplishment than earlier cultures had achieved. In writing, sculpture, and, many would say, building, the Maya surpassed the Mexica a half-millennium before Tenochtitlan began to rise amid the lakes of the Valley of Mexico. The coastal cultures of Peru, some of them still further back in time, outdid the Incas in artistry in cloth and clay. But no earlier culture, as far as can be told, had created political structures to equal those of the Aztecs and the Incas in complexity and physical size. The Spaniards, encountering these states, were fearful, and rightly so. To master such peoples, however, would bring wealth and glory beyond anything that America had so far offered.

[3] IBERIA AND AFRICA

VOYAGES AND ISLANDS

THE originality of Columbus's planning, and the enormous innovations that resulted from all four of his expeditions, cannot be denied. But equally undeniable is that his voyages were the outcome of two centuries of Iberian exploration and expansion. Many others had sailed at least parts of the ocean that he crossed. He, his captains, and their men drew on an enormous fund of knowledge and practical experience that Iberian seamen had accumulated in the Atlantic from about 1300 onwards. Hulls, sails, provisioning practices, navigational techniques for the Ocean Sea, as the Spaniards called the Atlantic, were, by Columbus's time, well tried and proved. Above all, perhaps, there existed a psychology of deep-sea voyaging. Ancient fears of impenetrable Torrid Zones and fatal Green Seas of Darkness had yielded to experience in the tropical waters west of Africa. Columbus's men became alarmed, to be sure, as he pressed ever further west in September and October of 1492. But that was not because they feared mysterious, mythical dangers (and much less dropping off the edge of a flat earth). Their concern was practical. They had sailed an unprecedented distance westward with the wind behind them. Would their ships and supplies suffice for the inevitably much slower return journey eastward?[1] (In the event, Columbus led them back in early 1493 by a more northerly course, again with following winds. His finding of that airstream from the west, and his consequent definition of a looping route from southwest Europe to the Caribbean, and back, were among his greatest feats; though even for this there was a partial precedent.)

Stirrings in the Iberian lands of movements to south and west can be seen in the late thirteenth century. Catalans, long active voyagers and traders in the Mediterranean, appeared at that time off the Atlantic coast of Morocco, and perhaps pushed further south as far as Senegal.[2] It was in those same final years of the 1200s that Genoese sailors are thought to have reached the

Canaries, perhaps also on their way down the African coast. From then on, the Genoese, among the greatest of Mediterranean merchant-venturers, were to be closely associated with Spanish and Portuguese voyaging in the Atlantic. In the early fourteenth century other Genoese explored the Canaries, and possibly settled there for several years. A Catalan chart of 1339 shows most of the Canary Islands correctly placed, along with most of those in the Madeira group, to the north. By 1350, Spaniards from Mallorca and Andalusia, and more Genoese, had visited the Canaries to trade or take slaves from the islands' population.[3] In the mid 1300s, also, the Azores may have been located, though the definitive discovery is usually placed in 1427, when a Portuguese from the Algarve (the southernmost province of the country) put the group on the map. It is impossible, though, to say for sure when these various island clusters were first sighted. Throughout the period so far discussed, and in fact long before it, fishermen from Portugal and the north coast of Spain had been pushing out into the Atlantic. They may have seen much that was never written down. It is absolutely certain, however, that they created a fund of experience on which later voyagers drew.

The movement out into the Atlantic coincided with a series of technological advances in ships and navigation that accelerated it. Some might argue that without these changes the expansion could not have happened; but it is worth remembering that the Norsemen had reached North America, via Iceland and Greenland, c.AD 1000, and perhaps maintained contact for several centuries after then, without the benefit of these advances.[4] And the voyages of Iberians and Genoese no doubt themselves forced the pace of change, in a typical example of the mutual influence that links technology with the historical environment in which it exists.

The importance of the magnetic compass for long-distance sailing needs no emphasis. The compass was possibly a Chinese invention. It was first described in Europe in the late 1100s, and was in use in the Mediterranean by then. The portolan chart, drawn from bearings taken by compass, and allowing plotting of a course between ports over the open sea, was being used by Italians by the start of the fourteenth century.[5] Ships could be more easily kept on course, and more easily maneuvered, if fitted with a rudder hinged to the stern-post. This replacement for the awkward steering sweep is supposed to have had Baltic origins, and had been adopted by Spanish shipbuilders by the 1280s.[6] Agility, and speed also in some wind conditions, were improved as well by adoption of the triangular lateen sail. The lateen had its origins in the eastern Mediterranean. Its use enabled a vessel to "point higher" – that is, to sail more nearly into the wind – than could be managed with the square canvas typical of Atlantic ships of medieval times. When, early in the fifteenth century, shipwrights in southern Portugal and southwestern Spain mated this sail to a new, shallow-drafted, dhow-like hull, Portuguese and Spanish sailors found themselves equipped with an almost ideal vehicle for exploration: the caravel. This was a nimble, speedy vessel, just as good for crossing oceans as for probing unknown coastlines. A crew of twenty could manage the three big lateens carried by the typical caravel of

30–50 tons. The hull was capacious enough to hold many weeks' stores for so small a crew. The caravel, though of cockleshell size, was a long-range vessel. It was an efficient tool which opened up the western and southern Atlantic to European access.

Having the right tool is an immense help in doing a job well; but it does not necessarily lead the holder to embark on the task. Motive must be present, and, preferably, propitious circumstances as well. In the late Middle Ages, circumstance and motive converged in the Iberian lands in a way that goes far towards explaining why this rather remote part of Europe became the base from which western expansion began.

First was geographical position. This simple, passive, fact should be given its full weight in accounting for the Iberian lead. First, Iberia stood as the junction between the ancient world of the Mediterranean and the nascent world of the Atlantic. And if there was a more definite place where those two worlds dovetailed together, it was the part of the south coast of the peninsula that faced the Atlantic: Spain west of Gibraltar, and the Algarve coast of southern Portugal (to which must be added, a little further north, the splendid harbor of Lisbon in the Tagus estuary). Here it was that Mediterranean technology in shipping was adapted to Atlantic conditions, and the resulting caravels taken to sea by men long accustomed to the greater scale and severer challenges of the great ocean. Here, also, Mediterranean merchant techniques and ambitions, carried westward by the Genoese and others, found an Atlantic home, and did their part to propel the ships of Iberian explorers outwards.

Again, the Iberian peninsula projects south and west into the Atlantic from the main mass of Europe, simply giving explorers sailing from it towards Africa or America a head start of 1,000 kilometers or more over men putting out from northern European ports. More important, ships departing on southwestern or southern headings from Lisbon, the Algarve, or southern Spain immediately found themselves with following winds and currents to carry them quickly to the Madeira group, the Canaries, and points south and west. Getting back, to be sure, was a slow business, at least until it was discovered that a north-west course from the islands eventually brought ships into the westerlies of the North Atlantic, which would return them swiftly to the north of Portugal or Spain. It was supposedly while taking advantage of this wind pattern that Portuguese boats encountered the Azores in 1427.[7] This circular track anticipated on a smaller scale the transatlantic loop that Columbus was to define at the end of the century.

Iberians, then, were well positioned, geographically and technically, for expansion. What of will and cause? The least complex aim was profit. Late medieval Europe was short of gold. Gold was known to come from Africa. It arrived on the coasts of Morocco and Algeria from unknown sources in the interior. As early as 1291 the two great Spanish kingdoms of Iberia, Castile and Aragon, made a treaty dividing between them rights to conquer and explore in north-west Africa: Castile in Morocco, Aragon in Algeria and Tunis.[8] Though the time was still not ripe for Spanish incursions into northern Africa, and little progress was made on this front for two centuries, the lure of gold remained strong, and was a powerful incentive for the Portuguese voyages of the fifteenth century that finally carried Europeans into the Gulf of Guinea and close to the origins of West African gold.

A more powerful drive for at least southward movement had been, however, deeply seated in the Iberian psyche long before gold began to exercise its draw. In AD 711, in what was perhaps the single most significant event in recorded Iberian history, Muslims had invaded the peninsula across the Strait of Gibraltar from Africa. Over the following two decades they occupied all but small, isolated areas in the north. For the next five and a half centuries, in the case of Portugal, and for almost the next eight, in the case of the Spanish kingdoms, gradual recovery of territory and reimplantation of Christianity – collectively known now as the Reconquista, the Reconquest – were rarely far from Iberians' minds. Progress was intermittent. But in the twelfth century, the example of crusades to the Holy Land took root in Iberia, and helped spur a renewed, and successful, assault on Islam. By 1300 Portugal was again entirely Christian, and only the emirate of Granada, in present south-eastern Spain, remained in Moorish hands elsewhere.

The model and spirit of crusade, now reinforced by successes in the peninsula, made Spaniards and Portuguese think of carrying the fight across the water into northern Africa. The freeing of Jerusalem itself came to seem a possible objective. (It remained one until much later; Columbus himself hoped that the wealth he might find would contribute to its liberation.) But, far short of that, any pressure or attack on Muslim North Africa would weaken Islam: direct assault, diversion of trading profits into Christian hands, piracy, plunder – all could be placed under the heading of crusade. The push down the west coast of Africa came to be included in this religious effort, because it held out the ultimate prospect, after an eventual rounding of Africa's southern tip, that Islam would be outflanked on the south. This would be an especially powerful move if contact could be made with the mythical medieval figure of Prester John, a Christian ruler reputed to hold sway in eastern Africa, or possibly some point still further east.[9]

Southward progress was, however, interrupted for several decades after 1350 or so, as problems that generally afflicted fourteenth-century Europe took their toll also in Iberia: the Black Death, war, and internal social conflict. Castile, by now by far the largest kingdom in the peninsula, and the Spanish territory that possessed Atlantic shores and experience, suffered severe political and social disruptions for a century. Portugal, already more organized and stable than its Spanish neighbors before the troubles began, recovered sooner. By 1400 it was centered under a powerful and popular monarch, John I (1385–1433), the first of the Avis dynasty. And, although exploration was not to be organized on a large scale by the Portuguese state until late in the fifteenth century, nonetheless this absence of internal struggle (and of the disorder and waste it caused) seems to have enabled the Portuguese to push outward throughout the 1400s with a determination unmatched by the Spaniards or any other European people.

PORTUGAL IN AFRICA AND THE ATLANTIC ISLANDS

A clear statement that the Portuguese had emerged from the doldrums of the late 1300s was their famous attack on the port city of Ceuta, across the strait from Gibraltar, in 1415. This was intended by John and his eldest son, Duarte, as the first step in a crusade-like subjugation of Muslim Morocco. John had in fact first thought of assaulting Islam in Granada, but desisted, apparently under pressure from Castile.[10] North Africa was a closer target, and Ceuta fell quickly, yielded satisfactory loot, and soon had a strong Portuguese garrison. Other Moroccan towns and territories, however, were more stubborn. Despite much effort, focused by another of John's sons, Prince Henry, over the following five decades, the Portuguese managed to do little more than set up a few fortresses on the coast south and west of Ceuta. Tangier, another early Moroccan objective of the Portuguese, did not fall until 1471.

Meanwhile, however, Portuguese seafarers pushed back the limits of knowledge of the African coast. That Cape Bojador, 1,500 kilometers south-west of Ceuta, had been reached in the fourteenth century is clear enough from a Catalan atlas of c.1375.[11] But it still, fifty years later, seems to have marked the boundary between the familiar and the fabulously hazardous zone of the tropical Atlantic. Finally in 1434 a mariner named Gil Eanes, dispatched by Prince Henry ("the Navigator," though in truth his own navigations were minimal), took his ship around round Bojador (after, reportedly, fifteen attempts).

From then on, progress quickened. Although Henry continued sending exploratory ships southward, most of the running was made by private expeditions in which hope of profitable trade was mixed in growing proportions with discovery. In 1444 the Portuguese reached Cape Verde, the westernmost projection of Africa. By the early 1460s, the explorers were almost around the bulge and faced a coastline that stretched before them south-eastward and then eastward. By this time Africa had long since proved itself a profitable venture. Sources of gold began to be found early in the 1440s; but the Portuguese quickly discovered that for them the richer prospects were in slaving. A man named Antão Gonçalves has the unenviable distinction of being the first Portuguese to ship African slaves back home from the mainland, after taking them in what is now northern Mauritania in 1441. He captured only two; but the example inspired more ambitious imitators, so that by the 1450s the number of slaves entering the European market annually through Lisbon and ports along the southern Portuguese coast had reached 700 to 800.[12] So began the grim story of Portuguese slave shipments from Africa to Europe, and then to America, that over the ensuing four centuries would run into the millions.

To handle the growing trade in slaves, gold, and other items such as red pepper, cotton, and ivory that became available as more of the coast was opened up, the Portuguese built along it from the late 1440s a chain of fortified trading posts. Only much later, and above all in Mozambique in the south east of the continent, did Portuguese colonization in Africa take the form of inland movement and occupation of the land. Neither in the fifteenth century nor later did Portugal have the men or the money to conquer, settle, and organize territory in most of its empire. But the trading post mode of colonization owed at least as much to the large Italian, above all Genoese, participation in Portuguese exploration and trade as it did to Portugal's own limitations. Small trading colonies were what the Genoese and Venetians had used in the Black Sea and the eastern Mediterranean to channel Asian goods into European markets. The castle or small fortified city serving to focus and protect exchange was the standard Mediterranean form of overseas settlement. The Portuguese, with many Genoese in their midst from the fourteenth century on, adopted it. It was the sort of colony that Columbus, himself a Genoese, still naturally expected to install on the large Caribbean islands, as late as the end of the fifteenth century.

In the Atlantic islands that Portugal reconnoitered at the same time as the African coast, however, things went differently. Here there was no native population – except in the Canaries, where a people often called the Guanches lived. These seem to have descended, rather distantly, from Berber and black origins in the north-west and west of Africa. They were part-nomadic farmers, arranged in tribes under authoritative lords who proved well able to organize them for fierce resistance to outside interference.[13] The Guanches' fighting abilities, though, were not enough to protect them from Europeans' desire for slaves. In the late 1300s, long before the first West African slaves were shipped to Portugal, Castilians, Frenchmen, and Italians, as well as the Portuguese, had been raiding the Canaries for Guanche slaves. Nonetheless, apart from slaves, the Canaries offered very little in the way of immediately available exports. Nor did Madeira, the Azores, or the Cape Verde Islands (also uninhabited), found by the Portuguese early in the 1450s.[14]

In the Azores, Madeira, and the Cape Verde group, then, the Portuguese had to settle in order to realize the economic possibilities that these territories gradually revealed. (There was no Portuguese settlement of the Canaries, partly because of native resistance, and partly because of Castile's strong competing claim to the islands.) Madeira, located before the middle of the fourteenth century, was the first target of Portuguese colonization in the Atlantic. The name means "wood" in Portuguese, and reflects the first impression that the islands left on early visitors. One sort of tree yielded a rich red dye. Both this and timber were sent back home by the first settlers, who took up residence in the 1420s. In the early days, fish was the basis of the islanders' diet. But, as woodland was cleared, farming began. Madeira's virgin soils, enriched by the ash from burned vegetation, proved excellent for wheat. By 1450 half the wheat grown was being exported to Portugal. Water mills had been built by then to provide flour locally. Cattle and grapes thrived similarly. But Madeira hit its full agricultural stride with the introduction of sugar cane, probably from Sicily or Valencia. The first refining mill was set up in 1452. In 1455 sugar production had reached almost 70,000 kilograms, and in the following year, sugar was first exported to England.[15] The creation of sugar estates on Madeira was a sign of things to come for centuries ahead in the Atlantic world (and outside it, in other westernized regions also, for that matter). These were the first plantations – the first demonstration that the tropics and the semi-tropics could provide, cheaply and abundantly, foodstuffs for which Europeans had a potentially immense appetite but could produce locally only with great effort and cost. Further, the sugar plantations in Madeira were the first to be worked by slaves, brought in from Africa and the Canaries in the 1460s to do the hot, heavy sort of work that Europeans shunned away from home.[16] These slaves added to a swelling population in Madeira that passed 2,000 in the 1460s.

In other matters, the colonization of the Madeira group was less innovative, but it still played an important transitional, or transmitting, role in the broader Atlantic progression. Both the wheat and the sugar trade were run in part by merchants from the Mediterranean (Catalans and Italians), as well as by Portuguese. That immensely important commercial and economic participation of Italians, especially Genoese, in all Portuguese expansion, is visible again here. Peninsular Jews also had their part in the sugar trade. When, a century later, the far vaster sugar industry of Portuguese Brazil began its growth, foreign participation, though now from north-western Europe, would again be central to its success.

Similarly, in administration, Mediterranean precedents left their mark in Madeira. Most of the responsibility for organizing government fell to Prince Henry of Portugal, after his elder brother, Duarte, by then king, made him in 1433 a lifetime donation of the islands. Henry in turn split them up into three hereditary and perpetual captaincies, to whose lords, titled "captains-donatary," he gave great powers, including jurisdiction (the administration of justice) and monopoly control of productive activities. The model for this system was in the eastern Mediterranean of post-crusading times, when the Italians, Catalans, and French had used similar procedures in creating settlements there.[17] The same system was set up in Brazil once Portuguese settlement started there in the early 1500s. Once more, as with technology, commercial practices, and the trading post mode of settlement, currents from the Mediterranean can be seen flowing into the Atlantic, with Portugal providing the conduit.

Things went very much the same way in the Azores, when finally, in the 1460s, thirty and more years after the initial discovery, the Portuguese began to settle this group in earnest. Wood and dyes, then cattle and wheat, provided exports and wealth. The cooler, more northerly climate, however, prevented the Azores from following Madeira into the sugar business. The close tie between slavery and plantation agriculture, strongly suggested by the early history of Madeira, is confirmed by the almost total absence of slavery in the Azores. Just as in Madeira, however, captains-donatary were appointed to the Azores, with the same sweeping administrative, judicial, and economic powers.

The Cape Verdes, too, were assigned to captains-donatary after their discovery in the 1450s. Here, though, in contrast to the islands further north, lack of rain hampered farming. Attempts to grow sugar had little success. Other resources were scant, and the islands were far from home. The Portuguese state had, consequently, to step in to some extent to maintain settlement in the late 1400s. The crown, for example, granted settlers a special permit in 1466 to trade in African slaves. The presence of Africans from Guinea, and the relative absence of Portuguese women, led quickly to race mixture. Three of the islands had stable, if small, populations by the beginning of the sixteenth century, with Santiago being by then the best-established colony. But no settlers were drawn to the other six islands until 200 or more years later.[18] The Cape Verdes were a useful way station for Portuguese shipping along the African coast. But their part in the broader Atlantic expansion of Portugal was small.

AFRICA

The part of the African coast that the Portuguese began to move along in the 1460s – the shores of the great western bulge of the continent that faced southwest or south – was, with its hinterland, soon to become so closely tied to Atlantic affairs in general, and American affairs particularly, that it is worth turning aside here briefly from Iberian matters to place it on the historical map. To that coast, and the many different peoples living along it, Europeans gave the name "Guinea." Beyond this Guinea coast, as the shoreline again turns south at the modern Cameroons, lay another part of Africa, first revealed to Europe by Portuguese explorations late in the 1400s, that would also be closely tied to Atlantic and American affairs. This is West Central Africa. It was not given any generic name to correspond with "Guinea." But the names of two large kingdoms there, Kongo and Ngola, became familiar to Europeans and to Iberians in America (each sited very roughly where the modern countries with similar names lie).

These African regions – Guinea and West Central Africa – were of interest to Europeans, and European colonists in the Americas, above all as sources of slaves. A commonly accepted generalization, both now and in the centuries of transatlantic slaving, is that the slaves from those parts of Africa were valuable because they could perform heavy manual work in hot conditions – something to which many native American people proved unsuited, or at least strongly averse. That ability was the result of their adaptation to tropical climates and environments.

The African areas from which almost all slaves came were indeed in the tropics. But it is important to recognize how wide a variety of environments was present there. The variety contributed to the slaves' possessing abilities and knowledge that made them desirable to potential owners for many reasons besides their physical strength and endurance.

The northernmost area from which slaves originated was the vast savanna – grassland with occasional trees – that lies to the south of the Sahara desert and stretches 6,000 kilometers across the continent from the Atlantic coast to the Red Sea.[19] Water supplies are irregularly available in the savanna. The most prominent source of water in its western half is the great Niger river, which rises only 300 kilometers from the sea in western mountains, loops up inland to the north-east through the savanna and briefly into the Sahara, and then, 300 kilometers east of Timbuktu, down again south-eastward to enter the Atlantic in what is now Nigeria. Rain also falls on the savanna, mostly in the months of the northern hemisphere's summer, and more abundantly in the south than up towards the edge of the desert. The rain is sufficient, obviously with regional variations, to make the savanna an enormous farming region. The staple foods traditionally grown were sorghum and millet, both domesticated in this part of Africa millennia in the past. Of the two, sorghum can thrive on less water, and so was commoner in the drier, more northerly, parts of the savanna. Those same northern areas, closer to the edge of the desert, were also used for raising cattle, and to a lesser extent horses (for military use) and camels and donkeys (for transport).

Millet and cattle were also important products of a different, far distant, savanna region, 1,600 kilometers to the south of the mouth of Niger and bordered, in fact, on its north side by another of the great rivers of Africa, the Congo. Though smaller than the northern savanna, this one, too, stretches deep into the interior – more than halfway across the continent, indeed.

Between the two savannas, and extending west along the Guinea coast, lay (as it still does) an imposing area of tropical rainforest, second in area only to Amazonia. Many of the peoples of these forests were farmers. Their major food crops varied from place to place. In farthest western Africa a native African variety of rice was grown, in fields watered by rain rather than in the paddies typical of Asia. Eastward along the coast, as far as the Cameroons, people grew and ate yams above all else. Then, to the south and east, in the forests of the Congo basin, bananas and plantains were the staples. The forest farmers also raised small domesticated animals, such as goats and poultry.

Thus slaves taken to America from West and Central Africa were not simply used to laboring in more or less hot and humid tropical conditions, but knew how to work the soils of such areas to produce food, and how to breed and tend animals, from goats to cattle, that would provide meat, milk, and hides. A slave from the forested coast of Guinea would be to some extent at home – in the sense of physical environment, at least – in the forests of eastern Brazil, northern Colombia, or southern Mexico. Equally, the slave from an upper area of the northern savanna would be to some degree in his element on the dry grasslands of northern central Mexico or of the Argentine pampas.

To the skills that either of those slaves might have brought from his homeland in raising crops on forest soils, or tending animals on grazing lands – the latter being a skill, it is worth remembering, possessed among American natives only by the camelid raisers of the Andes – should be added other abilities valued by European slave buyers across the Atlantic. One was woodworking, as demonstrated by a long history of wood carving in West and Central Africa. Another was clothmaking, from locally grown cotton spun into thread and then woven on hand looms, and often dyed. There were building skills in adobe, wood, stone, and thatch. But perhaps most attractive of all to potential buyers of slaves in America were Africans' abilities with metals. Both the northern and southern savannas produced and worked copper, sometimes also alloying it to make brass. Still more impressive was West African refining of iron, particularly on the northern edge of the rainforest, where abundant wood supported smelting of iron from local ores. Refiners there developed a type of furnace which used pre-heated air to yield iron of very high quality – which in turn was further refined into steel as good as anything that Europe produced in early modern times. West Africans made their good iron and steel into effective tools and weapons. Given this tradition of skill, it is no wonder that from the early sixteenth century onwards blacksmithing was a common occupation for African slaves (and soon freedmen as well) in Spanish America.[20] They already possessed knowledge that American natives had to acquire, either from them or from Spanish ironworkers. Middle and South American peoples had worked a variety of metals: gold, silver, copper (and, from it, bronze) – but never iron.

Another welcome trait of at least some African slaves taken to the Iberian colonies was their prior familiarity with Christianity. This was so mainly of slaves from Central Africa exported in the seventeenth century and later. The Portuguese in those parts made efforts to establish Christianity there that had some success. African religions were, generally speaking, quite different from Christianity – with, for example, varied local deities in contrast to the single Christian god, and attribution of powers to ancestors and multiple spirits. But Africans were perhaps more open than Europeans to new revelations of spiritual force, and ready to incorporate them into their beliefs. Thus Christianity, though alien, was not unacceptable to them – although, like American native people exposed to Spanish preaching, they would not accept it as a replacement for their own beliefs, but only as something to be added to them. So, for example, people in the kingdom of Kongo, where the Portuguese began teaching Christianity in the 1490s, came to believe that religious beings whom they had long regarded as local spiritual forces were, in fact, Christian saints and angels with universal existence and powers.[21] There were, nonetheless, other local spiritual entities that did not coincide with anything Christian, and they continued as objects of devotion as before.

Slaves from Central Africa were sent above all to Brazil (an estimated 180,000 between the early sixteenth century and 1650, and the vastly greater number of 3,135,700 between 1650 and 1820 – in contrast to only some 167,000 to Spanish America in the whole c.1500–1820 period.)[22] A great majority of all slaves taken to Brazil were, in fact, these partly Christianized Central Africans. In West Africa – the enormous but vague region of "Guinea" – the Portuguese were less active in conversion. Since Spanish America received far fewer slaves from Central Africa than from West Africa, its intake of slaves was less conversant with Christian beliefs, although far from resistant to absorbing them once in America. Those probably least inclined to do so were people originating from the northern savanna. Their homelands lay, by 1500, on the fringes of the world of Islam – a monotheistic and exclusive religion, similar in those respects to Christianity.[23]

Buyers of Africans newly shipped to America may have been happier when their purchases were already familiar with Christianity. But, of course, the primary identity of incoming Africans was not Christian, but slave. For many of those sold in Africa to the transatlantic shippers this was not a novel status. Enslavement had been common in Africa for many centuries before Europeans entered the trade in the 1400s. Some slaves had been held by other Africans, and had stayed more or less close to home, while others had been exported across the Sahara desert to North Africa, or eastward to destinations along the shores of the Indian Ocean. As Islam expanded southward into Africa, Muslim states in the north of the continent and in the Middle East, beginning in the period between the eighth and tenth centuries AD, took a growing part in the already existing export trade. They used male slaves as soldiers and adminis-trators, and some also as domestic servants. Women also were bought for domestic service, some of them becoming concubines. Many slaves were orig-inally captured in the frontier religious wars waged during the Islamic expan-sion, and then sent to be sold in central Islamic areas. Since the area of that expansion also included eastern Europe, the people enslaved came to include Jews and Christians as well. All slaves taken were regarded by their Muslim captors and owners not just as workers of one sort or another, but also as can-didates for conversion to Islam. Thus, as for ancient Greeks slavery served as a means of civilizing barbarians – and was therefore a positive condition for the enslaved – so in Islamic lands it was held to be a method of bringing the heathen to the true religion.[24]

Some slaves exported from West Africa northwards across the Sahara by Muslims were finally bought by Spaniards and Portuguese. As, therefore, Portuguese voyagers gradually advanced down the African coast in the first half of the 1400s, they looked for the sources of those slaves – and duly found them in West Africa. There, in fact, they inserted themselves into the export trade already set up by Muslims, creating a seaborne slaving route northwards parallel to the older trans-Saharan roads. The Portuguese quickly went further and began using their ships to carry slaves along the West African coast, buying them from Africans and selling them to other Africans. Then, in the early 1500s, having advanced farther southwards, they began an export trade from Central Africa, mainly from the kingdom of Kongo, that had no Muslim prece-dent, since they were now far south of the maximum expansion of Islam.[25]

European slave traders, then – first the Portuguese and later others – built on a long-existing familiarity in Africa with both export of slaves and enslave-ment itself. There is no question about that. What historians do debate, how-ever, is how much enslavement grew after the Portuguese set the Atlantic trade in motion, and how willingly Africans who were able to obtain and sell slaves – i.e. political, military, and economic leaders – participated in the export business.

The first question is hard to answer in one respect, and easy in another. It is not known how many slaves were held by other Africans in, say, 1400, shortly before the Portuguese arrived. One authority declares that there was an "enor-mous slave population" in Africa at that time, and another dismisses that asser-tion.[26] It is, then, impossible to say whether the Portuguese entry into the slave trade increased the number of people being enslaved in Africa. It might just have diverted into the export business slaves who would otherwise have been taken and kept in Africa. On the other hand, there is no doubt about the growth of slave exports in the longer term after Europeans entered the trade. Around 1450 it is estimated that about 2,800 slaves arrived yearly at their destinations across the Sahara, and some 880 at European and other Atlantic destinations. All these came from West Africa, since exports from Central Africa had not yet begun. Two centuries later, the total annual arrivals at destinations were about 13,200, with 9,100 from West Africa and 4,100 from Central Africa. It is notable that more than a third of the total (4,900) still went to trans-Saharan destinations, over the ancient routes across the desert. The arrival places of the others had become far more diverse than in 1450: Spanish America (3,600), Brazil (3,600), the non-Spanish Caribbean islands (600), and various points in Europe and the north Atlantic (500). A hundred and seventy years later, around 1820, the total of yearly slave arrivals at those same destinations had reached some 75,200 (with still 7,400 having crossed the Sahara) – more than five times the number in 1650. Summing up, it seems that between 1450 and 1650, a total of 1,652,600 African slaves arrived at various destinations in the Americas, the Atlantic, Europe, North Africa, the Middle East, and points further east than that. From West Africa there came 1,259,000, and from Central Africa, 393,600. For the period 1650 to 1820, the corresponding numbers are 9,834,300 (5,674,000 from West Africa, and 4,160,300 from Central Africa).[27] There is no doubt, then, of the growth of slave exports from Africa over almost four centuries from the first entry of the Portuguese into the trade in the 1400s.

The centuries-long existence and expansion of the export of slaves into the Atlantic trade and elsewhere suggest that, if there was resistance to that export within Africa, it was not wide, deep, or persistent. And indeed that seems to have been so. For an understanding of that lack of resistance, knowledge of the sources of slaves is important. Many men and women who finally found themselves on slave ships crossing the Atlantic were captives taken in the wars constantly fought between African states – some of them wars in which some large and regionally powerful state tried to increase its size by conquering its neighbors, others simply conflicts between two or more of the multitude of small polities existing in West and Central Africa. In addition to warfare, enslavement came, in the seventeenth century, to be seen as fitting punishment for criminals, witches, and other social misfits. And beyond that there was simple raiding and kidnapping, sometimes by local warlords who were outside the control of any state, for the purpose of selling the people taken captive into the slave trade.[28]

Generally speaking, then, slave export was the outcome of some sort of conflict or tension in African societies, whether formal or informal. For the most part, "Africans enslaved their enemies."[29] To that, however, must be added that fact that exporting slaves was profitable to Africans who were in a position to sell them, and that there were a very great number of people to sell. The population of West and Central Africa around 1500 was in the range of 50 to 60 million,[30] and although slave exports may have reduced it or slowed its growth after 1600, it remained large. Again, the goods that the foreign traders offered in exchange for slaves were tempting. Cowrie shells (originating in the Maldive Islands, west of Ceylon) were in wide use as money in West Africa, and were welcome as payment for slaves – as was cloth from India, brought back, like the shells, from Asia by the Portuguese and other Europeans. A great variety of luxury and consumer goods rare in Africa came also to be offered by slave buyers – fine European clothing, mirrors, needles, beads, alcohol, and tobacco, to name a few. Perhaps most welcome of all, given the ubiquity of war in West and Central Africa, were weapons: guns and ammunition, knives, swords, and horses (particularly valued by the states in the northern savanna because they commonly fought with cavalry). African political leaders were anxious to improve their military capabilities, and the rich merchants in their states stood to gain by exchanging slaves for arms. There were probably European suppliers who saw that offering weapons and horses might stimulate the supply of slaves for sale, but on balance it seems likely that African leaders exchanged people for arms by their own decision, for the rational purpose of increasing their military and political strength.[31] The case, however, of the kingdom of Benin and Dahomey, in the area of today's western Nigeria, shows that rulers also felt compelled to trade for slaves in order to obtain the firearms necessary to defend themselves from raiders who were already using such weapons. And as African polities obtained firearms, their neighbors sought still more advanced weapons – cast off from Europe in an era when European powers themselves were in an arms race to develop the most sophisticated firearms. In the early years of contact with the Portuguese, the rulers of Benin held back from taking part in the slave trade and from importing firearms; but in the end they had to do both to defend themselves.

The broad conclusion must then be that the Atlantic trade, through which Spanish and Portuguese America obtained some 5 million slaves between their beginnings and 1820, was a willing collaboration between European shippers keen to carry slaves to markets and African sellers who by means licit and illicit, in local terms, were in a position to send so many people across the ocean into chattel servitude. It cannot be over-emphasized, however, that during those centuries no sense of a common African identity existed. Slave traders mostly captured and sold people from other societies. When they did sell members of their own societies, they chose those defined as criminals or social misfits – even though the definitions perhaps became ever looser as the demand for captives grew. All these general considerations about the slave trade to Ibero-America apply equally, of course, to slaving to parts of the Americas that were not Iberian, and to the trade that continued to send slaves across the Sahara to North Africa and destinations further east.

SPANIARDS IN THE ATLANTIC

Spanish activities in the Atlantic lagged behind Portugal's for a very long time – almost until Columbus's day, in fact. This was not wholly for lack of interest. Spaniards from several parts of the peninsula felt the draw of the south, as the sally of the Catalans *c*.1300 to the Moroccan coast, and the Aragonese and Castilian interest of the same period in North Africa, show. Alfonso XI of Castile even went so far in 1345 as to declare to the Pope that he had a royal right to acquire the "kingdoms of Africa" by virtue of earlier Castilian rulers' successes against the Moors in the peninsula.[32] The outcomes of such interests and sentiments, however, in the fourteenth century fell far short of Portuguese accomplishments. In part this was because Spain, unlike Portugal, still had not become a political and religious whole. Whereas the Portuguese, after the expulsion of the remaining Moors late in the 1200s, now without distractions at home, could focus their attention on overseas affairs, Spain still lacked any such enabling unity. Politically, it was still split into the two distinct and often contending major kingdoms of Castile and Aragon. And religious division still persisted in fourteenth-century Spain in the form of Islamic Granada. With their house not fully in order, Spaniards were not yet ready to devote themselves to Atlantic ventures on the Portuguese scale. This unreadiness was prolonged, especially in Castile, by the long series of political and social struggles that developed after 1350.

There was one clear exception, nevertheless, to this inward focus: the Canaries. Here fourteenth-century Spaniards, especially again the Catalans, showed a clear interest in what would seem to be the conflicting aims of spreading Christianity, often at Rome's urging, and taking Guanche slaves. (As in America later, contemporaries may have seen no contradiction. Slavery after all brought pagans into close contact with Christians, and the gift of the true faith, it could be argued, far outweighed the burden of enslavement.) After several Catalan-directed expeditions of evangelizing friars, the Castilians finally entered the fray in 1393, with an exploratory force to the Canaries dispatched by Henry III. This brought back a profitable cargo of slaves and Canarian products.

The foray of 1393 certainly marks a quantum leap in Castile's attention to the Atlantic, and seems to have been followed up by other expeditions to the Canaries before the end of the century. Still, it is some indication of Castile's persisting tentativeness that when a decision to settle the islands was made later in the 1390s, the job was entrusted to Frenchmen, under the rather fitful leadership of Jean de Bethancourt, a nephew of the French ambassador to Castile. With his expedition of 1402, Bethancourt managed to take and settle some of the lesser islands. In due course Henry III pronounced him king of the Canaries, subordinate to the Castilian monarchy. But he spent little time in the islands, and finally was allowed to sell his rights in 1418 to the Castilian count of Niebla.[33]

Bethancourt's efforts lacked resolution, but they certainly strengthened Castile's claim to the islands. And this went along with a larger claim to Africa that Castile began to make in the fifteenth century – a claim that had far deeper roots in time than the earlier argument of kings' doughty strivings with the Moors. The new argument was that the Visigothic rulers of the peninsula of pre-Islamic times had been lords of the African shores, and that the kings of

Castile had inherited these powers.[34] This rising Castilian concern for Africa made for an ever sharper conflict of interests between Castile and Portugal in the eastern Atlantic. Portuguese colonization of Madeira in the 1420s was in part a response to a Castilian expedition to that group of islands in 1417.

Portugal replied in kind with a large expedition to the Canaries in 1424 or 1425, which was an attempt to take Grand Canary – an attempt justified by the contention that the island was not yet occupied by Christians.[35] Exactly how many Castilians there were in the islands in those years is hard to tell. And the titles to the islands granted by Castilian rulers to various of their subjects were overlapping and confused. Still, Castile doubtless had by the mid 1400s a stronger hold on the Canaries than Portugal, both through law and actual settlement. In the end the dispute with Portugal was settled in the Treaty of Alcáçovas of 1479, by which (among many other contested questions) Portugal accepted Castile's claims to the Canaries, and Castile in return recognized Portuguese rights in the Cape Verde group, Madeira, and the Azores – as well as on the African coast south of Cape Bojador. This was a rehearsal for the division of the hemisphere into eastern and western zones of interest, exploration, and conquest that was set up in the more famous Treaty of Tordesillas negotiated between Castile and Portugal fifteen years later.

THE CATHOLIC MONARCHS

The making of treaties about Atlantic (and other) exploration and settlement in the late fifteenth century is clear evidence of the Castilian expansionism that by then was strongly under way. It also marks the rise of exploration to the level of prime state business. Before, in both Portugal and Spain, discovery and settlement had generally been something of a sideline for government. But in these final decades of the 1400s there existed, for the first time in the Iberian age of exploration, a powerful and unitary Spanish state that could direct exploratory efforts and negotiate with authority about them.

This was the Spain of Isabella, queen of Castile, and Ferdinand, king of Aragon. The year 1469, in which these two married, ranks second only to AD 711 (and some might reverse the order) in its significance in Spanish history. At the time, neither was on the throne. Ferdinand was unchallenged crown prince of Aragon, and duly succeeded in 1479. But Isabella's claim to Castile was disputed by Princess Juana, daughter (or alleged daughter – and in that doubt lay much cause for contention) of the ruling monarch, Isabella's half-brother, Henry IV. After Henry died, late in 1474, a fiercely contested war of succession broke out. In this, Isabella's party was backed by Aragon. It had been in part to secure such support that Isabella had married Ferdinand. Juana, at first with fewer major Castilian figures behind her than Isabella, nevertheless soon found a champion for her cause in Afonso V, king of Portugal, who hoped to marry her and thus set his line on the Castilian throne.

After four years of contest, Isabella's party emerged victorious. The Treaty of Alcáçovas, of September 1479, was above all a closing of the war. With it

Afonso renounced his betrothal to Juana, and agreed that the unfortunate girl, still only 17, should be put away in a nunnery so as to destroy any threat she might pose to Isabella's occupation of the Castilian throne. There she remained until her death in 1530. The large concessions in the Atlantic that Castile made to Portugal in the 1479 treaty were, in fact, partly the price paid for the assurance that it gave of Isabella's position.

With, now, undisputed tenure of their respective thrones, Ferdinand and Isabella were able in effect to create a unified Spain. Technically speaking, there was still no single "Spanish" monarchy. But the two acted and ruled in such close accord that, to the outside world, Spain was now for the first time one political unit. It was a powerful unit, a rival for any other realm in Europe, and more than a rival for most. Aragon, which embraced Catalonia (and Valencia), under Ferdinand retained and expanded its deeply rooted interest in Mediterranean trade and politics. The Aragonese crown had, during the first half of the fifteenth century, incorporated Naples and Sicily. Ferdinand was already king of Sicily by the time he married.[36] During his marriage to Isabella, which ended with her death in 1504, he tended to concentrate on Aragonese affairs, especially his kingdom's long-standing combat with France over border issues and contested territories in northern Italy. But there was little that Isabella did in, and for, Castile that Ferdinand had no hand in, so that he, while not king of Castile during her lifetime, was very close to being its co-ruler.

Castile, with its larger territory (the whole peninsula except for Portugal, Aragon, the small Moorish remnant of Granada in the south, and the still smaller kingdom of Navarre in the center-north), and its larger population (probably *c*.4.5 million in 1500, as against Aragon's 1 million),[37] was the dominant force in the partnership. Late fifteenth-century Castile was also economically more vibrant than Aragon, above all because of its large exports of raw wool to northern Europe. The merchants of its northern cities, especially Burgos and Bilbao, were sophisticated and experienced overseas traders. The Castilian merchant marine was strong. Cantabrian shipbuilders on the north coast were internationally known for their abilities. Basque ironworkers were among the most advanced of the day.

Ferdinand and Isabella, therefore, found themselves facing an opportunity in 1479 that was without precedent in Iberian history: that of creating a unified state, under native government, that would embrace the great majority of the peninsula. This chance they seized eagerly, and with such success that their joint reign is generally seen as the beginning of modern Spain.

They were astute, able, and determined rulers. Ferdinand was taken as a model of the Renaissance prince by Machiavelli, and Isabella yielded little to him in the application of *raison d'état*. Their major aims, duly accomplished, within the peninsula were to concentrate power in the monarchy, and, by various measures, to advance the unification of Spain beyond the mere co-rulership that resulted from their marriage. Here, true enough, they had a firm popular basis from which to work. In the Middle Ages, inhabitants of many parts of the peninsula, though their strongest loyalty would be to some particular province, carried in their minds a notion of belonging also to a broader "Hispania."[38] It was an identity that Ferdinand and Isabella set about strengthening.

Much of what they did served both their purposes. Increasing the authority of the monarchy inevitably meant making it a more palpable presence in their subjects' lives, and so also provided a common point of reference for all "Spaniards." Isabella took care to make court life more splendidly ceremonial and formal than before, so as to raise the image of monarchy to a higher plane where it would be more remote from, and so more impressive to, the mass of the people. The court was still peripatetic, like its counterparts elsewhere in Europe. Many subjects had opportunities to lay eyes on the monarchs as they moved around the peninsula. But to increase the tangible presence of royal power Isabella added to the single supreme court of appeal that existed at the start of her reign (the *cancillería* of Valladolid) other high appeal courts: one in Galicia, in the north-west, and another in Ciudad Real, in the center-south. This tribunal, created in 1494, was moved to Granada in 1505.[39] Since the provision of justice was considered to be the highest obligation of Castilian rulers, this multiplication of royal tribunals increased not only the visibility of monarchy but also its legitimacy. The series of high courts was soon extended to the Canaries and then to America. In both the tribunals were known as *audiencias*, places where trials were heard.

The monarchs' intrusion into their subjects' lives was, of course, sometimes far from welcome. To bring Castilian towns, which had long been bases of autonomous regional power, into line, Ferdinand and Isabella greatly increased the number of them to which crown-appointed *corregidores* (literally "co-rulers") were assigned. Rural disorder was tackled by the creation of what amounted to a national police force for Castile, the "Holy Brotherhood" (Santa Hermandad), whose organization was set up in the summer of 1476, well before the war of succession ended. In fact, Isabella's initial purpose with the Hermandad was as much to gather fighting men for the war as it was to carry law to the countryside. After she came to the throne, the Hermandad remained as a sort of rural army, charged with enforcing law in the vast spaces between the local jurisdictions of towns. Members held powers of summary justice. Brigands and thieves could be, and were, executed or mutilated on the spot. Though the Hermandad's range and accomplishments may sometimes have been exaggerated, it certainly brought a governmental presence into country areas that had rarely felt it before; it was sometimes used (illegally) to pursue opponents of the monarchy into cities; and it contributed substantially to what was one of the monarchs' main achievements – to give Spain internal peace and order.[40]

The greatest challenge to royal authority in Castile undoubtedly came from the nobility, which over much of the previous two centuries had advanced its own power, status, and wealth at the monarchy's cost. The nobles' power-plays in the dispute over succession had added much fuel to the fire of civil war at the start of Isabella's reign. Historians long tended to exaggerate the crown's success in this central political contest of the reign, proposing, on insufficient evidence, that Ferdinand and Isabella came close to crushing the Castilian nobility over the twenty years following the war of succession. But recent reassessment of the question finds that at the end of Isabella's life the nobility had lost nothing in social standing, and little or nothing in wealth. The broad seizures of nobles' vast estates that were once thought to have happened have now been reduced to a return to the crown merely of royal lands it had lost since 1464.[41] Indeed, in 1505, nobles' hold over their estates was fortified by a general concession of the previously jealously guarded privilege of *mayorazgo*, or entail, which allowed landowners to protect their holdings from division during inheritance.[42]

Nevertheless, Ferdinand and Isabella did manage to trim the aristocracy's political wings severely by excluding nobles to a large degree from central government. New councils of state were created (or old ones substantially reorganized), and were staffed by preference with university-trained lawyers, generically known as *letrados*. High nobles might attend council meetings, and speak; but they had no vote. So began the construction of a professionally staffed bureaucracy that would grow over the next century into a great apparatus of state embracing not only Spain and sundry parts of Europe, but also the American empire. Aristocrats could certainly find a place for themselves in this apparatus, often occupying prominent positions as viceroys, council presidents, and the like. But they could not control it. It was under Ferdinand and Isabella, as one historian remarks, that "the time ended in which nobles made and unmade kings in Castile."[43] Now monarchy and aristocracy were in a mutually useful, if often uneasy and suspicious, alliance. The monarchs controlled central government. Nobles, provided they consented to that, might do as they wished with their great estates, and were free to pursue opportunities to increase their wealth.

If the nobility seemed the most urgent and obvious threat to royal power in the early days of the reign, Ferdinand and Isabella quickly saw that there was another equally potent, but more diffuse, challenge that must be met if Castile – Spain, indeed – were to become truly one, truly whole. This was the problem of religion, or, more precisely, of its variety in the peninsula. As long as Catholicism was not universal in the monarchy, ideological rifts would prevent unity from being achieved. The glaring exception to religious uniformity was, of course, the surviving Islamic presence in the emirate of Granada. It was obvious enough from the start that only force would bring a solution there; and, soon enough, force was applied. But even before that, Isabella moved against the other great variety of heterodoxy in Castile, which was Judaism.

Since at least early Visigothic times, nine centuries past, Jews had lived in the peninsula, and had become an integral part of its social and economic life. They had, indeed, been much better integrated, in both practice and law, than in other parts of Europe. Perhaps this was because, during the Reconquest, settlers were needed to occupy land recovered from the Moors. Jews were welcomed into these retaken territories. It is probably no coincidence that a consistent antisemitism developed in Spain only after the Reconquest had come close to its goal, with the compression of Islam into the single realm of Granada in the thirteenth century. Thereafter it grew and festered, bursting out in 1391 in pogroms in the Jewish quarters of Seville, Toledo, Valencia, Barcelona, and other towns. Pressures on Jews to convert to Christianity became intense, and the many thousands who submitted to them – becoming "the converted," or *los conversos* – found themselves in the fifteenth century the objects of suspicion by both Jews and Christians. Still, *conversos* continued to play crucial roles in society and economy, working, as their Jewish ancestors had done for centuries, as craftsmen, traders, financiers, doctors, and scholars, and also as administrators in church and state. Both Isabella and Ferdinand employed Jewish and *converso* financiers in high government posts.[44]

However valuable, though, such individuals may have been to the monarchs, it was clear that the *conversos* as a whole were a disruptive element in society. To resentments over their continued prominence as craftsmen and professionals was added a popular suspicion, often enough correct, that they secretly continued to practice Judaism. It was to investigate these doubts over genuineness of conversion that Isabella and Ferdinand, in late 1478, applied to Rome for a bull creating in Castile an Inquisition into heresy.[45] It was granted. The first inquisitors began work, in Seville, in 1480. Over the next decade, tribunals of the Inquisition were set up in many other Castilian cities. In 1482–3, Ferdinand revived the long dormant medieval Inquisition of Aragon. The outcome of these efforts was grim. Isabella's secretary, Hernando del Pulgar, estimated that by 1490 2,000 judaizers had been burned, and 15,000 others punished in attempts to "reconcile" them with the true faith.[46]

Unconverted Jews (and other non-Christians) were outside the Inquisition's jurisdiction; it existed only to investigate heresy among people supposedly faithful. But the 1480s were a decade just as harsh for Jews as for *conversos*. Popular prejudice found ever greater backing in law. In 1480 Jews were restricted to living in ghettoes. Many were expelled from Andalusia in 1482–3. Finally, in March of 1492, came Ferdinand and Isabella's notorious decree ordering all Jews to convert within four months, on pain of expulsion. It may be that the monarchs expected that the great majority would join the church and remain in Spain. A conversion campaign was waged to that end. But of the 100,000–200,000 Jews then in Castile and Aragon, only about half chose Christianity. (This number includes last-minute converts and Jews who later returned to Spain and became Christians.) The rest left in a great exodus that carried Spanish-speaking Jews to Portugal (a brief haven, since conversion was demanded of them there in 1497), Italy, North Africa, and above all to the lands of the Ottoman empire in current Greece and Turkey.[47]

The Inquisition and the expulsion were more the outcome of a mixture of political and religio-ideological causes than, as has sometimes been suggested, of class conflict between Christian Spaniards (whether workers or nobles) and an incipient "bourgeoisie" of Jews and judaizers. Isabella's piety, sometimes pronounced remarkable, now seems to have been no more than conventional, and Ferdinand's was even less. But both saw religious uniformity as a means, indeed a necessity, for the social and political cohesion of the new state. The forces of dissolution – nobility, towns, local legal privileges, deeply rooted regionalism – were still strong; an all-embracing Catholicism could serve to fuse what so far was joined through little more than the rulers' marriage. At a more practical level, the Inquisition, by its very structure, was a powerful political tool. Its central body, the Suprema, was one of the state councils reporting directly to the crown. Its local agents, or familiars, were numerous. What began as a device for investigating suspected crypto-Jews became a means of checking for any sort of deviation from religious, moral, and political orthodoxy.[48] While there is exaggeration in seeing traits of modern totalitarianism in the Inquisition,[49] its creation (like that of the Santa Hermandad) undeniably promoted the centralization of authority that Ferdinand and Isabella consistently pursued.

But whatever fame, or infamy, the Inquisition has conferred on Ferdinand and Isabella's reign, the creation of that Holy Office in Castile seems little more than an administrative maneuver by comparison with the major campaign they waged to restore uniformity of faith to Spain: the reconquest of Granada. The emirate had never presented any threat to the Christians' hold over the other Andalusian territories that they had retaken in the 1200s. But it proved a tough nut to crack. The final war of the seven-century Reconquest began in 1481 in a series of frontier skirmishes between the Moors and the Andalusian nobility. The monarchs quickly decided to join in. A dispute over succession in Granada provided them with a weakness that they were able to exploit, specifically through an on-and-off alliance with Boabdil, a leading contender for the throne. Still, the conquest soon became a slow grind of taking the emirate's towns one by one. Ronda fell in 1485, Málaga in 1487, Almería and Guadix in 1489, to name only the main places. Finally in April 1491 began the siege of Granada itself, with the Christians encamped before the city on a site they named, appropriately, Santa Cruz (Holy Cross). A surrender was signed in November of 1491, and Ferdinand and Isabella led a procession (in whose number went, incidentally, one Christopher Columbus) into the defeated capital on January 2, 1492. So ended the territorial Reconquest of Spain; and so began a year that would see Spaniards crossing the Ocean Sea to do to an enormous and unknown segment of humanity what had been done to them by the Moors almost eight centuries before.

Many motives drew Ferdinand and Isabella into the Granada war. Prime among them, certainly, was the wish to oust an alien creed from the peninsula and replace it with Christianity, for the same reasons as had inspired the assault on *conversos* and Jews. Moslem Granada, however, held threats that Jews did not offer. Over Christendom there loomed in the fifteenth century, ever larger, the shadow of the Ottoman Turks, who, four decades before the conquest of Granada, had taken Constantinople from the Christians. Islam was again on the rise, and in Spain it had a bridgehead in Granada. The situation was intolerable, not only for religious reasons, but because the Ottoman empire threatened Aragonese trading and political interests in the Mediterranean.[50]

At home, too, there were material gains to be had from a successful assault on the emirate. Granada offered rich loot (including slaves) for both crown and soldier. It had fertile land that could be, and was, granted to nobles still unrewarded for their support in the Castilian war of succession, or that could simply be added to the crown's domains. As the war progressed and its costs grew severe, such gains for the crown became a motive for pressing on until success was achieved. Again, Granada's silk trade was thriving, and was a tempting object for incorporation into the Castilian economy. Finally, a significant by-product of the war, though hardly a cause for waging it, was the creation, at least temporarily, of a national army. With men coming from noble estates, towns, and the ranks of the Santa Hermandad, Ferdinand by the late 1480s commanded a force of 45,000–50,000 foot soldiers and 10,000–13,000 cavalry, an enormous number for the day. This army quickly dissolved once Granada was taken. But from this point on, until well into the seventeenth century, the Spanish monarchy was well known, and feared, in Europe for its ability to put fearsome armies into the field.[51] At home, too, the close link of monarchy with military force that the war created could only contribute to the concentration of power for which Ferdinand and Isabella always aimed.

"Athletes of Christ," the Pope pronounced Ferdinand and Isabella to be after Granada fell, formally giving them the title of "Catholic Monarchs" (Reyes Católicos) by which they have been best known ever since. This was recognition as much of the blow struck against Islam in the wider world as it was of the "purification" of Spanish faith.[52] In the event, the monarchs did not at first put as much pressure on the defeated Moors to convert as might have been expected in the year of the expulsion of the Jews. Possibly inspired by the mutual toleration that had marked long stretches of the Reconquest, the capitulation terms gave guarantees of the religion, laws, customs, and property of the vanquished. In a foreshadowing of practices used in America a few decades later, local leaders were left in place, though under general Castilian supervision. Despite these concessions, many of the former emirate's people chose to leave, which may have been the crown's hope. From an initial total of half a million, 200,000 departed, many to North Africa. A further 100,000 had died or been enslaved during the conflict.[53] The roughly 200,000 remaining were subjected to conversion by persuasion: preaching, distribution of Gospels and catechisms in Arabic translation, and the like. The results were promising, but slow. And finally, in 1499, Francisco Jiménez de Cisneros, archbishop of Toledo and head of the Spanish church, grew impatient and persuaded the crown to order forced conversion. This policy brought a reaction of local revolts. And in reaction to that there came in 1502 in Granada a famous burning of Arabic texts. The monarchs had ordered destruction of copies of the Qur'an; Cisneros may have added other books to the fire, though he saved medical works for his new university foundation at Alcalá de Henares.[54] The same year Isabella resolved that all remaining *mudéjares* (Muslims living among Christians) in Castile should be given the choice offered the Jews ten years before: convert, or go. Most chose to convert.[55] Now, at least in principle, Castile was single in faith as it had in 1492 become single in territory. In Aragon, though, Muslims might still practice their religion. The events following from the Granadan war served to widen contrasts that already existed between Aragon and Castile: the first to a degree tolerant of political and ideological diversity; the second showing signs now of the austere rigidity that would make it later in the sixteenth century the temporal champion of the Counter-Reformation.

While they were trying to purge Spain of faiths that challenged Christianity, Ferdinand and Isabella also applied their purifying efforts to the Spanish church itself. The aim, as in much else they did in religious matters, was not so much to instill piety for its own sake as to use it as a tool for national unity. The church in Spain should not only be in partnership, spiritual and political, with the monarchy, but should be a disciplined and well-schooled body, able to play a unifying part in national affairs. It almost seems that the monarchs wanted to charge the spiritual batteries of the country so as to fill it with a crusading Christian energy. If there was one man particularly associated with this effort, it was again Francisco Jiménez de Cisneros. He had entered the Franciscan order at the age of 48. Eight years later, in 1492, Isabella chose him as her confessor. In 1495, the same year as he became primate of Spain, she instructed him to reform the Spanish church. He set about the task by raising the level of orthodoxy and austerity in its members, especially among the monastic orders and, among them, particularly in his own society, the Franciscans. In the last year of his life, 1517, the monasteries of the Conventual, or less strict, branch of the Franciscans were shut in Spain, leaving only the Observants, who closely followed St. Francis's vows of poverty.[56] The spiritual dedication of other orders in Spain underwent something of the same renewal. And it was the men of those orders, devout, dedicated, and educated, who formed the vanguard of the mission effort on the Spanish American mainland from around 1520 onwards.

COMPLETION AND INNOVATION

As in any treatment of "great" rulers or individuals, there is a danger in the case of the Catholic Monarchs of exaggerating their abilities, originality, and accomplishments. Spain had been in the process of fusion for a very long time. It had been coming together from, indeed, almost the moment of the Islamic invasion. Behind the slowly advancing Christian frontier, principalities had gradually grown into kingdoms, and kingdoms had drawn together under the rulership of Castilian and Aragonese monarchs. Then again, by the time of Ferdinand and Isabella, the Castilian and Aragonese crowns were already linked. Early in the fifteenth century, a cadet branch of the ruling Trastámara house of Castile had occupied the throne of Aragon. Isabella and Ferdinand had great-grandparents in common.

Similarly, several of the measures most associated with the monarchs were not original to them. An Inquisition had existed in medieval Aragon. Henry IV, Isabella's predecessor on the Castilian throne and her half-brother, had contemplated creating some special tribunal to watch over the *conversos* in Castile. He, too, had favored setting up new *hermandades* to bring peace and order to the countryside. Again, *corregidores* had long since exercised the monarch's authority into some Castilian towns. And if Ferdinand and Isabella were able, as they were, to strengthen the Castilian monarchy by vastly increasing its income, that was in good part thanks to a Castilian economic expansion already in process by 1469. Much of Europe, moreover, shared in that economic growth.

Still, in the emergence of a single Spain that is traditionally, and rightly, located in their time, they played an active part. They were like-minded rulers with complementary abilities and personalities. What might easily, in other hands, have become a jostling for individual power, or a covert contest between Castile and Aragon was, in theirs, a collaboration, so that the whole became greater than the sum of the parts. By the time Isabella died, in 1504, a genuinely Spanish state existed, and had indeed existed for some years, for all practical purposes. Disputes over the succession held back the fulfillment of its potential for a time. The monarchs' increasingly deranged daughter, Juana, was incapable of ruling Castile. Her husband, Philip of Burgundy, could have done so; but he died in 1506. Ferdinand thereafter governed Castile, though with much internal opposition, until his own death in 1516. Then, finally, with the accession of Juana's son, the 16-year-old Charles I (soon to become, in 1519, the Holy Roman Emperor Charles V) Spain took the dominant place on the European, and indeed world, stage for which the Catholic Monarchs had prepared it.

Spain's world role began in earnest with the Atlantic voyaging performed by Columbus and various of his associates and imitators in the 1490s. Their explorations built on the earlier Castilian probings into the Atlantic, particularly those directed at the Canaries. State-to-state negotiation between Castile and Portugal at Alcáçovas in 1479 provided Spanish seafarers with a reliable base or stepping stone in the Canaries. It also cleared the way for Spanish exploration westwards, since the same treaty, with its confirmation of Portuguese rights to the African coast, tended to focus Portuguese attention on the south. Exploration in that direction now came under state direction far more than ever before. The Portuguese king, John II, was quick, after Alcáçovas, to send a fleet to build a fortress-cum-trading post, the famous and long-lasting São Jorge da Mina, on what is now the Ghanaian coast. One who went with this fleet of 1482 was Christopher Columbus, then living in Portugal. Then followed a rapid push southward, much of it accomplished by Diogo Cão at the urging of his king, which took the Portuguese as far in five years as they had come in the previous seventy. Cão's report that he had in 1483 sailed around Africa to the beginning of the Arabian Gulf gave John immense pleasure.[57] The news was premature. But the king's rejoicing reveals what Portugal's aims now were in southern exploration. The allure of African products and African trade had long driven the voyages. But now the view had lengthened to take in direct trade by sea with India and the Orient, by a route around the tip of Africa, wherever that might be. Spices, silks, ivory, jade – all the high-priced goods whose entry into Europe the Italian traders had long monopolized – could be had at their source, so the Portuguese thought, once the way to Asia around Africa was opened. They were of course right. And soon another of John's expeditions, led by Bartolomeu Dias, did what Cão thought he had done, and rounded the southern tip of Africa, probably in the opening days of 1488. It was not for another decade that the first Portuguese fleet, under Vasco da Gama, went to India and back. But after Dias, Portugal's attention was firmly directed eastward. An additional attraction there, made more powerful by the looming Islamic threat in the eastern Mediterranean, was the improved possibility that circumnavigation of Africa gave of finding the legendary Christian ruler, Prester John, and other Christian groups and leaders, in Africa or the East. With such contacts made, Islam might be contained, or even attacked in its underside.[58]

Ferdinand and Isabella's attention was fully occupied, while the Portuguese were making these outward leaps in the 1480s, by domestic affairs, among them the war against Granada. It was not by chance that Columbus succeeded in getting their support for his own proposed westward exploration only after Granada had fallen. With that thorn finally, if painfully, plucked from Castile's side, and, indeed, amid the rejoicing following its removal, the Catholic Monarchs at last decided that Columbus's distinctly dubious project was worth backing.

PART II

APPROACHES

CHRONOLOGY

1451   Birth of Columbus in Genoa

1492   Columbus's first voyage to America

1493   Columbus's second voyage: settlement of Hispaniola

1496   Foundation of Santo Domingo, as capital of Hispaniola

1498   Columbus's third voyage: first certain European sighting of a South American coast

1500   World map of Juan de la Cosa. Pedro Alvares Cabral lands on Brazilian coast.

1501–2   East coast of South America surveyed by Amerigo Vespucci

1502–4   Columbus's fourth voyage: east coast of Central America surveyed

1502–9   Administration of Nicolás de Ovando, "founding" governor of Hispaniola

1503   Casa de Contratación founded in Seville

1506   Death of Columbus

1507   World map of Martin Waldseemüller, showing "America"

1508   From Hispaniola, Juan Ponce de León takes Puerto Rico

1509   From Hispaniola, Juan de Esquivel takes Jamaica, and Alonso de Hojeda leads an expedition to the Venezuelan and Colombian coast

1511   First Spanish town on the American mainland: Santa María la Antigua de Darién. Conquest of Cuba, from Hispaniola. *Audiencia* established at Santo Domingo, the first in America. Sermon of Antonio de Montesinos, OP, in Santo Domingo, criticizing colonists' treatment of Indians

1512   Arrival of first bishop (of Caparra, Hispaniola) in America. Laws of Burgos, regulating Spanish treatment of Indians

1513   Juan Ponce de León claims Florida for Spain. Vasco Núñez de Balboa crosses the Isthmus of Panama to the Pacific

1516   Death of Ferdinand of Aragon. Accession to the Spanish throne of Charles I (from 1519, Charles V, Holy Roman Emperor)

1517–18   Spanish reconnaissance from Cuba of eastern Mexican coast

1519   Mainland cities of Panama and Veracruz founded

1519–21   Hernán Cortés conquers the Aztecs for Spain

1519–22   First circumnavigation of globe, by Magellan's expedition

1529   Treaty of Zaragoza: Tordesillas line projected into the Pacific at *c.*145°E

1532–6   Francisco Pizarro conquers the Incas for Spain

1538   Foundation of Santa Fe de Bogotá

1541   Foundation of Santiago de Chile; permanent Spanish settlement of Chile begins

1542   Permanent foundation of Guadalajara, in western Mexico

1565   Northerly return route from east Asia to America found by Andrés de Urdaneta

FURTHER READING FOR PART II

Still excellent reading on Columbus is Samuel E. Morison, *Admiral of the Ocean Sea.* For more modern information see Felipe Fernández-Armesto, *Columbus,* and *Columbus and the Conquest of the Impossible* (Phoenix, London, 2000), and William D. and Carla Rahn Phillips, *The Worlds of Christopher Columbus*. For interpretation of Columbus's writing, see Margarita Zamora, *Reading Columbus*. For other Spanish explorers, see Louis-André Vigneras, *The Discovery of South America and the Andalusian Voyages*. Francisco Morales Padrón, *Historia del descubrimiento y conquista de América*, is a comprehensive, factual account of both Spanish and Portuguese explorations and conquests in America.

The standard work in English on the early Caribbean is Carl O. Sauer's *The Early Spanish Main*. In his *Conquête et exploitation des nouveaux mondes (XVIe siècle)*, Pierre Chaunu is characteristically interesting and idiosyncratic.

On the military conquests, the tales told by the conquerors themselves are by far the best starting point. For Mexico, see Bernal Díaz del Castillo, *The Conquest of New Spain*, and Hernán Cortés, *Letters from Mexico*. Hugh Thomas, *Conquest: Montezuma, Cortés, and the Fall of Old Mexico* is a splendid, detailed retelling of the Aztec conquest. For the Andean conquests, there is no Spanish chronicle quite on the same level as those written about Mexico, but John Hemming, *The Conquest of the Incas*, is an excellent modern account, drawing as it does directly and deeply on contemporary accounts.

For both the conquests and the sixteenth century generally, great riches are to be found in John H. Parry and Robert G. Keith (eds), *New Iberian World: A Documentary History of the Discovery and Settlement of Latin America to the Early Seventeenth Century*.

[4] COLUMBUS AND OTHERS

COLUMBUS

COLUMBUS had, in fact, been kept on hold for several years by Ferdinand and Isabella. He had first approached them with a plan for sailing west to the Orient in 1486. Since then he and the monarchs had played a sparring game: he threatening to take his scheme elsewhere if they would not support it, they refusing full backing, but providing occasional subsidies that partially maintained him and kept him hoping for more. Finally he secured the terms he wanted, and the trivial investment that they had made in him before 1492 paid off incalculably in the form of a vast empire in a "new" continent.

Christopher Columbus (Cristoforo Colombo, as he was in Genoa, where he was born in 1451) personified that blending of Mediterranean and Atlantic that, working especially through Portugal, contributed so vitally to the early expansion of Europe. Perhaps chief among his many remarkable qualities as a mature man was his seagoing knowledge, gained first in the Mediterranean as a youth, and then in the Atlantic after he began to live in Portugal in the mid 1470s. By 1492 he was as salt-soaked as any earlier explorer of the African coast or any voyager to the Atlantic islands. He had sailed to the east end of the Mediterranean on Genoese trading business, and in Portuguese ships to a variety of Atlantic ports ranging from São Jorge da Mina in Africa to Galway in Ireland (and perhaps to Iceland, though probably not). In Portugal he married into a rich merchant family, named Perestrelo, of Italian origins. His wife, Felipa Moniz, was the daughter of Bartolomeu Perestrelo, who had been in the 1420s one of the leaders of the expedition that settled the Madeiras, and then the captain-donatary of the island named Porto Santo in that group.[1] Columbus sailed often to the Madeiras on business. His voyaging made him familiar with both colonizing forms that the Portuguese used in the fifteenth century: commerce through trading posts, following the Mediterranean model, on the African coast, and actual settlement, for economic development, in the Atlantic island groups.

The notion of sailing west to Asia grew slowly in Columbus. When and where it first came to him is not known. Lisbon, his base after his move to Portugal, bubbled with navigational knowledge, reports, rumors, and ideas, including that of the westward passage. It was not, after all, so surprising a notion, given the prevailing general acknowledgment of the roundness of the earth. One man who contributed much to its currency in Lisbon was a geographer and merchant of Florence named Paolo dal Pozzo Toscanelli, who in 1474 wrote to the king of Portugal pointing out the possibility of sailing westward to China, via the island (soon to be shown as mythical) of Antillia, and Cipangu (Japan). Though this letter produced no immediate outcome in new Portuguese explorations, its content became a commonplace at the Portuguese court, where members of the Perestrelo family were often to be found.[2]

More original to Columbus than the idea of sailing west to Asia was his conception of the distance that would have to be covered. Combining several estimates, both ancient and modern, of the size of the earth and of the linear length of a degree of longitude, in such a way as to minimize distance, Columbus proposed that Cipangu lay roughly where Florida is – some 6,200 kilometers west of the Canaries. Expert opinion of the day held this to be a gross underestimate, as indeed it was (the actual distance being some 19,000 kilometers), and this is one of the reasons for Columbus's long failure to find royal backing. But his calculation was not far off the scale of distances admitted by contemporary opinion. Toscanelli himself had proposed a distance of *c.*8000 kilometers from the Canaries to China, and thought Cipangu lay far west of China, and Martin Behaim's respected globe of 1492, summarizing geographical knowledge on the eve of Columbus's first voyage, put Cipangu little farther from Europe than Columbus proposed it was.[3]

Columbus's distortions of geography were probably not, therefore, the only, or even the main, reason for his inability to persuade kings to put up the money for an expedition westward. His first approach seems to have been to John II of Portugal, in 1484. Portugal was the obvious choice, since it was the leader in Atlantic exploration, and voyages of discovery were now definitely seen there as state business. Finding, however, no support in Lisbon, Columbus next, in 1486, tried Ferdinand and Isabella. They, too, remained unconvinced even by his maturing powers of persuasion, though they were intrigued enough to promise to reconsider his proposal once the Granada war was over; and in the meantime supported him with occasional small cash grants. Columbus also made indirect approaches to Henry VII of England, and possibly to the French crown as well. Neither obliged; it is difficult indeed to imagine Columbus pressing these overtures, so much was he a man of the south – though both France and England had ample seafaring experience and interest.

Why did Columbus persist in seeking royal support? Many earlier expeditions, larger than anything he proposed, had been funded privately in Spain and Portugal. In fact, an offer of backing does seem to have come *c.*1487 from the Castilian duke of Medinaceli, who had, apart from the wealth necessary to provide the ships and crews that Columbus wanted, a variety of interests in the

Canaries and in Atlantic trade. Medinaceli later claimed to have maintained Columbus for a time in the late 1480s. But he seems to have withdrawn as a sponsor of any actual expedition because he wished to avoid interfering with whatever plans the Catholic Monarchs might have for Columbus.[4]

In any case, Columbus sought, besides money for ships and men, guarantees that only monarchs could provide. He wanted, in any place he might discover, powers of control and assurances of material gain, whether from riches found or trade that would follow. If these gains were to be secure, his discoveries would need a level of protection that only kings could provide.[5]

It may well have been, in fact, the extravagance of his ambitions rather than the flaws of his geography that dampened Ferdinand and Isabella's, and other monarchs', interest in him for so long. What he wanted, and finally obtained in 1492, for the proposed voyage itself – three ships, crews, and supplies – was modest enough; the necessary funds were squeezed without difficulty (and certainly without any pawning of Isabella's jewels) from the Castilian treasury. But there was no modesty in his demands for honors, positions, and material rewards if his voyage proved successful. It is still a puzzle to understand why the Catholic Monarchs granted so much to him in the famous Capitulations of Santa Fe, the agreement made at the camp before Granada, in April 1492, and in confirmations given in 1493 before his second voyage. Ferdinand and Isabella conferred on him noble status (something else that only kings could bestow), and made him admiral, viceroy, and governor general, under Castile, of any lands he might find to the west. The admiralty, above all a judicial post, was to pass to his heirs in perpetuity. One-tenth of any net profits from his explorations would go to him (and the rest to the crown). And he might put up an eighth of the cost of any ship trading with his discoveries, and receive an eighth of any profit in that trade.[6]

If Ferdinand and Isabella really believed that Columbus would open a westward route to the Orient, where rich and powerful polities were known to exist, they were, by these agreements, conceding to Columbus not only wealth beyond computation, but also political authority that they could not possibly hope to sustain. Perhaps the celebration and optimism following from the taking of Granada made them reckless, or careless. But it is hard to avoid the suspicion that they did not take him quite seriously; that in the euphoria of victory they simply decided to make what was, compared to the costs of the war, a minor investment, and see what it might yield. The outcome was, of course, totally unexpected. And although the Catholic Monarchs were never faced with the problem of defending claims to Castilian sovereignty in India, China or Japan, they did, within the decade, have to engineer Columbus's removal from power over the Caribbean islands that he found, and later contest the claims of his heirs.

Possibly, too, the experience of Granada moved Ferdinand and Isabella to back Columbus for another reason. With the Iberian peninsula now unified in religion, they were able to give full attention to repulsing Islam overseas. North Africa was the next obvious battlefield. But the prospect of a new front in the East was still enticing. Columbus himself offered this as a potential outcome of his explorations. He went further, indeed, by suggesting that a combination of an eastern attack on Islam and proper use of the wealth he hoped to find would enable Christians to recover Jerusalem. This connection of old crusading aims with his own scheme had occurred to him by 1492.[7] From this time the spiritual aspects of his ventures weighed ever more heavily with him, as he became convinced of his role of contributor, through spreading Christianity, to the approach of the millennium – the thousand-year reign on earth of the returned Christ. He was struck by the symbolism of his name's Latin basis: *Christum-ferens*, "Christ-bearing." He was now bearing Christ to the heathen across the Atlantic, and by doing so would quicken the return of Christ to the entire world. These beliefs coincided with a long tradition of millenarianism at the Aragonese court, predicting the conquest of Jerusalem and formation of a world empire specifically by the Aragonese kings. Those ideas may account in part for Ferdinand's interest in him.[8]

Columbus was a powerful mixture of the medieval and the modern, of the mystical and the practical, of the delusive and the persuasive (of both self and others). Being convinced at the start that he would reach Asia, he persisted in trying to fit the Caribbean islands and mainlands that his four voyages revealed into a model of the Orient that he carried in his head – a model that, with each new find, naturally grew more complicated. Till the end of his life, in 1506, he insisted that what he had found was Asia, even though other Europeans soon suspected that it was something quite new to them. Sailing along the coast of Venezuela on his third voyage in 1498, he reasoned quite logically that the presence of fresh water far out to sea implied the proximity of a great river. It was, in fact, the Orinoco. But then he went on to argue that this river must be the fourth stream that descended from the earthly paradise; and that therefore he was within reach of that blessed place. At sea, he was a magnificent intuitive navigator, but a poor handler of the instruments of celestial navigation. Aboard ship, or in royal courts, his persuasive powers could bend seamen and monarchs to his will. But as a governor of colonists in Hispaniola he proved a disastrous incompetent. He was, then, a being of apparent opposites. But for some purposes these contradictions served him well, pulling together in such a way as to set him apart from other great (but mere) navigators of his time. Medieval spirituality drove him to use his practical gifts as a seaman to their utmost extent. Illogic in geography inspired him to persuasive efforts that ultimately won monarchs, captains, and seamen to his side. Sometimes, though, even his rhetorical powers were unequal to the task. During his second expedition he surveyed, in 1494, the south coast of Cuba almost to its western end. This was no mean feat of sailing in treacherous waters. The length of the coastline convinced him that he had found a part of mainland Asia in which civilized people would soon appear; or almost so convinced him. Having announced to his ship's company that Cuba was mainland, he made them swear that what he had said was true, on pain of a large fine, a hundred lashes "for the ship's boys and such people," and having their tongues cut out.[9] Such suspicions that geography was betraying him might intrude once in a while; but they soon evaporated.

Spanish Voyages of Exploration

The quincentenary celebrations of 1992 made the events of Columbus's first voyage familiar: the sailing of the *Santa María, Niña,* and *Pinta* from Palos in south-western Spain on August 3, 1492; provisioning and refitting in the Canaries; departure from there on September 6; a swift passage westward before the north-east trade winds; a light sighted in the early hours of October 12; Columbus's bestowal, next morning, of the most Christian name San Salvador (Holy Savior) on an obscure Bahamian island; his claiming of it for the Catholic Monarchs; his meeting with naked native people; his explorations, over the next three months, of north-eastern Cuba and the north coast of Hispaniola; the wrecking of the *Santa María* on Christmas Eve; Columbus's reading in this accident of a providential sign that he should create a settlement; a fortress, named Navidad (Christmas), built from the wrecked ship's timbers, and garrisoned with thirty-nine men; the return to Spain of the *Niña* and *Pinta* begun on January 16, 1493; westerly winds encountered, but also great storms; the brief haven found in the Azores; more storms before landfall off the river Tagus, in south-western Portugal, on March 3; the return, after repairs in Lisbon, to Palos; and the triumphal reception of Columbus, now truly Admiral of the Ocean Sea, by Ferdinand and Isabella in Barcelona.

Columbus's three later voyages, begun in 1493, 1498, and 1502, are less well known, for reasons obvious enough; but each of them added immensely to European knowledge, and ultimately settlement, of America. The second was the largest of all his ventures, and was in fact planned as a colonizing enterprise. Columbus, now at what was to prove the apex of his career, found Ferdinand and Isabella keen to dispatch another expedition. Settlement would cement Castile's claim to what Columbus had found. Some 1,200 men sailed in seventeen ships from Cadiz on September 25, 1493: adventurers, artisans, farmers, soldiers, and (of particular concern to the monarchs) priests to turn the islanders to the path of salvation. Columbus dropped south of his first route, and entered the Caribbean through the Lesser Antilles. Heading north-west back to Hispaniola, he surveyed the south coast of Puerto Rico. Another new land was added to the European map. But then, successfully returned to Hispaniola, he found his fortress at Navidad destroyed and all those he had left behind eleven months earlier, killed. Though he had judged the Arawaks of Hispaniola docile and pliable, even they had been driven to violence by the demands, for gold and women, of those first European residents of the Caribbean. The immediately urgent business, though, was to find a site for a larger settlement; and this Columbus chose to place some 110 kilometers eastwards along the north coast, naming this first Euro-American town, in honor of the queen, Isabela.

The place was unworthy of its royal name. It was infertile and unhealthy, and had a bad harbor. Columbus chose it in impatience, partly because it seemed near possible sources of gold.[10] Isabela was a poor start to what became a calamity of colonial administration. Columbus had no fundamental interest in being a governor. He still, and always, was in search of the rich, civilized parts of Asia that he had originally proclaimed to be his goal. In April of 1494 he sailed westwards from Isabela to find them, feeling his way along the shallows of the southern Cuban coast, and then, on the return, locating Jamaica. Back at Isabela, in September 1494, Columbus found illness, hunger, demoralization. Some colonists had fled back to Spain in ships taken without his leave. Complaints quickly reached royal ears of the admiral's deficiencies, more of omission than commission. He further eroded his standing with the crown by sending native islanders as slaves to Spain, in an attempt to produce some sort of profit from settlement. With remarkable speed a royal agent arrived in October 1495, with orders to look into the complaints made. Columbus decided it was time to state his own case, and left for Spain in March 1496.[11]

So began his long losing battle with the crown to maintain his powers in the lands over which the Capitulations of 1492 had given him charge. As he, and soon others, extended their probings of the transatlantic shores, and it grew ever clearer that whatever this place might be, it was very large, and probably not Asia, the monarchs' impetuous alienation of control to a voluble Genoese visionary seemed increasingly undesirable. The method chosen to sap his position was bureaucracy. Interfering functionaries of increasing rank were dispatched to Hispaniola. His incompetence at, or lack of interest in, administration, provided a useful justification for this. The sharpest blow came in mid 1500, when a newly arrived royal inspector, Francisco de Bobadilla, put Columbus in irons and sent him back from Hispaniola to Spain. The monarchs of course ordered his shackles struck off as soon as he arrived; but this was a humiliation inconceivable only a brief time before.

By then, Columbus had completed his third expedition. In the summer of 1498, having crossed the Atlantic from Spain, he went even further south than on the second voyage. As a result he and his crew became the first recorded Europeans to lay eyes on the South American coast. His landfall was the island of Trinidad. He then passed between it and the Venezuelan coast, finding in the vast discharge of the Orinoco evidence both of a large landmass and of the proximity of Eden. But lacking time to explore upstream, he turned north and west for Hispaniola.

Up to this time, Columbus had persuaded the crown that the agreements of 1492 gave him a monopoly of exploration along the new coasts. But the combination of his South American find, his administrative failings, and perhaps also the swelling strain of prophetic religiosity in his reports, now moved the monarchs to give licenses for exploration to others.[12] Many were anxious to sail, including several who had been with Columbus on his earlier voyages. So began a new rush of European discovery. Four major expeditions in 1499–1500, led by Andalusian captains, surveyed almost all the north coast of South America.[13] Their findings appeared in a famous world map by Juan de la Cosa, a Spaniard who had sailed with Columbus in 1492 and 1493, and was one of the voyagers of 1499. This map, generally accepted as being of 1500, shows the entire northern shore of South America eastward to Cape São Roque (at the north-east tip of Brazil), as well as Hispaniola, Cuba, and a long North American east coast (reconnoitered in part by John Cabot, sailing for and from England in 1497). La Cosa was uncertain of the connection between North and South America, and also, so the map suggests, of the distinction between at least North America and Asia.[14] But his representation of an immense coast of northern South America, and of Cuba as an island, indicates a growing suspicion at the time that what explorers were encountering was something new.

In April of that same year, 1500, the first certain European landing on the east coast of Brazil took place. Pedro Alvares Cabral, commander of the second Portuguese fleet bound for India around southern Africa, sailed far west in the Atlantic and made a South American landfall. Not linking what he found with the north coast of South America, he named it the Ilha da Vera Cruz, the Island of the True Cross. Cabral sent a ship back to Lisbon to report the find, and the following year the Portuguese crown dispatched three caravels, under the guidance of a Florentine merchant and geographer, Amerigo Vespucci, to survey this new coast. Vespucci – yet another Italian beguiled by navigation, exploration, and the commercial opportunities they might reveal – had earlier, in 1499–1500, sailed on one of the Andalusian voyages to the north coast. Now, in 1501, he continued his efforts in what he called "the Indies" under the flag of Portugal, hoping to find a southerly passage to known Asia around the great land mass that was revealing itself.[15] His survey of the east coast of South America, possibly as far as the La Plata estuary, lasted into early 1502. He reported that he had seen a "new land," a "continent," but it is not clear whether he yet regarded it as something quite separate from Asia. The combination of his accounts, however, with the knowledge accumulating from other explorations, suggested ever more strongly that America stood apart from the Orient. And this notion found its defining statement in a world map published in 1507 by one Martin Waldseemüller, a priest and schoolteacher of Saint Dié in Lorraine. On the map a great ocean is set between America and the East. So renowned had Amerigo Vespucci's reports become (though much of what appeared under his name was forgery), and so long were the South American shores that he had coasted, that Waldseemüller, casting round for a name for the new continent, chose a feminine form of Vespucci's first name – "America."[16]

So Columbus was doubly deprived: he first lost the powers granted to him in 1492, and then the honor, surely deserved however wayward his geographical notions, of having the continent he had been the first European to see named after him. His worthiness in this respect grew with his fourth voyage of 1502–4. Here again he was a pioneer, this time in surveying the Caribbean coast of Central America from Honduras down to Panama. The rigors of this venture, especially a long stranding on Jamaica on the return voyage, sapped his strength. He did not live to know the humiliation of the misnaming of America, dying in Valladolid in the spring of 1506, some eighteen months after his patroness, Isabella.

After the burst of voyaging at the turn of the century, exploration lagged for a decade or more as the new revelations were digested, and Spaniards, if not yet the Portuguese, found they had plenty to do in adjusting, as settlers on Hispaniola, to New World conditions. The upper coasts of the Caribbean, from Honduras northward, were oddly slow in being reconnoitered. The first contact came in the east, in spring of 1513, when Juan Ponce de León, a Caribbean settler made rich by his conquest of Puerto Rico in 1508–9, sailed north-west under royal orders to seek the reported islands of Bimini. After threading through the Bahamas, he took possession of the mainland coast in April of 1513, naming it the Flowery (Florida) Isle (possibly an allusion to its abundant vegetation).[17] Ponce surveyed the whole of the east coast of Florida, and part of the west, before returning to Puerto Rico.

To the west, it was not until 1517 that a Spanish expedition first examined the Mexican coast (though it may have been cursorily scouted in 1508 for a passage to the Orient). In 1517 Francisco Hernández de Córdoba, another wealthy settler, but this time of Cuba, took a small expedition westward. His three ships progressed as far as the base of Yucatan on its west side. A second exploration, under Juan de Grijalva, was quickly organized in 1518. This expedition followed Hernández's track, and then pushed forward to a point halfway up the east coast of Mexico. In doing so, Grijalva and his men made the first recorded contact between Europeans and Aztecs. News of this encounter spurred the governor of Cuba, Diego Velázquez, to put together a third Mexico-bound expedition, in 1519. This force, led by Hernán Cortés, did nothing to extend coastal exploration; it did, of course, conquer the Aztecs in quite short order. The task of completing coastal exploration in the northern Caribbean between Mexico and Florida fell to Alonso Alvarez de Pineda, sailing from Jamaica on the orders of its governor, Francisco de Garay, between late 1518 and mid 1519.[18] By the time, then, that Cortés was planning his assault on the Aztec empire in the autumn of 1519, the entire Caribbean coastline from Florida round to Venezuela was known to the Spanish. They knew also the islands, large and small, of what was rapidly becoming their American Mediterranean; likewise the rest of the South America's northern shore down to the easternmost point of Brazil.

On the eastern side of South America, below the limits of Portuguese voyaging, Spanish exploration proceeded slowly. Its motive was less knowledge of the shores themselves than pursuit of that elusive goal, a passage to the Orient. Late in 1515 an expedition sailed from Spain commanded by Juan Díaz de Solís, an experienced sailor in American waters. He was charged with finding a passage through South America, and exploring the ocean beyond it. But sailing the Pacific was not to be his lot, for, after discovering that the Río de la Plata was not – as he briefly hoped – a strait but an estuary, Solís was killed on its shores in a skirmish with native people. The remnants of his expedition went back to Spain.

There, two years later, the government of the young King Charles accepted a proposal from a crabby Portuguese mariner, Fernão de Magalhães, to show a way to the Spice Islands of Asia around America. Magellan, to use the anglicized form of his name, seems to have been sure where this passage lay; but he, like Columbus, had not been able to persuade the Portuguese crown to back him, and, perhaps in retaliation, now brought his plan to Spain. He found receptive listeners there, especially since Spain was by now anxious to establish territorial claims in the Orient to offset those being made by Portuguese who had reached Asia by the route around Africa. In August of 1519 Magellan's five ships left Seville. There followed one of the epic voyages in the history of navigation: mutinies, storms, desertions, scurvy, sinkings – but as a result of it, the discovery of the Magellan Strait linking the Atlantic with the Pacific in southern South America, the first documented crossing of the Pacific, and, of course, the first circumnavigation of the globe. Any lingering doubts of the earth's sphericity were now exploded. Magellan was killed by native people in the Philippines, after meddling unwisely in local political affairs. Only one ship, the aptly named *Victoria*, carrying eighteen men (of the original 265 in the expedition) finally returned to Spain. It docked at Seville in October 1522, commanded by Juan Sebastián Elcano, a Basque who thereupon became one of the great heroes of Spanish maritime history.[19]

Though Magellan had finally found the western passage to the Orient, the discovery was long of little practical use. Whether by way of the intricate and reef-filled strait, or by doubling Cape Horn itself, fighting into the Roaring Forties and the great seas they stirred up, rounding the tip of South America was so daunting a venture that the route was little used for many years. Only in the eighteenth century, with technical improvements to ships, did this Atlantic–Pacific passage become a commonplace, if still daunting, piece of navigation.

One outcome of this was that the Pacific shores of America were explored largely from west-coast ports. The first of these, and the one from which the most influential voyages departed, was the City of Panama, founded precisely in the year in which Magellan sailed from Spain, 1519. Ten years before, a gold- and slave-seeking expedition had set out from Hispaniola for the coast of what is now Colombia. There it suffered most severely from native resistance. The survivors finally found refuge in 1511 near the base of the Isthmus of Panama, attaching themselves to a settlement of more welcoming Indians. To this place they gave the name of Santa María la Antigua de Darién. It was the first Spanish (if partly native) town on the American mainland. By this time a stowaway of much innate ability had risen to lead the group, by name Vasco Núñez de Balboa. Two years later Balboa took a party across the isthmus. And it was he, and not (*pace* Keats) "stout Cortez," who then stood upon a peak in Darien and surveyed the Pacific Ocean. Balboa waded out into this Southern Sea (Mar del Sur), as he named it, and claimed it and its shores for the crown of Spain. In good Spanish legal fashion, the act was notarized, with the members of the party as witnesses. The first to put his name on the document, after Balboa himself, was one Francisco Pizarro, who had been a member of the original expedition from Hispaniola in 1509.

Pizarro was already a leading figure among settlers of the isthmus. By the time the City of Panama was founded, in 1519, he was also growing rich. In the 1520s he put his resources into voyages of exploration down the Pacific coast of present Colombia and the shores of Ecuador. These probings, encouraged by rumors of rich people and lands far to the south, eventually, early in 1528, brought him into contact at Túmbez in northern Peru with coastal outposts of the Inca state. And this inspired him to undertake, beginning two years later, the conquest of the Incas. During the conquest, and in the years immediately after it, most of the rest of the west coast of South America was reconnoitered.

Coastal exploration of Central America, and inland settlement for that matter, also proceeded northward from the Panama base, running into southward expansion of Spaniards from Mexico in the late 1520s. The west coast of Mexico itself was the object of several expeditions from the early 1530s on. Hernán Cortés himself in 1535 crossed from the mainland to the southern tip of Lower California, which was still thought to be an island. The Gulf of California to this day, in Spanish, bears his name: the Sea of Cortés. Upper California's coast, almost to the present Oregon line, was surveyed in 1542–3 by Juan Rodríguez Cabrillo and Bartolomé Ferrelo, sailing from western Mexico at the order of the first viceroy of Mexico, Don Antonio de Mendoza.[20] Sixty years later, in 1602, Sebastián Vizcaíno gave that shore a more thorough examination and produced the first maps of it. In these northbound voyages the motive was not mere curiosity but also the search for a northern passage between Atlantic and Pacific – the Strait of Anian, as it was generally called in the seventeenth century. Fears that others, particularly the English and the Portuguese, might find this strait first gave the Spaniards an extra incentive to press northwards.

Western Mexico also quickly became a point of departure for ships bound for the Orient. Cortés, again, with the sense of potentially global Spanish empire that the Aztec conquest had inspired in him, was an early mover of such ventures. At his urging Alvaro Saavedra Cerón sailed in 1527 to follow up on the Magellan expedition's exploration of the Spice Islands. One of the three ships reached New Guinea, though none returned to Mexico.[21] The return to America from Asia – the eastward crossing of the Pacific – indeed remained for several decades an obstacle to the westward extension of Spain's empire into the Orient, where Magellan's voyage had given it claims. The westward voyage across the Pacific, though long, was not excessively hazardous. Ruy López de Villalobos managed it again, with a small fleet, in 1542; but none of his ships came home to Mexico. The North Equatorial Current and north-east trades that favored sailing west from southern Mexico to the Philippines effectively blocked the return at that latitude. Finally the key to communication between America and Asia was found in 1565, by the Augustinian friar Andrés de Urdaneta. He, in his youthful, pre-monastic days had spent several years in the islands of South-East Asia as a survivor of an ill-fated expedition from Spain that had reached the Orient via the Magellan Strait in 1525. In the late 1550s Urdaneta, now with a strong sense of where the return route should be sought, persuaded the second viceroy of Mexico, Don Luis de Velasco, to support a new trans-Pacific expedition, one of whose main purposes would be to demonstrate the eastward voyage. Late in 1559 the king, Philip II, ordered Velasco to organize exploration of the Asian islands. The commander of the flotilla formed as a result was Miguel López de Legazpi; Urdaneta was the navigator.

Their four ships left Mexico on November 21, 1564, and arrived in the Philippines on February 3, 1565. For the return, Urdaneta chose the fastest ship, and provisioned it for eight months. On June 1, 1565 he sailed from Cebu in the Philippines, striking far north of earlier attempts. In doing so, he picked up both the westerlies of the north Pacific and, doubtless without knowing it, the help of the Japan Current and then the North Pacific Drift. The voyage to Acapulco lasted four months; scurvy took a toll, with sixteen of the crew of forty-four dying.[22] But, like Columbus in the Atlantic, Urdaneta had mapped out an oval pattern of Pacific winds and currents that allowed reliable communication between Mexico and South-East Asia. Communication was the essential precondition for political control, if Spain wished to have it. And in fact, while Urdaneta was feeling his way back to America, Legazpi, as he had been instructed, began the Spanish occupation of the Philippines, keeping the Portuguese at bay, and often finding himself gladly enough accepted by native groups as an ally against the recent Muslim Malay invaders of the islands.

By the 1560s, then, Spaniards knew in some detail not only the coasts of the Caribbean, eastern and western South America, and western Central America, Mexico, and North America, but also those of the archipelagos of South-East Asia. They had made themselves familiar with conditions of winds and currents on these coasts, and were learning to move between them with minimum waste of time. In little more than half a century, Europeans' knowledge of the western hemisphere had grown vastly, beyond earlier conception. People alive in 1490 could hardly, in their wildest speculations, have imagined what was to be securely known as geographical reality seventy years later: not only an entire new continent, but one separated from the Orient by an ocean far broader than anything Europeans, even the Portuguese tracking the African coast southwards, had ever encountered. And by the 1560s not only was this new western geography known, but also to a surprising degree dominated – dominated by the efforts of European navigators of several nations, but chief among them, beyond question, Spain.

SPAIN AND PORTUGAL DIVIDE THE WORLD

While Spaniards circled half the world to the west, the Portuguese did the same to the east. The two movements met in the early 1520s in South-East Asia with Magellan's arrival in the Philippines under Spanish colors. Over the previous twenty years the Portuguese, advancing on Vasco da Gama's path-breaking voyage to India and back of 1497–9, had surveyed great stretches of the Asian coast and the Indian Ocean with astonishing speed: the Seychelles Islands and the Arabian coast in 1503, Sri Lanka in 1505, the Bay of Bengal from that year on, the Persian Gulf from 1507 on, the Malay peninsula, Sumatra, and Java between 1509 and 1512, and, farthest yet to the east, the Celebes, Timor, and the Moluccas (the "Spice Islands") in 1512.[23] By 1513, when the first European, Núñez de Balboa, looked out over the Pacific from its American shore, the Portuguese were at its western edge in Asia.

Magellan's expedition was the first European presence in the Philippines, immediately north and a little west of the Spice Islands. His appearance in the Orient in 1520 precipitated several years of military and diplomatic friction between the two Iberian states. The roots of the conflict go back to 1494, when Spain and Portugal agreed, in the famous (infamous, no doubt, to other Europeans) Treaty of Tordesillas, that lands lying in the Atlantic beyond a pole-to-pole line 370 leagues west of the Cape Verde Islands should be Spanish, and those east of such a meridian, Portuguese. The line was not randomly chosen. It was far enough to the west, the Portuguese thought, to preserve their access to Africa, while not so far, in the Castilians' view, as to allow the Portuguese into the Caribbean. Both sides knew that this division would be hard to place exactly on land or at sea. But it was precise enough for the purposes of the day; precise enough, for example, for there to be no doubt that the Island of the True Cross, encountered in 1500 by Alvares Cabral on his voyage to India, was Portugal's. Hence, among much else, Brazil speaks Portuguese.[24]

But if demarcation of Spanish and Portuguese zones might be debatable only on a small scale in the Atlantic, in the Pacific the question was wide open. Though the Tordesillas agreement was drafted, and could only have been drafted, with only the Atlantic in view, once the Pacific became known after 1512–13, the notion grew that the line should be projected into the eastern hemisphere. And once Spain made an appearance in the Philippines, with Magellan, and began also to claim rights in the Moluccas, thereby endangering Portugal's monopoly access, among European powers, to the riches offered by cloves and other spices, agreement on a division became essential. Finally, after several years of local skirmishing in the islands, and protracted negotiation at home, by the Treaty of Zaragoza in 1529 Spain and Portugal agreed on a continuation of the Tordesillas line into the Pacific at $c.145°E$. This placed all the disputed territories in the Portuguese zone. But Spain renounced claims to the Spice Islands only in exchange for the very large payment of 350,000 *cruzados* by the Portuguese; and although the Philippines now lay indisputably on the Portuguese side of the line, Spaniards still set much store by prior discovery, so that once Urdaneta made trans-Pacific communication a routine matter in the 1560s, Spanish colonization from Mexico proceeded quickly. Portugal could do little to stop it. Thus the Philippines became Spanish territory, and remained so until 1898.

Although the islands lacked the civilization and wealth of Japan and China, Columbus might have been happy enough with that outcome. For Spanish missionaries soon set to work in the Philippines, evangelizing the population, thereby setting up a barrier to the eastward spread of Islam, and contributing to the world-wide spread of Christianity. And Manila, the Spanish capital in the islands, soon proved to be the source of great wealth as the entrepôt at which oriental fineries, jewels, and spices were profitably exchanged for the silver of America.

[5] EXPERIMENT
IN THE CARIBBEAN

FIRST ROOTS

THOUGH Spanish exploration of American, and other, shores proceeded with impressive speed in the sixteenth century, settlement was a slower business, at least in its early stages. For a generation, almost thirty years, after Columbus first crossed the Ocean Sea, Spaniards on its western side chose to live only in the large Caribbean islands, and on the Isthmus of Panama. And Panama, until it became the base for conquest in South America early in the 1530s, might as well have been another large island, so isolated was it from other Spanish American places. Spanish occupation of the American mainland can properly be said to start in 1519, when Hernán Cortés went from Cuba to Mexico, and in two years conquered the Aztecs. His encounter with that great culture is almost on a par in its outcomes with Columbus's encounter with America, since it spurred a vast increase in interest in the new continent, a growth of emigration, a leap in expectations of economic gain, and, partly as a result of these, the emergence of the notion that America was truly the stuff of empire for Spain. The conquest of the Incas a decade or so later served only to reinforce all this.

Modest, though, as the Caribbean stage of Spanish occupation of America may have been, it was a period of essential learning – an apprenticeship for Spaniards in living an ocean's width from home, among people of a sort they had never before experienced, in tropical places whose plants, animals, soils, and climates were new. It was equally a period of apprenticeship for those back in Spain who were faced with the task of governing these territories so remote in space and time. All rose to this challenge of learning with astounding speed, so that by the time the occupation of the mainland began, many of the practices (administrative, fiscal, legal, economic, social, cultural) that were to characterize the empire over its whole span were in place in at least embryonic form. The process of learning was far from uniformly positive, to be sure: disasters occurred, or were allowed to occur, including the all but total destruction of the native people of the Bahamas and the Greater Antilles. Viewed from certain angles, indeed, this first Caribbean stage of Spanish colonialism is thoroughly deplorable. Nonetheless, for the formation of the empire, the Caribbean experience was crucial. It was a bridgehead into the new.

Spanish settlement did not extend beyond Hispaniola for sixteen years after it began there, at Navidad, in late 1492. That small fortress (in a really elemental sense a European settlement, since it was built partly from the timbers of the wrecked *Santa María*)[1] did not survive until Columbus's return on the second voyage, eleven months later. Finding it destroyed, and the forty or so men he had left there killed, Columbus chose to found the first true Spanish town on Hispaniola 120 kilometers further east, on a flat, barren site near a river mouth that offered some protection for ships. This was Isabela. Public buildings, a church, and perhaps even parapets and a moat were soon in place.[2] But the town never prospered. Its surroundings were not fertile. The European crops on which those first settlers counted, failed. Very soon there came hunger, sickness, and death. Many began to wish themselves back in Spain, and indeed left once an opportunity arose. In part to correct this initial mistake in settlement, Columbus chose another site on the south coast for a new town, 200 kilometers south-east of Isabela. There in mid 1496 his brother, Bartolomé, began the building of Santo Domingo, which has been the capital ever since. The harbor was good, the nearby land rich, well watered by rain, and densely peopled. A promising goldfield had already been found 50–65 kilometers inland, which was another reason for the founding. Survivors from the north coast quickly shifted to this better place, leaving Isabela all but abandoned by 1499.[3] By that time, two or three small fortresses had also been built in the interior, between Isabela and Santo Domingo, to discourage native resistance to Spanish settlement and its growing demands. But European numbers in Hispaniola were still falling. Though Columbus had come with 1,500 men in 1493, and ships had constantly arrived from Spain since then, by the end of the century the Spanish population of the island (still entirely male) was down to between 300 and 1,000.[4]

OUTWARDS FROM HISPANIOLA

Spanish occupation of Hispaniola in reality began almost anew in 1502, when 2,500 colonists arrived with the second royally appointed governor of the island, Nicolás de Ovando. Among them were the first European families to emigrate to America. Though, once more, many of the newcomers died, a continuing influx led to net growth, so that by 1508 some 10,000 Spaniards were in place, living in fifteen Spanish towns (*villas*) scattered throughout the island.[5] By then, indeed, Hispaniola was beginning to seem crowded; or, at least, the balance between settlers and useful resources was no longer as favorable as new emigrants expected. The resource most sought after was native labor, but by 1509 the Indian population had fallen, through the effects of war, maltreatment, social disruption, and disease, to some 62,000.[6] Though the size of Hispaniola's population before October 1492 is still hotly debated, it was certainly much larger than this: probably between 200,000 and 1,200,000, and just conceivably several millions.[7] So the expectations of immigrants that they could prosper from the surplus of native production were increasingly disappointed; and Spaniards in Hispaniola looked for new places to settle.

Now, therefore, Hispaniola became the center from which Spanish activities in the New World emanated, whereas before their source had still chiefly been the coast of Andalusia. This American base had been fifteen years in the making; now it had firm foundations. The first major outward movement came in 1508, when Juan Ponce de León, the later explorer of the Florida coast, was charged by the crown with following up on gold discoveries that he had made in an earlier reconnaissance of Puerto Rico. Back on that island, he created towns near the gold deposits in the south-west and north-east, and assigned the native Taino to settlers to wash gold. This resulted in a native revolt that Ponce fiercely suppressed. There followed a repetition of the miserable story already played out in Hispaniola: the disappearance within a few years of almost all the native population of Puerto Rico.

In the following year, 1509, the pace of expansion from Hispaniola accelerated. An expedition went to settle Jamaica, led by Juan de Esquivel, a man who had taken part in suppressing native resistance in south-east Hispaniola. The island revealed no gold. Its Taino people, however, when distributed among the incoming Spaniards for farming purposes, fared no better than their counterparts in Hispaniola and Puerto Rico who had been put to digging and panning gold. By 1519 the native Jamaicans were almost gone.[8] Jamaica never amounted to much under Spanish rule: a small community of farming settlers, off the beaten track. It is no surprise that it was the first large Spanish island in the Caribbean to fall to a foreign power. In 1655 the English took it, against little resistance.

Far more significant for Spanish imperial history was a second movement outward from Hispaniola in 1509. In December of that year, two expeditions left the island for the mainland, one under Alonso de Hojeda, directed at the coasts of what are today Colombia and western Venezuela, and the other under Diego de Nicuesa, bound for Veragua, that is, the Caribbean coast of Central America from the Gulf of Urabá at the lower end of Panama, northwards to Honduras. The purpose, as directed by the crown, was settlement, but settlement with the specific purpose of securing precious metals, of which the crown intended to take its royal share. The expeditions were large. Nicuesa took five ships carrying almost 800 men, Hojeda three with 200–300 men. In the end it was the smaller force that had the greater effect. Nicuesa's expedition was a disaster. Few, if any, of his people survived it. Columbus, on this Panama coast on his fourth and final voyage, had found gold, and, through his reports, created the impression that here was a zone vastly rich in metal. Nicuesa, in his hurry to find this wealth, split up his ships, ignored the navigational advice of men who had been with Columbus five and six years before, became lost, and exposed his force to native attack, and, even more deadly, to starvation. No settlement of Central America resulted from his enterprise.

Settlement was the outcome, on the other hand, of Hojeda's efforts. Preceding the final success was much fierce combat with natives on the Colombian coast, in the course of which the famed navigator and map-maker Juan de la Cosa lost his life, and Hojeda himself suffered wounds and privations that led to his early death after he returned to Hispaniola in the summer of 1510 to gather reinforcements. Poisoned arrows offered the Spaniards a severity of challenge in this territory that they had rarely faced before. The expedition was reduced at one point to sixty men. But under the final leadership of Vasco Núñez de Balboa, and also the doughty influence of Francisco Pizarro, the survivors eventually settled, more in exhaustion than triumph, on the fertile and welcoming western side of the Gulf of Urabá. The town of Santa María la Antigua de Darién was the immediate result; and in the longer term came the founding of the City of Panama on the Pacific side of the isthmus in 1519. It, in turn, became a new Spanish base, beyond Hispaniola, for exploration and conquest. Without this base, the conquest of the Incas would have been a distant, if not impossible, prospect.

The final outward leap from Hispaniola was to Cuba. The conquest and occupation of this largest of the Greater Antilles began in 1511, with a two-pronged attack led by men who had already honed their swords and skills as conquistadors elsewhere: Diego Velázquez in south-western Hispaniola, and Pánfilo de Narváez in Jamaica. Neither of them made any pretense about what they wanted for themselves and their followers: native labor for washing gold and growing food. The occupation of Cuba was a work of violence and terrorism, designed to intimidate the local population into submission. In that it was successful before the end of 1511. The best that can be said of Velázquez's and Narváez's vicious seizing of the island is that it had some redeeming effects in the longer term. Accompanying Velázquez, as a minor treasury clerk,[9] was Hernán Cortés, who a decade or so later in Mexico resolved that there should be no repetition in the land he had just conquered of the mindless destruction of native people he had seen in the Caribbean. And in Narváez's group was Bartolomé de las Casas, a recently ordained priest, but in most respects still a colonist with the standard ambitions of the time. The destruction wreaked by Narváez as he bludgeoned his way from south-east to north-west across the island – Las Casas later wrote "I do not remember with how much spilling of human blood he marked that road"[10] – led this future and greatest of defenders of the American natives to examine and write about the morality of conquest.

The invaders soon found gold in the streams descending from the highlands of central Cuba. A gold rush followed in 1512, drawing crowds of prospectors from Hispaniola. By 1515 six Spanish towns were in place. Cuba began to supplant Hispaniola as the prime Spanish base in the Caribbean. Only the western quarter of the island lacked a European settlement. Most of the towns were sited in areas of heavy native population: labor was always the great magnet. Indians sent to the gold placers died in large numbers, so that by 1515 workers were already in short supply. Cuba had in any case, by several accounts, been more lightly peopled before the Spanish came than Hispaniola.[11]

The rapid erosion of this slighter base was one reason for the relative brevity of the island's role as central Spanish focus in America. Only ten years after conquerors entered Cuba, Mexico became a far greater attraction; and Cuba, along with the other islands, receded into the background of the now genuinely imperial scheme of things Spanish in America.

GOVERNMENT

The Greater Antilles played the essential roles not only of bridgehead and psychological proving ground for that mainland empire, but also of territory for experiment in distant administration. A variety of governing mechanisms were tried; some were transferred to the mainland when the time came, others were discarded. Naturally enough, Iberian practices were the point of departure. One of Columbus's titles was viceroy (of the islands and mainlands he might discover); viceroys had been an essential part of Catalan–Aragonese regional rule in the Mediterranean since the fourteenth century. Then again, Columbus's brother Bartolomé, who tried to govern Hispaniola in the viceroy's absence in Spain between 1496 and 1498, did so as *adelantado* – a term coming from the verb *adelantar*, "to advance." The title was one of frontier governor, with strong military overtones, and had been frequently used in the Reconquest. In the fifteenth century it was given also to the conquerors of the Canaries. Those islands, in fact, saw several peninsular techniques of government tested overseas for the first time.[12] But as the Canaries were relatively close to Spain, and because settlement of them did not begin in earnest until the 1480s, administrative experience there did not teach fundamental lessons that could be applied to the Caribbean. Far off on the other side of the Ocean Sea, America had necessarily to be its own laboratory.

No royal agent sailed with Columbus on his first voyage. But on the second, in 1493, one was present, in the soon to be ubiquitous shape of a treasury official. (The term *real oficial*, or "royal official," quickly came to mean in America specifically an officer of the treasury: the royal interest in taxes was very clear from the start.) Columbus had proclaimed the potential wealth of the islands, and the crown wanted its share. This was the first intrusion of the state into Columbus's domain. Doubtless this interference would have grown with time in any case; but it was accelerated by Columbus's incompetence and lack of interest in governing, and by the effects of natural problems in settlement that the eager fortune hunters of the second voyage had not foreseen. By early 1494 hungry, sick, and dying men at Isabela were already blaming him for failing to prevent food from rotting, when heat and humidity were the main culprits. Columbus, rarely a subtle man, tried threats and violence to persuade the complainers, among them many courtiers and gentry, to work for their own salvation. "The outcome was hatred for the Admiral," Las Casas later wrote, "and this is the source of his reputation in Spain as a cruel man hateful to all Spaniards, a man unfit to rule. Columbus's prestige declined steadily from then on, without one day of respite, until in the end nothing was left of it and he fell utterly into disgrace."[13] Some of the gentlemen took their complaints to Spain. The result was that a royally appointed inspector arrived in October 1495, and began to act as if he were the chief authority in Hispaniola. Columbus returned to Spain in March 1496 to explain himself, leaving his brother Bartolomé, the *adelantado*, in charge.

Matters, not surprisingly, grew worse. Being another foreigner, and lacking Columbus's titles and his moral stature as discoverer, Bartolomé would have needed almost miraculous governing abilities to hold together the fractious Spanish community. Lacking such powers, in 1497 he found himself faced with a revolt led by a man named Francisco Roldán, whom Columbus had left as local governor (*alcalde mayor*) of Isabela, a town now rapidly nearing extinction. Roldán set up a rival regime in western Hispaniola, drawing into it by 1498 about half the Spaniards. Though Columbus, back on the island in 1498, was able to make peace with the rebels, he did so only through granting concessions, above all of control over native labor. These, though, did little to diminish Roldán's, and others', hostility to the Columbus brothers. Further complaints, sent to Spain in 1499, along with royal concern over the continuing cost to the treasury of the Caribbean venture, and with Isabella's anger at Columbus's granting of native slaves to Spaniards returning to Spain – by what right, she asked, did he give her vassals as slaves? – finally led the monarchs to send out a far more powerful administrator in mid 1500. This was Francisco de Bobadilla, a commander (*comendador*) of the military Order of Calatrava, and a well-tested servant of the crown. So ended Columbus's, and his family's, independent power in America, and so was revoked, *de facto*, much of the agreement made at Santa Fe in 1492; for Bobadilla held powers to remove Columbus as governor, and promptly proceeded to do just that on his arrival. The departure, in chains, of the admiral and his brother for Castile followed soon after. Adding insult to injury, but showing very clearly where royal sympathies now inclined, Bobadilla pardoned the rebellious Roldán.

After two years of comparatively peaceful administration, Bobadilla was recalled to Spain, perhaps because he had offended the crown by temporarily cancelling mining taxes in an effort to stimulate gold production. In this he succeeded. Much of the metal gathered was, however, lost when a hurricane laid waste the fleet carrying it back to Spain in July 1502. Both Bobadilla and Roldán were drowned. That may have given Columbus some bitter satisfaction, especially since he, approaching Santo Domingo on his fourth and final voyage to America, read the signs of the storm's approach and warned Bobadilla. Ignoring the advice, Bobadilla set sail, and perished.

In April 1502 there had arrived in Santo Domingo Nicolás de Ovando, a knight-commander (*comendador mayor*) of the Order of Alcántara, and the first fully fledged governor of Hispaniola belonging to the royal bureaucracy. He had accepted a term of two years, but stayed seven. In them he made the island a royal domain. With the new emigrants that his fleet carried, the European population of Hispaniola jumped from perhaps as few as 300 to around 3,000. From this reinvigoration, a confident occupation of the island followed. Under Ovando gold production rose, partly in response to cuts ordered from Spain in the royalty tax charged on it, from the 50 percent payable until 1502 to the 20 percent conceded in 1504.[14] Ovando further boosted mining by assigning native labor to it. He did the same for Spanish-run farming. A growing supply of foods familiar to Spaniards, particularly beef and pork, was just as encouraging to potential settlers as the prospect of gold. Cattle, pigs, and horses brought in from 1493 onwards, and allowed to multiply wild, had by Ovando's time become very numerous. He imported more breeding stock at his own cost. A growing supply of horses was one reason for the rapidity of Spanish conquest of other Caribbean islands from 1508. Hispaniola proved an excellent breeding ground, offering virgin grassland that was free of predators, and still without diseases and parasites to threaten stock. The precipitous fall of the native population released ever more land for grazing. Though large private landholding had not yet begun, the land for the moment being regarded, both popularly and legally, as public domain open to all, nonetheless here in Hispaniola the model of the New World ranch was being created.[15] Meat quickly became more abundant than it was in Spain, and its price dropped. Lard, tallow, and particularly hides began to be exported, providing some needed variety, beyond gold, in the island's marketable products. Sugar cane was introduced in Ovando's time, though sugar was not yet exported.[16] True enough, the Spaniards' staple grain, wheat, was never successfully grown in the islands. But the colonists bent enough towards native culture to accept bread made from manioc flour as a basic food.

The growing Spanish population gathered into new towns (*villas*), or, more precisely, was moved into them, since Ovando had come with royal orders to create new settlements and people them with Christians from Spain. Here is an early realization in America of the Spanish conviction (drawing on a long European tradition) that civilization was essentially something that developed and belonged in towns.[17] Spaniards were not, Ovando was urged, to be allowed to live scattered about the countryside.[18] Most of the fifteen towns that existed in Hispaniola by 1509 seem to have been founded in 1504–5. They were concentrated in the eastern half of the island, but five were on or very near its western end.[19] By the time Ovando left, in 1509, Santo Domingo was becoming a recognizably Spanish town in its physical form, with stone houses (some of them roofed and floored with tiles from Spain) built by drafted native laborers under Spanish artisans' supervision. The first luxuries were beginning to appear by then, reflecting a rising prosperity: imported musical instruments, candles, damask tablecloths, and silverware. Among the first colonists to prosper were lawyers, repeating in America the rise in wealth and status that they had enjoyed in Spain under Ferdinand and Isabella.[20] But wealth also began generally to show the socially elevating power that it exercised throughout colonial times in Spanish America. Distance from Spain weakened the traditional determinants of social standing in effect there, so that colonials found that mere money could bring them a far greater social lift in America than it could in the peninsula.

Santo Domingo and the other towns were not to have just Spanish populations, but populations of married Spaniards. The family seemed the natural social unit, and marriage was seen as likely to solidify settlement. Anticipating later general policy, Ovando particularly favored (with grants of native labor, for instance) married immigrants, insisting that men who had left wife and family in Spain should bring them out within three years. The better to root unattached Spanish males, he encouraged them to marry native women. His efforts had some success. In 1514 a partial but probably fairly complete count of householders (*vecinos*) in Hispaniola found 392 of them living in the island's fifteen towns. Of these, about a quarter (92) had Castilian wives; and about an eighth (54), native wives.[21] Many others probably lived unmarried with native women. The children born of these unions can only have added a stabilizing weight to the social structure. More important still, for the genetic and cultural future of Spanish America, was specifically the early appearance of children of mixed blood – the first of the *mestizos* (literally, the "mixed") who have come to form most of the Spanish American population. Encouragement of intermarriage of Spaniards and natives (nearly always Spanish men with native women) became normal policy later, at least during the founding phase of the mainland empire.[22]

Another of Ovando's tasks was to audit the accounts of Columbus's government of Hispaniola. To improve collection of royal income in the future, a full set of four treasury officials was appointed to the island in 1501.[23] They were the first component installed of what was to become an enormous bureaucratic machine of government in the Spanish Indies. Two years later, in another step in that machine's assembly, these officials became the American agents of the first governmental body set up in Spain to deal specifically with Indies affairs. This was the House of Trade, or Casa de Contratación, created in Seville in 1503 to supervise trade with the Caribbean, collect duties, and act as court of first appeal in trade suits. The Casa rapidly developed into much more than this, however, becoming not only the channel through which royal orders flowed to Hispaniola, but also the supreme advisory, and even executive, body for America. Its head, the cleric Juan Rodríguez de Fonseca,[24] was immensely influential in early Caribbean affairs, and remained so until a fully fledged royal Council of the Indies (Consejo de Indias) came into being in the early 1520s. At that point the Casa reverted to its concentration on trade, which, however, embraced communication with America and control over emigration.

The state's crossing of the Atlantic was marked, among other things, by the creation in Ovando's time of a branch of the Casa in Santo Domingo, staffed by the treasury officials.[25] Ovando worked in other ways, backed and directed by Ferdinand and Isabella, to impose the weight of government on Hispaniola. The independence of municipalities had long been a thorn in the royal side in Spain. To forestall any such annoyances in America, the crown gave Ovando powers in 1504 to name first-instance magistrates (*alcaldes ordinarios*) and constables (*alguaciles*) for towns on the island. By tradition, these were elected offices; complaints about Ovando's meddling with them went to Spain, but to little avail. Above the municipal level, royal justice was in the hands of two superior magistrates (*alcaldes mayores*). From them, appeals went to Ovando, who judged rigorously.[26] A strict austerity, indeed, allied with remoteness and personal morality, formed his hallmark. With it he stamped his efforts, which were successful, to remedy the chaos of the 1490s, impose royal authority on Hispaniola, and make the island productive enough both to attract new settlers and to satisfy the crown's (especially Ferdinand's, after Isabella's death) thirst for new American income.

Ovando was less careful of natives' interests on Hispaniola than he was of the colonists', or the monarchy's. He asserted Spain's presence by suppressing what remained of native polities. He began with the island of Saona, off the south-east tip of Hispaniola. Here Spaniards had senselessly provoked Indian hostility, which Ovando read, some say with malicious intent, as rebellion. The ensuing campaign destroyed Saona's native population.

A far larger native state survived in the west of Hispaniola, ruled by a queen named Anacaona. Late in 1503, the region's *caciques* (chiefs) assembled to meet Ovando during what seemed to be a friendly Spanish visit. In the midst of festivities and displays of arms, he ordered his men to attack the native leaders. A rumor of native plotting may have been behind this assault.[27] Whether this was so or not, Ovando took the opportunity to remove the native leadership. By one report, he hanged eighty-four chiefs, and Anacaona too.[28] The following year, 1504, he made the Higuey peninsula in south-eastern Hispaniola his target, and the final large independent chiefdom of the island disappeared. Though there is disagreement about Ovando's motives and procedures in these attacks, they seem to have been examples of what was already, and what was long to be, a prime Spanish tool of conquest: terrorism. Columbus had used it in his time, and in the other large islands, and then on a vaster scale on the mainland, succeeding waves of conquistadores made use of it. It was an easy way of attracting native allies. Those already defeated, and sometimes those still unconquered, sometimes joined the Spanish and "fought strenuously, such was their fear of the Spaniards whom they accompanied and their desire to please them… ."[29]

Part of Ovando's reason for eliminating native governments was that he was keenly aware of the importance of native labor for producing wealth, both public and private, from Hispaniola. The persistence of native political systems might well complicate access to that labor. Further, holding the gift of labor added enormously to his own political strength. Although he received orders from Spain about assigning Indian workers to colonists, he had, as governor and man on the spot, much discretion in this key matter.

Grants of Indians had first been made by Columbus in 1497–9, for farming land that he also distributed among early colonists.[30] He had quelled the Roldán rising in 1498 partly by making such grants. Indians intended for agriculture soon found themselves gathering gold, a far heavier task. These early allocations were termed *repartimientos* (from *repartir*, to distribute). Natives in *repartimiento* were not considered slaves, since they were not the property of the Spaniard to whom they were assigned, but continued under the control of their own leaders – who, generally, were made responsible for supplying the decreed number of workers. But they were certainly forced laborers, subject to the whim of their Spanish masters. This quickly made them an object of concern to Isabella, who from the start inclined to see Indians as inherently free. On the other hand, it equally quickly became obvious that Hispaniola would not yield income to the monarchy, nor would Spaniards be persuaded to settle the island, unless native people were forced to work. It was a dilemma met with over and over again in the sixteenth century as the Spaniards occupied the mainland, and one that persisted to some extent until the end of the empire.

In 1503 the monarchs, in orders to Ovando, tried to have matters both ways. In March he was told that it was proper, for maximum gold production, that Indians work in mining; but they must do so of their own will, be well treated, and be paid. The crown's ideal from these earliest days was, indeed, voluntary wage labor by Indians. But neither now nor for several decades on the mainland did this come about. In December 1503 a far more severe order was issued. Ovando should compel Indians to work for colonists, in building, farming, and mining; though they should be compelled "as free people, which they are." He should set wages and see that workers were well treated.[31] Whatever the contradiction here, this command established, once and for all, the principle of state compulsion of native labor.

Ovando was in fact well prepared to put such arrangements into effect. His military order in Spain, Alcántara, had during its participation in the Reconquest received many grants of frontier places and people, with obligations to administer them, and rights to collect taxes and services that otherwise would have gone to the crown. These grants were called *encomiendas* (from *encomendar*, to entrust or commend). They did not give ownership of land.[32] On Hispaniola, once he had undone the large native polities in 1504–5, and following this familiar notion of trusteeship, as well as the 1503 orders from Spain, Ovando assigned Indians to settlers who showed a need for them for mining, farming, and other purposes. Some he allocated also to royal mines and lands. The numbers granted are unclear. Thus the crude distribution (*repartimiento*) of Indians started by Columbus became, in principle at least, the entrustment (*encomienda*) of native workers to deserving settlers, who were expected to pay and care for these Indians. In reality, nothing changed in the laborers' treatment, which was at best harsh. The continuation in common use of the term repartimiento, instead of *encomienda*, suggests how little changed (though the recipients of Indians were known henceforth as *encomenderos*). It was perhaps this, among other things, that prompted Las Casas, the fiercest foe of forced native labor, to describe Ovando as a good governor, "but not of Indians."[33]

Ovando's successor as governor was Columbus's son, Diego, who had for some time been pursuing the rights and powers granted in perpetuity to his father in 1492–3, but then taken from him. His case was helped by his marriage to a noblewoman, María de Toledo, a cousin of Ferdinand, and by Ovando's effectiveness in bringing Hispaniola so firmly under state control that Ferdinand ran little political or economic risk in returning the governorship to the Columbus family. From 1509 to 1511, Don Diego had only the title of governor, not viceroy. Nonetheless, when he arrived in Hispaniola in 1509 with his wife (the first Spanish noblewoman in America) he set up something of a viceregal court in Santo Domingo. It was perhaps an attempt to compensate, in pomp and ceremony, for what he lacked in authority, for although he received some of the Indies' income promised to his father, his powers were largely confined to Hispaniola. He argued with Ferdinand particularly about jurisdiction over Panama and Puerto Rico, both of which drew his and the king's attention on account of their strong promise of gold. These disputes, exacerbated for Ferdinand by Don Diego's duplicity in failing to report vacant *repartimientos* of Indians and assigning them to settlers without royal knowledge, led to his recall in 1515.[34] He was restored as viceroy and governor of the islands from 1520 to 1523, but again was called home to answer charges about his administration. He died in 1526, aged about 46. His wife continued the battle with the crown over the family's rights in America. Finally in 1536 a compromise was struck by which Diego Columbus's descendants kept the title and privileges of Admiral of the Indies, but gave up all other claims in return for the titles of duke of Veragua and marquis of Jamaica, a small estate in Panama, a fiefdom of the island of Jamaica, and a perpetual annuity of 10,000 ducats.[35]

Though Don Diego had seen the major threat to his authority and rights as coming from autonomous governors in Puerto Rico and Panama, a far more serious challenge, in the long term, to colonial chief executives' authority was the sort of body that appeared in 1511 in Santo Domingo: the *audiencia*. Just as Isabella had used high courts of appeal to carry her authority through Castile and to the Canaries, now Ferdinand created one for the Indies precisely to limit Diego Columbus's freedom of action.[36] The judges were ordered to meet regularly with him and the treasury officers to read and reply to royal letters and to discuss local executive questions.[37] Until the late 1520s, when another *audiencia* was created, in Mexico, the court in Santo Domingo was the chief tribunal in Spanish America. It was the first of many such courts, all of them combining judicial, executive, and some legislative functions, and serving in reality as the main channels for the transmission of royal will to America.

CHURCHMEN IN THE ISLANDS

Another innovation of Diego Columbus's time, with still more profound effects for Spanish America in the long term, was the effective arrival in the Indies of the Catholic church. Priests there had certainly been in Hispaniola before: five came in 1493 in Columbus's second expedition, and others with Ovando in 1502. But even in his time the church's presence had been slight. The few priests in the island seem largely to have tended the colonists. Evangelization of the natives, which was an obligation laid upon the Catholic Monarchs by the papal bulls of 1493–4 conceding them temporal powers in America, languished. In part this was possibly an outcome of Ovando's own formation. His order, Alcántara, while definitely a part of the Church Militant, had not in the Reconquest taken on an evangelizing role. That was the church's business once the unfaithful had been conquered in the field.[38] But a far stronger reason was that Ferdinand, before allowing a large clerical apparatus to develop in the Caribbean, was determined to ensure that Spain, not Rome, controlled it.

For this purpose, he sought an extension to the Indies of the powers of royal patronage (*real patronato*) that Rome had given the Spanish monarchy in Granada in 1486. A first concession came in 1501. But only with bulls of 1508 and 1511 did the papacy give Ferdinand what he wanted: a very large degree of control over the creation of churches and monasteries, over the appointment of churchmen of all ranks, and over the collection of church taxes.[39] With these powers in hand, Ferdinand presented candidates for bishoprics in Hispaniola. At the same time church building accelerated in the island. By the time Ovando left, in 1509, various churches existed. He himself had also endowed a Franciscan friary in Santo Domingo. By 1509 that central house had developed three branches in the island, and a total of twenty Franciscans were present.[40]

In 1512 the first bishop arrived in America to occupy his see at Caparra in Puerto Rico. In 1513 came the second, to Concepción in Hispaniola. Santo Domingo had no resident bishop until 1519. The first prelates, it is true, did not stay long in place. Both were back in Spain, in absentee status, by 1516. Both had found the resources assigned to them, mainly Indians in *repartimiento*, too slim to support their establishments. But if the religious commanders proved short in resolution, the rank and file, in the form of regular clergy (members of religious orders), were another matter. In 1511 the Franciscan force grew by twenty-three, and more joined it in 1513. Some, at least, of these men were products of the reform currently being applied to the Franciscan order in Spain by Archbishop Jiménez de Cisneros and others. As such they were more educated, disciplined, and evangelical in inclination than many of their fifteenth-century predecessors. Spiritual energy in Hispaniola received another charge in 1510 with the dispatch by Ferdinand of a small group of nine Dominican friars to the island. His alleged purpose was that they should root out reported heresies in the island, a task for which their order's devotion to orthodoxy especially fitted them. The presence of Dominicans, noted for their dedication to preaching and intellectual matters, was quickly to add a strong and distinctive tone to the church's voice in America.[41]

The incoming friars soon moved beyond Hispaniola. Two or more Dominicans were in Cuba the year its conquest began, 1511. By late 1515 a Franciscan and a Dominican mission existed on the coast of Venezuela.[42] Thus in Diego Columbus's years as governor, though little of it was his doing, the church expanded its base in America as both institution and mission. From that foundation Catholicism spread rapidly in the following decades, so that by the end of the sixteenth century most of the native people in Spanish territories from Chile in the south to New Mexico in the north had at least heard its message.

SPANIARDS AND ISLANDERS

There are historians of the Spanish American colonial church who would date the start of evangelizing Catholicism in the empire to a precise day, December 21, 1511. On that Sunday before Christmas, Antonio de Montesinos, one of the Dominicans who had come to Hispaniola in 1510, preached in Santo Domingo undoubtedly the most famous sermon in Spanish American history. He, like his brother Dominicans, had been less struck by individuals' heresies in Hispaniola than by the colonists' mistreatment of natives, which to some extent was certainly the outcome of public policy. This "very choleric and most effective" preacher, as Las Casas described him, harangued his congregation, among whom were notables who held Indians in *repartimiento*, in biblical tones:

> I am the voice crying in the wilderness ... the voice of Christ in the desert of this island ... [saying that] you are all in mortal sin ... on account of the cruelty and tyranny with which you use these innocent people. Are these not men? Have they not rational souls? Must you not love them as you love yourselves?[43]

The arrival of the Dominicans may not have marked the beginning of liberation theology in America, as one historian would have it.[44] But their protesting was certainly the first resounding shot fired by the pro-native side in a long conflict among Spaniards over the treatment of Indians in the empire. Montesinos's sermon stirred up an angry buzz of complaint in Hispaniola, which soon reached Spain. Ferdinand briefly took against his favored Dominicans, since criticism of colonists' treatment of Indians was clearly likely to undermine production and taxation in Hispaniola and other islands. On the other hand, he heeded the friars' warnings from Hispaniola sufficiently to put together a commission, consisting of senior ecclesiastics and lawyers (who lacked, it should be said, personal experience of America), to look into Spanish–Indian relations.

This junta met at Burgos in 1512. Before ruling on the treatment of Indians, it first felt obliged to consider (as did several later bodies confronting the same questions) the basic standing of the American natives. Like Isabella a decade before, and many other authorities in later years, it declared them to be free. Nevertheless, the junta said, Indians were vassals of Ferdinand, who for that reason might order them to work, provided that laboring did not interfere with their evangelization, and was beneficial to them and to the public interest.[45] In December of 1512 the commission drew up a series of regulations in accord with these principles. These Laws of Burgos, as they are known, were the first attempt at a broad code of Spanish–Indian relations, although, reflecting practical reality in the Indies, the central objects of attention were labor and Christianization.

The authors of the Laws of Burgos saw in the obligatory labor system of *repartimiento* a means of fusing work with conversion. Indians should be removed, forcibly but gently, from their villages and resettled near their *encomenderos*. These should build a church in each new village, and instruct their people in the basics of Christianity. The old villages should be burned, so that natives should not be tempted to return to their traditional places and idolatries. Bishops should ensure a supply of priests for services in the village churches, confessions, baptisms, and the like. Indians were, then, to be gathered together (*congregados* became the standard term for this much-used practice in the sixteenth century) for better evangelization. At the same time, the new villages were to be a source of labor. Indians must mine gold for five months of the year, after which they should have forty days free to cultivate their manioc. No woman more than four months pregnant, or within three years of giving birth, should mine gold or plant manioc, but should be given light tasks in the *encomendero's* household. *Encomenderos* should feed their people during work periods, supply them with hammocks, pay them a gold peso a year to buy clothes; see that men had only one wife; and send the sons of caciques to the local Franciscans for four years of education. Indians should not change masters. No *encomendero* might be granted more than 150 Indians, or fewer than forty. Finally the laws ordered regular official inspections of native villages.[46]

The Laws of Burgos were an ingenious design for combining conversion of the Indians with labor extraction. For the modern observer they also reveal the educated Spaniard's image of the Caribbean native people twenty years after they had first entered the European consciousness. Indians were seen as idle and given to vice (the preamble to the laws says both); if not supervised they would relapse into idolatry and promiscuity; unless given a hammock and money to buy clothes, they would sleep on the ground and go naked (both signs of lack of civilization). Though soon modified to a degree by contact with the high mainland cultures, this early-established definition as a backsliding, lazy primitive clung to the native henceforth. It was one point of departure for official thinking about Indians, as was also a conviction that the indigenous peoples, however backward, were free, and also the special responsibility of the Spanish monarchy. The tension between these views accounts for some of the contradictory waverings in sixteenth-century, and later, policy on native matters.

The Laws of Burgos remained largely unenforced. That is, *encomenderos* continued to use native labor, but the provisions for conversion and welfare were ignored. The Dominicans' indignation about native treatment, of which Las Casas, although not yet a Dominican, rapidly became the most vociferous and influential exponent, was not calmed. In 1515 Montesinos and Las Casas together went to Spain to argue the Indians' case. Las Casas contrived an interview with Ferdinand, who, however, died soon after, on January 23, 1516. Cardinal Cisneros, becoming regent on Ferdinand's death, was Las Casas's next target. He proved remarkably open to persuasion.

Las Casas proposed that *repartimiento* (or *encomienda*, as the practice was now increasingly termed) should be ended, Indians freed, and administration of the Indies given to ecclesiastics. Cisneros immediately adopted the third point, naming an administrative committee for the Indies consisting of three Jeronymite friars. None of them had any American experience. They were to observe without preconceptions, and decide how the Caribbean natives should be managed. Were they capable of living in a satisfactorily civilized way under self-government? Did they need some sort of Spanish supervision, perhaps in newly created villages? Or might the *encomienda* system, suitably modified and properly subject to the Laws of Burgos, be preserved?[47]

The Jeronymites arrived in Santo Domingo in December 1516, and stayed for three years. This was the only period in which the Spanish American empire was governed wholly by priests. (From 1517 to 1520 the audiencia of Santo Domingo was suspended, leaving the friars free of even the judiciary.) It was a daring and noble experiment, perhaps possible only at a time of political fluidity at home, as the shift took place from the Trastámara dynasty to the Hapsburgs.

In the event, though, local conditions were already so firm that the Jeronymites not only changed little, but finally proposed changing little. They took away the Indians of absentee *encomenderos*, to general approval; but they found it politically impossible to abolish the *encomienda* system. They judged Indians incapable of self-government in the Spanish style. They recommended the import of African slaves to ease the Indians' labor load. They thought that with enough incentive (gifts of animals and seeds, for example) poor Spanish farmers might be encouraged to emigrate. They built some thirty new villages for the "congregation" of Indians, in line with their instructions and with the Laws of Burgos. But in the end, and with their assent, the *encomienda* and its abuses remained. Las Casas, whom Cisneros had named "Protector of the Indians," raged in disappointment. Even the new Spanish king, Charles, on the friars' return to Spain, disdained to receive them.[48]

In Charles, indeed, Las Casas found a sympathetic audience. At a meeting at Barcelona in 1518 he had expounded before the young king his convictions about American native people: their capacity to receive the faith and live virtuously in self-government, their inherent liberty, their openness to reason. He went on to win many of Charles's advisers to the anti-*encomienda* position. The outcome was that in May 1520 Charles ordered limited trials of native self government, despite warnings that the suppression of *encomienda* that this implied would drive colonists from the islands. He went further in July, issuing an order (*cédula*) that declared his conviction of the Indians' freedom, and therefore of the wrongness of their being "entrusted" to anyone. Indians allocated to absentee *encomenderos* should immediately be declared free under the administration of their *caciques*. To avoid "difficulties," other natives in *encomienda* should not be freed immediately, but only as they became "vacant" – that is, as their *encomenderos* died.[49] In this way, the *encomienda* would gradually disappear.

In fact, it did not. As Charles gave his orders in 1520, Hernán Cortés was halfway through his battle with the Aztecs. A year or so later, to reward his successful conquerors, he began, unaware of Charles's ban, to distribute Mexicans among them in *encomienda*. The same happened a few years later as Spaniards penetrated South America. And the *encomienda* in the huge frame of the mainland was to give the Spanish authorities far graver political and moral headaches than it had in the islands. Still, Charles's rejection of the institution in 1520 concludes the first Spanish confrontation of the Indian perplexity: that set of questions about the native people's nature, moral and legal status, and rights that so exercised Spaniards in the sixteenth century. The king had concluded that Indians were free and should therefore live only under self-government (though with clerical oversight). The conclusion was admirable, the product perhaps of youthful idealism. Inasmuch, though, as it ignored the question of how the Indies were to be kept settled with Spaniards if colonists were deprived of easy access to cheap native labor, the conclusion was impractical and short-sighted.

THE CARIBBEAN BALANCE

The story of the Spaniards' first quarter-century in America lends itself to strong and contradictory judgments. On the one hand, the period was crucial for the making of Spanish America. On the eve of the expansion into Mexico in 1519, Spaniards could claim to occupy in America an area (roughly the size of Castile) of some 300,000 square kilometers, two-thirds of it in the islands, and one-third in Tierra Firme (Panama and nearby parts of present Colombia and Venezuela).[50] In that area a multitude of experiments, formal and informal, conscious and unconscious, were tried by people of all sections of the nascent colonizing society, from governors and bishops down to artisans and farmers. This Caribbean experimentation was crucial to the formation of the Spanish American empire. The Caribbean, indeed, was never again to play such a large role in Spanish imperial affairs. Much that was tried, failed; as a result, many Spaniards died, or went back home in despair. After twenty-five years, however, few in Spain or the Caribbean doubted that Spaniards should be in the Indies. Indeed, the sense that America was God's gift and revelation to Spain was by then firmly rooted. And some (the persistent, the well-connected, and the lucky) had by 1519 discovered that the distance, both physical and psychological, of the Indies from Spain meant freedom: freedom to do as one wanted, freedom to gather wealth and land, freedom to rise, through wealth and deeds, in the social scale with a speed that the conventions of peninsular life made impossible.

On the other hand, much of this freedom came at the expense of the native Caribbean people. The most drastic example of this was the fate of the Lucayos, the inhabitants of the Bahamas, or Lucayas, as the Spanish called them. These people, the first to meet the Europeans in 1492, were the first to be destroyed. At Ferdinand's order, given in 1509, Ovando began to bring Lucayos to Hispaniola to offset the decline in labor supply there. They were then either sold as outright chattel slaves or distributed among colonists as servants bound for life, a status for which the local term *naboría* was used. The crown took a very profitable share of this business. By 1513 the Bahamas seem to have been emptied of people.[51] In Hispaniola, the population of 62,000 or so in 1509, already only a fraction of the pre-contact figure, continued to fall: to c.28,000 in 1514, 15,600 in 1518, and a few hundred, or practical extinction, by 1540.[52] Parallel losses afflicted the other large islands. Some of the smaller islands fared a little better: island Caribs still could be found in the Windwards in the eighteenth century. Reasons for the terrible collapse are not hard to find, but are much less easily ranked. Disease probably played a powerful part.

No devastating epidemic to compare with those that later mowed down the mainland peoples can be definitely identified in Hispaniola until 1518, when smallpox struck the island (although the possibility of smallpox there in 1493 has recently been raised). But waves of severe disease, among them perhaps influenza and typhus, certainly attacked the Spaniards from the earliest years, and the natives cannot have escaped them.[53] Campaigns of conquest, with their accompanying episodes of terrorism, undoubtedly killed many more. Yet more probably succumbed to intense Spanish demands for unaccustomed labor, in extracting gold, carrying heavy loads, building in stone, and raising new crops. The *repartimiento*, especially in its first and totally unregulated form before 1500, gave Spanish masters complete control over Indians at a time when the supply of labor must have seemed limitless. The resulting treatment of workers can only be surmised. *Repartimiento* under Ovando was more controlled, but largely in the sense of being more efficient in moving native people around Hispaniola, especially to maintain gold production; and hence more disruptive of community and family.[54] Again, as the demand for natives' effort grew, their diet deteriorated. Production of the staple manioc seems to have held up; but natives could no longer hunt or fish as before, and so lacked protein and fat.[55] Work therefore weighed even more heavily on them, and disease found easier entry. Probably, also, children were less likely now to be conceived; a physiologically caused infecundity was added to reluctance to bring offspring into a disrupted world.

Intentionally and unintentionally, then, the Spanish trampled the Caribbean natives into the ground as they strove to gain a foothold in the New World. Some, a few, saw what was happening and called for a halt, or at least for moderation. But the lure of gain was too strong for much to be changed. The state looked to the Indies for territory, income, and the greater weight and power in the world that these would bring. Individuals saw unprecedented chances for wealth, social advance, and the status that fame could confer. All these ambitions would be carried to the mainland, there to repeat their effects on a continental scale. But there most native cultures proved ultimately more resistant to the invasion, and so, although seriously altered and damaged, escaped extinction.

[6] MILITARY CONQUEST

MEXICO

IN 1516 there began a movement towards Mexico that sparked off the explosive growth of Spanish America. Within three decades the Spanish territories grew from being a set of exotic, but thinly settled, islands and Central American forests into the first great European-based empire of modern times. This movement started as a private venture. A hundred or so footloose men of Cuba, including some who had originally gone to Tierra Firme and returned, finding themselves frustrated by being denied the *encomiendas* that were the best source of economic and social advance, bought three ships to try their luck to the west. They invited a rich settler-*encomendero* of the island, Francisco Hernández de Córdoba, to lead them. Diego Velázquez, the conqueror and now the governor of Cuba, gave his approval, hoping to profit from any incidental enslaving of native people that the party might undertake.[1]

In 1517 this expedition reconnoitered the north and the upper west coasts of Yucatan. Hernández and company found several surprises there: large towns of masonry buildings; evidence of more complex religious practices than anything the Spaniards had seen before in the Caribbean; small, but enticing, examples of gold; and a confident, abundant native people. It was soon clear that one source of their confidence was fighting ability, deployed, moreover, with notable cunning. The Spaniards found themselves lured into hot contests with arrow-shooting Indians armored in padded cotton. They had run up against the distinctly fractious Post-Classic Maya. Hernández suffered a wound from which he died after returning to Cuba.

The discoveries of 1517 prompted Velázquez to fit out and dispatch a four-ship expedition the next year. This, led by Juan de Grijalva, surveyed all western Yucatan and most of the Gulf coast of Mexico proper. Now the Aztecs came into view, with more and greater surprises: ornamental copper axes; much more gold; evidence of great political power, centered somewhere inland; towns and temples, with clear proof of human sacrifice in them; and, most tantalizing of all, hints of a sophistication of culture never yet encountered in the Indies.

Once the new reports reached Cuba, interest in westward exploration began to grow fast. Velázquez sent to Spain for permission to trade and conquer, hoping to forestall others' efforts. He had a powerful friend there in Juan Rodríguez de Fonseca, head of the Casa de Contratación. But even before approval came, he gathered ten ships for a new approach to Mexico. The choice of leader was difficult. A capable, authoritative man was needed; but from the first Velázquez feared that such a person, once in charge of a large force, might strike out on his own. Despite precautions, this is precisely what happened with Velázquez's final selection for the job, Hernán Cortés.

Spirited independence cannot have seemed, on past record, a great danger in Cortés. He was a man of 34 who in fifteen years in the Indies had proved himself a solid citizen, and conventional to the extent that any of those pioneering colonists was conventional. He was the son of minor gentry of Medellín, a small town in Extremadura in south-western Spain. In Hispaniola he had acquired Indians in *repartimiento*. He then went to Cuba in 1511 as a subordinate of Velázquez in the conquest of the island. Again he did well, acquiring Indians, mining gold, prospering modestly, serving twice as a local magistrate, and remaining, with occasional lapses, on good terms with the governor.

Although Cortés must initially have seemed a safe choice to command the 1519 force, Velázquez began to have doubts about him even before the flotilla sailed. Bernal Díaz del Castillo, the great soldier-chronicler of the Mexican conquest, comments that once Cortés was appointed, "he began to adorn himself," wearing "a plume of feathers, with a medallion and a gold chain, and a velvet cloak trimmed with loops of gold. In fact he looked like a bold and gallant Captain."[2] As the date of departure came near, Velázquez tried to remove Cortés from command, but was unable to stop him from sailing. The expedition left, then, under a leader who was already insubordinate; and so he remained.

The story of the conquest has been brilliantly told several times: in the sixteenth century by Bernal Díaz, by Cortés himself in his letters to Charles V, and by his early biographer, Francisco López de Gómara, and then in the nineteenth century by William H. Prescott. It is an astonishing tale. The bare bones are as follows.

Cortés sailed from Cuba on February 18, 1519, with 11 vessels carrying some 600 Spaniards, 16 horses, and 14 small pieces of artillery.[3] He followed the track of the two earlier expeditions. At Tabasco, at the base of Yucatan, his force had its first, and stiff, engagement with Mexicans. It prevailed. The defeated Tabascan leaders presented Cortés with twenty women, among them a noble captive of theirs, Malinaltzin, named Marina by the Spaniards (and now usually referred to in Spanish as La Malinche). She was to become Cortés's mistress, mother of one of his sons, and, most important, a crucial linguistic and cultural interpreter of the Aztecs for the invaders. Going northwards now up the Gulf coast, the Spaniards reached a rare sheltered spot, later named San Juan de Ulúa, in mid April. There, on Good Friday (April 22, 1519), Cortés put ashore and made camp.

He stayed at this base for four months, making essential preparations for a move inland. He had first to consolidate his own force, which was divided between his own adherents and men loyal to Velázquez. It is not clear exactly what the governor had first intended the 1519 expedition to do, and Cortés kept his plans veiled for a time, perhaps as he developed them. But the men evidently saw themselves faced with a choice from the start between Cortés and Velázquez. Cortés won over enough to give him an operative authority. Opulent gifts of gold, featherwork, and cotton cloth descending on the Spaniards from Tenochtitlan helped him make a case for staying and conquering. There was unimagined wealth to be had here. At one point, he threatened to pull up stakes and go back to Cuba. This caused uproar among his supporters, in the midst of which he persuaded the party to name him its chief justice and captain-general (and, as such, recipient of a fifth of all booty gathered).

With these powers in hand he resolved to found a town. This was done with full Spanish formality. And once the place, the Villa Rica de la Vera Cruz (Rich Town of the True Cross), had been created, and equipped through his appointments with a full complement of urban officials, Cortés pulled off what has always seemed his most blatant piece of chicanery. He resigned his powers to the town council and magistrates – in full confidence that they would immediately pass them back to him, as they duly did after grave and formal debate. Here Cortés drew on Reconquest practice in Castile, by which newly recovered frontiers were politically solidified through the creation of towns. Towns, in such circumstances, also took on an identity of their own that he doubtless aimed to create in the case of Vera Cruz. A chartered town in Mexico was a legal and political body that could at least make pretense to independence from the governor of Cuba, and deal directly with the monarchy. Cortés, holding powers given to him by the town, both distanced himself from Velázquez and gave himself some cover against charges of rebellion.

From Veracruz (to adopt the modern spelling) Cortés also probed for information about Mexico in general and in particular, as he became increasingly aware of it, about the Aztec state. Moctezuma II, informed from the start of the aliens' presence, sent envoys to look, converse, and report. Cortés realized quickly that Aztec power was not monolithic. Much resentment festered on the recently incorporated periphery over Tenochtitlan's tribute demands. The Spaniards saw this at first hand among coastal communities near Veracruz, and from these places took their first native allies, promising them support if they resisted the Aztecs.

Encouraged by these evident fissures in the Aztec imperial polity, Cortés began a cautious advance inland in mid August 1519. To mark this new departure, both physical and psychological, and perhaps to stiffen the resolve of remaining waverers, he declared the ships unseaworthy, and beached them. They were not burned, as the story sometimes has it. He left a garrison of 150 or so at Veracruz. The rest of the party, accompanied by local Indians carrying supplies and pulling cannons, began crossing the tropical coastal plain towards the highland escarpment. The direct distance to Tenochtitlan was some 330 kilometers. The Spaniards moved circumspectly, taking three months for the journey, but on the way had notable adventures. The most important was a contest with Tlaxcala, a city-state 90 kilometers east of the Aztec capital that had long resisted imperial domination. The Tlaxcalans fought Cortés's force several times. In these battles he could count himself the victor, in the sense of having survived the attacks of vastly greater numbers. The Tlaxcalans were impressed enough by the Spaniards' weapons and doggedness to see in them useful partners against Tenochtitlan. This was the crucial alliance of the conquest for Cortés. Tlaxcala from this point never failed to offer men, and a base on which he could fall back. Its example persuaded other foes of the Aztecs to join the Spanish against them.

After surviving an attempted Aztec ambush at Cholula, between Tlaxcala and Tenochtitlan, the Spaniards entered the Valley of Mexico, and reached the capital on November 8, 1519. Moctezuma welcomed them into the city and lodged them in one of the palaces of the past Aztec rulers that surrounded the central temple compound. Ten days later, Cortés took Moctezuma captive, confining him to the Spanish quarters. This, obviously enough, was a risky blow to attempt. But Cortés had well enough gauged the emperor's uncertainty about the Spaniards' intentions and nature as to judge the risk acceptable. He may also have calculated that Aztec power was so densely concentrated in the supreme ruler that if this figure were neutralized, the rest of the upper political system would suffer paralysis. This certainly proved to be so, at least for several months after Moctezuma's capture.

During those months of the winter of 1519–20 and the following early spring, Cortés kept his force in Tenochtitlan, where the Aztecs continued to feed it, though with growing ill grace. He gathered information about Mexico, partly from the natives and partly through small forays of Spaniards dispatched to explore.[4] Beyond this, Cortés seems now to have been awaiting a royal reaction, presumably approving, to a report on his activities he had sent to Spain the previous July. Unexpected responses to his doings from much closer at hand, however, forced improvisation on him, and changed the pace and course of the campaign. It proved no bad thing for the Spaniards; Cortés was at his most creative when improvising.

The ship sent with the report to Spain had, contrary to Cortés's order, touched on Cuba. News of his venture spread quickly there. Velázquez put together a large force (900 men) under Pánfilo de Narváez, a seasoned campaigner from the Cuban conquest, to bring his errant underling to heel. Narváez arrived off Veracruz in late April 1520. When word of this reached Cortés in the capital, he decided on a forced march to the coast with some of his men, a surprise attack, and then reliance on his persuasive powers to bring the chastisers over to his side. In all this he was brilliantly successful, and so more than doubled the strength he could put against the Aztecs.

And strength he now needed. For the man he had left in charge in Tenochtitlan, a senior lieutenant named Pedro de Alvarado, had been anything but successful in keeping harmony between invaders and natives. By this time (May 1520), to be sure, organized resistance to the Spanish was finally developing among part of the native nobility. The paralysis of Moctezuma's capture was wearing off. A plan was perhaps made to attack the Spanish party during the major religious festival named Toxcatl, held in May. It was a feast of Huitzilopochtli, a particularly fitting time for retaliation since he was the Mexicas' tutelary god. Sensing danger, Alvarado had attacked gathered lords and warriors in the temple compound at the start of the celebration. Many of them were killed, which weakened the Aztecs' ability to resist from then on. But this fight marked a change in the nature of the Spaniards' struggle with the rulers of Tenochtitlan. The time of psychological maneuvering and mutual measuring was over. It was clear that the final outcome would now result only from physical confrontation.

The Aztecs allowed Cortés to re-enter Tenochtitlan with his enlarged army. Their plan, simple and obvious enough, was to trap him. Cortés wished only to unite his force and escape. For several weeks the Spaniards failed in their attempts to break out. They finally succeeded one night in late June or early July, fighting their way, down the shortest causeway, to the western shore of the lake. Many of them died. (Moctezuma died also, possibly at Spanish hands, possibly of a wound suffered earlier as he had tried to dissuade Mexica warriors from attacking the Spanish.) Most of the horses and all the artillery were lost. This was the "Noche Triste," or gloomy night, of the conquest. Cortés's only hope now lay in Tlaxcala. His safest, though not most direct, way to it lay around the north end of Lake Texcoco, where settlement was sparse. On the journey the Aztecs again brought him to battle, at Otumba. It was a fierce fight, but the Spaniards struggled back to Tlaxcala, whose leaders, after some debate, agreed to take them in.

For Cortés, this was the nadir of the assault on the Aztecs: his force diminished, its technological edge (of guns and horses) blunted, hostility still looming at his back in Cuba, his standing in Spain still uncertain. He seemed totally at the mercy of Mexicans, both his Aztec foes and his Tlaxcalan allies. Now, though, he turned with amazing success to diplomacy outside the Valley of Mexico. During the second half of 1520 he used a mixture of military threat (supported by Tlaxcala) and persuasion to pry local communities in southeastern Mexico loose from Aztec control. Small places were easily intimidated, and success built on success, so that, despite the Spaniards' expulsion from the valley, they soon again seemed potential victors against Tenochtitlan. An alien ally now also began its grim work. Smallpox, in an extension of the 1518 outbreak in Hispaniola, had reached Mexico with Narváez in April 1520. By the autumn its effects were severe. Many local native leaders died. Cortés found communities coming to him for advice on government.

By January 1521, when Cortés judged the time ripe for a new approach on Tenochtitlan, the Aztec empire outside the valley had dissolved. He decided to mount his attack from Texcoco, 25 kilometers east of Tenochtitlan, across the lake. Texcoco had once been part of the Aztec Triple Alliance, but, only a few years before the Spaniards' arrival, had been alienated by the Mexicas' imperious behavior towards it. From this base in early 1521 Cortés subdued Aztec subject towns around the lake shores. Then, in May, he began to move in on Tenochtitlan along its causeways, and also by water, using thirteen brigantines assembled near Texcoco from components cut outside the valley. By now new arrivals of men whom rumors had drawn from the islands had raised the Spanish force to some 900, along with several dozen horses, and new cannon. Much of the final fighting on the causeways, however, was done by the multitude of native allies, whose fury against Tenochtitlan had sometimes to be restrained by the Spanish. Perhaps even deadlier help in this final siege came from smallpox. Many defenders of the city died horribly from it, the toll of the disease being worsened by starvation in the last weeks. The resistance was heroic. Cortés had almost to raze Tenochtitlan in order to take it. But finally the city yielded on August 13, 1521, as the last independent Aztec leader, Cuauhtémoc, was captured.

So ended the military conquest of the Mexican heartland. Never again, in fact, in what Cortés now controlled – essentially the Aztec imperial territory – did the native population pose any martial threat to Spanish presence. The rest of central Mexico also quickly fell to the invaders. The Tarascans of the center-west, who had stoutly held the Aztecs at bay, collapsed before the Spaniards, perhaps overawed by their success against the empire. Northern Mexico was another story. There the mainly nomadic tribes of the plateau, and various small sedentary groups in the western Sierra Madre, resisted the European invasion long and hard. It was not until about 1600 that Spaniards could move around the *altiplano* without danger of surprise native attack. The subjugation of the north took half a century, and cost the Spanish far more in lives and money than the Aztec episode. The north-western mountains always remained a breeding ground of native revolt; but those distant risings posed no threat to Spanish control of the whole, and so were no more than passing flurries of concern to the colonial government.

THE ANDES

The same pattern held true in the rest of mainland Spanish America. The major conquest in South America was of the Inca empire. This was a larger and in some ways more forbidding enterprise than overcoming the Aztecs. The Incas were more organized fighters, and their mountain world was more daunting in terrain and climate than central Mexico. Yet in Peru the Spanish in essence repeated the Mexican exercise, twelve years later. Here Francisco Pizarro, another product of Extremadura, was the leader. He, like Cortés, was a veteran of the Indies. He was, in fact, a tougher and more senior veteran, since he had lived and fought through the hazardous reconnaissance and settlement of Tierra Firme from 1509 on, and by the early 1520s was one of the leading *vecinos* of Panama. He was a little older than Cortés, having been born *c*.1478, and was a more rough and ready character – he was the illegitimate son of a minor noble of the Extremaduran town of Trujillo, illiterate, and lacking Cortés's sophistication and legalistic turn of mind. But he was, for all that, a compelling expeditionary leader, and no mean judge of native political affairs.

He was, too, a methodical man. He approached Peru slowly, responding to rumors of rich lands to the south by probing by sea from Panama in the mid 1520s. This was done with the consent of Pedrarias Dávila, the governor of the territory, whose reputation for erratic ferocity perhaps reinforced Pizarro's natural caution. Having finally proved the rumors by reaching an outpost of the Inca state at Túmbez in northern Peru, Pizarro then went to court in Spain to make a contract (*capitulación*) with the crown for the conquest. Such contracts were the legal rule in the Spanish occupation of America; Cortés's impulsive decision to attack the Aztecs was an exception testing the rule. In July of 1529 Pizarro's agreement was concluded. He undertook to equip an expedition at his own cost; in return he was to be *adelantado*, governor and captain-general of whatever he might take.[5] The titles gave him supreme civil and military powers, subject only to the monarchy.

Having gathered followers from Extremadura, including several of his brothers, Pizarro returned to Panama. From there he departed south with some 180 men at the end of 1530. His three ships reached the equator in thirteen days. But it was not until September 1532 that he began the march up into the Andes that brought him face to face with Inca power. In the interim he surveyed part of the southern Ecuadorian and north Peruvian coasts, gathered information, seized booty (from Túmbez, for example), and created a base and port, San Miguel de Piura, a little further down the coast.

Other Spaniards arrived meantime from Central America. But the party that Pizarro led inland had only 168 in it, 62 of them horsemen. These were quickly to become the most famous of all conquistadores; for if Pizarro was more cautious than Cortés in approaching the center of native power, once there he acted even more urgently. The Spanish party entered Cajamarca, a major town in the northern Peruvian Andes, on November 15, 1532. The next evening, in the enclosed town square, they attacked and captured the Sapa Inca, Atahualpa. Pizarro had invited the ruler, who was camped outside the town with a large army, to this meeting. He planned an ambush. Atahualpa, suspecting nothing, or if suspecting, made careless by the imbalance of numbers between his army and the Spaniards, came. He was offered – briefly, formally, and unintelligibly – a chance to accept Spanish authority and Christianity. This he not surprisingly rejected. The Spaniards hidden around the square attacked. Their handguns and few small artillery pieces sowed panic. Perhaps 2,000 of Atahualpa's company died. No Spaniard did, and only one was injured. Atahualpa was captured. The Spaniards held him in Cajamarca before executing him in late July 1533. He had attempted to buy his freedom with a famous promise to fill a large room with gold and silver. The promise, equally famously and to the Spaniards' surprise, was fulfilled. But a Sapa Inca seemed too dangerous a figure to release. Finally, though, by the time the invaders were preparing to move south from Cajamarca to Cuzco, Atahualpa's value as a hostage was clearly falling, and the simplest course was merely to destroy him.

The seizing of Atahualpa in November 1532 was by no means the end of the Peruvian conquest. But although the Spanish had to fight considerably for the territory, against forces led by surviving Inca lords (most notably in 1536, when a brother of Atahualpa named Manco almost succeeded in ejecting them from Cuzco), as in Mexico their permanent presence was never seriously threatened once they had dealt that first heavy blow to the center.

As in Mexico, too, areas close to the imperial center fell quickly and quite easily. Forces spreading from Peru brought what are now highland Ecuador and Bolivia under Spanish control in the late 1530s, and by the early 1540s central Chile too. Sebastián de Belalcázar led the Quito, or Ecuadorian, campaign; Hernando and Gonzalo Pizarro, younger brothers of Francisco, directed the incorporation of Charcas, the future Bolivia; and Pedro de Valdivia commanded the expedition that settled central Chile. All these areas had been part of the Inca empire. In some of them, residual Inca resistance persisted, and had to be quelled. Anti-Inca feelings in the local populations sometimes helped the Spanish in this. On occasion, though, those same populations blocked the Spanish advance; but they did not hold out for long.

Curiously enough, at first sight, the areas that took longest to conquer were those beyond the frontiers of the native empires. In part this was because such places were usually poor in soil, hostile in climate, and thinly peopled. The Spaniards tended for obvious reasons to leave such places to last. Generally only late arrivals or men who for some personal or political reason had been squeezed out of the major conquests showed an interest in tackling these fringes, hoping to gain something, if only status. A more telling reason, however, for the peripheries proving so hard to subdue was simply that they lacked political centers. There was no single head whose removal would paralyze the entire body, as in the Aztec and Inca cases. Small groups, often mobile and able to live off the land as they moved, had to be suppressed one by one. The effort was often not worth the result. Examples are the forests of southern Chile, the plains of Uruguay and Argentina, much of the interior of Venezuela and Colombia, and Yucatan. Northern Mexico would have been one of these lightly attached peripheries had it not proved to be a rich source of silver. The prospect of that reward spurred Spanish incursion, exploration, domination, and settlement from the 1540s on.

The mainland conquests, then, expanded from two main foci. From the middle of Mexico, once it was secured by Cortés, lesser leaders went out south to upper Central America (Honduras, Guatemala, and El Salvador), and then Yucatan, in the 1520s and 1530s; others went west to Michoacán and the west coast in the same years; yet others, in a far more protracted effort, gradually pushed northward, drawn mainly by silver, until, c.1600, New Mexico, the most remote of the provinces of colonial Mexico, came into being. New Mexico has, since 1848, belonged to the USA. Its capital, Santa Fe, founded in 1609, is a very close contemporary of Jamestown in Virginia, and Quebec in Canada. In South America the source of expanding conquest was the Inca heartland taken by Pizarro. Lesser centers of conquest elsewhere were Panama, whose settlers moved upward through southern Central America, eventually to run into the wave descending from Mexico, and the Río de La Plata, from which, after the collapse of an initial attempt to found Buenos Aires in the mid 1530s, settlers moved upriver to begin Spanish colonization of Paraguay.

North-western South America, far from both Peru and Mexico, underwent its own, distinct process of conquest and occupation. The Venezuelan case was the most unusual. The coast had early attracted attention, both as a source of pearls and as a mission field. But by 1520 or so the pearls were mostly gone and the missions had failed. With no prospective conquerors and settlers in view, Charles V turned to the Welser banking company of Augsburg to undertake exploration and settlement. As Germans, the Welsers were citizens of the Holy Roman Empire, and therefore Charles's subjects. They could legitimately be allowed into Spanish America. Besides that, Charles owed them money. So in 1528 a contract was made for the Welsers to colonize Venezuela and defend its coast, in return for the profits of trade. In the event the profits were scant. What the Germans most avidly sought was gold, and they found little. Pursuing it, however, they sent six expeditions inland. The great lure was already, as it was long to remain for explorers of north-western South America, the tales of El Dorado, the reputed golden monarch of the interior. These German expeditions made the first European surveys of the interior. Apart from that, though, the Welser experiment produced little and proved mutually unsatisfactory to crown and company. The Germans failed to profit as they had hoped. They also failed to found towns and pay taxes as contracted. They maltreated both natives and such Spaniards as were in Venezuela. In 1548 Charles revoked the 1528 agreement, and a slow, purely Spanish settlement of the land began. Caracas, the colonial and present capital, was founded in 1567.

One of the Welsers' expeditions, led in a famously hazardous Andean crossing by Nikolaus Federmann, had strayed in 1539 into what is now Colombia. There in the interior it ran into a Spanish expedition that had come up from the Caribbean coast. In this north-western corner of South America conquest was slow. The only Spanish presence by the mid 1530s consisted of two small towns, Santa Marta and Cartagena, on the Caribbean. Endless rugged ranges, the valleys between them blanketed in equally endless wet forest, discouraged inward exploration. But, about 1535, native tombs not far inland revealed gold almost on the Peruvian scale. Interest and resolve grew enough for substantial expeditions to be organized. Of these, the critical one was an 800-man force led by Gonzalo Jiménez de Quesada in 1536 up the Magdalena valley. That was one of the few possible passages to the highland interior, though one that was hot and unhealthy. After many tribulations, 160 survivors finally clambered up the valley side to the grassy plateau where the Chibcha culture flourished. In 1538, using the well-tried combination of intimidation, warfare, and politics, Jiménez subdued the Chibcha. Hardly had he done so when there appeared not only Federmann and his German–Spanish band from Venezuela, but also another Spanish company from the south, an offshoot of the force that had taken Quito under Belalcázar. Jiménez had best claim, however, to the interior highlands. He bestowed the name New Granada on the region, and founded on the site of the Chibcha center a Spanish city, Santa Fe de Bogotá, that remains capital of Colombia to this day. Though by the late 1530s many South American regions still awaited European exploration, the domination of the Chibcha nevertheless completed a major phase of Iberian conquest, for this was the last area of high culture to succumb in South America, or indeed in any part of Latin America.

EXPLAINING THE CONQUESTS

The period of the major military conquests by the Spanish, roughly 1520–40, must rank as the most tumultuous twenty years in the history of the Americas. Never before or since can so many lives have been so thoroughly shaken. The Spaniards' actions may be admired or deplored; but those on both sides of that moral question continue to be fascinated by them, and by the manner of their execution. How could so few dispose of so many? Why did such mighty political structures collapse at what, comparatively speaking, was a mere touch?

The answers are many, and no generally accepted ranking exists of their importance. Any list must, though, include the Spaniards' technological advantages. Their steel swords and steel-tipped pikes were more durable and generally more damaging than any hand-held weapon that they faced. Swords and long pikes probably gave them a greater advantage in close combat than even firearms provided. The guns, both the few light cannon and the more numerous arquebusses that they had, were slow to reload. The alarm caused by their noise and smoke may well have been of greater effect than the injuries inflicted by the shot. But even this scare value was transient; after the first few encounters, native warriors grew used to gunfire. More fearsome were clearly the Spaniards' animals of war: large mastiffs, used especially in the islands to pursue and bring down foes, and, of course, horses – "The mighty horse, which, with mounted man, a monstrous beast appeared, six footed."[6] The Mexicans, lacking large domestic animals, were particularly awed by these, and tended to regard them as touched by the divine. Horses gave the invaders the tremendous advantage of height in combat; riders could strike down on the Indians. After battle, horses enabled pursuit at speeds unknown to the native people. (Though hardly martial creatures, pigs should not be omitted here. Live pigs carried aboard ship, then driven along with the conquering bands, provided the Spaniards with protein in a familiar form.) Finally, the invaders had the great advantage over the natives of being able to move themselves and their equipment over water with ease and relatively great speed. Ocean-going ships were fundamental to the expansion of conquest. And, in the particular case of the Aztec contest, the ingenious building of brigantines for use on the lake was central to Spanish success.

The Spanish also had the advantage of better battle tactics. Native attacks were mainly mass charges, whereas the Spaniards fought in disciplined ranks, with pikes facing forward. As the first Indians fell before these, the efforts of men behind them were blocked. Again, and more telling, at least in Mexico, the two sides fought with different purposes: the Spaniards to kill, the Aztecs to take prisoners for sacrifice.

Then there were contrasts of strategy. The Spaniards developed in the islands the practice of the knock-out blow: they aimed from the start to destroy whatever central command the opposition might possess. First, of course, it was essential to identify and locate this authority; hence in part Cortés's and Pizarro's long delays on the coast before their inland advances, as they probed as best they could the politics of their targets. Once the goal was in view, the invaders acted with a purposeful directness that the native side usually lacked, or did not develop until it was too late.

Another, connected, political aim was to identify the enemy's internal foes, to find the strains in the political structure. Cortés was possibly the most adept at this of all conquistadores, but to play native rivals off against each other was the aim of all Spanish leaders. Even Pedro de Alvarado – not, to judge by his performance in Tenochtitlan in May 1520, the most subtle of political calculators – managed it with great success in 1524 against contending Maya groups in his conquest of Guatemala. In Peru, Pizarro did not receive as much active native aid as Cortés in Mexico. But he benefited greatly from the enmity between Atahualpa and Huascar, contenders for the Inca throne. Huascar's base and support were in Cuzco; Atahualpa's were in Quito, far to the north. Pizarro's force came on the scene as Atahualpa, prevailing in the war of succession, was advancing south towards Cuzco. Even after his capture by the Spaniards, Atahualpa was able to order Huascar executed. Consequently, Huascar's followers tended to see Pizarro, if not as a friend, at least as the enemy of their enemy, and did not resist the Spaniards' further advance into Peru. At least two Andean ethnic groups, moreover, did fight with the Spaniards against Inca resistance, avenging, as they saw it, earlier defeat and humiliation by Cuzco. These were the Chachapoyas people of northern Peru and the Huanca of the center. Again, in 1534, Pizarro's lieutenant Belalcázar, campaigning to subdue Quito, which remnants of Atahualpa's forces still controlled, found an active ally there in the Cañari Indians. These had suffered severely at Atahualpa's hands. Like parallel groups in Mexico resentful of the Aztecs, they fought now for the Spanish "with savage glee."[7]

To these quite concrete advantages of weapons, native supporters, tactics, and strategy enjoyed by the Spanish must be added another physical element, although one over which they had no control. This was disease. That Tenochtitlan's defense was weakened by smallpox during the final siege is quite clear. In fact Mexican resolve had been increasingly undermined over the previous twelve months, after the arrival of the disease on the mainland in April of 1520. It is thought that the epidemic of smallpox that began then in Mexico swept down through Central America and into northern South America during the next few years, very possibly killing the ruling Inca of the time, Huayna Capac. His death precipitated the succession war of the late 1520s between Huascar and Atahualpa, a war that left the Inca empire badly weakened just as the Spanish came onto the Peruvian scene. For that reason, smallpox may have done even more to facilitate Spanish conquest in the Andes than it did in Mexico.

To all this should be added intangibles of psychology, especially of the Indian perception of the invaders. One of the most tantalizing questions about the

Aztec defeat is whether, as some sources report, Moctezuma took the Spanish as agents of the man-god Quetzalcóatl, who, legend had it, had departed eastwards from Mexico several centuries earlier, promising he would return to claim the land as his inheritance. The year of Cortés's arrival was, by some accounts, the appointed date. Similar predictions were made by several other native cultures that the Spanish overcame.[8] It is possible, even likely, that such stories were post-conquest inventions of the vanquished, intended to explain, or explain away, their defeats. Nonetheless, often enough the Spanish were ascribed some degree of divinity when they first appeared. This is no surprise. The native cultures they overcame generally did not make any solid distinction between the earthly and the divine. The Spanish, being unfamiliar in appearance and speech, possessing ships, guns and horses, and acting in unconventional and mysterious ways, were good candidates for some measure of deification. This made wariness in treating them still more advisable; hesitation thus plagued native decisions about dealing with the invasions.

Enormous advantages may have come to the Spaniards simply because they acted, unwittingly, so unconventionally. War in Mexico, for instance, was ruled by protocol. Foes announced their coming attacks, sending ambassadors. The Spanish did not. Wars did not begin in the late summer, the time of harvest. Cortés started his march on Tenochtitlan in August. Splendid gifts of the sort that Moctezuma kept sending to Cortés were intended to convey Aztec wealth and power, and hence to dismay the enemy. The Spaniards were simply drawn onward by them. There was no apparent reason why the Spaniards should attack. Mexicans understood war as a contest between the populations of cities, who fought to gain tribute, and captives to be offered to the gods. The Spanish, men of no city, had no place in such a pattern. They sought not to capture, but to kill, and from there to proceed to absolute domination, a notion alien to Mexicans. For all these reasons, and others, it is possible that Moctezuma made the ultimately fatal mistake of letting the Spanish into Tenochtitlan simply because confusion prevented him from conceiving how dangerous they were. In South America the Incas suffered from similarly fatal misapprehensions. One was that no serious threat could come from the coast. Atahualpa had no precedent to warn him of the possibility of reinforcement over the sea. The sea, conversely, had always seemed a limit to the possible power of the coast. The Incas' world, the territory of their empire, was the Andes. That, with few exceptions, was where redoubtable enemies were. Pizarro, approaching up the mountain slopes from the Pacific, was not ignored, but tolerated, even seen as entering a trap. But the disaster befell the trappers, not the intended victim.[9]

The conquests, then, give the impression that the native peoples (especially, perhaps, the advanced ones) were at a greater psychological than technological disadvantage. They simply could not comprehend quickly enough the threat that suddenly confronted them. Patterns of behavior and thought – military, religious, political – bound them to an inadequate set of responses to the new, exotic challenge. There were, naturally, some exceptions, especially in more immediately practical matters. The Aztecs learned to avoid cannon fire by running in zig-zags rather than straight lines; they tried, with some success, to destroy horses by digging pits lined with sharp stakes. Going further still, the Inca leader Manco by 1536 had learned to ride a captured horse in battle. But at the deeper, vital level of understanding the invaders, their actions, and their aims, the native leaders largely failed. Their responses to invasion were therefore slow, hesitant, and confused. The Spanish did not understand the native cultures either, of course, in any profound sense – the intricacies of Aztec religion, or of Inca succession, for example. But they had little need to do so. The simplicity of their purpose (kill, take booty, and above all seize the center) gave their efforts a focus that the opposition lacked. Their technological superiority, in weapons, methods of fighting, and transport, enabled them to realize their purpose. The Spanish had the immense advantage of being on new ground. In total contrast to the Indians, they were away from the familiar surroundings that restrained or conditioned action. Here is another of the liberties that Spaniards found in the New World.

Historians have commonly, and properly, seen much that is medieval in the organization and practice of Spanish exploration and conquest. A clear example is Cortés's exploitation in 1519 of the traditional prerogatives of Spanish towns to bolster his own political and legal position. But in a broader sense the leading conquistadores seem post-medieval – fully men of the Renaissance, imitating, if unconsciously, the political style of Ferdinand: pragmatic, subordinating means to ends, agile extemporizers rather than servants of tradition. The same contrast between incisive invaders and bemused non-Europeans recurred time and again over the following three or more centuries as the European expansion proceeded. The Spanish were simply the first to bring what proved to be the terrible weapon of empiricism to bear on non-European cultures – the empiricism that was one of the enduring mental products of the late Renaissance.

The conquests, especially those on the mainland, need therefore a many-sided explanation. The native states were certainly populous, but their peoples were not united. The states existed as structures sustained by many counteracting tensions. If only a few of these strains were altered, the whole edifice tottered. The native people managed to blunt some parts of the Spanish technical edge; but in aggregate that edge remained throughout a crucial advantage. Above all, the invaders brought an advantage in mentality, one that allowed them to apply their technical superiority to maximum effect, and which, more important, overtaxed native powers of adaptability. The Spaniards acted and fought in ways that broke the American rules; the Indians could not decipher and absorb the new, alien rules quickly enough to save themselves.

Still, when all the explaining is done, the conquests remain a conundrum. The overwhelming of the Aztecs and the Incas remains an amazing, barely credible, feat, to be wondered at, if not approved. Despite the flaws in native polities, the Spaniards often found themselves fighting vastly larger forces. How could several thousand Tlaxcalans, for instance, fail to crush Cortés's few hundred by simple weight of numbers? Time after time, the Spanish escaped being crushed, though they were sometimes badly bruised. Each escape, each campaign, seems a close-run thing when seen in isolation. Failure seems an imminent possibility in nearly every case. Yet failure never came. And if the period of military conquest is regarded as a whole, an opposing view emerges: one of the inexorability of Spanish advance. On the ceiling of the Hospicio Cabañas in Guadalajara, the twentieth-century Mexican muralist José Clemente Orozco painted Cortés as a man-machine, a striding figure of steel with great bolts for its joints. Perhaps he had in mind the post-conquest vision that the Mexica retained of the Spaniards' entry into Tenochtitlan in 1519: "some came all in iron; they came turned into iron; they came gleaming."[10] Certainly, nothing could convey more dramatically than Orozco's picture the relentlessness of Spanish advance through the Indies that the story of the conquests as a whole conveys.

The contrast between looming failure in particular campaigns and broad success in the conquest as a whole is perhaps a false one. Every disaster avoided, and every threat finessed, reinforced in the Spanish an energizing sense of the rightness of their actions, fortified by the belief that God blessed their enterprise – that, indeed, they were enacting divine will. And as among the conquistadores this belief in divine justification grew, so among the natives sureness of their cause, of their gods' power, indeed of their understanding of the universe and its workings, dwindled. This shifting balance of confidence was the invaders' final advantage.

PART III

DOMINATION

CHRONOLOGY

1484   Birth of Bartolomé de las Casas in Seville

1501–38   Rome grants to the Spanish monarchy patronage and other controls over the church in America

1503   First sugar mill built in Hispaniola

1511   First American *audiencia* established, at Santo Domingo

1513   See of Darien created

1516   Las Casas named Protector of the Indians

1522   Papal letter *Omnimoda* entrusts evangelization of natives in Spanish America to regular clergy

1523–6   Cortés is official governor of New Spain (i.e. Mexico)

1524   Arrival of first bureaucrats (treasury officials) in Mexico. Foundation of the Council of the Indies (Consejo de Indias)

1526   See of Tlaxcala, the first in Mexico, created

1527   First *audiencia* established in Mexico City (refounded with new judges in 1530). See of Mexico City created

1528–30   Cortés in Spain. He is named marquis of the Valley of Oaxaca

*c.*1529   First sugar mill built in Mexico

*c.*1530   First silver strikes in Mexico

1530s   Treadle looms imported into Mexico

1532   Vasco de Quiroga's first *hospital*, Santa Fe de los Altos, founded near Mexico City

1535   Arrival in Mexico of the first viceroy, and founding viceroy, Don Antonio de Mendoza

1537   First Peruvian see created, at Cuzco

1538   *Audiencia* placed at City of Panama (re-established 1564)

*c.*1540   First sugar mills built in Peru

1540   Cortés returns to Spain from Mexico

1541   Assassination of Francisco Pizarro in Lima by Almagrists. See of Lima created

1542   Promulgation of the New Laws, reforming Spanish government in America, and controlling the *encomienda*

1543   *Audiencias* established in Lima and Guatemala

1544   First viceroy, Blasco Núñez Vela, arrives in Peru. Revolt of Peruvian colonists, under Gonzalo Pizarro, begins

1545–64   Council of Trent

1545   Silver ores found at Potosí

1546   Silver ores found at Zacatecas: start of mining in northern Mexico

1547   Death of Cortés in Spain. *Audiencia* established at Guadalajara. Grammar of Nahuatl, the first of a Mexican language, produced by Andrés de Olmos, OFM

1548   Defeat and execution of Gonzalo Pizarro: end of Peruvian rebellion against royal rule. See of Guadalajara created

1548–50   Government of Peru by Pedro de la Gasca

1549   Royal ban on *servicio personal* by Indians (i.e. the use of Indians in *encomienda* for labor)

1550   Debate between Las Casas and Sepúlveda at Valladolid in Spain

*c.*1550   Beginning, in Mexico, of state-imposed draft labor by Indians

*c.*1555   Beginning of silver refining by amalgamation in Mexico

1556   Abdication of Charles V (died 1558). Accession to Spanish throne of Philip II

1559   *Audiencia* established at La Plata

1563   *Audiencia* established at Quito

1566   Death of Las Casas

1568   First Jesuits in Spanish America, at Lima

1569–81   Administration of Don Francisco de Toledo, fifth, but "founding," viceroy of Peru

1570–1   Tribunals of the Inquisition set up in Lima (1570) and Mexico City (1571)

1575   Silver refining by amalgamation begins at Potosí

1573   Ordinances for New Discovery and Settlement

1574   Ordinance of Patronage (Ordenanza del Patronazgo)

1583   *Audiencia* established at Manila

1598   Death of Philip II of Spain. Accession of Philip III

FURTHER READING FOR PART III

Volumes 1 and 2 of Leslie Bethell (ed.), *The Cambridge History of Latin America*, contain numerous chapters on the topics raised here. The two essays in volume 1 by J. H. Elliott are especially elegant. A classic work is Clarence H. Haring, *The Spanish Empire in America*. Two academic texts, distinguished by their intelligence, are James Lockhart and Stuart B. Schwartz, *Early Latin America: A History of Colonial Spanish America and Brazil*, and Lyle N. McAlister, *Spain and Portugal in the New World, 1492–1700*. Also enlightening are Mario Góngora, *Studies in the Colonial History of Spanish America*, and Enrique Semo, *The History of Capitalism in Mexico: Its Origins, 1521–1763*. Good monographs dealing with the aspects of domination discussed here include: Noble David Cook and W. George Lovell (eds), *"Secret Judgments of God": Old World Disease in Colonial Spanish America*; Susan A. Alchon, *A Pest in the Land: New World Epidemics in a Global Perspective*; Inga Clendinnen, *Ambivalent Conquests: Maya and Spaniard in Yucatan, 1517–1570*; Sabine MacCormack, *Religion in the Andes: Vision and Imagination in Early Colonial Peru*; Jacqueline Holler, *Escogidas Plantas: Nuns and Beatas in Mexico City, 1531–1601*; Karen Vieira Powers, *Women in the Crucible of Conquest: The Gendered Genesis of Spanish American Society, 1500–1600*; John L. Phelan, *The Millennial Kingdom of the Franciscans in the New World*; Peggy K. Liss, *Mexico under Spain, 1521–1556*; Charles Gibson, *The Aztecs under Spanish Rule: A History of the Indians of the Valley of Mexico, 1519–1810* (but mostly concerned with the sixteenth century); Susan Schroeder, Stephanie Wood, and Robert Haskett (eds), *Indian Women of Early Mexico*; Susan Socolow, *The Women of Colonial Latin America*; Steve J. Stern, *Peru's Indian Peoples and the Challenge of Spanish Conquest: Huamanga to 1640*; James Lockhart, *The Nahuas after the Conquest: A Social and Cultural History of the Indians of Central Mexico, Sixteenth through Eighteenth Centuries*; Herbert S. Klein and Ben Vinson, *African Slavery in Latin America and the Caribbean*; and Anthony Pagden, *The Fall of Natural Man: The American Indian and the Origins of Comparative Ethnology*.

[7] *Administration: The Power of Paper*

Conquerors as Governors

FROM the military conquests of the mainland there followed a bureaucratic domination of the regions seized. This came more quickly in some areas than in others, but with the same feeling of inexorability as the conquests give.

The shift from the military commands of the conquest to civil government did not, however, happen easily. The contracts that leaders of conquering expeditions made with the crown typically granted them titles of governor, so that a nominally civilian chief executive was immediately in place once the fighting was over. He was, moreover, the man who probably had the best knowledge of the region under his control, and his military expertise fitted him to direct the mopping-up operations and expansionary efforts that usually followed from the conquest of some major center of native culture. But once all this was over, or even before, tensions often arose between conqueror-governor and the home authority, precisely because the crown feared that it had given away too much power, and too much potential for profit. The richer the region conquered, the sharper such fears would be.

No region promised greater wealth at the time of conquest than Mexico, and in most respects the story of Cortés and his role in governing the new colony is a representative one. It is of course exceptional in that between crown and Cortés no contract existed; he was, as a conquistador, technically a rebel. But nothing succeeds like success. After what must have been a nerve-racking period of waiting for royal response to his calculatedly persuasive reports on the conquest, and to the gifts that he had chosen to suggest Mexico's wealth and artistry,[1] Cortés received in September 1523 his appointment as governor, *adelantado*, and captain-general (i.e. military commander) of New Spain, as he named the conquered Mexico. It had been issued in October 1522. Both Diego Velázquez and his influential backer, Juan Rodríguez de Fonseca, long the chief of American administration at the Spanish end, died in 1524. Chagrin over Cortés's success is said to have hurried them to the grave. Certainly both departed under a cloud of disgrace, after being found guilty of grave distortion of Cortés's record in Mexico, and Fonseca of having accepted payments from Velázquez.[2]

Briefly, now, Cortés was officially in sole charge of New Spain. He showed himself to be, for the time, an enlightened governor. True enough, he distributed native Mexicans in *encomiendas*. He began to do so before he knew of his appointment as governor, and in ignorance of Charles V's suppression of *encomienda* in 1520. When the king duly objected, and ordered cancellation of the grants, Cortés argued that he had had no other resources besides "deposits" of Indians with which to reward many Spaniards who had fought in the final stages of the attack on Tenochtitlan. And, he said, for the longer term, if settlers were not granted the tribute and labor of Indians through *encomienda*, they would leave. Then New Spain would be lost to Spain, and many souls to God.

These were typical arguments of colonists wanting *encomiendas*. But Cortés believed that *encomienda* had been much to blame for the destruction of the Caribbean islanders, and was determined that New Spain should not suffer the same fate. Many of the men settling New Spain, he saw, "expect to do with these lands as was done in the Islands when they were colonized, that is, to harvest, destroy and then abandon them."[3] To avoid repetition of that calamity, he issued rules for the treatment of the Indians he had "entrusted" in *encomienda* to the conquerors. These ordinances, given late in 1524, restated many of the main points of the Laws of Burgos of a decade earlier (the obligations, for example, of *encomenderos* to provide religious instruction and food for their charges), but they especially stressed the agricultural employment of the Indians. Their use in mining was banned; only native people who were legally slaves were to be assigned to that.[4] This was a great contrast to the Laws of Burgos. Cortés was indeed much concerned to develop farming in New Spain, and made efforts to import seeds and livestock from the Caribbean islands to that end. He forbade *encomenderos* to leave New Spain for eight years after being granted their Indians and, like Ovando in the Caribbean, hoped to fix Spaniards in the land by binding them with family ties. *Encomenderos* should marry within eighteen months or, if they were already married in Spain, they must bring their wives over within the same period "so that the desire which the settlers of these parts have to remain should be made more manifest."[5]

Cortés, then, despite his misgivings about the *encomienda* in the Caribbean, clearly saw it as at bottom a useful and practicable means of promoting settlement and creating wealth in his new colony. He also had a strong personal interest in the existence of *encomiendas* in New Spain; he may have hoped to make the people of Tenochtitlan itself his own holding, and certainly assigned to himself the populations of Texcoco, Chalco, Otumba, and Coyoacán, all of them major towns close to the capital in the Valley of Mexico.[6] Cortés, indeed, rapidly became the richest man in the Indies in the years following the Aztec conquest, and, as governor and conqueror of the colony, was undoubtedly the most powerful. The more the crown learned of New Spain, the more evident and troubling the extent of this power seemed. Equally fraught with potential problems seemed Cortés's creation of a large group of men with lordly pretensions[7] – the 350 or so ex-conquistadores to whom he gave *encomiendas*. They were all in their varying degrees Cortéses in miniature: men with the pride of the conquest to swell their egos, and with Indians to rule and make them rich. In the wake of recent regional insurrections in Castile – the revolt of the *comuneros* in 1520–1, when many towns, with some initial noble backing, had challenged royal power – and, before them, the long contest the Catholic Monarchs had waged with the Castilian aristocracy, the rise of such power and wealth far away across the western sea was worrying indeed to the government in Spain.

Cortés, therefore, was not long left to rule alone. A series of governmental officials, of ever greater seniority, began to arrive in New Spain. The first to be sent, as in the islands, were *reales oficiales*, officers of the treasury. Four arrived early in 1524. At first they jockeyed for Cortés's favor, looking as much for their own profit as for the crown's. But then an unexpected opportunity for influence presented itself to them. In October 1524 Cortés decided to leave the capital, México-Tenochtitlan as it was now called, to make an overland journey to Honduras. His ostensible purpose was to subdue a rebellion by a man who had been one of his major commanders in the Aztec conquest, Cristóbal de Olid. Cortés had sent Olid to take Honduras and seek a strait from the Caribbean to the Pacific; but en route Olid had succumbed to the temptation, perhaps encouraged by Diego Velázquez, who sniped at Cortés from Cuba to the end of his days in June 1524, to try Cortés's own trick and make himself the independent conqueror of Honduras. But quashing Olid was certainly not the whole purpose of the exercise, for the force of several hundred that departed southward contained not only Spanish and native armed men, but pages, musicians, jugglers, falconers, and cooks. Several high Aztec dignitaries were also forced to join the party, among them Cuauhtemoc, the last Mexica king, and the pre-conquest rulers of Tacuba and Texcoco. The expedition was, then, akin to a royal progress, designed to exalt the magnificence of Cortés's power.

It was also a disaster. In the mountainous rainforests of southern Mexico there was no food for so large a group. Men and horses died. Cortés suspected plotting among the native nobles; he therefore cruelly executed Cuauhtemoc and several others. When finally he reached Honduras, he found Olid already removed – beheaded – by men loyal to himself. And Honduras (literally the "Depths") proved poor, isolated, and certainly without a strait.

Meanwhile, the cat gone from central Mexico, the four royal mice began to play, or rather, to squabble ferociously among themselves. Latent tensions among the early settlers also broke to the surface, some over grants of Indians, though a more general source of trouble was continued mistrust between supporters of Cortés and those of Velázquez. This rivalry, which had its roots in Cortés's break from the governor of Cuba in 1519, bedeviled New Spain throughout the 1520s. Rumors of Cortés's death on the expedition undermined order still further, since those loyal to him could now no longer appeal to his distant authority, or threaten consequences on his return. Spaniards died in something approaching civil war, and others in an Indian rebellion in the south.[8] The governor's orders on the treatment of natives were disregarded. Enslavement and other maltreatment of Indians grew. Of this chaos Cortés was duly warned in Honduras, but he was oddly hesitant to return to quell it.

If his purpose in delaying was to show his indispensability, the plan backfired. For though he re-entered New Spain from the Gulf coast in late spring 1526, to general and joyful acclaim (especially from the Indians, who fêted him in México-Tenochtitlan in the manner accorded to Aztec emperors), disorder in his territory was the best of reasons for the crown to seek increased control. In midsummer 1526 there came from Spain a young magistrate named Luis Ponce de León to conduct an investigation (*residencia*) into Cortés's administration since the conquest, and look into various specific accusations against him, among them the assumption of regal privileges, an intention to withdraw the colony from the monarchy, and the possession of excessive rents. Ponce was also to inquire into the doings of the treasury officers and, finally, to compile a full account of New Spain's people, features, and resources (with particular attention to mines). While doing all this, he was to be acting governor. A re-enactment seemed imminent of Bobadilla's confrontation with Columbus in Hispaniola in 1500.

It was not quite that, for Ponce died within a fortnight of reaching México-Tenochtitlan. Rumors flew that Cortés had poisoned him, but many others succumbed to the same fever. Cortés did not now regain power, however. Ponce had appointed an ancient and fragile lawyer, Marcos de Aguilar, to assume the governorship and the task of investigating Cortés. After Aguilar in due course himself expired, in February 1527, the only one of the miscreant treasury officers still in office became chief executive. Some of Cortés's supporters, including the ever-faithful native leaders of Tlaxcala, urged him to seize power and even, by Bernal Díaz's report, to declare himself king of New Spain.[9] But he, now recovering the political acuity that had apparently been eclipsed by arrogance in 1524, decided his best course was a personal appearance before the emperor in Spain. He sailed from Mexico early in 1528, with, once more, a number of senior native nobles in his party.

It was a shrewd move. As he left, an order summoning him back to Spain was issued. His unexpectedly early arrival, and his voluntary "surrender" to royal authority, seem to have produced a good effect. His foes were thrown off balance. His reception at court was splendid. An order went out that his properties in New Spain were not to be disturbed. But there were limits to the crown's practical favors. Cortés hoped for restoration of his governorship, but he had still not secured that at his death, in 1547. What he did get was reinstatement as captain-general of New Spain, and ennoblement as marquis of the Valley of Oaxaca. As physical expression of this title, the Emperor Charles gave Cortés what was undoubtedly the largest *encomienda* of all time, and moreover one that was unique in that it included land as well as people. The grant consisted, formally, of twenty-two Mexican towns, containing 23,000 tributary Indians (that is, adult males). In reality, the towns were far more numerous, their tributaries perhaps close to 100,000, while the associated lands covered more than 65,000 square kilometers.[10] The towns were not only, or even mainly, in the Oaxaca valley, but scattered over a large area stretching from the Valley of Mexico, down through present Morelos, to both the Gulf and Pacific coasts.[11] The grant was perpetual, and was made an entail (a *mayorazgo*) in what was, at the time, a rare concession of that privilege. While in Spain, Cortés remarried. His first wife had died late in 1522, shortly after her move from Cuba to Mexico. His new bride, as befitted an empire-building marquis, came from a noble family, the Zúñigas, of the highest rank and distinction. Her uncle, the duke of Béjar, was a member of Charles V's Council of State.[12] He was also one of Cortés's keenest backers at court.

With wife, title, and grant, the captain-general returned to New Spain in the summer of 1530. The enthusiastic welcome given by Indians and some Spaniards was doubtless gratifying. But Cortés soon realized how far he had been displaced from the center of the colony's affairs. A clear mark of this was that the marquisate's lands did not include most of the leading towns in the Valley of Mexico, the heart of the Mexican heartland, that he had held before 1528. Still more serious was that during his absence an *audiencia* had been installed in México-Tenochtitlan, with a president exercising full governing authority. Though this court had already shown itself to be miserably corrupt and inefficient, Cortés could not wrest executive power back from it. When, in 1531, the *audiencia* was refounded with far more able and honorable men, the power to govern became even more remote, and Cortés moved his household south from the capital to Cuernavaca, close to his largest and richest landholdings, on which he raised sugar cane. The palace he built for himself there stands to this day. In Cuernavaca he lived out his remaining decade in New Spain, immensely wealthy, but increasingly a mere symbol of the conquest's triumph, ever more distant from power. Even his military role was eroded when the first viceroy of New Spain took office in 1535, for viceroys were *ex officio* supreme military commanders. In 1540 Cortés returned for a second time to Spain, again to make his case to Charles V. In 1541 he tried to prove his continued worth by taking part in a large Spanish attack on Algiers; but his reduced status in Spanish government by this time was shown by his exclusion from the council of war directing this campaign.[13] After that, he pursued the royal court, seizing chances to attack the current authorities in New Spain, but gaining nothing. In 1544 he presented himself to the emperor as a man now "old, infirm and encumbered with debt," who had passed forty years of his life "with little sleep, bad food, and with his arms constantly by his side": an embarrassing set of exaggerations. Finally he gave up, and prepared to go back to Mexico to die. But death took him, ignobly, of dysentery, in late 1547 as he waited to sail at Castilleja de la Cuesta, a small town outside Seville.

For two decades, then, Cortés had remained something of a thorn in the crown's side, as he struggled, ever more feebly, against the bureaucratizing of colonial government. He had certainly promoted that process, however, by in effect abdicating his power in 1524–5 during his absence on the futile expedition to Honduras. Even the disreputable and self-seeking officials to whom Mexican government was given in those, and immediately succeeding, years managed to prevent his resurgence. To a certain degree the leading conquistadores of the other great mainland prize, Peru, also unintentionally simplified the installation of the machinery of royal government; though they did it differently, by killing each other in factional conflict.

Civil wars among the Spaniards are, indeed, the outstanding feature of colonial Peru's early political history. They happened because divisions in the conquering forces were deep, far more severe than the Cortés–Velázquez split in Mexico. The Peruvian conquest had two major leaders: Francisco Pizarro and Diego de Almagro. Almagro was the junior partner. In Panama he had been the manager of Pizarro's lands and business. He was an expert and natural man of business; Pizarro was not. The abilities of both men combined well to carry off the Pacific coast explorations opening the way to Peru in the 1520s. But Pizarro, when in Spain in 1529 arranging the contract for the conquest, kept all the important titles and potential rewards for himself, very largely ignoring Almagro's interests and earlier services. This was the seed of future hatred. For the moment, however, though angry, Almagro remained in the enterprise. Then, when the conquering force left Panama in late 1530, he stayed behind to attend to business matters and organize reinforcements. When he, with some 200 men, finally caught up with Pizarro at Cajamarca in April 1533, he found that he and his party were excluded from sharing in Atahualpa's gold and silver ransom, since they had taken no part in the Sapa Inca's capture the previous November. Now the discontent was not Almagro's alone, but spread and festered among a large group of Spaniards.

Still no open conflict erupted, because Almagro and his followers hoped to find some other prize in South America to equal Incaic Peru. Seeking it, in July 1535 he set off, in one of the epic marches of the conquest, leading a force of some 570 Spaniards and a multitude of native carriers southwards past Lake Titicaca, across the Bolivian *altiplano*, over the coastal Andean ranges, and down to central Chile. Though the land was fertile there, and the climate good for living and farming, Chile had no advanced native culture, no cities, no arts and crafts to compare with those of the Inca heartland. Almagro, much disappointed by not finding new high cultures, but then animated by the news that he had been granted the governorship of part of Peru, moved back northwards up the Chilean coast. In doing so, he and his men made the first crossing by Europeans of the Atacama desert. If, on the way, he had become aware that large gold deposits existed in northern Chile, and had stopped to exploit them, the history of Spanish Peru might have been happier. But he did not, and pressed on, reaching Arequipa early in 1537 and then marching up into the mountains. There fighting between Pizarrists and Almagrists now finally broke out. Almagro took Cuzco and held it for a year. Eventually, however, at the battle of Las Salinas just outside Cuzco in April 1538, he was beaten and captured; and later, in July, the Pizarrists executed him by garroting.

The Almagrists now rallied around Almagro's young *mestizo* son, Don Diego *el mozo* ("the lad"). In June 1541 they plotted, and successfully carried out in Lima, the assassination of Francisco Pizarro, who was still governor and now also ennobled, like Cortés, as a marquis. Young Diego's followers then pronounced him governor of Peru. But the time of unfettered exercise of authority by the original conquistadores was coming to a close. The earlier ructions had led the authorities in Spain to send to Peru as aide (and bridle) to Pizarro a judge of the *audiencia* of Valladolid, Cristóbal Vaca de Castro.[14] At the time of the assassination, Vaca had already reached southern New Granada. The Pizarrists in the central Andes quickly rallied to him; the Almagrists fell back on Cuzco. Royalists and rebels came to battle on September 18, 1542 near Huamanga (present Ayacucho), a large mountain town halfway between Lima and Cuzco. *El mozo* was soon after captured near Cuzco, and beheaded. Vaca de Castro assumed full governing powers.

With the prime leaders dead, struggle between the original factions abated at this point; but conflict, often violent, soon resumed in Peru, now in a struggle between settlers and royal government that lasted well into the 1550s. Its general cause was an aversion to royal interference, very evident now with the presence of a governor (and soon an *audiencia* and viceroy as well), among settlers who for a decade had done much as they pleased. The immediate reason was restriction of access to native tribute and labor. Like Cortés – and in what, in fact, became standard practice on the mainland – Pizarro had distributed Indians in *encomienda* to his followers. Little, if any, control had been placed on the treatment and use of the natives "entrusted" to Spaniards in this way. In 1542 the crown, inspired partly by anxiety about the well-being of its native American subjects, partly by fears that *encomenderos* were becoming a menacingly rich and powerful colonial elite, tried once more to regulate the *encomienda*. The new rules were part of what is probably the most famous piece of Spanish colonial legislation, the New Laws and Ordinances for the Government of the Indies.[15] Clause 30 of this code forbade the issue of new *encomiendas* by royal administrators in America, and ordered that, when present *encomenderos* died, their Indians should come under royal administration. This was a stunning blow for the holders, who generally saw their Indians as the economic basis of long-lasting family dynasties: as recently as 1536 they had been told that the holdings were hereditary. The anger and alarm of Peruvian *encomenderos* were particularly provoked by another clause, number 29, which ordered that anyone found notably culpable in the Pizarro–Almagro conflict should lose his Indians. This was a severe threat, since almost all *encomenderos* in the central Andes had been involved to some degree in that struggle.

The New Laws had also called for greater order in the government of Peru, which was hardly surprising given the in-fighting of the late 1530s, and growing realization in Spain of the new colony's size and wealth. A viceroy should be installed in Lima, and preside there over an *audiencia*. The person chosen for this task was Blasco Núñez Vela, an experienced naval commander and town governor in Spain, but a man, it quickly proved, quite bereft of political skill and remarkable mostly for his inflexibility. He sailed in 1543 with the first three *oidores*, or judges, of the new *audiencia* of Lima. After landing in northern Peru in March 1544, he immediately proclaimed the New Laws, incensing *encomenderos* and their many dependants. When he reached Lima, the *cabildo* appealed to him withhold the laws. But he refused, "saying he was merely their executor, and that although he might be boiled in a vat of oil, he could do nothing but implement the said ordinances as they were written, to the letter."[16] The outcome was an armed rising of many colonists, led by Francisco Pizarro's youngest half-brother, Gonzalo. He was a brave and personally attractive man, but of the several Pizarros active in the early colony, the most obtuse.[17] The new *audiencia* in Lima, already at odds with the viceroy after quarrels on the journey, was inclined to sympathize with the *encomenderos'* protests over the New Laws. The judges' sympathy increased, perhaps, as Gonzalo Pizarro's army drew nearer to Lima. In September 1544 they arrested Núñez Vela on the grounds that he was a danger to government, and put him on a ship for Panama (and Spain). He, however, managed to get ashore in northern Peru, and gathered a royalist force in the Quito highlands. There, finally, in January 1546 a showdown came between the viceroy and Gonzalo Pizarro. At the battle of Añaquito the rebels defeated and captured Núñez Vela. Soon after they beheaded him. It was the only case of a viceroy's being killed by colonists (or anyone else, for that matter) in the history of the Spanish American empire.

From the viceroy's departure from Lima in September 1544 until early 1548, Gonzalo Pizarro was the effective ruler of Peru. The *audiencia* needed little persuasion to name him governor and captain-general in October 1544. After defeating the viceroy in Quito and placing agents in Panama, Pizarro nominally controlled the whole west coast of South America. His more ardent supporters, like Cortés's in New Spain twenty years before, wanted to see him as king of Peru, and titled his illegitimate *mestizo* son "prince." But most colonists did not want to go so far as setting up a rival to the king of Spain in Peru.

In reality, Pizarro's hold on the Peruvian colonists was increasingly tenuous. His keenest supporters were impetuous men whose loyalty, for that very reason, was unreliable. He tried to buy support by granting *encomiendas*, but the claimants were so many that some of the allocations were very small, leaving the recipients resentful, and the Indians harshly burdened. Pizarro was driven to threats, violence, and executions to maintain his position, so that the last year of his regime was a reign of terror as he and his grim henchman, Francisco de Carvajal, sought to root out disloyalty.

That is part of the reason why Gonzalo Pizarro's rebellion, so energetic in 1544, simply petered out in less than four years. Still, the events themselves did not lack surprise and drama. Realizing, perhaps, the limits of the practicable, the home government made no attempt to send an army across the sea against the rebels. Rather, in 1546, it dispatched to Panama a single lawyer, the Licenciate Pedro de la Gasca, arming him with wide powers to pardon and reward those who rallied to the royal cause. He also brought news that Charles V had revoked the offensive clauses 29 and 30 of the New Laws. Slowly La Gasca moved southward in 1547 towards Peru, playing on the underlying loyalties and self-identification of settlers with Spanish values[18] that had enabled the viceroy to assemble a royalist force in Quito in 1545–6. Pardons, and redistribution of the Indians from *encomiendas* taken from rebels, gradually brought people over to the king's side. When La Gasca's force finally confronted

Pizarro's army in April 1548 at Xaquixaguana, near Cuzco (always Cuzco, the node of highland affairs), that process of absorption reached its climax. There was no fight; the Pizarrists simply deserted to the king. Gonzalo was taken and beheaded. He was buried in Cuzco, in a chapel of the Mercedarian monastery where the bodies of the two Almagros also lay.[19] Thus the factions came together in death.

BUREAUCRACY RISING

And so also ended the age of the conquistador in Peru. It had persisted far longer than in New Spain, where Cortés's departure for Honduras late in 1524 cut it prematurely short. In Peru, the conquerors had almost uninterrupted control for fifteen years. The difference comes in part from the greater remoteness of Peru. Authorities in Spain were slower to get to know Peru, slower to learn of events there, and hence slower to provide remedies for them. Equally telling, probably, was the contractual, legal nature of the Peruvian conquest, dissuading the crown from interference in Francisco Pizarro's domain. Cortés, though soon granted the governorship of New Spain after his success in conquest, always remained politically suspect.

After Gonzalo Pizarro, royal officers of one rank or another governed Peru. First, briefly, was La Gasca, as president of the *audiencia* of Lima. After his return to Spain in 1550 there followed almost two decades in which either viceroys or the *audiencia* held executive power. The quality of government in these years was certainly uneven, but never again did the crown lose control. A briefly threatening flurry did occur in 1553–4 when a group of highland *encomenderos* led by Francisco Hernández Girón rose to protest against a law of 1549 forbidding use of *encomienda* Indians as laborers. (Only tribute in cash or kind might now be taken from them.) Suspension of the law by the *audiencia* quickly defused this rising. Finally, the arrival of Don Francisco de Toledo, fifth viceroy of Peru, in 1569 began a run of viceregal administration that continued almost uninterrupted until independence, two and a half centuries later.

In other parts of the empire, with, of course, variations of circumstance and pace, the shift from conqueror to bureaucrat, from military to civil government, followed the patterns seen in New Spain and Peru. Naturally, outside those great central regions of the empire, where native population and potential wealth were concentrated, the issues and contests of control were less urgent. Or, at least, they were so for the crown, which was relatively little concerned if conquerors and their *encomendero* descendants took a large portion of the slight product of, say, Paraguay or Yucatan.

There was one particular circumstance, however, that made the military-to-civil transition less complete in some outlying regions of empire than in the centers. That was the persistence of native opposition. In New Mexico, raiding by Navajos, Apaches, and, in the eighteenth century, Comanches, was a constant threat.[20] In Yucatan, until the late seventeenth century, the possibility of native resistance from the deep interior hung over the towns and estates clustered in the north and west of the peninsula. The sedentary Paraguay of Spaniards and Guaraní was menaced by the people of the Chaco.[21] But the exemplary case is southern Chile, where the Araucanians constantly fought Spanish advance to a standstill until the early seventeenth century. Then the Spaniards stopped trying to push southward, and relinquished the half of Chile below the river Bío Bío to the natives, who were not finally crushed until the late nineteenth century, long after Chile had ceased to be a Spanish colony. In the sixteenth, they had killed Pedro de Valdivia, the colony's founding governor, in 1553; after several decades of successful guerrilla fighting, they killed another governor, García Oñez de Loyola, in 1598; and then in a broad rising lasting several years they destroyed or forced the abandonment of all Spanish towns south of the Bío Bío. From 1541 to 1664 the fighting killed some 20,000–30,000 soldiers and settlers on the Spanish side, and probably far more Araucanians.[22] In an effort to punish the Indians, encourage settlers, and maintain Chile's labor supply, the crown reversed its quite definite sixteenth-century policy trend on Indian slavery, by, in 1608, specifically permitting enslavement of "rebellious" Chilean natives. This, not surprisingly, aggravated the conflict.

Frontier hostilities are not of merely incidental interest. The Spanish American empire was a large area that, during its three centuries of existence, was strikingly free of war. Once the military conquests were over, most of its people never felt the direct or indirect effects of conflict that plagued much of the Old World: no sieges, no invasions, no blockades, no armies living off the land. So peaceful, indeed, was most of colonial life that it is hard to find in it any roots of the militarism so visible in post-independence Spanish America. One such root, however, clearly enough was the martial culture of various imperial frontiers, where European settlement was in constant friction with nomadic or at least mobile native peoples. Here the mentality of the conquest, even of the Iberian Reconquest, found an environment to sustain it.

Peripheries apart, however, by the 1550s order was beginning to descend on Spanish America. The main conquests were long over, and the contests that conquistadores and early settlers had waged among themselves – no happy bands of brothers, these, but fierce and treacherous competitors for booty, Indians, and land – were yielding to the relentless bureaucratization that emanated from Spain.

The administrative system of the mainland drew on experience in the Caribbean. There, the authority of the second viceroy, Diego Columbus, had been curbed in 1511 by the creation of the *audiencia* of Santo Domingo. Although that court did not play a strong role in the islands' government, and was eclipsed by the Jeronymite troika of 1516–19, *audiencias* were the tools of government that in due course the crown found most useful for the mainland. As, in their origins, high courts of law, they provided, first, a unity of judicial and executive functions that mirrored the nature of Spanish monarchy itself. They also offered rule by committee. The court's president generally acted in consultation with the *oidores*, and all were assisted by staff lawyers. Thus the risks of an individual holding full executive power were reduced.

And, again, the precedent of government at home, where councils of state advised the monarch and in effect made both policy and executive decisions, was followed.

The first mainland *audiencia*, that of New Spain, was created late in 1527, as part of what was by then a clearly necessary effort to bring order and royal authority to that rich new colony. Like sixteenth-century *audiencias* in America generally, it had four judges. Its president, named early in 1528, was a man then in office as governor of the province of Pánuco, a coastal region in northeastern Mexico which by this time was considered distinct from Cortés's jurisdiction. This was Beltrán Nuño de Guzmán. He was chosen as president of the *audiencia* because of his familiarity with Mexico, and because he was a known foe of Cortés, having in the past been an ally of Diego Velázquez in Caribbean affairs. Authorities at home hoped he would therefore dig deeply into Cortés's alleged misdeeds. He proved, however, a dreadful choice, "a natural gangster" whose "demonic energy ... enabled him to command and hold together whole armies of lesser scoundrels."[23] Two of the *oidores* died soon after reaching New Spain. The other two seem to have joined their president in the sack of Mexico that he immediately began. More than investigating Cortés's conduct, Guzmán simply seized his property and Indians, and those of known Cortés supporters, and distributed them among his own backers. Generally the native population suffered greatly under the rule of what is generally called the "first *audiencia*" of New Spain, although it was really the dictatorship of the president. Guzmán encouraged slaving of Indians. The native people allotted in *encomienda* to his allies found themselves burdened with vast tribute demands. Guzmán tried to stop news of all this from reaching Spain by censoring outgoing mail. Finally, though, a protest by the first bishop of New Spain, the Franciscan Juan de Zumárraga, was smuggled out, and in 1530 Guzmán was removed from his presidency. The two surviving *oidores* were also removed, sent to Spain, tried, and put in jail, where they died. Guzmán, however, seeing the direction of the wind, had in 1529 left México-Tenochtitlan at the head of an expedition to extend Spanish conquest in western Mexico. This he did successfully, roughly from Lake Chapala up to Culiacán, though again with a great cruelty to the west coast peoples that caused a lasting hostility towards the Spanish there. After ruling for several years what was in effect a personal satrapy in the west, to which he gave the name New Galicia, Guzmán was finally returned to Spain in 1538. He died in prison in 1544.

In 1530 the *audiencia* of New Spain was reconstituted with a new staff. The president was Sebastián Ramírez de Fuenleal, previously bishop of Santo Domingo. The four *oidores* were serious and distinguished administrators and churchmen. This court is remembered for remedying its predecessor's misdeeds towards the native population, punishing colonists who had mistreated Indians assigned to them or otherwise acted against the royal interest, and starting to strengthen royal authority across New Spain by appointing local administrators. From now on, until independence in 1821, the *audiencia* was a fixture of the Mexican capital, its judges and other officers being replaced as they were moved, retired, or died. Gradually, as its business expanded, the court grew in size. In the eighteenth century the *oidores* numbered ten. The other American *audiencias* underwent a similar expansion.

Nine more high courts were created in the sixteenth century. Next after New Spain came Panama (1538), where an *audiencia* was seen as needed to hear cases from the rapidly growing number of settlers of Tierra Firme (the Spanish Main – that is, the Caribbean coast from Venezuela west and north to Nicaragua). The intent at this point was also that appeals from all of west-coast South America should go to Panama.[24] But then, four years later, the New Laws called for a separate *audiencia* in Peru, at Lima, and another to attend to cases from Guatemala and Nicaragua.[25] The court at Panama was therefore abolished in 1543, but then reinstated in 1564, in recognition of Panama's immense strategic and commercial importance as the crossing point for people and goods between the Atlantic and the Pacific.

Peru and Guatemala received their *audiencias* in 1543. Next came the high court of New Galicia, or Guadalajara, in 1547, to deal with litigation and affairs particularly from the silver-mining settlements that were appearing in western Mexico. In the same year, an *audiencia* was created for Santa Fe de Bogotá, to attend to the growing settlement of New Granada. Then, in 1559, came that of La Plata, or Charcas (modern Bolivia), again largely in response to local rise of silver mining and its associated population, specifically at Potosí. Quito became the seat of a high court in 1563. Two years later one was ordered for Chile, at Concepción on the Indian frontier. It was, however, disbanded in 1575, because the undiluted authority of a military governor was thought necessary to deal with the Araucanian threat. The Chilean court was reinstated, permanently, in Santiago in 1603. The final *audiencia* created in the sixteenth century was at Manila, in the Philippines. The placing of a court there in 1583 reflected the rapid growth of the city's importance as Spain's outpost in the Orient, and its crucial commercial role after the opening of the trans-Pacific trade to New Spain in the 1570s. Only three more *audiencias* were added to the eleven set up in the sixteenth century: Buenos Aires, briefly from 1661 to 1672, then permanently in 1783; Venezuela, at Caracas, in 1786; and Cuzco, in 1787.

The *audiencias* were all founded in response to a need perceived by the monarchy for strong judicial and executive authority in particular regions. Aside from that, as in Spain under the Catholic Monarchs, *audiencias* served as highly visible symbols of royal power – physical outposts of the monarchs' authority in remote American places. The regions in which they were installed were ones in which there were notable concentrations of either population, both European and native, or wealth. Usually population and wealth coincided. Some *audiencias* were set up in towns that had long been native power centers, and in which the conquerors thought that the same function could be usefully preserved: México-Tenochtitlan, Santa Fe de Bogotá, Quito. Others were in towns of essentially Spanish making, such as Guadalajara, Panama, Lima, or La Plata, that had some new, post-conquest, political or economic reason for existing. The territorial limits of the courts were at first vaguely defined. Jurisdictional disputes were the frequent outcome of that. But over time these, and simple matters of practicability, fixed the boundaries. In several cases, the territories of the independent Spanish American countries of the nineteenth century were the same as the those of the colonial *audiencias*, or very close to them. The *audiencia* of Lima, for instance, became Peru; that of Charcas, Bolivia. The territories of the courts in Quito and Santa Fe underlay those of present Ecuador and Colombia, and since these *audiencias* were sited in important pre-conquest centers, a direct line can be drawn in these instances from pre-conquest native polities to present states.

After the energetic burst of *audiencia*-founding between 1538 and 1563, most people in Mexico, Central America, and the colonies in western South America were within possible, if not easy, reach of a high court. South Americans living away from the west coast had further to go. Venezuela remained in the jurisdiction of the Santo Domingo court, and the Río de la Plata and Paraguay in that of Charcas. But whatever the distance, as political bodies the courts functioned to a notable degree as intended. For most people in the empire the local *audiencia* was the highest representation they would ever see of Spanish power. People of all ranks and ethnic origins had access to the *audiencia* as court of law, though, unsurprisingly, it was mainly white colonists' legal business that ended up there. Still, the ceremonial surrounding the courts' workings, and the public presence of robed judges and crown attorneys, worked continuously to remind colonial society of the distant existence of the royal court and the authority attached to it. Nor was this reminder limited to the *audiencia* cities, for individual *oidores* constantly went on tour – not to try cases, but to investigate administrative problems, and to suggest and enact new regulations.

As law tribunals, *audiencias* were primarily courts of appeal, hearing cases previously tried by lesser justices, and various administrative courts, such as those of the merchant guilds (*consulados*) or the mints. In criminal cases the decisions of *audiencias* were final. Civil cases, if large enough (over 10,000 pesos, after 1542), could be referred to the Council of the Indies, in Spain.

Much of a court's time went to hearing litigation. Two days a week, for instance, were usually given over to suits between Indians, or between Indians and Spaniards.[26] But the administrative function of the body was still more crucial than the judicial one to the running of the empire. Broadly speaking, the further an *audiencia* was sited from a viceroy (and until well into the eighteenth century, only two viceroyalties existed, based in Lima and Mexico City), the greater was the executive and administrative authority that it possessed. The precise division of authority between *audiencia* and viceroy, and the degree of administrative independence with which a court could act, varied over time, and from place to place. Quite often, in fact, independence of action varied according to the strength of will of the officials involved. A set of stubborn and experienced judges could, and did, face down a viceroy in decisions about their own area. And no matter what administrative regulations might say, the president of a remote *audiencia*, such as Charcas or Quito, was an immensely influential figure in his own territory, with a range of executive, legislative, and even military, powers much like those of a viceroy. This was inevitable. Slowness of communications between viceroy and provinces meant that some local officer must hold independent power to make urgent decisions. The obvious candidates were the heads of the *audiencias*.

The *audiencia*, then, whose potential as a tool for extending royal authority was clearly seen by the Catholic Monarchs in Castile, fully realized that promise in the Indies. It became there the prime channel of the Spanish monarchy's force, of that distinctive intertwining of dominion with law. For the longer term, most *audiencias* generated around themselves in their provinces a political geography (in some cases reinforcing what had existed in native times) that over the centuries of colonial rule solidified, and then endured after Spain was gone. Thus, in the early independence years, it was barely conceivable that any city beside La Plata should be capital of Bolivia, or any city other than Quito of Ecuador. It is still so. Nearly all *audiencia* seats, of the sixteenth century and later, are present national capitals.

The sole administrative superior to the *audiencia* in the Indies was the viceroy: literally, the man in place of the king. The office had long been used by Aragon to govern its Mediterranean possessions in medieval times, and in the unitary Spain of the sixteenth century Aragon, Catalonia, and Valencia themselves were run by viceroys. Once viceroyalties were created for New Spain and Peru, the total of these units in Spanish realms became nine: the five just mentioned, and Navarre, Sardinia, Sicily, and Naples besides.[27]

The decision to raise New Spain to the rank of a viceroyalty was taken late in 1529, while Cortés was still in Spain. The recommendation came from a special junta convened by Charles V to advise him on government in Mexico, and particularly on Indian policy. The man chosen for the position was Don Antonio de Mendoza, a member of one of Castile's most distinguished noble families. But a series of delays meant that he did not reach New Spain until 1535. In the interim the re-staffed *audiencia* did valuable preparatory work, calming and ordering a population that Guzmán's depredatory antics had agitated. Mendoza remained in Mexico until 1551. A sixteen-year tenure was extraordinary in later colonial times. But Mendoza was seen at home as the "founding" viceroy of what soon became known as the "realm" (*reino*) of New Spain; and his conduct in office argued for his being kept there as long as possible. Indeed, in 1551 he went back not to Spain but to Lima, as second viceroy of Peru, charged with the same settling of affairs there, in the wake of Núñez Vela's blunders and the Pizarro rebellion, as he had managed in New Spain. What he could have done will never be known, for he died in Lima less than a year after his arrival.[28]

Mendoza's prime accomplishment in New Spain was precisely to have averted violent reaction to those of the New Laws that attacked the *encomienda* – the regulations applied in Peru by Núñez Vela at the cost of precipitating an uprising among the colonists. He himself took a practical attitude towards the *encomienda*, seeing it, rather like Cortés, as a political and economic necessity if Spaniards were to settle in America, but also as a system wide open to abuse, and therefore in need of careful vigilance. Though he had no particular esteem for Indians, he took his duty to guard their interests seriously, and they came to regard him, again like Cortés, as their protector.

Word of the New Laws' ban on the inheritance of *encomiendas* and on the making of new grants of Indians went ahead of the promulgation of the code in New Spain. When a royal agent, Tello de Sandoval, arrived there in 1544 to enact the laws, he was met with howls of protest. But no violence followed, thanks to Mendoza's prevailing on Sandoval to suspend application of the clauses the settlers most disliked, while an appeal on them went to the Council of the Indies. Mendoza was supported in this temporizing by the heads of the three religious orders present in New Spain at the time, the Franciscans, Dominicans, and Augustinians. The council, and the emperor, bowed to the advice of the men on the spot, and in October 1545 removed the offending regulations. Thus tensions were kept in check in New Spain, and the foundation was laid for the crown's recovery of Peru.

That was the most dramatic challenge that Mendoza faced. But his many other actions in New Spain may have had a more formative effect in the colony. He ousted incompetent officials from the lower ranks of the *audiencia*; improved tax-collection, and account-keeping in the treasury; founded a mint in México-Tenochtitlan in 1536 so as to promote trade through the provision of a trustworthy medium of exchange; promoted the production of raw silk, and from it the weaving of cloth; and imported, once more like Cortés, seeds and stock so as to expand European-style agriculture. Mendoza himself acquired several large landed properties on which he bred the Spanish merino sheep, in the traditional style of the Spanish nobility from which he came. (Engaging in profitable enterprises was a concession granted to these early, founding, administrators that later officials were denied, at least in principle.) He directed the building of roads for carts and mule trains – roads that fanned out in all directions from the Valley of Mexico to Taxco and Oaxaca southwards, Michoacán and Jalisco westwards, and Pánuco and Veracruz eastwards. In his time, also, began the Spanish expansion into the north that ultimately yielded one of the most radical changes in Mexico resulting from the Spanish conquest: the "civilization" of the *altiplano*, and its incorporation into the political and economic life of the center. The start of northward movement was linked to a native rebellion that began in New Galicia in 1540, a rising known as the Mixton War that briefly seemed a serious threat to the Spanish hold on New Spain in general. The rebellious Indians lived in the canyons north of Guadalajara, and on the west coast at the same latitude. They belonged to several distinct groups, but had in common that they were on the margin between the developed sedentism of central Mexico and the simpler, sometimes nomadic, cultures of the north. Their attack on the Spanish was, then, a transient example of the frontier refractoriness that the colonizers encountered in Chile or the far Mexican north. It was also a delayed reaction to the spoliations of Nuño de Guzmán and his followers in this region in the early 1530s. The rebellion began with Indian attacks on *encomenderos* and mission friars. With much effort, the infant city of Guadalajara was defended. The viceroy arrived, responding to appeals for help from the acting governor of New Galicia, Cristóbal de Oñate, with 450 Spaniards and, reportedly, 30,000 Aztec auxiliaries.[29] The rising could not long resist such force, and subsided in 1542.

In its aftermath, Spanish expeditions, organized by Oñate and others, pressed further than before up the canyons. The critical outcome was that in 1546 they found the silver ores of Zacatecas. This strike was the first of many made on the *altiplano* over the following century that turned Mexico into one of the world's prime sources of silver, as it still is.

Mendoza did not live long enough to see the mining potential of the north fully revealed. But New Spain's promise as a silver producer was clear to him from the start. In 1536 he issued his first mining regulations. These emerged finally in 1550 as a considerable mining code, which remained in force until 1577. In general he gives the impression of having achieved a mental mastery of Mexico – of its geography, developing colonial economy, politics, and at least the European part of its population. He remarked, in the memorandum to his successor that all outgoing viceroys were expected to write, that he had found the Spaniards of Mexico easier to govern than any he had encountered in his career. But they had respect for neither wealth nor rank if not treated as *caballeros*, gentlemen, that is, of noble quality.[30] Here is a glimpse of colonials' touchy pride, founded in the achievement of conquest, or, for newcomers, in the status that they thought they had gained in merely risking the Atlantic crossing. Do little, Mendoza recommended, and do it slowly. He had not, in fact, done little himself; quite the opposite. But for all his activism, he had certainly applied, as one notable student of Spanish colonial government observes, "a policy based on prudence, tenacity, concessions on points of detail and occasional rigor" to draw the conquerors under bureaucratic control.[31]

Mendoza's particular deeds suggest what a viceroy's broad powers were. He was first the chief executive officer in his region. As such he could issue regulations for it, though for these to become permanent law they had to receive final royal approval. He was military commander of his territory, normally bearing the title of captain-general. He was also *ex officio* president of the *audiencia* in his capital city, and might sit as president of other *audiencias* in his jurisdiction; though, unless a lawyer, which was rare, he could not participate in judging in the court. Nonetheless, he could exercise, if he wished, much influence over the operation of the high courts. In addition, he was vice-patron of the church in his realm, just as the monarch was its patron throughout Spanish territories. This gave his opinions on church matters weight with even archbishops and heads of orders in the Indies. Also, and no less telling, vice-patronage gave him power to present candidates for posts in the lower priesthood. Beyond all this, the viceroy, as chief executive, was automatically head of the treasury system in his jurisdiction. He was also in principle the chief defender of natives' interest, since he was particularly charged to "have special care for the good treatment, conservation, and increase of the Indians," and might indeed hear cases between Indians as a first-instance magistrate.[32]

For all that viceroys could do, and often did do, they remained remote figures for most of those they governed. This was in part intentional policy, for viceroys, like monarchs themselves, should gain authority in aloofness. They occupied large and splendid palaces on the main plaza of the colonial capitals. In these the ceremonial of the royal court was reproduced as far as possible, so that the aura of monarchy should surround the viceroy. For the same reason, most viceroys were chosen from the upper ranks of the nobility; if they were related to the royal family, so much the better. Their arrivals and departures in America were occasions for elaborate ritual, as were their rare travels within their viceroyalties.[33] Most of a viceroy's time was spent in his capital.

The outstanding exception to this normal immobility was Don Francisco de Toledo, fifth viceroy of Peru. In his long tenure (1569–81) he played the "founding" role in South America that Mendoza had performed in New Spain. Though some of his success derived from his intelligence and personality (he was an energetic, impatient, and authoritarian man), it was also the outcome of his intimate knowledge of at least the heartland of Spanish South America: Peru and Charcas. And this he gained by inspecting the territory in person, in a five-year journey that took him and a retinue of aides through Huamanga, Cuzco, Potosí, La Plata, Arequipa, and back to Lima. In the course of this *visita general* Toledo imposed a number of socio-economic changes in the interior that impinged especially on the native people. He continued and expanded the process of resettlement, or *reducción*, of Indians into new towns that had started in Peru in the mid 1560s. The aim was greater efficiency in the government of natives, in their evangelization, and in extraction of their labor. He enlarged and formalized the *mita*, or draft labor system, that supplied Indian workers to Spanish mercury and silver mines at Huancavelica and Potosí. And he hastened the adoption by Peruvian miners of amalgamation, a new and economical method of refining silver ores developed in New Spain in the 1550s. One broad effect of these and other measures was to add to the Indians' burden of labor and tribute. Toledo has therefore often been seen as a scourge of the central Andean Indians, and with some justification. He was probably less careful of native interests than Mendoza had been in New Spain. But he governed in a different time, one in which Spain's fiscal needs were far more urgent than they had been before 1550. The ruling monarch, Philip II, had dedicated his empire to defending the true faith against insurgent Protestantism, and in so doing plunged Spain into endless European wars. Potosí seemed divinely revealed to fund these contests; and Toledo knew that he must make Potosí yield. The well-being of Indians was secondary.[34]

For the breadth of change that he brought about, Toledo has been called the Solon of Peru. He was a legislative dynamo, throwing off code after code of regulations as he traveled. His mining ordinances superseded Mendoza's for the whole empire, and remained in effect well into the eighteenth century. He was voluminous on the *mita*. He ordained on Indian government, on the organization of hospitals, on the sale (forbidden) of wine to Indians, blacks and mulattoes, on the public fountains of Lima, on the sale of adobes, on the inns of Charcas, on coca, and on more other issues than can easily be imagined. A recent collection of his regulations runs to 950 pages of fine print.[35]

This, of course, was exceptional, indeed unique, and was the result of Toledo's being particularly charged to set Peru straight after what seemed, to Spain, two decades of timid administrative shilly-shallying. The usual source of legislation for the Indies was not viceroys, or any authority in America, but the Royal and Supreme Council of the Indies, a body firmly resident in Spain, and closely attendant on the monarch. This council came into existence in 1524, partly as a response to the rapid expansion of the American territories produced by Cortés, and partly in a broad upgrading of Spanish central administration by Charles V's grand chancellor, Mercurino Gattinara.[36] Before then, Juan Rodríguez de Fonseca, once Isabella's chaplain, and later bishop of Burgos, had long held the reins of the Indies in his hands, though from 1516 on members of the Council of Castile had also taken up American business.

Short of the king, the Council of the Indies was, from its founding until the early eighteenth century, the ultimate authority in the government of America. As the Indies' importance to Spain grew more obvious, the council became one of the most senior of the state councils that the Spanish Hapsburgs used to rule their wide possessions. At the start it had a president and four or five councilors (normally lawyers and clergymen), and a small staff of lawyers, accountants, scribes, and the like. In the seventeenth century the number of councilors rose to ten. Oddly enough, at first sight, few councilors – only a dozen or so before 1700 – were men with American experience.[37] Disinterested detachment was held to outweigh the possible advantage of personal experience.

Nothing in American administration fell outside the council's purview. It was the final court of appeal from *audiencias*' verdicts. It was the central executive and law-making entity in the empire. Its authority extended to military matters, trade, finance, and, via the royal patronage, to the church. It was the destination of nearly all official, and many private, communications from the Indies. Reports and letters might be addressed to the monarch; but with rare exceptions the council read and screened them. If they conveyed a substantial problem or bore on some question of policy, the councilors and their staff would send their own, generally succinct, memorandum – a *consulta* – to the monarch, often with suggested courses of action. Back it would come with the royal preference indicated in marginal notes or a separate written statement. The council's staff then drafted a suitable royal order, to be signed by the monarch (not with a name, but simply *yo el rey*, or *yo la reina* – "I the king," "I the queen"), and sent off to the proper person or body in America. This system functioned most energetically in the time (1556–98) of Philip II, the most dedicated royal servant of the bureaucratic system that Spain had necessarily created to manage its broadly scattered realms. He, at the apex of this new "government by paper,"[38] spent countless hours awash in the river of documents flowing to him from a dozen state councils. His hurried marginal scrawlings have been the despair of researchers of his reign's history.

The Council of the Indies received correspondence not only from viceroys and *audiencias*, its immediate subordinates in the American bureaucracy, but from all lower levels of government (and indeed from private citizens who had some case to make or some favor to seek). Beneath *audiencias* were two more ranks of general administrators. The more senior was the governor.

Governorships lay physically within the bounds of viceroyalties and *audiencias*, but were generally frontier areas where a combination of remoteness and need for defense made the presence of a senior figure useful. The typical *gobernador*, therefore, was a well-tried military man, able to command in the field. He might carry the extra title of captain-general. He was also, however, chief civil administrator for his region, and its senior judge. Examples of governorships in the mature empire are New Mexico (capital: Santa Fe), New León, in north-east Mexico (Monterrey), Santa Cruz de la Sierra, in eastern, lowland Charcas (Santa Cruz), Paraguay (Asunción), and the Río de la Plata (Buenos Aires).

Smaller than governorships, and far more numerous, were *alcaldías mayores* and *corregimientos*. The heads of these areas, *alcaldes mayores* and *corregidores*, were the district officers of the colonies, and as such the crown agents most directly in touch with the people, of whatever rank or color. (The offices of *alcalde mayor* and *corregidor* seem to have been practically identical. The first title was more commonly used in New Spain, and the second in South America. Here, for economy, *corregidor* will be used to stand for both.)

It took time to create and staff this lower end of the colonial bureaucracy. The first district officers of the empire were, in effect, the *encomenderos*. An overlooked function of the *encomienda*, and one of the reasons the home administration tolerated it long after its dangers to native well-being were clear, was to spread Spaniards across mainland America, and so provide a rudimentary rural administration at a time when money, men, and knowledge were still lacking for creation of an official system. This, though, gave powers and opportunities for gain to *encomenderos* that in the longer term were intolerable. On the mainland, it was in New Spain that their replacement by local functionaries began most swiftly. The crown told the reformed *audiencia* to proceed with this task. The judges of the court indeed went at it eagerly, shifting 53 *encomiendas*, from a total of possibly 300, to the control of *corregidores* between 1531 and 1533.[39] Some of these new local officials, it is true, were ex-*encomenderos*, or even current *encomenderos*. But the *audiencia* preferred to appoint men who did not hold Indians, and often named as *corregidores* recent arrivals from Spain. Conquistadores and earlier settlers muttered about being excluded while newcomers lacking status, accomplishment, and wealth received positions. But marginalization of the men who had dominated New Spain in the 1520s, whether under Cortés or Guzmán, was precisely the official intent by this time.

By the mid 1540s, just as northward expansion was beginning, New Spain had some 150 *corregimientos*. By the early seventeenth century, the number had risen to about 200. Peru, at the same date, was divided into 88 of these jurisdictions. There the introduction of *corregidores* had begun only in the 1560s, delayed by the wars, and by the prolongation of *encomienda* that had been necessary to appease restive colonists. Viceroy Toledo carried the reform forward vigorously in the 1570s, seeking, as had been the aim in New Spain, to replace private with public interest at this most local level of administration.[40]

Corregidores were rarely, of course, the ideal and disinterested local governors that policy called for. Like greater administrators above them, they were not only executives but also magistrates and legislators for their areas, and few of them resisted the temptations that this combination of powers made available. Nearly all *corregidores* were administrators of Indian districts. In these some battened on their charges just as harmfully as *encomenderos* had done before them. In remote districts of, say, Central America or the Andes, they governed almost unsupervised. The only nearby resident European to keep watch over them was the parish priest, and often enough priest and *corregidor* collaborated to their mutual advantage. *Corregidores* were, moreover, often the dependants or relatives of viceroys. They held office, by gift of their master, only for as long as his term of office. Many saw the position as a transient chance to enrich themselves. They seized the opportunity, and administration suffered accordingly.

A small minority of *corregidores* and *alcaldes mayores* were governors of Spanish towns in America – mayors, roughly speaking, although that term does not give a good sense of their powers since these officials, once again, were a combination of executive, law-maker, and magistrate. Normally, and particularly if the town were a provincial capital or a prosperous port or mining center, these men were carefully chosen royal appointees (as *corregidores* of peninsular cities had been in Isabella's time). They ranked with provincial *gobernadores*, and might well, like them, have a military background.

One of the tasks of such a *corregidor* was to preside over meetings of the *cabildo*, or town council. In doing so, he became the point of contact between bureaucracy and the sole administrative body dominated from the start by the colonists themselves. All substantial Spanish American towns had *cabildos*, consisting fundamentally of six or more aldermen (*regidores*), and two first-instance magistrates (*alcaldes ordinarios*). To these were usually added a variety of constables, jailers, standard-bearers, clerks of the works, legal representatives, and inspectors (of weights and measures, and prices, for example). All were local men, and none received any wage from the crown. They were not, then, colonial bureaucrats, though they certainly had an administrative function.

Historians have sometimes tried to present the colonial *cabildo* as an example and source of democratic practice in Spanish America, but the argument is sorely strained. Next to no record exists of the election by householders (much less by the whole city population) of aldermen. They were usually appointed by the viceroy or monarch, or, from the later sixteenth century on, tended to have bought their positions from the crown. *Alcaldes ordinarios* were co-opted annually from among householders (*vecinos*) by the aldermen; again there was no hint of popular election. Generally speaking, members of the council came from rich families with standing in local society. Its composition would change in parallel with shifts in distribution of wealth and status among the more prominent townspeople.

To the extent that leading families' interests coincided with those of the whole community, *cabildos* can be said to have represented their towns.

Certainly they made protests – to all levels of government, from the Council of the Indies down to the local *corregidor* – against anything seen as bureaucratic interference from the outside, on matters ranging from the imposition of new taxes to the sending of inspectors to look into local government. Sometimes, by adroit politicking, they won their point, and stopped higher colonial powers from meddling in municipal affairs. That apart, *cabildos* spent most of their time on internal matters: protecting town commons from incursions by neighboring communities, regulating prices, trying to ensure adequate supplies of basic foods (such as grains and meat), inspecting goods and food for quality, checking on sellers' weights and measures, and maintaining streets, bridges, and public buildings (above all the town hall, jail, and parish church). Their scope of action was limited because generally they were poor. Their fundraising capacity, from local fees and taxes, was limited by law. And much of their slight income tended to go on public acts – celebrating, for instance, the birth of a prince or the winning of a great victory. Putting on ceremonies was a central and valued function of a *cabildo*. The office of standard-bearer (*alférez real*) tended to command one of the highest prices once council positions came to be sold.[41]

Finally, to the administrators of America (in descending order, monarch, councilor of the Indies, viceroy, *oidor, gobernador, corregidor, cabildo* member) must be added the taxman. The treasury official was generally the first royal agent to appear on the scene of any conquest, and thereafter remained ubiquitous. By 1600, at least forty-seven treasury offices were functioning in Spanish America,[42] placed in any major town where tax income was enough to warrant the bureaucratic expense. The royal treasury system, or *real hacienda*, was therefore a large structure. It stood aside from the general administration, but was linked to it through the viceroy, who had a special charge to enforce revenue collection. A viceroy's performance, indeed, was measured partly by the amount of money that was sent to Spain during his tenure.

Obvious candidates for a treasury office were ports (for customs duties and sales taxes), mining centers (for royalties on gold and silver), towns amid large native populations (for tribute), and capitals both provincial and viceregal (for assorted taxes). Each office had its *caja*, or strongbox, fitted with three locks. Each of the three principal officers at any branch (treasurer, accountant, and business manager) held a key to one of the locks, so that the *caja* could be opened only when all three were present. This simple security procedure doubtless helped to keep the king's money safe in the strongbox, although there certainly were cases of treasury officials colluding to "borrow" royal funds for their own business purposes.

Many in the colonies experienced the personal attention of these *reales oficiales* of the treasury. They were not men to be taken lightly, for they had the force of much law behind them, and their bureaucratic status was not far below that of high court judges. And few escaped indirect contact with them, for almost all were taxed in one way or another. Indians were liable for tribute; most purchases were subject to sales tax; import and export merchants paid tariffs; miners paid a royalty on the metal they refined.

IMPERIAL MACHINERY IN MOTION

The Spanish American administration of the sixteenth century was a remarkable accomplishment. It had flaws, to be sure, some of which later became serious weaknesses. But, just as the military conquests can be explained but are still astonishing, so the rapid achievement of operating government can be described, but still, when the size of the obstacles is considered, is impressive. By the late 1500s, the Spanish Indies were the largest overseas empire that Europeans had ever possessed. The entire area was governed by a salaried bureaucracy, in America and the Philippines, that cannot have numbered much over a thousand: viceroys, *oidores*, *gobernadores*, *reales oficiales*, *corregidores*, and supporting staff. Skeptics might well object that the intensity and effectiveness of that government were low – and that is quite true by standards of today's advanced countries. But codes of law were in place and to some extent enforced. Crown prosecutors brought some offenders to trial. Awareness of the laws and the penalties for infringing them was widespread. Many native people had access to high courts, where salaried defenders of Indians sometimes represented them. Taxes and tariffs were collected, though, as anywhere and at any time, evasion was common. Roads and ports were built; coin was struck. As a result, trade flourished, linking regions economically that had been mutually unknown before. Information, as well as goods, flowed regularly and predictably from most of the Indies to Spain, and back again.

Above all, what impresses is that a continent-wide governing structure came into being where nothing comparable had ever existed before. To a degree, the offices and procedures used to create the structure drew on well-tried antecedents at home and in the Mediterranean. But much had to be adapted and invented to meet American challenges: unprecedented distances from Spain, and the resulting slowness of communication; vast and puzzling native populations, of widely varying cultural levels, not to mention languages; new seas, terrains, climates, soils, products. Whatever criticisms may be made of the administration's performance, great energy and creativity in setting it up must be granted to sixteenth-century Spain.

For such a system to function, a ranking of authorities and a clear chain of command were needed. The account given here of the administrative structure suggests it was rigidly hierarchical – and so it was in some respects. Movement of personnel between ranks, for example, was rare. Because viceroys were generally nobles and men of worldly action ("of cape and sword," as the standard phrase had it), while *oidores* were mostly commoners and by definition lawyers, *oidores* did not become viceroys; the limit of their movement was promotion to an *audiencia* presidency, or to a more senior and central court. Similarly, *corregidores*, not generally being lawyers, did not become *oidores*.

But in its working the system was far more flexible and adaptable than its fixity of structure might suggest. Communications did not have to pass upward, or downward, level by level. Town councils, for example, indeed even private individuals, could and constantly did send their petitions and complaints to viceroys and even the monarch (meaning, in practice, the Council of the Indies). Beyond this, and more important, the governing structure was from the start a political as well as an administrative system. The existence of rivalries between governmental entities, viceroys and *audiencias* for instance, and even between individual bureaucrats, meant that issues were not always resolved in ways predictable by law, and that skillful players, both inside and outside the system, could manipulate government to their advantage.

It is hard to tell how far this politicking was intentionally built into government. Certainly, jurisdictions were often left imprecise: physical ones, such as, for example, the boundaries between *audiencias*; or operational ones, such as whether, in a provincial *audiencia*'s territory, the viceroy or the court's president held military authority. In some cases, such blurring resulted from ignorance in the Council of the Indies, the body that set these various limits in America. But the imprecisions were tolerated and often went unresolved for decades because they generated tensions in the machinery of American government that, while sometimes the cause of inefficiency, also made administrators mutually vigilant. The outcome was streams of reports back to Spain from contenders in these jurisdictional combats; they were often indignant and strident reports that overflowed the issue at stake to give other information useful to the council. Officials at all levels knew, indeed, that they were expected to spy on their fellows, and should expect to be spied on. Private citizens of the colonies were quick, naturally enough, to turn this inbuilt rivalry to their own ends by allying themselves in various ways with the dominant bureaucrats of a particular moment, while sending back to Spain criticisms of others.

This spontaneous informing may well have been more valuable to the powers at court than the formal mechanisms put in place for checking on officials' performance and on broader conditions in America. For evaluating individuals, the *residencia* was the standard tool. It consisted of an inquiry by an incoming official into his predecessor's conduct. Criticisms were gathered from people subject to the man in question; he could then defend himself against charges lodged. Both sides could call witnesses, whose evidence was written down. In principle all this created a continuous record of the performance of a particular office. In reality, not surprisingly, collusion between arriving and departing officials was often an irresistible temptation, with a resulting whitewashing of the record; and many *residencias* were simply never taken. Similarly, the *visita*, or inspection of the general state of affairs in some region or institution, had inherent flaws that sapped its value. The inspectors, or *visitadores*, were generally named by the Council of the Indies. They were typically senior men, given powers to assume the functions of any officials they evaluated. The double task, of running normal administration while conducting a major inquiry, was too demanding in many cases, so that administration often became paralyzed while the inspection was half-baked. The cure was thus sometimes worse than the sickness.

The informality and flexibility apparent in these methods of information-gathering and internal regulation extended to other aspects of government. Though the councilors in Spain rained reams of precise rulings down on colonial governors, sometimes wasting time on absurd minutiae – a ban on the raising of chickens in coastal fortresses even made its way into the great summation, or *Recopilación*, of Indies law of 1681[43] – men on the ground in America had in reality much discretion to modify or ignore these orders. This is illustrated by the invariably quoted (though in fact rarely formally invoked) declaration available to viceroys faced with an impractical or unwelcome order: *Obedezco pero no cumplo* – "I obey but do not implement." This was, first, the system's acknowledgment that, given the immense space and time separating Spain from America, home authorities simply could not always issue suitable orders. A deeper principle revealed here is that the monarch, whose prime task was to make justice available to all, could not be conceived to have intended an injustice; therefore any order likely to produce injustice must be modified, postponed, or ignored. The whole administration was shot through with a similar pliancy, inevitably so given the size of the empire, but not, obviously, without dangers of abuse.

Informality extended also to the appointing of officials. It was often done by patronage. Many district *corregidores* were the friends or relations of viceroys, part of a retinue of dependants embarking with the great man on his journey to America and hoping to recoup costs and make profits in the few years of his tenure. Presidents and judges of *audiencias* had their own lesser influence in placing dependants in their particular courts and localities. Treasury officials and even *corregidores* could in practice select their assistants. Office-holding was to some extent regarded precisely as a chance to reward or support dependants – and, of course, to benefit oneself. Officials, particularly the humbler ones, still tended in medieval fashion to see their positions as property, to be used first for their own gain. At the same time, though, with the sixteenth-century burgeoning of bureaucracy in Spain there came also a definite professionalization of the upper officialdom.[44] It is little surprise that viceroys such as Toledo and his contemporary in New Spain, Don Martín Enríquez, took their duties so seriously; they were, after all, noblemen with a sense of public responsibility, and resources of their own to boot. But it is impressive to see with what energy, interest, and initiative many *oidores* of the late 1500s attacked their judicial and administrative tasks.

This is one sign of the maturing of colonial administration in Spanish America. Indeed, the growth of the quality and quantity of officials in the middle decades of the sixteenth century signals the appearance of a genuine apparatus of state in the colonies: a machinery of government capable of imposing policies decided in Spain with a high (though never perfect) level of effectiveness. Its largest and most obvious units were the two viceroyalties: New Spain, embracing Mexico, Central America (less Panama), the Caribbean (including Venezuela), and the Philippines; and Peru, covering all of South America (less Venezuela, and Brazil, of course a Portuguese territory), and Panama.

The most authoritative expression of Spanish dominion in America and the Philippines, however, lay not in the viceroyalties but in the eleven *audiencias* created over the course of the century, most of them in the middle years. The close union in these courts of judicial and governing functions made them particularly good conductors of the monarchy's power. And the lesser size of the *audiencias*' territories, in comparison with the viceroyalties, made them the natural units of administration and law to which colonizers and colonized turned, and with which they identified themselves. The various *audiencias*' territories were, indeed, in the Hapsburg polity, seen as separate realms – the "kingdom" of Quito, or of New Spain, for example – whose unity came not from being part of an empire or even of a viceroyalty, but solely from their subjection to the monarch. The monarch was the post to which all Spanish territories, whether in Spain, other parts of Europe, or elsewhere in the world, were moored. Only in their common connection to that mooring were they united. This discreteness increased the likelihood that colonizers of Chile, for example, would come to see themselves as Chileans first, and only second as citizens of the viceroyalty of Peru or of an even larger and less tangible Spanish empire in America.

Although some of them would soon work their way into the state machinery, the inhabitants of the American realms found it largely closed to them in the late 1500s. The only level of government available to them was the lowly one of the town councils, whose powers were small and local. Council members, further, were technically outside the state bureaucracy, since the treasury paid them no salary. This scanty role in administration for colonizers and colonized was matched by a similar lack of political representation. All, it is true, could, and a surprising number did, send petitions directly to *audiencias*, viceroys, or even the Council of the Indies. But no channel existed for sounding a collective voice. Spanish Americans had no place in the *cortes*, or parliaments, of the peninsula (except for the briefest moment early in the nineteenth century), much less any formal assemblies of their own.

On balance, in fact, the first century of Spanish government in America is striking for its success in excluding colonists from administrative and political influence, particularly so when the immense powers and potential wealth given to Columbus and later explorers and conquerors are recalled, along with the large part played by individual, rather than state, enterprise in the winning of Spanish America. The crown's path to control was far from even or straight. But by using and even encouraging factionalism among conquerors, by the relentless showering of law onto the new realms, by the gradual adaptation of known administrative forms to new places and conditions, by the creation of a new, paper-based, bureaucracy, the monarchy's will was made to prevail by the 1560s, at least in the rich, populous, and hence important areas. The resultant governing system was markedly authoritarian in design. Most of the early flickerings that can be glimpsed of representative process were doused.[45] Especially telling for Spanish American politics in the long term was the intentional combining in all levels of officialdom of executive, legislative, and judicial powers. Not all officials held equal balances of these powers, of course; viceroys were rarely fully qualified judges; *corregidores* could legislate only locally. But minimal effort was made to separate powers. Indeed, to do so would have been foolish given the need to create order. And beyond, or beneath, this practical aim lay perhaps a deeper concept of the nature and purpose of government – one deriving from Aquinas's view that the key purpose of kingship was to maximize the common good of the multitude.[46] This implied both a downplaying of individuals' rights, and a concentrating of authority for a good and beneficent ordering of the whole.

Whatever the motives, theoretical or practical, for bringing together governing powers, a good case can be made for saying that success in that process made Spanish America more closely and intensively administered in the late sixteenth century than at any other time in the colonial centuries, with the possible exception of the late 1700s. (During a long middle period of the empire government's hold loosened, for a variety of reasons to be seen.) Bureaucratic domination was one remarkable achievement of Spain's first century in America. But bureaucracy, of course, played mostly on the practical surface of the lives of colonists and colonized. A more subtle, more profound attempt at domination proceeded in mutual reinforcement with administration: that of religious belief. The story of Spanish Catholicism's implantation in America cannot properly be separated from that of colonial government's beginnings.

[8] CHURCH: FRIARS, BISHOPS, AND THE STATE

CHURCH AND STATE

COLUMBUS'S three ships of 1492 carried no priest. It was a curious omission even for a voyage of pure exploration, given the admiral's already marked religiosity. There can, however, scarcely have been a later Spanish fleet or flotilla bound for America that lacked a cleric. Certainly Columbus's colonizing expedition of 1493 had its complement of friars: a Benedictine, a Jeronymite, and three Franciscans.[1] Nonetheless, in the first, turbulent decade or more of colonization in the islands, the church remained unremarkable for its numbers or its actions. Then, in 1510–11, with the arrival in Hispaniola of Dominicans and a new group of Franciscans, it began to stir busily. The evangelizing of America by mendicant friars, the noblest aspect of Spain's entire imperial exercise, suddenly sprang into motion. If there was an awakening call, it was the Dominican Montesinos's excoriation, in his Advent sermon of 1511, of the citizens of Santo Domingo for their maltreatment of the native islanders.

Though many friars saw the task of Christianizing America as a personal challenge, and set about it as zealous individuals, in their labors they were inevitably agents of the Spanish state, collaborators with the growing bureaucracy in bringing the Indies into Spanish control. Though particular instances of conflict between church and state were legion, broadly speaking the two were linked in America in purpose, organization, and operation to a degree rarely matched in Christian history. The prime reason for this was the existence of royal patronage, or *real patronato*, of the Spanish American church.

Ferdinand's reluctance to see the church expand in the Caribbean before Rome had given him wide powers over it was one reason for its early feebleness. To his gratification, the concessions soon came. They extended a series of papal pronouncements inspired by earlier Spanish and Portuguese expansion, starting with bulls in the 1450s that granted legitimacy of occupation of Atlantic islands while raising questions about the conversion of the native people there.[2] Best known of all, and basic to Spain's entire imperial scheme, was the bull *Inter caetera*, issued in May 1493, very soon after Columbus's return from the first voyage. In it Alexander VI in essence ceded the crown full and perpetual dominion in America in return for an undertaking to bring its peoples into the faith: a bargain of which Spanish monarchs remained long, if intermittently, conscious. Rome soon followed with grants of control over the ecclesiastical forces needed to achieve this conversion. In 1501 Alexander bestowed on the crown the church tithes from America, so that there should be money to fund evangelization. Then, in 1508, Julius II, in *Universalis ecclesiae*, gave Ferdinand and his successors the right to present to Rome candidates, from archbishops downwards, for church posts in the Indies (with the understanding that one of the monarch's nominees would be chosen). Further, the crown was to have control over the building and endowment of cathedrals, churches, monasteries, and hospitals; tithe income was to be used for that purpose. Yet again, the monarch might control the movement of all churchmen to America. (Those approved had their passage paid by the royal treasury.) Finally, in 1538, the crown successfully claimed the right of inspection, with power of veto (the *pase regio*), of all papal dispatches to America.[3] In practice, the Council of the Indies exercised this vigilance, and, indeed, from its creation in 1524 ran the entire machinery of the *patronato*.

Rome's concession of powers was phenomenal, approached elsewhere only in a grant of patronage made to Ferdinand and Isabella for Granada and the Canaries in 1486. In Spain itself (except for Granada) Rome retained much influence in appointing clergymen until the mid eighteenth century. Part of the reason for its handing over the American church to the Spanish crown was precisely that the Indies were a challenge of evangelization on a scale that Rome could not itself meet. The task had to be delegated; *patronato* was the cost of doing so. Besides that, Alexander VI owed political debts to Ferdinand and Isabella; and he and later popes could scarcely ignore Spain's political power in Italy, made absolutely clear in 1527 by the sack of Rome by troops serving Charles V (Holy Roman Emperor, but also king of Spain).

The *real patronato* bound state and church in the Indies into a single entity. Notions of separation of church from state were of course scarcely conceivable in the Spain of the time; but the intertwining of the two (with the state always having the upper hand) was truly something original and unique to Spanish America. Once the crown gained its powers of nomination (in reality, of appointment), the American church establishment grew fast. Ferdinand sent Dominicans to Hispaniola in 1510; the number of Franciscans there rose rapidly soon after; and friars of both orders began to spread across the Caribbean. Cortés had priests with him in the Aztec conquest, both regulars (members of orders) and seculars (those not belonging to orders, but subject to bishops). And in the immediately following years others, mainly Franciscans, came to New Spain. Cortés, suspecting a potential for ostentation and wealth-seeking in the secular church, made efforts, while he was governor of New Spain, to attract friars to evangelize his domain.[4] Particularly remembered among these are the band of Franciscans who came at his invitation in 1524. In imitation of the Apostles they were twelve in number, as were other and later groups of missionaries, and as had been also St. Francis's first band of followers. It is related that after these men had walked up from the Gulf coast, Cortés, kneeling, greeted them as they entered México-Tenochtitlan by kissing the robe of their leader, Fray Martín de Valencia. The gesture reflected, perhaps, his own piety; but it also directly signaled to Spanish and Indian onlookers the respect with which he intended the church to be regarded in New Spain. If the conqueror and governor abased himself before barefooted and dusty clerics, how much more should lesser men heed them?

Cortés's objections to church hierarchy notwithstanding, New Spain soon had bishops. In 1520, even before the Aztec conquest was done, Charles V had decided that the territory merited a bishopric. He named it, presumably for lack of information about Mexican places, simply "Carola."[5] In the event, the first see was not formally created until 1526, and was placed at Tlaxcala. But México-Tenochtitlan clearly could not be left long without a bishop. In 1527 Charles V presented to Rome his nomination for that prelacy, a Franciscan named Fray Juan de Zumárraga. Such was the *patronato*'s authority that Zumárraga was in place in New Spain and taking energetic action against the misdeeds of the first *audiencia* at least a year before his diocese was formally created, in 1530. The crown quickly set up other sees as the Spaniards spread out over Mexico: Oaxaca (1534), Michoacán (1536), and Guadalajara, or New Galicia (1548). Late in 1547, México-Tenochtitlan was declared a metropolitan diocese, so that Zumárraga was briefly an archbishop before his death in 1548.

Elsewhere on the mainland, bishoprics were created just as quickly, following closely on Spanish movement into particular regions and the first budding of bureaucracy in them. The very first mainland see was not in Mexico but on the Isthmus of Panama, at Darien in 1513. Then came the first two Mexican foundations; and soon after them Guatemala, Nicaragua, and Honduras in 1530–1. Cuzco was the earliest Peruvian diocese (1537). Lima followed (in 1541, then was raised to metropolitan status, like México-Tenochtitlan, in 1547). Cities with *audiencias* rapidly became the seats of bishops; and so did various lesser provincial capitals. Of the 45 dioceses created in the entire colonial era, 22 were set up before 1550, and only 14 after 1600; and among those 14, only one (Buenos Aires, a see from 1620) was a notable administrative center of the church.[6] As with other sorts of organization of Spanish America, the sixteenth century saw the structure of the colonial church definitively assembled, and much of it was in place before 1550.

Bishops must have their cathedrals, built in the Spanish colonies with the tithe income that the *patronato* granted to the monarchy. They were, initially, small and simple buildings, though by mid century the foundations of imposing edifices still standing today were being laid. Cathedrals necessarily had their clerical staffs of deans, archdeacons, canons, and lesser prebendaries. These staffs, like other bureaucracies, started small but grew irresistibly. Evangelization, however, which was the prime task of the church in America, and one of the central purposes of Spanish colonizing, was rarely undertaken by cathedral chapters. It was mainly the work of the front-line troops of the ecclesiastical army: the priests in the *doctrinas*, or rural parishes.

Regulars as Missionaries

Parish priests, in Spain and elsewhere in Europe, were usually secular clergymen. Given the Spanish crown's obvious keenness to set up an episcopal church in America – a well-tried hierarchical chain of command consisting of archbishops, bishops, cathedral chapters, and local priests – seculars might well have been chosen as the true faith's trench warriors to battle America's indigenous paganism. But the young Charles V found his new kingdom's secular clergy slack in behavior and intellect. By contrast, at least portions of Spain's regular priesthood had been energized in mind and spirit by the reforms of the Catholic Monarchs and their indefatigable minister, Archbishop Jiménez de Cisneros. Hence Charles applied to Pope Adrian VI – who, as Adrian of Utrecht, had earlier been his adviser and then regent in Castile – to allow regulars, and above all Franciscans from the Observant, or stricter, part of the order, to form the evangelizing force that mainland America demanded. Permission came in the papal letter *Omnimoda* of May 1522. There Adrian also gave the regulars' leaders in America great independence of existing and future bishops, and authority in their mission regions even over the secular clerics.[7]

Thus in the early 1520s not only was the somewhat ad hoc evangelizing that friars had earlier performed in and around the Caribbean given Rome's formal blessing, but the door to the mission stage was flung open and mendicant brothers urged to pass through it. So came to New Spain in 1524 the apostolic Franciscan twelve, soon to be followed by others of their order, then by Dominicans (from 1526 on) and Augustinians (from 1533). Franciscans reached Peru with the conquest, expanding from there to Quito (1535) and to other parts of South America in mid century. Dominicans and Augustinians followed close on their heels. A group of twelve Mercedarians entered New Spain in 1530; but friars of this order found greater space for evangelization in South America. The last major order to send men to Spanish America in the sixteenth century was the Society of Jesus, founded by the Spanish saint Ignatius of Loyola, in 1534. The first Jesuits reached Lima in 1568 and New Spain in 1572. Most of their highly distinctive missions in remote parts of the Indies were, however, seventeenth-century creations.[8]

The friars were thinly spread over the immense task of conversion they had undertaken. In 1559, for example, only 380 Franciscans, 212 Augustinians, and 210 Dominicans were living in New Spain; and among these were many (lay brethren, novices, administrators, the infirm) not active in the field.[9] By the early eighteenth century, the number of Franciscans in the entire American empire stood at some 5,000. A century later it had risen to about 6,000, roughly a half of all regulars in Spanish America.[10] The Franciscans were always the largest contingent of regulars in the colonies, as they were in Spain itself in the sixteenth century.

The Franciscans of the conquest period were impelled not solely by some charitable desire to convert the pagan, but also by the urgent biddings of a millenarian utopianism they had inherited from the Middle Ages.[11] They saw themselves as central actors in the final conversion of the Gentiles – among whom were the American native peoples – to Christ. Once that task (and the conversion of Jews and Muslims also) was accomplished, so apocalyptic tradition rooted in the book of Revelation proclaimed, there would begin a thousand-year period of blessedness on earth, preceded, or perhaps followed, by the second coming of Christ. To this line of belief many Franciscans (though not all) were drawn from the very foundation of their order in the early thirteenth century. Among those who later found it compelling were some of the dozen Franciscans who arrived in New Spain in 1524. Their order had been the subject of the most intense spiritualizing reform in early sixteenth-century Spain, and they were among the products of that effort. One of the twelve, Fray Toribio de Benavente, recorded that their leader, Fray Martín de Valencia, on contemplating the question of converting the heathen and the return of Christ, asked himself: "When will this be? When will this prophecy be fulfilled? Shall I perhaps be worthy to witness this conversion? For we are now at the evening and the end of our days and in the last age of the world."[12]

Driven by this sense of the end's imminence, and of their role in bringing it to pass, the Franciscans in New Spain set furiously about the work of conversion. They set about learning native languages in order to preach, studying native religion so as to know what was to be overcome, inquiring into native history in an effort to place their charges on the cultural map of humankind, founding schools to impress faith and European civility on the sons of native leaders (in the hope that the lessons would filter down to their subjects), designing and building churches, traveling, catechizing, and baptizing. By 1533 the Franciscans estimated that they had baptized 1,200,000 native people in New Spain; and 5,000,000 by 1536, when they themselves numbered perhaps sixty. Clearly little teaching preceded baptism. Dominicans and Augustinians objected strongly to the Franciscans' wholesale approach to baptism – holy water applied from a jar to thousands of heads per day.[13] But baptism was the sacrament that brought admittance to the church; and that was the urgent and overriding goal.

The effort truly verged on the superhuman. The Franciscan who late in the sixteenth century recorded the deeds of his brethren in New Spain, Fray Gerónimo de Mendieta, wrote:

> In Spain we know it for a common thing that when priests have to preach a sermon they are so tired and in such a sweat that they have to change their clothes ... And if after he had preached, a priest were told to sing a Mass or comfort a sick man or bury a dead one, he would think it the same as digging his own grave. But in this land it happened every day that one lone friar would count the people in the morning, then preach to them and sing Mass, and after that baptize both children and adults, confess the sick no matter how many, and then bury any dead there might be. And so it was for thirty or forty years, and in some places so it is still.[14]

Singly, or more typically in pairs, Franciscans fanned out over central Mexico, then the west, and the north, where late in the sixteenth century they contributed much to the pacification of the Chichimeca, and in the seventeenth became the sole order active in New Mexico. But towns offered challenges of conversion, too, and in them, above all in México-Tenochtitlan, Franciscans distinguished themselves in native education. In this the model was Fray Pedro de Gante, a highly educated product of the Flemish Renaissance who arrived in New Spain as a Franciscan lay brother in 1523. He immediately set up a school, though not in Tenochtitlan, which was being rebuilt after its razing in 1521, but east across the lake at Texcoco. Its first pupils were the Texcocan nobility, many of whom were baptized once the twelve friars of 1524 had arrived. In 1526 Gante moved his school to the resurgent capital, opening it now to native boys of all social ranks, as it remained, under his direction, till his death in 1572. His aim was primary education in the catechism, reading, writing, numbers, and singing. All teaching was in Nahuatl, which Gante quickly learned to speak, and then, among the first to do so, wrote down in Latin letters. He used plays, pageants, and music to convey Christian teachings. Thus European music and musical instruments of the time were grafted on to the native musical tradition. Later a craft school was added to the establishment, where, again, European practice came to blend with native skill in, for example, stoneworking and tailoring.

Gante's school demonstrated and confirmed the Franciscans' early confidence, soon to be shared by the other orders, in native Mexicans' intellectual and artistic capacities. This assurance appeared again in their foundation of a college of secondary and higher learning for Indians in Tlatelolco, the northern section of the capital. It was opened on January 6, 1536, the feast of the Epiphany, and a day traditionally linked to the manifestation of Christ to the Gentiles (personified in the Magi). Over this symbolic ceremony presided Viceroy Mendoza, attended by Bishop Zumárraga and the president of the *audiencia* of New Spain.[15]

The Tlatelolco college was designed for sons of the native nobility from all parts of New Spain. In it the Franciscans hoped to form a Europeanized native leadership capable of serving as a wedge between Indian society as a whole and the colonizing Spaniards. Only in such separation did the friars see a chance of preserving the native population in physical and spiritual safety. Other orders shared this view. The regime imposed on the boys in the college must have had the friars' own training as its model: sleeping in a large dormitory, rising at dawn, communal eating, regular church attendance, a curriculum of reading, writing, music, Latin, rhetoric, logic, philosophy, and – here a New World innovation – native medicine. No Spanish was spoken – only Latin and Nahuatl. From all this at least some remarkable native scholars emerged, skilled Latinists and translators of Nahuatl who collaborated crucially with the friars in putting Christianity into native terms, and in creating the great compilations on Mexican history and culture that are the most enduring legacy of the early Franciscans in New Spain.

The Tlatelolco college flourished, however, for only a decade or two. It was worn away by a strengthening current of anti-native sentiment among colonials, a current combining several streams: fears that Indians were incorrigible heretics, that to educate them would simply make their heresy more dangerous, and that it would also lift them out of the servile position to which ever more settlers wished to consign them. More telling, though, than even these misgivings was the objection to indigenous Christian priests, whom the Franciscans had particularly hoped to train at Tlatelolco. Rome was not against a native Catholic priesthood; but it was a notion that most of the colonial church and population could not stomach. Until very late in colonial times no Indian priests were to appear in New Spain, or, indeed, anywhere else in Spanish America. Underlying all specific objections to the Franciscans' efforts at Tlatelolco, and similar efforts by them and other orders elsewhere, was doubtless, by the mid sixteenth century, the growing disdain for Indians felt by a colonial society that contained ever fewer members who had seen native culture in something like its pre-conquest splendor. As that vision faded, native survivors of the conquest found the horizons of their existence – social, political, economic – relentlessly shrinking.

The other orders established early in New Spain rivaled, if they did not quite match, the Franciscans in efforts of evangelization and Indian education. Schools were often attached to the monasteries that sprung up as the friars spread out in all directions from the center of the colony. In the South American colonies the Franciscan primacy is less clear. There were Franciscans, Dominicans, and Mercedarians in Peru in the opening year of the conquest, 1532; after this, the Dominicans were perhaps the quickest to increase numbers and extend their ministry.[16] The Jesuits, once they arrived in Spanish America c.1570, entered the fray with an energy befitting the youth of their society. Seeing, though, that primary teaching was already well attended to, they immediately applied themselves to higher education, and, similarly, finding no lack of missionaries and parish priests in the colonial heartlands, decided to take the word to the frontiers. In the western Sierra Madre in Mexico, the inner slopes of the Andes, the western fringes of Amazonia, and Paraguay, they became the prime evangelists, and so remained for two centuries.

The mission effort also included women, at least initially. The first religious houses for women appeared very soon after the mainland conquests. In New Spain, for example, Bishop Zumárraga created a *beaterio* (lay convent) in México-Tenochtitlan to house six Franciscan laywomen whom he had brought in from Spain to teach Indian girls.[17] More *beatas* – pious women who took simple vows under the rules of the third orders of Franciscans and other similar societies[18] – soon followed, creating a number of schools for the religious and practical education of *indias*. Churchmen were at first enthusiastic about the *beatas*: in 1537, Zumárraga wrote of his desire to create a colony-wide network of Poor Clare (reformed Franciscan) convents, with "as many houses of girls … as monasteries of friars."[19] However, this enthusiasm waned by the early 1540s, when few of the *beatas* and students remained within the schools. So, by the time of the first fully conventual foundation in the Americas, a more conservative spirit carried the day; Mexico City's Nuestra Señora de la Concepción, founded in 1540–1, admitted daughters of the Spanish elite under the relatively relaxed Conceptionist rule. In Cuzco, on the other hand, city fathers established the convent of Santa Clara for young *mestizas*; however, there too the convent became dominated by Spanish women with the passage of time.[20] Through subsequent foundations, the Conceptionist order remained strong in the Indies, though Franciscan, Augustinian, Dominican, and Carmelite houses for women were also soon in place in the major towns. Following the trend of white exclusivity already established, most convents enacted either formal or tacit policies that barred non-whites from professing as choir nuns.

Though nunneries were clearly the most prominent of such communities, other houses that could be called "semi-religious" were also established during the sixteenth century in many areas of Spanish America. These were often founded for reasons of social exigency, often to shelter and educate vulnerable white and *mestiza* girls. In Mexico City, a school for *mestiza* girls was established in 1548. During the second half of the sixteenth century, city fathers in Lima established lay schools, and a school for white female foundlings, Santa Cruz de Atocha. These institutions were a source of pride and an object of devotion for the colonial population, but were also vulnerable to takeover or even extinction. Mexico City's *mestiza* school, for example, was dominated by Spanish girls by the 1590s. In Lima, by the end of the century, lay schools had virtually disappeared, while newly established convents had taken up the slack and were educating girls.[21] By 1600, Spanish nunneries were the dominant – and most stable – expression of feminine religiosity.

Although historians of the later colonial period have given much attention to the secular side of convent life – the luxury in which some nuns lived, the episodes of improper behavior in the locutory, and, more seriously, the considerable part played by nunneries in local economies – there is no questioning the true religiosity of many nuns. The founding period of many of the houses, the second half of the sixteenth century, was also a time in which the value of contemplation, often deeply tinctured with mysticism, was stressed by the church. It was the time, in Spain, of St. Teresa of Avila, and of St. John of the Cross, both ascetics, and indeed the restorers of the initial austerity of their order, the Carmelites. Moreover, the early years of most colonial convents were not particularly luxurious. In Mexico City, for example, constant financial trouble beset sixteenth-century convents. Only a return to European-style foundations backed by wealthy patrons put women's communities, by 1600, on a firm financial footing. Sixteenth-century nuns could not expect a particularly luxurious life. Thus the social reasons for the founding and growth of convents should not be overemphasized. It was not simply, or even mainly, lack of suitable husbands that led women to take conventual vows; but rather, for many of them, a genuine vocation.

By the end of the sixteenth century, many convents had been established in the capitals of Spanish America. These institutions would continue to grow and flourish in the seventeenth century, providing religious opportunities for the daughters of the elite, and serving as a central marker of Spanish urban identity and pride. Lost in the long process of creating and stabilizing women's institutions, however, was the original aim of Bishop Zumárraga and others who sought to establish the first convents in the Indies: the participation of religious women in the missionary endeavor, and the extension of a fuller Christian religious life to indigenous women.

THE REGULARS REINED IN

Not all was sweetness and light on the mission front, of course. Zeal could easily tilt into fanaticism, especially in men isolated from their religious brethren, not to mention from settler society as a whole. In 1562 the small band of Franciscans working to convert the Maya of northern Yucatan fell into a rage of disappointment when they discovered idol-worship among those they thought they had Christianized. In an effort to eliminate all such backsliding, they hoisted suspects up with cords around their wrists to extract confessions about the numbers and sites of idols. Such use of torture was not merely immoral but illegal; only secular government could apply it.[22] There was, alas, ample precedent in earlier church behavior in the Valley of Mexico, where there had occurred, for example, the notorious case of Don Carlos Chichimecatecuhtli. He, a nobleman of Texcoco and a product of Franciscan education, had been found guilty of keeping idols in his house and publicly defaming Christianity. After an investigation led by Bishop Zumárraga, himself a Franciscan and on that account doubly incensed, Don Carlos was garroted and burned in 1539.[23] This was extraordinary punishment. A offender of Don Carlos's rank had to be made an example. To native backsliders in religion who had less social and political prominence in the valley the Franciscans meted out beatings and perhaps a spell in private jails that the order had built.[24]

If the friars could slip from their ideals in their treatment of their converts, they were prey also to conflicts among themselves. The orders squabbled over mission territory, over methods of proselytism, and over matters of public policy, such as the pros and cons of the *encomienda*. They were subject, also, to a creeping worldliness; it would have been miraculous if they had not been. By the mid sixteenth century they were beginning to own property, in the form of land and houses, notably in New Spain. This was not through conscious acquisitiveness, for poverty and asceticism were still firmly rooted in most mendicants' minds, but more the outcome of gifts and bequests, some from conquerors and early settlers anxious to ease their consciences as they aged and died. Not that wealth was without its proper uses; it allowed, for instance, for more ambitious building of churches, and for some incipient richness of interior decoration. The Augustinians, in particular, thought it fitting to glorify the Lord with gold and plasterwork in the roofs of their mission churches. Late in the century, lofty and elaborate altarpieces appeared in churches even in native towns. Indeed it was particularly fitting that they should be in those churches, for such reredoses often incorporating statues of saints and church Fathers, along with paintings of biblical scenes, were not mere decoration, but illustrations of Christian belief and history to which preachers could point as they delivered their sermons.

Wealth, then, the friars could find good use for, even though they might not pursue it. What they did pursue, and what eventually brought charges of worldliness heavily down on them, was a political role in America. Their concern with Indians' wellbeing put them in the thick of politics almost from the start; again, Montesinos's sermon of 1511 was the signal event. The separation they aimed to create between natives and secular settlers was a threat to labor supply, and hence a threat also to both individual colonists' income and the state's taxes.

Nonetheless, for several decades the friars had the monarchy's backing. Christianization was at the heart of Spain's purpose in America; and, at a more practical level, the orders provided a useful counterweight to the *encomenderos*, who were, until the mid century, a far more potent political challenge to the crown than the thinly scattered mendicants. Then, however, the royal view of the friars grew slowly jaundiced. With the *encomenderos* weakened by legislation and events of the 1540s, and the American bureaucracy gaining strength and reach, the friars' ministry to the Indians began to seem like a usurpation of royal powers. Especially irritating was their assumption of jurisdiction (the right to try, judge, and punish Indians for civil as well as religious offenses) in their *doctrinas*. This was an intolerable intrusion into the Spanish monarchy's supreme function. The growth of royal disillusion coincided with the deliberations of the Council of Trent (1545–64), one of whose central themes, within its broad effort to stiffen Catholicism's resistance to the encroaching Protestant Reformation, was the subjection of the entire priesthood to the authority of bishops. This aim of reinforcing the church's backbone, that is, the hierarchy extending down from pope, through bishops, to parish priests, found a welcome in the Spain of the young king Philip II. Although the *patronato* in principle gave Spanish rulers authority over the regular as well as the secular clergy, the regulars' traditional autonomy as self-contained bodies within the church made them, in practice, less easy to influence. The prospect of their now being placed squarely under the thumb of bishops was a heartening one for a Spanish monarchy irritated, and even alarmed, by the growth of friars' influence over its native American subjects.

Philip II and his advisers were, then, in the 1560s distinctly inclined to rein in the regulars. The king's concerns and intentions were clearly expressed in the instructions given late in 1568 to the newly appointed viceroy of Peru, Don Francisco de Toledo. Philip wished the orders (Franciscans, Dominicans, and Augustinians) to be favored: they had, he said, been of great effect in the evangelization and conversion of the Indians. They had, though, resisted the authority of the bishops in Peru. Some of them, as individuals, had gathered personal property, and had even returned to Spain with money. Such acquisitiveness contravened canon law, the constitutions of their orders, and their own vows. They had tended to build their monasteries in fertile and comfortable places, leaving less appealing areas unevangelized. They were reported to have claimed secular jurisdiction in civil and criminal cases in the districts of their monasteries. They had, further, under the pretext of defending the Indians, interfered in matters of justice and executive government (*gobierno*), "seeking to meddle in [affairs of] law and sovereignty of the Indies, and other things that lead to much commotion, especially when they speak of these things from pulpits and in other congregations and pronouncements."[25]

The regulars, then, had done a good job; but not as good or as complete as it should have been. More parishes, the king pronounced, were needed in Peru. Toledo should create them, in consultation with the bishops and with the archbishop of Lima. These parishes would need curates; but there were too few secular priests available to man them. Since, therefore, the regulars were well used to parish work, they might continue to serve as parish priests. But they should no longer be appointed by their order or monastery, but be nominated by the bishops, for later presentation (to Rome) by the king. Once in place in their parishes, the friars should be subject to visitation and discipline by the bishops (something the orders had adamantly rejected before).

The king proposed also a concentration of the regulars in the major towns, in the sense that large, central monasteries should be set up there, to function partly as training schools in native affairs and languages. From these urban bases, friars should go out as parish priests to small houses in the country. Toledo was to consider reducing the existing number of big provincial monasteries, which were the cause of "certain disadvantages of much consideration."[26] Philip's discomfort here was probably the thought of large bodies of friars living far from the viceregal eye.

Regulars, then, might continue to do what they had done since the conquest: instruct and convert Indians in their villages across Peru. The monarchy was grateful for past efforts. But their freedom to convert where, when, and how they pleased was now curbed by a king who found their autonomy threatening, presumptuous, and conducive to slackness. They must now submit to the king's will. Regulars in parishes were, in effect, to be appointed by him (or, in practice, by his viceroy), since the bishops who were to nominate them were themselves, through the operation of the *patronato*, the king's men. The bishops would, likewise, be well placed to oversee the friars' new and enlarged houses in the principal towns. One prominent strand running through Philip's orders to Toledo on these church matters, in fact, is a reinforcement of the bishops' authority. In making that emphasis, the king both heeded Trent's resolutions and strengthened their implementation. He strengthened also, of course, his own directing role in the church's life in America.

The changes that Philip entrusted to Toledo for Peru in 1568 were generalized over the Indies by the Ordenanza del Patronazgo, or Ordinance of Patronage, of 1574. Here the king drew into one code many earlier orders bearing on royal control of the American church, with the aim of reinforcing his authority. Again, subjection of regulars to the bishops, and their replacement in parish work by seculars, were two of the main means chosen for achieving that end. Still, the secular-versus-regular issue was by no means closed in 1574. Such was the moral and political weight of the orders in Rome, Spain, and America, and such the momentum of their evangelizing in the Indies, that they managed to sustain their pastoral role for many a year. Even so late as the mid eighteenth century, in so central an area as the Valley of Mexico, friars tended to a large majority (59 of 72) of parishes.[27] The final ousting of the regulars from these, and their replacement by seculars, came only *c*.1770, as the effect of a far deeper sort of secularization than anything the Spanish world had previously felt. That was the reformism of the Spanish Bourbons, inspired by a centralizing regalism typical of the eighteenth century. Driven by that modern impulse, the monarchy took a degree of control over the entire American church that exceeded Philip II's most optimistic imaginings.

Nonetheless, Philip's campaign against the orders in the 1560s and 1570s, though it left friars in parishes, had had its intended effect. It had changed the terms on which the regulars worked and existed in the Indies, just as the anti-*encomienda* laws of the 1540s, though finally allowing *encomenderos* to stay in place, had changed the conditions of their existence by denying them free access to Indian labor and subjecting them to the crown's good will for extension of the grants. Both groups lost the immense freedom of action they had enjoyed in the early decades; both found themselves far more dependent than before, for their continued activity, on royal benevolence and approval. This said, it might seem contradictory that, even after the 1570s, many regulars appeared as bishops in the Indies. In the first half of the seventeenth century, indeed, slightly more than half (146 of 257) of men named to and holding bishoprics in America and the Philippines were regular priests.[28] But since, through the *patronato*, Spanish rulers completely controlled the appointment of bishops, the placing of friars (mostly Dominicans and Augustinians) in sees both indebted the orders to the crown and gave the government a direct access to the regulars' affairs in America that otherwise it would have lacked. By making friars senior members of the episcopal hierarchy in the Indies the crown thus tied the American church closer to government. And in reality the entire process of the curbing of the orders' independence in the 1560s and 1570s was another part of that solidifying of the Spanish state in America pursued for two or three decades before then. The change was a part of what led Gerónimo de Mendieta, an apocalyptical Franciscan historian of his order's deeds in sixteenth-century New Spain, to pronounce the reign of Philip II to be the Silver Age of the American church, in contrast to the Golden Age of Charles V.[29]

Another block laid in place in the state-building process of these years in America was the Inquisition. Bishops had in fact been energetically active as inquisitors in the Indies since shortly before 1520, and special papal dispensation had been given to regulars, as with parish work, to carry out inquisitorial functions. These generally aimed to promote religious orthodoxy. Indians being converted were an obvious source of concern, and indeed many were investigated and some even executed for backsliding into paganism. Blasphemy among Spaniards was another worry. The contention popular in Spain, for example, that frequenting prostitutes was a venial, not a mortal, sin (especially if one paid), had its adherents in America, and for such errors the early Inquisition pulled people in. But there were as yet in America few suspected judaizers, or foreigners perhaps carrying some virus of Protestantism; so the episcopal inquisition was an ad hoc, erratic affair.

As the Counter-Reformation gathered force, however, and the call for church discipline came loudly from Trent, and as the American administrative bureaucracy grew and strengthened, a parallel extension to the colonies of the inquisitorial machinery of Spain seemed useful. In 1565 Philip II ordered tribunals of the Holy Office to be set up in America; the personnel were in place in Lima in 1570 and in Mexico City in 1571. Indians were now exempted from the Inquisition's attentions. Vigilance over their faith was left to the bishops, who were, however, no longer inquisitors. But the rest of the colonial population, Spanish or mixed-blood, and, of course, any of the Protestant corsairs and privateers now prowling the Spanish American coasts in growing numbers who happened to fall into Spanish hands, were grist to the inquisitorial mill. The political effect of the system, though, was just as important as its doctrinal role. For the king controlled the naming of inquisitors in America, just as in Spain, and the Supreme Council of the Inquisition sat at court, under the royal eye. Thus this new American bureaucracy, on the borderline between church and state, gave the monarchy another channel through which to send commands to the colonies and gather information from them. Inquisitors, prosecutors, and scribes were in the viceregal capitals, close to viceroys, *audiencias*, treasury officers, and the upper church hierarchy. The Inquisition's local agents, or familiars, were scattered through provincial towns. They were on the lookout for not only religious, but also political, heresy.[30]

Evangelizers and Observers of Indians

The Christianizing of Spanish America clearly required an organized evangelical force, and this, despite contention among regulars, seculars, and monarchy, was what Spain provided. All saw, however, that conversion would be surer and quicker the better the targets of the campaign were known. Thus Indians became the objects of close study of a broadly anthropological sort. The people best placed to carry this out were the missionary friars, as the largest group of Europeans in close contact with Indians. The friars were also the majority of educated Europeans in America. Many of them had had university training in ancient languages and philosophy. Some were humanists in the best and full Renaissance sense of the term: men keen to recover and update the wisdom of classical European culture, and integrate it with Christian belief. For some such men, study of native culture and language became something to be pursued not only to promote conversion, but for its intrinsic fascination.

So many were the missionaries who strove to understand and record native affairs that a sampling of the more remarkable of them must suffice here. Brief recognition should first go again to Antonio de Montesinos, not because he is the source of much information about the Caribbean peoples, but because in his sermon of December 1511 he raised a crucial question about native Americans that became the topic of stormy argument for decades after. "Are these not men?", he asked his indignant congregation in Santo Domingo. "Have they not rational souls?" The degree of Indians' rationality – or, conversely, the degree and nature of their barbarism – soon became of intense concern not only to ecclesiastics seeking the most effective methods of conversion, but also to administrators and political theorists trying to decide how native people should be treated, and even what rights Spain had in America to occupy land, seize property, and dispose of its peoples' lives.

Settlement of the mainland raised such questions to new levels of dispute since, while the size and complexity of political organization of the great states, their elegant cities, their high craftsmanship, and so forth argued for rationality and civility, proponents of barbarism could support their view with such contradictions of advance as absence of writing, and Aztec predilection for human sacrifice. One who clearly never much doubted the rationality of central Mexicans was Pedro de Gante. His schools in Texcoco and Tenochtitlan showed from earliest post-conquest times, through the most practical of demonstrations, that young native children could learn precisely as Europeans did. Later Franciscan schooling at Tlatelolco and elsewhere simply confirmed this.

A similar confidence in native Mexicans' capacities, though not precisely in their rationality, appears in Vasco de Quiroga, one the most effective of pro-Indian activists of the sixteenth century. He came to New Spain as a judge in the reforming second *audiencia* created in 1530. The first and deepest impression that the Indians left on him was of their poverty and their defenselessness against the demands and maltreatment of Spanish settlers. Quiroga, who was a remarkable blend of idealism and practicality (the first energizing the second), decided quickly that a new type of native township was needed for the Indians' economic and general protection. This he called an *hospital*. The term implied refuge, broadly speaking; though a place for treating the sick was certainly a part of it. Workshops for native craftsmen were also included in the community, as well as land for communal farming. Government should be by native leaders elected by the families making up the population, under the supervision of a Spanish official. A Christian priest should oversee the religious life of the village. Particularly striking about Quiroga's *hospital* plans was that they were consciously modeled on Sir Thomas More's *Utopia*. That work, of 1516, had itself been inspired by the American discoveries of the early sixteenth century.[31]

Quiroga founded his first *hospital* near Mexico-Tenochtitlan in 1532, naming it Santa Fe de los Altos. A second, Santa Fe de la Laguna, followed in Michoacán after Quiroga completed an inspection of that western region in 1533. In 1538 he became the first bishop of Michoacán, receiving simultaneous ordination and consecration from Bishop Zumárraga of México-Tenochtitlan. From then until his death at a great age in 1565 he strove to protect the bodies and souls of the Indians of Michoacán, where, it is said, his memory lives on to this day. He created his most ambitious *hospital* town on the southern shore of Lake Pátzcuaro, intending it to become the city of Michoacán, the capital of the region, and the site of a great five-naved, star-shaped cathedral.[32] But the church plan was too large to be built, and the hostility aroused in settlers and also in Viceroy Mendoza by his strategy of protecting Indians through segregation brought the choice of Valladolid (now Morelia) as capital. Quiroga also set up in existing native towns of his bishopric 88 *hospitals* of a lesser sort: single buildings comprising a chapel, a space for treatment of the sick, and another for the use of the town's native government.[33] These *hospitals* were to be run wholly by Indians, and so conformed to Quiroga's intent to strengthen native defenses against Spanish inroads of all sorts.

Quiroga clearly saw central Mexicans as rational enough to run their own local government, in a colonial setting, under broad supervision from Spanish officials and priests. It was not, though, so much their intellect that drew him as their psyche. They seemed to him simple, humble, malleable – and perfectible. In 1535 he compared their pre-conquest existence to life in the mythical Golden Age of the Kingdom of Saturn. In both he found "the same customs and manners, the same equality, simplicity, goodness, obedience, humility, festivities, games, pleasures, drinking, idling, pastimes, nudity and lack of any but the poorest of household goods and of any desire for better ...."[34] (Quiroga limited his attention to the common people; neither Aztec nobles nor the many local *caciques* who survived the conquest could possibly have inspired such an assessment.) The Spaniards' restlessness, ambition, and cupidity left Indians astonished. In the right surroundings, which Quiroga thought would be native towns of 6,000 families, Indians would govern themselves well and convert easily to Christianity. He hoped, indeed, that in the New World, mass conversion of native people could re-create the early Christian church in its pristine purity.[35] No such thing was possible. But Vasco de Quiroga, with his potent blend of idealism, practicality, political skill, and determination, came closer to replicating it, in his diocese of Michoacán, than any other sixteenth-century reformer in Spanish America.

In the years, the 1530s, when Quiroga began his work in Mexico, debate about the nature of Indians and related political questions reached new levels of intensity and sophistication in Spain itself. Few years had passed without dispute of this sort since serious consideration began of Indian treatment with the drafting of the Laws of Burgos in 1512. One continuous thread in the discussion was the notion that Indians were "natural" slaves. An early and influential exponent of this view was Juan López de Palacios Rubios, a lawyer, but not a cleric, who in 1513 wrote of the Caribbean natives as simple primitives, living as gentle barbarians in harmony with nature. In this he seems to prefigure Quiroga. But the conclusions he drew from that diagnosis were very different from Quiroga's. Caribbean people were free while they were isolated. But contact with civilized men, such as the Spanish, revealed a disparity of human status that relegated Indians to service of their "natural" masters.[36]

These notions of "natural" slavery and mastery came from Aristotle. They received their closest examination, in relation to native Americans, in lectures given in the 1530s at the University of Salamanca by the Spanish Dominican, Francisco de Vitoria. Vitoria, assuredly among the finest intelligences of sixteenth-century Spain, was a founder of the intellectual movement known as the school of Salamanca, which made that university into the chief authority on scholasticism of its time. At Salamanca, Vitoria introduced Aquinas's *Summa Theologica* as the central theological text, and in so doing intensified study in Spain of Aristotle, whose thought Aquinas had played a large part in re-establishing in Europe.

It is no wonder, then, that the fraught and interconnected questions of the Indians' human standing, their freedom, their treatment by Spaniards, and indeed Spain's right to dominion over them and their territories, received their most thorough analysis in Aristotelian terms. Aristotle had pronounced that in humanity, as in the rest of the universe, there existed a duality, between those in whom reason dominated and those in whom passions prevailed. Human groups in which intellect failed to rule passions were naturally subservient to others in which reason was in command. These natural slaves were not without reason; but for some cause it was weak in them. The relationship between natural slave and master should not, though, be exploitive, but mutually beneficial: the slave should work for the master, and in doing so improve his exercise of reason.[37]

Identifying the natural slave, however, was not simple. A broad category proposed by Aristotle was people living in barbarity. Spaniards looking at native Americans, therefore, debated furiously whether Indians were barbarians. But this, naturally, drew them into further problems of categorization; and the theoretical exegesis of Aristotle could be drawn to so complex a fineness that almost any prejudice or conclusion could substantiated. Vitoria found the high American cultures deficient in reason – and hence barbaric – because, among much else, of their practice of human sacrifice and ritual cannibalism. Eating human flesh he regarded as not so much sinful in a Christian sense, but as reprehensible on Aristotelian criteria, because it showed unawareness of natural hierarchies. Human flesh was not proper food for civilized beings; no more were the insects that Aztecs were reported to eat. Animal flesh was the fitting food for the civilized. The Aztecs ate little of it. On the other hand, their highly organized city life, social hierarchy, and sophisticated trade suggested a well-developed humanity.

The contradictions proved almost endless. They also proved, when confronted by as powerful a mind as Vitoria's, the means for breaking the molds that Aristotle had cast for humanity. For Vitoria finally resolved the puzzle by arguing that the Indians occupied some middle ground between "natural" masters and slaves. Their rationality could not be denied; but it was still not fully developed, its potential still not realized. But, having rationality, Indians were essentially human. Their failings, like those of European peasants, were to be attributed to inadequate education, and, therefore, they were remediable. Or Indians could be regarded as children, whom Aristotle had seen as only potential humans, as yet quasi-animal, while their rational faculties were still growing. Applying this assessment to the matter of Spanish rights to America, Vitoria held that, until their raising to full rationality were complete, Indians must stay under Spanish control, as children under parents' formative guidance. One basis of Spain's title to America was therefore a duty to provide this guidance. On the other hand, the Salamanca school's opinion logically became that once the tutorial task was done, that claim to title lapsed; for Indians, as essentially rational, were essentially free.[38]

Vitoria's categorization of American natives coincided nicely with the ruling of Pope Paul III, in his bull *Sublimis Deus* of 1537, that they were fully fitted to receive the faith, and that anyone who denied this, proclaiming Indians to be "dumb brutes created for our service," was simply a "satellite" of the Devil.

It is no surprise that it was another Spanish Dominican, Bernardino de Minaya, who moved Paul to issue this and other pro-Indian edicts in 1537.[39] Equally unsurprising is that Vitoria's views were not welcomed by the crown, particularly as another of his radical notions was to challenge the long-established doctrine giving universal temporal powers – power over the affairs of the world – to the Papacy. Christ had not claimed such powers. How, then, could his vicars, the popes, hold them?[40] If they did not, Alexander VI's 1493 grant of general dominion in America to Spain was worthless; and Spain's first and strongest title to the Indies was undermined. Small wonder that in 1539 Charles V banned further debate on titles to America.[41] Nevertheless, the tiresome academics of Salamanca continued to think of the matters Vitoria had raised, and their school became broadly anti-imperialist.

By the 1540s, of course, the question of titles was, literally, academic. There was no practical prospect that Spain would abandon the Indies. Certainly few even of the missionaries in America would have welcomed such a move, however much they wished that secular settlers would leave Indians alone, the better to be guided to true faith and civility by the priesthood. In particular, the Franciscans' longstanding millenarianism had been reinvigorated by Spain's transatlantic expansion; at the same time, once in the Indies and striving to maximize both numbers and speed in conversion, they saw the secular settlers as a definite hindrance to their purpose.

One means by which Franciscans tried to separate their charges from the general run of colonists and from broad European contamination was to preserve native languages. If Indians did not learn Spanish, colonists could less easily influence and command them. This, as much as the desire to promote conversion, was the motive for the friars' monumental linguistic efforts in sixteenth-century Mexico. In the 1520s, forty languages were spoken in the parts of New Spain recently conquered, though, under Aztec influence and policy, Nahuatl had become a lingua franca in much of that area. In the sixteenth century, 109 works were published on or in native Mexican tongues; of these, the Franciscans produced eighty.[42] The first grammar of a Mexican language, one of Nahuatl, was put out in 1547 by the greatest of Franciscan linguists in New Spain, Andrés de Olmos, who was possibly the man whom Gerónimo de Mendieta had in mind when he later wrote of a Franciscan able to preach and write catechisms in ten or more Indian languages.[43] The friars' learning of languages, which they then duly set down in grammars and dictionaries, provided incidentally in some cases a record of tongues that have long since disappeared.

Language was, though, only one part of native culture that the missionaries preserved on paper. Olmos, for example, while evidently a supreme linguist, was also a student of native Mexican affairs in general, and in the 1530s wrote a *Treatise on Mexican Antiquities* – alas, a lost work.[44] An abundance of similar work by other Franciscans in Mexico survives, however, Prime among it is the great compilation of Fray Bernardino de Sahagún, the *Historia general de las cosas de Nueva España* (*General History of the Things of New Spain*). It, too, suffered initial perils, but survived to provide a view of unmatched breadth on Aztec and sixteenth-century native Mexico.

Having been a student at Salamanca in the 1520s, Sahagún came to New Spain in 1529. As he learned Nahuatl, he decided to produce an illustrated dictionary of the language.[45] This plan expanded as he turned to parish work, observed his surroundings, and began interviewing surviving native nobles. He taught at times in the Franciscan school in Tlatelolco. His pupils there added information to what he had gathered, and helped him write it down. Gradually his *Historia* was drafted, in Nahuatl; it reached its first stage of completion in 1569. A bilingual text followed, with Spanish and Nahuatl in parallel columns, and illustrations by Indian artists. This is now known as the *Codex Florentino*. Though Sahagún gathered much information himself, and recorded it in Nahuatl, much else came from his native collaborators. The *Historia*, then, both because of its sources and its initial compilation in the native language, gives a markedly "inside" view of Indian life, before, during, and after the conquest. Its twelfth and final book is the fullest available native account of the conquest of the Aztecs, written in the highly charged rhetoric of native formal speech. The sufferings of the dwellers in Tenochtitlan in 1520–1, first from smallpox and then from the Spanish onslaught are, for example, harrowingly portrayed: "Sores erupted on our faces, our breasts, our bellies; we were covered with agonizing sores from head to foot … The sick were so utterly helpless that they could only lie on their beds like corpses … If they did move their bodies, they screamed with pain."[46] This last book of the *Historia* is the most historical in content; the earlier sections form a great linguistic-cum-ethnographic compendium on native Mexican religion, thought, and society.

Sahagún had no doubts about Indians' intellectual potential. His native collaborators on the *Historia* from the Tlatelolco school were men to whom the Franciscans had successfully given an education in the European mold. But, by the time his great work was nearing completion, he, like other evangelizers of the later sixteenth century, was growing gloomy about the natives' moral resilience, and hence about the depth of their conversion. There were no Indians in the priesthood, in his view, because they were incapable of celibacy. The climate, abundance, and constellations of New Spain were conducive to vice and sensuality. Conquest, too, had broken the previously rigid moral backbone of Aztec society; now drunkenness and dissolution prevailed. Native religious belief persisted strongly, close to the surface. The Spanish occupation of New Spain might be best seen simply as a step on the way to the conversion of China, where Christianity might sink deeper roots.[47]

Two practical realities of the 1570s also served to depress Sahagún's spirits. One was the continued shrinking of the native population, made all too obvious by severe, if still unidentified, epidemics after 1576. Another, more personal, source of distress was growing official hostility to the sort of work to which he had given much of his life. In 1577 Philip II forbade research on Indian history and religion. Most of what Sahagún had written was confiscated (and did not again come into public view until the nineteenth century). This reversal of earlier governmental encouragement of inquiry into Indian matters had several sources. One was the urge to centralized conformity in the church expressed at the Council of Trent, the cleaving to a single line as a means of throwing back the Reformation. An outcome of this was Trent's ban on translation of the scriptures into vernacular tongues. The Bible, for instance, might be used only in its Latin Vulgate version. This led to the Inquisition's seizure in America, in 1576, of translations of sacred texts into native languages. In New Spain, the houses of the Franciscans, the most active translators, were inspected and religious works in Mexican languages impounded. The friars objected that evangelization would suffer; but the new orthodoxy prevailed.[48] The king's order fitted, also, with the official mistrust of the regulars in America that had arisen in the 1560s. The orders were in every way, including intellectual inquiry, too close to the Indians. The Franciscans in New Spain were particularly suspect for their Indian sympathies. More generally, Philip's banning of the study of Indians reflects the relegation of native people to a fixed and lowly place in colonial society that was largely complete by the 1570s. (What need was there to know more about common workers and tribute payers?) This relegation was in part the outcome of a growing Spanish tendency in some quarters, already visible in the 1550s, to see native cultures as full of undesirable, devil-inspired, influences. And, more broadly still, the ban is linked to the Spanish mind's closing to the alien and the unorthodox that had begun c.1530 and had become more obvious with each passing decade.[49]

A man who did more than any other, including Sahagún, to keep American natives in the Spanish government's view, especially when it would rather have forgotten about them, was the Dominican, Bartolomé de las Casas. He was a historian of early Spanish America, missionary, ethnographer, but above all else polemicist and propagandist on the Indians' behalf. Las Casas was born in Seville in 1484, saw Columbus there in April 1493 on his return from the first voyage, heard first-hand of Hispaniola from his father (who sailed with Columbus on the settlement expedition of 1493, and returned to Spain in 1498), went himself to the island in 1502 in Nicolás de Ovando's fleet, and there in due course became an *encomendero* who sent his Indians to till fields and mine for gold: nothing remarkable, except to the extent that being one of those early Caribbean settlers was itself remarkable. Soon, however, he became unusual, and his life (a long one, since it was 1566 before he died) took a new direction, for, it seems in 1510, he became the first Christian priest to be ordained in America. Why he took this step he does not explain. Nor is it clear who ordained him. Perhaps it was one of the Dominicans who arrived in Hispaniola in 1510.[50] Certainly the pro-Indian campaign that those Dominicans soon launched impressed him; as did, negatively, the suffering he saw inflicted on the natives of Cuba as Spaniards seized the island from 1511 onwards. Nonetheless, he was on good terms with the governor of Cuba, Diego de Velázquez, and received from him a share in a large *repartimiento* of Indians, whom he put, as in Hispaniola, to farming and washing gold. Then, early in 1514, meditating on biblical texts and his own earlier sermons, he was struck by a passage from the apocryphal book Ecclesiasticus (chapter 34), beginning "Tainted his gifts who offers in sacrifice ill-gotten goods. ... " He recalled also once being denied confession in Hispaniola by the Dominicans, who refused to absolve men who held Indians. Further reflection led him quickly to the conclusion "that everything done to the Indians in these Indies was unjust and tyrannical." It was a conviction that directed the rest of his life's activity. In the fullness of his outrage over Spain's iniquities he came to see pre-conquest America as a paradise that had become, under colonial rule, a hell.[51]

The next half-century saw him cross the Atlantic several times. In Spain he argued the Indians' case with officials, recruited missionaries, and, in his later years, wrote sprawling tracts and histories. In America he supervised schemes of peaceful colonization and conversion, wrangled with administrators and settlers (for whom he became "one of the most hated men who had ever been in the Indies"),[52] and exercised two offices: Protector of the Indians, which title he received from Cardinal Cisneros in Spain in 1516, and bishop of Chiapas, in southern Mexico (1544–50). In Spain, he had striking initial successes in influencing the decision to experiment with theocratic rule, under the three Jeronymites, in the Caribbean (1516–19), and then Charles V's condemnation of the *encomienda* in 1520. But his own experiment in peaceful settlement, limited to priests and Spanish farmers, on the Venezuelan coast failed in the early 1520s. In disappointment he entered a Dominican monastery in Santo Domingo in 1522, took his vows as a Dominican friar the next year, and for the next decade retired from active life. He used that secluded time to inform himself about theology, law, and the early history of the Indies – of which he began to write in what was to become his massive *Historia de las Indias*. Late in the 1530s, with other Dominicans, he attempted an innovative peaceful conversion of particularly hostile and resistant Indians in the province of Tuzulutlan, in north-east Guatemala. By agreement with the regional governor, secular Spaniards were to be excluded for five years, and no *encomiendas* could be granted in the area. Here Las Casas tried principles recently offered in his tract *The Only Method of Attracting All People to the True Faith*, in which he argued against the use of war against Indians, and in favor of conversion solely by appeal to reason and will. The experiment of Tuzulutlan (or, as Las Casas came to call it, the land of Verapaz, or True Peace) succeeded during the 1540s, in part because it incorporated maintenance of the powers of native leaders; with them, consequently, Las Casas was able to negotiate to allow undisturbed preaching by the Dominicans.[53] After 1550, however, for reasons that are unclear, revolts erupted.

Meanwhile, back in Spain in 1539 to recruit Dominican missionaries for his scheme, Las Casas was able to give added impetus to a pro-Indian current already strongly running, shocking the court with the outright propaganda of his *Very Brief Account of the Destruction of the Indies* (by Spanish settlers and officials, of course), and contributing powerfully to the opinions in imperial government from which the New Laws of 1542 emerged. He was, though, an uncomfortable presence at court. An offer was made to him of the see of Cuzco, which he rejected. But in 1544 he accepted the bishopric of Chiapas, since Verapaz lay on its southern side. In Chiapas – where, perhaps remembering his own experience long before with the Dominicans in Hispaniola, he proposed to refuse absolution to Spaniards who held Indian slaves or did not repay gains made from *encomiendas* – he was met with hostility, threats, and even rioting among the settlers.[54] The Indians of Verapaz, conversely, gave him a warm welcome. But the recently founded *audiencia* of Guatemala sided with the *encomenderos* and settlers, leaving him without governmental support.

It was not so much these setbacks, however, as the revocation of clause 30 of the New Laws, banning inheritance of *encomiendas*, that made Las Casas hurry back to Spain in 1546. He found that the court had undergone one of its periodic swings on the question of Indian treatment, alarmed by, among other things, the current revolt of colonists in Peru. By now Las Casas, through insisting that restitution must be made to Indians for what the conquerors, *encomenderos*, slaveholders and other Spaniards had taken or earned from them, seemed to be challenging not only Spain's use of the Indies, but also its right to be there at all, for his reason for calling for restitution was that the entire conquest and exploitation of native Americans had been unlawful.[55] Conquerors were *ipso facto* thieves. If Las Casas was made to explain himself in Spain, he can hardly have been surprised.

His influence at court, however, was still powerful, and was certainly instrumental in persuading Charles V, via the Council of the Indies, to order in 1550 a suspension of conquests in America until lawyers and theologians had ruled how they could be justly made. This led to what is undoubtedly Las Casas's most famous public appearance, arguing before an august council of fourteen in the summer of 1550, at Valladolid, not simply for conquest without force, but one entrusted to missionaries alone (at least in areas where the priests would be safe from danger). Underlying this was his belief that the Spanish monarchs' title to the Indies rested solely on "the extension of the Gospel in the New World, and their good government of the Indian nations."[56] He was, indeed, now approaching his late and extreme position that Spain's only purpose in America was to convert, holding even that if conversion could not be managed without force, it was better that Indians not be converted, and that Spain lose dominion in America, than that the native peoples be destroyed. Opposing Las Casas before the council at Valladolid was Juan Ginés de Sepúlveda, a translator and humanist writer whose defense of conquest by war, entitled *Democrates Alter*, Las Casas had blocked from publication in 1548. Sepúlveda argued, using Aquinas's reasoning, that war against Indians was just, because of their evident sins and vices, for better spreading of the Word, and because they were clearly slaves by nature, who would benefit in serving superior men, such as Spaniards. Aristotle's natural slave thus resurfaced at Valladolid, despite Vitoria's lifting of native Americans from that category of humans a decade before. He did not survive, however. Although no formal decisions emerged from the Valladolid meeting, Las Casas's views apparently won the greater support, and certainly, after then, conquest without force became the prevailing policy, if not always the reality. It was formalized in a set of ordinances that the Council of the Indies drafted in 1573 after consulting Las Casas's manuscripts.[57]

America saw no more of Las Casas after 1550. In that year he resigned his bishopric in Chiapas, and took up residence in Dominican monasteries in Spain, first at Valladolid and then Madrid, which became the fixed seat of Spanish government in 1561. From these bases, until his death in 1566, he devoted himself to the role of Protector of the Indians before the royal court, with all the effect that his abilities, experience, and relentless vitality gave him. He recruited Dominicans to continue the work in America. And he wrote voluminously, finishing his *Historia de las Indias*, and also producing, among much else, an *Apologética Historia* (Apologetic History), an ethnographic study of American native culture intended to refute the criticisms made of Indians since the first contact.

In his will of 1564, Las Casas stated that "God ... saw fit to choose me as his minister ... to plead for all those people of the Indies ... against unheard of and unimagined oppressions and evils and injuries received from our Spaniards ... and to restore them to the primitive liberty unjustly taken from them. ..."[58] Oppressed but fundamentally free: those are two certainties about Indians that Las Casas had striven to inject into policy-making for half a century. They were free because God had created all men free. But anyone who observed them could see that they were oppressed.

A third quality of Indians of which Las Casas was convinced demanded more elaborate proof: full rationality. He argued for this lengthily and intricately, drawing on whatever arguments, Classical or Christian, came to hand. The fundamental reasoning of the case was Aristotelian, and consisted of showing that Indians did not fit Aristotle's definitions of barbarity. There were awkward corners to negotiate: lack of true writing, for example, and human sacrifice. But outweighing these defects were the positive qualities of "excellent, subtle, and very capable minds." Most Indians were

> likewise prudent, and endowed by nature with the three kinds of prudence named by the Philosopher: monastic, economic, and political. Political prudence includes the six parts which, according to Aristotle, make any republic self-sufficient and prosperous: farmers; craftsmen; warriors; men of wealth; priests ... and sixth, judges or ministers of justice who govern well.[59]

In their government, indeed, and in observing "natural reason," Indians had even surpassed those most prudent of past peoples, the Greeks and Romans.

In comparing native American cultures to those of the Classical Old World past, and in trying to untangle the problem of the presence in any of them of contradictory behaviors (in the case of Mexico, for example, the building of large and elaborate cities in which human sacrifice was practiced), Las Casas concluded that human conduct was not the product of a particular people's fixed psychology, but rather a function of its progress along a path of development. Native Americans were generally not far along this track. Elements of ruder behavior persisted in them. (Human sacrifice, he noted, had once been widely practiced among peoples who now condemned it.) But – and here he came close to Vitoria's diagnosis of Indians as children, but educable children – progress was probable, even inevitable.

> We all have the need, from the beginning, to be guided and helped by those who have been born earlier. Thus, when some very rustic peoples are found in the world, they are like untilled land, which easily produces worthless weeds and thorns, but has within itself so much natural power that when it is plowed and cultivated its gives useful and wholesome fruits.[60]

Las Casas, then, from his effort to characterize native Americans in order to save them from exploitation, emerged with an evolutionary notion of human development of which only the seeds existed before.[61] This was a large conceptual contribution to the nascent art of anthropology that the European encounter with the American populations inspired.

Las Casas is Latin America's most renowned churchman, Vitoria the leading legal theorist on issues raised by Spanish overseas expansion, Sahagún the founding ethnographer of native American cultures. But many others, mainly missionary friars, thought and wrote on the matters that occupied these three in the early post-conquest decades. In New Spain there was Fray Toribio de Benavente, nicknamed Motolinía ("poor man") by the Indians for his extreme practice of the Franciscan vows of poverty. No less keenly did he adhere to Franciscan millenarian beliefs, and so took a leading part in his order's early efforts in mass baptism. Though critical of Aztec cruelty, which was, he thought, clearly the Devil's work, in his *History of the Indians of New Spain* (1541) he generally praised, like Quiroga, the Mexicans' gentleness and receptivity to the faith.[62] In South America there were fewer towering figures, in part because New Spain, being earlier conquered, had taken the best of the outstanding crop of Spanish regular priests trained early in the sixteenth century. Much of the recording of Indian culture done in Mexico by friars was, in the Andes, the work of laymen. One was Juan de Betanzos, an official interpreter in Quechua who married a woman of royal line from Cuzco. Another was Pedro de Cieza de León, a young Spaniard who observed and recorded acutely as he moved through the Andes in the late 1530s and the 1540s. The leading clerical student of the Andeans was the Dominican, Domingo de Santo Tomás, who arrived in Peru in 1540, and soon took up cudgels for the Indians in a distinctly polemical, Lascasian style. His long journeys through the central Andes gave him a first-hand knowledge of the mountains and their people. In 1560 he published the first grammar of Quechua. His major political campaign, waged in the 1550s, aimed to free the native Peruvians of the *encomienda's* burdens. He had only limited success. He was bishop of La Plata, or Charcas, from 1562 till his death in 1570.

The efforts of this variety of men had created by 1570 or so an immense knowledge of the native cultures conquered or encountered by the Spaniards in America. Whatever the motive for gathering information – surprise, simple admiration, intellectual curiosity sharpened by humanistic training, a desire to know native religion the better to attack it (and the Devil presumably behind it), a moral urgency to defend Indians from the ravages of conquest, or some political agenda aiming to change the entire form of colonization – the outcome was an intellectual incorporation of the Indian into the Spanish mental world that paralleled the physical and legal incorporation of American territory into the monarchy. It was, effectively, a mental domination of the Indian, a campaign in which ancient weapons of analysis taken from the arsenals of Greek and Roman thinkers, and of medieval churchmen, were found still indispensable – though they were unalterably modified by the novel use to which they were now put.[63] Few Spaniards in either Spain or America, of course, were fully aware of all that had been learned of Indians in that half-century after conquest. It was of concern mainly to administrators and clerics. Colonists, on the whole, formed their own views of Indians from practical experience. These in some respects coincided with the intellectuals' conclusions. Both groups found Indians generally to be simple people, docile, childlike, not yet fully formed in mind or morality. For the rank and file of settlers, this diagnosis provided both reason and opportunity for misuse and exploitation. For at least some leaders in both church and state, long into the colonial era, it was reason to work for defense of Indians against those abuses, though difficulties of enforcement, and the pressures of circumstance, often negated these protective efforts.

Understanding, and protection, of Indians carried, however, a deep irony. For the more the church sought to defend and even separate native Americans from settlers and the state, the more its efforts contributed to their domination by the invading culture, of which it was an elemental part. The orders of friars and the state may have had their conflicts in the post-conquest years over mission methods and sharing of authority over Indians. But as friars moved across the colonies, and their great mission churches, often fortress-like and assertively European in style,[64] rose to dominate the landscape, the message to the conquered was obvious enough: it was all invasion, no matter whether the outsiders wore chain mail or woolen robes, whether they bore swords or crosses.

[9] *Society: Old Orders Changed*

Population

It is arguable that nothing has marked the social history, indeed the entire history, of Middle and South America since 1492 more than the enormous loss of native population that followed the Europeans' arrival. That the loss was enormous there is hardly any doubt, although its exact size is impossible to calculate because the number of native inhabitants at the moment of contact is unknown, and will probably always remain so unless unimagined new sources of information appear.

For the Americas as a whole the best approximation of total population just before 1492 is 50 to 60 million, but honestly made estimates run from 8.4 to 112 million.[1] For individual regions, the range is similarly wide: for example, Peru (as it now is), 4 to 15 million;[2] central Mexico, 5 to 25 million; and Central America, 2.25 to 5.45 million.[3] These are the areas for which knowledge is most precise, though obviously not notably so. The enormous variability is partly the outcome of differences in methods of calculation. A common technique has been the backward extension of rates of decline from later periods (1550–1650, for example) – periods for which more, though far from wholly, reliable data are available. This is a simple mathematical operation; but there can be no certainty that the loss rate before a certain date in a particular area prevailed after that date. Other researchers have begun from the counts made by European explorers and conquerors. But these were inevitably rough and impressionistic. For central Mexico, late Aztec tribute assessments provide some guide, though presenting problems of completeness and interpretation. And then, beyond and perhaps more influential than these technical problems, come the effects of politics on the estimates, both old and new. Las Casas was the first of the determined "high counters," as they are now called,[4] with, for example, his notorious assertion that pre-Columbian Hispaniola held 3 to 4 million people.[5] It suited his political purposes to make the post-conquest loss seem high. Conquerors' glory, and their prospects of reward, were similarly enhanced by high estimates of the size of the native forces they had vanquished. Today, high counters tend (though there are honorable exceptions) to be nativists, or nationalists whose political or ideological ends are served by claims of high loss (and therefore of high initial numbers). Conversely, those who prefer to see European expansion in a positive light incline to play down its negative demographic outcome.

Loss rates after contact, then, are disputed, just as are the initial numbers from which the losses began. But no one disputes that some degree of decline took place; indeed, those who argue for small declines have the more difficult case to make. From the mid sixteenth century onwards, the growing Spanish bureaucracy in America counted tributaries in the colonies: adult Indian males on whom a head tax was imposed (as it was on commoners in Castile). These counts were not made at regular intervals across the colonies, nor with equal care in all places, and they are full of problems of interpretation (for example, by what factor to multiply the number of tributaries to arrive at a total population). But they do provide periodic tallies of the same category of people, which should reflect variations in the whole fairly consistently.

Calculating mainly from these tribute records, historians have posited native populations for central Mexico (roughly speaking, Mexico south of the *altiplano*, less Yucatan) thus: 1548, 3.6 to 6.3 million; 1568, 2.65 million; 1595, 1.375 million; 1620–5, 730,000.[6] By this estimate, the Indian population in the mid 1620s was 11.6 to 20.3 percent of what it had been some eighty years earlier. Since some decline had certainly taken place between 1519 and 1548, it is beyond reasonable dispute that the native population of central Mexico fell by over 85 per cent in the century after the military conquest. The 1620s seem to have marked the low point in Indian numbers. A slow, but accelerating, recovery began soon afterwards.

The story was similar in Peru, the other large area for which thorough demographic research has been done for the early colony. The first broad count of natives there was supervised by Viceroy Toledo in the early 1570s. It suggests an Indian population of about 1.3 million in 1570. By 1620 the number had fallen to about 700,000: a decline of 48.5 percent in half a century (and one of 83 percent from even the low 4 million estimate of the pre-contact total).[7] Thus, to the 1620s, the Peruvian decline may have been slightly less severe than New Spain's. But Peru had not yet reached its low point. This seems to have come in the mid to late seventeenth century, or perhaps even later; though estimating the true number of Indians in seventeenth-century Peru is complicated by their clearly enormous migrations. The Andes offered more refuges from Spanish reach than New Spain did, and many natives took advantage of a loophole in the law that made people who moved away from their birthplace to another community exempt from tribute and forced labor. Not surprisingly, there arose of multitude of these *forasteros* (outsiders), as they were called, and officials did not count them until the late 1600s. But despite this omission, there is little doubt about the downward trend of Peruvian native numbers over much of the seventeenth century.[8]

A growing number of local studies shows that great losses of native people, of three-quarters or more of the pre-contact figure, seem to have been the rule across most of Spanish America in the aftermath of conquest.[9] No large mainland area, it is true, saw the extinction of its pre-contact population that the Greater Antilles and the Bahamas suffered in the sixteenth century. (It is worth recalling, though, that the nomadic tribes of the Mexican *altiplano* had disappeared, first through warfare and then by cultural absorption, by the mid seventeenth century.) The only possible exception to this terrible trend is Quito, or present highland Ecuador, where research has indicated a strong recovery in the seventeenth century after grave losses in the sixteenth. But even this may be an illusion, the result simply of more complete counting by Spanish officials after 1600.[10]

The consensus is that only disease could have produced this demographic collapse. Great waves of sickness are known to have swept across the mainlands decade after decade in the sixteenth century. After this the epidemics were less frequent, but still wreaked havoc when they came.[11] Smallpox was probably the worst killer of Indians. It and the plague can be clearly identified from contemporary descriptions. Less surely present, but quite likely to have been so, were typhus, measles, mumps, and influenza.

These sicknesses were devastating, nearly all now agree, because they were new in America. If the American natives' ancestors in Asia had been subject to the bacteria and viruses causing these diseases, they had not carried them along in the migration to America. The migrating groups may have been too small for the germs to survive in them. Or, perhaps, the microbes had evolved in the Eurasian Old World after the departure of those who were to become native Americans, and had produced new strains of the illnesses. In any case, the diseases that the Europeans brought – unintentionally but unavoidably – to America after 1492 were novel there, and Indians seem consequently to have had little or no resistance to them. In the first attacks of each disease, at least, it is likely that all age groups in the infected population suffered severely. Children who survived an illness would acquire an immunity to it; most of them would survive subsequent episodes of the same disease. Death rates would stay high, however, among those not infected before: these would mainly be children born since the previous attack. But the destruction across age groups caused by the first assaults of a disease meant the disappearance of many people of reproductive age, and hence fewer children were born. This drop in births, added to mortality from the diseases themselves, suggests that the decline in total numbers was particularly steep in the early years after the conquests, when newly imported ills were constantly appearing. Experience elsewhere in the world with these so-called "virgin soil" epidemics, though fortunately never again on so vast a scale as in the Americas, shows that the exposed population takes three or four generations to develop a collective resistance to them. This finding fits with the slowing, and eventual reversal, of decline among American natives observable a hundred years or more after first contact with Old World outsiders.

The Americas were not edenically free of disease before the Europeans came, of course, though the number of serious epidemic ailments seems to have been much smaller than in the land mass of Europe, Asia, and Africa.[12] Internal parasites, bacterial pneumonia, and tuberculosis were present, as perhaps were yellow fever, malaria, typhus, and just possibly typhoid. The typical life-span of native Americans was not long. For the Mexica, for example, life expectancy at birth has been calculated at only fifteen to twenty years, and they were not unusual.[13] America held no pathogen, however, capable of exacting revenge on the Old World for what its bacteria and viruses did to the New. The one noteworthy exception may be syphilis. A virulent, quick-killing, form of it appeared in Europe directly after Columbus's first return. Whether it was caused by a new bacterium brought back from Hispaniola by his men, or by a coincidental mutation of the related yaws treponema already existing in Europe, has been the topic of a long, lively, but inconclusive debate. Innovative research on the question, by comparative analysis of yaws and syphilis genes, supports the notion that the disease had an American origin; but that is unlikely to be the last word.[14]

Epidemics were not the only destroyer of Indians in the sixteenth century. The case of the large Caribbean islands shows that Spanish arms could kill many. Intentional massacre of entire villages as a terrorist tool of conquest was used both there and later in the mainland campaigns. The "Black Legend" – the proposition that Spaniards were unusually cruel and destructive in their treatment of non-Europeans – had part of its origin in such episodes, publicized, it might be added, by Las Casas above all others. Early Spanish presence in Hispaniola, Puerto Rico, Jamaica, and Cuba also showed how disruptive to native culture and survival the settlers' post-conquest demands could be: Indian men and women put to unbearably heavy work, families split up by labor drafts for long periods, tribute taken in foods that the people themselves needed, land overrun and crops eaten by Spanish domestic animals. Of all this there is incontrovertible evidence, not only for the islands but for the mainland, too. Less easily shown, though highly likely, was the psychological damage done to American natives by the experience of conquest and domination: the revelation of their gods' powerlessness, the invalidation of world-view. Early friars and chroniclers give anecdotal reports of suicides, abortions, and infanticide. Some evidence exists that unwillingness to reproduce was a cause of falling birth rates after the conquest, though that is not the finding for sixteenth-century Peru, where birth rates seem to have risen after epidemics, as if communities were trying to make up their losses.[15]

There was, therefore, a variety of downward pressures on native numbers. But those just proposed do not seem enough to account for the vast losses suffered by the mainland peoples for so long after the military conquests. Spanish ignorance, carelessness, maltreatment, and cruelty were probably mostly to blame for the destruction of the Caribbean peoples. But administrators and, to a lesser extent, colonists learned from that experience, so that from the 1520s protective laws and practices began to have some effect. True enough, the mainland populations at first appeared to be so huge that, for many early colonists, squandering the Indians granted to them in *encomienda* seemed unlikely to pose any threat to their own, or the colony's, future. This led, for example, to the ill-treatment of Indians in New Spain in the late 1520s, when the grasping regime of Nuño de Guzmán had replaced Cortés's more protective rule. But laws had some effect. If they had not, the colonists' protests over the New Laws in 1542, and to the ban in 1549 on the use of *encomienda* Indians for labor, would have been less strident. Finally, however, once the process of domination was in action and the danger of native resistance receding, Spaniards had no interest in destroying Indians. Quite the reverse: Indians, as workers and tribute payers, were the root of the wealth that both state and colonists looked for in America. This was particularly clear in the high-culture regions. Their peoples had many skills immediately useful to the Spanish, and were accustomed, from pre-conquest times, to being organized into labor forces by government. It is a speculative thought – but perhaps the Caribbean people, had they seemed as full of economic promise as the Mexicans and Andeans later did, might have been spared the intolerable pressures that quickly destroyed them.

There will always be some doubt about allocating blame among causes for the deaths of those many millions on the mainland of sixteenth-century Spanish America – in part because crucial data do not exist (Spaniards did not, and probably could not, record how many succumbed to this or that epidemic), in part because the debate will probably long remain as much political as historical. A sophisticated inquiry, however (though it deals only with the Valley of Mexico) concludes:

> The catastrophic decline in the [valley's] Amerindian population was due to the combined effect of a series of epidemic crises, each of which reduced the population significantly. By far the most important factor in these crises were the profound short-term increases in mortality engendered by the "virgin soil" epidemics. No reliance need be made on the so-called Leyenda Negra [Black Legend] of Spanish cruelty to explain the holocaust.[16]

As native populations fell, numbers of Spaniards (once the late 1490s were past) rose constantly. The actual total of Spaniards in the early colonies is, though, hardly clearer than the total number of Indians. No head tax was applied to them, so there was no need to count them for that reason. And though licenses were legally required for traveling to America, many people clearly sailed without them; so the number of emigrants is uncertain. By about 1570 the total number of Spaniards in the Indies was probably between 125,000 and 150,000. They lived in some 225 towns.[17] During the sixteenth century as a whole, Spanish emigration to America was probably between 250,000 and 300,000 (a good deal of uncertainty about the number resulting from about half the migrants having crossed the Atlantic without licenses).[18]

In the conquest decades, most emigrants were young, single men (though families had begun to arrive in Hispaniola in 1502); some of these men married or cohabited with native women, engendering the beginnings of the *mestizo* population that in the end was to become so central a demographic and cultural feature of Spanish America. Among the earliest of such unions were those between Spanish conquerors and elite indigenous women, particularly prevalent in central Mexico. Several daughters of Moctezuma II married Spanish men. Doña Isabel Moctezuma, for example, married three Spanish husbands, among them Juan Cano; one of the Cano de Moctezuma sons eventually returned to Spain, where he built the lavish Palacio de Moctezuma in the city of Cáceres.[19] Exceptionally, among indigenous women, Doña Isabel was an *encomendera* who retained enormous wealth after the conquest; her riches and exalted origins made her an attractive marriage partner. Most Spanish men considered indigenous lineage a considerable disability, and therefore elite Indian women who wed Spaniards generally married down. This was particularly true in Peru, where few Indian noblewomen married *encomenderos* or other truly elite Spanish men. Still, even in Peru, marriage to a native aristocrat was a strategic move for an aspiring member of the upper elite, and could propel a Spaniard to upward mobility.[20] Spanish–Indian marriages were thus an important feature of early colonization, and in some regions, such as Puebla de los Angeles, formed a significant minority of all marriages.[21]

The relative rarity of Spanish–Indian marriages in this period does not, of course, indicate rarity of sexual contact. Quite early in the conquest of Mexico, the Spaniards were given women by their indigenous allies. These women might be slaves – as in the famous transaction that brought Cortés the interpreter Malinaltzin, or Doña Marina – or they might be daughters of chieftains, given in the hope of marital alliance. For the Spaniards, such women seem to have been regarded primarily as sexual partners, regardless of their station or the manner of their delivery. The conquerors were equally willing to take women by force. In just one example, Bernal Diaz describes an incident where conquerors argued over the best-looking female captives, a conflict which was only partially resolved when Cortés decided that the "just" outcome would be to sell all of the women at auction, offering all soldiers the opportunity to pay for the women of greatest beauty.[22] This attitude towards indigenous women persisted for some years after the conquest was complete, most infamously during the Mexican first *audiencia* of 1528–30, when indigenous women and girls were a significant part of the *oidores'* plunder; two judges amassed harems, going so far as to besiege a Texcoco cloister to remove an attractive girl who had sought refuge there.[23] Similar abductions of women occurred in the Andes.[24]

Many other sexual relationships between Spaniards and indigenous women had the characteristics of concubinage; that is, the relationships were not explicitly coerced, and persisted over some time. Most of these relationships ended when the male partner married. In some cases, however, Spanish men continued to cohabit with one or more indigenous women even after taking Spanish wives. Such was the case of the Lima *encomendero* Francisco de Herrera, who eventually bestowed much of his wealth on the two indigenous mistresses who had given him his only heirs.[25] Throughout the conquest period, then, Spanish men availed themselves of indigenous women of varying rank, occasionally marrying high-born women but more often engaging in consensual and coerced relationships of varying duration.

Once the conquests were over, Spanish families became more frequent, as a broader socio-economic range of men began to cross the ocean – artisans, lawyers, administrators – some of them with wives and children.[26] At the same time single Spanish women began to move to the Indies in growing numbers. The official emigration licenses suggest, in fact, that between 1509 and 1538 rather more adult single women than married women crossed the ocean. There was occasional official concern about the morals of some of these, and certainly among them were adventurous camp followers. But many were women who saw in the Indies the possibility of marriage, at a time when there was an excess of marriageable women at home.[27] Marriage also offered a chance to tap into America's economic promise. A story from Guatemala, about 1530, has a group of young Spanish women brought from Spain by Pedro de Alvarado, the governor of the province and an ex-conqueror of the Aztecs, discussing the prospect of marriage to unattached conquerors. To the objection that these were aging men, many of them maimed, or uglified by wounds, one of the group retorted: "We're not going to marry them for their looks, but to inherit their Indians. They're so old and worn out, they're certain to die soon, and then we can choose whatever young men we please instead of these dotards, like changing an old broken pot for a new whole one."[28] The tale may be apocryphal, but the young, wealthy widow of a conquistador or *encomendero* was not a rare figure in the sixteenth-century colonies.

Up to 1560 about a tenth of emigration licenses went to women. This was an average. The proportion was certainly smaller early in the century, and higher by the middle decades. In the 1560s women made up a quarter or more of emigrants from Spain. The actual populations may have held more women than the licenses suggest. In Peru, by the 1540s, the male:female ratio among Spaniards was seven or eight to one. In 1550, 1,000 Spanish women were in Peru, scattered through all the major coastal and highland towns. At the start of the seventeenth century, Lima alone is said to have had 5,359 Spanish women, giving them a slight edge over men (5,258), in a total population of 26,441.[29] The proportion was probably similar in other large Spanish centers. By that time, although emigration from Spain was still rising, many "Spaniards" (*españoles*) in the colonies were in fact locally born, in, presumably, almost equal numbers of females and males. Among Spaniards, what might be called the "demographics of conquest" – a large male preponderance – had given way to the gender balance of a normal population, with all that that implied for family formation and the decline of stable unions between Spanish men and non-Spanish women.

Most of those women were Indians. But, almost from the beginning, Spaniards had also taken African women as consorts. Such women were part of an African population, mostly slaves but some free, that by the end of the sixteenth century was a prominent feature in the social landscape of early Spanish America. Africans had been present in the Caribbean islands from earliest times. Seventeen black slaves, for instance, were sent to Hispaniola from Spain in 1505 to work in gold mining.[30] Then there were blacks in the expeditions of conquest on the mainland. They fought alongside the Spaniards, and so the first experience that Indians had of them was as part of the invading culture. The black conquerors had arrived with their owners from Spain. Soon, though, a flow of slaves began directly from Africa. By 1650 the total number of Africans who had arrived in Spanish America as slaves was about 213,000 – 123,000 from West Africa and 90,000 from Central Africa.[31] More specifically, the best estimate has at least 75,000 enslaved Africans being disembarked in the Spanish colonies between 1526 and 1600. About a half of them went to New Spain, where by 1570 they numbered some 20,000.[32] At most a third of those imported were women, since male slaves were in greater demand, and hence more profitable to traders. Consequently the slave community produced relatively few children. And that, added to high mortality, meant that new slaves had constantly to be imported from Africa. Though few African offspring were born, partly black children certainly made an appearance in the sixteenth century. There were mulattoes (black and Spanish) and *zambos* (black and Indian). Since a child took its mother's status, black men had reason to choose Indian women as mothers of their offspring, since Indians were free by law. Conversely, the child of a white father and black mother was a slave if she was a slave. But white fathers were often in a social and financial position to free their children.[33] Both circumstances reinforced the other obstacles to natural increase in the black slave population, while adding new dimensions to Spanish American ethnic blending, which had first consisted of only the white–native mixture. And as the numbers of *mestizos*, mulattoes, and *zambos* grew, so the possibilities of mixes of mixes also rose, accelerating and complicating miscegenation.

SOCIAL HIERARCHY

These various elements shook down into a structured society by the late 1500s. Though the structure that emerged was by no means rigid or compartmentalized, it was shaped by an innate notion of hierarchy. A passage from a memorandum of the Council of the Indies to Charles IV in 1806 shows how long this idea stayed embedded in the official Spanish mind:

> If it is undeniable that, for the maintenance and good order of a monarchical state, diverse hierarchies and spheres are of supreme importance, since their ranked and interlinked dependency and subordination produce and sustain the lowest vassal's obedience to, and respect for, the sovereign's authority; how much more necessary is such a system in America, on account of both the greater distance from the throne, and of the great number of those sorts of people who, owing to their wicked origins and nature, constitute a very inferior species, not to be compared with the common people of Spain; it even occurring that the known children or descendants of slaves sit down and fraternize with those who derive from the first conquerors or from families that are noble, legitimate, white, and free of all taint.[34]

Here is a splendid concatenation, indeed, of prejudice and ignorance from these mandarins of the late empire: the American population dichotomized into noble whites and a perverted remainder; the whites all pure-blooded and legitimate, the rest perpetually contaminated by an assumed bastardy somewhere in their origins. But overriding this distortion by far in historical significance was the assumption that such a population can be kept orderly only through hierarchical organization. People must have, and know, their place in society. They know it through their links of "dependency and subordination" with those above them. Those links also extend downwards to locate people lower on the scale.

The use of the image of links (*eslabón* in the original Spanish) in describing the needed social structure brings to mind the classical chain of being, along which all parts of creation were located, in proper and immutable order. This notion of society indeed had its origins in ancient thought. It also drew – hardly surprisingly, since he was the great restorer of Aristotle, prime among the ancients – on Aquinas's concept of society as "first ... a hierarchical system in which each person or group serves a purpose larger than any one of them can encompass."[35] Inequalities are an intrinsic part of this hierarchy, to be corrected only when Christian justice is threatened. The society's members should accept them as inevitable attachments to each rank and its role. These European notions of what a proper society should be were reinforced in the Indies, at least in the high-culture areas, by native precedent. Aztec and Inca societies were not one whit less hierarchical than Spain's in the conquest period; perhaps, indeed, considerably more so. In applying their assumptions about the natural working of a society to America, the Spanish found among the most valued of those they colonized, the peoples of the high-culture areas, no resistance of principle. Only the less developed cultures tended to egalitarianism; that was, in part, why the Spaniards found them hard to overcome.

Notions of hierarchy and inequality applied not only to individuals, but also to groups within society. Indeed, society's basic units were not, in the Spanish view, individuals, but groups of various sizes, each with its particular part to play in harmony with the others. It was a notion of social composition typical of medieval Europe. Equally medieval was the concept that secular society was divided primarily into two large and firmly separated segments: the noble and the plebeian estate.[36]

The society of estates persisted strongly in sixteenth- and seventeenth-century Spain. But only the expectation that this was how a society should be, rather than the specific forms it took in Spain, transferred across the Atlantic. There were, for example, hardly any titled noblemen in America for almost 200 years. Until late in the seventeenth century, almost the only title holders in the colonies were the viceroys, who were transitory figures. On the other hand, nobility as a concept was abundantly present in America. Colonists as a whole, indeed, thought of themselves as a nobility, in the sense that they made up the upper section of society that was occupied by the nobility at home. For some, also, braving the hazards of the ocean crossing was an experience that in itself demanded heroic qualities; and heroism was a noble trait. There was also a legal reason for the assumed noble status of whites in America. In Spain, commoners paid a head tax, or *pecho*. But in America all people considered white were free of such levies. Thus the peasant, carpenter or tailor arriving in the colonies suddenly possessed one of the most cherished privileges of the Spanish noble, and felt ennobled by that gain.

Thus in some measure an estate simply of "Spaniards," whether immigrants, *criollos*, or even *mestizos* who looked like Europeans, took the place in America of the noble estate in Spain. And the native population became the equivalent of a European common estate. The term "estate" (*estamento* in Spanish) was not used, however, for these groupings, but rather *república*. A colonial society consisting of two such republics, one Indian and the other Spanish, was, by the time of the mainland conquests, what administrators in Spain hoped to produce in America. The intent was that such a division would help protect natives from predatory Spaniards, promote their conversion, and simplify extraction from them of tribute and labor. It would also further the crown's political aims in America by blocking colonists' access to native possessions and labor, and so slow the growth of their political and economic power.

In certain practical respects, the policy of two republics failed from the start. It was undermined by race mixture. The crown itself, holding to the canonical principle that people should be free to wed whom they chose, did not ban Spanish–Indian marriages. These, it is true, were few, and did not produce many children. But outside marriage, *mestizo* infants appeared, after the requisite number of months, wherever Spaniards went. The clear waters of the two-part society were instantly muddied. Then the crown itself mortally wounded the policy of separate republics by allowing expansion of the *encomienda* to the mainland. Spaniards and Indians were thereby thrust together, rather than apart. Policy-makers were perfectly aware of this, but had to yield to the urgent need to fix settlers in the vastness of America. For a time, the *encomienda* seemed the best way of doing that. Then again, the presence of blacks in the colonies, and soon enough of mulattoes and *zambos* as well, meant that the two-republic model simply did not fit the developing social reality.

Nevertheless, true to the principle of estates, Indians and Spaniards did always remain legally and functionally distinct populations in the Spanish colonies. Though historians in recent years have discovered how widely and ingeniously Indians adapted to and resisted Spanish pressures, there is no denying that throughout colonial times they were the dominated, and that the Spanish, whether representing the state or as individuals, were the dominators. Most adult Indian men paid tribute, as the law required, and Indians supplied most of the physical labor consumed in the colonies, as law or economic conditions dictated. The broad assessment of American natives reached by Spaniards by the mid 1500s – that they were free, fully human in potential, but still childlike in intellectual and moral development – was expressed in laws that treated them as minors, needing legal protection.[37] For example, they might not, except under the supervision of a Spanish justice, sell fixed or movable goods worth more than 30 pesos (the price of 40–50 bushels of maize in the Valley of Mexico *c*.1580, or of three or four llamas in Potosí *c*.1590).[38] They were excused from paying sales tax (*alcabala*) except when trading Spanish goods. A system of legal defense was created, consisting of lawyers on the *audiencia* staffs specializing in native cases, and, in New Spain, a general Indian court in Mexico City.[39] Countless other regulations and practices could be cited to show that Spaniards, in Spain and America, saw the American natives, within the colonial regime, as being radically distinct, in social, economic, cultural, and legal senses, from themselves. They were certainly an integral part of society, but one whose function, like that of European commoners, was to sustain, through work and taxes, the higher components of society and the existence of the state itself.

The Spanish section of the American population inherited the role of defense that had belonged to the noble estate of medieval Europe, and briefly played it well enough. Defense of the realm was, in fact, a duty that *encomenderos* owed the crown in return for their grants of native services and tribute. They and other early settlers certainly took up arms against native insurgency in the sixteenth century. The Mixton War in western New Spain in the early 1540s was one example, and Chichimeca raids on early Spanish settlement of the Mexican *altiplano* another (though that was as much conquering as suppressing revolt). But as the age of conquest passed, and as changes in the law undercut the *encomienda* as the basis of a proto-seigneurial class in American society, settlers' martial inclinations atrophied. In truth, there was little to keep them exercised, except in the frontier zones where Indian raiding was constant, or on coasts, mainly in the Caribbean, where piratical attacks often fell. The prime function of settlers became, then, one of occupying, operating, and supervising (beyond the activities of government) the colonies. This function had a large economic component. It included working land and mines; trading, at every level from retail shops to transoceanic exchange; setting up communications and transport, over both land and sea; and establishing manufacture, from small craft shops to sizable cloth works. Some of this had been done by nobles in Spain. Raising sheep and cattle on large estates was the most characteristic productive activity of the upper nobility of the Castilian highlands and Andalusia. And holders of high titles were not above profitable participation in the Indies trade. But the settlers in America certainly went beyond what even the neediest Castilian *hidalgo* would stoop to when they dirtied their clothes, if not their hands, in supervising ore-cutting in a mine, or in running a blacksmith's forge. And there were many, as Spanish numbers grew in America, who actually put their hands to tools. Thus the analogy between the noble estate in Spain and a colonists' "estate" in America, while broadly valid, stops short of the bottom end of the settlers' group.

The notion of society as an assemblage of groups rather than individuals extended downward below the level of estates or republics. Function generally identified these groups, though function was always linked to some degree with status. Churchmen were the most obvious such unit. They were not considered a separate estate, as in medieval Europe, perhaps because of the exceptionally close binding of the colonial church to the state. But they were certainly a corporate body, unified by function, and possessing distinct legal privileges, such as their own courts. Other groups – merchants and miners, for example – saw themselves as similarly distinct, and deserving. They also, in time, gained their formal legal identity and privileges. So too did the military, once it was formally created late in the colonial era.

INDIAN SOCIETY

Neither native nor Spanish society in America remained fixed in its form or workings after the conquest. The sixteenth century brought profound developments for both Indians and colonials that set Spanish American social history on a course that it long pursued. Broadly speaking, native society became simpler in structure, and Spanish society more complex. Neither change is particularly surprising, given, for example, the enormous decline in numbers on the one side, and their growth on the other. But the processes are worth comment and illustration.

The most obvious, and dramatic, simplification of the high Indian cultures came during the military conquest, with the removal of their supreme rulers and their accompanying administrative and religious bureaucracies, staffed by their relatives and other high nobles. This decapitation of native states by the Spanish is a commonplace of the conquest, as is the broadly successful installation of new European heads on the American bodies in the form of triumphant conquering captains and their lieutenants and advisers. Left relatively undisturbed, however, at least politically, by the defeat of native states were the local lords of units that had been incorporated into the large polities quite recently – generally no more than a few decades before the Spaniards came. These men often welcomed the demise of the state structures; some, indeed, contributed to their downfall by helping the Spanish.[40]

The Spanish, extending a Caribbean term to the mainland, generally called these local lords *caciques*, or sometimes in the Andes, using a proper regional name, *curacas*. There was actually, as might be imagined, a wide range of local authorities in various regions and cultures; but to most settlers they were all *caciques*. Whether or not these men had aided the conquerors, they and their family lines tended to do well in the succeeding decades. The main reason was that the Spanish needed them. While knowledge of mainland Indians (of their productive capacity, tribute systems, administration, and psychology) was still being gathered, *caciques* were essential go-betweens. They, in turn, could profit from the new conditions. Free now from Inca, Aztec, or other comparable controls, they could act more independently than before, for their own and their communities' benefit. In the very early years, when tribute rates were unregulated, they could negotiate favorable payments with the *encomendero* to whom their people had been assigned. If *encomenderos* wanted native workers, it was largely through the *caciques* that they must get them, on mutually satisfactory terms. There were instances, certainly, in which *encomendero* and *cacique* conspired for their own gain against the interests of the mass of the people. Or *caciques* might use their restored autonomy for private advantage, declaring, for example, communal land to be their own property. Generally, though, they worked to protect their people from both Spaniards and competing native neighbors (for the downfall of the overarching native states had led to a resurgence of local rivalries).

For some decades after the conquest, then, these local lords did well socially and economically; better, perhaps, than most had done before it. The Spaniards generally regarded them as *hidalgos*, and applied the honorific "Don" to the more eminent of them. *Caciques* were usually able to keep the various slave-like and serf-like dependants they had held in the past, and in some cases may have added more. These servants were often exempt from tribute to the Spanish.

But the post-conquest high status of *caciques* was not to last. Various changes in the colonies' government, populations, and economic life in the 1500s led to clear deterioration in the lords' situation. They lost importance as intermediaries between Spaniards and natives as the Spanish bureaucracy grew in numbers and knowledge. Their subjects and dependants died in epidemics. And, because the Spaniards' tribute income went down as the population shrank, the colonial administration abolished exemptions, making almost all adult native males, except *caciques* themselves and officers of town government, into tribute payers. For this reason native lords lost many of the personal servants who had given them labor, income, and status. This decline of *caciques* can be seen in New Spain in the middle decades of the sixteenth century. In the central Andes it came later, towards the end of the century.[41]

Indian *caciques* there still were, nonetheless, until the end of colonial times. But their numbers fell, and many long-standing family lineages, with pre-conquest origins, disappeared. Some survived by adopting European-style economic behavior, going into some kind of market-oriented business to replace the material support they had once had from personal dependants.[42] But many old, lordly families saw themselves replaced by new men – Indians lacking pedigree but finding in themselves an ability to prosper by going into that same European sort of trading business, and using wealth to create political authority.[43] Whether from old family lines, or newly self-made, *caciques* sought to straddle the cultural gap between their own and the European world by dressing expensively in Spanish style, living in large town houses, petitioning the king for coats of arms, riding horses, having their portraits painted, drinking wine instead of a native brew, and much else. But despite their efforts to behave like, and to be regarded as, Spaniards, from the mid-to-late sixteenth century on these men found themselves sliding, willy-nilly, into the function that the Spanish ever more insistently thrust on them: that of agents charged with making their people produce goods or labor, and with siphoning off a large part of that production to colonists and the colonizing state. They themselves lost materially and culturally in the process. "The curaca became, in the eyes of his people, only a dim shadow of his former institutional self."[44] This comment refers specifically to the north coast of Peru in the mid 1500s, but it is valid to some degree for all the core regions of Spanish settlement, which coincided with the pre-conquest areas of high culture. Elsewhere, the less developed native culture had been (and post-conquest Spanish settlement therefore less dense), the lighter the pressures on local rulers were (and the smaller the changes in their status). But the more peripheral places tended to have more egalitarian social arrangements in the first place, and so local leaders there had less to lose.

In sum, then, by the early 1600s native societies had not only vastly fewer people than immediately after the conquest, but local leaders whom depopulation and Spanish pressures had broadly laid low, politically, materially, and culturally. Along with that depression of the upper reaches of surviving Indian society had also come a raising of its lower levels to what was now an almost universal category of tribute payers. What had been, in the regions of high culture, a broad, multi-striped band of social functions and privileges was now a narrow ribbon of what Spaniards, at least, increasingly saw simply as "Indians" or "natives" (*naturales*). Between the edges of that ribbon there survived, to be sure, though often outside Spanish view, an impressive range of genuinely native behavior; but it survived in a much-compressed social structure.

NATIVE WOMEN

To native women, the broad processes and changes just described certainly applied, but with some particular twists and variations. A significant post-conquest change, visible particularly in the central Andes and in central and southern Mexico, occurred in the realm of gender relations. Before the conquests, in both central Mexico and the Andes, traditions of gender parallelism existed alongside a largely male-directed state apparatus. Indeed, in many areas some elite women exercised considerable political authority. After the Spanish conquest, the *capullanas* (local female leaders) of north coastal Peru and the *cacicas* (female *caciques*) of many other areas were excluded from exercising duties relating to their offices, even while they maintained their titles for purposes of determining inheritance and succession.[45]

Still, in the immediate aftermath of conquest women were arguably less disadvantaged than men, for a number of reasons. First, in many areas women outnumbered men after conquest, and therefore had greater access to kin and family headship and similar positions of authority. Moreover, sexual liaisons with conquerors offered at least a minimal avenue for survival and social advance. Finally, the introduction of Spanish law increased women's individual power to some extent, and indigenous women were enthusiastic litigators.[46] One scholar has gone so far as to speak of a brief "golden age" for Mixtec noblewomen in New Spain, produced by the combination of the tradition of Mixtec gender parallelism with favorable legal conditions.[47]

In the long term, however, Indian women's status suffered, even while some women made short-term gains. In the Andes, for example, indigenous noblewomen received individual property rights over lands held by the royal descent groups, or *panakas*, rather than by any one individual. While some elite women undoubtedly benefited in that way, it has been argued, the process of privatization undermined Incan women's institutions, which had previously been supported by the proceeds of the fields now bought and sold freely for the benefit of individual noblewomen.[48] In central Mexico, though the litigiousness and apparent autonomy of Indian women continued to draw disparaging comment from sixteenth-century settlers, the post-conquest period saw the gradual disappearance of virtually all of the female-only institutions that had provided women some control over judicial, market, and familial affairs of relevance to their sex. Peasant women's status was diminished by the loss of these institutions; and even in areas where women's institutions had been limited and women's participation in public affairs sharply proscribed, colonialism brought some damaging consequences. Among the Maya, for example, peasant women were heavily burdened long after the conquest by tribute requirements that demanded textiles – women's product – rather than cash.[49]

Even more dramatic changes in indigenous gender relations were produced by Christianization. First, native women lost most of the parallel religious structures that had given them some participation in sacred life, but were not given the same – though certainly junior – opportunities for Christian observance extended to Spanish women. In Mexico, for example, Indian women could not become nuns until the eighteenth century. While Indian women had access to the semi-religious life of the *beata* (a pious laywoman) and participated avidly in religious confraternities, they were indisputably marginalized within Christian religious life. Though certain practices, such as the confession of women by women in the Andes, persisted through the sixteenth century,[50] the once relatively formal religious domain of women was virtually eliminated.

The reorganization of marriage by Christian missionaries brought further sweeping changes. Some of these at least appear ambiguous, such as the eradication of polygyny (marriages in which a man had two or more wives). In the long term, the imposition of monogamy may have brought benefits to some women; in the short term, however, the elimination of polygynous marriages left many elite wives and children "brutally shorn of the rank that was their due."[51] Other changes imposed even clearer disadvantages on women, as Spanish marriage law conferred new patriarchal rights upon men. Some shifts, more subtle perhaps, nonetheless had broad consequences. For example, as populations declined in the sixteenth century, marriages outside one's own community or kin group became much more common. Royal policy, particularly in the Andes, called for women to live in their husbands' communities, where tribute was collected. In this and many other ways, Spanish law and policy privileged male lineage over female. Though Indians retained elements of their pre-colonial systems of descent, the result was greater distance between women and their kin networks and a general weakening of women's economic independence.[52]

Sexuality was another aspect of human behavior in which indigenous life changed significantly in the sixteenth century. Christian missionaries sought to produce in indigenous societies a commitment to Christian sexual mores that began with confining sexual activity to Christian marriage. In central Mexico, this was one of the main goals of the Christian education given to the children of principal natives. In the Andes a particular effort was made, unsuccessfully, to eliminate the practice of *servinacuy*, or trial marriage, which most missionaries saw as a form of concubinage. Besides trying to establish the monopoly of marriage over sexuality, missionaries attempted to reform particular sexual practices. Churchmen and settlers alike were appalled by what they considered indigenous tolerance of unspeakable sexual vices, such as sodomy, in addition to a general sexual laxity.[53] Priests therefore sought to use the confessional to inculcate appropriate sexual behaviors and prevent sexual practices judged illicit by the church. These practices could range from the infamous – sodomy in any of its forms – to masturbation or sexual intercourse with the woman on top.[54] Both men and women had to contend with these changes to pre-Hispanic sexual regimes; on indigenous women, however, fell new burdens, including a hitherto unfamiliar emphasis on female virginity. Indigenous women had to deal with a new sexual regime that placed on women great responsibility for the maintenance of chastity and reputation, even while the emerging colonial culture cast *indias* as available sexual partners for men of all ethnicities and classes. Thus while some women, particularly elite ones, survived and prospered in the early years of the colony, the mass of women saw their status diminished over the course of the sixteenth century.

SPANISH SOCIETY

Spanish society in America after the conquest took a course that was the reverse of the dominant native pattern. It grew more complex and more stratified. The bands of conquistadores had certainly had their social rankings, some originating in Spain and some in America. Nearly a quarter (38 of 168) of the men who took part in the capture of Atahualpa at Cajamarca in 1532 were *hidalgos*, though mostly from the lowest margin of that category in Spain ("very small gentry," none using "don").[55] But length of experience in conquering and settling could override such imported status. By the time of the mainland conquests America was starting to supply its own determinants of social standing. On the whole, though, the conquerors fell within a narrow social range, most being commoners from the manual trades or lower professions.[56]

Taking part in a major conquest, such as those of the Incas and Aztecs, and to a lesser extent, of such areas as Guatemala, New Granada, and Quito, catapulted even the humblest commoner to high standing in the Indies. Such men became the senior mainland *encomenderos*. Their fame was, therefore, buttressed, at least for two or three decades, by abundant tribute from large numbers of Indians. Though these men, with the exception of the greatest leaders, did not gain noble titles or even the use of "don," they became, functionally, an incipient American aristocracy. Early, but immediately post-conquest, settlers – the *primeros pobladores* – also ranked high in the Indies, though below conquerors, for most of the sixteenth century. Many of them, too, became *encomenderos*, with wealth to back their status as, if not heroes, at least pioneers. If they could not have titles, *encomenderos* tried to surround themselves with the material trappings of nobles: large houses set on broad lands, and filled with a retinue of relatives and dependants.[57]

Soon after the conquests the social range of immigrants widened. The expanding clergy added a new dimension of educated people. There also came administrators, most of them university-trained lawyers, to form a new professional segment of the top of society. Viceroys soon arrived to become, among other things, the pinnacle of the social structure; that was one important reason for their selection from the high aristocracy. Larger numbers of fortune-seeking lesser nobles – untitled Dons – also appeared in the colonies once reports of wealth crossed the ocean eastward. Most of them, however, hoped to fill their pockets and then return to Spain better equipped than before to enjoy civilized life there. They were helped in this by the preference given to them in the distribution of *encomiendas*.[58] Many of them did go back, so that the social dominance enjoyed by this group endowed with a traditional sort of Spanish status did not last long. And, of course, besides these higher-ranking figures, the Indies-bound exodus of common people – men, and increasingly women also – continued and grew as the years passed. There sailed artisans, agricultural workers, merchants petty and not so petty, muleteers, the odd miner or man of arms. Once across the Ocean Sea, all jostled to find a place to live, a means of support, and a niche in the ranks of the developing society.

Broadly speaking Spaniards in the Indies in the sixteenth century arranged themselves socially less and less by Iberian criteria of rank, and increasingly by new American standards. Besides the fame and fortune accruing from participation in exploration, conquest, and early settlement, simple wealth gained from using America's human and natural resources soon became a strong influence on social standing. As the native population fell and the number of Spaniards rose, ever fewer immigrants could aspire to the seigneurial life that *encomenderos* had tried to re-create in the colonies. What America then offered, and much more liberally than Spain, was the chance to make money through personal effort. Engaging in commerce, farming, mining, or some trade then became not merely socially acceptable, but desirable. This was true to an extent from the start. There were early *encomenderos* who were not content simply to sit back and accept tribute, but who used the native workers granted to them to work land to produce food for markets, or mines to yield bullion that even in an uncoined state was money. But the emphasis shifted as the first century progressed. The prospect of tribute-based colonization faded, while active creation of wealth through entrepreneurship, whether at a high or low level, became both necessary and more appealing. A Spanish immigrant in Lima remarked in 1587: "People never ask [here] in what occupation a man has made money, but how much he has; and when they are told that he has something, they shut their mouths and are silent."[59] Those who succeeded rose in public esteem. The process was to be repeated often in later European emigrations. The migrants, probably above average in enterprise to begin with, found, in their new overseas freedom from the social constraints of home, a welcome chance to better themselves economically, and often enough socially as well.

Mestizos, Africans, and others

One of the novelties that America presented to arriving migrants was people of mixed blood. Though the presence of these was increasingly obvious as the sixteenth century advanced, precise numbers are still harder to measure than those of Spaniards or Indians. The presence of *mestizos* was one of the most immediate consequences of contact and conquest. On the mainland, one of the most noteworthy births was that of Don Martín Cortés, son of the conqueror and Doña Marina. Born in 1522, the boy was named for Cortés's father and, at the age of 6, taken to Spain to be reared at court. He never saw his mother again. Even before this, however, his upbringing had been entrusted to a kinsman of Cortés rather than to Marina. Francisco Pizarro also sired a child with an indigenous woman, in this case Doña Inés Huaylas Yupanqui, one of the daughters of the Inca Huayna Capac. The child, Doña Francisca Pizarro, was raised not by her mother but by a paternal uncle, and ended her life in Spain.[60] This pattern repeated itself throughout the first generation of elite *mestizos*; customarily absorbed into the Spanish world of their fathers, these mixed-race children gained admission at the cost of their maternal ties.

If this elite *mestizo* generation was subsumed by Spanish settler society, it is nonetheless more visible to the historian than the vast majority of mixed-race births. One historian's guess "that the Spaniards commonly left more pregnancies in their camps than they did casualties on the field of battle," and that it was neither "microbe nor sword nor mailed fist" that conquered Mexico but the conquerors' sexual rapacity,[61] is supported by much anecdotal evidence; but nobody counted the outcome. The most reliable estimate of these Spanish–Indian *mestizos* for any region of the sixteenth-century empire puts their number in central, southern, and western New Spain *c.*1568 at some 2,400. The total population of the same area at the time was about 2.7 million (besides the *mestizos*, some 2.65 million Indians, 63,000 Spaniards, and 23,000 *pardos*, or people wholly or partly black).[62] Only 0.09 percent of the whole would seem, therefore, to have been *mestizo*. But this is probably a severe understatement of the biological, if not the cultural, reality. Many of the mixed-blood children born early in colonial times were raised by their Spanish fathers. These "euromestizos" are included here in the Spanish category. The *mestizos* shown, then, are the remainder, or "indomestizos." And undoubtedly other people who were genetically *mestizo* are hidden in the Indian total. *Mestizos* are thus a difficult group to track, not least because there was often considerable fluidity in categorization and life course, even for children from the same family. One scholar studying the rural Andes has found, for example, that *mestizo* boys often were raised by their Spanish fathers or remained with their mothers only until reaching their late teens; girls, on the other hand, almost always remained with their mothers. *Mestizaje* therefore produced not only people who were hard to define socially and genetically, but also unpredictable life paths.

Though the *mestizos* were such a small part of the central Mexican population in the 1560s, they seem to have increased more rapidly than any other of its components thereafter. By 1646 they (that is, again, "indomestizos") had multiplied seven times, to some 17,000, or 1.1 percent of the total, whereas the number of *pardos* had grown by a factor of 2.3 (to some 62,000) and that of Spaniards (both European- and American-born) had only doubled (to about

125,000).[63] The higher rate of *mestizo* increase persisted after that date, as would be expected as the absolute number of mixed-bloods increased.

New Spain probably led the way among large regions of the empire in Spanish–Indian genetic mixing, for at least two reasons. First, the process started earlier there than anywhere else on the mainland, except lower Central America (above all, Panama). Second, the balance of the two ethnic components also tended to equality earlier in New Spain than elsewhere, which should, other things being equal, have maximized the rate of mixture: the native Mexican population seems to have fallen particularly fast, while the colony drew more immigrants from Spain (a third or more of the total) than any other in the 1500s.[64] Conclusive comparisons with other regions of the empire are impossible to make, however, for lack of trustworthy estimates of the non-Indian elements. But the limited example of Lima in 1614 shows that *mestizos*, as broadly identified, were then only 0.8 percent of that city's population (192 in a total of 24,650).[65]

Numbers of blacks are clearer, since they were a more easily identified element of the population than *mestizos*; though the imprecise counting caused by variable defining in the case of *mestizos* applies also to the mixed-blood offspring of blacks – mulattoes, *zambos*, and other mixtures less than half African. What is immediately striking about Africans is how many of them were present by the late sixteenth century in comparison with all other groups except Indians. This was clearest in New Spain, as would be expected since it had imported the largest number of slaves. According to a census of 1570, eight large towns in the centre and south of the colony, including Mexico City, then held 9,370 black slaves and 1,160 mulattoes, as against 9,720 Spaniards. The capital contained the vast majority of the African element – 8,000 black slaves and 1,000 mulattoes, among 8,000 Spaniards – probably because the wealth concentrated there made for common use of slaves in domestic service. By 1612, whites were heavily outnumbered by blacks in Mexico City: 15,000 Spaniards as against 50,000 blacks and mulattoes (and 80,000 Indians).[66] Another count, this time of blacks together with people partly black, puts some 22,600 of them in central Mexico *c*.1568 and 62,400 in 1646 (respectively 0.8 percent and 4.24 percent of the total population).[67]

Spaniards took blacks with them wherever they went in the Americas in the sixteenth century. But it was Peru, as the second main focus of Spanish settlement after New Spain, that was the other large market for African slaves. The result, as in Mexico, was that towns there quickly came to have a large fraction of blacks and part-blacks in their populations. In the mid 1550s Lima had perhaps 1,500 such in its citizenry – half of all those in Peru, and perhaps a number equal to the Spanish population of the town. By the 1590s the count had risen to some 7,000. The Lima census of 1614 shows 10,386 blacks, and 744 mulattoes (41.9 percent and 3 percent of the total population of 24,650). By 1640 the number had risen to around 20,000. Lima was, in fact, genetically almost half African (or part-African) from the 1590s to the end of the seventeenth century; and the same can be said generally of both coastal and highland towns in northern and central Peru.[68]

An even larger proportion of Africans and people with some African ancestry existed in the population of Panama by the late sixteenth century. This, of course, was a far smaller area than Peru or New Spain, but an important one nonetheless, since it was the crossing point between the Atlantic and the Pacific for people and goods going in either direction. In the mid 1570s the total population of Panama (excluding a very small number of native people) was about 6,400. Of these, only 800 were white – and the rest black or mulattoes. Slaves had been brought in – some bought by the City of Panama itself – from the 1520s onward to carry goods over the Isthmus separating the two oceans, and to work on the roads crossing it. Over the next few decades, black slave employment diversified into domestic service, driving the mule trains transporting goods, small farming, diving for pearls, cattle herding, and logging.[69]

Substantial numbers of blacks or part-blacks were present almost everywhere else in Spanish America by the late sixteenth century. When they are added to the growing number of other people who were not white, or American natives, it is clear that that Spanish American society was rapidly growing more complex. The two-part simplicity of the initial colonial population, consisting almost wholly of Europeans and Indians, was fast disappearing, and would never return. A third element, comprising blacks together with Indian–Spanish–black mixtures, was increasing in numbers to occupy, or more accurately to create, a social space between Europeans and native people. This element, genetically and culturally varied as it was, came to be seen as a third major grouping of American society. It is tempting to dub it an American estate. But it had no unifying legal definition. Rather the reverse was the case, in fact, since blacks, for example, were treated separately in law from genetically mixed people, and slaves differently from free men. On the other hand, people in this third group were legally distinct from Indians in being exempt from the state's forced labor systems, and also in practice from tribute payment. But, above all, *mestizos*, blacks, mulattoes, and all the other more complex intermixtures that appeared as time passed were lumped together because they were neither native American nor European. The generic term applied to them was *castas*. The word does not translate as "caste" in the usual English sense. Fluidity, rather than rigidity, of social and economic position, within certain limits, was the essence of being a black or mixed-blood *casta* in colonial Spanish America.

That fluidity could, though, make for discomfort. The clear emergence of the *mestizo* onto the social scene in the mid sixteenth century was met with suspicion, both official and private. Up to then Spaniards had been few enough for *mestizos* to be seen as allies, as part-Europeans collaborating in the domination of America. But as the white population grew, from immigration and natural increase, *mestizos* slipped in esteem. By the 1550s, in fact, there were enough obviously *mestizo* children to constitute a social problem; indeed, the term "mestizo" arose to describe, and was originally applied to, mixed-race children who were vulnerable, illegitimate, and abandoned, "wandering lost through the land with neither law nor faith," in the words of sixteenth-century Mexican archbishop Juan de Zumárraga. Concern over the fate of *mestizos* led, between 1548 and 1551, to the creation of religious institutions to "remedy" *mestizo* girls in both Mexico City and Cuzco.[70] The worry apparent over the girls' behavior and fate seems highly exaggerated, given the relatively small numbers of *mestizos* at the time; it perhaps comes from a growing association of *mestizos* and illegitimate birth.

A prime cause of Spanish disdain for *mestizos* was, in fact, that ever fewer of them were the product of marriage. Spaniards, made acutely, even pathologically, conscious of legitimacy and "purity of blood" by long coexistence with Jews and Muslims, increasingly tended to look down on *mestizos* for their irregular origins. Despite this, of course, Spanish males continued to sire children in casual or even lasting unions with Indian or *mestiza* women, and many of these offspring became the objects of both native and Spanish suspicion, and of Spanish scorn. "You are to expel mestizos from Indian villages and send them to the nearest Spanish towns, where they can learn trades and seek employment, instead of living as vagabonds and setting a bad example to the Indians, as they do" – so ordered the governor of Peru, Lope García de Castro, in his instructions of 1565 for newly created *corregidores de indios*.[71] This became the lasting and standard official view of *mestizos*: idle and drifting troublemakers, irritating misfits for whom the simple Spanish–Indian model of early American society had no clear place. Their Indianness, transmitted not only through their gestation by a native mother but also through her milk, was also cause for alarm. Might they not, resentful and often skilled in arms as they were, lead Indians against the Spanish?[72] They did, indeed; but not until the eighteenth century.

Despite the nervousness they inspired, as their numbers grew *mestizos* inevitably took a wider role in society. Though some, the more Indian, found few openings outside manual and menial labor, and others, the more European, managed to insinuate themselves into the lower reaches of the secular priesthood and the bureaucracy, most gravitated to a middle range of occupations. They might become, for instance, supervisors on farms and in mines, perhaps small farmers themselves, muleteers, petty merchants, or artisans. How *mestizos* ranked in the popular view is suggested by their treatment by guilds in sixteenth- and early seventeenth century Mexico City. The trades that considered themselves most elevated (armorers and swordsmiths, for example) clumped *mestizos* with free blacks and mulattoes, denying them any advance in rank. Less exalted crafts allowed *mestizos* to become masters, while limiting other non-whites to journeyman status. The least pretentious – candlemakers and cobblers – gave *mestizos*, free blacks and mulattoes alike access to all ranks.[73] Thus Spaniards certainly consigned *mestizos* to the *casta* mass; but they gave them a slight, though not definitive, preference of status within it.

Blacks and mulattoes were more easily and more precisely placed in society. To begin with, they were more distinctive in appearance than *mestizos* were. Second, the taint of slavery always clung to them, even if they had been freed or were the descendants of freedmen. Slavery had, at some point, been the mechanism responsible for the arrival of almost all blacks in America. Third, Spaniards felt towards Africans little of the lingering sense of responsibility that Indians inspired in them, even if faintly as time advanced, and that, via

Indians, applied even more distantly to *mestizos*. No pope had given Spain any obligation to convert and care for Africans. Their spiritual welfare, therefore, was of little concern to Spain (although both administration and church were naturally vigilant in trying to stop Africans from practicing any sorts of religious or spiritual activities that might threaten Catholicism.) For all these reasons, Africans and part-Africans were assigned the lowest legal rank in society.

In fact, blacks nonetheless proved so useful to Spaniards in America, from the conquest on, that the real position that many of them occupied in society – with one large exception – was higher than their legal place would suggest. The exception was the considerable number of field slaves who were working, by the end of the sixteenth century, on plantations producing sugar on Hispaniola, on the Peruvian coast or in southern Mexico, for example, or cacao around Guayaquil on the coast of Quito. But, these aside, the sense of alliance between Spaniards and Africans that is evident in the conquests persisted long after whites and blacks had ceased to be comrades in arms. Colonials tended to regard blacks and mulattoes, whether slave or free, as more able and more reliable than Indians, and so gave them tasks and responsibilities that set them higher on the social and economic scales than all Indians, besides *caciques*. Further reason for this is not hard to find. Many of the blacks in America in the 1500s came from regions of West Africa in which iron-working and cattle-tending were part of material culture. Their knowledge and abilities were immediately useful to Spaniards. Again, although blacks brought many parts of their African way of life with them, in America they were cut off from the roots of the cultures into which they had been born. For their own wellbeing, psychological comfort, even safety, they had no choice but to identify with Spaniards, and Spanish-colonial culture, to some degree.

It is no surprise, then, to find many blacks as personal and domestic servants of Spaniards after the conquests. Having as many such servants as possible was also, of course, an important mark of prestige for the settler. *Encomenderos* often kept a large retinue of them. Colonists might also set up their slaves in craft shops; African blacksmiths were particularly common in early post-conquest Peru,[74] but slaves were often to be found also making clothes, shoes, furniture, and much else. There are cases in which a slave master craftsman was sent off by his master to another city to set up an independent artisan shop there. The owner trusted the slave to send the profits back to him. African slaves, indeed, did a great deal to help the Spanish create the material base of the colonies in the sixteenth century. The term "auxiliary slavery" has been suggested to describe the many sorts of work that they performed in close collaboration with their owners – in distinction to the field labor on plantations that is more commonly associated with African slavery in the Americas.[75] It is a useful term, and idea – conveying well the sense of alliance that for the most part characterized the relationship between owner and slave in the early Spanish American colonies.

The confidence that the Spanish often had in their slaves is shown also by their use of blacks to supervise native workers. The lesson that Indians had learned during the conquests – that the African was part of the invading culture – was reinforced after the fighting was done by the colonials' frequently giving black slaves or freedmen authority over Indians in mining refineries, craft workshops, and on farms and estates. Spanish fears that Indians and blacks would unite against them were very rarely confirmed. In a slave revolt on Hispaniola in the 1520s there was some of that collaboration, and later, when escaped slaves set up independent communities, as they did in many parts of Spanish America, they might establish cordial links with nearby native towns. Also, naturally enough, at the personal level there were many friendships, affective relationships (brief or lasting), and even marriages between American natives on one side, and Africans, or men and women of African descent, on the other. These ties probably became more common as, with time, ethnic and cultural blending progressed, and both natives and Africans acquired more traits of the general colonial culture.[76] But, broadly speaking, black and Indian interests always retained at least some of the differences that marked them at the time of the conquests. Those differences remained large enough to nullify the possibility of a general alliance of the two groups against Spaniards.[77]

The growing presence of blacks nonetheless made many Spaniards nervous, especially as, after 1550 or so, the numbers of Africans in the main colonial towns equaled and then passed the numbers of Europeans. A law of 1551 forbade them to bear arms.[78] As with the perceived *mestizo* threat, these fears were exaggerated. But they were not groundless, for although no serious danger to Spanish settlement at even the regional level ever came from blacks, protests there were aplenty in the form of runaway slaves and their communities. Some of sixteenth-century Panama's numerous and hard-worked slaves, for example, fled into the rainforests of the isthmus. The English corsair Francis Drake, leading his first assault on the Spanish Caribbean in 1572, found these maroons (*cimarrones*) a useful ally. After the failure of an initial attack on Nombre de Dios, the Spanish port on the Caribbean side of the isthmus, he

> came to the sound [i.e. gulf] of Darién and having conference with certain Negroes which were fled from their masters at Panama and Nombre de Dios, the Negroes did tell him that certain mules came laden with gold and silver from Panama to Nombre de Dios. Who in company of these Negroes went thereupon on land and stayed in the way where the treasure should come, with a hundred shot, and so took two companies of mules ... and he carried away the gold only, for they were not able to carry the silver through the mountains.[79]

No other place in Spanish America offered runaway slaves such power to damage Spanish interests. Panama was a peculiarly tender spot, since South American silver on its way to Spain there crossed from Pacific to Atlantic. Maroons elsewhere were a nuisance, a disruption of order, but a thorn rather than a sword in the side of the body politic. One group in Esmeraldas, on the northern coast of Quito, originated *c.*1570 in the wreck of a slave ship. These blacks blended with the local natives, creating a large *zambo* population that never succumbed to the feeble efforts the Spaniards made to subdue it. The region was isolated and of small economic importance.[80] Another outlying area in which a largely autonomous local black culture took root was the south-western coast of New Spain around Acapulco. The Spanish regarded more seriously an African separatist presence that developed in central Mexico. Maroons, by the early 1600s, regularly threatened the crucial road between Veracruz, the main port on the Caribbean coast, and the interior. In 1609 these renegades were reported to have chosen a king, named Yanga. Rumors circulated of a plot to kill all Spaniards in Mexico City. The viceroy immediately put together a militia force of 600 to subdue the rebels. But their guerrilla resistance proved hard to suppress, and the authorities finally had to strike a bargain with Yanga whereby he and his people could live unmolested in the mountains so long as they stopped raiding. Two years later another, perhaps more substantial, plot was discovered to kill the white inhabitants of Mexico City. This was put down in 1612 with the execution of thirty-six supposed black leaders. There was more trouble in 1617, when maroons started raiding in the countryside again. They were easily suppressed by force this time; but the offenders were allowed to stay at large in a town of their own named San Lorenzo de los Negros.[81]

These episodes in central New Spain suggest the ambiguity of Spanish attitudes towards blacks in America. On the one hand was a feeling of the need to treat them cautiously, inspired by fear, certainly, but perhaps also by a lasting sense that Europeans and blacks were essentially on the same side, collaborating to control Indians and America itself. On the other hand was disdain, and even scorn, for a category of people long associated with slavery and heathenism. Spaniards' equivocation was reinforced by the economic and social desirability of owning black slaves. In the Spanish view, they did some sorts of work better than Indians could; and there was no question that possessing blacks conferred far more social prestige on an individual than employing Indian servants, even Indian slaves. A classic comment on the topic came from Bishop Mota y Escobar, of Guadalajara, visiting the silver-mining town of Zacatecas in the opening years of the seventeenth century. He found there some 800 black and mulatto slaves, men and women, and also a number of free blacks, "who come and go, and hire themselves out for work in cattle-raising, farming, and mining. And generally both slaves and freemen are bad and pernicious. But it is as they say here: 'Bad to have them, but much worse not to have them'."[82]

The ambiguity of Spanish attitudes is also suggested by the clear presence of free blacks and mulattoes in the colonies from the start. Spaniards wanted slaves, but, it would seem, were unwilling to bar them rigidly from freedom. Slaves who were put to craft work, for instance, might be allowed to keep some of the shop's income and slowly accumulate funds with which to buy their own liberty. Owners might free mulatto children they had themselves produced. They also sometimes freed slaves in their wills. They showed some tendency to prefer women in these bequests of liberty; that promoted freedom further, since subsequent children took their status from their mothers. It is true that owners gave up less in freeing women; male slaves had a greater economic value. And

SOCIETY

the males who were freed tended to be older and hence less valuable. But a long medieval tradition existed in Spanish law providing openings to freedom for slaves. One student of slavery in New Spain offers an apt assessment:

> The distinctiveness of colonial Mexico, and perhaps that of other Spanish colonies, rests not on the ease and frequency of manumission but rather on the absence of an environment which frowned upon freedom for black slaves. The Spaniards in Mexico never quite rejected the idea that slavery was contrary to natural law and reason and never quite embraced the view that Africans were created to be slaves in perpetuity.[83]

But freedom was always more likely to go to those who were less useful economically: children, women, the elderly.

TOWNS

The physical framework in which Spaniards and *castas* arranged themselves socially was above all the city. In Spanish America today, and indeed in Spain too, the notion persists strongly that cities are the proper place for the development and exercise of civilization. The country may be briefly visited for purposes of relaxation or refuge, or, in the case of landowners, of supervision, and the pleasures of proprietorship. But rare still is the educated person who would choose the country life over the urban because of a fascination with flora and fauna, or enjoyment of undisturbed natural rhythms.

This preference for city life doubtless has many sources. But one of them is the ancient Greek notion that true, civil, people must inhabit a city, for a city is the only possible environment for developed political and moral existence. Those who live elsewhere are probably barbarians, lacking the political order for which the city provides a setting, and which indeed is the essence of city.[84] At the other, pragmatic, extreme from this principle it is easy to imagine why early Spaniards in America (and, for that matter, Christians pressing back the Moors over the centuries of reconquest in Iberia) would gather in cities. Such places offered physical and psychological strength in their concentrated numbers, and served as defensible bridgeheads in new (and in the American case, alien) territory. Further, medieval experience in Spain had given the city a corporate identity firmly defined in law. A town had legal rights (for instance, to choose its administrators and justices, and to allocate land for building and agriculture) from which its citizens could benefit, and which far exceeded any privileges they might exercise as individuals. These rights came into effect as soon as the town had been legally founded, and even before it had any physical identity besides its bare site. Thus, in the notorious example, Cortés founded Veracruz at the start of his Mexican campaign, naming aldermen and magistrates, and renouncing his authority in the expedition to them. They, then, as representatives of the corporation, quite legitimately appointed him governor of the town. And. holding that office, he became in fact and law the supreme Spanish official in Mexico, head of an autonomous corporation, and as such was able to take independent command of the party that he had brought from Cuba at Diego Velázquez's order, and redirect it to the purpose of conquest.[85]

The typical Spanish American town was built on a grid pattern, with eight major streets running outwards from the corners of a central plaza. Around the square were ranged the major municipal structures (the town hall, or *casas de cabildo*, the jail, a treasury building if the Real Hacienda had a branch in the town), the parish church, and possibly, if space remained, houses of pre-eminent citizens. Generally speaking, the more important a family, the closer its house stood to the plaza. Many sources have been proposed for this distinctive chessboard design: native cities such as Tenochtitlan, medieval fortress towns of southern France and north-eastern Spain, the influence of the Italian Renaissance, and, behind that, Vitruvius, the Roman author of *De Architectura* of the first century BC. His precepts appear clearly in parts of the Philip II's *Ordinances for New Discovery and Settlement* of 1573. But the oddity is that many towns had been built on the grid pattern long before Philip's rules were issued. From the first, indeed, it seems that Spaniards, whether conquerors, settlers, or officials, carried to America the notion that a grid of right-angled blocks was the proper form for a settlement, even though most of them came from parts of Spain in which medieval towns with narrow, winding streets were the norm. Some "collective intuition" seems to have been at work,[86] perhaps with a distant source in Roman Spain. Certainly the grid was a simple, even obvious, design on which to lay out a new place, especially if the site chosen was more or less flat, as many were. Division of square or rectangular blocks into house lots was simply done. But some attempt seems to have been made to impose the grid model also on irregular sites, such as the narrow valleys in which some mining towns were founded.

Whatever its source, the grid plan was well fixed in the minds of explorers and conquerors, and, it has been suggested, not simply as a practical convenience, but as a physical metaphor of the orderliness and civility that cities ideally embodied. It is as if the Spanish sought to declare the civilization they believed they were carrying to America in laying out everywhere they went that urban pattern of central square, straight streets, and right-angled blocks. Naturally they tried to impose this same design on native communities, into which they hoped also to inject their version of civility.[87] The new communities into which many Indians were "reduced" from the mid 1500s onwards were planned in this way, in the hope that urban surroundings would foment in the native people the *policía* – good, legal order and behavior – that Spain sought to inculcate in them. In reality, even the newly created native towns resisted this imposed geometry; as did also the native *barrios* that generally grew up around the central grid of Spanish cities. In the "reductions," the plaza tended to be simply an open space in which the parish church was the sole marker of authority, while the correspondence between social position and distance from the plaza, so rigidly set in Spanish towns, was weak in native places.[88] In Indian *barrios*, the straight streets of the town center tended to dissolve into wandering alleys and randomly placed houses.

It seems no coincidence that the greatest symbol of Spanish imperial power, Philip II's monastery-palace of San Lorenzo del Escorial, should also have been built on the grid plan – although the method of St. Laurence's death, by roasting on a gridiron, is also worth recalling. (Is it, though, some hint of uncertainty, humility, or irony in the king that he should have chosen a place named "The Slag-Heap," the literal meaning of *escorial*, for this massive expression of the state?) Certainly, in America, Spanish towns were the symbols and the foci of colonizing power. The central cities were the seats of viceroys, archbishops, *audiencias*, the treasury, the Inquisition. In smaller towns the monarchy was represented directly by a *corregidor* or *alcalde mayor*. But the *cabildo*, the town council of aldermen and magistrates of first instance, while defending the municipality's interests before outside authorities, was also a part of colonial government. Most aldermen, after the early decades, in fact received their positions through royal grant or by purchase from the state. As long as it was in their interest to do so, they played their part in imposing the official will on America and its native people. And as, in general, powerful private colonials pursuing economic interests in and around their towns, they certainly contributed in the wider sense to Spanish domination of American territory. Other powerful men, too – landowners, merchants, miners – even if they were not council members, along with the lawyers, notaries, and clerks who organized their activities, clustered in towns, making these, in a graphic phrase, "centrifugal points of assault on the land and its resources."[89]

FAMILY AND FRIENDS

If the city was a crucial socio-political unit on the large scale in the success of Spanish colonization, so, on a smaller scale, was the family. Official policy favored the formation of Spanish families in America from the start, and for that reason encouraged women to emigrate. At the command of the Catholic Monarchs in 1498, 30 females were among Columbus's party of 330 on his third voyage to the Caribbean. In 1505 Ferdinand issued the first example of an oft-repeated command that married men in the Indies (Hispaniola alone, at the time) whose wives were still in Spain should go and fetch them, or arrange their passage across the Atlantic. The aim was to set a good example for Indians, to reinforce the Spanish colonial hold through population increase, and to strengthen the will of settlers to "reside and remain in these parts" – to use the words of Hernán Cortés, who in 1524 ordered that the *encomenderos* whom he governed in New Spain should bring over their wives in eighteen months, or lose their Indians. A true *vecino*, or householder, another royal decree of 1544 stated, lived with his wife and children. Men separated from their wives were not established in America; "they never perpetuate themselves, nor attend to building, to planting, to raising animals, to sowing, to doing the things that good settlers accustom to do ...."[90]

Despite the implication of these constant urgings, it seems that in fact many married men moving to America did take wives and children with them. There were, certainly, men who abandoned their wives in the Old World to engage in libertinage or bigamy in the New, continuing a pattern of abandonment familiar – albeit on a smaller geographical scale–in the Iberian peninsula.[91]

There were also wives who flatly refused to make the long and perilous journey to an unknown land.[92] Probably more common than such intransigence was the attitude of Puebla's Sebastián de Pliego, who wrote to his wife in 1581 with detailed instructions for her journey to the Indies, concluding with evident passion, "I wish to see you with my eyes before I die."[93]

Quite aside from the real existence of conjugal love, the family, for Spaniards, was a deeply held cultural value: the cornerstone of society, the guarantor of inheritance and lineage, and the repository of familial honor. As far back as the Reconquest, wives were critical to the identity of settled Christian towns and occupied a dignified position.[94] This position, to be sure, was not one of equality; as the foundation of civil society, the family expressed the divine hierarchical principle of patriarchy, permitting a man to govern, protect, and discipline the members of his household, representing in microcosm the orderly republic, and reproducing the relationship that bound subjects to the father-king.[95] A community constituted without the guarantee of marriage, without a nuclear family structure, and without male dominance was, for the Spaniard, "no community at all but a mere horde."[96] The Spanish did not waver from this view as they confronted new forms of family structure in the Americas; indeed, one student of colonial society argues that of all the Spanish cultural forms exported to the Indies, the ideal of the patriarchal family "changed least in transit."[97]

Informal unions were not unfamiliar in Iberia, but only Christian marriage officially constituted a family, guaranteeing both the inheritance of children born within it and the property protections granted wives under Spanish law. Marriage also ensured the continuation of lineage, a principal concern of both Spanish and indigenous cultures. This is why, though Catholic marriage rested upon the dual principles of sacramentality and individual free will,[98] the constitution of a family was not simply a decision involving two people, but generally involved parents and other concerned kin. Marriage and the family were thus critical to the creation of a recognizably "Spanish" colonial society, and to the creation of individual colonial lives. In reconstituting nuclear families, or creating new ones, in the Americas, Spaniards expressed continuity with traditions deeply rooted in the Iberian past.

If the nuclear family was critical to both social order and individual identity, family was also central to individuals' efforts to set themselves up, survive, and prosper in America. The Pizarros are a prime early example. Francisco Pizarro recruited three brothers (Hernando, Gonzalo, and Juan) and other relatives as assistants in the conquest of Peru. This turning to relatives is scarcely surprising. The conquest years and their immediate aftermath were a time of fierce rivalries and hence great temptations to betrayal. Kin were likely to be the most reliable subordinates. The principle endured once settlement was established. Who could be more trusted than a brother, a cousin, an uncle, or a nephew as a business partner, or as an agent to carry cash to Spain and do business there? Given that Spanish extended families generally had ambitious young men to spare, familial chain migration seemed to solve a number of problems. "What I would need now," wrote Andrés Chacón to his brother in 1570, "is what there is too much of there, a boy from among those nephews of mine ... because the blacks overlook nothing they can steal, and as to the Spaniards that I have there, each one looks after himself."[99] Extended families, moreover, were likely to straddle various occupations and social levels in Spain, and, in time, in America also. They became, then, networks on which their members could draw, for the particular expertise of a merchant or a lawyer, perhaps, or the influence of a well-placed official. A family connection might be useful simply for the status associated with it. A quite local reputation in Spain could carry across the Atlantic. A man named Alvaro de Paredes Espadero, for instance, son of an *hidalgo* family in Cáceres in Extremadura, and a relative of a member of the Council of the Indies, found that his family's name was the key to bringing off an unexpectedly good marriage in Mexico City in 1590. His bride was the sister of an official in the *audiencia*, and brought with her not only a dowry of 8,000 pesos, no small sum, but good political and social connections.[100]

The trust a settler placed in family members extended out in diminishing measure to friends, people from the same home town, and finally to those from the same region of origin in Spain. Again, this was very clear in the conquests and early settlements. Nicolás de Ovando, another native of Cáceres, while en route to Hispaniola in 1502 gathered fellow Extremadurans as members of his large refounding party. One of them was Francisco Pizarro, a native of Trujillo, a town some 45 kilometers east of Cáceres. Twenty-five or so years later, Pizarro himself went back to Trujillo and Extremadura to collect not only relatives but local compatriots for the conquering expedition to Peru. The ties of Spanish city and region long remained strong in the Indies. A Galician, for instance, from north-west Spain arriving in America would find a welcome, lodging, perhaps even work among fellow *gallegos* already established there. The most distinct of Spanish regional groups in the Indies were the Basques, who clustered together to become prominent in commerce and mining, among other things,. Galicians and Basques had a strong defining identity in their languages. This must have been particularly so with the Basques, whose language, quite unrelated to the Romance tongues of the rest of Iberia, must have seemed an exclusive code to other colonists. Certainly Basques were a frequent source of suspicion and annoyance to other Spaniards in America.

So, in a series of physical and notional frameworks, the Spanish spread themselves across America in the sixteenth century, creating a society that reproduced in good part of what they had come from, but added new elements to it that the American experience produced. The European noble estate became, with necessary adjustments, the republic of Spaniards. The Spanish medieval town of narrow, twisting streets became the rectilinear and rectangular American city – except on its Indian outskirts, where, perhaps symbolically, the older pattern re-emerged. To the trustworthy men and women of family, home town, or home province were added in some degree black slaves and freemen, bound to their owners and masters by the shared rigors of exploration and conquest. In the single American republic of Spaniards, colonists moved up the social scale, and probably down as well, more freely than in Spain, with wealth becoming a more powerful influence on standing. The Spanish common estate had its American counterpart in an Indian republic in which, long before the end of the century, both the numbers and the social range of pre-conquest times were severely narrowed. Then, to these familiar or partly familiar features of society were added, increasingly obvious as time passed, the uniquely American products of a three-way racial and cultural mixture – *mestizos*, mulattoes, *zambos*, and, in time, other intermediate *castas*. Their growing presence was to do more than anything else to move the society of the Indies away from its European, and native, origins, and make it, over the balance of the colonial era and beyond, distinctively Spanish American.

[10] *ECONOMY: SHIPS AND SILVER*

We order and command the viceroys, presidents, governors, and ministers of Our royal treasury to take the greatest care in seeking the profit and increase of all that belongs to Us in the provinces under their administration, and to apply their entire attention and diligence to the exploitation and working of the mines, to the collection of Our royal imposts and to the remittance to these realms of what is gathered; proceeding with great diligence, not allowing withholdings or delays in any sum from one year to another ... The good administration and lawful growth of Our royal income (which will be most pleasant to Us) is fitting to the service of God, our Lord, and to the preservation of these realms. And we charge Our viceroys and presidents that, considering that this is the nerve and spirit that gives vigor and being to the Royal Estate, they gather with Auditors, Royal Officials, Ministers and other persons who may seem most fitting to achieve this end, and that they discuss and treat these matters, and the reduction of expenses in so far as possible, so that by this means, and others that they may arrive at, Our Royal income is increased, so that We may use it to attend to the needs of Our Monarchy ...[1]

THIS exhortation from Philip III, directed in 1617 to his senior administrators in the Indies, suggests how crucial American income had become to the Spanish crown in the sixteenth century. The "service of God" was not just a rhetorical flourish, for American wealth, particularly in the form of surging silver production from the 1560s on, had been part of the inspiration for Philip II's commitment of Spain to the militant defense of Catholicism in Europe.[2] Indeed, the appearance of that wealth seemed providential, a sign that Spain should assume the role of temporal leader of the effort against the spreading Protestantism of northern Europe. By some measures American wealth was astonishing. Silver production from Potosí alone in 1592, worth about 5.6 million ducats, amounted to some 44 percent of the Spanish crown's average yearly spending on state business in Europe between 1593 and 1597.[3] It is true, of course, that the crown did not receive all the silver produced at Potosí (or anywhere else) but only the royalty tax on it of about 21 percent. But the crown's complete revenue from America, including mining royalties, sales taxes, Indian tribute payments, customs duties and many other levies, amounted, in years of high remittances from the Indies, to about a fifth of the total royal income during Philip II's reign (1556–98). And just as important as the absolute quantity of silver, or even more important, was the fact that a large shipment of bullion could reliably be expected every year – and indeed, until 1600, a shipment of increasing size. The predictability of the arrivals of silver made American "treasure" particularly valuable to Philip II as a source of financial leverage. With it as security he could raise loans to fund his political and military efforts in Europe.[4]

Though the full extent of America's wealth in silver was not apparent until the second half of the sixteenth century, the royal and individual hopes for bullion before then that grew from Columbus's initial reports on Hispaniola and Central America were not disappointed. The Greater Antilles, though the scene of much washing for gold in the first two decades of the century, do not seem to have yielded abundantly. But spoils from the mainland conquests were a different matter. Cortés's initial force in Tenochtitlan seized plentiful gold, but lost most of it in the lake during their flight from the city in mid 1520. Atahualpa's famous ransom in Cajamarca of the amount of gold and silver needed to fill a large room to the height of a raised arm was an even greater haul. Together with other booty it came to about 1.5 million pesos, the equivalent, perhaps, of 1.5 million ounces of silver. The king's fifth of this reached Spain.[5] Other regions that proved rich in loot of worked gold were the Peruvian coast and highland Colombia.

In the early years after the conquests, the looting mentality expanded into one of extracting wealth through tribute collection. The ideal of most early *encomenderos* was to preside over lordly households and lands while being sustained by the tribute, in gold, food, cloth and other products, of the native communities granted to them. But not all *encomenderos* found their tribute receipts sufficient in quantity and variety, and far from all were content in a role of passive receipt of their Indians' products. Given the obviously widespread presence of gold (and, it was soon clear, silver also) in the rock formations of the mainland, it is no surprise that mining was one of the first enterprises to which they turned. The crown, too, was deeply interested in the mining of precious metals. Bullion was money. For the monarchy, indeed, even more than for colonists, American wealth always meant mining more than any other sort of production.

MINING

Mining in New Spain began within a decade of the conquest. Although some gold was extracted, chiefly in the south, it was soon clear that Mexico was richer in silver ores than in gold. The first silver strikes came c.1530, at Zumpango and Sultepec. Taxco and Tlalpujahua followed c.1534. All these were in central Mexico, within 150 kilometers or so of the capital. They produced encouragingly, especially as there was still no more ambitious standard against which to set them. But the full extent of Mexico's silver wealth was not revealed until the mid 1540s, when Spanish exploration reached the first of great ore deposits of the northern plateau. This was at Zacatecas (1546), and from there other northern discoveries were made, at, for example, Santa Bárbara in 1567 and San Luis Potosí *c.*1592. At Guanajuato, on the border between central Mexico and the arid north, and well south of Zacatecas, silver ore seems to have been found *c.*1550. Guanajuato was overshadowed by other districts for almost two centuries, but finally rose to become the new Potosí of the empire, outstripping any other silver center in New Spain or South America by a wide margin after 1740.

The ores of Potosí itself, long the token of Spanish American wealth for Spaniards and other Europeans alike, came to light in 1545. The Spanish, with the Pizarro brothers in the forefront, had worked the nearby mines of Porco, itself a major pre-conquest source of silver, from 1538. The discovery of the Rich Hill of Potosí was an offshoot of that effort; and the scion very soon outgrew its parent. In the century after 1550, the Potosí district, with the Rich Hill always its main source of ore, produced about half of Spanish America's silver.

The Andes proved richer in gold than New Spain, with major mining centers developing at Carabaya (1542) in south-eastern Peru, Chachapoyas and Valdivia (*c.*1550) in northern Peru and central Chile respectively, and Zaruma (*c.*1560) in southern Quito. But it was New Granada that dominated gold production in the Andes, and everywhere in the empire, in the sixteenth century and later. Production began at Popayán, in the south, before 1540, and at Antioquia, in the north, in 1546. New Granadan gold output seems to have passed through a deep slump late in the seventeenth century, while still exceeding that of any other region, and then climbed strongly throughout the eighteenth.

At the beginning, Spaniards drew on native mining and refining techniques wherever they existed. In New Spain native knowledge of metallurgy was slight, except among the Tarascans in the center-west, who were skilled producers and workers of copper. From them early Spanish silver miners may have learned something. In the Andes the Spanish certainly took much from a long and developed native tradition of underground mining, smelting, and elaboration of refined metals. The Andeans were familiar with gold, silver, copper, and tin; from the latter two, they alloyed bronze. Silver was the Spaniards' main interest. Such was the native skill in producing it in the Andes that, until almost 1570, Spanish mine owners in effect rented their mines to Indian managers, who in turn hired workers to cut and refine the ore. Spanish iron and steel tools probably were an advance over native implements in work below ground. But the refining of silver in the central Andes, predominantly at Porco and Potosí, was done in long-standing native fashion using small furnaces of stone or clay named *guayras*. The Quechua word means "air," and the furnaces were so named because the fire inside them was fanned simply by the mountain winds rather than by bellows. The fuel used was either *ichu*, the rough grass of the highlands, or llama dung. This simple smelting method was cheap and efficient enough, when applied to high grade ores, to yield a profit for both native workers and Spanish mine owners.

In New Spain, silver was also produced by smelting for some years after mines were first opened. The technology here, though, was European, consisting essentially of a small furnace in the form of a hollow, square column of stone, 1.5 to 2 meters high. The charcoal fire inside was blown by bellows. The whole apparatus was cheap and simple. Even where powered bellows were used, with the energy coming from a waterwheel or animals, the necessary machinery could be built of wood on patterns familiar from European mills for fulling wool or grinding grain. Some early Spanish colonists, at least, would have known of these designs, even if, as seems likely, there were few experienced miners among them. Almost certainly there was as well some early flow of mining and refining knowledge to New Spain from Germany, the European region most advanced in metallurgy in the sixteenth century. Miners from Silesia crossed the Atlantic to Santo Domingo in 1528 as part of the Welsers' colonizing effort in Venezuela. But they never reached Venezuela. Some went back to Europe, but fifty or so seem to have remained in the New World, and quite possibly moved on to Mexico. In the mid 1530s the factors in Seville of the other great German banking house of the day, the Fuggers of Augsburg, definitely sent German smelters to New Spain to provide help with difficulties in smelting silver.

Germans possibly played a part in bringing about a radical advance beyond smelting that was achieved in New Spain in the mid 1550s. This was the introduction of amalgamation of silver ores, a refining process that revolutionized silver production in Spanish America and that may rank, in its world-wide effects, as high as any other technical innovation made in the Americas since Europeans first went there. The principle of amalgamation – the curious capacity of mercury to bind to certain other metals, even when they are in the form of ores – had been known in the Old World at least since Roman times. It had been long used on a small scale, as, for example, in the recovery of gold and silver filings from the sweepings from a silversmith's floor. It probably passed early to America, since mercury has been found in the remains of the first Spanish town on Hispaniola, at Isabela, which suggests that gold may have been extracted there from alluvial sand or crushed rock by amalgamation. But it was in New Spain that mercury was first used to draw silver from its ores on what could be called an industrial scale. A Spanish cloth merchant from Seville named Bartolomé de Medina is given the main credit for the invention. In 1555 the viceroy granted him monopoly rights in the process in Mexico for ten years. Clearly associated with Medina, however, perhaps particularly in developing the machinery for crushing ore to the fineness that effective amalgamation required, was a German named Gaspar Lohmann. Both were active in Sultepec and the newly opened deposits at Pachuca in the mid 1550s.

Large-scale amalgamation appeared in New Spain not simply as the outcome of Medina's and Lohmann's inventiveness, but clearly as a response to changing local conditions. By the 1550s ores rich enough to be smelted at a profit were becoming scarce. They had mainly been surface deposits enriched by weathering, and were soon skimmed off. Enormous quantities of ore remained, obviously enough; but they were of lower grade, and furthermore had to be brought up from increasing depths. The ores' yield, therefore, dropped, and at the same time their cost rose. Medina and Lohmann's amalgamation process, with its capacity to refine great volumes of poor ores quite cheaply, was the answer. How eagerly the process was seized on is shown by that fact that over 120 refiners took it up before 1555 was out.[6] In the following years it spread to nearly all Mexican silver centers.

For lack of records, amalgamation's immediate effect on Mexican production cannot be seen. But in Potosí it had demonstrably dramatic results. The same problems of declining ore yields and rising costs as had earlier afflicted Mexico were depressing output there by the late 1560s. Viceroy Toledo arrived from Spain in 1569 with orders to install the mercury process in Potosí. He indeed played an active part in its adoption there, but the miners of Potosí would doubtless soon have used it in any case. The first mills for refining by amalgamation were built in the town in 1572. That was also the year of lowest production since records began in 1549. But, with the help of the amalgamation process, output grew between 1572 and 1582 6.7 times (from 26,000 to 174,000 kilograms). By 1592, the peak year in Potosí's history, it had risen to almost 202,000 kilograms. Amalgamation, it is true, was not solely responsible for this boom. In the 1570s Toledo had also increased the labor supply, reorganizing the forced drafting of native workers to miners and refiners in Potosí. But without amalgamation those reforms would have served little. The extra workers might have mined much ore at low cost. But it could not have been refined profitably with either Andean or European smelting techniques.

Amalgamation processing was itself far from cheap to set up; but the large initial investment required paid off quickly. The fundamental need was for a means of crushing the ore finely, so that the mercury, when added, could come into close contact with as much of the mineral as possible. This was done everywhere with a mill consisting of four to twelve vertical, iron-shod stamps, which were lifted in turn by cams rotating on a heavy shaft. The motive power was a waterwheel, where sufficient flow and head were available, or teams of mules in dry areas, such as northern Mexico. Once milled, the ore was mixed with water and mercury, and sometimes other reagents, such as salt, iron filings, and copper sulfate, that empirical testing proved useful. In the Andes, the mixing was done in large tanks holding some 2,300 kilograms of ore. Sometimes these were heated from below to speed the reaction. In New Spain, wooden troughs served the same purpose in the sixteenth century. After then the common method was to spread the blended ore out on a paved court, a practice that led to the use of the term *beneficio de patio*, or "patio processing," for amalgamation in New Spain. After some weeks (the actual time depending on the ambient temperature and other, lesser, variables) the refiner would decide, from experience, that the combining of mercury with silver was complete. The entire mixture was then washed, usually in wooden vats, sometimes fitted with powered rotating paddles. The mercury–silver amalgam sank to the bottom, whence it was gathered up, and excess mercury physically squeezed from it. Heating the amalgam then made the remaining mercury evaporate off; a honeycomb of pure silver remained. Once amalgamation became commonplace, refiners tried with some success to minimize the loss of mercury in the process. They found it possible to recover some of it by carrying out the heating of the amalgam beneath a metal or clay hood. The mercury vapor condensed on the inside of the hood into the metal's familiar liquid form, which could then be collected. The practice also had the advantage of reducing somewhat the risk of workers' being poisoned by mercury vapor, which is highly toxic.

Amalgamation was a long, many-staged process, and in its complexity a far cry from earlier refining by smelting. The amalgamation plant, known in the Andes as an *ingenio* and in New Spain as an *hacienda de minas*, was a large and expensive affair, with its crushing mill and associate driving mechanism, tanks or patio, washing vats, store rooms, living quarters for workers and supervisor, and often enough a small chapel. The water-powered *ingenios* built in Potosí in the 1570s cost on average 50,000 pesos each, the price of 50 modest houses, or 5,000 llamas. Such installations were, along with mine workings themselves, and ocean-going trading vessels, the largest capital investments made by colonists in Spanish America.

This need for heavy investment meant that refining silver by amalgamation was a business pursued almost exclusively by the white portion of the colonial population. In New Spain, where from the beginning native people had done little more in mining than provide simple labor, the arrival of the new technique brought little change for Indians. But in the central Andes it meant an end to the control of extraction and refining of ores that many skilled native miners had enjoyed, along with some share of the profit, from the 1540s to the late 1560s. These men did not have access to the cash needed to build *ingenios*. Further, the technology of waterwheels, geared machinery, and iron and steel was an import, and alien to them. Indians in Potosí and elsewhere, then, did not become *azogueros* ("mercury men"), the owners of refining mills and the dominant force in silver production after the 1570s. Production of silver by Indians, nevertheless, did not stop at that point. *Guayras* long continued to burn on Andean mountainsides, smelting small pieces of rich ore that indigenous men, and women, picked out from mine tailings, or that underground workers took from the mines as part of their wages. In aggregate this smelted production may have been considerable, though it is impossible to estimate its amount. The same happened in Mexico, where Indians and *mestizos* were always to be found operating small smelting furnaces in and around Spanish-dominated mining towns.

By Spanish law, subsoil rights in America remained with the crown. Private possession of land included only the surface. But individuals might claim mines and then work them for their own profit so long as they paid a royalty to the treasury. The basic rate of the tax in the sixteenth century was a fifth of the metal produced, the *quinto real*. Reductions in the tax were granted from mid century onwards to stimulate mining. New Spain was seen as particularly needing this help, so that in the second half of the century (and later) the prevailing rate there was a tenth. It is mainly from these royalty records, which become more complete as the century progresses, that mining production has been calculated. The best such estimate to date places Spanish American silver

Table 10.1 Gold production in New Granada,
New Spain, and Peru, 1550–1620

Period	Amount (silver pesos, millions)
1561–70	2.75
1571–80	2.78
1581–90	2.28
1591–1600	4.77
1601–10	6.88
1611–20	6.98
Total	**33.11**

output from its start until 1600 or 1610 at 375–400 million pesos, or 10.6–11.3 million kilograms.[7] By far the greater part of this amount was produced after 1550, as Potosí and the north Mexican mines began to yield. The rate of increase of total Spanish American production in the period from 1560 to 1620–30 was the highest of any long period in the colonial era, at about 2.3 percent annually. Potosí, once amalgamation was adopted there, was mainly responsible for the high volume of output, and for a time for its growth also. Production at Potosí leveled off, however, in the 1590s and then began to fall in the new century, as ore quality declined and the costs of extraction rose with the increasing depth of the mines. But it was still the largest silver producer in the Indies, and its output did not subside to 1572 levels until the early eighteenth century. Production in New Spain continued to rise until the 1620s, before dropping slightly for perhaps forty years. There, several substantial mining districts were always in operation, and a decline in one or two of them did not much affect the total output.

Gold production grew also in the 1550–1620 period, but less quickly. The most complete estimate to date shows totals, converted to an equivalent value in silver pesos, for New Granada, New Spain, and Peru combined (table 10.1). Of the 33.11 million total for the whole period, New Granada produced 22.36 million, or 67.5 percent.[8]

Not only did gold output grow less quickly than silver's in the second half of the sixteenth century, but its value was far less. That remains true even if the earlier gold booty of the conquests is taken into account. The total amount of gold gathered by the Spanish in New Granada, New Spain, and Peru from 1521 to 1610 has been estimated at the equivalent of 48.46 million silver pesos.[9] That is only 12 percent of the proposed *c.*400 million peso silver production of Spanish America to 1610. It was probably at some point in the 1540s, when little gold was left to loot, that the value of silver mined passed that of gold acquired. The lure of gold may first have drawn Spain and Spaniards to America; but it was the reality of silver that kept them there.

The third economically important metal mined in the colonies was mercury, obviously a strategic material once amalgamation became the normal method of refining silver ores. Constant searches for mercury deposits in New Spain revealed no useful source there. But Peru was a different matter. From Huancavelica, in the mountains 240 kilometers south-east of Lima, native people had long taken cinnabar (red mercuric sulfide) for cosmetic uses, and the Spanish subsequently found that it was a deposit large enough to supply the mercury demands of Potosí and other Andean mines for most of the colonial era. Its output was not, though, sufficient to cover the Mexico's needs as well. Fortunately, Spain itself held one of the world's largest mercury sources, at Almadén, north of Córdoba. Mining there went back to Roman times, but much ore remained to be extracted. For most of the span of the empire, Almadén supplied Mexican silver producers with the mercury they needed. As the sources of a material of vital interest to Spain, the mines of both Almadén and Huancavelica were placed under state administration, although contractors from whom the crown bought mercury at negotiated prices actually worked them for many years (Almadén until 1645, and Huancavelica until 1782). The mercury produced was distributed through the royal treasury system, and sold at prices fixed by the government. This royal monopoly of mercury was created partly to ensure supply, partly to produce a profit, and partly to force silver miners to pay the royalty due on silver – since, in law, a treasury office would sell them no more mercury until they had paid the fifth or tenth they owed on silver previously refined. In practice this system was less than wholly effective. Some silver escaped taxation, though nobody knew, or knows, how much; and some mercury escaped from the monopoly into private trading channels.

By the end of the sixteenth century, silver-mining was clearly the most heavily capitalized productive activity in Spanish America, the one showing most pronounced specialization and division of labor, and the one in which imported technology played the largest part. (Amalgamation, though developed industrially in New Spain, is taken here as an imported technology, since it had no native American roots.) The large mining towns would be instantly recognizable to a time-traveler from the present as industrial centers: smoke, smells, polluted water, noise, bustle, contrasting opulence and poverty, sheer size. By 1600 Potosí had some 80 thudding refining mills in operation, spread along several kilometers of the small river flowing through the town. To prolong milling beyond the rainy summer months, a series of interconnected dams had by then been built in a massif to the east of the town: another large investment. In New Spain, Pachuca had 49 operating mills c.1597; Taxco, 47; Zacatecas, 20. The entire colony had 372 active refineries – *haciendas de minas* – in which were installed 399 animal-driven stamp mills and 205 powered by water. Almost all the *haciendas* with waterwheels were in the center and west, where substantial rain falls, at least in the summer.[10]

CLOTH

Among other productive activities in the sixteenth-century Indies, those closest to mining in their degree of technical innovation and their reliance on the formation of fixed capital were cloth- and sugar-making. In textiles, there was a native tradition to draw on almost everywhere, and some regions, such as central Mexico and coastal Peru, had for many centuries past produced cloth of outstanding fineness and design. The Mexicans spun and wove cotton, lacking any wool-bearing animal. The Peruvians also used cotton; but their most remarkable weaving was of llama, alpaca, and vicuña wool, which they first spun to an astonishing fineness, a quality all the more remarkable in that it was achieved on simple, hand-held spindles. For weaving there was the backstrap loom, and an even simpler arrangement in which the warp is simply stretched between pegs set in the ground.

These looms, and the simple spindle, remained in use after the conquest, and indeed can still be seen in the Andes; men driving llama trains, for instance, spin as they walk along, twirling the spindle with one hand and feeding the wool onto it with the other. But the Spanish saw prospects of profit in quicker production, and soon imported European apparatus for that purpose, notably spinning wheels and treadle looms. These were devices of thirteenth-century origin, and in Spanish America continued in use until the nineteenth, finally succumbing to the power-driven machinery typical of the Industrial Revolution. But in sixteenth-century America they were radically new, and led to greater division of labor and much increased output.[11] They first came to Mexico in the 1530s, and followed on the conquerors' heels to South America. Complementing this technical advance, and accentuating its alien quality, was the arrival of two new fibers, of which sheep's wool was the more important in the long term. Its availability was a radical departure everywhere except in the central Andean natural range of the American camelids. Viceroy Mendoza himself brought the renowned Spanish merino sheep to New Spain, and ran flocks for his own profit. The more coarsely fleeced *churro* sheep had arrived sooner, via the Caribbean islands, where it had been introduced early, though without prospering.[12] Indians in both Mexico and South America quickly took to raising the animals themselves. Mendoza also made efforts to create a silk-raising and -weaving industry in New Spain, drawing on the great silk-working tradition of Moorish Spain. In this effort, Cortés was another keen participant. Silkworms were imported and mulberry plantations created to feed them. For much of the sixteenth century the production of silk thread prospered, especially in the south, and weaving throve in Mexico City and Puebla. Finally, though, with the rise of the trans-Pacific trade in the 1570s, competition from oriental silks overcame the Mexican effort.[13]

The production of thread and cloth with the new Spanish machines tended early to concentrate in workshops, commonly termed *obrajes*. These were generally premises in which carding, spinning, and weaving were carried out under a single roof. *Obrajes* are mentioned at Puebla as early as 1539, less than a decade after the town was founded. The inventory of Cortés's estate, drawn up in 1549, shows that he had built one near Cuernavaca, his seat from the early 1530s. This establishment contained a water-powered fulling mill, four functioning looms, and 21 spinning wheels. The labor force of carders, spinners, weavers, and fullers is estimated at 40 to 50. They worked both merino and coarser wool.[14] Fifty years or so later, mechanized textile production was a salient feature of the Mexican economy. In 1604, between 98 and 130 *obrajes* and smaller workshops called *trapiches* were producing cloth. They were widely distributed across the center and west of New Spain, with large clusters in and around Puebla, Mexico City, Texcoco, and Tlaxcala. The workforce in each is thought to have averaged about 50, so that the total number making cloth by these imported methods was perhaps 6,000. This was two-thirds of the number of workers in Mexican silver-mining in the same years.[15] How much cloth was produced, both in absolute quantity and in relation to native production by traditional methods, it is impossible to say; but clearly spinning and weaving in *obrajes* had become, by the late sixteenth century, a major component of the European side of the colonial economy. It had grown with backing from the crown, which was keen to ensure an adequate supply of affordable cloth in the colony.[16] Late in the century qualms arose about competition with producers in Spain, but not to the point where effective restrictions were applied to Mexican production.

Obrajes appeared in Peru soon after the conquest and multiplied there, again with royal support, in the mid 1500s. The emigration of Spanish master weavers and accompanying carders, fullers, and so on was encouraged. Most major towns soon had their *obrajes*, where cloth continued to be made for the rest of the colonial period.[17] Still, it was not Peru but Quito that became the leading textile region of South America. The province's central highlands offered great expanses of good grazing for sheep. And once local gold production began to decline, from about 1560, cloth-making seemed to leading settlers (most of them *encomenderos* still, in this rather isolated region) a promising means of acquiring cash. Fabric was a product compact and valuable enough to bear the high freight cost of export from Quito. Quito, indeed, for the rest of the colonial period depended on external textile sales to earn the money it needed to buy goods from elsewhere, and particularly from Europe; without cash it had no entry into the transatlantic trade. Its textile makers found they could sell cloth northwards to New Granada, for gold, and southwards to Peru and Charcas, for silver. The opulent age of *quiteño* cloth production was the seventeenth century. But the first *obrajes* probably date from the 1560s, when *encomenderos* and *caciques* joined forces to set up the workshops in native villages. The Spaniards looked for cash gains from sales. The native leaders, in return for organizing labor, took a salary from the *obraje*. But equally attractive to them was the fact that some of the profit went to pay their subjects' tributes, for which they were personally responsible. Thus native "community *obrajes*" came into being in Quito. By the opening of the seventeenth century fourteen of them existed in the highlands. Some of them had been founded, at least, on a notably large scale, with 200 or more workers. They remained one major base of textile production in Quito until the early eighteenth century. The other base consisted of shops owned privately, as in Mexico or Peru, that landowners set up on large rural estates where the primary raw material, sheep's wool, was produced. Between 1601 and 1628 the crown granted thirty-eight permits for the building of such *obrajes* in Quito.[18]

SUGAR

If cloth manufacture was often sited in cool highland areas suited to running sheep, the warmth needed for growing cane meant that sugar production was generally a lowland activity. The Atlantic islands settled by Portugal and Spain in the 1400s had generally proven welcoming to cane, and sale of sugar to the mainland had become good business, as Columbus learned in visits to Madeira before 1480. Planting cane, then, was logically among the first ventures in commercial farming tried in Hispaniola. The first mill was built there, at Concepción, in 1503. It was only after 1515, however, that, with the yield of gold placers declining, and the sugar price in Europe rising, settlers on Hispaniola gave serious attention to sugar. A strip of coast immediately west of Santo Domingo was planted with cane. The first sugar refined emerged from a small, animal-powered mill, or *trapiche*. In 1517 the first water-driven mill (*ingenio*) came into action. The design of its essential component, the cane-crushing rollers, had its origins in Sicily. It had been used in the Canaries, from where men were now brought to build and run mills in Hispaniola. Two vertical wooden rollers, geared together in counter-rotation, were the crux of the design. The cane was drawn between them, and its juice squeezed out as it went.[19] This device passed to the mainland, although there a three-roller pattern seems to have been used from the beginning, with the central roller driving, through gears mounted above, two others on each side. This arrangement gave the outer rollers opposing rotations, so that a piece of cane could be passed through in one direction, and then immediately back in the other to squeeze more juice from it.

Hispaniola thus became the first American colony exporting (to Spain) a plantation product. The other large islands followed suit in due course. Sugar production in New Spain, conversely, was largely for local consumption. Cane and milling technology had been carried there by 1530 from the Caribbean. The lower valleys around Cuernavaca and the coastal lowlands near Veracruz were the first good territory found for the crop. Then, as the century progressed, sugar planting extended westward into Michoacán, and Colima on the Pacific coast. Cortés, again, is the most famous of the early Mexican sugar raisers. His first mill (*c.*1529) at Tuxtla, on the Gulf coast, was probably the first in the colony. He built another, with an accompanying plantation, near Cuernavaca in the 1530s. The area around Cuernavaca became the major producing region, from a combination of climate, fertility, and above all closeness to the great market provided by Mexico City. The sweet tooth that New Spain – and the rest of Spanish America – developed in the sixteenth century constantly amazed newcomers and visitors from Europe, though it was a time in which the demand for sugar in Europe itself was apparently insatiable, as the largest American exporters of all, the planters in Brazil, found to their benefit. Indians as well as settlers took eagerly to sugar in New Spain, the natives probably consuming the less refined forms and the by-products such as molasses, while the clayed, whiter end-product went to colonists who could afford its higher price. By the early seventeenth century, fifty or sixty large *ingenios* and *trapiches* were at work in Mexico, producing perhaps 3.5–5 million kilograms a year; and many smaller mills besides.[20]

Some early Mexican sugar also went to Peru, though this trade had subsided by 1560 as a result of rising local output and a consequent drop in price. The first small sugar *trapiches* in Peru date from *c.*1540. A reliable source, Pedro de la Gasca, states that four were running in 1549. From then on production rose to meet a local demand as impressive as Mexico's. (In 1542 the city council of Lima had banned the making of candied fruit because it caused harm to the republic and turned men into idle vagabonds. Underlying, perhaps, what seems a curious puritanism were the facts that sugar was dear, it was valued as a medicine, and that importing it from Mexico drained scarce coin from Peru.)[21] From the start, Peruvian cane-growing was concentrated in the irrigated river valleys crossing the north and central coast. The great age of the plantations that grew up in those green patches amidst the desert was the seventeenth century, when the Peruvian mills supplied sugar to much of the west coast of South America and the central Andean highlands also.

The sugar refinery was a plant as complex and expensive as a silver-refining mill. The roller mechanism for expressing juice from the cane was a simpler device than the stamp mill; but the drive trains needed to carry energy from the waterwheel or animal team to the crushing machinery were similar in both cases. In place of the patio or refining tanks the sugar mill had a boiling house, equipped with large copper vats, and a purging house, with possibly hundreds of molds, where the boiled-down juice was formed into loaves. (The process is described in some detail in chapter 13, below, on colonial Brazil.) The apparatus, the buildings needed to hold it, and attached store rooms and living quarters were a costly proposition. In sixteenth-century Mexico a sugar mill cost 50,000 pesos; in the mid seventeenth century, refineries owned there by the regular clergy sold for up to twice that sum.[22]

DYES

Sixteenth-century sugar-making in New Spain has been described as Mexico's "first agro-industry,"[23] and the same may be said of it for Peru. It was not the only such industry, though certainly the largest. From the early 1560s New Spain also produced indigo, a rich blue dye extracted from leguminous plants of the genus *Indigofera*. Production began near Cuernavaca, but soon spread southwards into warm southern areas and Yucatan. To extract the dye, the leaves had to be cooked and mashed. Preparing indigo on a large scale thus required boilers and crushing machinery, sometimes driven by a waterwheel. The mills, of which more than 48 existed in Yucatan by the late 1570s, were therefore substantial pieces of fixed capital, though an order of magnitude smaller than sugar refineries in cost. Mexico sent almost 7,000 kilograms of indigo to Spain in 1576. In 1609 the export was 132,000 kilograms, worth almost 550,000 pesos, a very large sum indeed.[24]

Another dye was a still more valuable export of New Spain from the early years. This was cochineal, a red powder made by crushing the dried body of a small insect living on the nopal cactus. The preparation of cochineal differed, however, from indigo extraction in that it used no mechanical processing, or indeed any imported technology at all. Pre-conquest practices persisted throughout the colonial period, with Indians tending, collecting, drying, and pulverizing the insects. Southern Mexico, particularly the Oaxaca region, was the producing region. Spaniards bought the finished dye, mainly for sale across the Atlantic. The first export to Spain was in 1526; the first Mexican cochineal reached Antwerp in 1552, and London by 1569. By 1600 or so, Spain received perhaps 113,000–136,000 kilograms of Mexican cochineal yearly, worth some 600,000 pesos.[25] Throughout colonial times the dye remained New Spain's second export in value, behind (though far behind) silver.

SHIPBUILDING

A very different product of southern Mexico, and one relying on, indeed embodying, imported technology, was ships. From 1522 to the late 1530s, Cortés organized shipbuilding at different places on the Pacific coast – primarily Tehuantepec and Acapulco – for projected explorations. That he could have found the necessary carpentry skills among his men so early might seem surprising. But that simply indicates how far bands of conquistadores were samples of the general Spanish population rather than professional soldiers. In 1521 Cortés had made excellent use of one carpenter-conqueror, Martín López, to build the brigantines that gave him control of the lake during the final siege of Tenochtitlan. It was not so much Mexico, however, as Central America that developed as the main shipbuilding area on the American west coast for most of the sixteenth century. The first vessels were made in Panama in 1517, at Balboa's order, for exploration. Others followed in the 1520s, including those that Pizarro used for southward exploration towards Peru. Then the pace of building rose c.1530 to supply the needs of a new trade in Indian slaves from Nicaragua to Panama. By 1533 over thirty ships were sailing the Pacific, half of them or more slavers. Nicaragua's being the source of the slaves was certainly the prime reason for shipbuilding's rise there; but the region also had abundant wood for hulls and masts, fibers for ropes, and pitch.[26] Wealth of raw material, particularly of wood, later underlay also the development of Guayaquil, in southern Quito, as a shipbuilding center. By the late sixteenth century it was a major producer of shipping. Since passage of Cape Horn was a fearful obstacle to the movement of Atlantic shipping into the Pacific until the eighteenth century, Guayaquil and Central America were long almost the sole suppliers of vessels for the considerable trade that developed up and down the west coast with the settlement of Quito, Peru, and Chile.

CRAFTS

Ocean-going ships were the among the most striking examples of European technical innovation in sixteenth-century America, far exceeding the canoes of the native Caribbean or the large rafts of pre-conquest north-west South America in their ability to move cargoes and use the sea as a relatively rapid, multi-directional highway. They were also the most obvious and imposing products of Spanish artisanry. But artisanry on a smaller scale had just as profound an aggregate effect on the lives of colonizers and colonized. The speed with which Spanish craftsmen appeared in America and went to work might at first seem surprising; but, given the opportunities for gain that the inevitable demand for familiar goods from *encomenderos* and other wealthy settlers offered, it is less so. Probably at least a tenth of Spanish settlers in Peru up to 1560 were active craftsmen, 800 or more of them.[27] In order of descending numbers, the following were present and at work: first, tailors and shoemakers; ironsmiths; builders; then lesser numbers of silversmiths, barber-surgeons, muleteers, pharmacists, confectioners, arms makers, candlemakers, and musicians – and even a bookbinder.[28] Some specialization and subdivision of trades was initially lost in the transfer from Spain; but by mid-century there was little available there by way of craft products that could not be made locally, if a little more roughly, in Lima, Mexico City, or other provincial cities. This was quite clear in the Peruvian civil wars of the 1540s. Most of the muskets, armor, swords, horseshoes, and pikes used by all sides were locally made. Builders and carpenters soon imposed a familiar and enduring appearance on towns. "By 1545 the outward aspect of Lima was already what it was to remain for centuries, long lines of bare adobe walls broken by splendid wooden doors."[29] Gonzalo Pizarro, during his rebel leadership of Peru in the 1540s, kept a band of players capable of performing Renaissance part music. Musicians might double as dance masters. In 1552 a resident organ maker built a substantial instrument for Lima cathedral.

Clearly most of the goods produced by these immigrant craftsmen went to Spanish settlers. Equally clearly, incoming artisans could and did draw on rich native skills in working stone and cloth, and in the Andean case, metal as well; and to that must be added the ironworking abilities of Africans. But still a powerful acculturating influence flowed through Spanish craftsmen in the opposite direction, for many of the apprentices trained by arriving Spanish artisans were Indians and blacks. Spaniards were impressed by the speed with which Indians imitated and put into practice the new techniques (in, for example, weaving with Spanish looms, and making European-style musical instruments).[30] It is easy to imagine the pleasure of a native stonemason who, after working for years with nothing better than a cutting tool made of some harder stone, or at best bronze, was suddenly presented with a steel chisel. Thus Spanish techniques, tastes, and standards were quickly diffused into the new, miscegenizing culture.

FARMING

Most craftsmen worked in towns. And colonial towns, with their imported architecture and layout, and the various representatives of state power that they contained, as well as the new techniques of immigrant artisans, were obvious concentrations of acculturative influence. But signs and forces of change flooded across the countryside, too, as Spanish farming practice expanded. If introduced micro-organisms made themselves felt all too soon in epidemics, far larger fauna were not far behind: hens, goats, sheep, pigs, donkeys, cattle, horses. These animals, in fact, established themselves in most parts of Spanish America before any definite farming began. In the Caribbean islands they ran wild from 1493 on, and multiplied into numbers that not only fed the island settlers but provided vigorous stock to occupy the mainland. The rangy Spanish pig was as telling an ally of the conquistador as the horse – indefatigable, omnivorous, adaptable to almost any climate and vegetation America had to offer, from tropical swamp to highland desert. The rough and tough cattle were equally invasive; though more selective in their feed than pigs, they were better able to range fast and wide in pursuit of the grasses and grains they sought. Horses did likewise. The result was that the natural pastures of the mainlands, notably in northern Mexico and the plains of the Río de la Plata, but in many smaller areas elsewhere, saw enormous herds of feral animals appear with astonishing speed. The grasslands, never grazed before, and free, like those earlier in the Caribbean, of natural foes of the new animals, whether microbes, insects, or large predators, offered conditions in which numbers could grow tenfold in three or four years.[31] This bovine and equine paradise was fleeting, to be sure; damage from overgrazing was apparent in northern Mexico in the closing decades of the sixteenth century. But the numbers, if no longer explosively increasing, remained high. In 1586, two cattlemen in the Zacatecas region branded 75,000 young steers on the large estates they had by then created to supply the mines with meat and leather, and to send stock south for sale in central Mexico.[32]

Some of that northern beef ended up in the diet of Indians in the center. Indeed, as cattle multiplied, and the price of beef fell, meat protein became widely available to the mass of the native people for the first time in their history. It was never cheaper, perhaps, than in the mid sixteenth century. That, too, was perhaps the time when milk, cream, and cheese began to assume the large part they now play in the Mexican diet, a part surprisingly larger than in the Spanish. Again, though Indians themselves rarely raised the large imported animals, they took quickly to keeping pigs, sheep, and chickens, so that beef was not the only flesh now available to them. In sum, then, for native Mexicans the arrival of European domestic creatures brought a distinct modification of diet, and some change in the manner of producing at least its protein content, from cultivation of beans to raising of small animals. The same goes, with regional variations, for American natives elsewhere.

The dietary gain (if gain it was) came, however, at a cost. Indians had never had any need to fence crops in New Spain, since there were no large grazing animals to eat them. That changed with the arrival of cattle. By the 1540s destruction of maize plots was a severe problem in central and southern Mexico. Viceroy Mendoza went so far as to ban cattle ranches (*estancias*) in the valleys around Oaxaca; and commented to Don Luis de Velasco, his successor,

"The Spaniards cry that I have ruined them, and they are right ... But ... if cattle are allowed, the Indians will be destroyed."[33] The difficulty was not just that cattle trampled and ate the maize, but that aspiring Spanish stockraisers had a strong motive to push Indians off their communal lands to secure grazing. This was a conflict wherever in America Indians farmed land that could feed cattle. In New Spain, Mendoza and Velasco, with crown backing, sought to mitigate it by urging the use of the northern plains for stockraising. To that end, Velasco issued land grants in the north during the 1550s. There was by then in any case the added attraction of the growing market for meat and hides in the northern silver mines, besides which it suited all Spaniards if cattle in any way disrupted the nomadic Chichimeca of the *altiplano*, who clearly posed a potential threat to Spanish presence there. This was not the only case in which cattle were explorers and conquerors alongside men.

Sheep could pose similar problems, especially since, in contrast to cattle, their main grazing areas remained in central and southern Mexico. Following the Iberian pattern, sheep breeders soon began to practice seasonal transhumance. By the late 1570s flocks totaling 200,000 or so moved for the winter from the surroundings of Querétaro to Michoacán; there was a similar movement from Puebla to the Gulf coast. Villages along these sheep runs suffered crop damage; indeed, a heavy concentration of sheep in a particular area could produce wider and more lasting damage in the form of soil erosion and loss of fertility.[34] Goats, too, with their predilection for eating plants right down to their roots, were a mixed blessing. They could thrive on steep, dry land where no other useful animal would, yielding meat, milk, and hides, but often, again, at the cost of erosion.

In general, indeed, it is hard to strike the balance of the pros and cons for the land and native people of the Spanish American empire of the introduction of European livestock. The equation inevitably contains too many imponderables for a clear answer to be evident. The gain of a new source of protein was offset by loss of crops and probably of some farming land (though some of the land occupied by grazing animals had clearly fallen largely or wholly vacant with the collapse of native numbers). Oxen, horses, donkeys, and then mules, complemented the sole American beast of burden, the llama of the central Andes. Elsewhere, they relieved humans of the age-old task of carrying freight, but again at a cost in land. The same was true of their provision of useful materials beside food. Leather for clothing, shoes and general use became cheap and plentiful, where it had largely been unavailable before. Wool there had never been before, except in the natural range of the Andean camelids, from Chile to southern Ecuador. The existence of some native groups was changed radically by the arrival of the new creatures. The nomads of the South American pampas became horsemen hunting the wild cattle that multiplied endlessly on those plains.[35] The Navajo of New Mexico and Arizona turned from raiding their farming Pueblo neighbors for a living to tending the *churro* sheep and weaving its wool. In the more central areas of complex culture the changes were perhaps less profound, more a matter of adding what was useful in the new than of radically changing the old. Nonetheless, a world with the European domestic animals present must have seemed quite distinct from the previous one without them; as distinct, perhaps, as the times in Europe before and after the arrival of mechanical means of transport.

Less dramatically obvious than introduced fauna, but equally pervasive, were the new food-yielding flora that the Spaniards imported: citrus fruits, peaches, pears, apples, grapes, melons, bananas; onions, olives, radishes; sugar cane; rice; and the standard European grains, with wheat pre-eminent among them for the Spaniards. These were not an equal exchange for what America gave the world by way of new foods, beginning with maize and potatoes. But they made their mark on the American landscape; and Indians, if they did not eat many of these new vegetable foods, assuredly were soon familiar with them as the colonists, beginning with the *encomenderos*, demanded that they grow them. It must have been a great relief to the Spanish to discover in Mexico so much good land for wheat. The Caribbean islands and Panama had been a disappointment in that respect, and there was little a Spaniard hankered after more than fine wheaten bread. Highland New Spain proved ideal for the crop. The first major area put to wheat, in the 1530s, was the vicinity of Puebla, and the nearby Atlixco valley. Then, as the northward mining movement started late in the next decade, wheat followed, and so, gradually, "the former wastelands of the Bajío [became] converted into the most important, prosperous, and modern agricultural area of New Spain."[36] Travelers from Europe were amazed by the high yields that wheat farmers extracted from the Bajío. Its farming for wheat, and maize also, was another aspect of that inclusion of the north into the mainstream of Mexican life for which silver-mining was the prime motor. In the more distant north, wheat- and maize-growing appeared near mining centers wherever suitable soil, and water for irrigation, could be found. Other, smaller, wheat areas developed in Michoacán and elsewhere in the west. By the end of the sixteenth century, colonists generally had all the white bread they wanted, and newcomers commented on its quality. More indicative of long trends in Mexican history, though, was the appearance in the north of the *tortilla de harina*, the tortilla made from wheat flour. Here was symbolized in food the distinctively *mestizo* culture of northern New Spain: the alien grain prepared in the thin, flat form of the traditional Mexican maize bread.

In South America, too, land for wheat was abundant, although what was to become the largest and most famous wheat area of all, the wet pampa of Argentina, was not planted with it until the nineteenth century, for lack of demand. On the western side of the continent that the Spanish mainly occupied, they were able to take advantage, like the native cultures before them, of the effect of varying altitude on local climate to create niches for wheat-growing. The coastal valleys of central Peru yielded enough of it, under irrigation, to supply the coastal towns in the sixteenth and seventeenth centuries. Cochabamba and other mid-altitude basins sent wheat to Potosí and other highland mining centers in Charcas. Central Chile, with its Mediterranean climate, proved ideal wheat territory, and exported large amounts of it to Peru in the eighteenth century. In the northern Andes, the elevated plains around Bogotá and Caracas gave the wheat that was locally needed.

Spaniards in America naturally began with a preference for familiar European foods, but where these were not available – and increasingly as the proportion of American-born settlers grew – they ate the New World's products as well. Maize became almost as basic for them as it was for natives; and in fact crossed the Atlantic to become a staple in north-western Spain in the seventeenth century. The potato was another American vegetable that Spaniards and colonists took to, after initial suspicion. Indeed it was the Spaniards who carried the potato from the Andes to Middle America, and also to Europe. Potato-growing began in the Spanish Basque country before 1600.[37] Other examples of American foods adopted more or less eagerly by colonials – chocolate, tomatoes, avocados, chile, and so on – are legion.

Nonetheless, it was the settlers' preference for their familiar European foods, rather than their consumption of American crops, that proved disruptive to Indians. Moreover, this disruption was magnified by their importing alien notions about the tenure of land on which crops and animals were raised. The concept of private landholding had scarcely appeared in native American cultures. Only in the Inca and Aztec polities, at the pinnacle of the nobility, was there any trace of it, and that was a late pre-conquest development. The prevailing concept of land was that it was communal property, whose use could be allocated to individuals or families as long as they worked it. The Spanish, by contrast, though expecting to find some land attached to towns for communal uses such as grazing and charcoal-making, thought of it first as something to be possessed individually and exclusively.

Legal possession came from the monarch, since, as in the Reconquest, all areas newly conquered were defined as *tierras de realengo*, or royal territory. The crown might itself grant the land away, or, as more commonly happened in America, for reasons of distance, delegate the granting to some colonial authority – conqueror, governor, viceroy, and often, in the early days, to town councils. Generally these locally made grants became permanent only when the crown confirmed them.[38] Many Spaniards in sixteenth-century America asked for and received land in this way, from urban plots for a house to great swathes of countryside for grazing. *Encomenderos* were among the earliest applicants, since their allocations of Indians did not include land. Far from all the land that Spaniards acquired in the 1500s, however, came to them in this state regularized way. Some was bought from Indians, generally from *caciques* wrongfully alienating communal territory for personal gain or to secure cash with which to pay their people's tribute. And some was simply occupied (as when, for example, cattle strayed on to unassigned land), or seized. Doubtless, *de facto* occupation became more tempting and simpler as land fell vacant through population loss. But how much of the native community land coming under Spanish control was already unused for that reason, and how much was torn from active cultivators, is impossible to say. The proportion certainly varied by region. On the coasts of Peru and New Spain, for instance, where population losses were particularly severe, a larger proportion of the land taken by Spaniards had fallen into disuse than in the highlands of either area.

In the 1590s the crown began to accept payments to regularize deficient or absent titles, in a program of "composition" that went along with a new policy introduced under Philip II of auctioning off, rather than simply granting, new land titles.[39] The change reflects not only Philip's always desperate need of funds, but also a growing demand for land in the Indies after the mid-century. Spaniards' interest in agriculture had risen slowly from a slender start in the immediate post-conquest years. At that time it seemed likely that Indians, working their own land, would supply as tribute most of what the colonists wanted by way of food. Some *encomenderos*, it is true, could be found even then who wanted land to produce food for sale, and still more of them, perhaps, whose desire for land sprang from a mixture of commercial and psychological motives, since landowning was part of the lordly lifestyle they aspired to create for themselves. But still, it was only when a blend of demographic decline and rising Spanish numbers made the notion of a tribute-based existence for settlers increasingly improbable that landowning became a general ambition grounded in economic reality.[40] This realization, in the middle decades of the century, coincided, furthermore, with the rise of the silver-mining centers in the central Andes and in northern New Spain. It was not hard to see in that development good possibilities for profitable sales of farm products.

And so there appeared in the latter part of the century a multiplicity of private farms, of varying sizes, owned mainly by Spaniards and *criollos* (American-born whites), but some also by blacks, *castas* (mixed-blood people), and undoubtedly some Indian leaders. In New Spain, the term *labor* was generally used for a small farm producing wheat and other crops for a local market. In the Andes, *chácara* (Quechua for sown land) had the same sense. In both areas, *estancia* meant land held for grazing. On many of these farms the owner might have been found physically laboring, though, if he were white, he would certainly rather not have done so. By the end of the century, the size of the holdings varied enormously, from a few dozen hectares of good arable land in a valley floor up to many thousands of sparse grazing on some arid plain. There was much buying and selling of land, so that farms' size and boundaries shifted constantly. With time, some of the larger holdings began to take on the look of the classic Spanish American rural estate, the *hacienda de campo*. But that term, and the institution itself – a sizable piece of land with a large house, laborers' living quarters, barns, stables, workrooms, and so on at its center, often self-supplying in foodstuffs and basic craft goods, indeed a rounded and self-contained community – belongs to the seventeenth century and later. The first colonial century saw the bases of the rural *hacienda* laid down in smallholdings. And in fact smallholdings remained an important social and economic element of the country scene of the colonies until the end.

Even the smallest private farm was likely to use European iron and steel tools to prepare the land for sowing, rather than the wooden digging sticks that were the most advanced native tilling tools. Larger places might well have steel-bladed plows (over 12,000 plowshares were sent from Spain to Mexico alone in 1597)[41] and oxen or mules to draw them, though clearly there were many steep fields in the Andes and elsewhere where they would not serve. Still, the great grain lands opened up by the Spanish in the first century, particularly those of New Spain, were worked extensively, as in Europe, rather than in the intensive American fashion. Yields per hectare were undoubtedly lower than the amazing levels sometimes achieved by native methods (with maize around the lakes in the Valley of Mexico, for example); but the use of animal-drawn tools raised the yield per unit of human labor expended on cultivation. The outcome was that European-style farming made inroads into even the supply of traditionally native foods. By 1630, for example, Mexico City's maize came largely from colonists' farms around it rather than from Indian communities. This rise of commercial agriculture was promoted still more by the use of animal-drawn carts. It was simple and relatively cheap to move farm products to market over considerable distances – tens, even hundreds, of kilometers – where the terrain allowed carting roads to be made. If it had not been so, the existence of the mining towns on the Mexican *altiplano*, for example, would have been distinctly more tenuous than it was. But where carts could not go, mule trains generally could.

By 1600, then, many fertile regions of Spanish America, and some regions that were not so fertile, were well scattered with privately held smallholdings, farms, and nascent estates. Few of the owners were native people. These lands were worked by predominantly alien techniques to produce predominantly alien crops; though with time those methods were applied also to some native crops. Large, imported, animals were a key part of the new agricultural method, putting non-human power for the first time at the service of American agriculture. Large tracts of private land, particularly those unsuited by climate, terrain, or fertility to tillage, served as grazing for these exotic beasts – not merely those used for draught, but a far larger number raised to give meat and raw materials, particularly wool and hides. Meat in the amounts now available was an innovation in the American diet. Similarly, wool and leather became unprecedentedly common. The animals' numbers multiplied prodigiously in the new environment (almost 1.3 million cattle in New Spain by 1620, by one estimate, and 8 million sheep and goats combined).[42] In among the private landholdings, to be sure, native communities survived, each with its communal lands, safeguarded by Spanish law, that its people still worked by pre-Hispanic methods. Native farmers grew crops for their own subsistence, and certainly also for cash sale, where marketing opportunities existed (as, for instance, in nearby colonial towns). But Indian towns and villages had lost at least some of their best land to Spanish purchase, theft, and incursion. They were also fewer than a century before, inevitably so as a result of demographic contraction, and of Spanish policies, enacted from the mid 1500s on, of gathering Indians into new "congregations."

Native Labor

One purpose of creating those congregations had been easier access to native labor. Indians were brought together so that they could then be more easily removed to work in tasks profitable to both colonists and the colonial state. This was one in a whole progression of schemes devised to exploit native labor. In fact, questions of how, and how much, Indians should work for Spaniards were among the most hotly debated issues of imperial governance in the sixteenth century. The questions were not merely the practical ones of how to use a rapidly shrinking resource, but also the moral ones of how to reconcile the required conversion, civilization, and good treatment of native Americans with the soon evident need to compel them to work if the colonies were to sustain their populations and produce profits.

On the mainland, *encomienda* was the first solution tried. *Encomenderos* were supposed to look to the spiritual and material wellbeing of the Indians granted to them in return for tribute received. That tribute, for several decades, might take the form of labor ("personal service" was the term used) as well as offerings in bullion or goods. The outcome, though, tended to be as in the Caribbean islands: excessive and uncontrollable demands from the *encomenderos*, and rare fulfillment of the obligation to enlighten and improve the Indians. That imbalance, among other causes, led to the crown's attack on the *encomienda* in the New Laws of 1542, and, seven years later, to a ban on personal service from Indians in *encomienda*. Though neither the *encomienda* nor labor exactions in it disappeared at this point, nor in some places for long afterwards, the 1549 order does mark the beginning of the end of *encomienda* as the prime source of native workers in the central colonial areas.

It was replaced in those regions by state-directed systems of draft labor, in which native communities were ordered to supply a small proportion of their grown men at fixed intervals for assignment to particular tasks. In the central Andes the mechanism was called *mita* (Quechua for "time" or "turn"), the term used by the Incas for their own system of obligatory state labor, and the Indians caught up in the Spanish scheme clearly saw in it a link with preconquest practice. Elsewhere the Spanish word *repartimiento* ("distribution") covered the draft system (one of several official uses to which that word was put in the colonies). In New Spain a parallel existed in the native institution of compulsory public work, *coatequitl*, which continued to operate in surviving Indian polities after the conquest, though the name was not applied to the Spanish draft system.

Examples of ad hoc drafts can be found in the mid-century. In 1550, for example, Viceroy Mendoza drafted Indians to work on Spanish wheat farms around the capital, to relieve a grain shortage. Again, after severe flooding in 1555 Viceroy Velasco put some 6,000 Indians to work in building dikes and diverting streams to protect Mexico City.[43] Similar cases occur in the Andes also in the 1550s and 1560s. But in both regions it was the 1570s that saw draft labor generally and uniformly set up, through the efforts of viceroys Toledo, in Peru, and Enríquez, in New Spain.

At first the drafts were not overwhelmingly onerous. In the Valley of Mexico, the "take" in the *repartimiento* created for farming was 2 percent of adult men during the growing season, and 1 percent in the rest of the year.[44] In the most notorious draft of all, the *mita* organized by Toledo for Potosí in the mid 1570s, some 16 percent of grown men from most native communities lying between Cuzco and Potosí were ordered to move to the mines and stay there for a year. The total number was some 13,500; but each man had to work only one week in three, so that some 4,500, or slightly over 5 percent, were actively laboring in mining or refining at any moment.

In their initial forms, these drafts may actually have spread the labor burden more evenly among the native population than the *encomienda* had done, since some *encomenderos* worked their people pitilessly, and others lightly. Another gain over earlier "personal service" was that draftees received a statutory wage. It was probably not a living wage for a family; but in the *encomienda*, with the rarest exceptions, no wage had been paid – the intended reward of instruction in Christianity and European ways was intangible, and rarely delivered. In principle, also, draft labor should have given Indians some protection from abusive employers, since the state, represented by an allocating official, stood between employer and worker. But the benefit in practice may have been small. From the administration's standpoint, drafts offered two economic gains. One was that the shrinking labor supply could be channeled to what was considered essential production, defined as "public works." These included, certainly, the building of roads, bridges, drainage works, churches, and other public edifices; but, more crucial to both state and individuals, they also included agriculture and mining. Second, drafts broke the close control over labor that *encomenderos* had exercised; now workers could be given to incoming Spaniards who might well be more entrepreneurial than aging conquistadores and their socially aspiring offspring.

In the areas of intense economic activity by the Spanish, *mita* and *repartimiento* proved, though, inadequate almost as soon as put in place. In New Spain, severe epidemics, possibly of typhus, shrank the remaining Indians' numbers drastically in the late 1570s. In the central Andes also, the native population continued to fall, while the demand for workers at Potosí and other silver mines, at Huancavelica (the source of the indispensable mercury), and generally for farming (to feed the booming mining towns), leapt upward. Constant immigration from Spain created further imbalance between supply and demand in labor. One outcome was that the draft quotas increased in the closing years of the century. By 1600 some draftees were working every other year at Potosí, instead of one in seven. A parallel result, clear in its economic logic, was that Spaniards needing workers hired them individually wherever they could find them. Since almost all adult native men were liable for drafting, such private hiring cut into the numbers available for forced work – from which Indians were ever more anxious to escape, of course, as the "take" increased. By about 1600, then, working for wages was well ensconced in regions and activities which had a high demand for labor. The numbers are clearest in silver-mining. In New Spain the total workforce was counted *c.*1597 at 9,143, of whom 6,261 were waged laborers (68.5 percent), 1,619 *repartimiento* men (17.7 percent), and 1,263 black slaves (13.8 percent). In Potosí, a few years later, the total daily workforce was about 9,900, of whom some 55 percent were waged. If other mines by then active in the Potosí district are taken into account, the proportion of wage workers rises, since those mines received no draft. Miners and refiners in the central Andes used hardly any black slaves; they reportedly succumbed too soon to disease in the high-altitude chill to make buying them a good investment. And in neither New Spain nor in the central Andes were any *encomienda* Indians working in mining by the beginning of the seventeenth century.

Hiring Indians for wages spread across productive activities controlled by colonials. Some native workers in textile shops, some on estates, and some in artisanry received negotiated cash sums for their labors. The evidence, though thin and scattered, is also that such workers' wages rose in the late 1500s, and rose in fact faster than prices, so that their real income grew.[45] The relative price of labor should certainly have increased as workers became scarcer, and as, under more or less permanent contract, they acquired skills valuable to their employers. So desirable did skilled workers become that employers competed for them, luring them away with offers of higher wages. In some cases advances on wages were given not so much to tie a worker through debt to a workplace as to attract him to it in the first place.

Thus, in the regions most heavily developed economically by colonists (which corresponded generally with the areas of prior high native culture, but expanded now by silver discoveries), employment of Indians moved in the sixteenth century from the retainer-like relationship of the *encomienda*, to the state-run (but salaried) draft of *mita* or *repartimiento*, to the private and individual contracts of wage labor. A variety of causes drove this progression: the crown's reliance on, then rejection of, *encomienda* as a method of settlement; rising immigration from Spain; and, most powerful of all, the effects of native depopulation in, first, shrinking the pool of available workers, and, second, forcing the colonists to start organizing essential production themselves.

Even in the core colonial areas of New Spain and the central Andes, however, the coming of a new stage did not necessarily mean the disappearance of a previous one. *Mita* labor was crucial to Andean silver-mining to the end of colonial times, because it provided a cheap and reliable supplement to wage labor. Similarly, in New Spain, although the then viceroy ended drafts for agriculture in 1632 because they had become unnecessary, *repartimiento* for silver-mining remained active, at least for mines in the center and south.

And in peripheral regions, where whites and their enterprises were fewer and less dominant, use of native labor took a variety of courses. A common feature was survival of the *encomienda* as a source of labor, despite the decree halting personal service in 1549.[46] In outlying parts of New Spain such as New Mexico and Yucatan, as well as in remoter regions of South America, such as Venezuela, New Granada, Paraguay, and Chile, it little mattered to the crown if the *encomienda* persisted in its initial form, since there was little to be lost there, politically or economically, to a well-rooted seigneurial elite in society. In fact, it suited the crown's purpose that the *encomienda* should continue to play its anchoring role in those more or less marginal places, holding settlers usefully in place on the land. It was typical of the peripheries, also, that unless some new economic resource or new export opportunity appeared, competition for labor was slight; hence the economic need to move from *encomienda* to draft was small, or arrived much later than in Peru and New Spain. Again, the marginal areas had had small, weak, or no state structures before the conquest, and little in the way of state-organized labor; so there was no precedent in them to help the Spanish to set up their own drafts.

A blend of *encomienda* and *repartimiento*, whereby *encomenderos* were the main recipients of draft labor, emerged in Paraguay and New Granada. In Chile, by contrast, while *encomienda* continued to provide laborers until the late eighteenth century, drafts were not used. Colonists not holding *encomiendas* rented workers from those who did, in a practice suggesting the reduction of *encomienda* Indians almost to chattel status. It was, in fact, precisely in Chile that outright enslavement of Indians persisted most strongly. After the great native revolt in the south beginning in 1598, slaving was specifically permitted; and until abolition in 1674, Indians taken in war were legally put to work as slaves. Indian slavery had generally been ended in the empire *c*.1550 because of its blatant contradiction of the principle, by then well established, that Indians were intrinsically free, and also, perhaps, because slavery was a labor system afflicted with the same rigidities as *encomienda*, when what was needed was the flexibility in allocating workers that the draft provided. But an old policy persisted that Indians who rebelled against Spanish rule could legitimately be enslaved. This meant continued Indian slaving not only in the southern extreme of the empire but in the far north as well, when Comanches and Apaches raided New Mexico. Calling this "rebellion" bordered on sophistry, since those peoples had never been under Spanish control. But it was a convenient fiction, for it provided a steady, if small, supply of slaves to northern New Spain on into the seventeenth century while also helping to sustain settlement in the distant north, since colonists profited from selling the slaves they took.

BLACK SLAVERY

In aggregate, though, Indians were far outnumbered as slaves by blacks in the sixteenth century, as slave imports from Africa rose with the passing years. And those blacks were an increasingly large supplement to native labor in its various forms, as the indigenous numbers fell. Their participation in higher-level occupations, such as management and artisanry, was important as a social as well as an economic phenomenon. But where they became all but essential to the colonial economy was in providing labor that native people could not, for whatever reason, supply. The extreme example is agricultural work, particularly in sugar, on the large Caribbean islands, where literally no indigenous people remained after the mid sixteenth century. Sugar cultivation was the work almost entirely of black slaves everywhere, for at least two reasons. The warmer, lowland areas in which the cane thrived, such as the Mexican and Peruvian coasts, had suffered more severe losses of Indians than the highlands; and, at least in the Spaniards' stereotypical view, Africans withstood hot, heavy work better than Indians. That same opinion, added to the generally low level of prior native political, and hence labor, organization in tropical areas, led also to black slaves' often being used to pan gold, since alluvial gold tended to accumulate in the lower reaches of rivers. Hence gold extraction in New Granada, the metal's main Spanish American source, became largely the work of blacks. So was the cultivation of cacao in southern lowland Quito and in Venezuela.[47]

TRADE IN THE COLONIES

The products of the variety of workers and of working arrangements found in sixteenth-century Spanish America reached a wide range of consumers. Indians farming their communities' lands produced largely for their own subsistence. But, when ordered by Spanish officials to work in *repartimiento,* those same men might find themselves on a colonist's estate plowing land to grow wheat that would be sent to a market a few, or a few hundred, kilometers away. One further profound difference between economic practice in 1500 and, say, 1600 (besides technology, forms of land tenure, labor systems, and the like) was an immense growth in exchange over distance. Such exchange had not been unknown in native times, of course. Columbus met coastal trading canoes off the Honduras coast in 1502; Aztec *pochteca* brought the products of northern Central America to Tenochtitlan; the Inca state directed movement of goods up and down the Andes. But the distances, as well as the size and variety of trade, grew vastly once the Spanish came. Peru had never before dealt directly with Central America and Mexico; nor the Andean province of Charcas with the Río de la Plata; nor the Greater Antilles with Panama. Clearly ships, carts, oxen, horses, and mules were the key to this immense expansion of inter-change, offering swift and relatively cheap carriage of large volumes. Also pro-pelling it, of course, was the belief, grounded in much European experience, that trade was the surest source of profit. Spanish American colonial experi-ence validated that belief from the earliest days until the last. Then again, trade over distance grew and thrived precisely because the possibility of moving goods encouraged settlers to look for places where this or that item could easily be grown or made. Thus they found and developed large areas enjoying com-parative advantages for some particular purpose. The Bajío proved ideal in soil and climate for wheat and maize, and the grain could be moved cheaply enough by cart to central Mexico or the northern mines to allow for profitable sale there. Southern Peru offered excellent conditions for grapes; wine produced there could be cheaply sent northward by ship to Lima and beyond (even to New Spain), and by mule to the Andean mines, where it competed success-fully by the late sixteenth century with Spanish wine that carried a still higher freight cost. Large and specialized zones of production were in clear evidence across the empire before 1600: the two just mentioned; the cattle lands of nor-thern New Spain; the sheep lands of Puebla, and of Quito in South America; the sugar areas of the Antilles, southern New Spain, and northern Peru; and the developing mule and cattle lands of Tucumán in present northern Argentina. In an impressive realization of the potential of economic geography, production fed trade and trade stimulated production in these naturally favored areas.

Most of the exchange of these agricultural products, and manufactures made from them, was within the colonies, either within single *audiencia* territories or between them. The most powerful magnets of trade were the administrative cities and the mining towns – especially the latter, because they both tended to have large populations and were the source of the most desirable commodity exchangeable for goods: silver (whether in unminted or coined form). By one historian's rough estimate, a little over half the silver refined in Spanish America went to buy goods produced in the colonies; and these regional purchases by mining centers amounted to 60 or 70 percent of the value of transoceanic trade to and from the mining areas.[48] If these calculations are right (and much descriptive evidence argues for them), bullion produced in America did not, as often assumed, flood directly out to foreign destinations in Europe and the Orient, but instead passed through and energized internal trade circuits before it left America. Moreover, far from all of it did leave, though the fraction remaining undoubtedly varied with time.

OCEANIC TRADE

What sixteenth-century Europeans saw, however, and East Asians soon after them also, as they looked towards Spanish America, was not a developing structure of internal exchange, but shiploads of gold and silver crossing the oceans towards them. The transatlantic trading system of Spain, and then the trans-Pacific commerce, have likewise long captured the attention of historians; and with good reason, since the these were maritime operations to rival in scale and pomp anything before or since, and economic movements that produced irreversible effects on Europe and the wider world.

The small groups of ships used by the explorers gradually expanded with discoveries and conquests into flotillas, then into fleets, and finally, in the second half of the century, into great armadas carrying people and European cloth, tools, wine, foods, and other exports to America, and silver, dyes, leather, sugar, and medicinal plants back to Spain. In 1526 sailings of single merchant ships to and from the Indies were forbidden. Convoys, for safety from enemy attack and for best use of the limited number of pilots capable of mathematically based navigation, were the rule from then on. By the best estimate, at least 85 percent of Spanish transatlantic sailing from 1500 to 1650 was done in convoy.[49] Security increased from *c.*1540 with the entry into service of galleons, ships initially of perhaps 250 tons (though they reached 800 by the end of the century) in which some of the fine line of Mediterranean galleys was combined with the seagoing ability of Atlantic trading vessels to produce a relatively fast and handy fighting ship that could also carry cargo.

By the mid 1560s the classic Spanish American "fleet system" was in place, undertaking the Carrera de Indias, the "Indies run," each year. Two fleets were the backbone of the communication structure between Spain and America: the *flota* (simply "fleet") sailing to and from New Spain, and the *galeones* (galleons), whose destination was the Caribbean side of the Isthmus of Panama. Both fleets might consist of several dozen ships, though as important as the number was the growing size of the vessels as the century wore on. And both fleets included galleons, for defense and for freight of the main return cargo, silver. The isthmus-bound *galeones* were so called because that fleet had a larger fraction of galleons, to bring back safely the larger fraction of American silver that South America produced.

The standard rhythm of the Carrera was, broadly, as follows: the fleets should leave Spain in the early to mid summer; cross the Atlantic via the Canaries, following Columbus's route; enter the Caribbean in late summer through the Lesser Antilles; proceed to their appointed destinations on the isthmus or the Gulf coast of Mexico (with some ships dropping away to the Greater Antilles and Venezuela); discharge cargoes and load homebound goods; winter in the Caribbean; combine at Havana in the late winter or early spring; and make the eastward crossing, via the Florida Strait and perhaps the Azores, and again following Columbus's pattern, in the spring and early summer. If they stuck to this timetable, the fleets avoided the late summer and early autumn hurricanes of the Caribbean and western Atlantic, as well as the winter storms further north. As the goodly number of wrecks off Florida and Bermuda suggests, however, the schedule was not easily followed. Delays in leaving Spain, enemy presence, slow arrival of cargoes (especially silver) for the return voyage, mere logistical complexity – all these could and did interrupt the rhythm of the Carrera. Nonetheless, broadly speaking the design functioned as intended, transporting hundreds of thousands of people, animals, goods, bullion, and, not least, information and administrative orders across the Atlantic in the sixteenth century.

If all went exactly as planned, the combined returning fleet reached Spain at around the departure date of the next sailing. The same ships, however, could not possibly be refitted and reloaded in time to sail again that same summer. So shipping was needed for four distinct fleets if the annual round were to be sustained. This meant much time spent lying in port. Ships in the *flota* to Mexico spent only a quarter of their time at sea,[50] and the proportion for the *galeones* must have been similar. The cost in idle capital locked in motionless ships and their cargoes was high. But that was the price of safety. Single-ship and small-group sailings were seen as simply too risky.

It was also the price of the monopoly structure of the trade. After the creation of the Casa de Contratación in Seville in 1503 to regulate communication with the Indies that city gradually became, in law and fact, the sole conduit for all Spanish contact with America. It was already a great trading center, with a powerful merchant guild, and branches of many European trading houses, especially those of Italy, the Genoese prominent among them. The merchants of Seville seized on the American trade as their own province. It suited them that fleets should sail only at long, predictable intervals, and that no other legal channel of trade with America should exist, for that enabled them to drive up prices by withholding goods from the transatlantic market. It suited them also that there should be only a few legal points of entry to the Indies, for that also helped them to control supply. All goods entering New Spain had to be unloaded at Veracruz, the sole destination of the *flota*; and all goods destined for Peru and elsewhere on the west coast of South America had to go in the *galeones* to the isthmus, for freighting across to the City of Panama, and loading there into a legally regulated Pacific fleet. Crown and merchants were in full agreement in these matters. What concerned the government above all was that its silver – the royal fifth and other taxes – should not escape from its grasp, and that customs duties on the American trade should be collected. Both aims were more easily achieved if contact with the Indies were concentrated into a few sailings, and funneled through a minimum of access points. If the crown should by chance lean towards a loosening of the fleet system, it would increasingly find itself reminded, as the years advanced, that the merchants of Seville were a valuable source of credit to the state, and that a weakening of the Seville monopoly would benefit neither them nor the treasury.

The closed structure of the Carrera in fact served crown and merchants well in the sixteenth century, better than in any later period. The trade grew in volume and value almost without interruption from 1505 to 1610 (*c.*23,000 tons of outward- and homeward-bound shipping from 1505 to 1509, and *c.*228,000 tons from 1605 to 1609).[51] The causes of the growth were several: growing demand in America for Spanish and other European goods as a result of emigration and natural increase of the colonizing population; rising bullion production, giving colonists the means of paying for imports; colonists' growing engagement in economic activities as time passed, creating a demand for European tools and materials, such as metals; increasing and spreading wealth among settlers, spent partly on European luxury goods; and underlying the whole transatlantic exchange, of course, Spain's domination of the sea. Pirates and semi-official raiders might slip into the Caribbean, as Frenchmen and Englishmen did before 1600, and snatch substantial prizes to the Spaniards' irritation and alarm. But no nation could yet seriously threaten the great trading fleets at sea. The failure of the Armada sent against England in 1588 was a warning of things to come; but the lesson was not clear until the new century was well begun.

Possibly the most serious threat to the transatlantic trade in the late sixteenth century was not a military one from Spain's growing number of European enemies, but a commercial one from colonials' enterprises in the Pacific. After the discovery of a practicable route between New Spain and the Philippines in the mid 1560s, entrepreneurial traders in Mexico City soon decided to try their fortune in the Orient. The mercantile gateway to the east was Manila, founded on the island of Luzon in 1571 as the Spanish capital in the Philippines. Oriental goods reached Mexico from Manila in 1573, carried by the first of the Manila galleons. Those were great sturdy vessels that were soon being built in the Philippines from local teak. What above all energized this trans-Pacific trade was the relative shortage, and hence high valuation, of silver in the East. The Chinese valuation of silver in terms of gold in 1572, for instance, was 150 percent of the Spanish American valuation (8:1 v. 12:1).[52] A broad range of goods bought in the Orient were amazingly cheap to those buying them with silver. And since the largest source of silver at the time was Peru, where Potosí was precisely in the 1570s experiencing its most spectacular boom of all time, the Mexico City merchants who started the Manila trade soon found themselves acting not so much as importers into New Spain as middle men in the exchange between Peru and Asia. Peruvian silver, transhipped into the galleons at Acapulco, spread from Manila throughout eastern Asia. Some of it was carried by Portuguese merchants working from the base at Macao that they had set up on the south China coast in the mid 1550s. The Portuguese bought silks at Canton nearby. These, together with porcelain, perfumes, ivory, gems, spices, and even iron and copper, arrived back in Acapulco after the arduous four- to seven-month arching traverse of the north Pacific; and thence much passed southward to Peru.

This trade grew with startling speed; indeed, for the authorities and the merchants in Seville, with thoroughly alarming speed. In 1597 the amount of silver leaving Acapulco for Manila was greater than the value of New Spain's trade with Spain. In 1602 the town council of Mexico City judged that 5 million pesos passed annually through Acapulco to the Philippines, 3 million of which came from Peru. (Potosí's production was some 6.9 million pesos a year at the time.) Various restrictions were tried: only two ships might ply between Acapulco and Manila, carrying westward a maximum of 500,000 pesos (1593); the two ships might not be larger than 200 tons (1604); only three ships, of 300 tons or less, might trade yearly between Peru and Mexico, and carry no silver (1604). Finally, in a desperate effort to stop the hemorrhage of South American silver across the Pacific, and at the insistence of the Seville merchant guild, the crown in 1631 banned trade between Peru and New Spain altogether. None of this had much effect, so powerful was the lure of profit in exporting silver. Trade was still allowed between Peru and Central America; transhipment of goods and silver from there to Mexico was simple.[53] The Manila galleon of 1646 proved, on investigation, to be carrying from six to fourteen times the amounts of silver that the consigning merchants had registered for export.[54]

The great sums committed to the Philippine trade show how much silver the substantial merchants of Mexico City, and Lima too, had at their disposal. Much of the profit of the colonies' productive activities came to rest in the coffers of the import–export merchants, above all because they, collaborating among themselves and also with exporters in Seville, could to a considerable degree set the price of goods from Europe, as well as those from Asia. No producers in America had a comparable power to fix the price of their wares, whether food, cloth, craft items, or anything else. They certainly tried to do so; some estate owners, for instance, sought to extend their lands not so much to grow more as to prevent others from raising competing crops. But generally the market structures of the colonies, small and inefficient as they mostly were, provided in all but the short term some regulation of prices.

The profitability of the import business was clear from the earliest years. In 1529 the *alcalde mayor* of Oaxaca, and *encomendero* to boot, Juan Peláez de

Berrío, wrote to Spain: "It seems to me that one of the good and most important businesses in this land is merchandise, for in that are the true mines, beyond what one can believe ... The profit is so sure and so large that a well stocked shop here is the richest thing in the world, alchemy itself ... Would to God I had brought a thousand ducats' worth of clothing, for, as things are here, I could easily send back four, or even five, thousand from it, such is the need of Castilian clothes."[55] With time, local production expanded to cover everyday needs such as clothes; but even then importing merchants could still charge premium prices for luxuries not made in the Indies (or, even if made there, lacking the European or Oriental cachet): silks, taffeta, satin, velvet, damask, linen from Holland, Rouen cloth, Spanish paper, Spanish wine, decorative trimmings of silk, silver, and gold, kid gloves, hose, laced buskins, saffron, spices[56] – among much else.

INVESTMENT

Their profits made merchants a leading source of credit in the colonies. They lent officially at the legally approved annual rate of 5 percent, but in reality often at far higher interest if the risk seemed greater, to investors in property, mining, and all other lines of production. While this credit-supplying role of merchants is broadly clear, however, precisely how they performed it in the sixteenth century is far less so; and indeed the general topic of investment and capital formation in the early colonies is the least known, because least visible, aspect of their economic history.

It is, though, clear enough that most investment in the Spanish Indies in the sixteenth century was generated in America. The main exception was the period of Caribbean settlement, when funds came from Castilian, Italian, German, and Flemish sources.[57] Even then, however, gold-mining and agriculture could provide sizable accumulations, as Pizarro's funding of the Peruvian explorations and campaign from his landholdings in Panama shows. Loot from the mainland conquests then gave the lucky and the careful an opportunity to gather large quantities of gold, though their full potential as investment funds depended on their being hoarded until the extreme inflation of prices (enormous amounts of gold pursuing rare European goods) of the immediate conquest had passed. Once *encomienda* was in place on the mainland, Indian labor became the major source in the creation of fixed capital. Houses, storage buildings, irrigation works, early smelting apparatus, local roads – all these could be built with *encomienda* labor with little or no cash outlay by the *encomendero*. Canny *encomenderos* could also amass liquid capital in the form of bullion by sending their Indians to mine gold or silver, or by selling, for cash, in local markets other tribute items, such as pieces of cloth, or food, that Indians had paid in kind. Evidently enough, the growth of mining was central to any gathering of funds for investment, with silver even in its unminted form becoming (from the 1530s in New Spain and from the 1540s in Peru) a convenient means of accumulating value as well as of enabling exchange. Coined silver, of more reliable value than the motley bits of metal that first served as money, became increasingly common with the foundation of a mint in Mexico City in 1536. Another mint was set up in Lima in 1565; but Viceroy Toledo moved its operations to Potosí, where striking of coin began in 1574.

Mining seems to have produced its own start-up capital (in addition to the stimulus given it by *encomienda* labor). Weathering had often raised the silver content of the surface ores that were usually the first to be worked. Not only, therefore, was their extraction cost minimal, but the early smelting was of mineral with a very high silver content, in places up to 50 percent by some reports. Initial profits could therefore be high, even if, as in the Andes, native workers received a large share of the product. Something similar happened when amalgamation began. Here the capital cost in milling machines and other apparatus was large. Typically, however, amalgamation processing was installed in places that possessed accumulations of already-mined ore that had proved too poor for smelting. Much of this material could be worked profitably with mercury. Thus the early amalgamators were spared the cost of extraction while they were building their refining mills, and plowed much of what they refined back into the producing apparatus. In the first five years of amalgamation in Potosí, 1571–5, records indicate that the miners reinvested some 42 percent of their after-tax production in building refining plant. Refiners using amalgamation also received help and, in effect, encouragement from the crown in the form of credit on the mercury they bought from the royal treasury, the sole legal supplier. The treasury tolerated large debts on this account until well into the next century. Those debts were, in reality, interest-free loans quite consciously made by the crown to boost silver production.

Rising silver output after the mid sixteenth century generally stimulated trade. In isolated regions far from mining centers and off the economic highways of the empire, barter persisted, and also the use of some non-metallic medium of exchange, such as cacao beans in southern Mexico. But, broadly speaking, the second half of the century brought a monetization, though uneven, of the Spanish Indies. From growing commerce, merchants, especially those in long-distance trade, extracted handsome profits. By one report there were in Lima soon after 1600 some traders with million-peso fortunes, many with 500,000, and very many with 100,000.[58] Merchants made loans from these hoards, becoming one major group of creditors in the colonies. The other large lender by that time was the church, and particularly the orders of regular clergy. They, in the second half of the sixteenth century, had grown stout, if not yet fat, on gifts and bequests in silver or property. Lending from these resources became a standard practice until the mid nineteenth century. Merchants and priests were, then, the closest approximation to bankers to emerge in the Indies. No true banks ever appeared in colonial times, though some of the large merchant houses in eighteenth-century Mexico performed many banking functions.

Wealthy merchants and the church were generally not in the business of making small loans to poor people. But local credit systems developed in towns and cities across the empire that did just that. The lenders were, again, typically merchants, but at the level of keepers of general stores (rather than of emporia selling expensive imported goods). They might sell on credit, or make small loans against the security of goods left by the borrowers; they were, therefore, acting as pawnbrokers. Particularly notable is the fact that many such lenders were women. In Potosí, where this petty-credit system has been closely studied, a good number of these women were Indians.[59] Their clients included both other Indians and Spaniards. Thus, before the sixteenth century ended, at the level of common, everyday existence there existed a remarkable integration in economic affairs between native people and colonizers. The case of Potosí also shows how quickly and easily native people could learn and adopt the new practices of monetized exchange and credit that the Spanish had introduced.

DOMINATION SURVEYED

Identification of resources, introduction of alien crops and animals, application of new productive tools and techniques, organization of labor, the mapping and plying of trade routes on land and sea, the opening of economic circuits through which flowed increasing charges of silver coin: all constituted a striking economic domination, even an economic re-formation, of Middle and South America in the sixteenth century. Economic matters were naturally linked with every other aspect of Spanish treatment of America and its native peoples in that first century. The church, while some of its members strove to protect Indians from labor exactions and the maltreatment that these often entailed, served broadly to bring native peoples into the Spanish physical and mental orbit. A parish priest might criticize *encomenderos* or the *mita*; but, at the same time, the more his efforts to protect Indians attached them to him, the more powerful an agent of Spanish presence he became. The state, too, was naturally and inextricably bound up with economic affairs. America's wealth, once identified in present and potential forms, became a central part of Spain's fiscal being. The government logically worked to raise its income from the Indies, as it gained the administrative means to do so, by modifying systems of production (in suppressing the *encomienda*, for example), maximizing the use of a dwindling labor supply (through setting up drafts of native workers), and adjusting taxes (lowering the silver royalty tax from a fifth to a tenth in Mexico, for instance, since the silver industry there, though productive, certainly did not boom on the scale of Potosí in the central Andes).

But Spanish domination was not by any means a simple imposition on America of alien methods and solutions. It was equally an adjustment and adaptation of European ways to New World conditions that sometimes came close to new invention. The American *audiencia* by the late sixteenth century had moved far from its Iberian source in becoming as much an executive as a juridical body. The estate structure of Spanish society shifted across the Atlantic, but the occupants of the estates changed, with ethnicity rather than function now becoming the determinant in placement. Spaniards' partiality for wheat resulted in the location of excellent wheat lands in New Spain and elsewhere; but colonists quite soon ate maize (and potatoes and manioc too) as well. The interesting, but unexploited, qualities of mercury long known in Europe were developed, in mid-sixteenth-century Mexico, into the basis of a silver-refining industry whose product had worldwide economic effects. Even long-accepted European notions of what constituted humanity necessarily expanded when Spaniards met people whose qualities contradicted the old patterns. In sum, the same capacity to learn, to improvise, to respond creatively to the unknown and the uncertain that had given the conquistadores a crucial edge over the native states persisted among early residents of the Indies, both officials and settlers, advancing the processes of domination that are the essence of Spanish American history between the conquests and the end of the sixteenth century.

PHOTO ESSAY

PHOTO 1

1 VIEW OF THE PERUVIAN MONTAÑA FROM MACHU PICCHU

Only 70 kilometers north-west of Cuzco stands the spectacular archaeological site of Machu Picchu, probably the most famous tourist destination in South America. The settlement is sited on a mountain saddle at a height of about 2,400 meters. It was probably built in the mid 1400s AD by the great Inca ruler Pachacutec, who may have created it as a private estate and retreat. Its purpose is in fact not clearly established. Another suggestion is that it was a military post from which a watch could be kept for invading people from the Amazonian plains.

This photograph shows only a tiny fragment of Machu Picchu's impressive stonework. Its intention is geographical rather than archaeological. Machu Picchu stands in an area of Peru called the *montaña* – a wide strip of forested foothills between the high Andean ranges to the west and the tropical plains to the east. The site is 600 meters above the course of the river Urubamba, visible as a bright patch near the bottom of the picture. The river flows on down the steep valley that it has cut for itself until it emerges onto the plain, and after several hundred kilometers joins the river Tambo to form the Ucayali, which in due course joins the Amazon. What may impress the visitor to Machu Picchu as much as its Inca buildings and its immediate site is the surrounding topography. All around, its peaks surge almost vertically upwards for many hundreds, if not thousands, of meters. On the day this photograph was taken, in the southern hemisphere's mid autumn, clouds of mist constantly boiled up and over the peaks – the moisture flowing in from the rainforest to the east. The wet season, which lasts several months, was coming to an end, but the moisture deposited here during the late spring, summer, and early fall is enough to sustain a thick growth of trees and shrubs on all but vertical rock faces. The only way through the *montaña* zone is along the valleys of the many rivers that cut through it – rivers that are fed by the summer rains and whose powers of erosion have produced the multitude of precipitous peaks of which the region consists. A narrow-gauge railroad carries tourists from Cuzco to a station near the river below Machu Picchu. The track follows the river's course for some kilometers. But it goes only a little farther. Building railroads down this valley, or any other in the *montaña*, to the Amazonian plain is beyond all practical possibility. Even today making roads to cross this region is immensely challenging; very few exist. In colonial times the only Europeans to travel down through the *montaña* – and the same holds for the similar territory in what are now Ecuador and Bolivia – were determined explorers and dedicated missionaries. By contrast, the high Andes were easy terrain for travel. The *montaña* in effect cut off Spanish settlement in central western South America from the interior of the continent. To find topography gentle enough to allow comparatively easy access to the interior from the Andes it is necessary to go 700–800 kilometers further to the south-east, to the region of Cochabamba in eastern highland Bolivia. At that latitude the seasonal inflow of moisture from Amazonia towards the mountains is lighter, with the result that rivers are fewer and smaller, and thus the landforms less eroded and less extreme. Nonetheless, the land journey from Cochabamba to Santa Cruz in the eastern savanna of Bolivia is still far from easy.

PHOTO 2

2 TERRACING AT PISAC IN THE VILCANOTA VALLEY, PERU

The small town of Pisac lies 15 kilometers north-east of Cuzco in the southern Peruvian Andes. It is one a series of towns and villages along the course of the river Vilcanota (which changes name, some 15 kilometers downstream from Pisac, to Urubamba). The steep-sided course that the Vilcanota/Urubamba has cut through the mountains is now known as the Sacred Valley of the Incas. Whether the Incas did in fact regard it as sacred is not known, although the name of the river in their time was Willkamayu, meaning "Sacred River" in Quechua. What is clear is that the Inca nobility of imperial times had private estates in the valley, which contains one of the largest areas of good farming land close to Cuzco.

Given the quality of the land, it is likely that the valley was cultivated for many centuries before the Incas appeared. It is an excellent example of an Andean ecological niche, equipped with a microclimate that favors crop-raising. The depth of the valley floor makes it a little warmer than the general surrounding terrain (although downward-flowing cold air could pose a threat of night-time frost to emerging plants in the spring). The river has filled the bottom of the valley with silt, providing workable and fertile soil. And, of course, the river provides water, although the water was not available for diversion into irrigation ditches in places where the river had cut a trench for itself.

It is known that the Incas, during the 1400s, improved the valley (from the agricultural standpoint) with a view to growing large amounts of maize in it. They drained swampy land, canalized the river for more than 20 kilometers, built irrigation channels to bring in irrigation water from streams that ran in smaller, transverse, valleys, and constructed terracing up the valley sides where, again, irrigation water could be tapped into. It is estimated the Incas created 800 hectares of new land for maize simply by canalizing the main river. The terraces added considerably more. This was not the only valley to be modified in these ways. Similar measures were applied to the Cuzco valley itself, and to various other valleys in the Cuzco region.

Source: Covey, *How the Incas Built their Heartland*, and personal communication.

PHOTO 3

3   PYRAMID OF THE SUN AT TEOTIHUACÁN, MEXICO

This is the largest pyramid on the Teotihuacán site, and indeed the largest in Middle America. Its sides are 215 meters long, and it is 60 meters high. It is a solid structure consisting of 1,175,000 cubic meters of adobe brick and rubble, covered with stone. Despite its apparently rather "touristy" name, it is in fact quite likely to have been dedicated to the Sun, regarded by the people of Teotihuacán as a god. The temple on the top of the pyramid, in which rites of worship were performed, has, however, long since disappeared. Some idea of how impressive rituals must have seemed to spectators below can be had from the smallness of the figures standing on the top of the pyramid in this picture, outlined against the sky.

Like most Middle American pyramids, this one was built in stages, enlargements being laid over previous structures as resources, and the significance of the structure, grew. The first stages went up in Teotihuacán's initial phase, probably during the first century AD. The site of the pyramid is likely to have had immense religious importance. In 1971 a tunnel 103 meters long was discovered, starting from the foot of the great stairway and ending in a four-lobed, roughly flower-shaped, cave under the middle of the pyramid. The tunnel is a natural volcanic formation. The people of Teotihuacán enlarged both the cave and the tunnel, and finished their surfaces. It is clear that they regarded both as holy. Ancient Mexicans often considered caves to be symbolic wombs from which gods, and the original humans, had emerged. Besides that, according to some later sources, Middle Americans saw in a four-petaled flower a symbol of the cosmos, consisting of a center surrounded by four cardinal regions. So it is possible that for Teotihuacán's people, this cave was an image of the universe, and thus sacred in the extreme. The pre-conquest place glyph for Teotihuacán was two pyramids over a cave – possibly a reference to this cave and the two great pyramids on the site (the other being dedicated to the Moon as god). It is logical that the larger pyramid would have been raised over the cave.

Sources: Carrasco, *Quetzalcóatl and the Irony of Empire*, pp. 107–8; Coe and Koontz, *Mexico*, pp. 106–7.

PHOTO 4

4   THE NORTH ACROPOLIS AT TIKAL (GUATEMALA)

Tikal, Palenque, and Chichén Itza are in modern times the most renowned of Maya archaeological sites. Of the three, Tikal is the largest – in fact among the largest of all known Maya sites, covering 15–20 square kilometers, and having more than 3,000 mapped structures (though many remain to be excavated). At its height, in the Late Classic period (after AD 700), Tikal's population reached possibly 90,000. Substantial settlement was present on the site from the Late Formative period (*c.*AD 0), and expanded from then on. The influence of Teotihuacan in central Mexico is apparent at Tikal during the fifth century AD, although its precise nature is not known. It may have been a case of trade and of Tikal's leaders admiring Teotihuacán, then the greatest single power in all Mexico; or it is quite possible that men from Teotihuacán actually assumed power in Tikal and founded a ruling dynasty. In the sixth century the influence of Teotihuacán in Maya lands declined. Tikal, after being conquered by a neighboring city (either Caracol or Calakmul) in AD 562, remained quiescent until almost 700. After that, however, in the Late Classic, it grew, became more splendid in itself, and extended its political power widely over its region. Like other great Maya centers, however, it declined, apparently rapidly and for reasons perhaps never to be fully understood, in the ninth century. By the late 800s squatters had moved into the palaces once occupied by rulers and nobles.

The North Acropolis, seen in this photograph, mostly dates from between AD 300 and 600. It is a multi-level assemblage of temple-pyramids built over the tombs of rulers. Facing each other across the great plaza in front of the Acropolis are two large pyramids, typically Maya in being steep and slender. This photograph is taken from the stairway of one of them, Temple I. At the inner edge of the plaza (and the bottom of the picture) are stelae (stone posts) erected by the ancient Maya to display, in glyphs, the history of the site.

Sources: Coe, *The Maya*; Schele and Freidel, *A Forest of Kings*; Martin, "In Line of the Founder."

Photo 5

5   FRANCISCAN CHURCH AT TEPEACA (MEXICO)

The missionary church at Tepeaca, 30 kilometers east of Puebla in central Mexico, still stands firm c.450 years after it was built. A mess of ugly modern building covers most of its once spacious churchyard, leaving open only the long approach to the facade.

Tepeaca, today a middling town, had an early colonial history that shows well the fluid changeability of Mexico just after the Spanish conquest. There was a native fortress, Tepeyacac, on a nearby hill. But in late 1520 Hernán Cortés made the place into a Spanish town, naming it Villa Segura de la Frontera – "Safe Town on the Frontier." He intended it as a Spanish stronghold against any local native rising that might take place – and threaten the all-important road between México-Tenochtitlan, the capital, and Veracruz, then the only port on the Gulf coast. (Cortés may well have chosen the name thinking of a series of towns that fortified the boundary in Andalusia between Christian territory and Moorish Granada in the fourteenth and fifteenth centuries, such as Jerez de la Frontera or Arcos de la Frontera.) But that initial Spanish settlement quickly dwindled in population.

Franciscans came from the neighboring town of Huejotzingo to attend to the spiritual needs of the few people left in Tepeaca. By 1529 a chapel existed there in which the friars said Mass. By 1535 there was a church dedicated to St. Francis. But that was not the church seen here, which was built on a lower, flatter part of the site in the 1540s. To this second church was attached (on the right side, as seen here) a Franciscan monastery, which was still under construction c.1553. By that time the town was more firmly established, since the surrounding countryside was becoming part of the large wheat-growing area centered on the nearby Atlixco valley.

The facade now visible was built in the eighteenth century. The original one was very probably plainer. The body of the church behind the facade is one of the great stone boxes – in this case 22 meters high, 54 long, and 13 wide – that Franciscan, Augustinian, and Dominican missionaries put up across central Mexico, mostly between the 1530s and 1570s. The friars designed the churches, and organized Indians of the towns to build them. Many of them have a rather military appearance, with turrets or battlements along the tops of the walls, and small, high windows that would resist entry. Historians disagree, however, on whether these were castle-churches, designed as refuges for Spaniards in case of native revolts, or whether the friars were just adding simple elements of the Gothic architectural decoration that they knew from Europe.

The churches were built large because there were at first so many native people to convert and teach: those who would not fit inside could stand in the broad, paved churchyards and hear sermons preached from outdoor chapels. But with disease and the other woes of conquest and domination native numbers slumped, and, after the late sixteenth century, the great churches were long unfilled.

Sources: Chevalier, *Land and Society in Colonial Mexico*; Cortés, *Letters from Mexico*; Gerhard, *Guide to the Historical Geography of New Spain*; Kubler, *Mexican Architecture*; Ricard, *The Spiritual Conquest of Mexico*.

PHOTO 6

6 DETAIL OF THE MAIN PORTAL OF THE MONASTIC CHURCH OF SAN FRANCISCO, LIMA

The first Franciscan church in Lima was built in the mid-sixteenth century. But it collapsed in an earthquake in 1656. The church now standing was designed by a Portuguese architect, Constantino de Vasconcelos, and constructed between 1656 and 1678. The church is opulent in its interior, but its most striking feature is the main portal, part of which is seen here. Art historians consider this portal to be an "altarpiece facade" – in other words, it looks as if the richly decorated structure (the *retablo* in Spanish) typically placed behind an altar has been taken out and installed on the facade of the church. The portal has in fact been called the first important such facade in Lima, and a model for others built later in the city. Their purpose was to attract attention, and sometimes to act as backdrops for religious ceremonies, and theatrical and musical performances, taking place in front of them.

The portal of San Francisco is full of Baroque drama and energy, but also has some classical balance and symmetry to it. Over the door is a triumphal arch, and, just above, the crossed-keys insignia of the Pope. In a large, elaborately framed niche above that stands a marble figure of the Virgin of the Immaculate Conception – a manifestation of the Madonna to which seventeenth-century Spaniards had a particular devotion. Kneeling in reverence on her left is St. Francis and, on her right, St. Dominic. The top of the niche, over the Virgin, is in the shape of a conch shell – a conventional form in Baroque architecture, but perhaps a reference to St. James, the patron saint of Spain, of whom that shell is a symbol. The conch form is repeated, or alluded to, in the tops of the two saints' niches, and in the arches of the story above. Many of the surfaces around the Virgin and the two saints are densely and minutely decorated, for the glorification of such holy figures. The portal as a whole has multiple planes, with the Virgin standing forward most prominently, and the two saints a little behind her. All three figures, however, are pushed forward by the series of receding pilasters behind the saints' backs. The varying depth of the arches and other elements of the upper story produces characteristically Baroque contrasts of light and shadow – and, with a little stretching of the imagination, a stony evocation of clouds above the Madonna.

Sources: Bailey, *Art of Colonial Latin America*; Donahue-Wallace, *Art and Architecture*; Kelemen, *Baroque and Rococo in Latin America*; Kubler and Soria, *Art and Architecture*.

Photo 7

7 ANTONIO JOSÉ DE SUCRE ALCALÁ, 1795–1830: BRONZE STATUE, PLAZA MAYOR, SUCRE (BOLIVIA)

Sucre was Simón Bolívar's right-hand man in the final stages of the liberation of South America from Spanish rule. From 1821 until 1825, during the struggle against the Spanish in Ecuador, Peru, and Bolivia (to use the modern country names), Bolívar placed great reliance on Sucre's talents in both logistics and command of troops in the field.

Sucre, like Bolívar, was a Venezuelan, born in the eastern town of Cumaná in February 1795 to a locally prominent family. He received some education in Caracas, but at the age of 16 was already a lieutenant in the rebel force starting the fight for independence. He continued in that struggle throughout the 1810s, reaching the rank of brigadier general when he was 23. In 1817 he joined the staff of Bolívar, who admired his methodical qualities – "the scourge of disorder," he called him (Lynch, p. 138). There was perhaps an attraction of opposites: Bolívar all bravura, and Sucre retiring, though capable of prickliness.

In January 1821 Bolívar showed his confidence in Sucre by appointing him to lead a force from Colombia to Guayaquil, on the Ecuadorian coast, with the aim of extending the independence movement southward. Sucre suffered his only defeat in battle while on that campaign, but went on to overcome the Spanish at Pichincha, near Quito, in May 1822. A year later he arrived in Lima, sent by Bolívar as Colombia's representative to the Peruvian government, which was still unable to organize a final expulsion of the Spanish military from its territory. In the following year, independence forces defeated the Spanish twice in Peru – first at Ayacucho, with Bolívar commanding, in August 1824, and then definitively at Junín, under Sucre, in December. Sucre continued southward, dispersing remnants of Spanish troops in Bolivia in early 1825. The new Bolivian congress persuaded Bolívar to accept the presidency of the new country (named after him). But in December 1825 he passed the office to Sucre, who exercised it with reluctance, though honorably and progressively, for more than two years. His being a foreigner, however, brought rising internal opposition to his presidency, while growing disorder in the occupying Colombian army, and Peruvian military intervention, destabilized Bolivian politics. Sucre left office in April 1828. He returned to Colombia, where in 1829–30 he joined in Bolívar's unsuccessful effort to preserve the union of Venezuela, Colombia, Ecuador, and Peru as Gran Colombia. Association with the now reviled – and dying – Bolívar led to Sucre's own death. He was assassinated in June 1830 near Pasto in southern Colombia as he was returning to Quito, his wife's home city.

Sucre has been judged "in strictly military terms ... a better general than Bolívar" (Bushnell, p. 149). His memory lives on in Bolivia, where the members of the constituent congress of 1825 renamed the old colonial capital, Chuquisaca, after the man who finally expelled Spain from their incipient nation..

Sources: Bushnell, *Simón Bolívar*; Lynch, *Simón Bolívar*; Robertson, *Rise of the Spanish-American Republics*, ch. 8.

PART IV

MATURE COLONIES

CHRONOLOGY

1559   Beginning of royally approved sale of office (notarial posts) in Spanish America

1566   Beginning of Dutch revolt against Spanish rule

1586–1617   Life of Isabel Flores de Oliva (Santa Rosa de Lima)

1588   Defeat of the Spanish Armada sent against England

1590s   Rise of foreign incursions into the Caribbean

late 1590s   First Dutch settlers on Guiana coast of South America

1606   Royal decree permitting purchase of almost all local offices. Beginning of silver boom at Oruro (lasting until *c*.1630)

1609–21   Truce between Spain and the Dutch

1610   First Jesuits *reducciones* (missions) among Guaraní in Paraguay

c.1611–*c*.1681   Life of Diego Quispe Tito, prime early painter of the Cuzco school

1621   Death of Philip III of Spain. Accession of Philip IV. Foundation of Dutch West India Company

1624   English seize St. Kitt's in Leeward Islands

1628   Piet Heyn captures a Spanish treasure fleet off Cape Matanzas (Cuba)

1633   Beginning of sale of fiscal offices in Spanish America

1634   Dutch seize Curaçao

1635   French seize Martinique and Guadeloupe

1648?–95   Life of Juana Ramírez de Asbaje (Sor Juana Inés de la Cruz)

1655   English seize Jamaica

1660s   English settlement of mouth of Belize river

1665   Death of Philip IV of Spain. Accession of Charles II. France sends official governor to Tortuga: beginning of colony of St. Domingue, later Haiti

1677   Sale of *corregimientos* and *alcaldías mayores* permitted

1680–93   Revolt of Pueblo Indians in New Mexico

1687   *Audiencia* offices put up for sale

1700   Death of Charles II, last Hapsburg ruler of Spain

1701   Accession of Philip V, first Bourbon king of Spain

1701–14   War of the Spanish Succession

c.1710   Zacatecas overtakes Potosí in silver production

1712–13   Peace of Utrecht

1714   Ministry of the Indies created by Philip V

1717   Casa de Contratación moved from Seville to Cadiz

1728   Caracas (or Guipúzcoa) Company founded in Spain

1730   *Mestizo*-led rising at Cochabamba

1739   Viceroyalty of New Granada established

1739   Rising at Oruro, opposing tax increases

1739–48   Wars of Jenkin's Ear and of Austrian Succession

1742   Beginning of Juan Santos Atahualpa's rising in Peruvian Andes

1743   *New System of Economic Government of America*, by José del Campillo y Cossío

1746   Our Lady of Guadalupe proclaimed patroness of New Spain. Death of Philip V. Accession of Ferdinand VI

1748   Last sailing of *galeones* to Isthmus of Panama

1756–63   Seven Years War

1759   Death of Ferdinand VI. Accession of Charles III

1763   Peace of Paris

1764   First American ports opened to single ship trade. First intendant placed in America (Cuba)

1765   Rising in Quito against growing fiscal pressure

1765–71   Gálvez's inspection of New Spain

1767   Expulsion of the Jesuits from Spanish territories

1776   Last *flota* sails to New Spain. Viceroyalty of the Río de la Plata established

1777   Arrival in Peru of José Antonio de Areche as general inspector

1778   Regulations and Royal Tariffs for Free Trade between Spain and America promulgated

1778–9   The Inconfidência Mineira in Brazil (Tiradentes' plot)

1780–1   Revolt led by Túpac Amaru II in Peruvian Andes. Clavijero's *Ancient History of Mexico*

1781   Siege of La Paz (Bolivia) by Túpac Katari. *Comunero* revolt in New Granada

1783   Birth of Simón Bolívar

1785   Foundation of the Academia de San Carlos (of fine arts) in Mexico City

1787–8   *Audiencia* established at Cuzco

1788   Death of Charles III. Accession of Charles IV. Birth of José de San Martín

1791   Slave revolt in Saint Domingue (Haiti)

1795   Peace of Basle between France and Spain

1797   Spain forced to allow colonies to trade with neutral countries

1798   "Tailors' Plot" in Salvador

1803   Louisiana sold by Napoleon Bonaparte to the United States

1804   Seizure by the crown of the church's *obras pías* in America

1805   French–Spanish naval defeat at Trafalgar by Britain

1806   Miranda tries, and fails, to start rebellion in Venezuela

1807   Franco-Spanish invasion of Portugal

1808   Abdication of Charles IV of Spain. Accession and abdication of Ferdinand VII. French occupation of Spain. Joseph I placed on Spanish throne by Napoleon. British expeditionary force sent to Spain. Emergence of Spanish national junta. Viceroy deposed in New Spain by *audiencia* of Mexico. Arrival of Portuguese royal family in Rio de Janeiro

1809   Risings in Buenos Aires and Quito

1809–10   Independence declared in La Paz (Bolivia), but quickly suppressed by Spanish forces

1810   Declarations of self-government in Caracas, Santiago de Chile, and Buenos Aires (effective permanent independence of Río de la Plata). Viceroy deposed in New Granada. Return of Miranda to Venezuela. In Mexico, the "Grito de Dolores," and multiple risings in the north. Treaty of Navigation and Commerce between Great Britain and government in Brazil

1810–14   Deliberations of *cortes* (parliament) of Cadiz

1811   Defeat, and execution, of Hidalgo in Mexico. Effective achievement of independence by Paraguay. French expelled from Portugal

1812   Constitution of Cadiz

1813   French expelled from Spain. Morelos captures Acapulco

1814   Ferdinand restored to Spanish throne. First Mexican constitution issued, at Apatzingán

1815   Final defeat of Napoleon Bonaparte. Execution of Morelos. Brazil raised to status of kingdom, constitutionally equal with Portugal

1816   Death of Miranda

1817   Battle of Chacabuco. Republic of Pernambuco briefly declared in Brazil

1818   Battle of Maipú. Independence of Chile

1819   Battle of Boyacá. Independence of New Granada (later Colombia)

1820   San Martín lands on Peruvian coast, at Pisco. Military revolt in Spain, and restoration there of liberal constitution of 1812. In Portugal, military revolt, adoption of Spanish constitution of 1812, and declaration of constitutional monarchy

1821   Battle of Carabobo. Independence of Venezuela. San Martín named Protector of Peru. Plan of Iguala in Mexico, and subsequent independence. Return of John VI from Brazil to Portugal

1822   Battle of Pichincha. Independence of Ecuador. Confidential meeting of Bolívar and San Martín at Guayaquil, and San Martín's withdrawal from the independence movement. In Brazil, proclamation of Peter I as emperor, and independence

1824   Battles of Junín and Ayacucho. Independence of Peru

1825   Independence of Bolivia

1828   Effective independence of Uruguay

1830   Death of Bolívar

1844   Independence of Hispaniola (Dominican Republic), from Haiti

1850   Death of San Martín

FURTHER READING FOR PART IV

General works on the seventeenth century in Spanish America are few. An exception is Ruggiero Romano, *Coyunturas opuestas: La crisis del siglo XVII en Europa e Hispanoamérica*. Again, the first two volumes of Leslie Bethell (ed.), *The Cambridge History of Latin America*, contain fundamental readings, as does the first volume of Victor Bulmer-Thomas, John H. Coatsworth, and Roberto Cortés Conde (eds), *The Cambridge Economic History of Latin America: The Colonial Era and the Short Nineteenth Century*. D. A. Brading, *The First America: The Spanish Monarchy, Creole Patriots, and the Liberal State, 1492–1867*, offers a wealth of insight into seventeenth- and eighteenth-century attitudes. J. H. Elliott, *Empires of the Atlantic World: Britain and Spain in America, 1492–1830*, in comparing British and Spanish colonization, places many features of Spanish America in unusually sharp focus. Louisa S. Hoberman, *Mexico's Merchant Elite, 1590–1660: Silver, State, and Society*, is the most complete treatment of New Spain for the seventeenth century. Consult also J. I. Israel, *Race, Class and Politics in Colonial Mexico, 1610–1670*. For both the seventeenth and the eighteenth centuries, William B. Taylor, *Landlord and Peasant in Colonial Oaxaca*, and *Drinking, Homicide and Rebellion in Colonial Mexican Villages*, say much about the interactions of Indians and Spaniards. For Peru, Kenneth J. Andrien, *Crisis and Decline: The Viceroyalty of Peru in the Seventeenth Century*, Karen Spalding, *Huarochirí: An Andean Society under Inca and Spanish Rule*, Kenneth Mills, *Idolatry and its Enemies: Colonial Andean Religion and Extirpation, 1640–1750*, and Nicholas Griffiths, *The Cross and the Serpent: Religious Repression and Resurgence in Colonial Peru* are all full of interest. See also John L. Phelan, *The Kingdom of Quito in the Seventeenth Century: Bureaucratic Politics in the Spanish Empire*. For New Granada, Anthony McFarlane, *Colombia before Independence: Economy, Society, and Politics under*

Bourbon Rule, is a valuable contribution, as, for colonial Ecuador, are Kris Lane, *Quito1599: City and Colony in Transition*, and Kenneth J. Andrien, *The Kingdom of Quito, 1690–1830: The State and Regional Development*. Susan M. Socolow, *The Women of Colonial Latin America*, is a general account. Many of the essays in Asunción Lavrin (ed.), *Sexuality and Marriage in Colonial Latin America*, deal with the seventeenth and eighteenth centuries, as does Patricia Seed, *To Love, Honor, and Obey in Colonial Mexico: Conflicts over Marriage Choices, 1574–1821*, a study which has as much to say about social history as it does about marriage. More recent works on women's history include Kathryn Burns, *Colonial Habits: Convents and the Spiritual Economy of Cuzco, Peru*; Kimberly Gauderman, *Women's Lives in Colonial Quito: Gender, Law, and Economy in Spanish America*, and Martha Few, *Women who Live Evil Lives: Gender, Religion, and the Politics of Power in Colonial Guatemala*. Two central studies of Africans and their descendants are Frederick P. Bowser, *The African Slave in Colonial Peru, 1524–1650*, and Herman L. Bennett, *Africans in Colonial Mexico: Absolutism, Christianity, and Afro-Creole Consciousness, 1570–1640*. A recent work that integrates Spanish American art history well with general history is Kelly Donahue-Wallace, *Art and Architecture of Viceregal Latin America, 1521–1821*.

For the eighteenth century, Nils Jacobsen and Hans-Jürgen Puhle (eds), *The Economies of Mexico and Peru during the Late Colonial Period, 1760–1810*, ranges widely. Richard Garner's *Economic Growth and Change in Bourbon Mexico* is a thorough study of Spanish America's most prosperous region in the eighteenth century. For Indian risings, see Scarlett O'Phelan Godoy's notable *Rebellions and Revolts in Eighteenth Century Peru and Upper Peru*, and Steve J. Stern (ed.), *Resistance, Rebellion, and Consciousness in the Andean Peasant World* (as well as Taylor, *Drinking, Homicide and Rebellion in Colonial Mexican Villages*). For Bourbon innovations, Colin M. MacLachlan, *Spain's Empire in the New World: The Role of Ideas in Institutional and Social Change*, and Gabriel B. Paquette, *Enlightenment, Governance, and Reform in Spain and its Empire, 1759–1808*. For Bourbon efforts to discipline popular culture, see Juan Pedro Viqueira Albán, *Propriety and Permissiveness in Bourbon Mexico*; and for the local effects of Bourbon policies on the church, William B. Taylor's exhaustive *Magistrates of the Sacred: Priests and Parishioners in Eighteenth-Century Mexico*. John Lynch, in *Bourbon Spain, 1700–1808*, says much about Spanish America and its general relationship with the metropolis. John R. Fisher, Allan J. Kuethe, and Anthony McFarlane (eds), *Reform and Insurrection in Bourbon New Granada and Peru*, conveys the rise of tensions caused by Bourbon reformism in the eighteenth-century Andes. Many of the biographical sketches in Kenneth J. Andrien (ed.), *The Human Tradition in Colonial Latin America* are of late-colonial figures. Jane G. Landers and Barry M. Robinson (eds), *Slaves, Subjects, and Subversives: Blacks in Colonial Latin America*, samples recent research on its topic, some of it on the eighteenth century. A good new treatment in English of colonial Paraguay, with much on Jesuits in the eighteenth century, is Barbara Gannon, *The Guaraní under Spanish Rule in the Río de la Plata*. For Bourbon policy on American natives, and generally much about colonial frontiers, see David J. Weber, *Bárbaros: The Spaniards and their Savages in the Age of Enlightenment*. For a particular frontier region, see Cynthia Radding, *Wandering Peoples: Colonialism, Ethnic Spaces, and Ecological Frontiers in Northwestern Mexico, 1700–1850*. Again, J. H. Elliott, *Empires of the Atlantic World*, offers views of Spanish America made especially clear through contrasts with British North America.

[11] THE SEVENTEENTH CENTURY: A SLACKER GRIP

CHALLENGES TO SPAIN

FOR political and military achievement the sixteenth century has no rival in Spanish history: the New World brought to heel in the west; the Turks kept at bay in the east; Protestant heresy assaulted in the north; an empire created spanning two-thirds of the world's circumference, from Manila at 120°E to Lower California at 120°W. Spain's feats seemed superhuman, and so indeed Spaniards sometimes thought them to be, seeing divine inspiration and appointment in their nation's acts. The cost, though, was great; and what was built was not as sturdy as it seemed to other Europeans awed throughout the 1500s by Spanish power. By the end of that century of imperial explosion, those at its center began to feel a hollowness around them. That sensation, strengthened increasingly by tangible reality, was to dominate the new century.

PROBLEMS AT HOME

The reasons for Spanish gloom and disillusion, and for the real decline that accompanied them, are as varied as they are numerous, and almost as debatable now as they were then. Was the fault in part America's? Clearly colonizing did not drain Spain of money; the flow was overwhelmingly in the other direction. But did, perhaps, the American enterprise deplete Spain's reserves of men of energy and initiative? Did it reinforce in Spain medieval notions of glory won through feats of arms, at the expense of the adoption of the idea arising elsewhere in Europe that strength resided in the humdrum and steady pursuit of trade and industry? Neither point can be proved; but neither can be dismissed out of hand.

What is clear, however, is that Spain's possession of America and the receipt of American wealth encouraged a depth of engagement in European affairs that soon left the country overextended. This was particularly so in Philip II's reign

ILLUSTRATION 11.1 *The Annunciation,* by Cristóbal de Villalpando (Mexico, *c.*1650–1714). Even in a monochrome reproduction, the characteristically Baroque use of dramatic contrasts of light and dark is clear. Private collection.

ILLUSTRATION 11.2 *Archangel with a Matchlock Gun, Salamiel Paxdei* ("peace of God"): one of many such paintings of military angels, dressed in Spanish aristocratic style, from the central Andes. Late seventeenth century, Circle of the Master of Calamarca, Lake Titicaca School, Bolivia. New Orleans Museum of Art.

ILLUSTRATION 11.3 *Archangel Michael Triumphant.* "And there was war in heaven: Michael and his angels fought against the dragon; and the dragon fought and his angels, and prevailed not; neither was their place found any more in heaven. And the great dragon was cast out, that old serpent, called the Devil, and Satan ..." (Revelation 12: 7–9). Seventeenth-century polychromed mahogany sculpture, by an unknown artist of the Cuzco school. New Orleans Museum of Art.

ILLUSTRATION 11.4 *Our Lady of Pomata.* A painting of the miracle-working statue of the Virgin of the Rosary at Pomata, a small town on the west shore of Lake Titicaca in Peru. 1675, Circle of Quispe Tito, Cuzco school, Peru. Brooklyn Museum of Art.

ILLUSTRATION 11.5   St. Augustine, defeating heresy, represented by Martin Luther, who is held down by the saint's foot. Early eighteenth century, by unknown artist, Bolivia. New Orleans Museum of Art.

ILLUSTRATION 11.6   Biblical prophets in front of the church of Bom Jesus de Matozinhos, at Congonhas do Campo, Brazil, sculptured in soapstone by O Aleijadinho (Antonio Francisco Lisboa), 1800–5. *Top,* copyright Sue Cunningham; *bottom,* copyright South American Pictures.

VISTA DE LA PLAZA DE MEXICO, NUEVAMENTE ADORNADA, PARA LA
CARLOS IV, que se coloco en ella el 9 de Diciembre de 1796, cumple años de
por Miguel la Grua, Marques de Branciforte, Virrey de Nueva España, quien
gratitud y consuelo general de todo este Reyno, é hizo grabar esta Estampa, que

ESTATUA EQUESTRE DE NUESTRO AUGUSTO MONARCA REYNANTE
la Reyna Nuestra Señora MARIA LUISA DE BORBON, su amada Esposa a
solicito y logro de la Real Clemencia erigir este Monumento para desahogo de su
dedica a Sus Magestades, en nuevo testimonio de su fidelidad, amor y respeto

ILLUSTRATION 11.7 View of the Plaza Mayor of Mexico City, 1797, by José Joaquín
Fabregat: neoclassical reordering imposed on Mexico City by the government of Charles IV
(mounted, center). The Baroque cathedral stands in the background, with the parish church
of the Sagrario attached to the right of it. On the extreme right, part of the viceregal (later
national) palace. Benson Latin American Collection, University of Texas at Austin.

ILLUSTRATION 11.8 An early example of the invasion of north European taste: Mexican-
made chairs (1750–1800) in the "Mexican Chippendale" style. Brooklyn Museum of Art.

ILLUSTRATION 11.9   An eighteenth-century Peruvian table, of cedar. Dense Baroque decoration was not confined to churches. Note the spiraling Salomonic legs and the lacy carving of leaves and fruits. Brooklyn Museum of Art.

(1556–98), four decades in which American silver production, propelled by amalgamation, boomed. If Philip had been content to scale his European plans to the growing current of silver crossing the ocean to Spain, all might have been well. But instead he used it as the basis of still larger enterprises, borrowing heavily at home and abroad to finance them on the security of silver receipts to come. Among the outcomes was a series of state bankruptcies, or repudiations of debt, in 1557, 1575, 1596, and then, early in the reign of his son, in 1607. The first, it is true, was not of Philip's making. But the others reflect his over-commitment of Spain's resources, not so much despite as because of the American cornucopia. It seemed that this wealth had been divinely delivered to Spain to enable it to become the leader in defending Roman Catholicism from its religious and political foes, a task to which Philip remained wholly committed throughout his reign.[1] From duty and conviction, but also with misgivings, he devoted himself to what proved in reality a limitless and impracticable venture.

The main foes were the Dutch, in a revolt from 1566 against their Spanish rulers inspired by religion and national feeling. It was for Spain an endless, sapping war. Philip's efforts to draw in French Catholic help against the Netherlands embroiled him in France's civil wars to no good final effect. His attempts to eliminate English support for the rebels and more broadly to nip the vigorous growth of Elizabeth I's Protestant England were outright and costly failures. The first and most telling of these was the disaster of the Armada of 1588, when 40–50 of 130 ships were lost, along with some 15,000 men.

Spain soon made up the lost vessels. But the defeat by a combination of arms and storms was an arresting psychological blow.[2] The great charger of state, thunderously advancing for so long past, seemed suddenly to have crashed to the ground. Spain's foes were heartened, and the Protestant cause advanced.

Philip's final decade was therefore one in which Spain lost its earlier certainties of rightness. Not only were there more blows in the external world – England's brief holding and sacking of Cadiz in 1596, the failure of another fleet sent against England in 1597, the unavoidable granting of secession to the Netherlands in 1598, a peace, from weariness, with France at Vervins in May of that same year, five months before Philip's death – but also growing evidence of strain and decay within the country itself. Lack of funds in the treasury led in 1590 to the imposition of a new tax, the *millones*, on a Castilian peasantry already heavily burdened by increases earlier in the reign. Despite this, in 1596 the repayment of crown debts was suspended. This further weakened a Spanish economy that was now visibly in difficulties. The market and industrial towns of northern Castile, prosperous early in the century, were in decline, and their population drifting southward. More general, still, than this was a shift of population from the country to towns, not so much, it seems, because of attractive economic opportunities in them but because of the intolerable cost of staying on the land. Taxes, tithes, and rents took more than half the value of a peasant's product.[3] Most Castilian peasants were tenants, and more became so during Philip II's reign, as he, again to raise money, sold not only communal lands but also, with papal permission, some of the church's as well. Hence, curiously in a reign often thought of as prematurely absolutist, control of land tended to pass from the crown to rising and existing nobles. Great estates grew up, especially in the south.[4] More and more peasants of Philip's time, therefore, fell under the private jurisdiction of lords, and subject to whatever demands for rent and labor services their masters might make. The social outcome was exodus from the land; and the economic one a growing shortage, and rising price, of food. The absurdity arose, then, in the late years of the sixteenth century, of the country's importing staple grains that it had all that was necessary – soil, climate, land, and labor – to produce in abundance. It was an early example of the economic nonsenses, inspired by idiosyncratic social and cultural norms, that were increasingly to puzzle outside observers of Spain over the next several centuries. That this economic irrationality could have clear practical effects was soon demonstrated. Malnutrition and urban crowding made Spain a fertile ground for epidemic disease, as the country's seventeenth-century history repeatedly shows. Now there is no doubt that the population was falling, rather than simply migrating. The first attack came in 1596, when bubonic plague entered at the northern port of Santander. Over the next four years, perhaps half a million Spaniards fell victim to the disease.[5]

FOREIGN INCURSIONS IN AMERICA

Across the Atlantic, too, the 1590s brought disquieting signs that past certainties might not last. That was the decade in which foreigners began to show ominous naval and commercial strength in the Caribbean, which the Spanish had considered to be their own lake. Before, to be sure, there had been pirates and privateers: LeClerc and other Frenchmen before the Treaty of Cateau-Cambrésis in 1559, and more notoriously Francis Drake in the 1570s and 1580s. But in the 1590s foreigners began to look for a more regular, though of course contraband, trade with the Spanish colonies. Particularly interested were the arch-enemies, the Dutch, whose herring industry at home needed a reliable supply of salt. Their earlier source, Setúbal, just south of Lisbon, had been closed to them by Philip II. Another source of supply was the Cape Verde islands. But Araya on the eastern coast of Venezuela, though further off, was more attractive. A ship sent there could not merely load salt, but trade with settlers along the Spanish Main and in the islands, attack intercolonial trade, and even possibly pick off a ship separated from a transatlantic fleet. The venture had its risks; in 1593 the Spanish captured ten ships carrying Caribbean dyewood and other goods off eastern Venezuela.[6] But the prospect of profit combined with undermining Spanish trade and confidence was something a Dutchman could hardly resist. Besides the primary business of salt-digging, trade of Holland and English cloth for pearls and tobacco from Venezuela grew. Turning north, the Dutch soon also found Hispaniola and Cuba to be good sources of hides and sugar. Settlers and even Spanish officials were pleased to trade on the terms the Dutch offered – terms that were generous but so profitable to the Dutch that around 1600 they were sending 120 ships a year to the Caribbean. So disturbing did this commerce soon become to the higher authorities that in 1603 orders came from Spain to hinder it by the desperate measure of removing Spanish settlement from the north and west coasts of Hispaniola. Villages and sugar estates were duly abandoned – some of them being burned to force their inhabitants out – though for some people the allure of the contraband trade was so strong that they stayed.[7] Worse, northern, and especially north-western, Hispaniola became open territory for Dutch, French, and English settlers. Notable among them were the piratical French *boucaniers* – the original buccaneers. Their bases gradually became permanent in the first half of the seventeenth century. Thus the foundation of French-speaking Haiti was laid in western Hispaniola: a problematic history originating in Spanish panic.

Among the Dutch, also, rising trade soon brought thoughts of settlement in its wake. Their first attempts (and some English ones, too) seem to have been made on the "Wild," or Guiana, coast between Venezuela and the Amazon. Raleigh gave an enticing account of this in 1596; but by then the Dutch were already planning trading posts on it, which were in place before 1600. There was hope of precious metals; but gums, oils, and dyes proved to be the more mundane reality. Notwithstanding, Dutch trade in the Caribbean and South America at the turn of the century was highly profitable to them, and highly expensive to the Spanish, who had to divert ever scarcer funds to efforts to thwart the interlopers. They had some success. But so large were Holland's naval reserves by now that small setbacks were taken in their stride. And soon the same could be said of France and England as well. It was clear, as the seventeenth century opened, that Spaniards could no longer assume, as most had since Columbus, that the Caribbean was exclusively theirs.

It was amid the confusion and rivalries of the Thirty Years War (1618–48), however, and after the end of the Spanish–Dutch truce of 1609–21, that foreigners began to make truly serious inroads into the Spanish hold on the Caribbean. In 1621 the Dutch founded their West India Company, a blend of private and state enterprise, to trade and, if necessary, administer in America, and broadly to harass Spain in the Atlantic. The company's most spectacular success came only a few years later, in 1628, when its squadron, commanded by Piet Heyn, captured a returning Spanish fleet off Cape Matanzas in northern Cuba. It was the first time one of the great Spanish Atlantic fleets had been taken, and another staggering blow to Spanish martial confidence, as well as to the treasury. The resulting haul of 6 million pesos (170,000 kilograms of silver) went in part to fund a successful Dutch attack on north-east Brazil in the following year.

By the time of Matanzas Spain had also begun to lose islands in the Caribbean to foreigners. The English, seeking bases for trade with Spanish colonials, and sites for growing the tobacco for which there was now rapidly rising demand, seized San Cristóbal (soon to be renamed St. Kitt's) in the Leeward Islands in 1624, and Barbados in the Windwards in 1627. Despite Spanish attempts at reconquest, sometimes briefly successful, other islands in the Lesser Antilles quickly fell to the English, and also to the French (Martinique and Guadeloupe, for example, in 1635). These were islands that the Spaniards had generally regarded as "useless," and had left unsettled. In 1634, though, the Dutch took a place that was both occupied (if scantily) and far closer to Spanish mainland centers: Curaçao. Losses in the Greater Antilles followed within two decades. An English force sent by Cromwell against Hispaniola in 1655 failed in its attack on Santo Domingo, the capital town. But on the rebound it took Jamaica, where some 150 Spaniards lived. Jamaica remained under English control until 1962. Meanwhile the *boucaniers* had continued their hunting and smuggling in western and northern Hispaniola. The island of Tortuga, just off Hispaniola's north-west coast, had become notorious as a base for these French pirates. In 1665, Louis XIV's administration dispatched a governor to Tortuga to impose some order among the raiders, and also to supervise a more peaceful settlement, with farms and ranches, of nearby parts of Hispaniola. This followed as planned, and the formal French colony of Saint Domingue began to extend over the western end of that large island. Less formal, but still more insolent a challenge to the Spanish, was the largely English incursion into the Caribbean coasts of Central America in the mid-century. In 1642 came the capture of Roatán Island in the Bay of Honduras, a good base for piracy and smuggling, and also for dyewood cutters active in what is now Belize on the eastern side of the Yucatan peninsula. The Spanish built expensive forts to repulse these intruders. But in such thickly forested and thinly peopled areas there was little hope of success against men impelled by a profitable trade. The English woodcutters set up a base at the mouth of the Belize river in the 1660s, the seed of what was until 1981 a British colony. They also came to exercise much, if intermittent, control on the eastern coast of Nicaragua, as the persistence there to this day of English place-names suggests. The first English attempts at settlement of that Mosquito Coast date from the mid 1630s; only in the 1780s did Spain finally manage to drive the interlopers out.

With the exception of the Guianas, over various pieces of which the Dutch, French, and English haggled throughout the 1600s, creating some small settlements, no part of Spanish South America fell to foreign control in the seventeenth century. That north European trio of scourges of the Spanish contented themselves in South America with piracy and smuggling. The main target for illicit trade was Buenos Aires, a port almost completely closed by law even to Spanish shipping, in an attempt to stop the escape from it of silver produced in the Andean mines. But as with the attempted restrictions on trade between Peru and New Spain, and on trans-Pacific exports, the prospect of profit swept the law before it. There was no plugging the drain of silver through the Río de la Plata, exchanged for African slaves and European goods of various sorts bound mainly for the highland mining towns. The west coast of South America was protected by geographical isolation from such constant commercial attention. But European raiders occasionally penetrated the Pacific to attack ports and shipping on the west coast, sowing alarm far disproportionate to their numbers. The Dutch sent powerful, state-dispatched, squadrons around Cape Horn in 1615, 1624, and 1643. The latter two had among their aims the creation of trading posts on the west coast. But the Spanish prevented that, and damage and losses were on balance slight. There followed almost forty years in which the west coast saw no foreigners. Then came English filibusters across the isthmus from the Caribbean, seizing small Spanish ships in the Pacific and using them to raid ports and harry shipping, always in pursuit of silver. The first piratical onslaught was in 1680–1; the second, from 1685 to 1689. In these two episodes the Spanish lost over 50 ships and more than 200 men. The greatest damage may have been, though, in disruption of the lively Pacific coastal trade. Not only were its ships captured but, in an effort to deter the pirates, ports were closed and goods withdrawn inland. Finally colonists, despairing of the government's ability to defend the coast, subscribed to the purchase of two armed frigates. These turned the tide against the intruders.[8]

The seventeenth century was the great age of piracy in the Caribbean too. Officials in the new foreign settlements there, and their home governments, were for several decades tolerant of it. The main victim was Spain. But as the island colonies became more formal, and their populations grew (which some did with spectacular speed, Barbados's rising from 1,850 to 37,000 whites between 1628 and 1643, for example),[9] and as they also rose in economic importance to their home countries, especially with the shift from tobacco to sugar and other tropical crops after the mid-century; the official French, Dutch, and English view of corsairs became more critical. The Spanish were able to bargain in some measure with the intruders, offering recognition of the foreigners' island holdings in exchange for help against pirates. This was one reason, though political and military reality was the larger one, for a series of treaties granting territorial titles that began in 1648 with the cession of Curaçao and St. Eustatius to Holland, and ended in 1697 with the recognition of French Saint Domingue. Spain acknowledged all English claims, except that to Belize, in 1670.

So it was that, well before the end of the seventeenth century, Spain ceased to be mistress of the vestibule to the great edifice of the American empire. Robbers now lurked in the main portal of the Indies. That was more important than the loss of Caribbean territory, for in reality not much that Spain valued for its productive capacity had gone. The newcomers, certainly, produced richly where Spain had never tried; but there was land enough for sugar still in Peru, New Spain, and Cuba. Nor, strategically speaking, did the losses to the French and the Dutch much matter over the remaining century or so of the colonial period. By 1700 Holland was no longer a major European power. And, through the Bourbon connection set up by the War of the Spanish Succession (1700–13), Spain and France were generally allies in eighteenth-century wars. But the English, France's rivals for European and world power in the eighteenth century, were a different matter. To have them ensconced in the Caribbean was a severe handicap; their already formidable naval power was made still more menacing by the existence of their bases in Jamaica and the Lesser Antilles. Wars in the eighteenth century came to mean for Spain frequent breaks in contact with America caused by English naval activity in the Atlantic, with resulting disruption of trade and government. The final English insult came in Simón Bolívar's taking refuge in Jamaica in 1815, before starting his slow but finally successful campaign to free northern South America of Spanish rule.

With the rarest of madcap exceptions, such as a Portuguese scheme to seize Potosí from the Atlantic coast in the 1640s,[10] foreign powers did not plan major assaults on the Spanish American mainland in the seventeenth century. It was far less troublesome and costly simply to tap into the Spanish American trade from offshore settlements in the Caribbean. Viceroys and *audiencia* presidents, therefore, rarely had to ward off anything more serious than piratical attacks. That was just as well, since the military establishment was small and ill prepared except on the empire's periphery.

CREOLES ASCENDANT: COLONIALS IMPOSE THEIR WILL

If, though, the external threat to Lima or Mexico City was in reality slight, royal officers were increasingly conscious of a more insidious, and ultimately far more powerful, challenge from within. This came from the ever-rising number of American-born whites, congregated mainly in the cities and towns of the empire – the creoles (*criollos* in Spanish, from the verb *criar*, to raise or rear). The term *criollo* was often applied in the sixteenth century to American-born blacks. But it was used early of whites as well. "There gathered in this city the sons of householders [*vecinos*], who by another name are called *criollos*," reported one of the crown prosecutors in the *audiencia* of Lima in 1567.[11] From the start administrators regarded these white Americans with suspicion or even trepidation. They seemed footloose, proud (of their ancestors' participation in the conquest), idle, and troublesome. The youthful group in Lima in 1567 had disrupted a religious procession in the nearby port of Callao, tearing down decorative cloths hung out for the occasion, then mocking and injuring a magistrate who tried to stop them. European-born Spaniards in America –sometimes referred to as *peninsulares*, or "peninsulars" in English – remained until the end uneasy about creoles: people who thought themselves equal with Spaniards, but who were not quite Spaniards; lacking European culture; perhaps tainted with some Indian or black blood; perhaps made idle, frivolous, irresponsible by the climates or the environment of America; softened mentally and physically by the tropics. The antagonism was mutual. Some creoles, even before the sixteenth century was out, tended to regard incoming Spaniards, whether officials or private immigrants, as usurpers of positions, wealth, and status that properly belonged to families gloriously descended from conquerors and first settlers.[12] "O Indies! Mother of strangers, a shelter for thieves and delinquents, a homeland for foreigners, sweet kiss and peace for newcomers. O Indies! Stepmother to your own children and exile for your native sons, a scourge and knife for your own people ...," exclaimed a Mexican creole apologist for his kind in 1604, perhaps providing too easy confirmation for peninsulars already persuaded of creole foolishness.[13] The sense given here of creoles' strong attachment by this time to their American birthplace is, however, real.

For lack of discriminating censuses, the balance of numbers between peninsulars and creoles in the sixteenth and seventeenth centuries is unclear. One estimate for New Spain gives $c.6,600$ peninsulars against $c.11,000$ creoles in 1570, and $c.13,800$ against $c.169,000$ in 1646.[14] This last figure seems high; but a heavy *criollo* dominance in Mexico, or elsewhere, by 1600 would not be surprising, given the large number of Spanish women present in the Indies since the mid sixteenth century. By the end of that century, as would be expected, the creole segment of society had acquired its own internal social ranking. This was most developed in Mexico, the earliest of the major mainland colonies. There, at its head as the century turned, stood a sole titled family: the marquises of the Valley of Oaxaca, the descendants of Cortés. Three other rich, landholding families received titles in the first half of the seventeenth century. Beneath these in status, though not necessarily much lower in wealth and property, was a larger group of what had become aristocratic creole clans, stemming from conquerors, early *encomenderos*, and sixteenth-century senior administrators. By the early 1620s some fifty of these families in New Spain had created entails (*mayorazgos*) to protect their holdings in urban and rural property, proprietary offices, mortgages, loans, and assorted goods. They had become tightly interlinked by marriage. Some had blood ties to the upper Castilian nobility. Many also had close connections with the colonial administration; it was common enough for senior officials, who had high status without matching income, to marry the daughters of this untitled Mexican nobility in an exchange of influence for money.[15] Below these wealthy and high-ranking families came all sorts of creole traders, lawyers, priests, doctors, stockraisers, artisans – shading off into *mestizo* society, similarly differentiated at its own lower level.

As this sketch of Mexican creole society suggests, many American-born whites were not content to yield profitable offices and occupations to immigrants. The gripers about peninsulars taking the best positions were mainly from the ranks of the *beneméritos* – the "deserving" grandchildren and later descendants of conquistadores and *encomenderos* who came to hold what may seem an almost comical belief – though it was not in the least so to them – that their forefathers' heroism entitled them to the monarchy's perpetual support and gratitude. But even some of these, and certainly many of those who lacked such an illustrious background, were active enough in pursuing money. Some also pursued political power, for its own sake and for the social and financial returns it could bring.

In the sixteenth century, creoles found political opportunity mainly in town councils. Before the 1590s, most *cabildo* (town council) posts were distributed by royal gift, and once adult creole men appeared on the scene they began to receive positions, in recognition of their services or perhaps of ancestry. While a council's authority was certainly local, it was not trivial for the townspeople in question. It included levy of local taxes, regulation of the supply and price of grain and meat, and control over building lots and municipal commons. *Cabildos* proved adept at resisting viceregal and even royal orders that seemed harmful to a town's (or, more exactly, the local economic elite's) interests. They could and did send representatives to the viceregal and royal courts. Finally, councils were in practice, if not in constitutional intent, a distinct force in the application of law, since it was the aldermen who selected, at the beginning of January every year, a town's two *alcaldes ordinarios*, or magistrates of first instance. These were generally drawn from the same social and economic group as the aldermen themselves; so the leading citizens of towns, through the *cabildo*, gained an influence over jurisdiction, the most central and precious of the monarch's functions. An *alcalde ordinario* was not likely to rule consistently against the interests of peers who had chosen him.

In the seventeenth century, creoles added to their domination of *cabildos* some movement into *alcaldías mayores* and *corregimientos*, the local governorships that were the lowest rung of the salaried royal bureaucracy. Viceroys and *audiencia* presidents generally made these appointments, sometimes as a means of placating disgruntled *beneméritos*, sometimes because of personal ties – credit received, or children intermarried, for instance – with creoles. The positions often gave these local governors good opportunities to profit from near-monopoly sale of goods to rural Indians. Local office, however, was by no means the limit of creole bureaucratic advance. Late in the sixteenth century, to take one example, a son of one of the wealthiest and most eminent creole families in Mexico became royal treasurer in the capital. And between 1610 and 1687, creoles received almost a quarter of the senior appointments (as staff attorneys, prosecutors, or judges) made to colonial *audiencias* across the colonies. The availability by then of advanced legal education in American universities, particularly those in Lima and Mexico City, may account in part for this surprisingly high figure.[16] Again, though, local ties between high administrators and high creole society led to such appointments being made.

For those without influence or some family claim on royal gratitude, the crown opened another door to office by making an expanding range of positions purchasable. This began in 1559 when, scraping for money after the recent state bankruptcy, Philip II ordered notarial offices sold in the Indies.[17] As fiscal woes deepened, the variety of saleable positions grew. Offices in the two mints in New Spain and Peru could be bought after the late 1560s.[18] In 1591, struggling with the cost of the failed Armada of 1588, Philip put up for sale various of the positions in town councils, principally the *regimientos*, or aldermanships. These had in fact been transferable by private sale for decades past, after the monarch's initial bestowal of them.[19] But now the standard way to a *regimiento* became simply to buy it. Then a decree of 1606 made almost every local office purchasable, not simply for a lifetime, but in perpetuity. The holder might, on payment of a tax of half the post's value, pass it to another person, and he to another; and so on. As a result of this ruling, the accounting year 1606–7 brought the largest proceeds ever in colonial Mexico from office sales: the weighty sum of 300,342 pesos.[20] Still, though, fiscal needs pressed. Philip IV's administration took the drastic step of extending sales from municipal to bureaucratic positions. In 1633 appointments in American treasury offices, and in the auditing tribunals (*tribunales de cuenta*) created early in the century in Mexico City, Lima, and Santa Fe de Bogotá, were offered. In the 1640s, the infection spread to the Spanish end of the imperial administration, with the offer of lower positions in the Council of the Indies to buyers. Under Charles II the process was completed. First, in 1677, *corregimientos* and *alcaldías mayores*, and then in 1687 posts in *audiencias*, including the judgeships themselves, were put on the market. The crown thus weakened, for cash, its exercise of jurisdiction at the highest American levels. This was an even more striking surrender to fiscal expediency than the sale of the viceroyship itself, which indeed took place soon after. In the mid 1690s, the count of Cañete bought the post of viceroy of Peru.[21]

Creoles took advantage of the sales to enlarge their presence in government. After 1591 their hold on *cabildos* tightened. They dominated the councils of Mexico City and Lima, and certainly almost everywhere else, in the seventeenth century. While, for example, before 1599 only 19 percent of the *alcaldes ordinarios* of Lima were Peruvian creoles, the proportion rose to 71 percent in the 1600s, and to 81 percent in the 1700s. Again, it was very largely sale that produced a growing creole presence in the fiscal system. Peninsulars heavily dominated both the auditing tribunals and the treasury until selling of posts in them began in 1633. Then creoles began to buy their way into these bodies at every level, so that the collection of royal income was increasingly entrusted to men who had ties of friendship, marriage, and business with the leading families of the empire's major towns. The result was a clear fall in the quality and training of fiscal officers. Increasingly a high offer became the main reason for making an appointment. Worse still, future tenure of a position was also put up for sale, so that men bought offices for younger relatives to assume at a later date; and there was no knowing how capable they might be. For the accountant's post in the auditing tribunal at Lima, multiple sales of "futures" led to there being six buyers in line in 1653.[22]

Selling of fiscal, or other bureaucratic, office had other drawbacks. It weakened the viceroy's powers of patronage. It damaged morale and performance by interrupting patterns of promotion; officials who could have expected before that honest and efficient work would take them over the course of a career from provincial to central posts no longer had that incentive. Perhaps most obviously self-defeating of all was that bureaucratic offices were paid salaries. In seventeenth-century Lima, for instance, the price of treasury posts ranged from 5,375 to 18,750 pesos. The accountant's annual salary there was 3,000 pesos at mid-century.[23] Thus sales meant a brief surge in royal income in exchange for certain future loss – and that in addition to whatever the inefficiency or outright dishonesty of the buyer might cost.

Purchase did not increase the number of creole *alcaldes mayores* and *corregidores*. The reverse, in fact: after selling of these local executive posts began in 1677, creoles perhaps received fewer of them than before, possibly because merchants in Spain bought the appointments for peninsulars who, they hoped, would market exported goods profitably among Indians. The same was not true, however, of *audiencia* offices. From a little under 25 percent before 1687, the year the positions were first offered for cash, creole representation in the high courts rose to 44 percent in the period 1687–1750. Then, with attempts precisely to reduce American influence in the high courts, it dropped back to 24 percent in the second half of the eighteenth century.[24]

American-born colonists thus multiplied their influence over imperial administration in the seventeenth century, either through pressure informally placed on bureaucrats, or by becoming bureaucrats, through appointment or purchase, themselves. What this meant for the efficiency and honesty of government it is impossible to say exactly. Perhaps there were public-spirited creoles who sought appointments because they felt they could do a better job than peninsular bureaucrats. Far more numerous, though, in all probability were those who saw acquisition of office as a profitable investment, with the return coming in salary, commercial opportunities, possibilities of "borrowing" royal funds for personal use, and chances to favor family and friends; and, of course, in gain of status, and the simple exercise of power. Not all, by any means, of colonials' assumption of state business was illegal or immoral, though it all tended to be costly to the crown. The treasury, for example, resorted to local farming of taxes as a solution to shortage of staff. Tithes, customs duties (*almojarifazgo*), and the sales tax (*alcabala*) were often collected in this way. The gatherers, typically town councils or groups of local merchants, naturally bid less for the contract than they thought they would collect, and kept the difference. Clear illegalities, on the other hand, resulted from the large involvement, partly through purchase of positions, of private citizens in the minting of coin in both Mexico City and Potosí: the illegal minting of untaxed silver in the first case,[25] and severe adulteration of coins, through adding copper to the silver, in the mid-century in the second.

An example of a wider sort of distortion of government brought about by close association of bureaucrats and local people can be found, again in Mexico City, in 1621. The senior *oidor* and other judges of the *audiencia*, which temporarily held executive power in New Spain in the absence of a viceroy, concocted a scheme with the creole-dominated *cabildo* of the city, and others, to corner the city's market in wheat and maize. They were briefly successful in driving up the prices as planned. The racket was halted by the incoming viceroy, the marquis of Gelves, who was a man appointed precisely to carry to Mexico the tautening of government, not least of its fiscal aspects, that Philip IV's reforming minister, the count of Olivares, had begun to apply to Spain itself. The matter of the grain sales was, in fact, only the opening round in a two-year battle between the viceroy and the *audiencia*. Into this conflict all major forces in government, church, and society in Mexico City were drawn, on one side or the other, for a variety of causes. The archbishop at first sided with Gelves, but the two soon split over their contrasting view of creoles, whom Gelves lumped together in iniquity with the *audiencia*. Tensions mounted until finally the viceroy banished the archbishop from New Spain. The archbishop ignored the order and retaliated by excommunicating Gelves and closing all the churches in Mexico City. Finally, in January of 1624, riots broke out. The *audiencia* and leading creoles made, it seems, no determined attempt to contain them. The result was a sacking of the viceregal palace, from which Gelves allegedly escaped with his life only by mingling with the mob and joining in its cry of "Kill the viceroy."[26] He was quickly relieved of office; and reform of government lost momentum in New Spain.

Though it was a complicated, many-faceted affair, the confrontation between Gelves and the *audiencia* of New Spain, and its outcome in the viceroy's humiliation, suggest how firm the link between creoles and bureaucracy had become quite early in the seventeenth century. The time had passed when reforms threatening colonists' interests could simply be imposed by fiat from Madrid. Gelves's style was doubtless abrupt; he was something of a puritan. But his failure showed clearly to anyone willing to observe that government of the Indies was now more than ever before a matter of negotiation rather than command. A new role for governors was that of brokerage between the aims of the monarchy and those of the colonials.[27]

This tendency strengthened as the century progressed, to the point where a new "colonial pact" emerged, expressing the monarchy's weakness in America (as in Spain also) on the one hand, and the rising real power (founded in wealth and political influence) of upper creole society on the other.[28] What the crown wanted from America above all else in the seventeenth century was money (a fact symbolized by the uniting under one president of the Councils of the Treasury and of the Indies in 1678). Since silver production was no longer rising as it had before 1600, and as at least the legal transatlantic trade was declining, with a parallel fall in silver imports and duties collected, new or higher taxes seemed necessary. But these the creoles would in general not countenance. Therefore, in a forced shift to pragmatism, the crown raised funds by selling what creoles would buy. Offices, of increasing seniority and jurisdictional weight, were their first preference. But there was much else: titles of nobility (notably from the 1670s on), "compositions" replacing and legalizing missing or defective land titles, extensions of *encomienda* grants, pardons for a variety of transgressions, legitimizations of natural children, and, not least, bonds (*juros*) issued by the home government. These sales at once strengthened the notion that government was something that could be manipulated by money and that wealth was political influence, and also the idea, firmly established in America in the previous century, that wealth underlay social status.

These ideas were not unique to the colonies, of course. If in America they were partly the result of fiscal pressures imposed from Spain, they were all the stronger there, across the Atlantic, where the fiscal strains originated and were most acutely felt. ("A mighty knight is Sir Money" – *poderoso caballero es Don Dinero* – wrote the satirist Francisco de Quevedo, "for he makes equals of the duke and the drover.") It can be no chance that the seventeenth century saw the addition of "wealthy" to the basic sense of "powerful" that *poderoso* had long carried. Olivares was quick to blame the penury and weakness afflicting Spain by 1630 precisely on the *poderosos*.[29] Spanish politics is marked ever more clearly as the century advances, and central authority atrophies, by the emergence of rich and powerful regional oligarchies. The same term has sometimes been applied to leading creole groups in America. But it is too strong. Oligarchies in Spain, full of titled nobles, had a self-assurance, grounded in a deep sense of family and provincial history, that creoles still lacked. Colonials, however strongly attached to place of birth, still finally sought a sense of self-worth, of social validation, in a Spanish framework – hence, in part, their pursuit of senior offices, and of noble titles. They knew also, though perhaps unconsciously in most cases, that their own standing in every way depended on Spain's imperial presence in America. There appear in seventeenth-century America only the faintest glimmerings of separatism – nothing remotely comparable, for example, to the grievances that led Catalonia to revolt against Castilian rule in 1640, or the complaints of any other Iberian region overburdened by Castile's demands and undertakings. Creoles' disloyalty was limited to feathering their nests at the monarchy's expense, to subverting government to their own advantage, and broadly to making their own contribution to the "dissipation of effective sovereignty" that so weakened the seventeenth-century Spanish monarchy.[30] And most would have vehemently denied any lack of loyalty, regarding their gains as the due of the leaders of colonial society – but definitely *Spanish* colonial society.

PRODUCTION, TAXES, AND TRADE IN AMERICA

Sale of office was one means used by the crown to tap into the rising prosperity of least the central areas of Spain's American empire. That rise in production and wealth seems to have persisted from the late sixteenth century for several decades into the seventeenth, though the evidence is patchy and somewhat contradictory. The firmest information is on silver-mining. Even there doubts exist, certainly, because production has been calculated from royalty records, and some evasion of the tax clearly took place. But, precisely for that reason, the estimates of output are minimum possible amounts, and hence useful indicators.

MINING AND TREASURY INCOME

Royalty receipts by the treasury show, broadly, that in the central Andes and New Spain silver production rose in the early 1600s. Potosí's decline, it is true, began almost with the new century. Never again after 1605 did taxed production there exceed 1,500,000 pesos, as it had done several times since 1592. Potosí's decline in registered output lasted until the 1720s, with only occasional resurgences as important, but always lesser, ore deposits were found and worked at various sites on the Bolivian *altiplano* and in the nearby eastern Andean ranges. It was an initial boom at Oruro, the largest of these places, from 1606 to *c.*1630 that propelled central Andean production upward until about 1620. After then decline at Potosí became the dominant force; and from the 1630s to the 1660s Oruro followed it downward. Potosí's decay seems mainly to have been the reverse side of the coin of its success. What was so extraordinary about its Rich Hill was the dense concentration of rich ores that the peak contained. But the great mass was easily worked – and therefore quickly exhausted. Enormous amounts of poorer ore remained beneath the peak. Not only, however, did this ore yield less silver, but it also cost more to extract. Deep shafts, and galleries for drainage and ventilation, were expensive undertakings.

In New Spain it now seems, against earlier views, that silver production did not fall in the seventeenth century, except for a dip *c.*1635–65. The trend of Mexican output over the whole seventeenth century is, in fact, quite steeply upward, thanks to strong growth after 1670 that persisted, always of course with interruptions, until 1810.[31] Mexican production was spread among six or more districts and centers, so that local decline had only a small effect on the whole. The difficulties of the middle decades were in any case largely external to mining. They were partly the result of a governmental decision to divert the flow of mercury originating in Almadén from Mexico to Peru, which was short of mercury on account of decline at Huancavelica. At the same time, the treasury began collecting Mexican miners' accumulated debts for mercury distributed in the past. The double blow of shortage of money and of the essential reagent for refining ores shook Mexican mining for three decades. But it emerged fitter from the trial, with more discriminating investment than before from large merchants in Mexico City, and also a partial return to the smelting techniques of pre-amalgamation days. This technological shift, though how it happened still remains puzzling, clearly gave some protection against future shortages of mercury.

By *c.*1700 rising output in Mexico was enough to reverse the generally downward trend of total silver production in the colonies that had begun some

Table 11.1 Royal income at Lima

	Amount (pesos)
1607–10	16,432,000
1611–20	34,377,000
1621–30	33,399,000
1631–40	38,101,000
1641–50	35,809,000
1651–60	37,910,000
1661–70	19,935,000
1671–80	35,893,000
1681–90	24,995,000

seventy years earlier. Around 1710 Potosí finally yielded its leadership in output to Zacatecas (with taxed totals, respectively, of 1,220,000 and 1,560,000 pesos for 1710–14). By then silver production was rising fast in almost all Mexican districts; but fastest and most consistently in Guanajuato, which overtook Zacatecas c.1730 to become the new Potosí of Spanish America for the rest of colonial times.

In the seventeenth century, however, the original Potosí, even in decline, gave so much more silver than other mines that its waning was enough to produce a falling trend in colonial silver output – taxed output, that is to say – as a whole, c.1630–1700. What is surprising is that even in Peru this did not bring an immediate drop in treasury income. Receipts in the Lima treasury office, into which the balances from the regional offices in the central Andes flowed, did not reach their seventeenth-century peak until the early 1640s, and remained strong until the mid 1650s. The decadal totals of royal income at Lima (rounded to the nearest thousand pesos) indicate the broad pattern (table 11.1).

There was, it is true, some sleight of hand in these sums. A large and growing part of royal income at Lima from the 1630s on was in "soft" money (gifts and loans to the crown, sales of *juros* and offices) rather than in solid tax revenue. From 1643 to 1649, for example, no less than 22 percent of receipts came from loans.[32] Nonetheless, the fact that colonials, largely creoles, were able to put up such sums suggests an enduring prosperity among them for a long time. Only in the 1660s did receipts from loans in Lima drop, and very markedly. At the same time remittances to Lima from regional treasury offices also fell sharply; particularly so from Potosí, Oruro, and La Paz (near Oruro), in reflection of the persistent slump in mining.

The trend of income at the Mexico City treasury office, whose accounts included local income as well as the balances of the regional offices of New Spain, has similarities to Lima's in showing an initial rise in the seventeenth century, and then a fall. The fall, beginning perhaps c.1630 was, though, slight (see table 11.2).[33] In general these Mexican figures seem to follow the trend of silver production more closely than do those from Lima. Especially notable is the resurgence of income after the 1660s, a time of revival of registered silver production. The coincidence is probably not a matter of chance.

Table 11.2 Income at Mexico City treasury office

Date	Income (pesos)
June 1605–June 1615	20,784,000
July 1615–May 1625	22,343,000
(July 1625–June 1630)	9,882,000
Nov. 1636–Feb. 1645	19,550,000
Feb. 1645–June 1655	20.413,000
Apr. 1660–Mar. 1671	18,882,000
Apr. 1671–May 1681	24,173,000
June 1681–June 1690	24,867,000

For the penurious Spain of the seventeenth century, rising American treasury receipts in the early decades (and the late ones also in New Spain) were helpful. But they were less so than the numbers suggest, because a growing fraction of American fiscal income stayed in the colonies. Some went to payment of loans, interest on *juros*, and salaries of offices sold. But far outstripping these was the great and rising cost of defending the colonies, and transatlantic shipping, from aggressive and intrusive foreigners. Fortresses, arms, garrisons, and naval shipping absorbed huge sums in the seventeenth-century Indies. Between 1607 and 1610, only 16.5 percent of the Lima treasury's spending was on defense, some 2.6 million pesos. From 1611 to 1650, the proportion rose to around 25 percent – an average of 8 or 9 million pesos per decade. In the 1660s and 1670s, a third of expenditure went to defense; and in the 1680s, no less than 43 percent (10.3 million pesos). These, and other, costs reduced Lima's remittance to Spain from 51 percent of money sent out from the treasury office in 1607–10, to 35–40 percent for 1611–60, to 14.9 percent in the 1660s, 16.9 percent in the 1670s, and a paltry 5 percent in the 1680s. In actual silver, the decade of highest remittance to Spain was the 1640s, at almost 15 million pesos. In the 1680s, the Lima treasury sent home only 1.27 million.[34]

It was much the same elsewhere. Having supplied 1.37 million pesos to Spain in the first decade of the century, the treasury in Santa Fe de Bogotá managed only 48,000 pesos in the period from 1685 to 1700, mainly because of the cost of defenses at Cartagena on the Caribbean coast of New Granada. From 1672 Santa Fe was ordered to send annual defense subsidies (*situados*) to that crucial port, where the *galeones* generally wintered after unloading their goods, and collecting Peruvian silver, on the Isthmus of Panama. Certainly Santa Fe's remittances to Spain had dwindled constantly for assorted reasons; but it was military expense that finally reduced them to almost nothing.[35]

Mexican treasury remittances to Spain likewise fell drastically through the 1600s, from a high in the first decade of 10 million pesos to a low, in the last, of 2.7 million. The average over the century was some 5.7 million pesos per decade. New Spain carried a very large load of defense charges, not so much for its own coasts or the northern interior as for the Caribbean and also the Philippines. Between 1618 and 1621, for example, 1.65 million pesos of crown funds were sent to Manila for military purposes (possibly in anticipation of Dutch attacks there), while only 1.14 million (plus a large amount of cochineal on royal account) went to Spain.[36] *Situados* of unknown amount were also dispatched to Havana, Santo Domingo, Puerto Rico, and Florida in those four years, as they were to be repeatedly after then. Exactly how much New Spain spent on defending the eastern approaches to the empire is hard to say, since many disbursements were recorded under "miscellaneous" account headings. But it seems that after 1640 at least a third of total outgoings from all Mexican treasury offices went for military purposes in the Atlantic and the Caribbean. Not only did New Spain supply funds for fortresses, arms, and garrisons in the Greater Antilles and Florida, but it also ended up paying much of the bill for naval protection of the transatlantic fleets. The additional cost of supporting administration and defense in the Philippines was extraordinarily high. Between 1581 and 1700 New Spain sent to Manila no less than 23 million pesos in public funds, almost a third of the amount (76.2 million) dispatched to Spain in that same 120-year period.[37]

The monarchy's receipts from America, then, shrank in the 1600s, and particularly after the mid-century. The trend in private shipments of silver to Spain was, however, quite different; or so the weight of evidence, none of it wholly reliable, suggests. The reports of Dutch merchants, French consuls, and other unofficial sources in seventeenth-century Spain give a very different view of incoming American bullion from what Spanish treasury records show. By these estimates total arrivals (public and private) remained roughly level until the mid 1640s. Then came an abrupt drop until the late 1650s (but the records are incomplete for the entire period 1635–60, so that arrivals may have been higher). There followed in the 1660s and 1670s a sharp upsurge, to sums far higher than any ever received before (171.5 million pesos in the 1670s, for example); and then a leveling off from 1680 to 1699, but still at a very high average (13.8 million pesos annually, a figure never approached before 1670).[38]

Since there is no doubt that crown remittances from America fell drastically in the second half of the century, the arrivals of significant amounts of bullion reported after 1660 must have been largely private shipments. Most of them clearly were sums sent by colonial merchants to buy European goods. They were also almost all undeclared to the authorities, so as to avoid duties and levies for defense, as well as possible confiscation as forced loans to the crown. (The Spanish treasury's practice of seizing private silver coming in from the Indies, to reduce the crown's deficits, had grown rather common after 1600, as royal finances went from bad to worse.) The unofficial sources for silver arrivals reported total bullion inflows of 665.2 million pesos between 1650 and 1699, of which only 43.6 million (barely 6.6 percent) were registered. Some of this silver never touched Spanish soil. It was transferred from the incoming fleets to foreign ships waiting offshore. Some of it – much, indeed – went directly into the coffers of the numerous French, Genoese, English, Dutch, Flemish, and German merchants living and trading in Seville, Cadiz, and other Spanish towns. The crown was well aware of the fraud but, for lack of means and fear of reprisal for attacking powerful foreign interests, did little to stop it.

In what became its characteristic seventeenth-century practice across all Spanish territories, the government, faced with problems that it could not possibly control, sold pardons for blatant infractions of the law. The merchants willingly paid negotiated amounts, in what amounted to a form of self-regulated taxation.[39]

The size and pattern of the unofficial bullion receipts throw into doubt the long accepted decline of Spanish American trade after 1610–20. There was certainly a fall in number of ships and total tonnage in the official transatlantic fleets after then, and the decline became steeper as time passed. Between 1600 and 1650, 6,573 ships participated in the Carrera de Indias, as against only 1,835 (22 percent of the century's total) from 1650 to 1700.[40] The probable weakness of bullion receipts around the mid-century certainly fits with the drop in the Carrera's volume. But the recovery after then plainly contradicts it. The conclusion must be that the value of the trade did not fall as much as its volume, and that after 1660 its worth actually rose, with a growing fraction of it consisting of high-value, low-volume, non-Spanish products (fine cloths and hardware, for example), exported either by foreigners or Spanish merchants working with them. Decline of total exchange between Spanish America and Europe seems even less unlikely to have happened if contraband in the Caribbean is taken into account. How much this amounted to will never be known for sure. But it can only have grown as the Dutch, English, and French settled into their island bases after the mid 1620s.

The trends in unofficially reported bullion arrivals in Spain fit partially with known patterns of taxed American silver production in the seventeenth century: strong to 1630, weaker in the 1640s, 1650s, and 1660s. There is contradiction, though, in the 1630s (arrivals up, production down), and from 1670 onwards (arrivals sharply up, production at best in a gradual total decline, though with New Spain resurgent, and Potosí's rate of descent slowed, c.1665–90). Some combination of two possibilities seems for the moment most likely to explain the discrepancies. Colonials may for some reason (war, unfavorable terms of exchange) have held back bullion exports for years or even decades. Second, silver production may have been higher than the royalty record shows, and exports of untaxed silver likewise. It is clear, for instance, that untaxed silver from mines flourishing in the south of the Potosí district c.1680 escaped through Buenos Aires. Tax evaders did not, though, have to use a back door like Buenos Aires to slip silver out. In 1654 the largest galleon in the South Sea Squadron, the 1,200-ton *Jesús María*, ran aground near Guayaquil. Inspection showed the ship to be carrying at least 2 million, and possibly up to 9 million, pesos in untaxed, unregistered silver.[41] That was the equivalent of 250–800 percent of the Potosí district's annual official output at the time. The squadron (the Armada del Mar del Sur) was a state-funded flotilla created to defend maritime trade and communication between Panama and Peru. Guarding silver exports from the likes of the Dutch was, of course, among its main purposes. But native enemies were now in the heart of the system. Here was a royal vessel being used, necessarily with some collusion from its officers, to defraud the crown of perhaps more than 100,000 pesos in income.

The shrinking volume of the Carrera de Indias has often been taken as evidence of economic decline in Spanish America in the 1600s, parallel with economic contraction in Spain itself and other parts of Europe. The fleet trade dwindled because the colonies produced less to export – so went the argument. By the same reasoning, the strength of bullion receipts in Spain – indeed, over the century, their rising trend – for which there is now persuasive evidence, goes against notions of colonial decline. It is not enough to refute those notions, since silver was far from being the colonies' only product, and the links between silver production and the broad economic state were many and complex. But it is a noteworthy pointer.

TEXTILES AND FARMING

The direction of that pointer is confirmed by recent research on a number of productive activities across the American empire. The best known of these, after mining, is cloth-making. One of the two major textile areas, highland Quito, saw clear expansion in the seventeenth century, with the number of legally established *obrajes* rising from about 55 *c.*1620 to 117 *c.*1690 (and 57 other unlicensed mills then also). Although actual output is elusive, there seems no doubt that it grew until about 1690, when production probably reached its maximum for the whole colonial period.[42]

Quito was unusual in seventeenth-century South America in having stability, or possibly growth, in its native population, largely as a result of immigration. Thus part of its textile expansion was a response to rising internal demand for clothing, though it continued to export fabric north to New Granada and south to Peru. In the second important textile region in the Indies, central New Spain, Indian numbers continued their post-conquest fall until the 1620s, and then began a slow increase. Here again, it may be that demographic shifts influenced the fortunes of textiles. Output in Puebla, for example, an active textile center almost from its founding in the 1530s, turned downward in the 1580s, in part precisely because of rising production in the Andes, which had been an export market for Mexican cloth, but also perhaps in response to falling demand locally. By contrast, the Valley of Mexico, above all the towns of Coyoacán and Tacuba, produced strongly, especially in the mid-seventeenth century. A little further north, near the parts of the *altiplano* to which sheep-raising had shifted from more central pastures, the 1600s saw Querétaro become the main wool-weaving center of New Spain. In 1640 it had six *obrajes*, and in 1718, twelve, and other smaller *trapiches*. Querétaro grew in response to rising demand from Mexico City, and from Zacatecas and other northern towns as mining revived in the late 1600s. Its output in part replaced imports of Spanish woolens.[43]

Agricultural production in the seventeenth century (or any other colonial period) is hard to assess, for lack of firm and continuous information. Tithes would seem the best source. But they were often farmed, so that the amounts collected did not necessarily bear a fixed relation to production. Further,

Indians paid no tithe on what they produced on communal lands granted or confirmed to them by the state, so that no record remains of much of the food raised by the largest group in the population. Indians' total production of food certainly fell from earliest colonial times, more or less in line with population decline; fewer people needed less to eat. A positive outcome of that decline would logically be that food production generally was concentrated on the better land that any community or area held. Hence, other things being equal, a certain quantity of labor put into farming should have produced more food than before. Any such rise in labor productivity would have lifted the living standard of the drastically shrunken population that survived.

Commercial agriculture is easier to observe than subsistence farming, since its transactions are far more likely to have been recorded in writing. An intensive study of the Lambayeque region of coastal Peru, 700 kilometers north of Lima, shows that it was a prosperous source of both sugar and cattle in the seventeenth century.[44] It declined only under the influence of the earthquakes and volcanic eruptions that brought decline to much agriculture on the Peruvian coast after 1687. The main market for Lambayeque's sugar and wheat was Lima. The prosperity of the producing area suggests economic vigor in Lima, to the extent that can be read in its demand for food. Another Peruvian region that suffered in 1687 was Arequipa, in the far south. This was above all a wine-making area. It did well from sales to Lima and to highland cities such as Cuzco and Potosí from the late 1500s. That was a time when Peruvian wine was displacing imported Spanish wine in South America by undercutting its price. Other southern Peruvian regions suited for growing grapes, such as Tacna, Sama, Moquegua, Pisco, and Nazca, followed Arequipa's example. As a result wine became cheaper in the 1590s. Despite this, and the beginning of competing production in what is now western Argentina soon after 1600, Arequipa remained a major source of wine throughout the seventeenth century. It did not flourish as before, but neither did it fade.[45]

New Spain made little wine in the seventeenth century, but, like Peru, grew much sugar. The plantations set up earlier near Cuernavaca and in Michoacán particularly prospered from about 1620 in response to the demands of the Mexican sweet tooth.[46] In northern Mexico, *haciendas* continued to raise great numbers of cattle and sheep, though they certainly found local demand dropping for meat and hides during the contraction of mining after 1635. This led to the sale, whole or piecemeal, of some estates. With the later recovery of mining, however, different owners put together new, large landholdings to meet the revived demand in the silver-mining centers. Individual *haciendas*, as created in the late sixteenth century, might not survive; but the model of the great northern estate emerged intact and strong from the difficulties of the middle decades.

The monopoly in cacao production held by southern Mexico and northern Central America was broken in the seventeenth century with the spread of cultivation to Venezuela and Guayaquil. Both became exporters of the chocolate bean – first Venezuela legally to New Spain in rapidly rising amounts from the 1620s to 1650, and then Guayaquil, through contraband, to the Dutch in the Caribbean after the mid-century.[47] An even more vibrant contraband trade was, however, that of tobacco, grown on plantations developing all along the Venezuelan coast and on some offshore islands, and bought by the Portuguese, Dutch, and English from the early 1600s.

Broadly speaking, then, commercial agriculture is a prominent feature in Spanish American economic life in the seventeenth century. The impulse for it varied: local demand in some cases, intercolonial trade in others, and international trade, increasingly through contraband, in yet others. Of large regions only Central America lacked a profitable commercial crop or animal product. Cacao had played that part there, at least in the north, in the sixteenth century, but its place in the Mexican market was taken after then by Venezuelan chocolate. The Central American provinces, however, do seem to have produced adequate food for their own small markets and subsistence needs after 1600.[48]

Evidence on various sorts of production in seventeenth-century Spanish America is, as these examples show, scattered and partial. It will be a long time, if indeed it can ever be done, before production of, say, wheat or sugar is as firmly established as silver output has become (and some doubt remains even there because of tax evasion). Still, the weight of available evidence is on the side of increase, or, at the least, stability in output of foods and goods over the span of the century. Subsistence food production, of course, presumably continued to fall in the large regions where losses of Indians persisted, since fewer people needed less to eat. But foods that reached consumers through markets seem to have normally been in adequate supply, even as the number of buyers rose with the growth of non-Indian parts of the populations. A combining of this with evidence about silver production, treasury income, bullion exports, and trade (legal and contraband) suggests that at the very least Spanish America avoided the economic gloom that enveloped Spain itself for most of the century. Conditions obviously varied from place to place, and may have become generally harder in the middle decades. But, broadly speaking, a Spaniard looking for a comfortable life would probably have been wise to choose America over Spain after 1600. And it may be that the Indian peasant's lot was easier than that of his peninsular counterpart.

TRADING LINKS AND SELF-SUFFICIENCY

Underlying this relative prosperity of the colonies was a continuation of processes that had begun in the sixteenth century. Trade between colonies, and over long distances within them, seems to have flourished in various instances, despite some official attempts to block it when it threatened Spanish interests (as in, for example, the draining of Peruvian silver to Asia via Mexico). Broadly speaking, then, in the seventeenth century the Spanish American colonies continued to move towards becoming an integrated economic system, in which areas with natural advantages for producing one commodity or another – wine, cacao, wheat, beef, and so on – were able, through increasing exchange, to capitalize on those advantages. Venezuelan cacao exports to Mexico, trade of

Quito cloth to Peru and New Granada, and great cattle-drives from the Río de la Plata up to the Andean mining zone, are examples of this integration. Clearly there were limits to trade. Transport costs, especially on land, worked against exchange of cheap, bulky goods. But where boats could be used – for freighting sugar or wheat to the cities of west-coast South America, for example, or carrying Paraguayan *yerba mate* down the Paraná to the towns of the Río de la Plata – trade was particularly active.

The rise of exchange and of regional specialization of production, each reinforcing the other, contributed to a growing economic self-sufficiency of Spanish America in the seventeenth century. Transoceanic imports, whether from Asia or Europe, increasingly consisted of goods that were luxurious, novel, or status-conferring. American sources, near or distant, could provide most of the basics. This economic independence had varied origins. It was the outcome of Spaniards' learning the economic geography of America in the sixteenth century. It was a natural product of time, as numbers of craftsmen and farmers in the European mold grew with immigration and with the training of blacks and Indians in Spanish methods. It was probably advanced after 1600, though in ways still to be traced, by the growing retention in America of royal income, a change that seems likely to have produced multiplier effects.[49] Some part of the treasury's great disbursements for defense inevitably came back to American merchants, whether importers or local traders; and their profits were a source of credit for colonial investment. The second part of the century certainly offers evidence of colonials' willingness to invest productively. The revival of mining in the Zacatecas district after 1660, for instance, drew more deeply on Mexico City capital than it had before. Profits from wool-weaving in Querétaro were reinvested locally in the final decades.[50] Andean miners' clubbing together to buy ships to expel English pirates from the Pacific in the mid 1680s was another form of productive investment.

Again, creoles' growing numbers and self-awareness made for a greater desire to control their economic existence, and to reduce outsiders' gains from it. The classic case here is the rise of the *peruleros*. They were traders and factors from Lima, increasingly creole in origin, who about 1600 began to insert themselves into the fleet trade across the Atlantic. Their aim was to short-circuit the working of the Carrera de Indias to their own advantage. To do this, they reduced their purchases of goods brought by the *galeones* to the Isthmus of Panama. The great fairs held there on the ships' arrival had been, during the 1500s, Lima's source of European goods. Now the Lima men started to travel to Seville themselves on the fleets returning to Spain, taking large sums in silver to buy there directly from suppliers. In this way they avoided duties charged on the isthmus and took for themselves the profits of the Seville exporters. These, naturally, complained loudly about the intrusion. In 1626 they petitioned the king to "remedy the great excess that has come about … with ten or twelve barefoot men who come in the *galeones* [bringing] a third of the silver that [the ships] carry" to buy on behalf of Peruvian importing merchants.[51] There was, though, no stopping these crude colonials, who, however bare of foot, were only too sharp of eye in seeing how much the clumsy structure of the official Atlantic trade had been created and adapted to favor crown and Spanish exporters. Such contorted machinery cried out for simplification, and if Spanish officials and merchants would not attempt it, creoles were glad to do it for them. The final simplification of the Carrera, of course, was to stop using it altogether, and to buy from, and sell to, foreign contraband traders. This was step that growing numbers of colonials took in the seventeenth century, and it was in itself a form of economic self-determination.

INDIANS IN THE HEARTLANDS: MAKING THEIR OWN SPACE

Indians, too, in the seventeenth century were looking for greater self-determination; they did so, of course, within the broad limits set by the colonial state and society. Those limits were generally, in the 1600s, less closely controlled by the imperial government than they had been in the previous century, and this gave native people expanding room to open up for themselves as comfortable a place as possible in the colonial scheme. Their probing for independent action took place mostly in the central zones of the empire, since it was there that native people had most to avoid or adjust to in the way of burdens and imposed changes. On most of the periphery the relative lightness of Spanish presence, both official and private, meant that the Indian–Spanish relationship stayed closer to its sixteenth-century beginnings.

PHYSICAL MOVEMENT

Just moving from one place to another was the Indians' simplest form of self-determination. Though an early decree, of 1536, declared them to be generally free to move, except from places to which they had been "reduced," later regulations restricted that freedom.[52] Certainly, the practical assumption was that Indians would remain in the place on whose tribute list (*tasa*) they figured. Normally this was their birthplace. There were exceptions, the most obvious of which was that men assigned to forced *repartimiento* or *mita* work generally had to travel to do it. If they had to go far, for a long period, wives and children might go with them. Also exceptional were those unattached to any native community, men known as *naborías* in New Spain and *yanaconas* in the Quechua-speaking parts of the Andes. In pre-conquest times these men had generally been the personal dependants and servants of native lords; after the conquests many of them moved into a similar connection with leading Spaniards. With time the meaning of the terms grew broader. *Naboría* came to mean an independent, salaried worker, and *yanacona*, a permanent employee, sometimes salaried, of a Spaniard. But both were expected to be more mobile than members of native communities.

By 1600 or so, however, many natives besides forced laborers, *naborías* and *yanaconas* were showing a resistance to staying where the Spaniards thought they should be. The forced labor systems themselves, in fact, encouraged long-term or even permanent movement of people. For example, much of the enormous native population inhabiting Potosí by 1600 had originally been brought there by the mining *mita*, the single largest draft in the empire. After their year in the town, many men, having exhausted whatever supplies of food and clothing they had brought with them, apparently preferred staying on as workers in mining, refining, or something else, to the prospect of a long journey home with their family. Others moved out of the town to nearby valleys, apparently as subsistence farmers or workers on *chácaras*. The boom at Oruro after 1606 was another lure to Indians who had learned mining and refining in Potosí after being forced to go there by the *mita*. In fact, Oruro drew off *mita* men who were on their way to Potosí. They worked in Oruro as contracted wage laborers, since the authorities made hardly any *mita* allocation to Oruro. The other lesser mining centers that rose and fell in the Potosí district after 1600 were similarly *mita*-less, and had only the attraction of wages to hold workers – some from Potosí, some from native towns.

Thus those who were first moved by the mechanism of forced labor might then become permanent migrants through the lure of waged work. An initial uprooting by a labor draft was by no means essential, however. At the start of the seventeenth century, Lima's native population of about 3,000 included some 1,730 migrants, 34.5 percent of whom came from northerly regions of Peru, and even in a few cases from Quito and New Granada – places outside the catchment area of the *mita* draft that the city, like many others in the Indies, received for purposes of upkeep. A big attraction for these outsiders was clearly the income, in cash and kind, they could make as craftsmen, domestic servants, laborers on nearby smallholdings, muleteers, and the like.[53]

Clearer still was the case of Indian workers in the silver mines of northern Mexico. There, no *repartimiento*, or draft, ever functioned, mainly because the thin local population of nomads could not be organized into a workforce. Instead, from the start around 1550 at Zacatecas, migrant natives from central and western Mexico worked the mines and refineries for wages. From Zacatecas, as from Potosí, skilled men then spread out as other ore deposits were found, drawn by the high rewards that the initial mine workings usually yielded. San Luis Potosí in the 1590s and Parral in the 1630s were two major new silver centers that drew skilled Indian workers from Zacatecas. So there arose a permanent, mobile corps of native silver miners and refiners in the north. At the same time, though, new native workers continued to move up from the south, especially when new strikes made prospects for earnings seem good. This flow of Indians into northern Mexican mining continued into late colonial times.[54]

The large towns of the empire, all of which came quickly to be focuses of Spanish control and culture, were the first places to offer waged work to Indians. These settlements, most of them administrative or mining centers with substantial white populations, produced the most intense demand for labor, and it was therefore in them that forced labor arrangements were first likely to prove inadequate. Hence the appearance in them of individually contracted, native waged workers well before 1600 is unsurprising. What is striking, however, is the spread of wage labor into the countryside soon after its appearance in towns. Again, the growing need for workers is the reason, the outcome of a varying combination of population loss, local demand for food, and the inadequacies of draft systems. The white owners of wheat farms in the Valley of Mexico, for instance, were hiring Indian laborers in the 1580s to grow grain for the capital.[55] The process was self-reinforcing. Even if the native population had not still been falling – as it was – the use of waged workers would have shrunk the pool available for drafting, giving employers further reason to go out and hire. Since native Mexican numbers in fact went on falling until the 1620s, the negative effect of hiring on the draft was intensified. So great, indeed, was the shift to waged labor on the growing number of *haciendas* in New Spain that in 1632 the colonial administration ended the *repartimiento* for agriculture (though leaving it in place for mining). The wage system grew so quickly because it suited not only employers, but also Indian villagers. The rising shortage of laborers worked in their favor by driving up rates of pay. As they earned more on colonials' farms, they could more easily pay tributes. And by, in many cases, leaving their communities and taking up residence on those farms they could do even better – perhaps avoid tribute altogether, and also the demands of the *repartimiento*. Wage labor thus encouraged native migration not only to towns, but also to country estates, some of which now began to be village-like themselves, with permanent small dwellings for resident workers added to the basic plan of owner's house, chapel, stables, barns, and other storage buildings.

The combination of push and pull causes that led Indians to leave their own communities seems to have operated even more strongly in the central Andes than in New Spain. By 1690 almost half the population of the bishopric of Cuzco, covering much of southern highland Peru, consisted of *forasteros* – Indians who had left their places of origin for other native villages, estates, or larger towns. In the province of Charcas, directly to the south, *forasteros* were similarly numerous. Across the central Andes generally, in fact, native towns and villages could be found in the late 1600s where 80 percent of the population consisted of *forasteros*.[56] A great initial impetus for all this movement had come in the 1570s from Viceroy Toledo's concentration (*reducción*) of natives into new communities for ease of administration, religious instruction, and enforcement of tribute and labor levies. This was a far more wrenching reform, affecting perhaps as many as 1.5 million people, than any relocation program attempted in New Spain. Its success, however, is questionable. The new places were sometimes badly sited for farming, or for access to the people's scattered lands. Indians left the "reductions" to return home. Others left to become resident workers on colonials' farms and estates. Others simply fled into the Andes' numberless hidden places. All wished to avoid the mining *mita* – an expectable outcome, though a disappointing one from the Spaniards' point of view, since a prime purpose of setting up the *reducciones* had been to create a large pool of recruits for the mining draft. And by a quirk of Toledo's legislation, those living away from their own communities (including the *reducciones*) were exempted from *mita* service. Further, those who moved could probably avoid paying tribute as well. Indians had, then, every reason to leave their home towns and villages. And colonials who were not miners quickly came to realize that they also had good reason to harbor the fugitives and to resist the attempts made by later viceroys to reinsert them into the *mita*. For, just as in New Spain, a falling native population meant a general shortage of labor in the central Andes. As in New Spain, also, an outcome of the shortage was rising levels of waged employment, both in the urban labor market of Cuzco and out in the country. The degree to which wage labor – a practice far from the traditional Andean conviction that work was a matter of reciprocal duty in a community – penetrated labor relations is clearly revealed in a contract of 1666 by which an Indian undertook to work for pay on an estate belonging to his own *curaca*.[57]

As these examples of native migration, and its connection with different forms of work, show, the Indians' response to colonial pressures (demands that they provide labor, pay tribute, and submit to being moved) was varied and complex in the late sixteenth and seventeenth centuries. Refusing to be "reduced," some Andeans fled to where Spaniards could not find them. Others took refuge precisely among colonials on rural landholdings or in large towns. Some chose to support themselves by subsistence farming. Others took the opposite course of embracing the European economic system of markets in which goods and labor were sold for money, and plunged into sorts of work – crafts, silver-refining, domestic service – that were defined by European standards. Clearly the particular circumstances, abilities, and inclinations of individuals had much to do with their choices. Clearly, also, what they did might depend more on communal needs than on their own preference. It suited Andean *curacas*, for instance, that some of their people be hidden away in places unknown to the authorities. The tribute demand on the *curaca*'s community would be lessened (because the population would be recorded as smaller than it really was), while he would have subjects to draw on to fulfill *mita* requirements, perhaps, or to put to his own use in some sort of production or trade. But whatever the course chosen, the overwhelming impression is of the Indians' adaptability and flexible responsiveness. In the sixteenth century the leaders in the high-culture areas had quickly shown these qualities. In the seventeenth, the people as a whole did likewise. There was little passivity here. "If you can't beat them, join them" might seem to have been the attitude of many Indians; and to a degree it was. But the procedure was in reality more subtle. It consisted of meeting the demands of colonial state and society at some level close to the minimum they would accept; of playing the European economic game to the degree necessary to ensure material survival; of taking on a European disguise the better to defend the native identity. It was, perhaps, a case of taking one step forward (into the colonials' world) in order to safeguard two back (into the native world); of *sauter pour mieux reculer*.

It was, of course, impossible to preserve everything. Voluntary migration further sapped community identity and practices that had already suffered heavy blows before 1600 from depopulation, labor levies, and *reducción*. The seventeenth-century trend was one of a weakening of traditional ethnic identities – of native people's belonging to the culture of a particular community or small region – and the emergence of a more homogeneous Indian peasant mass. This has been particularly emphasized for the central Andes, but must be true of any area in which native people were intensely subjected to Spanish demands for tribute and labor.[58] Working for a wage under conditions set by individual contracts pushed native people in the direction of personal autonomy, and away from both the collective practices of Indian communities and the political authority of traditional rulers. Indians who moved permanently or even temporarily to large towns, especially to new foundations such as the mining towns where Spanish ways were so dominant, were likely to become cultural *mestizos*. As they did so, they would to some degree imitate Spaniards and colonials in making money, and purchasing what it could buy, a stronger criterion of social standing than it was in traditional native communities. And as that happened, it has been said, Indians began moving away from social ranking by caste and toward ranking by class.[59] That change was long and slow, and indeed is not yet complete in areas where native peoples are still plentiful. But it had visibly started by 1600, and grew ever clearer after that date.

MENTAL SELF-DEFENSE

Decisions about migration and taking a job for pay were largely a conscious matter, though the individual taking them might not be fully aware of all the forces inclining him or her to make the choice. In less tangible and conscious aspects of life as well, however, incorporation of various aspects of Spanish culture into native life can be seen to be proceeding fast after 1600. Language is one example. Research on the absorption of Spanish into the Nahuatl of central Mexico shows that in the sixteenth century borrowings were nearly all nouns, and that native pronunciation and grammar barely altered. But then "the dam broke."[60] Indians began bringing Spanish verbs into Nahuatl, and Spanish prepositions too, which is still more striking since Nahuatl did not possess prepositions as discrete parts of speech. Another borrowing was the Spanish (indeed, European) means of showing plural by adding a distinct suffix to a noun. This began to be done not only with borrowed words, but with some Nahuatl nouns as well. There is suggestive evidence also that native speakers began to use sounds that Spanish possessed but that Nahuatl did not. Thus, under the influence of spoken and written Spanish, central Mexicans drew into their language not only borrowings that dealing with Spaniards, colonials, and their speech made necessary, but also elements of Spanish (prepositions, for example) that were simply of linguistic use.

More fascinating still as evidence of native mental approach to, and incorporation of, what was Spanish are the idiosyncratic native documents from central and southern Mexico called *titulos* (titles), all apparently dating from after 1650, though written in archaic styles to make them seem to be from before 1600. Their purpose was, apparently, to bolster Indian communities' claims to land; but they are not land titles of a legal sort, but a blend of local myth and history intended to solidify a community's sense of its lasting individuality and occupation of its land. They draw on popular, oral culture. They give little sense of passing time; quite the opposite – they aim to convey timelessness, and a deep and constant mythical identity. In doing so, they blend native elements with Spanish. Spanish authorities as well as native ones are appealed to without distinction as part of a group's past, with no sense of one being more legitimate or favorable than the other. Indians as well as Spaniards may figure as hostile intruders in a village's past. Christianity and indigenous beliefs are given equal weight in the people's spiritual identity. "Oh my dear children, you must entirely understand that CortésDonLuis deVelasco Marqués brought us the true faith,"[61] went one writer's exhortation in the late 1690s. Here the blur simply runs together the conqueror of the Aztecs and the second viceroy of New Spain; but elsewhere the melding extends to combining the pre-conquest and the post-conquest into one historical entity. If the *títulos* are really a true reflection of Indian commoners' view of their past and of their current, late seventeenth-century, identity, they show a great capacity for syn-thesizing contrasts and changes in quite recent history, and a truly amazing acceptance of the culture and beliefs of the invaders. It was not, though, a pas-sive or resigned acceptance, but rather an active integration of the culture the Spanish had imposed on a mental world still very reminiscent of the Aztecs' vision of the supernatural as a mesmerizing swirl of spirits and gods.

The incorporation of Spanish into native languages has been studied closely only for central Mexico, and *títulos* may be unique to the center and south of New Spain. But both the linguistic borrowings and the historico-cultural blendings shown in these two phenomena fit with a pattern, visible across the areas of high native culture, of creative response to various sorts of invasion and intrusion – of taking from European techniques, practices, and beliefs what could be usefully adapted to native life under colonial rule.

A notable Andean instance of this sort of adaptability can be seen in *curacas*' attitude towards the Spanish king. For them, their own legitimacy depended on their being attached to some universal ruler. Before the conquest, that ruler had been the Inca emperor (and, before there were Incas, other hazily recorded holders of wide power). But now the Inca emperors were gone. So the *curacas* turned to the Spanish king as their universal superior – not merely out of respect or for political gain, but because without his existence their own genuineness as local rulers was lessened.[62] This attitude has something in common with the blending of native and Spanish authority visible in the Mexican *títulos*.

Even clearer examples of adaptive borrowing by native people are found in religion. Indian spirituality remained in the seventeenth century, as it still does, a complicated blend of the native and the imported. Many friars in the early post-conquest evangelizing campaigns had had hopes of displacing native beliefs and religious practices with Christianity, inspired perhaps by the view of Las Casas and others that indigenous religious history could be read as an approach to the true faith, a progression that keen Christian evangelizers could now complete. But this optimism was fading by 1600 as the persistence of pre-conquest belief became clear. And soon, under perhaps the influence of the same Counter-Reformation intolerance that had taken hold of Spain itself, clerics in Spanish America began arguing for an attack on native "idolatry," as it was often seen to be. Campaigns of "extirpation" were mounted, particularly in the central Andes, where they lasted, on and off, throughout the century. Special inspectors were sent out to native communities to dig out offending practices and punish their perpetrators.

The inspectors' reports confirmed the church's worst fears. Ancestor-worship was still common. If necessary, people went back to the pre-*reducción* sites of their communities to make offerings to mummies still preserved in caves. There was perhaps still some ritual sacrifice of children in the early 1600s. Offerings were still being made to *huacas* (to, for instance, stones believed to be the petrified forms of humans or animals). The extirpating priests might try to suppress such practices by destroying the physical objects of worship; but the people tended simply to replace them, since the spirit of the deity in question persisted even when the "idol" was smashed or burned. The priests failed to realize, or could not accept, that "Spanish colonization was an endless series of negotiations and compromises with Indian reality," as one recent historian has aptly observed.[63] The Spanish inquiries uncovered, in fact, a vibrant continuity in native beliefs and practices from the pre-conquest into the sixteenth century, and then on into the seventeenth; and for the Indians this persistence was more a matter of what was natural to them than a show of defiance.

Into these survivals Christianity had been woven, with an intricacy that was the despair of the investigating Catholic priests. Seasonal festivals of the Andes became entangled with Christian feasts, so that images of saints might be offered the traditional gifts of coca, *chicha*, and guinea pigs. Conversely, sacred objects might be hidden in Christian altars, to be worshiped surreptitiously while people were in church. The old Andean feast of Caruamita (the "time of yellowing" when maize ripened) was blended with the feast of Corpus Christi. Under cover of the Christian celebrations, Andeans made their own, ancient sort of confessions and sacrifices to local deities so that the crops would be protected from the threat of frosts that June brought.[64]

Almost all Indians had been impressed from the start by the evident power of the Christian god – their defeat was clearly in part his doing – and out of fear and also a desire to gain access to that power themselves, had taken up worshiping him. Evangelizing friars, then, had that great force on their side, besides whatever personal powers of persuasion they might be able to deploy. Under the friars' instruction, Indians also came to revere Christ, the Virgin Mary, and what seemed to them the lesser Christian deities, the saints. To Andean native people the saints, in fact, seemed the closest analogy to indigenous local spirits (*huacas*); like *huacas*, saints came to be seen as full of sacred power.[65] Thus it was common for a saint to be the immediate object of worship in small places, each parish church holding an image of its patron figure.

Despite the deep devotion to saints that Andeans had developed by the seventeenth century, it may be that this devotion, and indeed the hold over Indians that Christianity had gained by then, was still stronger in New Spain. Why this should have been so is unclear: perhaps a longer period of uninterrupted evangelization after the conquest, by more numerous and dedicated friars; perhaps the greater geographical accessibility of native communities in Mexico; or perhaps a greater keenness in those towns and villages to build a church and acquire a patron saint as marks of local identity and status. Whatever the cause, in the final years of the sixteenth century the cult of Spanish saints put down deep and lasting roots in the high-culture areas of New Spain. By the opening of the seventeenth century, Indians clearly regarded their images as the source of miracles, just as Spaniards did.[66]

Yet just as it seems that Indians had accepted some piece of Christianity in a more or less "pure" state, complications intervene. In late sixteenth-century Mexico City, native craftsmen made glazed incense burners in the form of male and female saints – certainly not following, in doing so, any Spanish Christian pattern. To celebrate St. Francis's day in 1593, again in Mexico City, other artisans showed the saint astride an eagle perched on a cactus[67] – the latter being the defining symbol of native Tenochtitlan, since the Aztecs had reputedly received a divine command to found their city on a site where an eagle was so perched. Repeatedly, then, native myth, history, and cult intertwined with the imported faith. One result is that it is impossible to know exactly what Indians did believe. There is no doubt that they accepted Christianity sincerely; but for almost all of them it was never more than a part of their faith, something to be absorbed into earlier beliefs, just as the deities of native invaders had typically been added to a conquered people's pantheon of gods in pre-Columbian times. As in those earlier days, the Christian invaders' faith may have continued to seem alien, something ultimately belonging more to the outsiders than to the vanquished native people. But it was certainly too powerful to be dismissed, too full of potential benefits to be ignored.[68]

A Christian figure with whom natives of Mexico, at least, found it particularly easy to identify, perhaps because she seemed the closest approach to the idea of the mother-goddess so strong in their own beliefs, was the Virgin Mary. The Virgin of Guadalupe has long been taken as the obvious example of this affinity. The time-hallowed story of her appearance to the Mexican Indian Juan Diego in 1531 traditionally made her the protectress of native people from earliest colonial times, and, in due course, of Mexico as a whole. Her tie to native affairs was strengthened by the fact that the apparition reportedly took place at the Hill of Tepeyac, a site near Mexico City sacred to the Aztec goddess Tonantzin, "our mother." Regrettably, though – for the niceness of that linkage and for the tenderness of the story – research shows neither any record of an apparition in 1531 nor any indication that the cult of Guadalupe, which certainly existed by the 1550s, was particularly Indian. Quite to the contrary, in fact: Spaniards were its main followers, which is not surprising considering the immense devotion they had long given to the image of the Virgin enshrined at Guadalupe in Extremadura. The cult of the Mexican Guadalupe was, further, mainly limited to Mexico City and its close surroundings until the mid seventeenth century. And though by the early eighteenth century Tepeyac was the prime pilgrimage site in Mexico, it was only after

1746, when the Mexican bishops and cathedral chapters proclaimed Our Lady of Guadalupe to be the patroness of New Spain, that her cult became colony-wide. Only then did a broad Indian linkage with her begin, far more as the result of teaching than of any earlier devotion. It may even be that the eighteenth-century promotion of the Guadalupe cult was the conscious doing of creoles seeking some symbol of proto-national Mexican unity. The story of the Virgin's appearance in 1531, in Mexico, and to an Indian, no less, certainly gave them reason to believe, and proclaim, that God had seen fit to create a specifically Mexican church. Mexican Catholicism was not simply, they could argue, a transfer from Spain of an established church, but a new creation, in New Spain, brought about and marked by the Virgin visiting the land.[69]

But if the idea of the Virgin of Guadalupe as a specifically Indian version of the Madonna no longer holds good, it remains true that Indians found the figure of Mary immensely appealing and comforting. She was, after all, the greatest of Christian saints, and as Indians turned to saints in the late 1500s, they embraced her among them. Like Christians from earliest times, they viewed her above all as intercessor, a loving mother pleading for them before a paternal but stern God. The medieval Spanish mind linked her closely with the land and its fertility; some native female deities had the same association.[70] The Virgin, then, was perhaps the easiest and most attractive of Christian figures for Indians to fuse into their spiritual life. Among the various aspects of Christianity that they made their own, she stood out prominently.

Another part of imported Christianity taken up enthusiastically by many Indians was the confraternity, or *cofradía*. This was a form of local organization, a religious brotherhood linked to the cult of saints and of the Virgin Mary. By the early 1600s Indians were keenly creating and participating in these religious societies. A *cofradía* was usually organized in a particular parish, and associated with devotion to a particular saint of which there was an image in the parish church. The religious function of the brotherhood was to preserve, dress, and decorate the image, and beyond that to celebrate its existence, and that of the saint himself or herself, by taking part in religious processions within the town or village. These celebrations, for which the images of saints would be typically brought out of the churches and paraded around the streets by the respective brotherhoods, became defining events in a community's yearly calendar (as they still are today in some places). They were expressions not only of the brotherhood members' religious devotion, but also of communal purpose and coherence.

Cofradías also had a more secular, everyday purpose: they functioned as local insurance societies. Members counted on each other for help in difficult times, or to see to burial at the end of their lives. If members contributed money to a fund organized by their *cofradía*, that cash could be used for the same purposes. It is easy to see why native people in the Andes adopted this Spanish-style brotherhood so eagerly (the priest of a parish near Cuzco remarked, critically, in 1609 that "there is no end to the novelties and bribery added every day to the confraternities' costly festivities, nor to the new flags, nor to the solicitation of funds") – it coincided perfectly with the traditions of reciprocity that were deeply rooted in their culture, and indeed reinforced them. But native *cofradías* were to be found throughout the Spanish American colonies, not just in Peru.[71]

A similar adoption was that of the Spanish practice of *compadrazgo*, or godparenthood. It was understood in this arrangement that the godparents chosen by the biological parents for their offspring became, at the baby's baptism, ritual kinfolk of the child's family. Again, much reciprocity developed as these relationships became common in a community. Each family was tied, through them, to others, for purposes of mutual help. The links would normally be with other families of similar status and wealth. But a rich or powerful *compadre* was especially sought after, and sometimes found. In that case, *compadrazgo* might become a means for redistributing wealth, in what amounted to patron–client relationships.

Across the whole breadth of life's practices and activities, then, from the economic to the spiritual, Indians, by or during the seventeenth century, absorbed from the invaders much that was useful for their own gain or comfort, often with the aim, intentional or unconscious, of using the alien as best they could in order to protect themselves from it. Clearly the borrowing was heaviest in the empire's central areas, where Spanish numbers and cultural weight were greatest. Elsewhere it varied, broadly according to the weight of Spanish presence, although colonials' influence on Indians depended not only on numbers but also on the local conditions within which that influence operated.

INDIANS ON THE PERIPHERIES

Seventeenth-century New Granada is a case in point. This was a large area, roughly within present Colombian boundaries. It was strongly regionalized even from before conquest because, first, of a brokenness of terrain unusual even for an Andean territory. Partly because of its array, or rather disarray, of valleys, basins, rivers, and rainforests, even the largest pre-Columbian polity (the Chibcha) was tiny by Aztec or Inca standards. The other native groups, largely agricultural and sedentary, were politically as well as geographically separate. The Spanish occupation brought little increase in unity, in part because of these pre-existing diversities, in part because it too was diverse, with competing expeditions coming in from different directions and settling in independent groups. Thus New Granada was born fissile, and so it has stayed. The *audiencia* of Santa Fe de Bogotá (1547) in reality had little authority outside the center-east of New Granada. The other two major centers of power were Cartagena, on the Caribbean coast in the north, and Popayán, overseeing a vast area in the south. New Granada, then, while peripheral to the empire's heartlands, had its own internal centers and peripheries.

Indians' colonial fortunes varied with this regionalization. Everywhere in New Granada the *encomienda* was the prime relationship before 1600 between settlers and natives. *Servicio personal* – Indians in *encomienda* actually working for their *encomenderos*, rather than just paying tribute to them – continued as the standard labor system thirty years or more after its decline began in Peru and New Spain. Only in 1597–8 was *repartimiento* (the system of state-organized draft labor) set up in New Granada (twenty to thirty years later than in Peru and New Spain), and then only in the central highland zone dominated by Bogotá. By then *encomenderos* were so much in social and economic control of that region, with rural estates set up to provide grains and meat for the city, that they managed, through connections with officials, to channel to themselves most of the drafted Indian workers. Others were assigned to urban building, silver-mining, household work, and cloth-making in a small number of *obrajes* that began to appear in Bogotá about 1600. The labor burden on Indians in the seventeenth century was heavy, as the native population continued to dwindle after its severe reduction in the 1500s, and as New Granada achieved some degree of the economic diversification and autonomy that were more obvious in the imperial heartlands. But at least in the region controlled from Bogotá there was some oversight by senior officialdom.

THE PERSISTENT *ENCOMIENDA*

Away from that central area the lot of seventeenth-century Indians was harder still. In many of these outlying areas *encomienda* persisted after 1600 in its original form, as the prime means of obtaining native labor. This was so, for example, in the great plains to the east of the Andes – the remote *llanos* of New Granada –where a few *encomiendas* survived until the early nineteenth century, although most had gone by 1750. Indians were notoriously badly treated by the holders of those grants, and open but completely illegal slaving of natives took place there. Gathering and selling Indians as slaves was more profitable than the dominant activity in the *llanos*, raising cattle.[72]

Encomenderos in New Granada also put their Indians to work in extracting gold. New Granada reached its first peak of gold production, from several fields, between 1580 and 1620. The richer miners began importing black slaves before 1600 to meet a need for labor that the shrinking Indian population could not supply. But slaves were expensive, so those who had access to the remaining natives, above all the *encomenderos*, used them to the fullest. Gold output leveled off or subsided after 1620, and did not revive until about 1700. But metal was still available in amounts large enough to lubricate internal trade (a mint was created at Bogotá in 1620) and to pay for goods bought from Dutch and other smugglers on the Caribbean coast. Throughout the century, then, *encomienda* Indians found themselves pressed into mining and washing for gold. The *encomenderos* of Popayán had their people farming as well as mining, under conditions described as "virtual enslavement" in the late seventeenth century.[73] Treatment was no better in other gold areas further north and west. Indeed, in the 1680s a royal inspector found severe exploitation of Indians in places near Bogotá. By then law on Indian labor was being ignored under the very nose of the *audiencia*, such was the loss of administrative control that the crown had suffered in New Granada.

On the periphery, then, and even more on the edges of the periphery, Indians stood to suffer from weakness or negligence in government. A common trait of these imperial fringes was persistence of the *encomienda*, often with its labor privileges still attached, as in much of New Granada. This might seem the result simply of governmental carelessness about areas deemed both physically and economically marginal. And perhaps it was to some extent a matter of neglect. But continuation of the *encomienda* also served practical ends. For on the edges it still usefully played the role it had had everywhere in the beginning, as a means of anchoring settlers in places where, for reasons of isolation or poverty, they would otherwise not have stayed. As a result, the imperial fringes presented anachronistic social and economic traits in the 1600s. In particular, Indians often found themselves subject to a sort of seigneurial control by settlers that had been weakened elsewhere by the rise of draft and wage labor. Where demand for natives' work was high, as it was in some outlying regions of New Granada, Indians found themselves at the unregulated mercy of their *encomenderos*, especially as these continued to be the prime economic and social power in the land.

In these respects, Venezuela resembled New Granada in the first half of the seventeenth century, with the difference that the work to which *encomienda* Indians were put was cacao production. The strength with which *encomienda* persisted here as an institution, and a social ideal for colonials, is suggested by the fact that most of the best grants on the coast near Caracas were held, in the mid 1630s, not by descendants of sixteenth-century original settlers, but by recent immigrants who had gained them by marriage. These men, successful entrepreneurs, were the first of the *grandes cacaos*, or lords of chocolate, who in the next century were to dominate Venezuelan society so thoroughly, and ultimately present powerful opposition to Spanish rule in the region. But the earliest of them, before 1650, built their wealth on the basis of *encomienda* in its sixteenth-century, labor-yielding, form. After that, it is true, as cacao production grew, they increasingly replaced natives with black slaves, as a source both of labor and of social standing. The growing numbers of blacks on the expanding estates of the Caracas coast resulted in a displacement of natives, and their gradual replacement by mixed-blood *zambos*. In 1691 the crown finally put an end to *servicio personal* in Venezuela, without great protest from the remaining *encomenderos*. Black slavery had proved the more satisfactory source of labor for growing cacao.[74]

FRONTIER MISSIONS: FRANCISCANS AND JESUITS

On the remoter fringes yet another feature of early sixteenth-century colonization tended to persist: a large role for churchmen, particularly friars in the regular orders, in what was in reality Indian government. The clerics' formal task may have been simply spiritual care; but since they were often the only outsiders in regular contact with natives, they inevitably came to be seen by their charges, and to see themselves, as agents of imperial power. This was also true, to be sure, of priests ministering to parishes in the central colonial areas. But on the edges, where other officialdom was sparse, the clerics' influence and authority were that much greater.

A classic case was New Mexico. The evangelization of Pueblo people here was entrusted to the Franciscans soon after settlement began around 1600. Conflict between the friars living in the native communities and the crown's governors seated in Santa Fe was at the center of New Mexican history for most of the century. The friars' ideal, never achieved but certainly approached, was sole domain over the Indians. The governors strove to sustain royal authority against this pretension among the Franciscans. *Encomienda* lived on in New Mexico, with holders, as elsewhere on the periphery, dominating local society and such small economic activity as existed, principally farming. *Servicio personal*, it is true, was not part of the New Mexican *encomienda*. But *encomenderos* used their local prominence simply to force Indians, quite illegally, to work for them. Naturally the Franciscans opposed them in this, not only for the Indians' wellbeing, but because they themselves also needed workers for the lands that sustained the missions. Though Spanish secular settlers were few (only 170 able-bodied men in 1679, for example),[75] the resulting pressures on the Indians were heavy. And after the Franciscans began making vigorous attempts to stamp out native "idolatry" around the mid-century, the distress created among the Indians by the combined pressures of friars and *encomenderos* slowly rose to breaking point. In 1680 they seized Santa Fe and drove out both settlers and priests from New Mexico. It was the most serious rebellion against colonial rule in seventeenth-century New Spain. The Spanish did not recover Santa Fe until December 1693.

Another outlying area in which the Franciscans' role remained large in mid-colonial times was Yucatan. As late as 1737 they still held twenty-nine of the sixty native parishes in the peninsula.[76] Here, though, the pressures were less intense than in New Mexico. Native numbers were greater so that the few thousand resident Spaniards and creoles (1,300 heads of household *c.*1670, for instance, against a native tributary number of some 33,600)[77] were able to realize on a small scale that general early Spanish aim – an empire sustained by Indian tribute. Draft labor, by *repartimiento*, operated in seventeenth-century Yucatan, but seems to have impinged only lightly on native communities. Colonials, happy enough, apparently, to base their subsistence on the Indians' tribute offerings of maize and beans, showed little economic verve. Small cattle-raising *estancias*, from the 1580s on, and limited to the north and west of the peninsula, were their main attempt at production, and these needed little native labor. Yucatan, then, in the 1600s was among the imperial areas to see least disruption of the native living patterns that had emerged from the previous century. It was a period of respite, for the Mayas' experiences in that earlier time had been far more trying.

The Franciscans might seek complete authority over their wards on the imperial fringes. But the religious who came nearest (very near, indeed) to gaining it were the Jesuits. Because of the Society's late arrival in Spanish America, *c.*1570 – by which time other priests and friars were already attending to the central areas – it turned its evangelizing efforts from the start to the frontiers. In the 1600s Jesuits could be found where hardly any other Europeans, clerical or lay, would care or dare to go: in the north-western sierras of New Spain; on the interior slopes of the Andes, from New Granada down to Charcas; and in eastern Paraguay.

The Jesuits' Paraguayan *reducciones* are the most renowned of all evangelizing attempts in Spanish America, precisely because of the high degree of organization that the priests managed to impose on the Guaraní whom they gathered into their missionary villages – thirty of them by the early 1700s[78] – and the independence with which they worked. The communities lay in a large area between, and on both sides of, the Paraná and Uruguay rivers, south-east of Asunción, and extending into the present Misiones province of northern Argentina, and a little way into southern Brazil. The first Jesuit *reducciones* among the Guaraní date from 1610.[79] They were new towns, built on the grid-iron plan laid down in Spanish colonial law. The central plaza was dominated by a large church, generally made of mostly of wood, which was carved and painted in the interior to provide a measure of sumptuousness. Next to the church stood the residence of the two or three priests who generally ran each *reducción*. Indians' dwellings lined the streets extending out from the square. Past Guaraní practice had been to live in large houses containing extended families, and to some degree this continued, at least in the case of village leaders. With the rest of the people, the Jesuits may have had greater success in imposing their ideas of proper Christian living arrangements: single nuclear families, one per house. The priests brought European music and its instruments for use in church services and celebrations. They taught their charges European crafts, even training some as printers to produce religious texts in Guaraní. *Reducciones* were equipped with hospitals offering a blend of European and local medicine. Some land was worked communally, and some as private, family plots. The grains and cotton grown on public land were held in a store-house to supply the needs of the those who could not farm for themselves, to provide seed for the next year, and to ensure some reserve of goods that could be exchanged for European imports. From the common lands came abundant livestock: cattle, horses, mules, sheep, and oxen (for farm work). Tens of thousands of cattle could be found around some missions by the late 1600s. They yielded one major export, hides, which was sent down river to Buenos Aires and shipped thence to Europe. The other product for which there was a large outside demand was *yerba mate*, mostly gathered wild in the seventeenth century, and cultivated after then around the missions under Jesuit supervision. The market for *mate* extended over the Río de la Plata basin, and up into the Andean mining settlements. With the cash earnings from sales of hides and *mate* the Jesuits paid their Indians' tributes to the crown, and bought tools and materials needed in the reductions.

As far as they could, the Jesuits isolated their mission areas from secular settlements and their administrative authorities. In Paraguay they largely succeeded in this, despite much predictable opposition from colonials in and around the Paraguayan nucleus at Asunción. Those people resented the removal of large numbers of natives – the population of the *reducciones* reached a high point of about 141,000 in 1732[80] – from the potential labor pool. In one notable episode, however, the *reducciones* were drawn deep into the state's affairs, and not without the Jesuits' consent. Early in the 1630s their more northerly Guaraní *reducciones* came under attack by roving slave raiders, the *bandeirantes* of the southern Brazilian town of São Paulo. The missionaries took the survivors southwards into the Misiones area; and then, in the practical and militant manner of their society, got leave from the Council of the Indies to arm their Indians. In 1641 a force of some 4,000 Guaraní, commanded by the governor of Paraguay, beat back the *paulista* raiders, not only defending the *reducciones*, but in effect blocking one front of Portuguese expansion into Spanish territory. Thus the Jesuit *reducciones* played the part assumed by other outlying missions – but here with a vigor all of their own – of stabilizing the empire's frontiers. In the 1680s and 1690s, indeed, *reducciones* were re-established in the region abandoned sixty years before.[81]

If the mission relationship between priests and Indians was extraordinary in Paraguay, so was the interplay of Guaraní and secular settlers a little further west. From the start the position of the Europeans in Paraguay had been unusual, since the first to arrive there had been fugitives from the failed settlement of Buenos Aires in the mid 1530s. The 350 or so refugees, among them Portuguese, Germans, and Italians, arrived in Guaraní territory in a peculiarly accommodating frame of mind, found the Indians far less hostile than the plains people who had attacked Buenos Aires, and set up the town of Asunción in 1537. There was, then, no military conquest of Paraguay; and the domination that certainly did occur was achieved with far less inequality developing between the two sides than anywhere else in the Spanish colonies.

The Guaraní found in the Europeans useful allies against their nomadic enemies in the Chaco to the west. The colonists' gain from this alliance was to receive the status of headmen in native society. As such, they acquired native women – and in that culture it was women who did the agricultural work. Thus the Europeans found themselves well provided with both concubines and farm workers. With the women came relatives who swelled the foreign-led households. All these native people constituted, quite informally, something between a set of personal dependants, along the lines of *naborías* or *yanaconas*, and an undeclared *encomienda*. In fact, the term *encomienda originaria* was applied to these arrangements. Then, in the 1550s, *encomienda* was formally created in Paraguay. The typical arrangement that developed from that received the name *encomienda mitaya*. Native communities up to 200 kilometers from Asunción were included in it. They gave tribute less in kind than in labor, again performed largely by women. Although the intent of the *encomienda mitaya* was that workers would come by turn from their villages to work for their *encomenderos*, the earlier pattern of Indians, especially women, becoming attached to a colonist's household persisted. As the native population dropped, indeed, through disease and precisely through the removal of women from their communities, colonists in the seventeenth century sought female workers avidly, even exchanging them among themselves for goods such as horses and clothing.

Relations between settlers and natives did not sour, however, as much as this chattel-like treatment of women might suggest. One reason, clearly, was that precisely because the Europeans had possessed large female households from the start, miscegenation had progressed unusually fast in Paraguay. After the founding generation, most "Spaniards" were in fact *mestizos*. And even though these continued to be the controlling minority in the society, that minority adopted the material culture, the habits, and even the language of the natives far more fully than any parallel group elsewhere in the Indies. There was little Spanish immigration into Paraguay, since the place had little to offer economically, except for modest profits from *yerba mate* exports. Hence the leadership of local society remained *mestizo*. Even to the present day, Paraguay is freer of a sense of divisive contrast between European and native than any other Spanish American country. Guaraní is an official national language and is spoken at all social levels, albeit sometimes with a strong Spanish influence.[82]

Indians living on the fringes in the seventeenth century, then, generally found themselves living in social and economic arrangements that had largely disappeared in the imperial centers. These holdovers could be amazingly persistent; some small examples of the *encomienda mitaya*, for instance, still functioned in Paraguay in the 1780s. Where falling Indian numbers and settlers' economic activities combined to place a heavy labor demand on the native population, as they did in parts of New Granada, Venezuela, and New Mexico, Indians could suffer severely under these antiquated systems, especially because the rule of law grew generally feebler with distance from the large administrative centers. In other peripheral places, though – Yucatan and Paraguay are, in their different ways, examples – the position of natives was, with inevitable exceptions, broadly less burdensome (although Paraguay, in both its secular and mission settlements, was so distinctive in its own particular ways that it can hardly be included in comparisons).

AFRICANS

For Africans in Spanish America, and people of some degree of African descent, the long seventeenth century was also a time of variety and change. Their numbers are a useful starting point. Between 1580 and 1640 it is thought that 289,000 slaves arrived in Spanish America from Africa (in contrast to the much smaller number of Spaniards crossing to America: 188,000). Those sixty years were probably the time of the highest level of slave imports in the whole colonial era. They were the decades in which a union of the governments of Spain and Portugal gave the Portuguese open access to the Spanish colonies; they took advantage of the opportunity to expand greatly their existing slave export trade from West and Central Africa. After 1640, the pace of Spanish American imports slackened by half: between then and 1700, 141,000 enslaved Africans arrived (against 158,000 Spaniards). Then another expansion took place, so that from 1700 to 1760, 271,000 new slaves landed (and 193,000 Spaniards).

These gross estimates of the arrival of slaves are easier to state than the actual slave populations present at any particular place and time. The figures for populations tend to be scattered, but some are nonetheless worth noting. Mexico held some 20,000 black slaves by 1570. In the early seventeenth century that number had risen to no more than 45,000. By 1645 it had possibly reached, at an extreme maximum, 80,000. But by then the total number of Africans and part-Africans in Mexico was around 150,000; thus it seems that by the mid 1640s at least a half of Africans and part-Africans in Mexico were free (as a result of buying their liberty, being set free by their owners, or being the child of a free mother). A great many black, and partly black, people had been born in Mexico over the previous eighty years or so. In 1570 the colony held only 2,437 of such *criollo* blacks; by 1646 that number had risen to 116,529. Another general conclusion about the black presence in Mexico by the mid-seventeenth century is therefore that more than two-thirds of it (roughly 116,000 of the total of some 150,000) was native-born, and this despite the fact that the first forty years of the century saw the largest import of slaves from Africa in the whole colonial era.[83]

For Peru, reported numbers of slaves are scarcer than those for Mexico. An added difficulty is that some reports are of slaves, and others of Africans and part-Africans, whether slave or free. The assumption must be that with time the proportion of those who were not slaves grew. Those cautions noted, some of the available figures are as follows. During the conquests in the 1530s and the civil wars of the 1540s, almost 2,000 slaves had been present. By the mid 1550s, the number had risen to some 3,000, half of whom were in Lima. In 1586 Lima had about 7,000 slaves in its population, and by 1640, some 20,000 slaves and free blacks and part-blacks. In Potosí, *c*.1600, about 5,000 blacks and part-blacks were present (in a total population probably exceeding 100,000); they were a mixture of slaves and free people. Some of them had certainly entered South America at Buenos Aires, the southernmost Atlantic port of the viceroyalty of Peru. Between 1606 and 1625 no fewer than 11,262 slaves are recorded as arriving at Buenos Aires, most of them destined for the mining zone of the central Andes and perhaps some for Chile, over the mountains to the west. Far to the north, on the Caribbean coast of New Granada, Cartagena served a similar function as the entry point for many slaves who would soon find themselves at work along the Spanish Main, and in the highlands of New Granada and Quito.[84]

The scattered nature of these figures, in time and place, and the fact that some of them refer to slaves alone, and others to total black and part-black populations, slave together with free, make for difficulties in interpretation. But the broad points are clear enough. African and part-black slaves came to America with the earliest explorers and conquerors. In the sixteenth century and the first half of the seventeenth, Mexico and Peru imported more slaves than the rest of Spanish America. But all the colonies received slaves from Africa. By the mid-seventeenth century, the black and part-black presence in Spanish America had expanded greatly and was still growing. Anyone visiting a Spanish American city or town in the 1600s (or in the next century, for that matter), expecting to see a population of whites, Indians and *mestizos*, would have been surprised by the number of people of African origin in the streets. By one estimate, in Mexico City, Lima, Quito, Santa Fe de Bogotá, Caracas, Cartagena, and Buenos Aires, black slaves made up on average, during the colonial era as a whole, 10 to 25 percent of the total populations.[85] To those slaves in urban places must be added a generally growing number of free black and part-black people. In fact, the visitor might well have been doubly surprised to learn that free men and women outnumbered the slaves. But he would quickly have noticed that almost all blacks and part-blacks, whether slaves or free, moved openly and easily around the streets, some of them accompanying masters or mistresses, others on business of some sort for their employers or pursuing their own affairs. And if he had ventured out into the countryside, he would also have found blacks and part-blacks, slave or free, in many areas; some, especially in hot regions, laboring as field slaves on plantations, but others, almost anywhere, supervising farms, working their own small plots of land, driving mule trains, herding cattle, making tools in village forges – busy, in fact, at any number of tasks.

In the sixteenth century the term *criollo* ("creole" in English) started being applied to blacks born in Spanish America, at least as early as it was used to denote American-born whites. By the mid-seventeenth century, in many Spanish American places, creole blacks and part-blacks outnumbered African-born men and women substantially. And along with the notion of birthplace, the term "creole" had gained a cultural force – the sense that Africans born in the colonies, while still retaining some of their African ways and beliefs, had also been influenced by the local environment in which they had been raised. To describe such influences, the modern term "creolization" has been used.

The process of creolization was complex, and far more nuanced than the simple importing and installing of African culture in America that historians once thought had taken place. It was, in fact, analogous to what happened to American native cultures once they came into contact with the invading Europeans. In those, there was not simple mixing of prior Indian and European practices, but various degrees of fusing and blending of the two cultures, so that what emerged was different from either of the originals.

So it was also with Africans and African culture – or, rather, with African cultures, for in reality the slaves shipped to America came from such a large area of Africa that they had been raised with widely varying languages, religious practices, political assumptions, and means of sustaining their lives. An immediate effect of the slave trade was to simplify that variety. The transatlantic shippers were generally not in a position to choose slaves from a particular region in Africa to carry to this or that part of the Americas. Nor were the buyers in America generally able to specify the region or nationality of the slaves they took from the shippers. Rather, the shippers received batches of slaves from the African sellers; and the batches generally contained men and women from different places.[86] This had the effect of starting a blending of African cultures even before the slaves crossed the ocean. Shiploads of people speaking a single language, or practicing a single religion, did not typically arrive in the

Americas. They might seem to do so, because slaves were often named by the port from which they left Africa. But they had generally come to that port from many different places inland.

For this reason the basic transporting of slaves simplified cultural diversity, and contributed to combining such traits as religious beliefs and languages into new but more widespread forms. African lingua francas emerged in America, as blends of African tongues with the European language spoken in a particular region (and undoubtedly to some extent with native American tongues as well). In fact, this process had started in Africa, where from the fifteenth century people over a good deal of West Africa, and later central Africa also, had been acquiring some Portuguese, and adding it into their own languages. Thus, slaves from quite different language areas might arrive in America, and find they could communicate to some extent through their various versions of Portuguese. The same went for Christianity. Portuguese teaching of Catholicism in Africa from the late fifteenth century onwards gave scattered African peoples some elements of shared faith; and this, again, in America was something that otherwise unconnected people might find they had in common. Christianity became, indeed, something of a cultural glue for transported slaves across the Atlantic. That is probably why Africans in America were generally receptive to the religion.[87]

Their Christianity was, nonetheless, far from conventional Catholicism. It had clear African elements. But those elements were not necessarily the strongest elements of religions in Africa. Gods and spirits that were associated with particular places or circumstances in Africa might not make the passage to America; nor might beliefs that were linked to specific social or political powers. On the other hand, spiritual forces and practices with close ties to family life might well carry across the ocean. And in America, as in Africa itself, when people sensed a parallel between their own deities and Christian saints they might combine the two into a single spiritual entity, neither purely African nor purely Christian, but a new fusing of the two in what has been termed "syncretic absorption."

Less elevated, and more popular, African spiritual practices, such as witchcraft and magic, may have arrived in America, and briefly persisted there, in their original forms. They were certainly practiced in the Spanish colonies by blacks from their sixteenth-century arrival onward. But here again cultural strands were soon entangled. First, Africa itself had myriad magics, which in America tended to blend together. Second, slaves naturally drew on the Spanish folk magic that they encountered in the colonies, for the same reasons as they drew on their owners' Christian faith. (And, in fact, slaves who had lived in Iberia or perhaps the Iberian-settled Atlantic islands sometimes picked up Spanish and Portuguese folk magic before they arrived in the colonies.) Third, once in America, blacks added local native sorcery to their magic practices. The outcome was, once more, something uniquely African-American – though, of course, never homogeneous, but with its own regional variety.[88] The apparent contradiction of blacks' professing Christianity at one moment, and then using magic the next, exasperated Spanish colonial authorities (as did similar behavior by American native people). One answer was to subject Africans in Spanish America, whether slave or free, to the Inquisition – as indeed they were from the time when the formal Inquisition was first installed in the colonies, around 1570. By contrast, Indians were free of the Inquisition's attention because, unlike Africans, they were considered childlike and therefore not mature enough to be responsible for their own actions.

The religion of Africans in America, then, is a prime example of their cultural creolization – of their fusing of the lifeways of Africa (which themselves underwent a process of combining as they crossed the Atlantic) with those of Europeans in America and of native American people. The same general trend is visible in much of Africans' life in America. For instance, very few African food plants were brought across, so, no matter what their staple diet might have been in their African area of origin, newly arrived slaves had to adopt and adapt what the Americas had to offer. In art, music, and dancing there was a similar compression of African styles and forms in the Atlantic crossing, and then a resurgence and re-expansion of those activities, now with American elements fused into them.[89] A particularly striking example of creolization, and one of great practical use to many Africans in Spanish America, was their learning and practicing of Spanish rules of one sort or another. In both church and civil courts, blacks suffering maltreatment by owners quickly learned to employ Spanish laws regulating the conditions of slavery. By doing so they could, and did, protect themselves to some degree from physical and verbal abuse, denial of conjugal rights, deprivation of food and shelter, and so on. In late sixteenth-century Quito, slaves on occasion used the courts to bring official displeasure down on their Catholic owners, saying that the masters forced them to work on Sundays, and prevented them from going to Mass. Notably ingenious was the practical use to which some slaves learned to put blasphemy. They might shout out some blasphemous exclamation or curse while being beaten or otherwise abused by their owners – knowing that the owner's religious duty was then to stop the punishment and hand the slave over to the Inquisition. There was a risk, naturally, that blaspheming would simply infuriate the owner further; but in some cases it did lead to an appearance before the Inquisition, which gave the slave a chance to denounce the abusive master. The slave would do all he or she could, also, to seem to be a pious Christian who had been driven to blaspheme only by extreme suffering.[90]

It would be reasonable to expect creolization to be least established, and original African behaviors most completely preserved, in black runaway communities – those villages, towns, and even small states of escaped slaves that existed, perhaps hundreds in number,[91] across the Americas by the mid seventeenth century. In Spanish America those communities were often called *palenques* (a word meaning "stockade," and indeed some of the communities were fortified), and their inhabitants, *cimarrones* (maroons, in English). In addition to the black community in the Panamanian forests in the late sixteenth century, or the one ruled by Yanga in central Mexico in the early 1600s, quite numerous maroon sites existed in the seventeenth century in Venezuela and northern New Granada, and others elsewhere. Slaves' prime aim in running away and forming *palenques* was to escape harsh treatment and to live as free peasants. Most maroons were therefore, not surprisingly, people whose lives had begun in Africa. Creole blacks, being by definition better adjusted to colonial conditions, had less urge to escape into freedom.

Hence "Africanness" was certainly to be found in maroon communities. The often military nature of the places was one aspect of it. Many *palenques* came under attack by colonial authorities, and so had to be ready to defend themselves. Among the maroons were many men who had actually fought in Africa before being made slaves – in fact, they might well have been enslaved after being captured in war. The leadership of maroon communities also tended to be on a military model. Since in Africa military prowess was one route to political power and social standing, men who led effective defenses of *palenques* might well become the leaders of the communities. In the larger ones, they were titled "king," on the African pattern; some of them were indeed from an African nobility. And, even though in the American circumstances it might be expected that social organization in maroon sites would tend to be egalitarian, in fact the social inequalities often found in Africa were generally replicated there – to the extent that superior members of the community would hold others as slaves. African religions and spiritual practices were also to be found in *palenques*; although it is noteworthy that in many of them Christianity was also practiced (but then it had been also in Africa).[92]

In *palenques*, then, aspects of African life certainly lived on vigorously in Spanish America. But those maroon communities held a very small fraction of the total number of blacks and part-blacks in the Spanish colonies. The large majority, being more or less exposed for most of their lives to Spanish and Indian ways, absorbed those ways willingly or unwillingly. A recent piece of research provides a striking example of how that could happen in an apparently unlikely setting.[93]

That setting was a remote region of South America called Mizque. The area is part of the inland ranges of the Bolivian Andes, and consists of deep valleys and rugged mountains that fall away eastward to the plains of the Amazon. Today it is an isolated and inaccessible place. But in colonial times, from about 1550 onward, though obviously no easier to reach than it is now, it was part of the economic system that provided supplies for the inhabitants of La Plata, the seat of the *audiencia* of Charcas, and – far more important – for the enormous population of the silver-mining city of Potosí.

The valley floors of Mizque were fertile, and well watered by the rivers that flowed down them toward Amazonia. Native people had long used the valleys to grow food, and Spanish colonists were quick to scent profits in a continuation of that use once La Plata and Potosí were established and growing. At first the farm work was done in Mizque by Indians in *encomienda*. But, as almost everywhere in Spanish America, sixteenth-century diseases killed many of the native people. The Spanish landowners in Mizque then realized that their sales to Potosí were profitable enough to warrant replacing their native workers with black slaves. Thus, well before 1600, Mizque had started to acquire an African population. Most of its slaves came into South America at Buenos Aires, and then trudged the 2,000 kilometers northwards over the *pampas* and up into the Andes. Their purchasers in Mizque were owners of land producing above all sugar, wine, and cattle. Some of the slaves, however, sooner or later became domestic servants; and others, mostly the descendants of the first arrivals, expanded the range of blacks' work in the seventeenth century to become town officials, town criers, militiamen, and overseers on landholdings large and small. Of particular note, however, are the ways in which they combined, biologically and culturally, with the remnants of the local Indian population. For instance, in the 1600s blacks and mulattos appear on lists of farm workers as *yanaconas*. That term had pre-conquest origins, and denoted servants personally attached to powerful people. It passed into the colonial era with much the same meaning of permanent, personal servant, except that the *yanaconas'* masters were now Spaniards. But the *yanaconas* themselves were Indians, or so the assumption has been. The records of Mizque reveal, however, that, by the seventeenth century, they could also be wholly or partly African. Blacks, or part-blacks, were stepping into Indians' cultural and social roles. Still more surprising is the expanded meaning that the word *mulato* took on in Mizque. In standard Spanish American terminology, that word meant someone of mixed black and white parentage, but in Mizque a *mulato* was a blend of black and Indian. And, in a final surprise, on one farm in 1683 a mulatto appears with the title of *curaca*. The term is native Andean, always assumed to refer to an Indian (or just possibly a *mestizo*) town leader. But here in Mizque it had come to apply to the manager of a farm, and to the person of partly African origin who held that job.

Creolization of Africans, therefore, proceeded robustly in Mizque in the seventeenth century. The incoming slaves had mixed, through marriage and more or less permanent cohabitations, with the native survivors of the great epidemics, producing children who clearly lived in a setting in which Andean ways impinged on them ever more strongly. This remote Andean province provides vivid instances of an empire-wide process that, having begun in the 1500s, advanced with growing vigor in the next century: the Americanization of Africans, their conversion into creolized inhabitants, whether slave or free, of Spanish America.

WOMEN

NATIVE WOMEN

In the seventeenth century movement of Indian women from rural villages into colonial towns was common across the empire. As men went to towns under the dictates of draft labor or to find waged work, their wives often accompanied them, seeking occupations that would supplement the man's income. Domestic service was a common choice, though often a hard one, since once in a household a servant might find it hard to escape. Cases are known of women being held in service for years for non-payment of small debts, while in the Quito region women were regularly abducted and forced into domestic work.[94]

Somewhat better off, if not economically at least in independence, were the many native women who took up some sort of petty trade, such as preparing food, or *chicha* or *pulque*, and selling them on the street, or retailing vegetables and fruit from a small shop (*pulpería*). Some, but fewer, Indian women, usually those of higher standing, perhaps with family links to local native leadership, owned and rented out houses and shops in white-dominated towns. These women are difficult to distinguish from *mestizas* doing the same thing. Indeed, prospering *indias* might come to be seen as *mestizas*, as the economic definition of ethnicity and status did its typical work in mid-colonial times.

Native women working in large colonial towns were important mediators between native and foreign culture. That role was epitomized by the many who looked after children, and especially by those who worked as wet-nurses. In seventeenth-century Cuzco, *indias* cared not only for the children of colonists (and of the hispanized descendants of Inca nobility), but also for those of black slaves, and orphans.[95] Such women inevitably gave their charges some familiarity with native language, mentality, beliefs, and, of course, aspects of material culture such as food and clothing. They were doing what, in the reverse direction, Spanish women in America have long been seen to have done after the conquest: acting as conduits through which one culture flowed into another.[96]

While many indigenous women were drawn into the colonial cities by force, choice, or circumstance, other women, particularly those of the high nobility, attempted to keep alive the indigenous traditions of the past. As late as 1600, some Andean women held the title of *principal*, or local leader, and when one noblewoman claimed the *curacazgo* of Magdalena near Lima in 1804, she was able to marshal evidence that women exercised political and economic authority not just in the ancient past, but during the colonial period.[97] Noblewomen, then, like the common women who migrated to Spanish areas, engaged both with indigenous tradition and with the policies and practices of colonialism.

With movement and migration so frequent among Indians in central areas in the seventeenth century, producing among other results a growing presence of native women in towns, it may be that *indias* then became more important than white women as cultural intermediaries. For, as they entered an expanding range of working roles that put them in constant contact with colonials, it seems that the set of activities open to white (and almost-white) women may have narrowed, at least in comparison with conditions soon after the conquest, when the rules and traits of settlers' society were still fluid and in formation. This was partly the result of Spain's sending to America its assumptions that families were hierarchical units in which ranking males had decisive, patriarchal, power, and that women were physically, psychologically, and morally fragile, and therefore in need of male supervision and protection.[98]

WOMEN, FAMILY, AND GENDER

By the seventeenth century, these notions about family and gender dynamics were widely shared among the various social groups that constituted colonial society. The implications of the embrace of patriarchal values were, for women, many. First was that prevailing assumption that a woman should be under some form of masculine authority. In marriage, according to law and custom, a woman was junior to her spouse, and was expected to show the appropriate deference and accommodation to his wishes. Disobedience by a wife, like the disobedience of any other underling, was punishable by physical discipline. The senior role of the husband also meant that mothers were in theory outranked by fathers when it came to the authority to make decisions concerning minor children. Finally, wives required their husbands' permission, either through a general power of attorney or through specific licenses, to engage in economic transactions. To the degree that Spanish law enshrined the headship of men and the obedience of women as the cornerstone of family life, the colonial Latin American family can truly be described as patriarchal.

Nonetheless, other parts of the Spanish tradition gave certain categories of women some freedom of action; and, as was generally the case, American conditions tended to loosen Iberian norms. By Spanish law, women retained ultimate control of property they owned before marrying. Given the Spanish custom of dividing inheritances among heirs – that is, the custom of "partible" inheritance – most women could expect to receive some share of their parents' property. The share often took the form of a dowry at the time of a daughter's marriage. Such property was to be itemized in notarized dowry contracts, which would provide documentation when the wife's property was once again parted from the husband's (as, most commonly, upon his death). Dowry was intended to help a newlywed couple with the costs of getting set up in life, but it was not to be exhausted, nor was it ever legally the husband's property. For that reason, though the husband administered the dowry during his life, it reverted to the widow after he died. A woman to be married might also receive from the groom, particularly if he were from the elite, a bridal gift, or *arras*. Such a gift was to amount in value to no more than 10 percent of the husband's property. Whatever the value of the *arras*, that too reverted to a wife on her husband's demise. Legally, a woman's property was also protected while her husband was still living; a wife who suspected her spouse of squandering or mismanagement could sue for the return of her dowry portion. Her property, furthermore, could not be taken without her permission (in legal terms, was inalienable) to pay her husband's debts. In 1682, in the province of Quito, Doña Catalina Ponce Castillejo's husband died while imprisoned for debt despite his wife's possession of land, livestock, and houses, which she jealously defended as dowry property and therefore inalienable without her specific and documented agreement to act as guarantor of his debt.[99] Those familiar with the doctrine of coverture will note that, in colonial Spanish America, "the legal and economic personality of the woman was not absorbed by marriage".[100]

Many of these legal protections were of primary benefit to those women wealthy and canny enough both to own property and to ensure that they protected it through the creation of formal dowry contracts at time of marriage. Where husbands squandered their wives' property and that property had not been inventoried in a duly constituted dowry agreement, there was little legal recourse. Still, women seem to have been aware of their rights, and even lower-class women created contracts to protect their property. This is not surprising given that plebeian women, unlike elite women, were almost universally economically active in their own right both within and outside of marriage.

Indeed, while both legal and cultural prescription recognized women's need for protection in matters economic, and therefore assumed their incapacity, most women were of necessity economic actors at some point in their lives. Elite women were trusted by their husbands to manage affairs in their absence, and were quite often given general powers of attorney to manage their own property during marriage. Economically active widows of varying social station were similarly no rarity, to be found running estates and farms, and a wide variety of productive and marketing businesses. Neither were mature, unmarried women barred by law or custom from the same sorts of work, or from other such respectable means of supporting themselves independently as, say, sewing or teaching. Women of the middle classes, like elite women, generally shunned economic ventures that required them to be in public, but more prosperous middle-group women, married or widowed, might own shops, taverns, or workshops without actually working in them, thus maintaining their respectability. Other respectable women might take in boarders, conduct a small business from their home, or engage in small-scale home-based production. Wives of artisans were expected to work in their husbands' workshops, though women were formally barred from membership in virtually all guilds and only exceptionally gained admission.[101] Still, women's skill was recognized in provisions that permitted artisans' widows to continue operating their husbands' businesses. Moreover, a few masculine trades seem actually to have welcomed women: the colonial printing business is particularly noteworthy for having significant numbers of female bookbinders and printers.

Certain occupations were also dominated by women or exclusive to them. Midwifery remained a female activity throughout the colonial period, largely because of colonial conceptions of decency. Regarded with suspicion by the medical profession, colonial midwives were drawn largely from the lower classes, and were often *indias*, *castas*, or blacks. Their practices, like those of many other illicit healers, blurred the distinctions among medicine, magic, and religion. As a result, midwives were sometimes suspected by their clients, and by the Inquisition, of illicit practices.[102] Another exclusively feminine and often reviled occupation was wet-nursing, participated in by all ethnic groups but undoubtedly dominated by indigenous and *casta* women. Women also predominated in the food business in many colonial cities, serving as both preparers and sellers of food, and working in bakeries. Women worked in the weaving industry, both at home and in workshops, and also as laundresses, seamstresses, and embroiderers. Finally, the largest area of women's employment was domestic service, an occupation generally judged fit only for single women and, by the seventeenth century, for those who were not white.[103] Though domestic service in particular and women's work in general were often poorly paid, women were still capable of survival and even prosperity. When one Mexican mulata married in the late seventeenth century, she did so with the impressive dowry of 5,000 pesos (enough money to buy, for instance, several moderate houses). She said that she had amassed this sum "through my skill."[104] Thus, while colonial prescription cast women as insignificant economic actors, most women found themselves having to work at some point in their lives, and women's work was significant to both society and local economies.

One striking feature of women's existence in the 1600s might be read as evidence of freedom of choice and self-determination taken to an extreme, but had in fact other causes. This was the extraordinarily high rate of illegitimate births, above all in the large towns. In Lima, for instance, between 1562 and 1689, the rate for white and *mestizo* children was never lower than 40 percent, and for Indians, blacks and mulattos, between 1618 and 1649, a little over 70 percent. In seventeenth-century Mexican cities illegitimacy stood at over 40 percent. At the end of the century, Guadalajara had rates of 61 percent for mulattos and 39 percent for whites.[105] These were levels of illegitimacy higher than those in Spain at the time, which were in turn above those elsewhere in western Europe. Indeed, it seems that, by the seventeenth century, Latin America had, in this respect, gone beyond replicating Iberian society, to establish itself as a distinct society with its own sexual and marital mores. While legitimacy and legitimate marriage remained social ideals, there were many pragmatic reasons for the high number of births out of wedlock. They included, in the case of *casta* women, the frequency of informal cohabitation, often long-lasting (*amancebamiento*), with men of similar origins or with married and unmarried men of higher rank; and, for white women, a relative shortage of men of equal social standing, which allegedly led them to yield sexually to males in the hope of assuring a marriage. There was no lack of opportunity for them to do that: seduction was a widely practiced art among colonial men, particularly among plebeians, who exchanged stories, charms, and advice relating to seduction, and who occasionally even made pacts with the Devil to gain greater access to the physical charms of women.[106]

Seducers could not, however, operate with complete impunity. Again, Spanish precedent had an effect. According to canon law, the exchange of a promise to marry (*palabra de casamiento*) was a solemn vow and a binding commitment. And a man who promised a respectable woman marriage, and then had sexual relations with her, became responsible for her honor before both the law and the church. *Palabra de casamiento* was, in fact, regarded by all classes as a pledge that legitimized sexual relations, and could also serve as a strategy by which young people could force reluctant parents to accept a marriage. And yet the practice of beginning sexual relations with a marriage promise was highly ambiguous, setting up a gendered game in which women risked their reputations to secure a promise of marriage, while some unscrupulous men offered false promises of marriage in order to gain sexual access to women. In the earlier colonial period, most men who had given promises to marry felt themselves bound by conscience and honor; by 1670, however, men in Mexico at least were increasingly willing to break their word.[107] The game became more complicated: to ensure that a marriage promise was as watertight as possible, women might demand gifts (*prendas*) from the suitor, or secure witnesses.

On the other hand, men whose aim was obligation-free seduction might attempt to avoid these markers of legitimacy, and could always resort to defamation of a woman's character should they seek to avoid legal sanctions.

Still, amid a shortage of suitable men, many women evidently thought the concession of sex a risk worth assuming to secure a partner. Given the shortage, however, such women then may have become satisfied with the second-best arrangement of a lasting but informal union. Many others found themselves abandoned, often after impregnation or birth, by partners who contracted marriage with other women. The outcome was many illegitimate children. Illegitimacy rates were, conversely, lowest, and rates of marriage highest, in Indian rural communities, where numbers were more evenly balanced, and where, perhaps even more tellingly, adherence to traditions of marriage was stronger than in the socially more tumultuous cities.

A group among which marriage was without doubt the rule was the Spanish elite, the small group of leading families at the pinnacle of society. Indeed, this group's identity as honorable people (*gente honrada*) rested in part upon its commitment – distinctive in colonial Latin America – to legal marriage and presumed legitimacy of births. Nonetheless, even at this elevated social level some of the same issues that dogged the lower classes appeared again. Like their social inferiors, elite men and women recognized the validity of *palabra de casamiento* as a legitimate beginning for honorable sexual intercourse. And elite women, like their lower-class counterparts, enjoyed no immunity from less "legitimate" seductions. In cases where elite women succumbed to the advances of men who then proved either unable or unwilling to marry them, elite families resorted to "private pregnancies," colluding to conceal a woman's shame and protect her reputation. Such protection, however, came at a steep cost: elite unwed mothers could never publicly recognize their children, and in many cases were forced to renounce them altogether.[108]

Though elite women paid more dearly, perhaps, than most to preserve their family's honor, honor was cherished at every step of the social ladder. Within the context of the patriarchal family, honor was both honor-status, an expression of one's "quality" (*calidad*) and lineage, and honor-virtue, an expression of how one conducted oneself in everyday life in accordance with the prescribed norms of one's society and station. One student of honor has referred to it as an "account"; one received "deposits" from one's parents at birth, and one either added to or diminished the balance through one's own actions over the life course.[109] Both men and women inherited honor from their families, yet the nature of the virtue demanded of the sexes was quite distinct. Men's honor resided in manliness, loyalty, honesty, and zealous concern for the reputation of their families. Sensitivity to insult was a requirement for the maintenance of honor, since anyone's honor could be diminished if not defended. Thus the system of honor undoubtedly bred masculine violence, as men at all levels of society sought to defend their (and their family's) honor from real or imagined slights.[110] Women's honor, by contrast, was primarily conceived as *vergüenza*, or shame, a quality that manifested itself in modesty, sexual propriety, and, among the higher social classes, *recogimiento*. This term, originally used to describe a particular form of contemplative practice, during the sixteenth century evolved a second meaning as a "gendered moral virtue" associated with honorable women.[111] Associated with enclosure and quietude, it also expressed a kind of moral containment opposite to the laxity and "looseness" so common among plebeian women. To be *recogida* or *vergonzosa* expressed the highest standard for female behavior.

Perhaps it is here, in the system of gendered virtue entrenched within the honor-bearing family, that we should look for the true potency of patriarchy. For while the Spanish legal system was abundant in protections for women's property, the principal model for their behavior within marriage was obedience. The often large age differences between men and their spouses, particularly among Spaniards, accentuated the authority of the paterfamilias.[112] In theory, of course, the conjugal ideal was reciprocal. Men had the right to be obeyed, but in exchange they had the obligation to love, protect, and avoid excess in disciplining their wives. In practice, men's right to "moderate" correction of their wives' "disobedience" often led to domestic violence, and even to what contemporaries called a "bad life" for women: *la mala vida*. Being hit by one's husband did not, in itself, constitute a *mala vida* for a woman; hitting was part of many relationships, and women themselves were known to hit and beat servants, slaves, and children. Rather, a *mala vida* meant excessive abuse, or abuse coupled with other serious infringements of the marital bargain.[113] Some women attempted to prosecute their husbands for abuse before criminal courts; they also sought ecclesiastical divorce, which was a rare phenomenon that permitted separation in cases of heresy, contagious illness, or extreme abuse. Finally, some women fled abusive marriages and sought new partners. There is little evidence that any of these strategies was either highly successful or widely adopted relative to the ubiquity – and sometimes shocking severity – of marital violence. The most useful strategy a woman could follow, perhaps, was the cultivation of a network of sympathetic kin, neighbors, and others who might intervene when beatings became severe. To the degree that women could find protection, it lay not in law but in a popular moral economy of marriage that asserted women's rights in exchange for their subordination.[114]

Many women in colonial Latin America, of course, had little expectation of marriage. Foremost among these were women of African descent. Many of these women spent much or all of their lives free from the male supervision and protection considered desirable for women by colonial society. This situation should not be romanticized; if enslaved, women were supervised by owners and experienced a harsher form of dominion that included beatings, but also, commonly, sexual abuse. If living in towns, many slave women were also engaged in prostitution in addition to their other jobs. (Indeed, the threat of sexual abuse dogged all unprotected women and girls, even more in rural areas than in towns.) Still, slave and free women of African descent also engaged in consensual relationships, many of them with Spanish men, and for some women this could be almost a career option. In the middle of the seventeenth century, the free mulatta Beatriz de Padilla was tried for malefice (sorcery) by the Mexican Inquisition. Beatriz had begun her life as a slave, but had been manumitted by her owner. As a teenager, she had become mistress to a well-off priest who also served as the local Commissioner of the Inquisition; another of her conquests was mayor of a nearby town, while yet another was a member of the local bureaucratic elite. Despite being a single mother with four children (by three different fathers), Beatriz managed to live in some comfort; moreover, she was able to achieve acquittal by the Holy Office.[115] While Beatriz may not have been a typical mulatta, her story shows how some women, disadvantaged in many ways by their color and legal status, were nonetheless able to survive and prosper despite lacking the protections of marriage and family. Colonial society's dictum that "a woman needs a husband or a wall [convent]" should therefore not be taken as evidence that colonial women were overwhelmingly married, that marriage was women's only option for survival, or indeed, that marriage was always protective. Nonetheless, the belief that women needed to "take estate" persisted through the colonial period, especially among the elite.

NUNNERIES

One outcome of this belief, coupled with a lack of eligible spouses for the daughters of well-to-do colonial families, was a growing number of nunneries in the seventeenth century. Conventual foundations spread from central to provincial towns. The nunneries' populations grew also, so that in the late 1600s, for instance, each of the six senior houses in Lima, the *conventos grandes*, may have had a thousand women within its walls. Far from all of these, perhaps a third to a half, were professed nuns, with the balance consisting of slaves, servants, novices, and girls temporarily resident for schooling. The total of thirteen nunneries in Lima are said to have held at one point a fifth of the city's female population. On the other hand, in Mexico City there were only 888 professed nuns *c.*1800, although the number had been higher before the mid 1700s.[116]

The seventeenth-century convents remained largely contemplative institutions, at most taking in a number of girls to be educated (mainly in what was needed to run a household). No convents of teaching orders appeared until the mid eighteenth century. Still, in the absence of a formal schooling system for girls, convents served as the main centers for female education. Convents admitted girls both as boarders and as day pupils. Among the pupils in the 1600s were many daughters of creole families prosperous in fame and fortune, of merchants, government officials, landowners, successful miners, lawyers, and doctors. In exchange for an admittedly idiosyncratic education (dependent largely upon the skills and inclination of the nuns in question), students provided the convent with much-needed income in the form of fees, and furthered the connections between convent and colonial elite. Despite, however, the nunneries' need for money and the social utility of the educative services they provided, nuns' participation in education was regarded with some distrust by the church. Convents were under constant pressure, from the late sixteenth century on, to limit the number of "secular persons" within their walls. The presence of children, in particular, was considered disruptive to nuns' love for and prayer to their divine spouse. Because of official disapproval, convents had little motivation to record (and perhaps had some motivation to under-report) the number of children schooled within the cloister. Data are thus scant. Nonetheless, nuns evidently not only schooled the children of the elite but raised foundlings, relatives, and the children of their slaves. In Lima in 1695, an inspection of the convent of Santa Clara found twenty-one children under the age of 6 living in the convent full-time, of whom seven were white. In addition, there were four "little slave girls" between 2 and 5 who lived elsewhere, but spent their mornings in the convent, as though going to kindergarten. Foundlings too arrived, either at the convent turnstile or via the foundling hospitals.[117] It is a reasonable assumption, therefore, that seventeenth-century convents contained a significant number of children, and that teaching children was an important part of nuns' labor. At the very least, nuns were highly resistant to attempts to limit the numbers of or remove the children within convent walls.

Thanks to the fees paid by pupils' families, to the dowries required of novices, to bequests and to gifts, many convents found themselves growing richer in cash as well as spirit as the seventeenth century advanced. Late in the century some began to make loans from spare funds, mostly to safe borrowers in the moneyed sector of society. Then they also took to investing in city property, to such effect that towards 1800 eight large convents in Mexico City were worth over 7 million pesos in various urban buildings. Nunneries were by then the largest property owners within the church; and the church held almost half of all the city's property.[118]

Although no women's order in the Indies devoted itself wholly to education until the eighteenth century, it is certainly true that before then nunneries offered the best conditions for cultivating the mind available to women interested in doing so, and that nuns were, collectively, the closest approach to a female intellectual community in Spanish America. The outstanding example is Juana Ramírez de Asbaje (1648?–95), better known and celebrated as Sor (Sister) Juana Inés de la Cruz. She was the illegitimate daughter of a woman from a creole family that owned land a little south of Mexico City. Nothing certain is known of her father.[119] As a child she showed great mental precocity, reading from the age of 3 in the books in her family's collection. Part of her later childhood she spent living in the viceregal palace in the capital, invited there by a vicereine astonished by such a prodigy. Then in 1668 she became a Jeronymite nun; not, it seems, out of any strong calling, but precisely because the convent seemed to her the place most conducive to the life of thought and writing that she had by then decided to make for herself. She wrote voluminously, particularly poetry and plays (works both of morality and comedy), using with much skill the conventions of the Spanish conceptism of her time, which loaded words and phrases heavily with multiple and often uncertain meanings. She was an able and moving poet in this metaphysical mode, and has been described as the final luminary in Spain's greatest literary period, the Golden Age of the seventeenth century.[120]

Among her best known poems are those telling of unrequited or misdirected love. One of them begins:

> Who thankless flees me, I with love pursue
> Who loving follows me, I thankless flee:
> To him who spurns my love I bend the knee,
> His love who seeks me, cold I bid him rue ...[121]

Such lines very probably do not refer to actual affairs of the heart, given Sor Juana's firmly declared aversion to marriage and her often repeated dedication to the intellectual life. They have, rather, been persuasively read as disguised confessions of mental and even psychological conflict within her – of her feeling of being torn between, on the one hand, commitment to the values and learning, if not profoundly to the faith, of the church she belonged to, and, on the other, her love of writing and of mental exploration of a broad range of worldly topics. Her interests included, apparently, the new scientific knowledge and method of the time, in the attenuated form in which they crossed the Atlantic from Europe. She gained some familiarity with them through many conversations, in her convent's locutory, with New Spain's leading male savant of the late 1600s, Don Carlos de Sigüenza y Góngora. He had been a pupil of Fray Diego Rodríguez, the first holder, from 1637 on, of the chair of mathematics at the University of Mexico, and a teacher who had included the findings of Brahe, Copernicus, and Kepler in his courses. When, finally, Sor Juana came under criticism from church authorities for both the unwomanly nature of her dedication to writing and intellectual inquiry, and for applying her superior mind to them rather than to matters of faith, she argued for the value of secular subjects such as history, architecture, geometry, arithmetic and physics for a full understanding of theology. But there was no deflecting her critics; nor her self-criticism, for her unorthodoxy clearly inspired guilt in her, not to mention a sense of alienation and even despair. "Let not the head which is the repository of knowledge expect any other crown than that of thorns," she wrote, under attack. Finally in 1694 she yielded, renouncing all her possessions, including her books and her musical and scientific instruments. She spent the last year of her life, before dying in an epidemic in April 1695, in contrition and self-chastisement, though never, it seems, formally abandoning the study of humane letters.[122]

Sor Juana, it could be said, was broken over the divide between the old and the new in Spanish America, between the Baroque, which harbored within it sundry medieval remnants, and the Enlightenment, which in her thirst for worldly knowledge she prefigured. That tension was so damaging to her precisely because she was a woman; a male religious with her interests would have met with less intolerance, if any.

The ideal of creole womanhood, and specifically of religious womanhood, can be found at the opening of the seventeenth century, and in the other viceregal capital, Lima. There in 1586 was born Isabel Flores de Oliva, on whose infant cheeks appeared one day the images of two perfect roses. The connection with the "rose without thorns," the Virgin Mary, was soon made. In 1597 the child was confirmed under a new name, Rosa de Santa María.

Throughout her short life (she died in 1617) Rosa was at the center of social life and religious cult in Lima. She became a *beata* at an early age, first using the Franciscan habit, and then in 1606 taking the vows of the Dominicans' third order. She continued to live at home, in a cell in the garden, where she sewed and embroidered for the high-society ladies who came often to talk with her. She changed the words of popular love songs to those of divine love, and accompanied herself on the guitar as she sang them. A reputation for working small miracles gathered around her. Then, shortly before her death, a more profound sign of her sanctity appeared, when a portrait of Christ before which she was praying began to sweat – and persisted in doing so even after two Jesuits from their neighboring college twice wiped the moisture from the paint. After her death, adoration of Rosa intensified. People of all ranks regarded her cell as a shrine. Despite some initial concern by the Inquisition over the authenticity of this cult she was beatified in 1668, and, as Santa Rosa de Lima, canonized in 1671 (becoming the first New World saint) and declared patron of America.

Sketched thus, it seems a gentle, simple life, recalling in its sweetness many depictions of Mary by Spanish and Spanish American painters in the seventeenth century. But there was a grimmer side of Rosa, recalling equally those many other works of the time emerging from painters' and sculptors' workshops that exalt the suffering of the saints, not least the Virgin. This was an age of Mariolatry in Spain and the Indies, and Rosa's quick canonization may have resulted from her identification as a revival of the Madonna.[123] Like the Virgin she suffered, though necessarily by self-imposed trials: a diet of bread, water, herbs, juices, and ashes; chile rubbed on her eyelids; fierce self-flagellation; sleeping on a bed of three knotty willow trunks; praying while hanging by her hair from a peg in the wall; bleeding from a crown of thorns pressed into her scalp. The self-discipline perhaps spilled over the line, often difficult to fix, between the devout and the psycho-pathological, and possibly had sexual undertones. That, too, may have been behind the Inquisition's hesitation.

ARTS, FORMAL AND POPULAR

THE BAROQUE

In its tension of light and dark, Rosa's existence seems a good example of the Baroque quality that some have ascribed to the seventeenth century in Spanish America.[124] Whether anything useful can be meant by applying the Baroque label to a whole culture is debatable, especially since the term is such a capacious and undefinable catch-all. But some of the traits of the Baroque in various forms of art – a fascination with the manipulation of shape and space, a celebration of complexity and contrast, a delight in opulence and grandeur, a certain thrilling to the macabre – can be seen, transmuted, by anyone inclined

ILLUSTRATION 11.10   The Metropolitan Cathedral of Mexico City. The facade is Baroque, but the body of the church was begun in 1563, before the Baroque age started, and the bell-shaped finials of the towers date from 1786–93, at the very end of the Mexican Baroque. Copyright Tony Morrison, South American Pictures.

ILLUSTRATION 11.11 The Capilla de los Reyes (Chapel of the Kings), 1718–37, in the Cathedral of Mexico City: a tall, gold-leafed cavern with walls encrusted with such complex and fractured decoration that it is hard to find any patterns in it. Copyright Tony Morrison, South American Pictures.

ILLUSTRATION 11.12 The facade of
the cathedral of Zacatecas, in mid-
northern Mexico, c.1750. This could be
a richly decorated altarpiece removed
from the interior and applied to the
front of the church, except that it is cut
from stone.

ILLUSTRATION 11.13 San Francisco, at
Acatepec in central Mexico, c.1730. The entire
facade, and the bell towers, are covered in the
glazed, multi-colored tile made in and around
Puebla.

ILLUSTRATION 11.14 The Santuario de la Virgen (Sanctuary of the Virgin), at Ocotlán (near Tlaxcala in central Mexico), c.1745. Here, in contrast to Acatepec, the tile is all of one red-orange color, contrasting brilliantly with the whitewashed stucco of the towers and the center of the facade. The effect is of an elegant, rococo lightness that is unusual in Mexico.

ILLUSTRATION 11.15 The central portal of the church of San Lorenzo, Potosí (Bolivia), 1728–44. The surfaces of the stone are covered in delicate decoration in the Andean style sometimes called "Mestizo Baroque".

ILLUSTRATION 11.16 The mission church of Yaguarón, near Asunción (Paraguay), 1761–84. The building is a large, plain, but elegantly proportioned shed held up by many wooden columns.

ILLUSTRATION 11.17 Yaguarón, interior view. The urge to decorate in the Baroque style reached even this remote corner of Spanish America. Note the painted imitation of spiraling on the square wooden columns.

ILLUSTRATION 11.18
Chapel of the Third Order
of St. Francis at São João
del Rei, Brazil, by O
Aleijadinho, 1774. Penguin.

to view things in that way, in such varied phenomena of the seventeenth-century colonies as complexity of social ranking, hot ecclesiastical pursuit of "idolatry," love of ceremony and processions, and savage fights for precedence by both churchmen and bureaucrats in their respective settings.

In the arts, the Baroque of course is unmistakably present. It is the dominant tenor from the mid seventeenth to the late eighteenth century. Sor Juana's poetry and other writing are one example among many in literature. It is even clearer in the productions of the host of painters active in the larger colonial towns, churning out work from their studios in response to orders for personal portraits, portraits of Spanish monarchs, landscapes, and, above all, devotional pictures for private houses, monasteries, convents, and churches. Among the most accomplished were Cristóbal de Villalpando (1645–1714) in New Spain, and Melchor Pérez de Holguín (c.1665–1724) in Potosí, who was perhaps the leading painter of colonial Spanish South America. On both of these the influence of the Seville school was heavy, with Villalpando in the debt of Juan de Valdés Leal, notably the creator of somber still lifes in the *memento mori* line, and Holguín aspiring to the level of Francisco Zurbarán, who was certainly a less gloomy spirit, but one immune from frivolity.[125] Equally profuse was the production of formal music, for use above all in the cathedrals, and written by organists and choirmasters either imported from Europe or trained in European canons in America. It was, however, in music that the Baroque influence was slowest in appearing. For most of the seventeenth century the older tradition of polyphony persisted.

The most obvious surviving evidence of the Baroque is in architecture. From roughly 1650 the eclectic mixture of Romanesque, Gothic, Renaissance (particularly in its Spanish plateresque offshoot), and simply ad hoc pragmatic invention that had appeared in civic buildings and monastic and other churches yielded to an American version of the Baroque. This tended to simplify its European sources, paying more heed to the modeling of surface than to manipulation of masses and volumes. This modeling could be complex and dramatic, as for example in the facade of one of the greatest of Spanish American churches, the cathedral of Mexico City, dedicated in its present design in 1667. In this case there are massive pilasters projecting out from the main plane of the facade, linked to it above by great, curling brackets of stone, and set back from it are the doorways to the nave and the two side aisles. But the addition of smaller decorations, such as spiral columns flanking sculpted panels, detracts from the play of masses, and makes for a slight sense of jumble that saps the undeniable grandeur of the whole. In many lesser churches of the Spanish American Baroque an appliqué of decoration to the exterior is the only claim to distinction. A highly carved facade, and perhaps two decorated belfries flanking it – all striking enough, certainly – may be applied to a building that is otherwise little more than two tall intersecting boxes with a dome over their crossing. It is above all this decoration (together with the massive, intricate, and gilded altarpieces in the interior that reached their full splendor with the eighteenth century) that the term "Baroque" has come to mean when applied to Spanish American churches.

POPULAR ARTS

As in architecture so with other art forms, or at least those of high art: Spanish colonial Baroque, broadly speaking, differs from its European models mainly in taking only part of their content and intent. Its originalities are small. But the opposite is true of popular arts in mid-colonial times, where Indians and *castas* made rich additions to the European base. Music was a large element in the evangelizing armory of the early mendicants. They organized native choirs for their churches, and taught Indians to accompany the singing on European instruments – viols, trumpets, sackbuts, fifes, and the like. Some traits of native music, especially perhaps rhythms, were woven into the European forms. To this blend of European and American was added in the seventeenth century a large African contribution. Again rhythm was a strong influence. By 1600 African drumming was more often heard in Mexico City than that of Indians, and after that varieties of rhythmic songs known as *guineos*, *negros*, and *negrillas* entered the musical repertory in both Middle and South America. Their texts were in an Africanized Spanish. One *negro* from Cuzco has the title *Bamo, bamo en bona fe* (*Vamos, vamos en buena fe*, "Let us go, let us go in good faith"), and another, *Caia guinea bailamo lo congo* (*Calla, guinea, bailamos el congo*, "Hush, man from Guinea, and we'll dance the congo"). Clearly these songs and dances had currency outside the black community, since Spaniards and creoles wrote words, in dialect, for them. Sor Juana was among those to do so, producing *negros* and *negrillas* for use as *villancicos* (popular songs associated with some religious festival, especially with Christmas).[126] She also wrote Nahuatl words for Indian *villancicos*.

There are parallels to this popular music in painting and architecture. The most obvious in painting is the Cuzco school of the late seventeenth century and onwards, generally considered to have originated in the work of the Indian artist Diego Quispe Tito (*c.*1611–*c.*1681). The forthrightness of the Cuzco canvases – there is more to them than a naive charm of primitiveness – has made them the most widely known product of colonial painters outside Spanish America. They typically show archangels dressed in the most sumptuous secular attire of the time, wielding swords or even firearms, and Madonnas viewed face-on, with vast, triangular, gold- and jewel-encrusted robes. The flatness of the style, the simplicity of composition, and the frequent use of decorative gold leaf on the canvases combine in an alluring mixture of simplicity and opulence. But the work is not wholly Indian. The figures are adaptations from European engravings, and, in the case of the angels, specifically from French military manuals.[127] In architecture, popular influence is even more widely visible, particularly in decoration. Many churches of the central Andes, from Quito southwards to Arequipa and Potosí, have flat ornamentation resembling embroidery or woodcarving, cut deeply into the stone of their facades. Whether this decoration has its roots in native or European patterning has been debated; but the masons were Indian or *mestizo*, and to the viewer the work has a strong native American feeling. This "highland planiform decoration"[128] began to appear about 1650, and was used until the end of the next century. Its essence is distilled in the door surround of the small church of San Lorenzo in Potosí (1728–44). From a high niche, a squat St. Michael oversees the entrance. Stylized foliage, in stone, covers much of the portal. In the upper corners, sun, moon and stars appear, and two mermaids playing guitars. The effect would be of coralline rococo encrustation, were it not for the weight of two large spiral columns, topped with heavily skirted stone caryatids, that flank the door itself. In New Spain a similar feeling of Indianness clings to various churches of the southern, or Puebla, style, despite arguments that its inspiration is, again, European. This style, too, dates from the mid 1600s. One of its many peaks is the parish church of Santa María at Tonantzintla (*c.*1700), close to Puebla, whose interior is so convoluted and complete a mass of polychrome stucco relief – leaves, fruits, cherubs' heads, scrolls, twisting columns – that all but the most general shape of the building is lost. It is a glory of gaudiness that may have sources in southern Spain; but even Andalusia falls short of this merry exuberance.

CREOLE NATIVISM

In the mid-colonial era, then, a creativity abounds in the popular arts, or the popular side of the formal arts, that is weak in the paintings, buildings, and music that come straight from European models. Creole high culture, it could be said, was not markedly innovative. One exception to this must, however, be made. And that is that some creoles of the middle period, especially in Mexico, wrote histories that began to link the native, pre-conquest, past with the colonial present in such a way as to suggest that there existed at least a proto-national identity between the two. This was partly a revival of the enthusiasm for Indian culture expressed in some early post-conquest writings, most clearly those of Las Casas. One of the first of these historians, the Franciscan Juan de Torquemada (not strictly a creole, but raised in New Spain from early childhood), drew on Las Casas, and also on Sahagún. The view given by his *Monarquía Indiana* (1615) of the Aztecs was certainly less than wholly positive. He thought that the Devil had first entered Mexico in the guise of Huitzilopochtli, their tribal god. But broadly Torquemada saw the Aztecs as equals in civilization and morality with Greeks and Romans.[129] As the century advanced a few others, some in South America, found admirable qualities in pre-conquest, and even present, Indians. But the creole most notable in this line of thought was Sor Juana's intellectual companion, Don Carlos de Sigüenza y Góngora. It was love for his fatherland (*patria*), he declared, that moved him to delve into Mexico's native past. Following European hermetic speculations of the day, particularly as developed by the Jesuit Athanasius Kircher, Sigüenza argued for the descent of Mexican Indians from the founding rulers of Egypt, from whom all wisdom had ultimately come. Egyptians had colonized Atlantis. It was only a short onward leap to Mexico. Similarities of pyramids, glyphic writing, clothing, and so on supported the Egyptian connection. Sigüenza gave physical form to his high esteem for ancient Mexicans in a triumphal arch he designed for the entry into Mexico City of a new viceroy, the marquis of La Laguna, in 1680. On it were displayed statues of the dozen native rulers of Tenochtitlan from its early fourteenth-century foundation to the conquest, each of them representing some particular political virtue. Sigüenza hoped that this would contribute to a revival of the deserved fame of those native rulers, by his time unjustly ignored.[130]

It was, naturally, easier to find admirable qualities in distant Aztec kings than in the downwardly leveled native commoners of late seventeenth-century New Spain. These inspired in Sigüenza a deep distaste. Nonetheless, his arch signals an early stirring of movement towards a conscious converging, from the creole side, of the native with the imposed culture. It is a movement that has continued to this day, not only in Mexico but in other Spanish American regions that have a strong native cultural base, such as Paraguay and Bolivia.

VARIETIES OF MESTIZAJE

Even without any such conscious effort, the seventeenth century advanced the mingling of American and European in the Spanish colonies. Though the fraction of people calling themselves *mestizos*, or so called by officialdom, was still small in most colonial populations (though always rising), they gained a prominence out of proportion to their numbers. This was because *mestizos* were increasingly regarded as misfits. In the 1500s, they had mostly been absorbed into either white or Indian society. The direction they took depended largely on their parentage. The child of a high-status Spanish father and native mother would likely be raised as a Spaniard, whereas the child of a poor Spaniard and Indian would more probably be brought up as an Indian. By the late sixteenth century, however, clear distinctions in parentage were becoming rarer, especially as *mestizo* parents produced their own children and it consequently became more difficult to assess a child's parentage from his or her appearance. Growing numbers also made absorption more difficult. So, by the early seventeenth century, *mestizos* had emerged as a distinct, and increasingly separate, component of colonial societies.

They found themselves with disadvantages and advantages. Against them was a rising hostility from Spaniards and *criollos*, visible in late sixteenth-century regulations excluding them from various roles and positions: the priesthood, inheriting *encomiendas*, and holding public office, for example. (Because of the increasing difficulty, in practice, of defining who was a *mestizo*, these exclusions had limited real effect. For the same reason, governmental attempts to make *mestizos* pay tributes also failed.) By 1600, *mestizo* was a distinctly negative term. Spaniards, and Indians also to some degree, regarded *mestizos* as subversive. They caused discomfort and mistrust because they had no clear, assigned place in society – and because, lacking such a place, they increasingly created roles for themselves in ways that white and native people found threatening. In the seventeenth-century Andes, for example, *mestizos* insinuated themselves into native communities as *curacas* – and so, in the native view, corrupted and weakened the authentic culture of those places. Broadly speaking, *mestizos* in the Andes could be found, in the 1600s, occupying "ill-defined plebeian positions," on the border between European and native society and culture.[131]

But at the same time they expanded that border to open up social and economic spaces for themselves – further disturbing Spaniards and Indians as they did so. In the lower-status crafts in towns, *mestizos* increasingly displaced poor Spaniards and *criollos*. On mountain roads in the Andes, *mestizo* mule drivers partly took over the freight-carrying business dominated earlier by Indians and llamas. In small-scale commerce, urban and rural, *mestizos* competed with both Indians and white people. Above all, the *mestizo* advantage was one of mutability and adaptability. In the right circumstances, a *mestizo* could exploit his Indian heritage, including language, to become the chief authority of a native community. But by speaking Spanish, dressing in European style, and working and behaving like a Spaniard, he might pass for a poor Spaniard, at least, in a city. Finally, *mestizos* had – despite the complaints of government, and periodic attempts to change this state of affairs – the enormous advantage over Indians of being exempt from exactions of tribute and forced labor (*mita* and *repartimiento*). Indians, in fact, increasingly tried to pass as *mestizos* in order to enjoy the same exemptions.

For all the tensions that expanding *mestizaje* created from the late sixteenth century onward into the seventeenth, it was nonetheless a key process in the creation of Spanish America. In the 1600s genetic and cultural fusion was in full swing, as developments in religion, conceptions of the past, language, and the arts show. And the Euro-American blend was enriched and complicated by many African additions, across the board from religion to clothing. Cultural mixing was undoubtedly pushed forward by the demographic changes of this middle colonial time, particularly by the growing tendency of Indians, under various pressures, to leave their traditional communities for creole-dominated towns, *haciendas*, and mines. There, to the degree that they adopted alien ways, they became less Indian. And Spanish America as a whole was becoming less Indian; for, although native populations generally tended towards stabilization in the seventeenth century after the grim losses of the 1500s, and indeed rose in New Spain, native people became an ever smaller fraction of the whole as other segments of the population grew around them.[132]

After 1600, then, the blending of people and cultures for which the foundation had been laid in the previous century, and which is among the salient qualities – perhaps *the* salient quality – of modern Spanish America, moved beyond any point of possible reversal. That is the chief accomplishment, for the long term, of the seventeenth century in Spanish American history. At the same time, ethnic and cultural mixing could only increase the divergence taking place between Spain and its American colonies – a splitting that was then more obviously visible in a range of practical changes in the operation of the empire: the growing role of creoles in their own administration, the fall in Madrid's receipt of American revenues, contraction in the official trade across the Atlantic, increasing commercial contacts with foreigners, and growth of an autonomous American structure of production and exchange. These were problems, from the metropolis's point of view, that even the disorganized and unstable governments of the enfeebled Spain of Charles II (1665–1700) could not fail to notice. Nothing much could be done about them in that anarchic time of oligarchical adventurism in the peninsula. But the new Bourbon monarchy that after much effort finally brought order, if never greatness, back to Spain during the eighteenth century had no choice but to engage with them.

[12] EIGHTEENTH-CENTURY SPANISH AMERICA: REFORMED OR DEFORMED?

SPAIN at the opening of the seventeenth century suffered twinges of self-doubt. Spain at the opening of the eighteenth suffered sword thrusts of invasion and civil war. The death in 1700, without heir, of Charles II, the last Hapsburg ruler of Spain, was quickly followed by the outbreak of the War of the Spanish Succession. The great European powers wrestled mightily for the Spanish crown; or more precisely for access to American wealth that possession of the throne should bring. Laughably trivial, indeed, if anyone remembered them, must have seemed the soul-searchings of the early 1600s, when in 1706 all the major cities of Spain, Madrid included, were occupied by forces of the Anglo-Austrian-Dutch Grand Alliance that was one of the contenders for control of the Spanish world. The most recent alien occupiers of Spain before then had been the Moors. The Alliance found internal support in the peoples of the Iberian periphery: Aragonese, Catalans, Valencians, and Portuguese seizing the chance to avenge themselves of earlier slights and impositions from Castile and, in the case of the three Spanish regions, to seek greater separation in the future. Opposing the Alliance was the Bourbon France of Louis XIV, whose grandson, Philip of Anjou, had been chosen by the moribund Charles II in his final days as his successor. Castilians accepted their former king's choice, and with it, necessarily, an alliance with France that from the start was a subordination.

The war, begun in 1701, dragged on, inside the peninsula and far beyond its bounds, until 1714. The allies were not able to hold for long what they occupied in 1706; but neither could France and Castile undo the Alliance. In 1712–13, in the multiple treaties of the Peace of Utrecht, compromises were negotiated that reflected the stalemate of the war. Philip was to keep the throne, being confirmed as Philip V of Spain, but only on condition that he abandon rights of succession in France. Spain was to keep its American territories, but was stripped of its European lands. Minorca and Gibraltar went to Britain, Sicily to Savoy, and Flanders, Naples, Milan, and Sardinia to Austria. The British in addition gained a long-desired legal access to Spanish American markets through the concession of the *asiento de negros*, or monopoly right to sell African slaves to the Spanish colonies, for thirty years. With this went what was to prove the lucrative right to send with each Spanish trading fleet a ship of 500 tons (no small vessel by prevailing standards) carrying goods for sale at the trade fairs of New Spain and the Isthmus of Panama. With silver from the sale of slaves and merchandise in Spanish America, the British aimed to quicken the growth of their trade with the Far East; again that endless oriental appetite for silver was working its effect on the western world.[1]

For Spain, the War of Succession and Utrecht were both end and beginning. The end – the formal, unequivocal end after a century of decline – was of Spain's standing as an autonomous world power. The beginning was of a period – a long period that has lasted until recently – of subordination to others' influence and will. It was now clear that Spain had gone from player to played-upon. In the eighteenth century the main external directing force was France, to which Spain was tied by the Bourbon family link (though, true to Utrecht, the crowns were never united). Over and again in that century, and particularly in its second half, Spain was drawn in France's wake into costly conflicts. The enemy was usually Britain, with which France engaged in a century-long series of wars for world pre-eminence. Whatever weight Spain retained in European affairs came largely from its possession of the American empire. The Spanish state became a paradox: a second-rate European power holding the world's largest overseas colonies.

That Spain did continue to hold those colonies resulted from several causes. First was the sheer size of Spanish America. Even its sub-units, such as the *audiencia* provinces and frontier governorships, were too large for any external power to bite off (without, at least, local collaboration, which was not offered). Again, America proved capable in the 1700s of providing funds and men for its own defense. Third, the sharing of wealth and administrative power with the monarchy that the colonies (or more precisely, the *criollos*) had achieved over the seventeenth century was conducive to preserving the status quo. At first sight, the absence of any colonial bid for separation during the War of Succession, when Madrid was powerless to thwart it, may seem striking. But in reality whatever gains such an attempt might have brought to the colonists were far outweighed by the risks of the unknown; much better to remain settled in the comfortable accommodation with the monarchy that long but largely gentle friction between rulers and ruled had produced over the previous century. It is in any case unlikely in the extreme that any colonist possessing political influence contemplated, even fleetingly, separation from Spain in the early 1700s. Only the experience of the Enlightenment and of reform would make the time ripe for such notions.

After the War of Succession, Spanish affairs could hardly do other than improve; and so they did, slowly. Under the admittedly erratic leadership of Philip V (1701–46) and his successors Ferdinand VI (1746–59) and Charles III (1759–88), and under the French absolutist influence that the Bourbon line brought into Spain, the authority of the central government grew, that of the nobility declined, and limited economic recovery took place.[2] These changes were also in part the outcome of an intellectual renovation fanned by winds of change that entered the land, even if much attenuated in their crossing of the Pyrenees from their source in the French Enlightenment.

The American empire, too, propelled Spanish recovery, with its growing contributions to the treasury. America was, in fact, notably more vibrant in all material respects than the home country throughout the eighteenth century, as almost all regions put behind them whatever contraction or stagnation they had known during the 1600s, and areas that had been economically marginal became profitably productive.

PEOPLE, PRODUCTION, AND COMMERCE

TRENDS IN POPULATION

Underlying this advance, first, was population growth. This is clearest for New Spain, where the total population grew from about 1.5 million in 1650, to 2.5–3 million in the early 1740s, to some 4.5–5 million in the 1790s, to above 6 million in 1810. These numbers suggest a rate of growth increasing with time. The same quickening increase can be seen in northern and central Chile (1 percent annually in the first half of the century, 2 percent thereafter), taking the population from *c.*95,000 in 1710 to *c.*583,000 in 1815. In New Granada a similar pattern seems likely, although the number of inhabitants early in the eighteenth century is unclear. During the 1770s the combined population of the *audiencias* of Santa Fe de Bogotá and Quito rose at the remarkable yearly rate of some 2.3 percent, and at perhaps 1.7 percent annually in the next decade. For Peru and Charcas demographic data are, unfortunately, still sparse for the eighteenth century. All indications are, however, that the population grew between 1700 and 1800. Crucial to that increase, whatever its pace, and to the clear acceleration of demographic growth in New Spain, was recovery of the Indian populations, founded above all on native peoples' improving resistance to the diseases that had for so long been so devastating. Native numbers rose particularly strongly after 1700 in Mexico, since that curve had touched its low point as early as the 1620s and was rebounding strongly by the end of the century. Standard opinion has long had the native population of the central Andes on a downward course until the 1720s, with a fierce, though unidentified, epidemic of 1719–20 dealing a blow that reduced numbers to their minimum in colonial times. Recent, if very local, evidence, however, suggests that the low point may have come before 1660, and that the epidemic of sixty years later, while undoubtedly severe, did no more than interrupt what was by then sturdy Indian growth. In the 1700s mixed-blood people multiplied fast almost everywhere. It is said, for example, that New Granada then became "a fundamentally *mestizo* society." In Chile, too, *mestizos* flourished, but there it was the white portion of the population (including a mixed element generally regarded as white) that truly prevailed, laying the basis for the present nature of the country's population.[3]

Eighteenth-century demographic growth in Spanish America was also raised by numerous new arrivals of slaves from Africa. Indeed, the term "re-Africanization" has been suggested as fitting for Spanish America in the 1700s, to indicate the upsurge in slave imports that took place then, after a decline in the second half of the seventeenth century.[4] In reality, however, it was not so much a case of "re-Africanizing" the areas that had received most slaves earlier as of greatly increasing the African slave population of several regions that now underwent – though at different times – quite sudden economic expansion. These were New Granada, Venezuela, Costa Rica, Cuba, and the Río de la Plata area. With the exception of New Granada, where the eighteenth-century boom was in gold-mining, these areas' new prosperity came from the land. The traditional heartlands of Spanish America, New Spain and Peru, certainly continued to import slaves after 1700, but not in such large numbers as these newly rich regions.

Under the *asiento de negros* that the British gained from the Utrecht treaties of 1712–13, they carried 75,000 slaves to Spanish America over the following twenty-five years. Roughly 16,000 of these went to Buenos Aires (and, from there, onward inland to the Andean mining areas and other inland destinations); the remainder went to the Isthmus of Panama (for sale in Central America or down the west coast of South America) and to Cartagena, on the Caribbean coast of New Granada (for sale mainly to gold-miners in that colony). Other slave traders continued shipping Africans to those same destinations after the British *asiento* came to an end with the outbreak of the War of Jenkin's Ear in 1739. The subsequent growth in slave shipments by various holders of the supply contract culminated in 1789 in the Spanish government's proclaiming free trade in slaves to its American colonies by suppliers from any country. This largesse – surprising in view of the constant policy, though not reality, of closed trade for centuries past – resulted from a desire to boost colonial production by any available means.

Expanding slave arrivals in the 1700s are visible in numbers from various regions: 2,000 African slaves mining gold in the Chocó area of north-west New Granada in 1720 – and 7,000 in 1782; 64,000 slaves in Venezuela by the end of the century, with almost 40,000 of them working in producing the raw material of chocolate on cacao plantations; in Cuba some 10,000 slaves early in the century, about 40,000 fifty years later, and 65,000 in the 1780s – mostly producing sugar, and by the late decades also coffee, on plantations. For Costa Rica, numbers of slaves are unclear, and they were certainly smaller than those in Cuba and Venezuela. But African slaves cultivated cacao – indeed, all but controlled the production of cacao – on estates in the Barbilla and Matina valleys near the Caribbean coast of the province. In growth of slave numbers, eighteenth-century Mexico and Peru stand in contrast with these areas of rising slave presence. Peru had around 90,000 black slaves early the century, and the same number at the end. By the late 1700s, New Spain's slave component had fallen to a far smaller number, at only 5,000 to 10,000; but it had perhaps 116,000 free people with some degree of African origin.[5]

By the close of the eighteenth century, the total population of Spanish America stood at some 12.6 million. By region, it has been reckoned as shown in table 12.1.[6] Three points call for comment here. First is the preponderance of Mexico, with almost half the total population of Spanish America by 1800.

Table 12.1 Population of Spanish America by region at the end of the eighteenth century

Region	No. (millions) *	% of total
Mexico	5.84	46.4
Central America	1.16	9.2
Caribbean islands	0.55	4.4
New Granada	1.1	8.7
Venezuela	0.78	6.2
Quito	0.5	4.0
Peru	1.1	8.7
Charcas	0.56	4.5
Chile	0.55	4.4
Buenos Aires and Tucumán	0.31	2.5
Paraguay	0.1	0.8
Uruguay	0.03	0.2
Total	**12.58**	**100.0**

* Figures are rounded to the nearest 0.01 million.

This is an accurate indicator of its general, and especially economic, prominence in the empire in the eighteenth century. Second is the growth of the total population in that century. Although reliable figures are available for very few regions in the early years of the century, almost every sign is of increase. And, given the great weight in the total of Mexico, for which estimates are available at least for the mid seventeenth and mid eighteenth centuries, it is likely that the whole Spanish American population grew between two and three times between 1700 and 1800. But, despite that, it should lastly be recalled that, before Cortés's arrival in 1519, the population of central and southern Mexico alone may well have surpassed the 12 million or so shown here for Spanish America as a whole. The gross demographic balance of the colonial period was definitely negative.

PRODUCTION

As in earlier times, it is in mining that growth is most incontrovertibly seen in the eighteenth century, thanks to the existence of continuous records of royalty taxes paid to the treasury. All major silver and gold regions managed an almost unbroken increase of production over the century. In silver output, the central Andes, after a steep decline throughout the 1600s, achieved an average growth of production of 1.2 percent annually in the eighteenth century. New Spain's rate of increase was the same or slightly higher from 1725 to 1810, and this was a continuation, after a brief dip in the early 1720s, of steady growth from about 1670 onwards. In the closing years of the seventeenth century Mexican silver production exceeded Peru's for the first time. Mexico stayed ahead, such that c.1800 Mexican mines yielded some 25 million pesos yearly, against the central Andean total of 8–9 million. The combined amount was more than double the highest previous American yield of silver, achieved in Potosí's heyday *c.*1600. In fact, that earlier maximum was first passed between 1710 and 1720, and was exceeded in every year between 1750 and 1810.[7]

The reasons for such a general swelling of the silver stream flowing from Spanish American mines were diverse. Some were particular to certain places, such as the continuation at Potosí of the state-run supply of cheap native labor through the *mita.* The recovery of Potosí's and Oruro's taxed production also fits with a cut in the royalty rate charged in the central Andes from a fifth to a tenth of output. Miners in Potosí had for a century or more pleaded for this reduction, which would make their tax load equal to the royalty charged in New Spain. Their petitions were finally answered in 1736. Mexican miners seem likely to have benefited from stable, or possibly even falling, labor costs that resulted from population growth in eighteenth-century New Spain. Generally encouraging to silver-mining everywhere early in the century was the high valuation of precious metals in Europe at the time. Other broadly vitalizing influences were the spreading adoption of subterranean blasting, from about 1670 in the Andes and after 1700 in Mexico, and the greater availability of mercury resulting from new finds of ore at Almadén in Spain early in the eighteenth century. Blasting seems likely to have lowered the cost of both seeking silver ore underground and removing it once found. Increased mercury output at Almadén eased the tightness of mercury supply that had often hampered silver-refining in the 1600s, and offset falling production at Huancavelica in Peru, the only substantial source of mercury in Spanish America.[8]

The general buoyancy of silver production in the eighteenth century brought rising revenues to the crown in royalties, sales of mercury, and taxes on general sales and trade. It stimulated the colonies' commerce, both internal and external, legal and contraband. Worth particular notice is the growth of silver output in the first half of the century that research has shown in recent years. The Mexican silver boom of the late 1700s, and the relatively modest recovery of Potosí at the same time, were always obvious to historians, who tended to see them as the outcome of a planned revival of mining through policies applied mainly under Charles III. These included cuts in royalty rates and the mercury price, state-sponsored technical education, state-organized credit banks, the creation of privileged mining guilds, and social rewards to successful miners in the form of noble titles. These measures certainly had positive effects. But now it is clear that late eighteenth-century growth of silver was also a continuation of a vigorously rising trend that had begun around 1670 in New Spain and perhaps fifty years later in the central Andes. This trend owed little to policy (except for the royalty reduction granted to central Andean miners in 1736), and much to the economic circumstances in which the industry operated, such as the technological advance of blasting, stability or possibly even decline (in Mexico) in the cost of labor, and a rise in the value of precious metals.[9]

Propelled by that same rising valuation, gold production in Spanish America also trended strongly upward after 1700. Much gold was found intermingled with silver ores in New Spain. It became there an important by-product of silver-refining in the eighteenth century, especially at San Luis Potosí. With some interruptions, the largest in the 1780s, taxed gold output in Mexico grew by an order of magnitude between 1701 and 1710 (c.70,000 oz in the decade) and 1801–10 (c.765,000 oz). Chile also produced much gold in the eighteenth century. Spanish America's best gold source remained, however, New Granada, where, according to records of both royalties collected and gold coins struck, the mines' output multiplied four or even six times between the early and late decades of the century. The royalty record, for instance, indicates an annual output for 1715–19 of gold worth c.440,000 silver pesos, against c.1,890,000 yearly in the 1790s. Apart from the rising worth of the metal, increased availability of labor seems to have underlain this mining growth in New Granada. Black slaves did much of the mining work, and imports of these were raised above earlier levels first by the French Guinea Company during the War of the Spanish Succession, and afterwards by the British South Sea Company operating the slave *asiento* under the terms set up at Utrecht. Population growth in general may also have provided new prospectors and workers, particularly for the important mining region of Antioquia in the center-north, where wage labor rather than slavery prevailed in gold extraction.[10]

Gold's value being so much more compact than silver's (the ratio of value of the two metals, weight for weight, in mid-eighteenth-century Europe was about 15:1), gold was the easier of the two, and the more tempting, to smuggle. Hence production estimates drawn from royalty accounts are more likely to understate gold's production than silver's. Even so, the margin between the output of the two metals in the late Spanish colonies is worth noting. By official record New Granada, the main gold-producing region, yielded gold worth a little less than 2 million pesos a year in the 1790s. New Spain, the main source of silver in the final colonial century, gave in the same decade some 25 million pesos annually. Silver remained to the last, as always, the prime metallic product, and the main export, of the American empire.

With the scale of its production, complexity of technique, and large formation of fixed capital in refineries, shafts, and adits, Spanish American silver-mining can properly be called an industry. The size, bustle, noise, smells, dirt, and environmental degradation of such places as Potosí from the late sixteenth century, and Guanajuato from the mid-eighteenth, would make a modern viewer see them as industrial centers. But, in that, mining was unique. The only other type of production that even approached industrial status was textile manufacture; and that only in New Spain.

Cloth, mainly rough woolen stuffs, and cottons where the fiber could be grown, continued to be made anywhere local demand existed. Native villagers spun and wove wool (from llamas, alpacas and sheep in the Andes, and sheep alone elsewhere) for domestic needs, as many still do today. Rural estates often had a weaving shop making cloth for residents' use. Regions particularly suited for raising wool-bearing animals tended to develop concentrations of *obrajes* for weaving. Conditions for production and sale might be favorable enough to lead local merchants and landowners to invest in these weaving sheds and the looms they contained. In South America the main such area after 1700 continued to be Quito. But the densest grouping of *obrajes* (and smaller establishments known as *trapiches*) in the eighteenth century was at Querétaro in the Bajío region of New Spain. While cloth output dropped in other Mexican textile zones, notably the Valley of Mexico and the Puebla area, it rose at Querétaro for most of the century, encouraged by population growth that provided abundance of both demand and labor. In the 1740s Querétaro had forty *obrajes*; though the number fell after then, production was maintained by a multiplication of the smaller shops. The number of working looms rose until the independence wars began in 1810. There were 290 in that year.[11]

That concentration of weaving capacity undoubtedly made Querétaro the textile capital of Spanish America. But it was hardly an industrial town. *Obrajes* were not factories, and *trapiches* even less so. A large *obraje* was one with twenty looms. No power was used besides that of human operators. No technological advance is visible in eighteenth-century cloth-making in Spanish America. As generally with Spanish American production in late colonial times, larger output was achieved by increasing inputs (in this case, of labor and wool), and not by improving productivity through technical change. Even at the best case of Querétaro, then, textiles were a matter of a proto-industry comprising proto-factories. The result was that Spanish American textile production was increasingly undercut as the century advanced by ever cheaper cloths dispatched by the ever more efficient powered mills of Europe. So great were the price differences that finally developed that in the century's closing decades no regulation was capable of blocking contraband imports of those cloths, particularly printed cottons from England. And so began a long period, still continuing in some degree, in which Latin America found its possibilities for economic growth and change cramped by its degree of technological lag behind First World producers.

Another activity on the border between craft and industry that continued strong in the eighteenth century was the building and repair of ships. Notable yards were at Guayaquil and Havana, and also on the Paraguay river, a few miles downstream from Asunción, where vessels were built to carry the growing river traffic of the Río de la Plata system. Suitable wood was at hand at all three sites.[12]

The processing of tobacco also came, in New Spain at least, to be a business impressive in scale, if again its techniques did not go beyond standard craft practices. Beginning in 1717, the Bourbon regime moved gradually to capitalize on the healthy American appetite for cigars, cigarettes, and snuff by creating state monopolies on tobacco. In most regions the state controlled only the sale of the leaf. But in the Philippines and New Spain it became not just the single buyer (at regulated prices) of leaf, but the maker of the end-products. The Mexican monopoly, indeed, dating from the mid 1760s, oversaw manufactories in Guadalajara, Puebla, Oaxaca, Orizaba, and Querétaro – as well as a central plant in Mexico City, which in the mid 1790s employed over 7,000 workers, 60 percent of them women. Four out of five of them rolled cigarettes by hand.[13] Without mechanization this massing of labor, however impressive in numbers, brought few economies of scale. Like the *obrajes*, the tobacco-processing plants were still proto-factories.

Crafts practiced in the traditional small shops in every town continued to provide most of what most people wanted or needed by way of clothing, tools and utensils, household decorations, riding gear, and so on. The import trade, licit and contraband, brought in the luxurious and the novel; but now increasingly it also supplied what was more commonplace but simply cheaper, as in the case of factory-made cloth.

Spanish America's slowness in moving towards larger-scale manufacture was arguably above all the outcome of a resistance to innovation and change, and a parallel unreceptiveness to science and technology, that may be traced to Spain's embrace of the Counter-Reformation, and deviation from many lines of European development, in the sixteenth century. As a result, the economic soil had not been prepared in the seventeenth century for the changes in productive methods that the eighteenth brought to the countries of north-west Europe. Bourbon attempts at innovation in production in Spain itself were, with rare exceptions, no more successful than America's. The Indies' lag was, though, also in part an outcome of policy. Since the late sixteenth century a thread of opposition to American manufacturing had run through the imperial policy. The fear was that goods made in the colonies were goods they would not buy from Spain, and, besides, that any degree of economic autonomy could only promote political unruliness.[14] The thread was never prominent in Hapsburg times, however, because of the impracticality of policing American production, and the unreasonableness of expecting colonials to import basic goods that they could make easily and cheaply themselves. But, in the Bourbon urge to reform, it was picked out again, as a central element in a new formulation of the entire imperial economic structure. One strong advocate of reform, Philip V's secretary of finance, war, the navy and the Indies in the early 1740s, José del Campillo y Cossío, argued in his *New System of Economic Government of America* (1743) that the colonies must be seen as markets for Spanish goods, and that therefore factories and industries were "the only matter that must absolutely be forbidden in America."[15] Other influential planners were less insistent on this point. Nonetheless, orders were certainly given later in the century for the closing of *obrajes* and smaller textiles shops operating without viceregal permits. Although it is not yet clear how widely these commands were enforced, it is certain that a prospective colonial entrepreneur wanting to invest in some productive activity outside mining or agriculture was unlikely to find enthusiastic official backing for his efforts.

Along with mining, farming and stockraising were clearly the most dynamic elements of the eighteenth-century colonial economy. Total food production necessarily rose with the general trend of population growth, under all types of land use and holding, from the communal subsistence fields of native villages to the large, privately owned estates. It may well be, however, that, at least in the more densely peopled regions, it did not quite keep up with the increasing numbers. For just as it is likely that, in the seventeenth century, drastic shrinking of populations and their demand for food generally meant that farming was concentrated on the most productive soil, so conversely in the 1700s growing population and increasing demand for food forced the use of progressively poorer lands. There followed a drop in the general productivity of both land and farm labor. Similarly, where land came into high demand to meet a large local call for food, smaller and weaker owners or tenants might find themselves forced out by the owners of larger tracts. For these two reasons, demographic recovery therefore brought falling living standards to at least some people at the lower end of society. But farming for consumption in the colonies broadly and inevitably expanded over the century. It did so using the same techniques as before, and the same range of land units, from native communal plots, through various types of smallholdings held by Indians, *castas* and whites, to *haciendas* modest to vast.

Even greater, however, was the growth of commercial, export-directed agriculture. This, indeed, was where true innovation in land use came in the eighteenth century; for although agriculture had yielded exports almost from the start (sugar, dyes, and cacao, for instance), these flows now grew so much that quantitative change became qualitative. In addition, regions which before had been minor producers now began to export heavily.

Chile was one such place. Its production of livestock and arable crops (mainly wheat) grew almost without interruption by a factor of seven or more between 1700 and the early 1800s, partly as a response to rising demand for Chilean wheat on the coast of Peru. Annual exports of wheat through Chile's main port, Valparaíso, rose, for example, from some 66,000 to 120,000 *fanegas* between 1705 and 1735 (a *fanega* is about 1.5 bushels).[16]

Another rising exporter was Paraguay. In the final third of the eighteenth century, the province's long-established export of *yerba mate* to the downstream regions towards Buenos Aires expanded tenfold. Shipments of tobacco, wood, sugar, and sweetmeats also rose substantially. All these goods were carried on ships built and crewed by Paraguayans, whose province for the first time became economically integrated into its broader Río de la Plata region.[17]

A leading reason for that linkage was the economic growth of Buenos Aires itself, founded on the export of leather from the cattle roaming the town's *pampas* hinterland. Here since the sixteenth century herds of wild cattle had thrived. Hides had been carried away by the small official trade – and larger unofficial one – in and out of Buenos Aires, some of them by Portuguese merchants operating from Brazil. In the War of the Spanish Succession, however, the major buyers were the French, to whom the new government of Philip V had granted the slave *asiento* during the war. Taking full advantage of this legal access, French ships sailed to Spanish American ports in large numbers for the first time. With their arrival in Buenos Aires there began an expansion in the export of leather that persisted through the century. From 1708 to 1712 some 175,000 hides may have been exported. After Utrecht, and the transfer of the slave-importing *asiento* to the British, the South Sea Company carried African slaves to Buenos Aires, and hides (and silver) from it: in 1715, some 45,000 hides, in 1718, some 40,000, in 1724, some 60,000. By the 1760s Buenos Aires was exporting 150,000 hides each year, and from 1779 to 1795, about 330,000. With this growth came expansion of Buenos Aires's control over the interior plains. The highly mobile Indians native to them were pressed inland, away from water and the better pastures. To do so was no easy task; the *pampas* peoples were a constantly moving target, and easily eluded attacks by conventional military expeditions. In the early 1780s the Spanish authorities settled on strengthening and adding to a line of forts inland from Buenos Aires as the best practicable means of containing the Indians.[18] The *cabildo* of the city began to grant *estancias* (not privately owned large tracts, as the term later came to mean, but rights to use grazing and water in specified areas). As shipments of hides multiplied, so began Buenos Aires's progression from small, isolated townlet to metropolitan city.[19]

Another region that after 1700 began to realize its long-apparent agricultural potential was Venezuela. Today Venezuelan coffee is renowned; but in colonial times the province's famous caffeine-containing product was cacao, exported mainly to New Spain in the 1600s, and later to Europe as well. Production was rising fast by the start of the eighteenth century, to judge by the number of cacao trees growing in the province of Caracas: half a million in 1684, 3 million in 1720 (and over 5 million in 1744). Until about 1730 Caracas-based growers and shippers rapidly enriched themselves from the sale of the booming bean, prized in Europe not only for its flavor but its supposed medicinal merits. The home government, its attention caught by these profits, decided to tap them for the peninsula's benefit by chartering in 1728 a commercial organization, the Guipúzcoa (or Caracas) Company, equipped with monopoly trading rights with Venezuela. In fact the company's monopoly was never watertight. Venezuelans fiercely resented the imposed attempt to make it so by, among other means, selling cacao to European contraband buyers. And the British South Sea Company, supplying black slaves to the Venezuelan cacao growers under the *asiento* until the War of Jenkin's Ear broke out in 1739, discovered that it was highly profitable to exchange slaves for cacao in Venezuela, and then sell that cacao at Veracruz, in New Spain, for silver.[20] So Venezuelan chocolate found its various ways into the cups of imbibers on both sides of the Atlantic.

North from Venezuela, Caribbean islands large and small had shown themselves by the eighteenth century to be unmatched in soil and climate for growing sugar cane. The Spanish had ignored this opportunity. Although they had been the first to plant cane in the islands, in their earliest years on Hispaniola, the lure of mainland riches had distracted them from the islands' potential. Hence it was the French, English, and Dutch who drew sweet profits from the Caribbean as they occupied, in the seventeenth century, islands undefended or readily abandoned by Spain. By the mid 1700s Saint Domingue (now Haiti) was by far the largest American sugar producer, followed by Brazil, then Jamaica. The leading Spanish source was Cuba, ranking eleventh in America, below Dutch Guiana, Guadaloupe, and Barbados. English and French colonies provided over 80 percent of European sugar imports.[21]

From the mid 1760s, however, Cuba grew more sugar, as the Bourbon monarchy sought to develop the island's possibilities. The aim, apart from a general effort to increase royal income from America, was to create wealth locally to pay for improved defense of the island. The need for this had been made quite clear by the British capture of Havana in the closing stages of the Seven Years War in 1762. Over the next three decades Cuba's sugar output increased two and a half times (from some 6 million kilograms in 1760 to 15 million in 1792). Puerto Rico also became a substantial grower. By 1792 Cuba was the third-largest American source, after Jamaica and Brazil. Saint Domingue had vanished from the ranking. The French Revolution inspired a slave rising there in 1791 whose effects reduced sugar exports from 74 million kilograms in 1791 to 24 million in 1804, and a mere 900 kilograms in 1825.[22]

The rise of agricultural exports from eastern regions of Spanish America was the most striking change to occur in the colonial economy in the eighteenth century. Many causes underlay it. Perhaps least important of them was the Bourbon developmental intent and policies visible over the century. More influential were improvement in the performance and capacity of ships, so that freight of bulky goods became cheaper; the inevitable rise, both legal and illicit (in the Spanish view), of foreign commercial contact with the colonies, as Spain's power waned and that of European rivals, and latterly of the United States also, waxed; and, overriding all else, the growth of population and wealth in western Europe, especially as industrialization and, with it, urbanization took hold in the closing decades of the century. There then emerged the massive First World appetite for the foodstuffs and raw materials produced on tropical and subtropical plantations that has been one of the motors of the world economy for two centuries past. Thus in Spanish America, though precious metals were still the major export in the aggregate, for the first time large regions lacking silver or gold found their prosperity and populations increasing. And along with that material growth went first a growing sense of local identity, and then one of future political potential.

TRADE

The fact that much of the rising demand for the products of Spanish America's land came from outside Spain complicated one the central aims of Bourbon reform for America, which was to recover control of the transatlantic trade for Spain. The problem was twofold. First was the matter of goods arriving in America in foreign bottoms, whether smuggled or under some legal arrangement. Second was the predominance, even in the official transatlantic commerce by fleets, of foreign goods (a predominance clear in the late seventeenth-century revival of the value, if not the volume, of the fleet trade). Neither difficulty had an easy answer. But the first was the less challenging of the two. Foreign ships could be excluded by law backed by force. Providing that force in the form of naval defense might be costly; but it was far less costly, and less demanding of profound economic innovation, than replacing alien goods with Spanish products, for that would require a wholesale modernization of Spanish manufacture, to match other economies already set on the road to mechanized industry.

The foreign presence in the Indies trade, in the form of ships actually docking in American ports, was huge at the start of the Bourbon era. France's holding of the slave *asiento* from 1701 to 1713 vastly stimulated a French interest in the Spanish American trade that had already been quite clear before 1700. Improvement in ships and navigation now permitted safe and regular passage around Cape Horn for the first time. French merchants took such quick and sure advantage of this that no less than 68 percent of Peru's foreign trade is thought to have been carried in French vessels between 1700 and 1725 (twelve years after the British secured the *asiento* for themselves at Utrecht). French traders were equally active in New Spain from 1700 to 1710.[23]

Then, after Utrecht, the British also shouldered their way into the Indies' markets on a scale they had previously only dreamed of. Not only could the South Sea Company smuggle in goods on its slave ships, but additions to the Utrecht Treaty permitted the dispatch of 500 tons of goods in a ship accompanying any annual Spanish trading fleet bound for America. It was a concession that the British exploited to the full. From trading premises (*factorías*) that it was allowed to build at eight major colonial cities, including Buenos Aires, Havana, Portobelo, and Veracruz, the company distributed not only slaves but British goods. Spanish officials estimated that by 1728 the British-held slave contract was the conduit for a third of the contraband entering America. In the late 1750s, long after the *asiento*, if not the company, had disappeared, the British were still smuggling goods vigorously into the Indies to the tune, by Spanish calculation, of 6 million pesos a year.[24]

By that time, changes were under way in the working of the official American trade that were intended to make it more resistant to interlopers and more rewarding to Spain. These changes were, to be sure, peculiarly slow in coming. The sluggishness resulted, it seems, mainly from the strong conservative influence over the government held still by the merchant houses handling the Indies trade in southern Spain. Their value as a credit source for the crown, and their control over a commerce seen as vital to national interests, preserved their weight in Madrid.

Hostilities during the War of Succession had reduced the fleet trade almost to nothing, completing the decline in official transatlantic shipping that marked the late seventeenth century. Reinvigoration of the fleets was the government's main hope for recuperation of the trade for several decades after the war. This approach, given the costly and clumsy rigidity of the structure, surely all too obvious from the successes of interlopers using single ships, seems a self-defeating policy. But pursued it was, with energy. One sensible change, by contrast, was the removal of the Casa de Contratación in 1717 from Seville to Cadiz; though even this relocation of the official base of the trade was simply recognition of a real shift that had been taking place for decades, as the Guadalquivir silted up between Seville and the sea.

A new master design for the fleets, the "Plan for the Galleons and Fleets of Peru and New Spain" of 1720, laid down that a fleet for each destination should sail yearly, at specified dates. This, in the event, proved no more practicable in the eighteenth century than it had in the sixteenth, with the result that for two further decades the fleet system did no more than sputter along. Suggesting, however, that something had been learned from the contrabandists, the 1720 plan also proposed the use of specially licensed single vessels to supplement the fleets, and especially to relieve any shortages of goods that might arise in particular places. To these "register ships," as they were called, colonial ports on the Atlantic side of America were declared open.[25]

The combining of sporadic fleets with occasional register ships brought a slight increase in the tonnage of the Carrera, from some 9,000 tons of total shipping annually in the 1720s to 11,000 in the 1730s and early 1740s. Over those same years, also, Spain built up a defensive presence in the Caribbean. This considerably annoyed the British, who came to view their habit of sailing where they pleased in that sea as a proprietary right. It was, reputedly, the Spanish interception of a ship commanded by a British captain named Jenkins, and the cutting off of his ear in the subsequent skirmish, that sparked off the War of Jenkins' Ear in 1739. The conflict was in reality a more general one, about access to Spanish America's trade as Spain's naval forces in the Caribbean began to display some teeth. It merged into the War of Austrian Succession (1740–8). During the decade of fighting, Spain gave further signs of recovered strength in the Caribbean, succumbing in some instances to massive British naval attacks, but beating off others, notably Admiral Vernon's assault on Cartagena in 1741.[26]

It was, too, with the end of the war in 1748 that a vigorous expansion of the legal trade began that lasted for forty years. By the early 1770s the annual transatlantic tonnage had risen to some 28,000 tons. This largely consisted of register ships. During the War of Austrian Succession no fleets had sailed, and after it they were unable to meet the challenge of the increasingly well-established single-ship trade. Indeed, no *galeones* went to the isthmus after 1748, and in 1776 the last *flota* sailed to New Spain, only the fifth since 1748.[27]

As in silver-mining, where the bulk of Bourbon reform was applied after many decades of expansion, so in the Atlantic trade the administration finally in the 1760s and 1770s gave legal form to what had long been increasingly successful practice. A series of concessions, beginning in 1764, gradually opened up major ports around the coast of Spain itself to single-ship trade with, first, destinations in the Caribbean, then others on the fringes of the mainland, and lastly those in the old, central colonial areas. The reforms were finally condensed into what is, after the New Laws of 1542, the most famous legal code applied to America by Spain in colonial times: the Regulations and Royal Tariffs for Free Trade between Spain and the Indies of 1778.

The aim of the code was precisely to liberalize trade between Spain and America, while excluding foreigners. The "freedom" of trade proclaimed in the title was only freedom inside the Spanish system. And, as the inclusion of "tariffs" in the title suggests, even exchanges between metropolis and colonies were not to be untaxed. Because another intent of the code was to bring about what Campillo y Cossío and others had long since advocated – that Spain should be the manufacturing center of the empire, and America the source of the raw materials to be processed in Spain's factories – tariffs were now revised to favor the movement of American primary exports to Spain, and of Spanish manufactures to America. True, a hodgepodge of petty taxes on the Indies trade was eliminated, leaving only customs duties and the sales tax in place.

One broad purpose of the Regulations, that of removing red tape hindering Spanish transatlantic exchange, was certainly achieved.

The 1778 law brought some gains for Spain, although not for long. It did not really take hold until 1782, towards the end of Spain's engagement, in alliance with France, against England in the War of American Independence. And its effect ended in 1797 when England, at war with a French–Spanish alliance, blockaded Cadiz and effectively cut Spanish contact with America. In the fifteen-year interim, however, exports leaving Spain for America rose, on an annual average, to four times their level in 1778. And the Spanish share of this expanded export grew: Spanish goods made up, on average, 52 percent of the value embarked, against 38 percent in 1778. More striking still was the rise of colonial exports to Spain. Their yearly average value rose more than ten times over the period, compared with 1778. The abundance of primary products now pouring from the land in Spanish America (tobacco, cacao, hides, sugar, cochineal, indigo, cascarilla, and others) were worth 44 percent of the total export, more than ever before; the rest was gold and silver.[28]

The greater increase in Spain's imports from America than in its exports to the colonies also suggests (Spanish re-exports being ignored) a rising metropolitan gain from the transatlantic trade. But, if the 1778 Regulations were apparently effective in raising the value of the trade, and Spain's share in it, they fell short of other aims. Most of the rise in Spanish exports consisted of agricultural products of the sort shipped to America since the early days of the colonies: wine, brandy, flour, olive oil, preserved fruits, nuts, and the like. Even the improved selling possibilities in America under the new trading regime, therefore, failed to stimulate Spanish manufacture. The sole, clear exception was Catalonia. There, direct trading between Barcelona and American ports, legal now for the first time, quickened the growth of the already established mechanized production of textiles. Barcelona was the second-ranking dispatcher of exports to Spanish America in the 1782–96 period. Its share, however, was only 10 percent of the total value. Cadiz still dominated the trade, with 76 percent of America-bound exports. There was, therefore, little redistribution of the export business among Spanish ports. Andalusia still controlled the transatlantic trade, as it had from the start.[29] And in Cadiz, foreign merchants still prospered, handling the transhipment of manufactures from many different European origins to America.

The trading link with the colonies was an early, and then constant, target of Bourbon reformers for obvious enough reasons. The century had begun with commercial disaster for Spain in America as, during the War of Succession, foreigners enlarged their already majority share of the business. But at least, after the war, the commercial problems it had made particularly clear could be partly tackled close at hand, in Spain itself, through an attempted renovation of the shipping system. Hence naval and trade reform was pursued energetically in the 1720s. A broader reason for the close attention given to colonial commerce was that increasing Spain's control and share of it seemed, in itself alone, an obvious and direct means of economic, indeed national, recuperation. In that way Spain could secure a larger share of America's economic product, even before policies to mold and expand the colonial economies were devised and applied. All in all the final outcome was positive, for while it is likely that more could have been done, and more quickly, if past practice (for example, the fleet system) had been abandoned sooner, nonetheless the Bourbons' reforms did finally expand Spain's share of exchange with America. If we set this in the context of prevailing economic circumstances, especially Spain's growing lag in technology and financial organization behind the leading European economies, then those commercial measures may perhaps be seen as surprisingly successful, an example of what policy can achieve against the odds of reality.

BOURBON REVISIONS OF RULES AND PRINCIPLES

GOVERNMENT

Bourbon reformers also tried, naturally enough, to renovate government, both at home and overseas; they were fully aware that the imperial system would not yield the fiscal fruits so essential to general Spanish resurgence unless the gaps and slackness in colonial government obvious by the late 1600s were remedied. For several decades, however, Spain itself absorbed most of the energy and attention of ministers. With one large exception, revision of colonial administration was limited to what could be done at home; and the major body with American tasks there was the Council of the Indies. As part of a general streamlining of government that had started in late 1706,[30] long before the War of Succession ended, most of the old Hapsburg councils of state saw their powers and functions passed to individual secretaries. Government by committee, safe but inherently slow, was now replaced by ministerial decision. Louis XIV's administration in France was the model followed here. Among the councils losing executive force, in matters financial, military, commercial and governmental, was that of the Indies. A Secretary of the Indies and Marine now exercised those powers, overseeing both the colonies and the transatlantic link with them. Of its former functions, the council kept little more than those of giving advice and acting as a final court of appeal from the judgments of American *audiencias*.

The one large reform in government made in America before the mid-century was the addition of a third viceroyalty, New Granada, to the two (New Spain and Peru) founded soon after the military conquest. This was first attempted in 1718–19, partly to remedy disorder and inefficiency in the *audiencia*, at Santa Fe de Bogotá, that had previously run the region, and partly to strengthen Spain's capacity to collect taxes in a colony where gold production was rising, and to hinder foreigners from smuggling that gold out across New Granada's Caribbean shores. But that first attempt failed. The man chosen to be viceroy, Don Jorge de Villalonga, displayed a mixture of personal extravagance and incapacity to control contraband that in 1722–3 resulted not only his own removal but also the dropping of the entire viceregal scheme. Perhaps it was still simply too soon for the post-war administration in Spain to take on such a major innovation in America. Sixteen years later the viceroyalty was successfully recreated, for the same purposes, though now made more urgent by the threat of the war that would break out in 1739.[31]

No such delay interrupted the formation of the fourth, and final, viceroyalty of Spanish America, that of the Río de la Plata, in 1776–7. The motives for this creation were similar to those behind New Granada's: the rising economic and commercial weight of Buenos Aires and its hinterland, and leakage of trading profits to foreigners, in this case the Portuguese in Brazil. An important Portuguese trading base on the north shore of the La Plata estuary, Colônia do Sacramento, long a thorn in the Spanish side, was seized once and for all in 1777 by the man sent out to be first viceroy, Pedro de Cevallos. Cevallos then took charge of a viceroyalty embodying major jurisdictional revisions in southern South America. Not only Paraguay came under his command, but also the *audiencia* of Charcas (an area known in the eighteenth century as Upper Peru).[32] Charcas had previously been firmly under Lima's thumb. Its transfer into the new viceroyalty had, particularly, the telling economic effect of diverting from Lima to Buenos Aires the silver flowing overseas from Potosí, Oruro, and other mines. The merchants of Lima complained bitterly. But at last, after 230 years, economic rationality prevailed, as Charcas's silver was legally permitted to follow its most direct channel, southward over the plains of the Río de la Plata, into the Atlantic trading system.

By the time this new southern viceroyalty was formed, administrative change in America had been gathering momentum for some fifteen years. While stirrings of activity can be found before 1760, it was really the dire consequences of Spain's late participation in the Seven Years War (1756–63) that made reform in America seem an urgent necessity. In 1761–2 Charles III, a king too ready to try war as a means of foreign policy – in this case to weaken the British in North America – allied Spain with France against Britain in that conflict. He grossly underrated British strength, and the outcome was the reverse of his hopes, a fortifying rather than a sapping of the British presence in America. The Peace of Paris of 1763 passed Florida (previously Spanish) to Britain, western Louisiana (previously French) to Spain, and all other French territory in North America to Britain. Thus France, Spain's natural ally through the Bourbon tie, was ejected from the North American mainland, and Spain was left alone there to face a British presence more massively menacing than before. By comparison, Britain's easy capture of Havana and Manila in 1762 (both returned to Spain by the treaty) was a minor blow, though certainly a clear display of how strong Britain was growing at sea.

So there now arose in Madrid a new determination to stiffen resistance, and, with respect to America, to cultivate and draw upon the colonies' wealth to an extent, and with a degree of purposeful design, that had no precedent in either the Bourbon or the Hapsburg eras. The increased yield of America would support both its own defense and Spain's military sallies in Europe. The trading reforms already in process and later drawn together in the Regulations of 1778 were one facet of this comprehensive intent; the stimuli applied to mining late in the century, another; the creation of the new southern viceroyalty, a third. But there was scarcely a place, person, or activity, however marginal, in Spanish American lands that remained untouched by at least some ripple of reform over the final third of the century.

The first step to making America more profitable was to gather current information about it. To this end reliable officials were sent from Spain to carry out through inspections, or *visitas generales*, of the major areas; the bureaucracy in place was seen as inherently unreliable and hence incapable of full and trustworthy reporting. The first region subjected to inspection was New Spain. It was thoroughly scrutinized over six years (1765–71) by a man, José de Gálvez, who came to epitomize the reforming effort in America, especially on account of his term (1776–87) as Minister of the Indies in the last decade of his life. As minister, Gálvez sent visitors in the late 1770s to Peru (Juan Antonio de Areche) and New Granada (Juan Francisco Gutiérrez de Piñeres) to imitate the data-gathering and disciplining of government that he had carried out earlier in Mexico.

Gálvez was typical of many of Charles III's high administrators: a lawyer, though not one trained in the leading colleges of the ancient Spanish universities that had traditionally supplied such officials, but a provincial from a family without social distinction. Reliance on men made zealous by their lack of conventionally privileged background and training was one aspect of the centralization of power pursued by Charles, whose reign represents the Spanish monarchy's closest approach to absolutism. Gálvez himself came to show the opinionated impatience of the self-made man; some around him found him "personally aggressive, ill-tempered, and intolerant, a bigot in the age of Enlightenment."[33] One prejudice that served well his own and the crown's political aims was the scorn he developed in Mexico for the colonial white population. They, the creoles, he judged to be "of a quick humor and understanding, but superficial and unreliable in judgment, even though remarkably presumptuous ... They are of little spirit, being timid and submissive."[34] This disdain of the colonies' social and economic elite was fully shared, and reinforced, by his appointees to senior posts in America.

The reformers' contempt for creoles fitted well with what was, from the Spanish standpoint, a change that had to be made in American administration if it was to serve Spain's purposes well: the weakening of its American-born component. Chiefly through the purchase of judgeships permitted from 1687, creole *oidores* were by the 1760s a majority in several *audiencias*, notably those of Mexico City, Lima, and Santiago de Chile. Creole numbers were large also, of course, in other branches of American government. Sales had already ceased in the 1750s, but the heavy American presence had by then been in place for decades. Among Gálvez's first acts as Minister of the Indies in 1776–7 was to enlarge the *audiencias* by adding 34 judgeships to them. Only two of those appointed to the new posts were creoles. In the entire period 1751 to 1810, 266 appointments were made to the American high courts: 203 of them went to peninsular Spaniards, and only 63 to creoles.[35]

Taking back the *audiencias* from the creoles was the most dramatic piece of renovation in American administration performed by Gálvez, his subordinates, and his successors. Perhaps more important, though, was the broader policy of replacing the patchwork structure of American government, bequeathed to the first Bourbons by the Hapsburgs, with an efficient and professional bureaucracy. This Gálvez and others achieved by establishing promotion patterns and paying adequate salaries. Not surprisingly, there were limits to their success. The features of the old system could not be completely erased. Creoles remaining in it could, and did, through ageless means of bureaucratic obstructionism, counter threats to themselves. And indeed the bureaucracy as a whole, even in its renovated state, could resist changes that seemed too radical or menacing to its interests. This is among the prime reasons for the essential failure of the largest innovation attempted in colonial government by the Bourbon reformers, the installation of a system of intendants.

Intendants were a new sort of regional governors, holding broad executive and judicial powers, and charged especially with developing local economic activities and extracting income from them for the crown. Their model was in officials of the same name and function in Louis XIV's France. They were used in Spain to good effect, in the crown's view, from the mid eighteenth century. The first American intendant was placed experimentally in Cuba in 1764. Gálvez saw in this species of official the answer to the ossified disorder of American administration, and was the most powerful, even fanatical, advocate of its installation in America. During his tenure as minister he placed intendants in La Plata, Peru, and New Spain. Only New Granada and Quito finally remained without them.

The purpose was to centralize authority through an executive structure parallel to, and indeed short-circuiting, the old one of viceroys, *audiencia* presidents, *gobernadores*, and lesser local officials. The intendants, resident in provincial towns (eight in Peru, twelve in Mexico, for example), were to report to the minister through superintendants placed in the viceregal capitals. But the new structure failed, essentially because the traditional bureaucracy, notably the viceroys, resented and resisted such a blatant sapping of its authority. Removal of the superintendants followed quickly on Gálvez's death in 1787, and with them went the new system's crucial link with Madrid. The intendants remained in place until the end of colonial times, gathering information useful to government, overseeing economic activities and tax collection, and in many cases modernizing their cities with lighting, new tree-lined avenues, and improved water supply and drains – fine practical stuff of the Enlightenment, of which many intendants were by education and inclination good agents. But a clean sweep of colonial administration they never were.

This undermining of Gálvez's design notwithstanding, the general tautening of administration that he and others before and after him accomplished, along with tax increases, the efficient use of royal monopolies, and the placing of new treasury offices in economically growing areas (notably in New Spain), produced the desired result. Royal income in the colonies rose. While the fiscal yield of almost all regions had grown from early in the eighteenth century, reflecting mainly a broad economic expansion, the rate of growth accelerated dramatically in period 1760–80[36] as the new efforts to raise revenues took hold. New Spain was the star of the fiscal stage, as its notable demographic and productive growth (especially in mining) would give reason to expect. Exactly how much the royal income did expand there, particularly from the 1780s, is still uncertain because the accounts are hard to interpret. But a cautious estimate is that the crown's receipts rose from some 3 million pesos annually in the century's early years to 20 million near its end. Other considered calculations suggest that the average yearly growth in royal income in Mexico for the whole century was 2.6 percent, with, however, an acceleration to 5–6 percent from the mid 1780s to 1800, and, remarkably, a further doubling of the yearly rate from then to 1810. Part of the rise in these late decades, which far surpassed economic and demographic growth, was the result of heavy borrowing by the treasury from individuals and institutions. This constituted a deeper tapping by the state of late colonial Mexican wealth than even the revised and expanded structure of taxes and monopolies could achieve. On the other hand, inflation increasingly undercut the value of fiscal income as the century wore on. By one estimate there was no real growth at all in royal receipts in New Spain between 1793 and 1810, even though the number of pesos collected doubled.[37]

New Spain is reckoned to have yielded two-thirds of the crown's income in America in the 1700s.[38] Much of this cash, however, never entered the coffers in Madrid, because the rise in American defense costs that began in the seventeenth century only accelerated in the eighteenth. Raising funds for local defense was, of course, precisely one of the aims of reform, particularly from the 1760s onwards. The fiscal yield of New Granada, for instance, grew strongly after the 1750s through the success of the royal monopolies on tobacco and *aguardiente* (brandy), and with the direct collection, rather than farming, of the sales tax. But with growing expenses for defense on the Caribbean coast, and other administrative charges, it was not until the 1790s that New Granada had royal funds, and modest sums at that, to send to Spain. In Lima, from 1750 to 1800, 40 percent of treasury income went to defense; very little remained for remittance to Spain. Having a much larger income, the Mexico City treasury could dispatch more, and more consistently, to the peninsula. But Mexico carried the defense costs not only of its own coasts and its vast northern frontier, but also of the Philippines and parts of the Spanish Caribbean. Given the size of what needed to be defended and administered, it is testimony to the reforms' efficacy that the American colonies, led by New Spain, were able to supply, in direct remittances, 15 to 25 percent of the crown's income in Spain in the closing decades of the eighteenth century.[39] To this contribution should be added a variable, but often large, amount collected at Cadiz in taxes on the transatlantic trade, and in fees, fines and loans deriving from America.[40]

For one Councillor of the Indies in 1804, the colonies had become "those lands from which we seek to extract the juice."[41] The crudity of the comment perhaps reflects Spain's desperate fiscal state by that date, enmeshed as the country was in the Napoleonic conflicts; but the phrase was no more than a plain statement of the prime aim of Bourbon policy towards America, formulated before the mid eighteenth century and applied mostly after then. The Hapsburgs too, of course, had wanted to draw wealth from America, and had done so successfully, particularly in the time of Philip II and Philip III. But, partly through difference of imperial concept, and partly through force of circumstance, Hapsburg exactions had seemed less severe. The prevailing notion before 1700 that the peninsular and American "realms" were united only in their subservience to the monarchy obscured the contrast of status between metropolis and colony. In principle, colonials served and supported the personal monarch rather than the abstract transatlantic state. And, in practice, they saw themselves as playing that role. Besides that, the rise of creole wealth and presence in American government made the final century of Hapsburg rule a matter of politicized negotiation with colonials rather than of sending them orders. Further yet, Spain's preoccupation with internal problems in the seventeenth century caused her governing of America to become more a process of reaction than of proposal.

All this the Bourbon regimes sought to reverse. For planners instructed in the orderly ways of the Enlightenment, the American realms were to be treated more as a unit than as discrete and idiosyncratic territories. Their part, as that unit in the empire, was above all to support the imperial state. To the extent that reality allowed, they were all to be subject to the same broad schemes of development, taxation, and control: creoles excluded from administration, intendants inserted into it, new taxes and tariffs uniformly imposed. The rules and ethos of empire thus changed radically between the late seventeenth and the late eighteenth centuries.[42]

CHURCH AND STATE

Clearly displaying the new Bourbon manner was the monarchy's attitude to the church after the mid-century. For Charles III and his ministers the church was to be the servant of the state; and it should provide that service, moreover, strictly within its own spiritual and pastoral sphere. To this extent, the older, indeed ancient, notion, preserved under the Hapsburgs, of church as the partner of monarchy in governance (though in the Spanish case, a well-controlled partner) was now eroded. The monarchy still certainly saw the church as its ally; but as an ally with its own set of separate tasks, fighting on a different, spiritual, front.

In this desire to restrain the church lay little anti-religious feeling. The portions of the Enlightenment that Spain imported barely included freethinking. Rather, the motive for change was the regalism typical of the absolutist monarchies of the day.[43] In the Spanish case, that desire to assert the monarch's supremacy in ecclesiastical affairs was combined with a highly practical notion. This was that the church's great wealth in land and other property tended to deflect clerics from their proper spiritual duties. They would do their job far better if the crown took that wealth, or at least some of it, to meet its own fiscal needs.

With one exception, however, transfer of church property to the government did not begin until the century's end. Before then, the crown worked to control the clergy and reform it in the direction of zeal and spirituality. For both purposes, an essential tool was a Concordat negotiated with Rome in 1753, granting to Spanish rulers essentially the same powers of nomination of clerical candidates in Spain as had been conceded for Granada and Spanish America around 1500. Some 50,000 benefices in Spain, including bishoprics, now came under royal control; Rome's political influence in Spain and its ability to siphon money from the Spanish church were reduced. Gaining on both these counts, the monarchy saw the added authority won in Spain through the Concordat as an almost revolutionary advance.[44] Over the following decades, control over appointments brought into office in Spain many bishops who approved of the crown's desire for a leaner, purer, politically detached church.

In America change on this scale was not possible, as the crown had already long controlled appointments through the royal patronage. There the main tool chosen for renovation was the convoking of provincial councils – the first, in fact, since the late sixteenth century. These met in the sees of archbishops (Mexico City, Lima, La Plata, and Santa Fe) in the early to mid 1770s. Perhaps because the American church had undergone no organizational upheaval comparable to what Spanish clerics had experienced, these assemblies of bishops and parish priests showed little inclination to reform themselves. The councils' achievements were minor.

If little change came from within the Spanish American church, however, its members certainly found themselves the objects of reforming orders from Spain. The lower clergy – the parish priests – became a particular target for change, because they were many and they had great influence over the mass of the people – their parishioners. It seemed to the government in Spain and its officials in the colonies that the parish priests had grown far too slack in their spiritual work, and far too engaged in local matters that were not spiritual, such as acting, in effect, as civil administrators, and even judges. (Bourbon criticisms of parish priests are, in fact, very reminiscent of the criticisms made of missionary friars two centuries before by Philip II. In both cases, they were thought to have usurped powers that belonged to the monarchy and its representatives.)

Bourbon controls on parish priests began, in fact, to be applied around 1750 – well before the arrival of the major tide of reform in the 1760s. They continued until the 1790s. The following is a brief sample of the measures imposed in those forty or so years. Fixed schedules of fees were issued for priests' services (such as baptisms, marriages, and burials). The amount of work they could demand of their parishioners was defined (and reduced). The part of their stipends paid from the treasury was cut (their living costs should be covered by their ecclesiastical superiors, the bishops, not by the king). They were to be removed from their parishes if they could not speak the language of their native parishioners. They should no longer have any part in running elections of town officers. They should not criticize the government. They should not so freely give asylum in their churches to offenders pursued by the law. They should not leave their parishes without permission from a royal official. They were to reduce the number and cost of celebrations of religious feast days. And so on and so forth – the reformers fired a long and broad barrage of restrictions at parish priests, all with the characteristic Bourbon aim of promoting central control, order, uniformity, efficiency, and economy.[45] A desire for those qualities in administration, indeed, was what lay behind all the commands sent out to the priests – and not any general anti-clericalism. But some of those on whom the barrage fell felt it as an attack on the clergy in itself, and grew resentful. (It should be said that the particular measures mentioned here were applied in New Spain; but they are typical of general Bourbon attitudes and purposes.)

Under this sort of pressure, the colonial clergy, though unhappily, became more responsive to royal command as the second half of the eighteenth century progressed.[46] A loud warning shot across the colonial church's bows, fired by the crown early in the reform effort, doubtless contributed to this deference. In 1767 the Society of Jesus was expelled from the Spanish empire, as it was from Spain itself. In decreeing the expulsion, Charles III was following the example of rulers in Portugal and France, who in 1759 and 1764 had done the same in their realms. The Jesuits were suffering the effects of energetic regalism in Europe, where monarchs determined to take centralized control of their states were suspicious of what seemed an autonomous, secretive, international society. The distrust resembled the feelings sometimes inspired in small nations today by the presence of multinational corporations. To those organizations, in fact, the Society had some remarkable likenesses. The Jesuits' special allegiance to the papacy simply reinforced the distaste they inspired in European monarchs.

In America, the Society's efforts and achievements laid it open, in a time of political centralization, to suspicion and even charges of subversion. Its control of large mission areas (particularly eastern Paraguay, viewed by authorities as almost an independent state within a state), its possession of many prosperous *haciendas*, and its operation of most of the best schools and universities in the colonies, combined to make it the target of both the crown's distrust and its envy. It supervised the education of many creoles; thousands of Indians lived under its tutelage; it was rich. "That pest," Charles III called it. In Spain its autonomy was not so obvious, but it was still seen as sapping the monarchy's power. There, with minimal justification, the Jesuits were accused in 1766 of encouraging popular riots in Madrid, troubles produced in part by the high price of bread, and probably whipped up by conservative nobles opposed to current reformism.[47] The expulsion followed a few months later. From Spain itself some 2,800 Jesuits were banished, and from America 2,200, among them many creoles. The loss was far more damaging than the numbers would suggest. Those expelled included many dedicated missionaries, hard-working estate managers, and educated teachers. The missionaries had held 300,000 Indians in their charge, in 220 missions scattered over the remoter parts of north-west Mexico, eastern Peru, eastern Bolivia (as it is now), Paraguay, and southern Chile.[48]

In the year after the expulsion, the crown called the rest of the regular clergy to order. The friars were still generally more resistant to the king's control than secular clerics, as they had been in the sixteenth century. And indeed in what seems a replaying of Philip II's campaign to control the Regulars precisely two centuries earlier, the crown in 1768 ordered friars in America to restore their communal monastic life, fulfill their vows of poverty, abandon commerce, and study assiduously. They were, furthermore, urged to "inspire in those most faithful vassals [the people living in the Indies], as a fundamental maxim of Christianity, respect and love for the Sovereign, and obedience of the Ministers who in His Majesty's royal name rule and govern those provinces ... ."[49] This duty extended to the friars' ministering to even remote Indians. In some previously Jesuit missions in the Moxos region of south-eastern Bolivia, in addition to the king's and queen's birthdays being celebrated as important holidays, priests were to make their charges submissive to the crown with the following exchange:

> "Who are you?" – "I am a loyal vassal of the King of Spain."
> "Who is the King of Spain?" – "He is a Lord so absolute that he recognizes no greater temporal authority."
> "And where does the King derive his royal power?" – "From God Himself."[50]

The estates and other possessions of the Jesuits in Spain and America passed to the crown after the expulsion. Most were sold at auction over the next forty years. This was the first large confiscation of church property by the Bourbon reformers. The next did not come until 1798, during times of fiscal crisis caused by war with Great Britain. In that year Charles IV ordered that various sorts of church-related property in Spain should be disentailed, seized, and auctioned. The former owners were to receive 3 percent interest on the money raised. That money went into a fund intended to repay, or consolidate, earlier loans the crown had received for war costs. Against those loans had been issued bonds, called *vales reales*. By 1808 about a sixth of church property in Spain had been taken by the government.[51]

Fiscal conditions worsening, from 1804 part of the American church's property, its *obras pías*, was seized for the same purpose of consolidating the *vales reales*. These "pious works" were in fact large cash funds containing centuries' worth of donations by the faithful for the creation of chantries, chaplaincies, and the like. The funds had soon come to function as sources of loans, credit banks in effect, for colonials. Thus this category of church wealth now consisted largely of outstanding loans rather than land, buildings, or even cash. When, therefore, in 1804 the crown ordered the expropriation of *obras pías* in America, economic damage extended far beyond the church into civil society. For many of those who had taken loans from the *obras* funds were forced to sell real property – buildings and land – to repay them; and widespread simultaneous selling depressed prices. The Consolidation decree of 1804 thus caused widespread bitterness in America, especially in New Spain, where it was more thoroughly applied than elsewhere. By late 1808 New Spain had yielded some 10.2 million pesos on this account; Peru, by contrast, produced only 1.2 million. In that year, the decree was cancelled.[52]

Bourbon regalism thus drew on the physical resources of the church in America, after having tried to renew the clergy's spiritual energy as well for better service of the state's ends. That attempt to create a church militant in the royal service had limited success, especially once the leaders in spiritual militancy, the Jesuits, considered too active to be safe, had been cast out. But the crown did at least achieve what could be called a "church compliant."

MILITARIZATION

The reformers were, on the other hand, more successful in raising the level of conventional militancy in the colonies; though the process of creating a useful and reliable armed presence in vast regions that had lacked one for two centuries was inevitably slow and difficult. From the start, the Bourbon regime had a more military cast than the Hapsburg. Except for Navarre, those Spanish provinces that had been governed by viceroys came, with Philip V, under the control of captains-general. These officials also presided over regional *audiencias*, so that jurisdiction at the highest level was under strong military influence.[53] Then came from the 1720s the effective restoration of Spanish naval presence in the Atlantic, and in the mid-century an expansion of land forces also. A growing military presence in the Indies followed from the lessons learned in the Seven Years War. By 1771 some 43,000 troops were supposedly in place in Spanish America (doubtless many were there only on paper), mostly in garrisons in and around the Caribbean. Fear of internal disorder as well as a repetition of the foreign assaults inflicted during the war was, though, an impetus to expand the ranks. In New Spain, for example, substantial protests in 1766 in Guanajuato against new excise taxes, and then in 1767 about the expulsion of the Jesuits (into whose splendid church the city's wealthy had recently put much money, and the poor much work), were met by Gálvez, then visitor general, with hangings and multiple imprisonments. Then, to control "the perpetual disturbances and scandalous unruliness which the populace have maintained for so many years," he formed a new militia regiment with men from Guanajuato and nearby towns, as well as a quasi-military police force for street patrols.[54]

Militias of Americans, rather than regular army units of Spaniards, inevitably became the majority of the growing soldiery henceforth. Only a few and, it was hoped, exemplary troops could be spared for America from Spain, given the home country's many European engagements in the late eighteenth century. And those men went preferentially to the exposed Caribbean garrisons rather than to the mainland. Nor could the colonial treasuries, even that of Mexico, fund the import of troops. Hence, local militias must do the job. But raising them was fraught with problems. As popular risings had suggested, and continued to suggest, it was potentially dangerous to arm the colonial poor. Governors hesitated particularly to give weapons to Indians and those with any degree of black origin, the latter always feared as possible troublemakers. On the other hand, the *castas* resisted being drafted and disciplined; desertion was rife. Hence creating substantial and reliable militia units was a slow affair. Numbers given in reports exaggerated effective forces.[55]

However difficult it was to keep the mixed-blood rank and file in uniform, there was no lack of creoles anxious for commissions. In the century's closing years, especially in the Andes, the motive in some was a conservative desire to help suppress further social disturbance. But improved status seems to have been the most general aim. One visitor to Venezuela at the turn of the century remarked of the rich creoles: "At present they seek an epaulette with as much avidity as they did formerly the tonsure." Of Peru, the most renowned traveler of Spanish America in its final colonial years, Alexander von Humboldt, noted: "It is not the military spirit of the nation but the vanity of a small number of families ... that has nourished the militia in the Spanish colonies ... It is amazing to see, even in the small provincial towns, all the businessmen transformed into colonels, captains, and *sargentos mayores*." Commissions could be bought. Rich white colonials spent heavily on them, thereby helping support military growth in the colonies. By the decade 1800–9, creoles were 60 percent of the officer corps (including cadets and sergeants) in Spanish America, up from about 34 percent in the period 1740–69. Almost all other officers were peninsular Spaniards.[56]

Creoles, then, could soothe their frustration over exclusion from the higher bureaucracy by gaining a commission, a uniform, a title of rank. Allowing, even encouraging, this martial self-expression of creoles was, however, a dangerous policy for the crown. Selling army positions was just as foolish a short-term expedient as the sale of administrative office had been a century before. For though this apparently frivolous embrace of the military life by creoles signals no particular rise of Spanish American praetorianism before 1800, nevertheless the outcome was that from 1810 many creoles found themselves suddenly transformed from salon soldiers into real men at arms. Most, initially, fought for the monarchy against revolutionary insurgents; a very few chose the independence cause from the start. But, with time, growing numbers changed sides, until royal armies in America found themselves at war with forces of independence led, in many instances, by creoles whom Bourbon reform had first drawn into the military life, and whose true martial abilities had been revealed, then honed, by combat on Spain's side. Reformers who had worried over arming the poor might reasonably have been expected to be equally cautious about creating the basis of a creole officer corps.

SOCIETY: CHANGE AND PROTEST

CREOLES, MESTIZOS, AND OTHERS

If, though, Spanish administrators saw creoles as acceptable soldiers but unacceptable bureaucrats, that was simply one instance of the mutability of white colonials' existence in the eighteenth century. Their numbers certainly rose. Despite the rarity of censuses until the late 1700s, there is little doubt that creole populations maintained a growth, strong in most regions, that had begun long before. Between 1646 and 1774, for example, the number of *vecinos*, or white householders, in eleven provincial Mexican cities (excluding Mexico City itself) grew eightfold, from 2,690 to 28,288. Assuming six people on average in each family, these urban whites, most of them creoles, increased from some 16,000 to about 170,000. A more complete comparison can be made between the mid 1740s, when creoles were about 9 percent of the total Mexican population, and *c*.1803, when they were 18–20 percent of it. (Both percentages included some *mestizos* counted as white.) In the first decade of the nineteenth century, New Spain held some 5–6 million people altogether; hence in the final colonial years creoles numbered a million or more. New Spain's prosperity in the eighteenth century had favored their increase. Elsewhere, though multiplying, creoles were fewer. In the central Andes, for instance, eight major cities (including Lima) experienced a rise of only 1.4 percent in their number of *vecinos* between 1628 and 1764. A census of Peru in 1792 found a total population of 1,076,122. Of these, 13 percent, about 140,000, were "Spaniards" (that is, either creoles or peninsular Spaniards, these being in a small minority). The rising export zones of eastern South America, by contrast, while having smaller populations by far than New Spain, equaled or passed it in demographic growth. The city of Buenos Aires, for example, quadrupled in size between 1740 and 1776 (from some 5,000 to 20,000 inhabitants). Since in 1778 three-quarters of the population of the Río de la Plata basin was white, mostly American-born, creole numbers were clearly rising fast there.[57]

With these increases, the American-born part of the colonial white population further enlarged its long-standing majority. The number of migrants from Spain to America was smaller in the eighteenth century than in the previous two, at about 53,000. Most of these people crossed the Atlantic in the later decades, attracted by economic growth. For that reason a disproportionate number went to New Spain. But even there the peninsular population *c*.1800 was no more than 15,000, outnumbered sixtyfold or more by creoles. In Peru, with fewer Spanish immigrants, creoles were probably similarly dominant, though censuses did not count them separately from the peninsular-born.[58]

Creoles, then, increasingly outnumbered Spaniards in America, while, from the 1760s, becoming ever more the object of at least official Spanish scorn. They found themselves assailed also from below, by the lower, and largest, segments of colonial society. This, first, was the outcome of the full ripening of the processes of ethnic mixing in the eighteenth century. Briefly stated, the number of mixed-blood people was now rising exponentially, most of them the offspring not of two individuals of a particular ethnic identity, but rather of parents who were already of mixed origins. Hence in early nineteenth-century New Spain, by one estimate, mixed-blood people were 22 percent of the total, against 18 and 60 percent respectively for whites and Indians. (The mixed category here includes blacks, but they were a small part of it.) The Peruvian census of 1792 showed 27 percent mixed (again including blacks), against 13 and 56 percent white and Indian. In the two old central zones, therefore, whites (very largely creoles) were now simply outnumbered not only by American natives but also by the mixed-bloods.

With mixing rampant, ever more of its products could not be securely or easily placed in any definite socio-ethnic category. A sign of the difficulty is seen in many series of paintings of *castas* done in eighteenth-century Spanish America (mostly in New Spain). The pictures typically show families of three, with each parent of a particular basic identity or mixture, and their offspring of yet another mixture. Indian and black engender a *zambo*, for example; white and *mestiza* produce a *castizo* ("well bred," but not quite white). In their striving to identify subtle ethnic variations, these paintings may seem relics of a medieval mentality; or they can just as well be seen as a product of the categorizing urge of the Enlightenment. Very likely, as one art historian has suggested, they were done to convey a sense of steady, hierarchical order in colonial society, which would be reassuring to creoles.[59] But in the everyday world the fine distinctions they show were not, and could not, be used. Genetics working as it does, a *mestizo* father, say, and a mulata mother might produce children varying in appearance anywhere within the bounds of a black-Indian-white triangle. Appearance was thus a poor guide to parentage, and so the attempt to make fine ethnic distinctions from looks alone could only fail.

For purposes of social ranking, color, facial features, and body proportions still mattered, of course, as they do to this day in Latin America. But, increasingly, they could be overridden by other, acquired, traits. An Indian who spoke Spanish, and adopted the dress and short haircut typical of a *mestizo*, might well be generally reckoned *mestizo*. If he worked in a town at some task typical of *mestizos*, such as petty trade or a craft, rather than as a rural peasant farmer, he would almost certainly be so considered. Conversely, someone who was known to be of definitely *mestizo* parentage, but who married an Indian and lived among Indians, might for those reasons be considered, and even legally defined, as Indian.[60] Thus arose a partially cultural defining of ethnic identity, which has continued to strengthen ever since.

There were, it is true, limits to this "passing" from one attributed identity to another. An ethnic Indian who dressed as finely as a viceroy and who lived in a large house around the corner from the viceregal palace would not thereby be whitened, or generally be thought to belong to the gentility (unless he descended from the ancient native nobility, and the higher the better). Nor would a white ever be thought Indian or black, no matter how like them he or she might behave. But a poor white, living by manual labor as an artisan, a small farmer, or a servant, might well be taken for a *mestizo*. And in the eighteenth century the number of such poor whites rose.[61]

The lower border of white colonial society became increasingly frayed in the eighteenth century, as the *mestizo* population grew (and grew faster even than the white element). The fraying was exacerbated by the persistent influence of wealth on status; or rather the generalization of that influence now from whites to other sorts of people. With the growing difficulty of locating individuals socially by their looks, the part played by what they could buy – housing, clothing, food – in indicating their status also expanded. Beyond this, some general shift from honor to wealth as the prime source of status, perhaps in distant accord with the pragmatic spirit of the age of enlightenment, may have been under way. Such, at least, has been proposed for eighteenth-century New Spain.[62] In any case, the easier accessibility of social standing now made available by money, to *castas* as well as whites, inspired in leading creole families a strong desire to maintain and mark their social superiority. (The fact that very few such families were completely free of mixture in their past can only have sharpened that desire.) One means of doing so was to acquire titles of nobility, for which they showed a keen appetite. The Bourbons greatly expanded the issue of American titles; and Charles III was the most generous of the Bourbons with them, granting 23 to New Spain alone during his three decades on the throne. The marquisates and countships were not sold, but awarded for notable service, mostly either military or economic. Hence rich mining entrepreneurs were rewarded for their success (and particularly, no doubt, for the cascade of silver into the treasury that resulted from it). Titles went both to creoles and to Spaniards living in America. But as many of the Spaniards founded families, or married into creole families, most of the titles remained there. In 1790, 49 titled nobles graced Lima alone. New Spain, between 1810 and 1820, had 54 titled families.[63]

If some families were socially ascendant, many colonial families were increasingly out of step with Spanish ideals. Marriage remained a key ideal of Spanish American society, despite what had become a culture in which many never married. The ideal of feminine enclosure remained strong even while, throughout the eighteenth century, the number of households headed by women grew, particularly in urban areas.[64] As the number of female single parents grew, so did women's employment outside the home; by 1753, fully a third of the labor force of Mexico City was female.[65] In the late eighteenth century the Bourbons consciously fostered female employment in tobacco factories throughout Spanish America under the auspices of the royal tobacco monopoly. From 1769 on, women were employed as cigarette rollers, by 1809 accounting for a large majority of such workers in Mexico.[66] Though the factory displaced the women who had previously engaged in home-based production and sale of tobacco, new employment was opened for some lower-class women, who preferred factory labor to domestic service. Women's employment was further diversified in 1799, when a royal decree struck down New Spain's guild restrictions barring women, as had been done on the peninsula fifteen years earlier.

Women's employment, however, was a very partial and unattractive solution to the problem of family disorder. Increasingly, a chaotic marriage regime based on impulse and passion was blamed for social ills. One response was the Pragmatic Sanction of 1778, an edict by which Charles III proposed to remedy "the lack of order that has slowly been creeping into society."[67] The edict transferred jurisdiction over marriage from church to civil courts, and required parental permission for the marriage of minors. Parents were specifically empowered to deny permission to marry in cases of "substantial social inequality," defined as racial disparity. The edict can thus be read as an anachronistic attempt to impose a caste hierarchy upon an increasingly wealth-determined society. Parents nonetheless used the language of social inequality to argue, sometimes successfully, against a perceived disparity in "morals," honor, or any other attributes they considered essential to conjugal harmony.[68] Though canon law permitted the marriage of children at 12 (girls) or 14 (boys), parents also attempted to use age as a rationale for denying permission to marry, for example when a teenage son or daughter wished to marry someone significantly older.[69] Despite the vagueness of parents' claims – and the broadness of judges' interpretations – of "social inequality," the crown deemed it necessary to extend parental rights further; thus, in 1803, parents were given an absolute veto on the marriage of children younger than 23 (if female) or 25 (if male). This exaggeration of the power of the patriarchal family would endure longer than the colonial state that instituted it.

While parental authority was strengthened by Bourbon family reforms, parental responsibilities were also more fully described. In 1790–1, the crown published a circular comprising recent edicts relating to the family. Among these were orders empowering local functionaries to intervene in the education of children and ensure the inculcation of useful occupations and habits of industry in cases where parents were neglecting their responsibilities.[70] The idea of children as future citizens who were to be trained for a life of utility, an artifact of Enlightenment, was exemplified by Charles IV's dramatic ruling, in 1794, that from then on all foundling children would be considered legitimate.[71] If the Pragmatic Sanction of 1778 was a prop to old notions of caste hierarchy, the 1794 ruling appears an axe-blow to its very roots. In social policy, as elsewhere, the Bourbon reforms were a curious admixture of modernization and reaction.

Bourbon attempts at social hygiene extended beyond the family to the streets: that is, to the wider life of colonial subjects. Popular entertainment and amusements, never judged favorably by monarchs, were subject to new restrictions, culminating in attempts to regulate and even ban spectacles considered inappropriate. Bullfights were first restricted, from 1767 on, before finally (if briefly) being banned in 1805.[72] The theater was viewed more positively as a potential force for education; but it too was regulated. Bernardo de Gálvez (viceroy of New Spain, 1785–6) issued new regulations for the censoring of plays; as an emblem of the new role of colonial theatre, Gálvez had printed on the curtains of the New Coliseum verses that proclaimed the duty of drama "to correct mankind."[73] Other restrictions aimed at the regulation of public drinking, carnival, games, and dances, which were seen as emblematic of declining deference and social order.

Social protest

Some of these new restrictions undoubtedly irritated colonial elites, adding to their sense of being under increasingly heavier pressure from the Bourbon thumb. But restraints on the behavior of the growing lower-class masses in cities were generally welcomed by the upper end of society. Popular urban unruliness only added to the concern about creeping invasion of their social space from below felt by the white (very largely creole) segments of the late colonial populations. There was, however, a good deal more for them to worry about in the eighteenth century than upstart *castas* behaving above their station, and drunkenness in the streets: it was in that century that popular revolts first threatened central regions of the empire.

It is true that the previous century had not been wholly free of troubles. The mountains of north-west Mexico, for example, were always a center of native resistance to missionary intrusion and economic burdens (specifically the demand for mining labor), and liable to ignite in revolt, as the Tarahumara Indians demonstrated several times in the late 1600s. Further north still, in 1680 the Pueblo Indians finally reacted to almost a century of unregulated pressures from settlers and evangelizing Franciscans by violently expelling them all from New Mexico for a dozen years. Such risings were, however, comfortably far from the heartland of New Spain. Right on high creole society's doorstep, by contrast, was the very noisy *tumulto* of June 8, 1692, in Mexico City. A mob of Indians and assorted *castas* invaded the main square and set fire to the viceregal palace, the town hall, and nearby shops. The central cause of this was the shortage and consequent high price of wheat and maize, resulting from excessive rains in the summer of 1691, followed by blight in the crops later in the year. The viceregal administration actually tried hard to remedy the scarcity with grain imports from other Mexican regions; but the results fell short, giving rise to resentment against a government popularly thought to have failed in its duty to the public good and to have refused to heed justified complaints. The riot was, then, an expression of suffering, with loud overtones of anti-government sentiment. The administration heard these, and reacted with harsh punishments, including several executions.[74]

In the 1700s popular risings became more frequent in the colonies and, in the central Andes, bigger also. New Spain experienced only a few substantial movements. In 1712, for example, over twenty highland Maya villages erupted in rebellion, protesting at the church's suppression of a new cult that was based on apparitions of the Virgin Mary to young Maya women and that defended syncretic Maya Catholicism.[75] And in 1761, the Maya further north, in Yucatan, rose at the behest of a leader who claimed to be a prophesied king who would oust the Spanish and begin a new phase of history. Though decisively and brutally repressed, and far from the heartland of colonial Mexico, the rebellion was nonetheless a warning to government and to high society.[76]

Mexico City suffered no repeat of the eruption of 1692, despite several later episodes of crop failure, rising maize prices, and subsequent outbreak of disease.[77] On the other hand, in central New Spain worrying discontent in native villages provided constant and unsettling background noise throughout the 1700s. In areas partly covered by the present states of Oaxaca, Puebla, Hidalgo, and México, at least 142 minor revolts flared up between 1680 and 1811. It is true that these risings remained local. They were, it seems, less the result of any general discontent with the colonial order than the product of specific grievances in particular native communities: a new *corregidor* who raised taxes, a priest who increased his fees for baptism, marriage, and burial, authorities who pushed up labor demands, or, particularly, violated what the village thought of as its rights of self-government. Indian villagers took violent exception only when what seemed unreasonable and unusual demands were newly thrust on them. The colonial authorities generally responded intelligently by negotiating with villages and punishing only the leaders rather than the whole community – and them leniently. (Only in the time of Gálvez's inspection of New Spain in the late 1760s did punishment grow fiercer, as, for example, in the violent suppression of scattered protests at the expulsion of the Jesuits, and that is hardly surprising given Gálvez's authoritarian bent.[78]) Nonetheless, the continual rumble of trouble emanating from the countryside in the eighteenth century did not contribute to upper-class colonials' peace of mind, reinforcing as it did a growing concern about the unruliness of expanding *casta* populations of towns and cities.

If such worries became common in New Spain in the eighteenth century, creoles and peninsulars living in South America had far graver cause for concern. The central Andes were the scene of as many risings in the eighteenth century as in southern and central Mexico, with the difference, however, that some of the Andean movements became regional affairs that made the upper reaches of society more than merely nervous. These more widespread Andean revolts were often the work of *mestizos* as much as of Indians. That, indeed, is a strong reason for their extension: they were not limited to the local concerns of single native communities. An early, if minor, example was the *mestizo*-led rising in Cochabamba, spreading to the neighboring province of Oruro, that took place late in 1730. This seems to have been a reaction to a new population count, made by order of the Peruvian viceroy of the late 1720s, the marqués de Castelfuerte, for the purpose of upwardly revising assessments of tribute and forced labor levies. To that end, since *mestizos* were exempt from tribute and forced labor, some attempt to reclassify them as Indians was made. This naturally raised hackles, and an armed rising that led to the death of a government official was the outcome. Again, in Oruro itself in 1739, objections at all social levels to tax increases led to a planned rising including not merely *mestizos* and Indians, but creoles as well. In fact, the leader was a creole – and this shows how malleable ethnicity had become by the eighteenth century – who asserted his descent from the Incas and planned to be crowned as Andean ruler at Cuzco, the ancient Inca capital. The plan was indeed for a joint creole, *mestizo* and Indian fighting effort against the Spanish.

The Oruro plan has been described as "the first genuine rebel programme of the eighteenth century" in the Andes, and one that may have served as model for later movements, including the mighty shaking of the colonial order that Túpac Amaru II caused in southern Peru four decades later.[79] What is new in it is, first, a sense of a multi-ethnic Andean unity reacting to attempts to impose change by outside forces, specifically the imperial government represented by the viceroy on the Peruvian coast. The blending of creole, Indian, *mestizo*, and other *castas* in at least some of these Andean movements distinguishes them from concurrent rebellions in New Spain. Second, the Oruro plan of 1739 brings out the messianic streak common in the Andean plots and risings, the theme of a restoration of Incaic rule that would rescue all those suffering under colonial oppression. There is far less sense in eighteenth-century Mexican risings of any comparable vision of salvation through renewal of, say, Aztec power. The greater physical isolation of native peoples in the Andes, favoring the maintenance of memories, may account for some of the contrast.[80]

Andean messianism soon became vividly clear in a more fully Indian, but still multi-ethnic, movement that arose on the forested inland slopes, or *montaña*, of the central Peruvian Andes in 1742. Its leader was a man named Juan

Santos Atahualpa, who claimed descent from the Atahualpa captured and killed by Francisco Pizarro in 1532–3. Juan Santos titled himself Apu-Inca, or "Inca Lord." He was a *mestizo*, Jesuit-educated, who viewed the world as properly divided into three kingdoms – Spaniards in Spain, Africans in Africa, and God's "children the Indians and *mestizos*" in America.[81] His own contribution to making this schema real was to begin in the eastern Andean forests, spread to the highlands, and end in his being crowned as a new Inca ruler in Lima. The blending here of Incaic restoration with the reality of colonial rule (acknowledgment, in a concept completely alien to the Incas, that power in Peru emanated from a coastal city) is most striking.

In the event Santos Atahualpa had limited success. To the Spaniards' great frustration, he was able to repel four military expeditions sent in the 1740s to defeat him in the *montaña*; and he indeed achieved a long-lasting reversal of Spanish mission penetration of that zone of forested foothills. But in the highlands themselves he managed to gain only a brief and tenuous foothold on their eastern rim in 1752. On the other hand, the simple persistence of his movement away in the east may well have encouraged several other highland plots and risings in the mid-century. Notable among these was one in 1750 at Huarochirí, a region directly inland from the capital. This was, in fact, the continuation of a scheme devised by Indians living in Lima to destroy Spanish authority in the city by killing all officials, and, indeed, all Spaniards except priests. News of the plot got out, and it was suppressed. But its extension to Huarochirí over several weeks brought the death of most of the Spaniards in that province.[82]

Thus the Andes of what are now Peru and northern Bolivia became in the eighteenth century a seedbed for local revolt and broad sedition. The mountains, like those of north-western Mexico, but on far larger scale, were ideal ground for this – their ruggedness as always blocking events from Spanish view, hindering attempts at control, and providing refuge for schemers. A crucial distinction from Mexico was that here the mountains stood close to the main centers of Spanish power and white population on the coast. The political menace they embraced was thus near to home. From the mid-century the rate of insurrection (mostly, it is true, minor) quickened: 1750–9, 13 events; 1760–9, 16; 1770–9, 31; 1780 alone, 22; 1781, 14 (including the start of Túpac Amaru's revolt in November). The pace increased in New Spain also, but less than in the Andes.[83]

The rising rebelliousness of both regions reflected the ever heavier fiscal pressure that the Bourbon monarchy applied to the colonies after the mid-century. The greater unruliness of the Andes was probably the expression of lesser capacity to meet the crown's demands. Economic expansion there was smaller and later in starting than in New Spain, in part because the post-conquest recovery of the native Andean population had lagged behind that of Mexico. Growing tax loads therefore weighed more heavily on the Andean population, and they did so to the extent, indeed, that not only Indians, but also *mestizos*, and even some creoles, were driven to protest. Native people, however, were certainly those who suffered most. They were the poorest; they alone paid tribute to the crown; and they alone were subject to a form of forced subsidizing of the administrative and commercial system known as the *reparto de comercio.*

Reparto simply meant the forced sale of goods to Indians by local governors. During the seventeenth century *corregidores* and *alcaldes mayores* had slipped into the habit of supplementing their salaries by using their authority to force the Indians under their control to buy various sorts of goods. Indeed, they often became monopoly suppliers by keeping other sellers out of their jurisdictions, and so controlled the selling price. The goods in question might be American products, such as mules or everyday cloths, or imported items for which few Indians had any desire or need. In time, supply networks developed between merchants in the colonial capitals and the local governors, so that the merchants' livelihood came also to depend in part on the *reparto* system. The practice became more abusive of Indians in the 1720s, when the crown, still striving for economies after the War of Succession, stopped paying salaries to most *corregidores* and *alcaldes mayores* in America. The *reparto* then became these local officials' prime source of income. It even received the crown's legal license in the 1750s, though by then its abuses were well known, having been famously condemned in a report on affairs in the province of Quito written in the 1730s by two visiting officers of the Spanish navy. They, Jorge Juan and Antonio de Ulloa, found it a "system ... so cruelly wicked that it appears as if it were imposed on those people as a punishment," and declared that "A more tyrannical abuse could not be imagined."[84] The *reparto* inspired the same objection in Gálvez during his long inspection of New Spain thirty years later. His hostility to it was one source of his almost fanatical advocacy of the intendant system of local government during his decade as Minister of the Indies. Intendants and subdelegates (district officers within the intendancies) were to replace the previous local governors, and to receive salaries so that there would not longer be any need for exactions like forced sales. In reality, late eighteenth-century attempts to uproot the *reparto* showed it to be less than wholly pernicious in its nature and effects; by then, though inherently exploitative of Indians, it was bringing supplies of some goods to remoter places that other trading links could not or would not reach. For this and other reasons it was never eradicated.

Still, for most native people most of the time, *reparto* was definitely one of the multiple burdens of support of the colonial state that they carried: head tax (*tributo*), formal forced labor, *reparto*, and the illicit labor demanded by both local officials and parish priests. The legalization of *reparto* in the mid eighteenth century seems to have made that particular part of the load more irksome, especially for the relatively poor Andean natives, and for that reason legalization may have contributed to the surge of local rebellion after the 1750s.[85]

The great Peruvian storm of the early 1780s, however, while drawing energy from this native discontent, became large and regional because it was driven by the anger of *mestizos* and creoles as well as Indians. Resentment rose rapidly in the 1770s as the full flood of Charles III's reformism struck Peru, and especially after José Antonio de Areche, a man of the same rigid cast as his master, Gálvez, arrived as general inspector in 1777. Among the changes were these: increases in the general sales tax (*alcabala*) rate from 2 to 4 percent in 1772, and to 6 percent in 1776; fuller collection of the *alcabala*, by the treasury rather than by tax farmers; the imposition of a 12.5 percent tax on brandy (*aguardiente*) in 1777; application of the 6 percent *alcabala* to coca in 1779; establishment of customs houses in several major towns, to collect duties on internal trade; and in 1780 a royal command, intended to simplify tax-gathering, that all artisans must belong to a guild.[86] These measures struck hard at many small and middling economic interests – *mestizo* and creole craftsmen, traders, muleteers, and small farmers. The customs houses were a particular target of ire; local revolts often followed their creation. The tax on brandy affected the same groups; that on coca, mostly Indians, who were the main chewers of the leaf.

In November 1780 began the most conspicuous reaction to this tightening of the fiscal screws, indeed what is now the most renowned revolt in the Spanish empire's entire history. Its leader was a *mestizo* named José Gabriel Condorcanqui, a *curaca* and landowner from the Cuzco district who claimed direct descent from the Incas. During the 1770s he sought formal recognition of this claim by the Spanish, and also pursued a Spanish title of marquis. Late in the decade he joined in the rising resistance to Spanish demands, finally taking the Inca name Túpac Amaru ("Royal Serpent" in Quechua) in intentional evocation of the last Inca noble, of the same name, to hold out against the Spanish in the sixteenth century. After his capture in 1572, that first Royal Serpent had been executed at Cuzco by order of Viceroy Toledo. He remains to this day a powerful symbol of native resistance to European invasion.

The rising led by the second Túpac Amaru began at the native town of Tinta, in the south of Cuzco province, on November 4, 1780, with the seizure and execution of the local *corregidor*. This man, Antonio Arriaga, was a notorious abuser of the *reparto* system, and was therefore an exemplary victim. In early December the rising turned south, to the area around Lake Titicaca; and then, late in the month, north again towards Cuzco, which Túpac Amaru briefly and unsuccessfully besieged in early January 1781. Another southward thrust followed, with an attempt, again fruitless, to drive the Spanish from the important trade center of Puno on the western shore of Titicaca. By then, however, the government in Lima had been able to send a large military force to the rebel area. Túpac Amaru was captured and, in May 1781, executed along with close relatives who had also been leaders of the rising. He then was drawn and quartered.

The revolt was remarkably violent, with much loss of life. It produced also much sacking of property, such as *haciendas* and *obrajes*, that belonged not to Indians but to creoles and *mestizos*. This destructiveness quickly deprived Túpac Amaru of most of his non-native support; most of the initial leadership had been *mestizo*, and there were creoles at first willing to back the rising in the hope of reducing the state's impositions on them. They were perhaps reassured by Túpac Amaru's early proclamations that he was acting in the king's interests, indeed at the king's orders, in ridding Peru of bad governors. There is here, as in many colonial risings, an element of the often cited cry "Viva el rey y muera el mal gobierno" – "Long live the king and death to bad government" – implying a separation between the monarch and his agents, and a sincere belief that a just king could intend no harm to his subjects.

But the movement was sapped also by complex political and ethnic currents among the native population of southern Peru and northern Charcas.[87] Túpac Amaru, as a rural *curaca*, failed to gain the support of the old Indian nobility, sure also of its Inca origins, of Cuzco itself. In fact, some of those noble *cuzqueño* families helped the Spaniards to suppress the rising. His self-proclamation as a restored Inca (late in 1780 he had himself and his wife portrayed in a painting as Inca king and queen), while fully in what was now a strong tradition of millenarian re-creation of Inca rule, alienated those greater lineages. And adding to the weakening effect of disharmony among the Quechua speakers of central and southern Peru was the ancient antagonism between them as a whole and the Aymará-speaking groups around Lake Titicaca and south of it. These, in the mid fifteenth century, had been brought into the Inca state by force; the Spanish conquest had freed them from that domination. And though now, three centuries later, they had common grievances with the Inca descendants against the Spanish, a full and easy alliance was not possible. An Aymará rising had indeed begun in Chayanta, in present northern Bolivia, in 1787, led by Tomás Katari, whose followers also saw in him a messiah. After Katari's capture and execution in January 1781, leadership of his movement passed to another Aymará speaker, who styled himself, like Túpac Amaru, "Royal Serpent" (Túpac Katari in that language). There was a strained alliance between Quechuas and Aymarás in a siege of La Paz, from March to October 1781, that was Katari's most severe challenge to Spanish control. That siege was finally no more successful than the earlier attacks on Cuzco and Puno, although it briefly shook Spanish, and creole, confidence to the roots.

The Aymará movement ended shortly after the relief of La Paz by crown forces in October 1781. The Spanish captured Túpac Katari, perhaps with Quechua help. Túpac Amaru's followers continued to be active well after their leader's death, as the siege of La Paz shows. They finally made peace with the colonial government in January 1782, although aftershocks of the rising continued to ripple through the center and south for months after that.

The troubles of 1780–2 in southern Peru and northern Bolivia have been called a civil war. Certainly their violence and their cost in lives (possibly 100,000) justify placing them in that particularly bloody class of conflict;[88] as does also the significance of their outcome. In the short term, the reaction to the conflict of the colonial regime, led by Gálvez as Minister of the Indies, was to meet various of the rebels' demands, once the leaders were punished. An *audiencia* was created in Cuzco in 1787–8, to provide the highland people with faster access to justice. Local government by *corregidores* was abolished and thereby, it was hoped, the *reparto* system also eliminated. (The hope was vain. The subdelegates within the intendant system, which was applied to Peru in 1784, continued using the *reparto* for their profit.[89]) But it was the longer-term outcomes that were most telling for the course of central Andean, and particularly

Peruvian, history. The war laid bare contrasts in mentality and material interest between natives and most of the rest of highland (and lowland) society. While many *mestizos* and even some creoles living in the mountains had been drawn into the Inca restoration current so clearly evident in the mid-eighteenth century, in its fully developed form that movement grew disquietingly extreme. It became messianic not only in the broad sense of Inca revival, but also in a narrower Christian frame – as, for example, Indian followers of Túpac Amaru began to view him literally as a redeemer who could raise the dead.[90] Although this fusing of Indian and Christian spiritual elements is wholly typical of native religion throughout colonial Spanish America, it was also, for conventional Catholics, heretical. But still more alienating of creoles, *mestizos* and other non-Indians was the destruction of lives and property that the war brought. Once the genie of native militancy had been unbottled, it could not, evidently, easily be restrained or recaptured. The resulting fearful distrust of native Andeans broke up the multi-ethnic highland unity that was emerging by the mid-century, made most Peruvians chary of political movement and change for the rest of colonial times, and deepened an existing hiatus in Peru between coast and mountains that still impedes the country's progress today.

If never on the Peruvian scale, most of Spain's other South American colonies experienced growing internal disturbance after the 1750s. The city of Quito, for instance, was shaken through much of 1765 by violent opposition from *mestizos* and Indians (backed by much of the white upper crust of the city, including some clergy) to a broad sharpening of Spanish fiscal tools begun *c*.1760. This has been identified as the first large rising in America provoked by Charles III's reformism, though it did not spread outside the city of Quito.[91]

A later movement, similar in its temporary conjoining of all social ranks, but far wider in geographical range, was that of the *comuneros* of New Granada in 1781. From March to June of that year a large region of the eastern range of the Andes north of Santa Fe de Bogotá effervesced with hostility to the tightening of the fiscal screws. Higher and better-collected *alcabala*, and the installation of royal monopolies on tobacco and *aguardiente*, which meant loss of profit to local growers and higher prices for local consumers, were the sorest points. In what was becoming a pattern, serious trouble started when a reforming visitor general, in this case Gutiérrez de Piñeres, enforced the new *alcabala* measures in March 1781. The focus of resistance was Socorro, a small town some 200 kilometers north of Santa Fe. Peasants there found the town's creole leaders, prosperous landowners in the main, quite willing to support the protest, disaffected as they were not only by fiscal demands but also, more gravely, by a sense that the crown's reformers were invading a political and social domain that they had long considered theirs alone. Inserting the state into places where it had rarely been a more than distant reality was, certainly, an aim of Bourbon reformism. That, precisely, was one of the purposes of the intendant system. In early May 1781, a large *comunero* force overwhelmed soldiers sent out from Santa Fe to suppress the protests. Later in the month 15,000–20,000 *comuneros* assembled to threaten Santa Fe; whereupon the authorities in the capital, notably the archbishop and the *audiencia*, decided that negotiation was the better part of valor. With the rebellion spreading into neighboring lowlands, the officials gave in on June 7 to most of the protesters' demands. Among these were the departure of the visitor general; a promise that no such officer should be sent again to New Granada; preferential appointment of creoles to administrative posts at all levels; reduction of tribute and *alcabala* rates; and abolition of the royal monopolies on tobacco and playing cards. All this, and more, the archbishop and judges conceded. The viceroy, who had been absent throughout on the Caribbean coast attending to its defense, later confirmed the agreement, and granted a general pardon.[92]

Like the Quito episode and the Túpac Amaru rebellion before it, and many other smaller movements, the *comunero* eruption in New Granada was above all a call for reversal of intrusive and exploitative change, rather than an attempt to destroy the system that had imposed that change. Although some historians in the countries concerned have liked to find early bids for national independence in these movements, they were not that. In that respect, the large South American insurrections and the local Mexican village risings of the eighteenth century have similarities. They aimed first to recover a status quo that familiarity had made tolerable. (Onto that basic purpose, certainly, radicals in Peru and Charcas grafted a desire to restore ancient, native government in the highlands. But that was far from a call to establish an independent Peruvian or Bolivian state.)

What is intriguing, indeed, about the New Granadan rising is its implicit appeal to an earlier political condition that was specifically colonial. In their public pronouncements, the *comuneros'* leaders referred repeatedly to the good of the *común*, the social community; hence the movement's name. And although upper-class sympathy with Indians and *castas* must seem opportunistic (and indeed usually evaporated at the first outburst of destructive violence), nonetheless those references to the *común* were more than mere rhetoric. For they suggest a memory of the corporate, organic, and hierarchical model of society implicit in the earlier Hapsburg organization of the empire, and of the underlying notion that, although differences of wealth and status were in the nature of a hierarchical society, the common good was the final concern of the ruler. It was to what they saw as neglect of, or assault on, that common good that the *comunero* leaders objected in 1781. They had a sense, not perhaps conscious, of the degree to which Bourbon reformism after 1760 was attacking the deepest social and political assumptions that had underlain the empire for its first 250 years.[93]

CREOLE SELF-AWARENESS: REJECTION AND RECEPTION OF EUROPE

Even though creole *comuneros* were, then, essentially conservative, in the sense of looking back fondly on an earlier mode of colonial existence, at the same time their dismay over the assault on that way of being in the late eighteenth century clearly implied danger for the Bourbon state. For the moment, they, like many other creoles elsewhere in America, might join with activists lower in

ILLUSTRATION 12.1 Santiago Matamoros (St. James the Greater in the guise of Moor killer). St. James was patron saint of Spain, and allegedly the helper of Spaniards in battles against American natives, as well as in earlier conflicts with the Moors. Cuzco school, Peru, eighteenth century. New Orleans Museum of Art.

ILLUSTRATION 12.2 Don Antonio de Mendoza, first viceroy of New Spain (1535–49).

BVEN GOBIERNO
DŌ FRAÑ DE TOLEDO

mayordomo desumag.s · bizorey diapogro dosteReyno

don fran deto ledo gouerno dusˀ yeel año de mill y quinien don
tenta y os ta el mes de julio delaño de mill y quinientos
ta y uno—entiempo del Rey felipo el segundo

ILLUSTRATION 12.3 Don Francisco de Toledo, fifth viceroy of Peru (1569–81). From Felipe Guaman Poma de Ayala, *Nueva Coronica y Buen Gobierno*, Paris, 1936.

ILLUSTRATION 12.4 St. Rose of Lima, canonized in 1671, the first American-born saint. She appears here as a Dominican nun, bearing the infant Christ on a bed of roses. Unknown artist, Cuzco school, late seventeenth century. New Orleans Museum of Art.

ILLUSTRATION 12.5 Sor Juana Inés de la Cruz, scholar and greatest of colonial Mexican poets. Miguel Cabrera, 1751; Museo Nacional de Historia, Chapultepec Castle, Mexico City.

ILLUSTRATION 12.6 Equestrian statue of Charles IV, in bronze, originally placed in the center of the Plaza Mayor of Mexico City. Manuel Tolsá, 1796. Copyright Tony Morrison, South American Pictures.

ILLUSTRATION 12.7
Simón Bolívar (1783–1830)
late in his career. Mary Evans
Picture Library.

ILLUSTRATION 12.8
José de San Martín (1778–
1850), with his staff.
Unknown artist, nineteenth
century. Copyright Corbis-
Bettman.

society in blaming supposedly perverse agents of the monarchy, rather than the crown itself, for injuries received and the ills of the society around them. They would look on approvingly as rioters still shouted "Viva el rey" while sacking a customs house. But each new departure from the old model inevitably brought them closer to a political stance from which some of them would blame the Bourbon monarchy, and not merely its officials, for the losses and problems they perceived.

Such a political shift among creoles was encouraged also by their growing self-awareness. Spanish officialdom's disdain of them was one cause of this. A second source lay in the opinions of America and its inhabitants published by several European writers engaged in gathering knowledge of the natural world, and categorizing it in accord with the Enlightenment's desire for orderly patterns. America fared badly in these efforts. Prominent *philosophes* tended to abandon scientific rigor, indeed common sense, when attempting to rank it among the world's regions. Thus the Dutch writer Cornelius de Pauw, drawing on a climatic determinism advanced by others, found that the American tropics had produced, in the native population, a "degenerate species of humanity," and, in creoles, people given to indolence and vice. Georges-Louis Leclerc Buffon, eminent naturalist as he was, held that America was both geologically young and excessively wet and swampy; with the result, he sagely opined, that America's fauna were fewer and smaller than those of the Old World (except for its snakes, lizards, and insects). With few exceptions, American native people were also the feeble product of the same pernicious environment. In arriving at these conclusions, de Pauw, Buffon, and several similarly minded confrères, twisted, or simply threw out, abundant contravening evidence.[94]

Creoles' reaction was twofold. They first sought refutations in America's nature and in the reality of its pre-conquest and colonial history. Among the most forceful of writers in this line were creole Jesuits in European exile after the Society's expulsion from the empire in 1767. These were men personally familiar with the regions they described. They were also, ironically enough, well equipped mentally with the new rationalism to argue their case; for the Jesuits had been the chief importers and teachers in Spanish America of the science and mathematics of the seventeenth and eighteenth centuries. It was simple for them to show the falsity of European assertions about American natives, flora, and fauna. The most complete of these refutations came from a Mexican exile in Italy, Francisco Javier de Clavijero, who produced in 1780–1 an *Ancient History of Mexico*, exalting a high culture that in his view began with the Toltecs in the sixth century after Christ and ended with the Aztecs. Clavijero also described the positive qualities, physical and mental, of present Mexican native people (while not denying their faults), and demonstrated, through an account of the geographical variety of New Spain, the absurdity of Europeans' gross generalizations about America's climate and landforms. But most striking was his praise of the politics, culture, rationality, and morals of the pre-contact cultures, which were comparable with those of Greece and Rome.[95] Clavijero here picked up threads first spun by the likes of Las Casas and, later, Sigüenza y Góngora. His work was a notable advance along the path, leading to the present, of incorporation of the pre-conquest cultures into Mexican national identity and consciousness. A further step in this process came in the 1790s, when Antonio de León y Gama, an official in the Mexico City *audiencia* as well as a mathematician, astronomer, and antiquary, published a study of two large Aztec stone carvings just found under the city's main plaza. These were two pieces that have come to stand as no others for the grandeur and complexity of the pre-conquest high cultures: the earth goddess Coatlicue, represented as a composite in stone of skulls, detached hands, and interwoven rattlesnakes, and the "Calendar" Stone, a symbolic depiction of the five "suns," or ages, of the pre-conquest history of central Mexico.[96]

The creoles' second response to criticisms of America and its inhabitants was to collect and publish new knowledge of their continent's physical and human reality. Here the true spirit of the Enlightenment was a help, its concern with methodical accuracy a useful impetus for inquiry. Creoles had learned the new science from the Jesuits. They had also read widely among Enlightenment authors, most of whose work reached Spanish America with minimal censorship, either civil or ecclesiastical, until almost the end of the century. In New Spain, then, creoles published information on the geography, climate, plants and animals, economic resources, and productive capacity of the territory in journals founded from the 1780s on. In Lima, the journal entitled *El Mercurio Peruano* carried the same range of data, among it the first year-by-year record of Potosí's silver production from the mid 1500s. In New Granada, Quito, Chile, and Buenos Aires the same spirit of practical inquiry arose. The outcome of this close attention to local conditions went beyond mere contradiction of European distortions of America, to produce among creoles a strengthening sense of regional identity and loyalty. Thus in the late eighteenth century there emerged a definite "creole patriotism" in Spain's colonies. The Mexican *Gaceta de Literatura* printed the phrase "our Hispanic American nation" as early as 1788.[97] Over the next two decades growing numbers of creoles came to share the sentiment contained in those words.

As their reactions to the Enlightenment suggest, creoles' intellectual awareness expanded in the eighteenth century. Whereas Spain had long been the natural point of reference, now, with the arrival of, first, the new science and then a wider range of innovative thinking and writing, much of the rest of western Europe began to loom larger on creoles' mental horizon. Much contributed to this shift: Spain's political subsidence in the western world, set against the rise, on every front of human activity, of France and Britain; the intrinsic allure of the new thinking, in its rationalism and even its inherent secularism; late in the century, practical demonstration of the Enlightenment's political possibilities in North American independence and the French Revolution. Creole receptivity was not always and wholly welcoming, of course. Given the deep roots of Catholicism in Spanish America, secularism dismayed far more white colonials than it attracted. And the French Revolution, particularly after its American manifestation in a notably destructive slave revolt in Haiti in 1791, had the effect of purging all but the most radically inclined creoles of admiration for wholesale political innovation. Nonetheless, the creoles – native-born leaders of their several colonial societies – by the early nineteenth century had come to look on Britain, Germany, and particularly France as the prime sources of intellectual innovation and cultural creativity in the widest sense. This esteem of what is European has continued in Spanish America, with the hesitations caused by the resentment that admiration can engender, down to the present. Added to the list of models, from the late nineteenth century, has been the United States.

The arrival of non-Hispanic European currents in the empire is clearly shown also in the music and art of the eighteenth century. In 1701 came the first known performance of an opera in Spanish America, *La púrpura de la rosa* (The Purple of the Rose), put on to celebrate the eighteenth birthday of the new king, Philip V. The libretto was by Pedro Calderón de la Barca, some would say the most profound dramatist of Spain's cultural Golden Age in the seventeenth century, and the score was by Tomás de Torrejón y Velasco, a Spaniard who was chapelmaster at Lima cathedral from 1676 to 1728. But opera as a musical form was an Italian invention of the late sixteenth and seventeenth centuries, and its arrival in the colonies therefore marks a rising internationalization of taste in Spanish America. The first operatic performance in Mexico City (and indeed in North America) came ten years later, with *La Partenope*, written by the noted Italian librettist Silvio Stampiglia and scored by Manuel de Zumaya, a Mexican-born composer who later became chapelmaster of the cathedrals of Mexico City and Oaxaca.[98] The Italian influence in Spanish American music remained strong for the rest of the eighteenth century, partly in reflection of the esteem which Italian composers and players commanded at court in Spain. Local composers, both American- and Spanish-born, tended to follow Italian forms and styles. In Peru, the Milanese Roque Ceruti was a dominant force in music from his arrival in Lima in 1708 until his death in 1760. A comparable figure in New Spain was Ignacio Jerusalem y Stella, from Lecce in Italy, who was chapelmaster in Mexico City from 1749 to his death twenty years later. Even the remotest provinces felt the Italian musical touch. Domenico Zipoli (1688–1726), first a Jesuit church organist in Rome, spent the final decade of his life at the Society's house in Córdoba, in present Argentina. There he wrote liturgical music in a fully Baroque style that Jesuits in the field carried to missions in Paraguay and Chiquitos (an area roughly corresponding with the Chaco of present north-western Paraguay). Not only did the Chiquitos Indians readily take to this music, but, having carefully recopied it over the years, they still perform it today for the annual feast of St. Ignatius of Loyola.[99]

In painting, sculpture, and architecture, the Baroque prevailed for most of the eighteenth century, with continued development of the regional variations that had arisen earlier. Touches of rococo lightness appear here and there within the Baroque. The two noted *mestizo* sculptors of eighteenth-century Quito, for example, Bernardo de Legarda (d. 1773) and Manuel Chilí (known as Caspicara), achieved this delicacy of touch: Legarda in his swaying "dancing Virgin" figurines of the Madonna, and Caspicara in a variety of gently done religious images from very late in the century.[100] In New Spain, the rococo is exemplified in architecture in the delicate facade of the Sanctuary of the Virgin at Ocotlán (1745), near Puebla, where slender bases veneered with red-orange tile support "two lacy sculptured belfries, shining in the whitest whitewash."[101] Elsewhere, however, the urge to decorate surfaces so typical of the Spanish American Baroque could yield a grandiosity that is far from rococo. The altar and reredos (1718–43) of the Chapel of the Kings in the Mexico City cathedral, for instance, form a massive gilded assemblage of architectural elements and vegetation-like decoration almost concealing a minor multitude of polychromed figures. In this "ultra-Baroque" agglomeration the contours of the structure dissolve; the intent is apparently to submerge the viewer in a many-dimensioned opulence.[102] Rather more organized, and more powerful yet, is the stone facade (1752) of the parish church, and later cathedral, of Zacatecas in northern Mexico. Here it seems that the architect decided to offer to all and sundry passing by in the street the spectacle of a reredos taken to the Baroque extreme. Into a display, over 20 meters high from pavement to pediment, of three orders of solomonic columns sharply carved with twisting grape vines, shells, and caryatides are inserted Christ and the Apostles, the four Fathers of the church, and, presiding, God the Father set amidst angels with musical instruments.[103]

From the 1770s, and especially in the major cities, some reaction to Baroque floridity appeared. Those creoles who were now busily absorbing European tastes turned from what they found provincial and popular. At the same time, the imperial administration sought to modernize and impose uniformity on public places in America. The aim was to impress on colonials the state's physical presence among them. Austere sobriety was the dominant note in the change. An early example was the new mint (Casa de Moneda) at Potosí, which, when finished in the 1770s, was among the largest secular structures in Spanish South America.[104] The facade has the bare simplicity of Spanish sixteenth-century building. Aversion to the Baroque, however, typically took the form of neoclassicism, then an ascendant style in Europe that was carried across the Atlantic mainly by migrant Spanish artists and architects. Another Casa de Moneda of the late eighteenth century, that of Santiago in Chile, is a clear instance of the new stylistic preference. Its success in symbolizing authority is suggested by the fact that in republican Chile it has served as the country's presidential palace. Santiago also received a new neoclassical cathedral, as did Santa Fe de Bogotá. In New Spain the cathedral at Puebla was adorned with an imposing neoclassical baldaquin. Its designer, Manuel Tolsá, a sculptor and architect from Valencia in Spain, was the first director of sculpture at the new school of fine arts, the Academia de San Carlos, that Charles III founded in Mexico City in 1785 to stimulate artistic revival in Spain's richest colony. Tolsá left several lasting marks on Mexico City: the royally instituted School of Mines (built 1797–1813), the final portions of the towers and dome of the cathedral, and an equestrian statue of Charles III's son and successor, Charles IV (1788–1808), modeled on that of Marcus Aurelius on the Capitoline in Rome. The statue was the centerpiece of a renovation (the same reworking as uncovered the Aztec "Calendar Stone" and sculpture of Coatlicue) of the

Plaza Mayor that another Spanish-born member of the Academia de San Carlos, Antonio Velázquez, oversaw in the early 1790s. The main architectural feature of the renewed plaza was a large elliptical balustrade, broken by four imposing iron gates, enclosing and isolating the king's statue. The effect was one of formal solemnity.[105]

THE EIGHTEENTH-CENTURY BALANCE

Tolsá's statue of Charles IV is long gone now from the main plaza, demoted to a more modest square nearby. With perhaps affectionate irony, present Mexicans call it El Caballito, the Little Horse, passing over the fustian presence of the tunic-clad, laurel-crowned monarch astride the animal's back. Well may they do so. For in hindsight there is truly a touch of absurdity in the representation of Spain's late colonial authority by the figure of Charles IV – a notably incompetent and inattentive king in whose reign Spain subsided into a mire of debilitating warfare that helped to precipitate the American empire's demise, and whose rule ended in ignominious abdication when France, under Napoleon, invaded Spain early in 1808.

Nonetheless, it was in Charles IV's time, the last decade of the eighteenth century and the first of the nineteenth, that Spain reaped the richest gains from the reforms applied to America by his grandfather, Philip V, his uncle, Ferdinand VI, and particularly by his father, Charles III. In the limited sense of producing more revenue for use in Europe and America, the wide innovations in taxation, officialdom, and territorial and administrative organization executed under the Bourbon kings were successful reforms. For colonials of all social ranks, however, and above all for the growing creole population that was becoming the political nation of Spanish America, the aim of the changes seemed to be as much deformation as reformation.

Broadly speaking, by the early 1700s Spanish America seemed set on a self-directed course, if not towards anything that could yet be called progress or development, at least towards creating an autonomous identity of its own. Abetting this process was the constitutionally equal standing of the individual colonies with the Iberian kingdoms (the Hapsburg monarchy consisting of separate realms, such as Castile, Aragon, New Spain, Peru, Quito, and so on). This equivalence, admittedly legalistic but no mere fiction, was in practice increasingly undermined by the Bourbons as the eighteenth century advanced. Concrete aspects of Spanish American selfhood plainly visible by the early eighteenth century included an expanding creole population which, through long and informal negotiation with Hapsburg administrators, had achieved a marked degree of political and administrative self-determination; wide freedom of access to foreign products both within the formal working of the Carrera de Indias and outside it through contraband; development of internal trade among and within colonies; and, in a less material aspect of life than all the preceding, a richness of religion in which Christian, native American, and African elements were fused in a varying proportions in different places and populations. More characteristically Spanish American than any of these, however, was the sort of society that was clearly established by 1700 in much of the colonized area – a society in which hierarchy was still an unchallenged structural principle, but in which ethnic and cultural mixture, and personal economic success, allowed a growing freedom of movement in status.

With various aspects of this selfhood the Bourbons proceeded to meddle, more or less effectively, at different times and places after 1700. There were various attempts to make the expanding mestizo population pay tributes – implicitly equating them with Indians and thus compressing the social scale. These attempts failed. But in the 1760s the assault on the central influence that creoles had long had in their own governing was a different story; and the assault expanded into an attack on their intellectual and moral capacity, with an implied opening of social difference between them and peninsular Spaniards. At the same time, a large degree of de facto freedom of trade was being replaced by a so-called free trade, operating strictly within and among Spanish territories, that was intended to subordinate the colonies more fully than ever to Spain's economic gain. And the economic interests of many, both high and low in colonial societies, suffered as taxes grew in rate and application, as internal customs houses proliferated, and as royal monopolies expanded, all stifling the local and inter-provincial trading that supported innumerable creoles and *castas* by the late eighteenth century. To this list of Bourbon distortions of the emerging Spanish American identity might be added measures taken not just to secularize the church (particularly as exemplified in the expulsion of the Jesuits, among whom were many creoles), but to change the way it functioned at the level of its parish roots, dividing the priest from his parishioners, and leaching vitality from its variety of local cult. Finally (in this list, at least, for much else could be included), the Bourbons reinserted a military strain into societies whose martial element had notably withered once the conquests were over in the sixteenth century.

Not all changes were unwelcome, of course. Most town dwellers benefited from the practical improvements in streets, lighting and water supply that many intendants brought to their provincial capitals. Those same intendants were a conduit by which new knowledge and ideas reached colonials, mostly creoles, living deep in the American interior. Almost all creoles were, finally, thankful for the presence of military forces that suppressed ructions in the lower reaches of society. But these were small compensations for the Bourbons' impositions on, exactions from, and manipulation of Spanish America. Soon enough the costs of that imbalance would become clear.

PART V

PORTUGAL IN AMERICA

CHRONOLOGY

1494   Treaty of Tordesillas

1497–9   First Portuguese voyage to India around south of Africa, led by Vasco da Gama

1500   Pedro Alvares Cabral, commanding second Portuguese fleet bound for India, touches on coast of Brazil

1501–2   Portuguese exploration of Brazilian coast

1504   First French ship on Brazilian coast

1516   Fortified Portuguese trading post founded at Pernambuco. First indication of sugar cultivation in Brazil

1532   Settlement at São Vicente by Martim Afonso de Sousa. Settlement also inland, at Piratininga, mid 1530s. Brazil divided into captaincies

1538   Probable date of first shipment of African slaves to Brazil

1548–9   Tomé de Sousa appointed and installed as governor general of Brazil. Foundation of town of Salvador (Bahia) as capital. Arrival of Jesuits. Appointment of first *ouvidor geral*

1555–67   French colony of "Antarctic France" at Rio de Janeiro

1557–72   Governorship of Mem de Sá

1560s   First serious epidemics of Old World diseases in Brazil

1570   Indians declared free by Sebastião, king of Portugal

1578   Death of King Sebastião at Alcácer Quibir

1580–1640   Portugal and its empire under Spanish rule

*c.*1600   Beginning of slave-raiding *bandeiras* from São Paulo

1606   Founding of first Brazilian *relação*, at Salvador

*c.*1610   Three-roller sugar mill introduced into Brazil

1615   French finally driven away from Brazil

1621   Maranhão declared a separate "state" of Portuguese America. Dutch West India Company founded

1630   Dutch capture of Recife. Beginning of Dutch occupation of north-east Brazil

1637–9   Expedition of Pedro Teixeira from northern Brazil to Quito and back. Brazil's boundary extended far westward

1637–44   Brazilian administration of Johan Maurits van Nassau-Siegen

1640   Portuguese revolt against Spanish rule

*c.*1640   Beginning of large-scale sugar-planting in non-Spanish Caribbean islands

1649   General Brazil Trading Company founded

1650–1700   Large inland movement of cattle

1654   Dutch leave Brazil

1661   Revolt of citizens of São Lus against Jesuits

1669   Fortress built at São José de Rio Negro, at confluence of Negro and Solimões rivers mid 1690s. Gold found in Minas Gerais

1703   Methuen Treaty

1720   Captaincy of Minas Gerais created. Abolition of General Brazil Trading Company. Chief executive in Brazil henceforth termed viceroy

1720s   Diamonds found in Minas Gerais

1724   Founding of the Academy of the Forgotten (Academia Brasílica dos Esquecidos) at Salvador, first of several Brazilian intellectual academies of the eighteenth century

1744   Captaincy of Goiás created

1748   Captaincy of Mato Grosso created

1752   *Relação* of Rio de Janeiro created

1755   Lisbon earthquake. Beginning of the reform program of the marquis of Pombal. Creation of Board of Trade, and of Pará and Maranhão Company

1756–63   Seven Years War

1759   Creation of Pernambuco and Paraíba Company. Jesuits expelled from Portuguese territories

1763   Capital of Brazil shifted from Salvador to Rio de Janeiro

1775–83   War of American Independence

1777   Fall of Pombal

1778   Treaty of San Ildefonso, fixing southern boundaries of Brazil

1791   Slave revolt in Saint Domingue

FURTHER READING FOR PART V

E. Bradford Burns, *A History of Brazil*, has much on the colonial period. For a native, if brief, account, see José Honório Rodrigues, *Brasil: Período colonial*. The multiple works of C. R. Boxer remain eminently readable: *The Portuguese Seaborne Empire, 1415–1825*; *Salvador de Sá and the Struggle for Brazil and Angola, 1602–86*; *The Dutch in Brazil, 1624–1654*; *The Golden Age of Brazil, 1695–1750*; and *Race Relations in the Portuguese Colonial Empire, 1415–1825*. To these should be added the works of Stuart B. Schwartz, notably *Sovereignty and Society in Colonial Brazil: The High Court of Bahia and its Judges, 1609–1751*, and *Sugar Plantations in the Formation of Brazilian Society: Bahia, 1550–1835*; those of A. J. R. Russell-Wood: *Fidalgos and Philanthropists: The Santa Casa da Misericórdia of Bahia, 1550–1755*, *The Portuguese Empire: A World on the Move*, and (as editor), *From Colony to Nation: Essays on the Independence of Brazil*; and Kenneth R. Maxwell, *Conflicts and Conspiracies: Brazil and Portugal, 1750–1808*. For the sixteenth century, see Alida C. Metcalf, *Go-Betweens and the Colonization of Brazil, 1500–1600*, and for the eighteenth, Caio Prado, Jr., *The Colonial Background of Modern Brazil*. John Hemming, *Red Gold: The Conquest of the Brazilian Indians, 1500–1760*, digs deeply into its topic.

[13]   COLONIAL BRAZIL: SLAVES, SUGAR, AND GOLD

EXPLORERS, INTERLOPERS, AND SETTLERS

BRAZIL is today by far the largest Latin American country. At 8.5 million square kilometers, it is not much smaller than Canada and the continental USA (respectively 9.9 and 9.4 million square kilometers). But its beginning was quite modest, and indeed the very existence of this large nation, the greatest concentration of Portuguese speakers in the world, has in its origins a certain air of chance. For in 1494, the year in which Spain and Portugal drew up the Treaty of Tordesillas, dividing the western hemisphere between them into separate zones of exploration, influence, and commerce, the geography of the western Atlantic shores was almost unknown. There was therefore no suspicion in that year that the placement of the demarcation line 370 leagues west of the Cape Verde Islands would give Portugal territory in America. That realization did not come until exploration of the South American coast revealed how far eastward the land extended. Then it became clear that the Tordesillas line sliced off for Portugal all of South America to the east of the mouth of the Amazon.

Even when the first Portuguese touched on the coast of Brazil, in 1500, they did not realize that they had reached a part of the American mainland. In that year, the second Portuguese fleet bound for India (the first had been Vasco da Gama's of 1497–9) swung far westward in the Atlantic en route to the Cape of Good Hope, propelled, so it seems, more by winds and currents than by any intent to explore. The ships came upon the Brazilian coast at about 16°S, and there rested for a week. The fleet's commander, Pedro Alvares Cabral, took the discovery for another island, to be added to the Azores, Madeira, and the Cape Verdes in Portugal's collection of Atlantic island colonies. He named the discovery "Island of the True Cross."

The island notion was soon dispelled. An exploratory flotilla sent from Lisbon in 1501 reconnoitered most of the eastern coast of Brazil. One outcome of this voyage was the permanent, if highly debatable, naming of the emerging continent. Aboard one of the Portuguese caravels was a Florentine explorer, merchant, and chronicler named Amerigo Vespucci, who in 1499 had already surveyed much of what in the end proved to be the north coast of Brazil. Vespucci's reporting –or rather the publication in Florence of inflated accounts based on it – led within a few years to the name "America" being attached to what in justice should be called after Columbus.[1]

The exploration of 1501–2 revealed the enormous length of the new coast, but found little else to engage Portugal's attention, with the striking exception of abundant wood yielding a red dye. Doubtless some remembered that the first saleable product of Madeira had been a red dyewood. So vivid a color did the American wood (*caesalpinia echinata*) give that it suggested to the Portuguese glowing coals – *brasas*. And after these the land soon came to be named (or so the most appealing etymology of "Brasil" – as the country's name is spelled in Portuguese – would have it). For the next four decades, Brazil wood was the main economic attraction for the Portuguese in this portion of South America that the luck of Tordesillas had given them. The crown immediately set up a royal dyewood monopoly, and then secured an income from it by licensing private traders to obtain logs from Indians and sell them in Europe.

But it was not only the Portuguese who came to load logs. From 1504 on, when a French ship happened on the Brazilian coast, merchants from several northern French ports made every effort to profit from the strong European demand for good red dyes. Competition between Portuguese and French for dyewood quickly grew into general hostility at sea, with each seizing the other's ships where possible. The presence of French shipping on the Brazilian coast was also a threat, in Portuguese eyes, to the safety of the fleets returning from India around the south of Africa. Hence some form of defense of the Brazilian coast was needed. In 1516 came the first royally directed attempt at this, with the dispatch to Brazil of coastguard ships, and the founding at Pernambuco, at the top of the eastern coastline, of a fortified factory, or trading post.

This was not enough to deter the French. In the 1520s French corsairs plagued Portuguese shipping not merely along the Brazilian coast but during the Atlantic crossing as well, taking perhaps twenty Portuguese vessels a year on average throughout the decade.[2] Behind the French persistence was not just the pursuit of profit, but also practical expression of resentment at their legal exclusion from America. The exclusion was in part the outcome of that Spanish and Portuguese agreement at Tordesillas to divide the non-European world between them. But underlying that agreement was the papal approval of the division, which rested in turn on the late medieval doctrine that popes possessed temporal powers over the entire globe. There were, by the early sixteenth century, theologians who regarded that doctrine with suspicion; in Spain itself Francisco de Vitoria publicly challenged it in the 1530s. And France, clearly for practical as well as theoretical reasons, joined the critics. Brazil offered an irresistible opening for a real test of the doctrine. It was easier to reach than the Spanish American territories, ensconced as they were in the

Caribbean, or lying beyond it. And Portugal, poorer in money and men than Spain, was a less dangerous adversary than its large Iberian neighbor.

Coastal settlement

The Portuguese, then, for the rest of the century, and indeed early into the next, found themselves continually obliged to swat at Frenchmen buzzing around this or that site on Brazil's vast coastline. The English became a smaller nuisance of the same sort late in the century, and on the north coast for some decades in the 1600s. There was, in truth, only one means of securing the coast, and Portugal's claim to Brazil, from such meddling, and that was to root settlements there. Portugal set about this in earnest in the 1530s.

Up to that time, with the exception of the factory at Pernambuco, which proved short-lived, and a few other royal factories built as collection points for dyewood, about which almost nothing is known, settlement of Brazil was unplanned and minimal. Most of the Portuguese in Brazil in the first three decades were deserters, castaways, survivors of shipwrecks, and convicts (known as *degredados*) exiled from Portugal. Indeed, Cabral had left two *degredados* behind in 1500, precisely so they might master the local language and culture and, eventually, facilitate further contact. Despite the uncertain fate of these two men, the Portuguese pursued a strategy of cultivating go-betweens throughout the early phase of colonization. In some cases, groups of indigenous people were taken to Europe; in other cases, Portuguese sailors were left behind in Brazil. The latter were, of course, all men. Some of them, from choice or necessity, took to living among Indians, sometimes becoming leaders of the natives' small communities. João Lopes Carvalho, for example, lived in Brazil for four years before serving as pilot of the *Concepción* at the beginning of Magellan's expedition of circumnavigation in 1520. Carvalho brought on that expedition his son by a local indigenous woman.[3] Even more important to subsequent Portuguese colonization was Diogo Álvares who, under the name Caramurú (meaning "Eel"), became prominent among the natives of Bahia. Álvares had relationships with several indigenous women, and married a woman called Paraguaçu. He took her to France, where she was baptized in 1528; she subsequently returned with her husband to Brazil. Years later, she and her daughters attended a Jesuit school for Christian instruction.[4] These early nativized settlers, and the indigenous women and kin groups that accepted them, set in motion the miscegenation that has ever since marked Brazilian social history. In learning one another's languages and customs, they also became ideal middlemen – cultural "brokers" – not only in the dyewood trade but also after formal colonization began.

The dawdling pace of Portuguese settlement in Brazil had several causes. One was certainly lack of economic allurement, apart from dyewood, the extraction of which barely required settling since the coastal Indians would happily cut it in return for trinkets and metal knives and axes. The Indians themselves were not such as to attract settlers. Brazil lacked the native states, large towns, elaborate works of art, and accumulated metallic wealth that drew the Spanish on across Middle America and western South America once they had encountered the Aztecs. Most telling of all, however, was that, by the time that Brazil made its appearance as a part of Portugal's Atlantic domains, that country's attention was already firmly fixed on West Africa, a rich source of gold and slaves, and even more on southern Asia. With Vasco da Gama's voyage in the late 1490s the Portuguese had achieved, after a century of dogged preparatory exploration, what Europeans had long dreamed of: linkage by sea, with all the potential for huge cargoes which that implied, with the fabled sources of pepper, cinnamon, cloves, and other spices, not to mention silks, ivory, and precious stones, of the Orient. With the vast profits of that trade in prospect, why bother with the Island of the True Cross, whose main claim to attention seemed to be a native people in whom naked innocence was disconcertingly combined with a propensity to roast and eat their captives?

If, indeed, it had not been for the interloping French, Portugal might have left Brazil to a few *degredados* and their companions for some time to come. But though Portugal had little urge to settle it, that anyone else should frequent it was intolerable. And so in 1530 John III's administration decided to create a permanent colony. Martim Afonso de Sousa, a well-tried naval commander, was sent off with five ships in that year to patrol the coast, explore the mouths of the Amazon and Río de la Plata to locate them relative to the Tordesillas line, and to set up a royal colony. His ships carried 400 settlers for that purpose. After extensive surveying, Sousa in 1532 chose São Vicente, close to present Santos in the south, as the settlement's site. His brother reported the allocation of land for farms, and the establishment of order and justice "to the great satisfaction of the men, for they saw towns being founded ... the celebration of matrimony, and living in civilized communion, with each man as lord of his own property ... and all the other benefits of a secure and sociable life."[5] Sousa may have chosen so southern a site because it offered the potential of easier access to the interior; and by this time rumors had filtered even to Brazil of the existence of a "white king" (the Inca) rich in precious metals who lived far inland.[6] Given that report, it is noteworthy that town-founding was not limited to the coastal plain. A small place, Piratininga, was also settled some 50 kilometers from the sea, facing inland from the top of the coastal escarpment. In the early history of Piratininga, and in fact in Sousa's settlement efforts in general, another nativized Portuguese, João Ramalho, played a notable part. Ramalho, who had lived in Brazil since 1512, had formed a lasting relationship with Bartira, daughter of the chief of the Tupinikin people of Piratininga, and had become, in effect, a headman. His power and connections later enabled him to supply slaves to São Vicente, drawn from local indigenous groups traditionally hostile to the Tupinikin. As late as 1552 he could supposedly muster 5,000 indigenous warriors in a day.[7]

In 1562 Piratininga, re-established in 1553 under Ramalho's captaincy, was united with a nearby Jesuit mission named São Paulo. It was therefore one parent of the town which centuries later would become Brazil's, South America's, and indeed the southern hemisphere's largest city, with a population, *c.*1990, of 16.7 million. In the much nearer future, particularly in the seventeenth century, São Paulo would also be the base for expeditions that explored much of Brazil's interior, and, in doing so, effectively push the colony's boundary far westward of the Tordesillas limit. Martim Afonso de Sousa, when he returned to Portugal in 1533, can have had no inkling of what he had set in motion in planting those urban roots inland from São Vicente.

Nevertheless, the São Vicente colony was only one small area of settlement on 5,000 kilometers of coastline. Occupying any large fraction of the rest with crown colonies was far beyond the monarchy's means. Hence in the mid 1530s John III resorted to an essentially private form of colonization. He divided Brazil into fourteen territories extending westward from the coast to the Tordesillas line, and granted these to twelve "captains-donatary," whose heirs could succeed to them in perpetuity. The captains were minor nobles and respectable commoners. Most them were military men and bureaucrats, in either case with good connections to the court. They received, as had comparable grantees of land in medieval Portugal, and in the Atlantic islands in the 1400s, vast powers.[8] Particularly notable was the king's permanent ceding of civil and criminal jurisdiction. The captains were empowered to name judges at all levels, execute criminals who were commoners, and exile those of higher social standing. They could found towns, and allocate lands to colonists. They themselves became owners of specified tracts of land, and received a small portion of the taxes due to the king on fish caught and dyewood cut in their territories. Fiscal control, including the royal dyewood monopoly and taxes, was, indeed, the sole major authority that the king retained. Notable in these grants is the lack of reference to Indians, except for a permit to send a certain number of them annually as slaves to Portugal, duty-free. Christianization of the natives receives no mention.[9]

Despite the immense opportunities for autonomous seigneurial rule which the captaincy plan offered to the donees, the project still did not, in general, promote settlement as the king had hoped. Colonizing was an expensive proposition, and only one of the captains was truly rich. Three of the appointees never made any attempt to settle their grants. Native resistance and the indiscipline of the people sent out (and of those already there) made the settlement of most of the others tenuous. Two captaincies, Bahia and São Tomé, that did well initially were abandoned in the mid 1540s as a result of native hostility. The Indians resented loss of land to settlers and, even more, the enslavement to which they were increasingly subject as farming began. The only true successes were in the far north and in the south, at Pernambuco and São Vicente. The first had the advantage of short sea passages to Europe, and also of able leadership from its captain, Duarte Coelho, who set about defending the coast and promoting agriculture with great energy. São Vicente benefited from being the site of Sousa's settlement a few years earlier. Although by the mid 1530s Sousa had become captain-general of Portuguese India, São Vicente was donated to him, and the capable lieutenants whom he left there ran it well. In both captaincies, also, the marriage of influential Portuguese – in Pernambuco, the captain's brother-in-law, no less – to the daughters of native headmen helped smooth European–Indian relations, and undercut the native hostility that became a severe hindrance to settlements elsewhere.[10]

The two exceptions were not enough, however, to offset the broad failure of the captaincies to raise the level of Portuguese presence in Brazil. By the late 1540s some fifteen towns and hamlets along the coast held a bare 2,000 settlers. Further direct royal intervention seemed indispensable, so in 1548 John III sent Tomé de Sousa, a cousin of Martim Afonso well tried in the royal service in Africa and India, to be governor general of Brazil. The failed captaincy of Bahia, between Pernambuco and São Vicente, was bought back from the heirs of its original grantee, to be established as a royal captaincy by this second Sousa. In 1549 he chose a site overlooking the entrance to the great Bahia de Todos os Santos – All Saints' Bay – for the capital of the new crown colony. The town that arose there, Salvador (often known itself as Bahia), became the capital of Brazil and so remained until 1763.

And so, almost fifty years after Cabral's landing, formal royal government finally came to Brazil. The governor general had supreme executive authority in Bahia, and broad, if ill-defined, oversight of the private captaincies. Some of these survived into the eighteenth century, with varying degrees of autonomy. Generally speaking, the crown and its colonial officials interfered least in those that were best run by their captains-donatary. Naturally enough, also, those that were simply furthest from the base of royal authority in Bahia tended to be left alone. Disputes between royal and private administration were common enough; but they were usually settled ad hoc by the crown itself without any damaging jolting of Portugal's hold on Brazil.

Defense, against both native and outside threats, figured largely in Tomé de Sousa's orders. Salvador itself should be built, of masonry, around a strong central fortress. Sousa was to see to fortification of the little towns already existing in various captaincies, and to the arming of their inhabitants. He was also to gather ships to drive away the French.

Military men were among the thousand people who went with Sousa to Brazil in 1549, his party instantly adding 50 percent to the existing colonizing population. Among the new arrivals were some 400 *degredados*, since Brazil had by now replaced the west African island of São Tomé as the main zone of exile for miscreants. Sousa also brought peasants and craftsmen; and, to staff his new government, lawyers and treasury officials. More serious attention was now given than before to the application and collection of taxes throughout Brazil.

INDIANS AND JESUITS

Most notable, however, among Sousa's founding force for the new crown colony of Bahia were six Jesuits. These were not only the first priests from the fifteen-year-old Society of Jesus to reach America, but a clear sign that the Portuguese crown finally intended to activate its long-proclaimed policy of protecting and evangelizing the Brazilian natives. From the earliest years of the century Portugal had held that its title to Brazil was justified in large part by Christianization. But missionary attempts had in reality been rare, the work of a small number of friars, some Franciscans among them. John III now decided that the new Society's blend of spirituality and worldliness fitted it to attack the long-delayed task. The number engaged in it was not large: by 1598, only 128 Jesuits had reached Brazil.[11]

Their work was twofold: to protect the native people from the settlers' depredations, and to make Christians of them. By 1549 the depredations had become severe, as is suggested by the native reaction to them in the form of attacks on colonial settlements in mid-decade. By then dyewood was no longer the sole profitable product exported from Brazil. Its rising rival, an introduced plant, was sugar cane. For cane to grow, land had to be cleared, then kept free of weeds. The cane had to be cut, and hauled quickly to a mill for extraction of its juice. All this demanded heavy physical effort, far more tiring, disciplined, and continuous than what was needed to fell the brazilwood trees and drag their trunks to the shore. The Portuguese were too few (and far too unwilling) to provide the necessary labor. Hence Indians must perform it. But in the dominant native culture of the coast, that of the Tupí speakers, agriculture was women's work. Moreover, it was a relatively light and intermittent task, since the staple food, manioc, grew abundantly with minimal attention. Money was no work incentive for Indians, since they exchanged only by barter – and they had accumulated enough of the tools and trinkets that the Portuguese and others had bartered for dyewood. Further, lacking any political structure larger than the village, the native people also lacked any centrally directed system of labor that the Portuguese might have adapted to their own use. (This was one large contrast between the Portuguese economic organization of Brazil in the 1500s and the Spaniards' exploitation of New Spain and the central Andes.) The outcome of all this, from the late 1530s on, was the Indians' enslavement.[12]

Thirty years passed before the crown finally came to grips with the question of Indian slavery. In the meantime, at least after c.1550, it entrusted the native people to the care of the Jesuits, who took on the challenge with all the enthusiasm to be expected of so young a body. Like the first Portuguese to see the Brazilian natives fifty years before, the Jesuits were initially struck by their apparent simplicity and receptivity. The Indians seemed to the Jesuits like sponges ready to soak up Christianity. The Jesuits' leader, Manoel de Nóbrega, wrote of them "They are not certain about any god, and believe anyone who tells them he is a god … A few letters will suffice here, for it is all a blank page. All we need to do is to inscribe on it at will the necessary virtues, be zealous, and ensure that the Creator is known to these creatures of His." Indians seemed superior to Christians in their practice of morality and natural law.[13]

Brief experience changed the tune. Although many native people came to the Jesuits apparently eager for teaching, and many thousands were baptized, it soon became clear that they were impelled as much by a hope that the priests would protect them from the settlers as by any thirst for the true faith. Further, and worse, the Christianity that they absorbed did not displace their own religious beliefs, of whose presence and complexity the Jesuits soon became all too aware. They "return to the vomit of their ancient customs" after being baptized, reported one. By the mid 1550s Nóbrega himself was disillusioned enough to call them, perhaps in a dark moment, "pigs in their vices and way of life."[14] There were evangelizing friars in the Spanish colonies, by that date, who would have had similar feelings about the Indians they were trying to bring to the Christian God.

From the start of their conversion efforts, the Jesuits saw their best chance of success in removing Indians from their communities and regrouping them in new villages (*aldeias*). One such place was set up in Bahia in 1552. But the Indians' natural urge to flee after they had been relocated, added to the settlers' objections to Indians being taken from the potential slaving pool, made the Jesuits uncertain about the village scheme for a few years. Then, though, realization that they were failing to convert native people in their own settlements revived the *aldeia* project in the late 1550s. From then on the villages were a standard feature of colonial Brazil. As in the Jesuit *reducciones* in the Spanish colony of Paraguay, in Brazil too the aim was both to pluck natives from a familiar environment that would tend to preserve traditional habits, and to deposit them in alien, essentially European, surroundings in which it would be easier to teach them new behaviors. So, for example, in the *aldeias* they should not live in multi-family long houses. In the small huts preferred by the priests, nuclear families would thrive, and the promiscuity supposedly encouraged by communal living would find no home. In the new environment of the *aldeias* the Indians would also, it was hoped, be more receptive to Christian teaching. The Jesuits went about the task by instructing young boys first, expecting that they would retain for life what they had learned at an early age. It was not so, however, for when the pupils reached adolescence the Jesuits saw them reverting to traditional beliefs and behavior. The *aldeias* also had a practical purpose, parallel to that of the *reducciones* that were beginning to appear in Spanish America at about the same time. That was to act as reservoirs of workers for hire by colonists. This might seem contradictory to the Jesuits' purpose – had they not wanted to gather the native people up so as to protect them from the colonists? But contracting workers out from the *aldeias* at least gave the priests some control over conditions and duration of work, and was certainly, in their view, far preferable to colonists' seizing Indians as slaves. Besides that, making *aldeias* into sources of cheap and accessible labor would incline colonists to regard them favorably – and stop seeing them as barriers put up by the Jesuits to block access to Indians. Colonists' early approval, or at least tolerance, of the *aldeias* also rose as they saw that removing native people from their original communities opened up land for farming.[15]

Support for the creation of *aldeias* certainly came from Mem de Sá, governor general of Brazil from 1557 to 1572, in both principle and action. On his arrival in Bahia, Sá quickly decided that the constant warfare among neighboring Tupí in the captaincy's interior must stop. He set out to achieve this through a mixture of force and enticement: peaceful Indians would be free and protected; those who insisted on fighting would be punished. The outcome for Indians who ignored Portuguese authority was quick and sharp. Sá attacked with great violence, his men's arquebuses mowing down native archers. By one report, thirty native villages were burned in Bahia; by another, from a Jesuit, 160. One outcome was that displaced and defeated Indians flocked to the *aldeias*. At the start of Sá's term these numbered two or three; by 1561, there were eleven, with a population in early 1562 of 34,000.[16] After his campaign in Bahia, Sá extended his disciplinary action to the north. There, between Bahia and Pernambuco, a particularly bellicose native subgroup named the Caeté fought not only other Indians but the Portuguese north and south of them. They had, moreover, in 1556 captured after a shipwreck the first bishop of Brazil, who was returning to Portugal from his see at Bahia; and, having taken him, they cooked and ate him. In 1562 Sá declared a general war of punishment on the Caeté. Anyone might attack them; any Indians captured could be enslaved. The outcome was the near-annihilation of the Caeté. Even those who had taken refuge in Jesuit *aldeias* were seized. Any who avoided capture fled into the interior.[17]

The 1560s were indeed dismal years for the natives of the Brazilian coast. After Sá's assaults, which were in fact the colonizing state's first large attempt to control the Indians, they next suffered what seems to have been the first major onslaught in Brazil of imported disease. It would be puzzling if Old World bacteria and viruses had not attacked the immunologically defenseless Brazilian natives earlier; and in fact the Jesuits reported high local mortality in the early 1550s.[18] But pandemic diseases, penetrating the interior far beyond European settlement, did not appear until *c.*1560. The first seems to have been a hemorrhagic dysentery, perhaps combined with an influenza that had afflicted Europe in 1557.[19] In 1562 both plague and smallpox, the prime killer of American natives in the sixteenth century, arrived. In these years between 25 and 60 percent of the *aldeias'* populations may have died. The Jesuits did what they could for both those in their *aldeias* and others who came for treatment. "I peeled part of their legs and almost all their feet, cutting off the corrupt skin with scissors and exposing the live flesh ... and washing that corruption with warm water. With which, by the goodness of the Lord, they were healed."[20] Concentrating Indians in *aldeias*, alas, encouraged the spread of the pathogens, and as more people were brought in to fill the places left empty, they too were infected and died. Village populations typically dropped from thousands to hundreds. With the many deaths inevitably came lack of food, since there were too few healthy people left to grow even the undemanding manioc. Most *aldeias* near Bahia and Olinda, the chief town of Pernambuco, disappeared. By the late sixteenth century, in fact, the future of the *aldeias* in Brazil seemed generally uncertain. Instead of furnishing the colony with Christians and workers, in one historian's view, "the *aldeia* system succeeded only in creating marginal communities of sickly, morose, and unproductive residents, hardly able to provide for their own survival."[21] Nonetheless, the *aldeia* did survive, and became, as it had always threatened to be, a contentious point between Jesuits and colonists, as each tried to draw Indians away from the other.

Reports to Lisbon on Indian matters by the Jesuits and the governor general, and a growing awareness that the Indians' decline meant lack of labor in Brazil at a time when sugar cultivation was rapidly expanding, now led to more serious thinking about the Indian question, particularly slavery, than ever before. On orders from Portugal, Mem de Sá called a junta in Bahia for that purpose in 1566. Its members were leading Jesuits, the bishop of Brazil, and royal judges. They found in favor of the *aldeia* system: Indians under Jesuit supervision would be protected from the settlers' demands. At the same time, though, the junta did not condemn enslavement, but merely urged that Indians not legally enslaved should be freed. These conclusions were sent to the king, Sebastião (1568–78), a young man predisposed to favor Indians, since, it has been said, if not king "he would probably have been a zealous missionary."[22] And in 1570 Sebastião issued the first statement to come from Portugal affirming the liberty of Brazilian native people. Indians might "on no account and in no way be enslaved." But, in recognition of the colonists' need for labor, the law immediately backed away from that ringing declaration, making exceptions of those found to be cannibals, those taken in just war (that is, war made by settlers in self-defense or retaliation), and those who repeatedly assaulted colonists or other natives. Such sinners and troublemakers might still be enslaved. In practice, even the crown's qualified ban on Indian slavery was quickly diluted still further in Brazil itself. The rising demand for labor, together with a loss of calm voices with the death of Nóbrega in 1570 and Sá in 1572, led to revocation of the 1570 law, and its replacement in Brazil from 1574 on by much laxer rules. The colonial authorities now decided that Indians taken by other natives in tribal conflicts, and in danger of their lives, might be bought out of captivity by colonists. This was a procedure known as *resgate* (a combination of ransom and rescue) that had long served the Portuguese as a means of acquiring slaves, but which had latterly drawn increasing official disapproval. At the same time the notion of just war was allowed to become so loose that almost any pretext sufficed for slave raiding.[23]

SUGAR

CANE AND MILLS

Many of the wounds that the Indians of the Brazilian coast were now suffering were inflicted, at a distance, by Europe's increasingly prominent sweet tooth. The Portuguese naturally experimented from their early years in Brazil with the profitable sugar cultivation that they, and Italians working from Lisbon, had begun in the 1450s in Madeira. As the first tentative colonization of Brazil was beginning after 1500, sugar-growing was starting to thrive also on the island of São Tomé, in the Gulf of Guinea of central West Africa, which Portugal had occupied in the 1480s.[24] In Brazil itself the first sign of sugar-making appears in 1516, when the colonial administration in Lisbon, the Casa da India, ordered the dispatch to Brazil of an expert capable of building a sugar mill. Brazilian sugar may have been sold at Antwerp as early as 1519.

It was, though, in the 1530s, those years when Portugal finally focused its attention on the territorial, administrative, and defensive ordering of Brazil, that sugar truly began to find its place in the colony. Among Martim Afonso de Sousa's people in 1532 were Portuguese, Italians, and Flemings who knew Madeira's sugar business. It was natural, as the idea of settlement prevailed over the earlier view of Brazil as a place mainly valuable for its bartered dyewood, that thoughts should turn to cultivable crops. And it was soon obvious that much of the east coast was ideally suited by temperature, rainfall, and soil to the raising of sugar cane. The two thriving captaincies among the dozen created in the mid 1530s owed their success largely to sugar: São Vicente in the south, and Pernambuco in the north. Sugar mills (engenhos) quickly appeared in both (and a few in other captaincies also). Pernambuco, for reasons of both climate and proximity to Portugal, developed into the prime sugar province of Brazil in the sixteenth century (By 1550 it had five engenhos running; in 1585, sixty-six.) Duarte Coelho, the founding captain of the territory, imported craftsmen from Portugal and from the Canaries, where in the sixteenth century the Spanish, also, grew sugar. He organized the sale of sugar in Lisbon, where a considerable degree of north European interest, mainly Dutch but also German, in the production, freight, and marketing of sugar arose as the century proceeded.[25] In Brazil the north-east became still more clearly the prime sugar region, when Bahia, after its re-creation as a crown colony in 1548, imitated Pernambuco in building engenhos. Tomé de Sousa, the first governor general, came with orders to set up mills and plantations. The land around the Bay of All Saints proved excellent for cane. Mem de Sá's subjugation of the Indians of the interior of Bahia in the late 1550s made planting that land safe. Sá himself built a large refinery. In 1570 the captaincy had eighteen mills, and by 1590 perhaps fifty. By then, Pernambuco and Bahia together yielded possibly three-quarters of Brazil's sugar. By the end of the century Brazil was producing some 600,000 arrobas, or c.8.8 million kilograms, annually, the great part of which was exported to Europe, drawn by the constantly rising prices that accompanied the incipient transformation of sugar "from a luxury of kings into the kingly luxury of commoners."[26]

With the sixteenth-century rise of sugar, Brazil took on the part of tropical agricultural exporter that it has played, with until recently only minor qualification, down to the present. Within the colony, the sugar engenho had become by 1600 the dominant economic and social unit, and was long to remain so. Its central position in the colony's existence put a rural stamp on Brazil as a whole. The colony was not one in which towns prevailed, controlling hinterlands, as in Spanish America. Rather, the defining trait was the rural plantation, with urban settlement secondary to it.

The sugar estate consisted of cane fields, typically under 1,000 hectares in total area, surrounding a nucleus of buildings. Of these the most important were the sheds housing the machinery for crushing the cane, and others, adjoining, that held the cauldrons and kettles in which the juice squeezed from the cane was boiled down to make crystalline sugar. The other major buildings were the workers' living quarters, the owner's house (often simply called the "big house," or casa grande), and a chapel.

Heavy physical labor went into every stage of sugar-making. Virgin ground being readied for planting was cleared with hand tools, and for almost all the colonial era further tilling and weeding was also done by hand, with little use of plows until the late eighteenth century.[27] The production process started with the planting of small pieces of cane. These took fourteen to eighteen months to grow to harvestable size. From the stump left after cutting, another cane would develop, although after three or four cuttings from the same root, the amount of juice yielded began to drop, and a new planting was needed. Once cut, the cane was quickly hauled to the mill on carts. If it was not crushed within forty-eight hours, the quality and quantity of the juice began to decline. The urgency of milling newly cut cane clearly placed limits on the practicable size of plantations.

The first type of crushing device used in Brazil was a simple millstone that rolled on its rim over chopped-up pieces of cane. An improvement on this was a machine consisting of two horizontal wooden rollers, geared together, and made to rotate either by the power of animals (oxen, horses, or mules), or by a water wheel where there was enough water at hand. Only around 1610 did the more efficient design present in New Spain in the sixteenth century reach Brazil. This had three vertical rollers, the middle one being turned by a shaft descending from above, while the two on each side, linked by gearing with the driveshaft, rotated in the opposite direction to it. This device was lighter, cheaper to build, and more effective in crushing cane than the earlier two-roller, apparatus. It was quickly adopted in *engenhos* after its appearance, and seems to have been the sole major technological advance made in sugar-processing in colonial times.

The juice from the cane flowed through a pipe or channel to the boiling house. There it was heated several times, to different temperatures, in copper vats of various sizes set over furnaces. The aim of the heating was to bring impurities and lighter sugars to the surface, where they could be skimmed off. From some of the skimmings alcoholic and non-alcoholic drinks could be made, though not rum (*aguardente*), which was distilled from the molasses separated from the sugar later in the refining process. After a final boiling in small kettles, the now thick syrup was poured into bell-shaped molds made of clay, and there left to cool. The molds were then set, narrow end down, in suitably pierced racks in the *engenho*'s purging house. There, over several weeks, the liquid would crystallize into a brown sugar. Further refining in the molds could convert part of their contents into white sugar. For this, a thin covering of wet clay was applied to the hardening sugar at the upper, open end of the mold. Water from the clay filtered down through the sugar, removing coloration and the last impurities from the upper layers. What flowed out of the hole at the base was molasses, which could be used as such, for distillation, or re-crystallization into a lower-grade sugar. After up to six clayings, the sugar in the top two-thirds or even three-quarters of the mold was white. Below it was a fine brown sugar called *mascavado* (muscovado in English). The solid loaf of sugar was tipped out of the mold, the white cut from the brown, and both pounded by hand with a mallet to a fine texture. Brazilian growers exported mainly muscovado and white sugar to Europe, where the latter was particularly esteemed.

Sugar-making was, then, a complicated and delicate process, whose many components had to intermesh closely if the optimal end product was to be obtained from the potential in the cane. Once the cane was cut, delay or interruption in processing would cause loss in quality or quantity up to the point where the molds filled with syrup were placed in the purging house. Optimizing the product required the use of skill and judgment by overseers in the boiling and purging houses. Cutting, hauling, and feeding the cane between the mill's rollers was hard and constant work; it was even dangerous, since inevitably hands and arms were occasionally caught in the machinery. Most striking of all was the continuous intensity of labor in sugar-making. Climatic conditions on the north-eastern Brazilian coast allowed the cane harvest (the *safra*) to proceed for at least nine months of the year. Since cane could not be stored, the mill had to be in operation for that time as constantly as possible. That meant, in practice, all but continuous work, day and night, in the boiling house, and milling stints of eighteen to twenty hours. The other hours went to cleaning and repairing machinery and cauldrons. For months at a time, then, apart from admittedly frequent religious holidays, workers had minimal opportunity for rest, and for gathering and preparing food.[28]

The *engenhos'* complement of buildings, machinery, cauldrons, furnaces, hand tools, and draft animals also made these plantations the most capital-intensive of productive units in colonial Brazil. One *engenho* in late seventeenth-century Bahia had copper cauldrons with a total weight of over 5,000 kilograms. All copper was imported from Europe.[29] Where water power was used, aqueducts were needed. Some growers built large storage tanks to provide a reserve of energy.

SUGAR WORKERS: SLAVES, INDIAN AND AFRICAN

A grower's largest investment, however, was in labor, since most of the work in sugar production was done by slaves. In the sixteenth century, these were mainly Indians, obtained by slave-raiding in the interior, or through *resgate*. As both Sebastião's 1570 declaration of natives' freedom and its subsequent dilution in Brazil suggest, the colonists' demands on the Indian population became constantly heavier in the middle decades of the century. The severe losses of people to disease in the 1560s resulted only in greater pressure on the survivors. The number of slaves taken did not fall; the reverse, in fact. Wars between groups of Indians that were traditionally hostile to each other became a major source of slaves. Before the Portuguese arrived, and in earliest colonial times, these conflicts had resulted in the taking of a few captives for sacrifice. But gradually they became slave-raiding expeditions. The Portuguese took advantage of these old hostilities by allying themselves – sometimes at the Indians' invitation – with one side. Their help, and their firearms, resulted in more of the opposition being taken captive, and, through *resgate*, a greater yield of slaves.[30]

By the 1580s many thousands of enslaved natives were at work producing sugar. The 66 *engenhos* operating in Pernambuco in 1585 used some 4,000 of them. In 1589 the 50 or so *engenhos* in Bahia had, by one estimate, some 9,000 Indian slaves.[31] By that time, it is true, not all natives working on plantations were slaves. Some, a minority, were free people paid in goods, such as metal tools, for their labor. They came either from nearby native communities, or, more commonly, from the Jesuit *aldeias*. In the early seventeenth century, by which time contact with colonists had made at least some natives familiar with European monetary practice, a few instances of actual wage labor appeared.[32] But this never became a standard type of employment in sugar (in contrast with labor arrangements in the Spanish colonies' major industry, silver mining).

While the numbers of Indians on plantations rose in the closing decades of the sixteenth century, sugar growers were also looking outside Brazil for workers. The soaring demand for sugar, the persisting toll of disease among the natives, the underlying opposition in Lisbon to Indian enslavement, and the rising cost of expeditions deeper into the interior to seize or ransom workers all united to persuade planters to turn increasingly to Africa for their workers. Powerful precedent for the use of blacks of course existed in the Atlantic islands on which Portuguese settlers had raised sugar, particularly Madeira from the mid fifteenth century and São Tomé in the sixteenth. Both had quickly become successful exporters of sugar. Slaves to grow it had been easily available from West African sources to which the Portuguese, as a result of their explorations and factory-building in the 1400s, had almost monopoly access. As experience with native slaves accumulated in Brazil, settlers there came to realize the attractions of Africans in comparison with Indians: greater technical skills in farming, animal tending, and even metalworking; greater physical strength and endurance; and greater resistance to disease.

Africans are reported as present in Brazil in 1535, working on early sugar plantations in São Vicente, though whether as slaves or free laborers is unclear. The date of the first shipment of slaves from Africa is probably 1538.[33] Until the mid-century, however, the African presence in Brazil was very small. After that it began to grow, as imports of slaves quickened. The import curve steepened notably after 1570, in response to the rise of sugar. There began in that decade a slow substitution of African for Indian coerced labor on the plantations that would take fifty years to complete. For a time, the great pace of sugar's expansion led to continued growth of the native labor force. But then the Indian component shrank, and Indians were finally, by the 1620s, all but wholly replaced by blacks in the cane fields and mills. The Africans transported to Brazil in the sixteenth and early seventeenth centuries came mainly from the enormous area of West Africa known to Europeans at the time as Guinea. By mid-century, however, the Portuguese were drawing more heavily on Central African sources of slaves in the Congo and Angola; and they continued to do so, in increasing measure, for the rest of colonial times. The numbers of slaves carried to Brazil are uncertain, except in their upward trend. By 1650, a total of 250,000 may have arrived, 70,000 from Guinea, and 180,000 from Central Africa.[34] The total number of Africans actually alive and present by then is not at all clear. Some idea of their increasing prominence is given by the fact that, in the late 1580s, 25–30 percent of slaves in Pernambuco and Bahia were black. Pernambuco's *engenhos* employed some 2,000 black slaves in the mid 1580s; in 1589, Bahia had 3,000–4,000 of them.[35]

PEOPLE AND GOVERNMENT

POPULATION TRENDS

Numbers are no clearer for other components of the population in the sixteenth century, or for most of the rest of colonial times, for that matter, since no official counting took place until after 1750. Unlike Spain, Portugal imposed no head tax on the Brazilian natives, so even that basic fiscal motive for keeping track of Indian numbers was lacking. Of the white population, the same in one respect can be said as of the African: that its growth accelerated notably after the mid-century. By 1570 the whites (very largely Portuguese) had reached some 20,700, concentrated, as would be expected, in the captaincies of Bahia and Pernambuco (each with some 6,000), and São Vicente (3,000). By the mid 1580s the white total had risen to 29,400. By then Bahia and Pernambuco, prospering from sugar, had both increased their share, to some 12,000 each, while São Vicente had fallen back to 1,800. It is likely, then, that by 1600 Brazil held some 40,000–50,000 whites, most of them in the north-east.[36]

Notwithstanding the lack of censuses, every indication is that over the sixteenth century the fall of the native population was far more dramatic than the rise of immigrant numbers. No one now doubts that there were more than a million Indians in 1500. A series of "educated guesses" suggests, indeed, that in the entire area of modern Brazil they may have then numbered some 2.4 million, and a reasoned proposal exists that Brazilian Amazonia alone may have held 5 million before the Europeans' arrival.[37] It is probable, as with blacks and whites, that only after 1550 did important changes begin. The first severe wave of alien epidemics struck in the 1560, their effects sharpened by the famine that followed them. Local outbreaks of disease followed in the 1570s and 1580s, and in 1597 came another broad onslaught of microbes on the coast, especially in the north-east. To be added to disease, of course, are the destructive effects of enslavement, and particularly of the raiding carried out to procure slaves. Though no reliable global figure for Indians is available for the late sixteenth century, the trend is clear in this contrast: in 1562 the Jesuit *aldeias* in the single captaincy of Bahia had 34,000 natives, whereas in 1585 the total of Indians in *aldeias* in Brazil as a whole was only 18,000. Flight to the interior may explain some of that fall; but disease and slaving were by all accounts the prime culprits.[38]

COLONIAL ADMINISTRATION

The growing complexity of Brazil and Brazilian issues in the late sixteenth century – among them, the rising urgency of the Indian question, the growth of African and European populations, the multiplication of settlements, and above all the expansion of sugar-raising and export – made the existing governmental arrangements seem inadequate. The Portuguese monarchy had throughout the century pursued centralization of power at home. To secure a hold on its Asian possessions it had installed in them some of the institutions tested in Portugal. Now, with Brazil proving to be far richer and therefore more attractive to settlers than had seemed possible for its first fifty years under Portugal, it was time to tighten the transatlantic reins as well.

Portugal shared with Castile a conviction that the supreme task of monarchs was to provide justice in their realms. Courts, judges, and lawyers, therefore, played just as prominent a part in the Portuguese world as they did for Spaniards. Judges, being the embodiment of royal law, also came to be seen, in the places to which they were appointed, as natural sources and appliers of new regulation. There was in Brazil, then, as in Spanish America, a fusing of the executive, legislative, and judicial tasks of government. In Brazil, the first legal figure with such powers was the *ouvidor geral* ("general judge," or high royal magistrate) sent out in 1549 with Tomé de Sousa, the first governor general.[39] A sign of the weight given to the office of *ouvidor* was that in 1554 it was combined with the post of *provedor mór da fazenda,* or chief treasury officer, in the colony. Judges were the men to entrust with gathering the king's Brazilian income.

Up to 1549 the law had been represented in Brazil by municipal magistrates, together with more powerful figures, also termed *ouvidores,* appointed, one per captaincy, by the donees. The new *ouvidor geral* heard appeals from these lower judges, and was also charged with visiting the various captaincies to monitor the application of the law. Naturally enough, those subjected to the inspections resented this intrusion by royal officers. This was one aspect of a broad resistance from town councils, the religious, and assorted colonials, to the imposition of royal authority in the second half of the century. The chief royal magistrates thus found themselves caught up in many sorts of business besides strictly legal questions. On occasion they became interim governors general. A small number found themselves leading military forays against Indians considered to be rebellious.[40]

By the 1580s it was clear that a single superior magistrate could not adequately oversee the exercise of law in such a vast territory as Brazil's, and among a population quickly rising in number and growing in wealth. This realization coincided with a radical change in Portuguese political affairs. For in 1580 began a period of sixty years in which the crowns of Spain and Portugal were united, and in which Madrid, at least nominally, became the master of Portugal's empire.

The union of crowns followed from the death, without heir, of the young King Sebastião during an assault on the Moors of Morocco in 1578. Sebastião, never in his young life an exemplar of stability and good sense, had been made foolhardy by a blend of religious zeal and imperial ambition. His somewhat rag-tag expeditionary army was routed at the battle of Alcácer Quibir by a much larger Moorish force, with great loss of men and at a total cost of six months' royal revenues. Several contenders for the Portuguese throne then presented themselves. The one who prevailed was Philip II of Spain. He was not only the son of a Portuguese princess, but the ruler of the first European military and political power of the day. And that power, of course, loomed over Portugal's land frontiers.

In the event, Spain left the administration of Portugal and its empire largely to the Portuguese themselves, under general supervision from Madrid channeled through a viceroy in Lisbon. But it is not surprising that the Spanish, in that Philippine age of newly achieved "government by paper," found defects in Portuguese administration both at home and abroad. One perceived deficiency was in justice. The remedy finally went as far as the promulgation of a new code of Portuguese law, the Ordenações Filipinas (Philippine Decrees), in 1603.[41]

The practical need to improve the exercise of law in Brazil, then, coincided in the 1580s with pressure for reform coming from Spain. The upshot was a decision to install in Bahia a high court of appeal, known in Portuguese lands as a relação. By the mid 1580s such courts existed in Lisbon, Oporto (in the north of Portugal), and in Goa (where one had been created in 1544 to enhance the legal and political presence of the monarchy in the Indian Ocean). Philip II had apparently concluded by 1586 that Brazil needed a relação, and three years later ten magistrates were chosen to staff it. The ship carrying most of them, however, was unable to make Brazil because of adverse winds. The judges were scattered, and no court took form. The setback gave opponents of the change, some of them high in Portuguese administration, the chance to marshal their arguments. Some feared that the presence of more senior judges in Brazil would only lead to more lawsuits. Others saw an easier solution in simply increasing the number of magistrates. The outcome was that the high court of Brazil was not founded until 1606. After then, except for a gap from 1626 to 1652, it was a permanent part of the colonial governing apparatus.

The relação of Bahia was founded with, at least nominally, ten judges. Most of these had the title of desembargador (literally, and rather optimistically, a remover of hindrance). Some desembargadores dealt with civil suits. Appeals from their verdicts, in cases worth substantial sums, went to the Casa da Suplicação in Lisbon, the senior relação in the Portuguese legal system. Other desembargadores were available for general assistance in trials where needed. Appeals in criminal suits were heard by the ouvidor geral, the prior senior magistrate in Brazil, whose office was now integrated into the high court. Cases involving royal interests, including of course treasury matters, went before a special judge, the juiz dos feitos da coroa e fazenda. These were the principal magistrates of the court. It was equipped also with a secretarial staff, a doctor, a chaplain, a bailiff, and a custodian, and at its head was a chanceler, or chancellor, who was finally responsible for the consonance of the court's rulings with existing law. His functions extended also, however, into executive business. He might examine regulations issued by the governor general to ensure their legality. He received and ruled on accusations made against the governor general. In the governor's absence, it was now he, rather than the ouvidor geral, who assumed executive command of Brazil.[42]

The *relação* at Bahia was the Portuguese parallel with the Spanish American *audiencias* that sat in viceregal capitals (until 1739, just Mexico City and Lima). They had a similar role of collaboration, but also inherent confrontation, with the colony's chief executive, in the Spanish case the viceroy. And, like viceroys in Peru and Mexico, the Brazilian governor general was the *ex officio* president of the high court, with a voice though no vote in its decisions. What Brazil lacked, however, was the series of regional high courts far from the colonial capitals that in Spanish America were such potent reminders of the monarchy's existence and authority. The absence of any such state agencies outside Bahia was a reflection of Brazil's smaller size and population, and particularly of the persistence of private colonization in most of the captaincies. Although Lisbon gradually pressed in on the donees' powers, the notion of private control and jurisdiction died hard in Brazil, whereas in Spanish America the crown had smothered it almost at birth by its rapid attacks on the authority of conquistadores.

Attacks on powerful and unruly local interests did, nonetheless, mark the first incursion of the Holy Office of the Inquisition into Brazil. From 1591 to 1593, Heitor Furtado de Mondonca conducted a visit (*visita*) to establish an inquisitorial presence in the colony. Among the many trials he conducted, those of powerful *mamelucos* and sugar planters are particularly noteworthy. Fernão Cabral, a prominent Salvador sugar planter, confessed to burning a slave woman alive, and was accused by others of sins as various as the illegal seizure of Indians, sexual advances toward a respectable married woman, and the obscene use of sacred words. His sins netted him two years' exile and a stiff fine.[43] Though the inquisitor's departure in 1593 marked something of a return to questionable colonial habits, and though the Holy Office never established a permanent tribunal in Brazil, the *visita* of 1591–3 nonetheless was a sign of the slow evolution of a bureaucratic structure.

As, then, Portuguese Brazil neared its first centenary it was at last acquiring an organizational form and a distinct identity that during the first half of the century seemed hardly to be developing. Sugar was now clearly the foundation of the colony's being, as its prime source of income and the reason for the existence of its defining social institution, the rural plantation. Sugar had caused colonists already in place to put down roots, and drew newcomers from Portugal. Its labor demands had shaped the treatment of the native people by colonists and colonial government alike, and ultimately driven rising numbers of Indians to flee from the coast to the relative, if only temporary, safety of the interior. Those same demands had energized the trade in African slaves, who, by 1600, were well on the way to supplanting native slaves on the sugar *engenhos*. By then, indeed, Brazil was firmly set on its road to becoming predominantly a society of whites, blacks, and, quite soon, mulattoes.

Brazil had lagged behind Spain's American colonies in acquiring a clear sense of self. Portugal's Asian orientation, perfectly reasonable given the wealth that it promised to yield, accounts in part for the difference in timing. A larger cause was the absence among the Portuguese of the almost crusading determination of sixteenth-century Castilians to bring American natives into the faith and culture of Europe. Neither that, however, nor any difference in governance or even ethnic and social development, was the deepest contrast between the two Iberian colonial presences in America. The most striking difference was, rather, Brazil's relative openness to the exterior. Its geographical position on the east side of South America, and the fact that its sixteenth-century settlement all took place within a few miles of the coast, made it a part of the Atlantic world in a way that no substantial piece of Spanish America would be until the eighteenth-century emergence of the Río de la Plata and Venezuela as rich agricultural areas. Spain's first major American territory, Mexico, lay shielded by the Caribbean and its barrier of islands. The second, Peru, was still further from other Europeans' reach, hidden away beyond Panama, beyond the South American rainforest and the inner Andean ranges. For purposes of religious purity and economic security Spain found this geographical arrangement most advantageous. And in the sixteenth century it was able, to a remarkable degree, to maintain a hermetic American empire, one linked to Europe by the narrow and sealed channel of the Carrera de Indias. By the end of the century, to be sure, the seals were clearly starting to leak; and from then on they did little but fail. But still, for that first century, in both aim and reality, comparatively speaking, Spain made a closed empire in America and Portugal an open colony.

OUTSIDERS: THE DUTCH, AND OTHERS, IN BRAZIL

The Portuguese did not, of course, indiscriminately welcome outsiders to Brazil. The French annoyance was a leading reason for the installation of royal government and defense from the 1530s. And after French Protestants founded, in the 1550s, a settlement that they named "Antarctic France" in the bay of Rio de Janeiro, Mem de Sá reacted forcefully, so that the colony lasted only twelve years (1555–67). But a less aggressive foreign presence was easily tolerated. From the start Italian, Flemish, and German capital flowed into the sugar business.[44] Dutch ships carried much of the sugar trade later in the sixteenth century, and even in the second decade of the new century Dutch merchants reckoned that their ships carried, with Portuguese approval, 50–75 percent of the trade between Brazil and Europe.[45] Another transatlantic trade was well developed by then, run by colonials themselves, as Brazil sent its tobacco to the west coasts of Africa to be exchanged for slaves.

A little later in the seventeenth century, beginning in the 1620s, Brazil found there was a price attached to its easy Atlantic accessibility, as it suffered the only major foreign invasion in its history to the present day. The attackers were the Dutch, who proceeded to ensconce themselves in the north-east of the territory for twenty-five years.

The origin of this change in the Portuguese–Dutch relationship, which until a few years before the attack was mutually beneficial, though certainly with its ups and downs, lay in the union of the Spanish and Portuguese crowns in 1580.

For although in everyday affairs the union's effects had been minimal since Spain's policy was to leave Portuguese officials and practices in place, at a higher political level the story was quite different. With the union, Portugal and its possessions had become part of the Spanish state. Enemies of Spain were now Portugal's too. Spain, from the late 1560s until the mid seventeenth century, had no foe more relentless than the Dutch. And the Dutch, correctly perceiving Portugal as the weaker and poorer part of the union, brought their firepower to bear on Portugal's overseas holdings. As themselves Europe's dominant new trading power, abundantly equipped with ships and deep-sea mariners, they would undoubtedly have been tempted to try their own fortune in business long controlled by the Portuguese. But the knowledge that a blow struck against Lisbon was also a blow against Madrid energized their efforts.

The Dutch aimed first at Portuguese interests in West Africa. On the Mina coast, at the western end of present Ghana, the number of Dutch trading vessels multiplied in the 1590s, so that by 1600 Hollanders had largely displaced the English and French as rivals of the Portuguese in the exchange of gold for European cloths and metal goods.[46] Further concentration on this area's trade culminated in 1606 in a Dutch attack on the venerable fortified trading station of São Jorge da Mina. The Portuguese, with the help of African allies, repulsed the attack. But the Dutch persisted with their exploitation of the trade and with their attacks on Portuguese positions, even during the truce between Spain and the Netherlands from 1609 to 1621. After the truce ended, neither the military nor the commercial situation improved for Portugal. Indeed, in 1637 the Dutch finally captured São Jorge, and in 1641 Luanda and Benguela also fell. These places Portugal recovered in a final peace with Holland in 1663. But the Dutch had taken and now kept control of the Mina coast. Portugal was now gone from West Africa, and could trade there only with Dutch license.

In Asia, Portugal lost far more to the Netherlands. The main Spice Islands went in 1605, though part of the loss was recouped in 1606 by a Spanish force from the Philippines. In 1622 Hormuz, on the Persian Gulf, fell, as did Malacca in 1641, and various Portuguese coastal sites in Ceylon between 1638 and 1658. Slightly to the west, Cochin and other points on the Malabar coast of western India succumbed to the Dutch in 1663. Macassar in the Celebes, to which the Portuguese driven from the Spice Islands had retreated to maintain their trade in spices and sandalwood, was finally taken in the late 1660s.[47] Having stripped Portugal of so many ports in southern and eastern Asia, the Dutch then took over the large share of the shipborne carrying trade in the Arabian Sea, the Bay of Bengal, and the China Seas that had so profited Portugal in the sixteenth century. Finally the Portuguese were left with just Diu, Damo, Bassein, and Bombay, in north-west India; Goa, half-way down the western coast; Macao, on the south China coast; and part of Timor in eastern Indonesia, where their sandalwood trade survived.

Dutch successes against Portugal in Africa and Asia had profound effects. One was to make the Netherlands an enduring colonial power in the east. Another was to leave Brazil as Portugal's pre-eminent overseas possession, a position for which the success of sugar had now well equipped it. The Dutch, naturally, did not neglect Brazil. Their West India Company, created in 1621 at the end of the twelve-year truce, was an organization designed to harass and profit from all and any Iberian lands in America. Brazil, as a result of Dutch familiarity with it, its accessibility, and its perceived weakness in defenses, was the company's preferred target. The first assault, on Salvador, came in May of 1624, directed by Piet Heyn. The townspeople fled in great panic. The Dutch held the town, though hardly any more, until April 1625, when a powerful fleet of Portuguese and Spanish ships ousted them. Salvador resisted two more attacks in 1627. But then in 1630 the company shifted its aim further north, to Recife, the chief town of Pernambuco. Now, with silver seized by Heyn from the Spanish at Matanzas in 1628, the company had funds to throw a force more than twice as large as that of 1624 (67 ships and 7,000 men, as against 23 and 3,300) against Brazil. Portuguese resistance was stiff. But the attackers prevailed; and so began a Dutch presence in the Brazilian north-east that lasted until 1654.[48]

At its maximum extent the Dutch occupation stretched 1,800 kilometers around the shoulder of Brazil, from a little south of the São Francisco river on the east coast to a little west of the Parnaíba on the northern. It went no further inland than the Portuguese had gone. Nor did it need to, for the West India Company had its eye on sugar above all else, and sugar was a coastal crop. By occupying Pernambuco, the Dutch took control of Brazil's leading sugar region. The West India Company, in its best years for sugar, 1637–44, apparently controlled at least a quarter of total sugar exports from Netherlands Brazil, and took taxes on the rest.[49] Most *engenhos* during the occupation stayed in Brazilian hands. Although a plan existed for emigrant European farmers to take up sugar cultivation, in the event time was too short even to reveal if this was practicable. Other exports were tobacco, hides, and, as ever, dyewood, on which the company set up a trading monopoly.

The broad impression remaining of the Dutch occupation of the north-east is one of rather open-minded civility on their part (despite Portuguese horror at heavy Dutch drinking). Not all, naturally enough, was harmony and light. Having resisted the Dutch invasion and expansion, the Portuguese colonists who chose to stay in the occupied area did so resentfully. On the edges of the Dutch zone there was continual skirmishing, with both sides working to attract Indian auxiliaries for their efforts in the field. Certainly, too, an undercurrent of religious hostility was present. The West India Company had been the creation of strict Calvinists, for whom abhorrence of the Catholicism of Iberoamerica was as much a spur to action as the political and economic damage the company might inflict on Spain. Nevertheless, despite the presence of zealous Calvinist preachers, the Dutch administration in Brazil was in practice tolerant of the exercise of Catholicism, even of the continued existence of monasteries and nunneries, supported by their traditional revenues.

The strong sense of enlightenment left by the Dutch regime owes much to Johan Maurits van Nassau-Siegen, from 1637 to 1644 governor general of Dutch Brazil, and a scion of the family that had produced William the Silent two generations before. Though a Calvinist and a soldier tempered by experience in the Thirty Years War, he officiated in Brazil more in the spirit of the humanistic education he had received. He developed much affection for Brazil; Dutchmen nicknamed him, indeed, "Maurits the Brazilian."[50] To indignant Calvinist preachers he promised repression of Catholicism; but he did little or nothing to effect it. He tried to diversify agriculture in Brazil away from sugar; but also cut taxes and made credit available to sugar planters for repair of *engenhos* damaged in the invasion. He set up town and rural councils, on which both colonials and Dutchmen should sit, in an effort to create representative government. In 1640 he went so far as to call a brief assembly of Portuguese settlers from the occupied zone, in an effort to give them a say in their government, and to hear and remedy their complaints about the behavior of the Dutch soldiery and local officials. The gathering has been described as "the first ... legislative assembly in South America."[51]

In the long term, though, Johan Maurits is best remembered for his efforts to gather and record accurate information about the people, fauna, and flora of Brazil. There he supported six artists, among them Albert Eckhout, who was particularly adept at painting humans and animals, and Frans Post, a specialist in rural views and scenes. He took with him to Brazil also one Georg Marcgraf, a German naturalist, who sent back to Europe collections of specimens of plants and animals. Marcgraf died young in Angola in 1644. But a compilation of his Brazilian notes was published in the Netherlands in 1648 as *Historiae Naturalis Brasiliae*, a work which provides the first systematic accounts of Brazil's flora and fauna, of native groups, and of the geography and climate of Pernambuco (with records of rainfall and winds).[52] The information gathered and reported by Johan Maurits' entourage was much better than anything previously collected, and remained central to the study of Brazil until the nineteenth century.

Across the Atlantic, late in 1640 Portugal rose against Spanish rule. Times had grown desperate for Spain. Military defeats on land in Europe were followed, in October 1639, by the destruction by the Dutch admiral Tromp of a large Spanish fleet in the Downs, off the south-east coast of England. In January 1640 another naval force, Spanish and Portuguese, sent to Brazil to oust the Dutch, was scattered by a smaller Dutch fleet near Itamaracá island, off the coast of Pernambuco. In May 1640 began the revolt of Catalonia against the centralized rule and tax demands of Madrid. The loyalty of other Spanish provinces seemed doubtful. And then in December the Portuguese proclaimed the duke of Braganza as their independent king, John IV.

Portugal and the Netherlands were now therefore united in hostility to Spain, and indeed they agreed upon a ten-year truce in June 1641. But it was a truce limited in practice to Europe. The Dutch continued to gnaw at Portugal's holdings in Asia and Africa; and they made no move to leave Brazil. Portugal, caught up in a war of national liberation with Spain that continued fitfully into the mid 1660s, could do little to oppose Dutch hostility overseas.

In Brazil, however, the events of 1640–1 had their effect. With the Dutch–Portuguese truce signed, the West India Company decided to cut costs in

Brazil by reducing its garrison there. It also recalled Johan Maurits, whose enthusiasm for Brazil had, so the company's directors thought, led to excessive spending on non-military activities. After protesting about both his removal and the risky economizing, he left Brazil in May 1644. With him went a powerful force for mediation between invaders and colonials, for there were many in all parts of the population – Dutch, colonials, blacks, and Indians – who had come to regard him as a just and trustworthy governor.[53]

In the mid 1640s, therefore, with the Dutch apparently hesitant, the guerrilla warfare that had always flickered on the edge of the occupied zone began to burn more steadily. Though it was the Portuguese governor general at Salvador, Antônio Telles da Silva, who first directed the anti-Dutch effort, its final success was very much the work of residents of Brazil, acting independently of Portugal, which remained focused on its own contest with Spain. The retreat of the Dutch to Recife and its close vicinity by 1648, and their final withdrawal in 1654, have been seen, moreover, as the doing of not only of white colonials, but of mixed-bloods, blacks, and even of Indians fighting alongside the others more or less willingly. For some more recent Brazilians, indeed, the process of ejecting the Dutch both encouraged and revealed the start of a sense of multi-racial national identity in the colony. And while it is rather easy to find signs of such sentiment where none may really exist, there is no denying that it was the colony and not the homeland that began and sustained the practical effort against the Dutch.[54]

In other respects, the Dutch presence was too brief to leave much permanent imprint on Brazil. One lasting change was that the great rise of population and commercial energy that the town of Recife experienced during the occupation persisted after the Dutch left. The external outcomes, however, range from the simply interesting to the historically fundamental. An example of the first sort is the departure from Recife with the Dutch, who had been notably tolerant of them, of a number of Jews who chose not to return to the Netherlands but to try their luck in Dutch territories in North America. Those arrivals in New Netherland in the mid 1650s became "The Pilgrim Fathers of American Jewry."[55] A far more telling movement was the extension, during the Dutch period, of sugar-growing from Brazil to the Caribbean. In Barbados, for example, where English settlers had first raised tobacco in the late 1620s, sugar-planting began in earnest c.1640. A rise in the European price of sugar after 1633, caused by disruption of Pernambuco's production after the Dutch invasion, was the first stimulus for the change of crop. The Barbadian English overcame their early problems in sugar-making by sending men to Pernambuco to learn the methods developed in Brazil.[56] Other islands, both English and French, took to sugar at the same time. And when the Dutch were driven from Brazil in the 1650s, they too began planting cane in their Caribbean colonies. Doubtless the new European colonists of the Antilles would in any case have developed the islands' potential for sugar sooner or later. But the easier access to Brazilian techniques provided by the Dutch occupation of Pernambuco quickened the process. The outcomes included Brazil's loss of its prior near-monopoly on the supply of sugar to Europe, and, conversely, vast and enduring gains in income for the northern European powers now building up their colonial presence in the Caribbean.

MOVEMENT INLAND: SLAVERS, PROSPECTORS, AND STOCKMEN

EXPLORERS AND BANDEIRANTES

While the north-eastern and northern coasts of Brazil were held by the Dutch in the 1630s and 1640s, the interior was finally, if slowly, starting to yield to a variety of probings by other residents of the territory. With these tentative inward movements began a process at least as important to the formation of modern Brazil as any multi-ethnic effort to expel the Dutch. For it was above all in the century between, roughly speaking, 1650 and 1750 that Brazil grew from its early coastal form to approximately its present size.

In the north a key event in this expansionary process was the final driving away of the French in 1615. Immediately after this a Portuguese expeditionary force was sent to found a settlement on the Amazon. On the Pará river, actually the southern arm of the Amazon estuary, this was done. A fortress was built, the nucleus of what soon became the town of Belém. Five years later, in 1621, the entire northern coastal region, generally termed Maranhão, was declared a separate *estado*, or "state," of Portuguese America, separate from the "state of Brazil," and with its own capital at São Luís, half-way along the north coast.[57]

From this new northern base area, exploration of the Amazon now proceeded, driven in large part by slaving of Indians along the river's banks. Native communities around the shores of the enormous estuary were all but destroyed. English ambitions for settlement along the Amazon were another spur, in the 1620s and 1630s, to surveying of the river.[58] Portuguese movement upstream was eased, too, by the union of crowns, because while Brazil was formally in the Spanish domain, Madrid seemed little concerned by what would otherwise have been violation of the Tordesillas Treaty. In fact, Philip IV encouraged exploration by the Portuguese and Brazilian colonials, and in 1637 went so far as to grant to Portuguese a hereditary captaincy extending some 400 kilometers up the north bank of the Amazon from the sea. It was in 1637, also, that a canoe bearing two Spanish Franciscans appeared at the mouth of the river. The two had left a failing mission attempt on the Napo river (in present Peru), and, fearless friars that they were, decided to see the Amazon rather than re-climb the Andes to the Spanish-settled regions. This feat moved the Portuguese governor at São Luís to send a strong expedition of 70 Portuguese and 1,100 Indians upstream to forestall any Spanish claim to Amazonia. Under Pedro Teixeira remnants of this force finally, in 1638, reached the city of Quito. Then, in 1639, Teixeira went back down the river, and, following orders, founded a settlement at Tabatinga on the Napo as the new marker between Spanish and Portuguese territories in the interior of northern South America. With this one astounding stroke the demarcation line was pushed almost 2,500 kilometers west of the old Tordesillas limit, where it has remained, at that latitude, until now. Tabatinga is at the modern convergence of the boundaries of Brazil, Colombia, and Peru. The Spanish, blocked by the Andean foothills from sending any large body from Peru, and now generally beset by far more urgent problems in the peninsula and elsewhere in Europe, did nothing to push the Portuguese back. In Teixeira's wake others began to use the Amazon and its tributaries for access to the saleable products of the rainforest, such as wild cacao, hides, wood, spices, and medicinal herbs.[59] A clear mark of growing colonial activity in Amazonia was the building in 1669 of a fortress, São José de Rio Negro, at the confluence of the Negro and Solimões rivers, near the present site of Manaus. Men from Pará explored the upper waters of Amazon tributaries in present Ecuador and Peru in the 1680s. Another variety of European presence along the rivers was the mission *aldeia*. Franciscans, and particularly Jesuits, tried as always to defend the forest peoples from the rising labor demands and the slave-raiding of the colonists. Carmelites seem to have been the most active evangelizers in western Amazonia, broadly speaking beyond the fort at São José.[60]

Some would see in Pedro Teixeira the very embodiment of the spirit of that classic and mythologized Brazilian type, the *bandeirante*. *Bandeirantes* were members of *bandeiras* – roving bands of armed men who traversed the interior of Brazil in the seventeenth century, hunting for sources of wealth (which they found mainly in the form of Indians whom they took as slaves), and in doing so exploring and extending westward the colony's territory. The word *bandeira* means, first, "flag"; but it was used in medieval Portugal as a term for a small armed unit, a raiding party detached from a larger company. In Brazil the word was current by 1635 to mean a group of backlands militiamen.[61] But the cultural implications that it has accumulated in more recent times are what has given it so much weight in Brazilian self consciousness. *Bandeirantes* set out on their journeys from several areas on the coastal periphery of Brazil. But the prototypical *bandeirante* was a *paulista*, a native of São Paulo in the south-east. And a distinctive trait of *paulistas* by the end of the sixteenth century was the degree to which they were the product of racial mixing – mixing not, however, of European and African, as was by then growing common elsewhere in Brazil, but of European and Indian. The term used for this combination, the Brazilian equivalent of the Spanish American *mestizo*, was *mameluco*. And what has made the *bandeirante* from São Paulo so important a part of Brazil's view of its past is that he was part Indian. It is perhaps through the phenomenon of the *bandeira* that the Indian has been most fully drawn into the Brazilian sense of self.

The *bandeirantes*, men of the seventeenth century, were the prime discoverers of Brazil, in the sense that what their journeys revealed in the interior was larger by far, and more varied, than what European explorers had found earlier on the coastal plains. With only minor exaggeration, in fact, the *bandeirantes* might be called the makers of Brazil, because it was mostly their roaming of the interior that established Portugal's claim to vast tracts west of the Tordesillas line.

The *mameluco* nature of São Paulo's people went back to the start of European settlement in the area where the town developed. The first Portuguese there, well before Martim Afonso de Sousa's arrival, was the warrior and head-man João Ramalho. Ramalho, it will be remembered, formed a union with Bartira, daughter of the local Tupinikin Indian chief. To avoid bigamy (he had a wife in Portugal) he never married in Brazil, but he remained attached to Bartira while engaging in relationships with other women. Thus, by the time of his death, Ramalho had innumerable children, grandchildren, and great-grandchildren.[62] Sire and progeny formed an influential group. Of Ramalho's twelve acknowledged daughters, all married Europeans. Three sons were knighted. The success of Ramalho's *mameluco* family was matched by the descendants of Jerónimo de Albuquerque, who fathered at least twenty children with several indigenous women. These children, later legitimated, became the foundation of the Pernambuco elite.[63] Thus, as in Spanish America, many early mixed-race individuals moved effortlessly into the colonial elite. In a few areas, most notably São Paulo, they would forge a distinctly hybrid culture that lasted well into the following century.

Piratininga, and São Paulo after it, did not draw large numbers of new arrivals from Portugal in the sixteenth century. Isolated as they were at 700 meters, just over the crest of the coastal escarpment (in fact the only colonial places so positioned until much later), they were less attractive to immigrants than the developing sugar areas further north. Early São Paulo had both the advantages and the drawbacks of its relative isolation: freedom from governmental meddling, but poverty in its apartness from the rising prosperity of the sugar-rich coast. Its own economy before, and after, 1600 was largely a matter of subsistence farming and the raising of pigs, cattle, and horses on rural estates.[64] There were typically patriarchal Iberian figures among the landowners and the leaders of town government (often the same men); but at the same time the simple and rough conditions of the plateau frontier made a man's standing dependent, to an unusual degree for the time, on his own efforts and ability.[65] By 1600 the town of São Paulo had some 120 houses and 2,000 inhabitants. Most of them were white, *mameluco*, and Indian, although by then some blacks were also present. It is a clear sign, though, of the region's ethnic and cultural nature that, even a hundred years later, the commonest language used by all those in and around São Paulo was not Portuguese, but Tupí.

The *bandeiras* of São Paulo are above all a seventeenth-century phenomenon. But the many defensive sallies launched by the *paulistas* in the late 1500s against hostile native people in the region around the town were clearly, in effect, rehearsals for them.[66] With the turn of the century came a distinctly offensive *bandeirismo*, aimed mainly at slaving, although two wide-ranging expeditions from São Paulo were organized in 1601 and 1602 by the then governor general of Brazil, Dom Francisco de Sousa, specifically to look for gems and precious metals in the interior. This was part of a continuing search for mineral wealth in Brazil that might match that of Spanish America. Later in the century *bandeirantes*, some at the colonial government's behest, were to make that their first object; and in the end their efforts yielded rich fruit.

For fifty years after 1600, however, the *bandeiras* from São Paulo were first and foremost slaving expeditions. Some of them were veritable small armies, in which a few dozen white *paulistas* commanded hundreds of *mamelucos* and even more numerous Indian auxiliaries. Slave-taking, indeed, often enough meant fighting. These forces went off into the interior for months or years at a time. As a practical guide to the territory they used its many rivers, following their valleys inland, down the slope of the plateau toward the major streams of Amazonia or the Paraguay–Paraná–Uruguay system. In this they perhaps imitated the travel patterns of native people of pre-contact times.[67] But it was not until the eighteenth century that explorers of the interior used boats on the rivers to move themselves and their goods. The seventeenth-century *bandeirantes* went on foot.

The slaves whom they captured were put to work locally on the plateau in and around São Paulo, or were sold on the coast for labor in sugar-making and other tasks. Although the proportion of African slaves in the *engenhos* was by this time rising fast, the vibrant growth of the sugar business still produced a demand for Indian slaves – especially so because the early 1600s were a time of growing Dutch interference at the sources of the slave trade in west Africa. Coinciding with this difficulty was the appearance of a tempting source of Indian slaves in the form of the mission reductions that the Jesuits were now starting to create east of Paraguay. The first of these, set up in 1610, were within 600 kilometers of São Paulo, almost due west of it on the southern bank of the Paranapanema river. Over the following decades the Jesuits gathered Indians into other *reducciones* further west and south, in what are now parts of eastern Uruguay, north-eastern Argentina, and southern Brazil (but, even there, areas that lay west of the Tordesillas line). There ensued a protracted battle between the Jesuits in these areas and the *paulistas*. The raiders on occasion found themselves abetted, if not aided, by the Spanish governors of Paraguay and even by the secular church authorities there, since both groups saw the Jesuits as intruders in their own jurisdictions. The missionaries resisted with unexpected, though thoroughly Jesuit, vigor and practicality, arming their neophytes and fielding them as surprisingly effective defense forces of their communities – and, for that matter, of this particular eastern limit of Spanish America, though the Spanish administration was not grateful. Finally, however, by *c*.1640, *paulista* pressure drove the Jesuits back behind the Uruguay and Paraná rivers. From then, also, Portugal's revolt against Spain inclined the local Spanish governors to take stronger action themselves against the *bandeiras*. In those forty years after 1600, nonetheless, the *paulista* raiders had in reality greatly extended Brazil's reach to the west, and southward into what is now Uruguay.

After the mid-century, the *bandeiras* broadly turned from a hunt for slaves to one for precious metals and stones. The reasons were several: the greater remoteness and defensive strength of the Jesuits' *reducciones* by then; the improvement of the African slave supply as Portugal took back a growing number of areas from the Dutch in Angola, though not in western Africa; and Portugal's need for a source of wealth and income to make up for losses in the sugar business to the new plantations on the Caribbean islands. And so, though slaving of Indians in the interior still continued to a degree, the *bandeirantes* now functioned mainly as prospectors. They were employed and organized as such, indeed, by the crown.

By 1650, the pursuit of minerals had already led to some spectacular incursions into the interior (journeys sometimes called *entradas*) from various coastal towns. From Bahia expeditions had gone west to the São Francisco river valley and ranged southward along it, covering many thousands of kilometers. One *entrada*, from Sergipe, just north of Bahia, had stayed in the interior for eight years around 1600. But it was after 1650 that these prospecting ventures ranged furthest, pushing the limits of Brazil (particularly of its central section between 10°S and 20°S) far westwards, in the sense of both the political boundary and geographical knowledge. Now *paulistas* trekked over areas that were to become known as Minas Gerais, Goiás, and Mato Grosso, 1,500 kilometers and more to the north and north-west of São Paulo. One of the most remarkable of them, Antônio Rapôso Tavares, spent the years 1648–52 on a formidable journey up the Paraguay river to some point in the eastern Andes, and thence back via Amazonia.

Gold

These explorations revealed enough gold to keep the prospecting effort at high pitch. But it was not until the mid 1690s that the great rewards came. They appeared, ironically enough, really quite close to home, not deep in the western interior but near the Velhas river, 500–600 kilometers north-east of São Paulo. Among several discoverers was Antônio Rodrigues de Arzão, who set out from Taubaté, near São Paulo, in 1693. A rash of strikes elsewhere followed in the next few years, some as far north as Bahia. But no other region proved to have gold in the amounts quickly found in the Velhas area. As a result, in 1709 the crown set up a new administrative unit, São Paulo and Minas do Ouro (Gold Mines) and revoked earlier limits on the number of slaves that could be sold for use in the mining industry.[68] In 1720 this gold zone was made a quite separate captaincy, Minas Gerais (General Mines), a name that persists to the present.[69] With the gold strikes began a new phase of colonial Brazilian history, a "golden age" lasting half a century or more (c.1700–60) in which Brazil imitated the central Andes and Mexico in exporting large quantities of bullion, and in which gold gave a superficial gloss of wealth to Portugal as well. During that period, as might be expected, prospecting continued with still greater energy, resulting in further major gold finds now far into the interior in Goiás and Mato Grosso. Large deposits of diamonds also came to light in the late 1720s in Minas Gerais, and others, though smaller, later in Bahia and Goiás.

With the gold discoveries, the pioneering work of the *bandeirantes* was done. Gold-prospecting soon gathered a momentum of its own in the interior, and mining brought more or less fixed settlement with it, so that for the first time towns appeared far inland. Fortune seekers, and supplies, were carried after 1710 or so to the mines and new towns by the *bandeiras'* successors, expeditions known as *monções*, or "monsoons" (so named, apparently, from the meaning of "season for travel" given to the word by the Portuguese).[70] These were freighting ventures, using long, dug-out canoes to take people, domestic animals, food, and other goods into the interior. Now the rivers flowing inland over the plateau proved their worth as means of transport, though their abundance of rapids and waterfalls made the freighting business slow and arduous.

In the early 1970s Embraer, Brazil's principal aircraft-building company, produced its first successfully exported airplane. It was named the "Bandeirante." The pathfinders of the seventeenth century occupy a place in the Brazilian memory comparable to that of cowboys in the USA or gauchos in Argentina, as the expression of an independent and hardy national spirit, and as the men who unlocked the nations' interiors. In truth, the *bandeirantes* fill this image far more completely than the other two types. They were active for better than a century; they ranged astonishingly deep and wide; their journeys were arduous without parallel. They were, of course, far from unsullied heroes. For fifty years they were out-and-out slavers, responsible for the uprooting, and probably the early death, of hundreds of thousands of natives of the interior.

The cattle frontier

Understandably less well remembered than the frontier-expanding *bandeirantes* of the 1600s are the cattle that moved into many of the opening spaces of the interior behind them. But the animals deserve recalling, because they were the most obvious alien presence in much of the *sertão*, or backlands, for a long time; and ranching drew colonists (landowners and herders, or *vaqueiros*) inland, admittedly in small numbers, long before the great inward flood of gold seekers took place in the early eighteenth century. Cattle were an important instrument of the European occupation of the land in Brazil, as they were also in the pampas further to the south, or in northern Mexico.

Martim Afonso de Sousa brought the first cattle to Brazil in the early 1530s. They multiplied on the coastal plain in step with the growth of the sugar industry, since the *engenhos* needed meat for food, and, more crucially, oxen to pull carts and turn crushing mills where water could not be used.[71] Hides served any number of purposes, and candles made from tallow were a basic source of light. As sugar output and the colonial population grew, cattle-raising spread inland from the coast, making good use of land that was too dry and infertile for cane. The easiest access to the interior was up the valleys of the rivers that cut through the coastal ranges, such as the Paraguaçu in Bahia, and above all the great São Francisco, which entered the sea half-way between Salvador and Recife, giving entry to an enormous area of the interior extending down almost to São Paulo. Throughout the seventeenth century, but mostly after 1650, stockmen and cattle pressed inland up the valleys. By the 1680s they had gone north from the São Francisco valley into the inner marches of the northern captaincies of Paraíba and Ceará. The land there is the epitome of what the word *sertão* brings to mind: arid, infertile, thinly covered with brush.[72] Only extensive ranching was possible on such land, and enormous estates came into being covering hundreds of square kilometers. On such areas the numbers of animals could, however, be very large. In the somewhat less forbidding interiors of Bahia and Pernambuco, 500,000 and 800,000 head of cattle were reported in 1711. Despite the existence of such numbers close to the large population centers of the north-east coast, great drives of animals from distant areas took place. In 1709, for instance, cattle were herded overland some 800 kilometers from Maranhão, which by then had become an active stock-raising area, to Bahia. Some, indeed, were driven a further 1,000 kilometers southwards, to feed the teeming gold-seeking population of Minas Gerais.[73] A northward flow of cattle also developed after 1700, drawn by demand in the mining areas. Stock estates appeared in the lowest reaches of Brazil, the Rio Grande do Sul of today, and sent their animals 1,500 kilometers or so north to the gold regions.

As in northern Mexico, native people in Brazil reacted fiercely to the bovine incursions. Cattle, large and easily hunted beasts, were a splendid new source of food. But this immediate gain was more than offset by the damage they did to farming land, and by the human presence and the taking of open territory for estates that came in their train. Resolute Indian resistance to the spread of ranching punctuated the second half of the seventeenth century, especially in the interior of Bahia and in the extreme north-east. Colonial governors of the region, driven to distraction by these risings, called in seasoned *bandeirantes* from São Paulo to suppress them. With much violence, the job was done.[74]

SEVENTEENTH-CENTURY SOCIETY

As the appearance of the *bandeirantes* shows, by the late 1500s Brazil was developing its own social types. The colonial society, indeed, was beginning to acquire its own identity, as, for example, *engenhos* multiplied and the imports of African slaves to work them rose. This growth of distinctiveness in the society and divergence from its Old World sources accelerated in the seventeenth century, and has continued since then.

It would be easier to follow these changes if the size of the several components of the population were better known. But in comparison with colonial Brazil even the Spanish colonies seem rich in demographic data. It is clear enough, however, that the Brazilian population was growing in the seventeenth century, as a result of both natural increase and immigration. The 40,000–50,000 whites present *c.*1600 had increased to perhaps 100,000 a century later. Scattered figures are available for particular places. The white population of Salvador early in the seventeenth century was perhaps 4,000; in 1709 the town had some 21,600 communicants, most of whom were probably white. The total population of the town *c.* 1700 was over 40,000, and is thought to have tripled between 1647 and 1717. Recife rose from a total of some 2,000 in 1639 to become the second town of the colony by the early 1700s, with 10,000 or so citizens in 1709. In 1646 São Paulo had 600 whites and *mamelucos* capable of bearing arms; in 1700, 3,000 of the same.

The ethnic make-up of the population is even less clear than its total size. In 1700, whites, at 100,000, were about a third of an estimated total, in the colonized areas, of 300,000. By 1680 the slave population (very largely black) may have reached 150,000, so that by 1700 it would have been rather more than half the total. The balance at that date of perhaps 40,000 presumably consisted of free blacks, Indians, and ethnic mixtures. The basic types of mixture were *mamelucos* and *pardos* (all those with some degree of African blood).[75]

As in Spanish America, social divisions and rankings went, with time and the increasing diversity of the population, from the simple to complex. At the start there were just Portuguese (and Portuguese mostly of low social or economic standing) and Indians (Indians, moreover, largely lacking the contrasts of rank, wealth, and power found in the high-culture areas of Spanish America). To these were added in the sixteenth century an African component. For an understanding of the social structure that arose from these basic elements, it is useful in the Brazilian case, as for the Spanish colonies, to suppose a transfer of the notion of estates from the home country. In America, all Portuguese and Spanish settlers, whether commoners or of higher rank, became the colonies' de facto nobility. In Brazil, Indians, then Africans also, took the role of the commoners, specifically of a commoner peasantry. These categories seemed at first distinct and fixed. But with miscegenation, acculturation, economic diversification, and the appearance of legal distinctions such as those between slaves and free people (whether black or native), the initial pattern lost its simple clarity. The free black artisan ranked higher, in both ascribed and real status, than the black slave domestic in the town house of a wealthy family. This domestic, however, was a social cut above the slave servant in the estate house of an *engenho*; who in turn saw himself, and was seen by all others, as superior to the field hand. Similarly, Indians in the seventeenth century who lived in villages near *engenhos* or towns, and who worked for wages in some craft or other task useful to the Portuguese, were in a quite different social category from those in mission *aldeias*. Generally speaking, ethnically mixed people, while subject to the same sort of suspicion about their morality and trustworthiness as was common in Spanish America, had an advantage in practical opportunity over pure blacks and Indians. An appreciable whiteness in appearance tended to make for access to the white segment of society and its economic offerings.[76] The *mamelucos* of São Paulo were a case in point.

Working and living conditions for the mass of commoners, the blacks, varied widely with their occupation and status. The free urban smith or carpenter had a material life not much different from his white or mixed counterpoint. On the sugar estates, field and mill slaves were worked hard and long, with some risk of injury from knives, crushing machinery, and furnaces. The combined tolls of heavy labor and disease undoubtedly led to a short life for most rural slaves, although life expectancy cannot be accurately calculated for the seventeenth century, nor is it clear how much shorter the slave's life was on average than that of other poor people. What is clear is that there was no natural increase in the rural slave population. If left to itself, indeed, it would have fallen. The rise in the number of African slaves in seventeenth-century Brazil was the result of large imports. The reasons for the tendency towards natural decline were several. A central one was the high cost to the owner of raising a slave child compared to the price of newly arrived captive from Africa. Owners were little concerned that their slaves should reproduce. They were therefore unwilling to buy many women. Consequently, fewer women than men were shipped to Brazil. Among such children as were born, early mortality seems to have been high, in part because mothers suffered the effects of hard physical labor and inadequate diet. The outcome was (in Bahia, at least) that from 1600 to the early 1800s, some 70 percent of slaves present at any time had been born in Africa. The constant influx – in fact, in the 1700s, a growing influx – of new slaves made for a steady reinforcing of African culture in Brazil, in religion and social custom, and a parallel slowing of the "Brazilianization" of the blacks (in notable contrast to the "creolization" of Africans in much of Spanish America in the 1600s). From the eighteenth century, for example, comes evidence that, in such church-consecrated marriages as did take place, ethnic and regional origin in Africa was influential; a man or a woman looking for a spouse clearly sought someone who had grown up in his or her own "nation," speaking the same language and sharing the same local culture.[77] As a result of such preferences, and of the upsurge in slave arrivals, Brazil, indeed, became notably more African in culture in the eighteenth century. One historian has written of Brazil (and of the Caribbean islands, which also imported great numbers of new slaves) that "in the eighteenth century African culture was not surviving: It was arriving."[78]

Blacks naturally produced a variety of reactions to their forced removal to Brazil and to the different hardships they suffered there as slaves. For most, religion gave comfort and a sense of community. African religions lived on in Brazil, and in fact continue to do so in vibrant, if transmuted, forms. Many slaves added to the beliefs they brought from Africa some elements of Catholic faith and practice, such as marriage by the church. Some undoubtedly found solidarity in sharing Christian beliefs. Besides that the church could actually offer some practical framework for community, such as religious fraternities that provided not only a sense of belonging but also funds for dowries, burials, and some insurance against hard times in life. More violent resistance to slavery and to specific ill-treatment was also common enough, though no slave rebellion took place before the nineteenth century. At the individual level, cases of abortion, infanticide, and suicide can be found. Many slaves also engaged in witchcraft and sorcery to prevent punishment, procure liberty, or harm owners' property. Occasionally slaves even sought to murder their owners, and sometimes their families too.[79] Much more common, though, was running away, which began to happen in the late 1500s. The coastal forests and mountains, and the *sertão* inland from them, offered plenty of hiding places. *Mocambo* was the name used in the seventeenth century for a community of escaped slaves; *quilombo* became the usual term after 1700. Such groups often survived by combining subsistence farming with assaults on estates, towns, and travelers. Because runaways were overwhelmingly male, their communities also organized raids to capture women. Most of these were probably black or mulatta, despite hysterical rhetoric concerning the abduction of white women.[80] Occasionally, women even took on leadership roles within the communities, as did Felippa Maria Aranha at the Amazonian *quilombo* of Trombates.[81]

Quilombos' existence naturally gave rise to considerable nervousness and irritation among officials, estate owners, and other colonials. Governors organized attacks on the runaway communities, often using friendly Indians as troops; a special rural police was set up to hunt escaped slaves. But the outlaws were resistant. The most famous community of escapees in Brazilian colonial times, Palmares in the interior of Pernambuco, existed for almost the entire seventeenth century. It grew to a size of many thousands. Its fortifications and well-organized militia held out against all attacks until in 1694 a tough force of *paulista bandeirantes* was sent against it, and finally prevailed, overthrowing its King Zumba. The depiction of Palmares and its fall in *Quilombo*, a film of 1984, reinforced its place in the Brazilian memory.[82]

A less drastic and more frequent reaction to slavery was to seek to escape from it by becoming free. A custom existed among owners of granting liberty in their wills to favorite slaves. Most of these were women. Black mistresses of *engenho* owners quite commonly were manumitted in this way, along with their children. Loyal male slaves also benefited from the custom, although for people past the prime working age the gain was dubious. In letting such slaves go, owners may have benefited more in saved maintenance costs than they lost in production. Slaves often also bought themselves out of servitude. Owners of sugar estates sometimes gave their more skilled slaves chances to earn small sums for extra work, apparently as a stimulus to productivity. Determined slaves might eventually save up enough to buy their liberty. Towns offered better earning opportunities, so that self-purchase was more easily managed there. Most freed slaves indeed lived in towns, for the same reason of more abundant work. Since mulattoes and Brazilian-born blacks (*crioulos*) were generally closer to the dominant European culture than those who were African-born, they were more able to find paying work. And so it was mulattoes and *crioulos* who predominated among the free. In the long term, since children born of the manumitted were also free, the cumulative effect of liberation was large, and notably offset the continued import of enslaved Africans. In the early 1820s, of Bahia's total population of half a million, some 170,000 were slaves, while 250,000 were freed men and women, or descendants of freed people.[83]

THE INDIANS AND FATHER VIEIRA

If seventeenth-century blacks had some chance of escaping from slavery, for the native people of Brazil the century offered only minimal chances of relief.

For some along the settled coast, there were opportunities for a meager independence as occasional wage workers or suppliers of food to colonists and the slave population. But for the great majority of Indians, living in the interior, the century brought only harassment by slave raiders, or at best well-intentioned disruption by missionaries. Philip III, king of Spain and Portugal in the first two decades of the century, in 1609 asserted that the Brazilian Indians were by nature free, though strictly as legal minors whose care he entrusted to the Jesuits. Of their own villages and lands, however, Indians were to have control; such land was inalienable. These rulings provoked a rising by the Bahian colonists, and reinforced an already well-established hostility between settlers and Jesuits, with the settlers accusing the priests of monopolizing Indian labor for their own gain in the *aldeias*. The protest was forceful enough to bring cancellation of Philip's rulings in 1611.

Slaving then proceeded without legal hindrance in the interior. The Jesuits found it particularly damaging in lower Amazonia, where the native population was exploited unmercifully by the newly arrived settlers of the Maranhão coast. That northern region was short in resources and economically isolated; throughout the century it was the poorest part of Brazil. Settlers there could not afford black slaves, so they seized Indians to work the small tobacco and cotton farms that provided the area's sole salable products. From the 1620s the Jesuits saw this exploitation of the natives as a challenge needing their attention, but for lack of numbers they could do little until the 1650s. Then they began in Maranhão and Pará a brief but furious pro-Indian campaign under the leadership of the most distinguished Jesuit to appear in colonial Brazil, Antônio Vieira (1608–97).

For his pro-Indian efforts, Vieira seems to the modern eye to have been the closest Portuguese equivalent to Bartolomé de las Casas. But his fame at the time had other more intellectual sources. He was born in Lisbon, but educated in Bahia by the Jesuits. There his brilliance emerged early, showing itself in his splendid oratory. His writing, and the record of his speaking, have sustained to the present his ranking as one of the greatest literary masters in Portuguese. His linguistic abilities extended to other languages; he learned Tupí (and also Kimbundu, a language of the Angolan blacks in Brazil). During the 1630s in Bahia he became the town's most renowned preacher. In 1641 he was one of a party chosen to go to Lisbon to congratulate the king, John IV, on Portugal's casting off of Spanish rule. The king was drawn by his talents, and sent him around Europe on secret diplomatic missions. John also heeded Vieira's accounts of the sufferings of Brazil's native people.[84] The king reiterated the principle of Indians' liberty, and tried to regulate their wages and maximum periods of work, though to little effect.

By 1650 Vieira was a preacher celebrated in various European lands, an influential diplomat, and a powerful courtier in Lisbon. The missionary vocation that he had felt as a young man still tugged at him, however, and he decided that northern Brazil was the place to exercise it. He reached Maranhão in 1653, and there proceeded to chastise the thousand or so white settlers of the north with sermons that seem to echo Antonio de Montesinos's excoriation of the citizens of Santo Domingo in 1511. On the first Sunday in Lent, 1653, he berated them thus:

> Christians, nobles, and people of Maranhão, do you know what God wants of you during this Lent? That you break the chains of injustice and let free those whom you have captive and oppressed. These are the sins of Maranhão; these are what God commanded me to denounce to you … All of you are in mortal sin; all of you live in a state of condemnation; and all of you are going directly to Hell. Indeed, many are there now and you will soon join them if you do not change your life.[85]

But he did not persuade them of their imminent perdition; nor that they should give up the labor of slaves and do the necessary physical work themselves. "It is better to live from your own sweat than from the blood of others."[86] But they thought not, and protested to the king about prevailing pro-Indian rulings. John IV thereupon gave new approval to slaving. Vieira saw no choice but to return to Portugal to lodge his protests in turn. The result was a temporizing decree in 1655 that gave the Jesuits charge over all native villages, and discretion to permit *entradas* to obtain slaves by *resgate*. Vieira in reality conceded that the combination of the north's poverty of resources with the ambitions of the settlers, largely Portuguese peasants, meant that some degree of native enslavement was inevitable. He granted that genuine *resgate* – the ransoming of Indians who were truly in danger of being killed by their native captors – was an admissible source of slaves, but strove to stop *resgate* from being used, as it long had been, as a blanket pretext for seizing all or any Indians.

His concessions did not, however, remove the tension between Jesuits and colonists, who still saw the mission presence as a threat to their access to labor. The intensity of the Jesuits' evangelizing efforts in the late 1650s only reinforced this feeling. Fifty-four *aldeias* were set up around the mouths of the Amazon, and filled with Indians persuaded to abandon their own communities along the shores of the rivers that flowed into the lower Amazon. But this exposed them to imported diseases, from which many died.

Finally, in 1661, the settlers' resentment exploded. The spark was perhaps provided by a severe epidemic of smallpox in Maranhão in 1660 that killed many natives, so shrinking still further the accessible labor supply. Settlers complained to the crown in January of 1661 of such penury that the daughters of "nobles" among them (those with most land, rather than title holders) had no suitable clothes to wear to Mass at Christmas.[87] In May of that year the citizens of São Luís revolted against the Jesuits. The settlers had the sympathy of other religious orders in the region, put in shadow by the Jesuits, and even of the governor, previously a backer of Vieira and his men. Vieira was confined, and with his fellows shipped back to Portugal. There his fortunes rose and fell erratically with political shifts in the court. But he never regained the authority he had held in the early 1650s. He later spent six years in Rome, confirming there in the pulpit his earlier European repute as a great preacher. In 1681 he returned to Brazil, where he persisted in the Indian cause until his death at a great age in 1697. He was never again, however, so influential a pro-native voice as before. The crown, inspired in part by his arguments, did once more forbid Indian slavery in 1680 and restored control of the northern *aldeias* to the Jesuits. But another rising by the settlers followed. The Society was again ousted. Vieira's strivings lived on mainly in the rules for running *aldeias* that he had created, and in the long term in his lasting fame as the chief champion of native interests active in colonial Brazil.

Jesuits, and smaller numbers of other missionaries, continued to minister to native people in the eighteenth century. In that century increasing numbers of non-Indians moved into Amazonia – soldiers exploring and setting up forts along the rivers, men traveling down the lower, southern tributaries of the Amazon to the new inland mining regions, collectors of spices, herbs, and other marketable products of the forest, missionaries, and, still, slave-raiders. For the numerous native groups of Amazonia, the effect of these growing incursions was almost entirely a continuation of the sorry tale of native Brazilians since the sixteenth century: flight, disease, and widespread death. People who had fled from the Atlantic coast in the 1500s and found refuge in forests as far away as the Andean foothills now suffered new pressures and attacks. They, and the multifarious original native groups of the forests, some-times welcomed missionaries as protectors, and sometimes attacked them. Some fought fiercely against incursive soldiers and civilians. Some, as from the beginning on the coast, joined in colonists' slaving expeditions to attack tradi-tional enemies. The Manao on the middle Rio Negro – whose name passed to the modern city of Manaos – were particularly enterprising slave traders, by 1720 supplying not only the Portuguese but also the Dutch on the north coast of South America in what is now Surinam (1,000 kilometers away).[88] Villages along great stretches of rivers' banks were depopulated and abandoned. In some cases, new people migrated down the rivers to occupy the now empty zones. In sum, the outcome was not simply loss of numbers, but loss of cul-tural variety – offset by complex recombinings of native lifeways.

GOVERNMENT AND ECONOMY IN THE SEVENTEENTH CENTURY

COLONIALS PURSUE THEIR INTERESTS

While Indians generally continued to suffer at the base of seventeenth- and eighteenth-century Brazilian society, the white segment of the population diversified in wealth and standing, as it did in Spanish America. The growth of towns provided an expanding range of opportunities for Brazilian-born and immigrant whites in crafts and in services such as small trading. In towns the possibility of social ascent through economic gain was probably greater than in the plantation-dominated countryside.

Particularly striking in the seventeenth-century history of Brazil's white population is the rise in political power of its upper end. As in the Spanish colonies, this clearly happened because of the increase, by 1600, of the number of locally born whites who had known nothing but Brazil, and also because of Portugal's difficulty, given such challenges as the union with Spain and the Dutch assaults in Asia, Africa, and Brazil, in administering Brazil as tightly as it might have desired.

As towns grew in size, the *câmara*, or municipal council, became a useful vehicle for the expression of colonials' wishes, likes, and dislikes. It was such councils in the north that sent protests to Lisbon about the Jesuits' activities. Aldermen and town magistrates were elected by local property holders, with the result, predictably enough, that members of *câmaras* everywhere in the colony tended to be men prominent in local economic affairs. In Bahia, for example, the councils were dominated by sugar planters and merchants. Since the crown depended for its colonial income on the prosperity of these leading groups, it had a political interest in heeding the wishes of town councils. This, together with the absence in Brazilian provinces of any powerful agencies of royal will to compare with the Spanish American *audiencias*, perhaps explains why these Brazilian councils seem to have had more political weight than their counterparts in the Spanish empire, the *cabildos*.

In the 1600s Brazilian colonials influenced government also by joining the bureaucracy in growing numbers, and at ever higher levels. By mid-century they held many of the mid-level posts that had previously been filled by European-born men, becoming "treasury officials, customs collectors, market inspectors, probate judges, scribes, and watchmen."[89] Such offices could be bought or inherited. Then in 1653 the barrier to the highest level of the judiciary was breached, with the appointment of the first Brazilian-born *desembargador*, Simão Alvares da Penha Deusdará. Alvares was the son of one Manoel Alvares da Penha, a leading citizen of Pernambuco during the time of the Dutch occupation, and a man who had given supplies to anti-Dutch forces there. This activity had brought him the nickname, subsequently added to the family name, of "Deusdará" ("God will give"), and a grateful king had granted him a title of nobility as well. The son's appointment to a judgeship in the high court at Salvador also probably followed from the father's patriotic services. The fact that he was the husband of a sister of Father Vieira, then at the height of his influence at court in Lisbon, can only have brought him further favor. This was the first of ten namings of colonial-born men as *desembargadores* before the mid 1700s.[90]

Even without Brazilians on the bench, however, leading colonials had, from early in the seventeenth century, close connections with the judges of the high court that gave them influence at the top of the colony's government. Despite rules to the contrary, the judges in the *relação*, like the *oidores* in Spanish American *audiencias*, were keen participants in the colonial economy. Some lent or borrowed money; some traded; some bought land. These and many other dealings inevitably created close ties with colonials, who used them to sway judgments in their favor. More personal links also developed from the start. Again ignoring regulations to the contrary, some *desembargadores* married into local families. Their high status and power made them desirable candidates for the hands of daughters of even the most prominent of colonial families; while the wealth of such families, and the potential that their local contacts offered for making money, made such alliances attractive to the judges, who were generally not rich. Almost a fifth (32 of 168) of the *desembargadores* appointed to the court at Salvador before 1759 married Brazilian women.[91] The children of such unions were well placed, in turn, for office and influence. Another strong family linkage was *compadrio*, or ritual co-parenthood, into which a person from outside the family might be drawn by acting as a marriage witness or a godparent. The connection was thought almost as close as a blood tie. High court judges were much sought after as *compadres*. And since a person might connect himself in this way to any number of families, the potential for locals' influence on government was even greater here than through matrimony.[92]

From the early 1600s, but especially after the mid-century, marriage ties developed between judges of the *relação* and some of the powerful and extended families, almost clans, that had become by then a salient feature of Brazilian society. Some of these families had branches in several regions of the colony, which they used for wide-reaching business and political purposes. The seventeenth-century extended family in Brazil has indeed been described as a corporation, in which the creation of wealth (and typically clannish feuding with other families) was seen as a collective rather than an individual enterprise.[93] One powerful northern family that linked itself early to the *relação* was that of the Cavalcanti de Albuquerque, who traced their descent in part from the sixteenth-century proprietary donees of Pernambuco, the Albuquerque Coelhos. A Cavalcanti daughter from Pernambuco married Manoel Pinto da Rocha, whose term as *desembargador* in Salvador began in 1609. Later in the century, three other judges in the high court married into the Cavalcanti, who in turn had marriage ties with other major families. Ownership of sugar estates was common in these groups. Judges also married the daughters, and sometimes the widows, of those other families. And so the supreme judicial body in the colony was extensively linked with the producers of Brazil's main export crop. This, broadly speaking, suited the interests of both crown and colonial leadership. The sugar barons, as they may perhaps be called, could count on the support of the high court in legal disputes, and the crown could thereby hope to promote the output of the product that was the prime source of fiscal income from Brazil. By modern standards, the judges' patterns of behavior – in marrying into local wealth and power, and in using their positions to advantage for private business and gain – were clearly corrupt. At the time they were acceptable if not taken to excess. By the early eighteenth century, the point of excess seems to have been reached, at least in the crown's perception. In the 1720s various judges were investigated for illicit business activities, and two actually removed from office. But the attempted reform was not harsh enough, or the temptations too strong. Later *desembargadores* continued to trade.[94]

The *relação* of Salvador was suspended between 1626 and 1652. Several reasons led to the removal of the court. The main one was the need to find funds to divert to defense after the initial wave of Dutch attacks in the early 1620s (which had, of course, resulted in the attackers' year-long occupation of

Salvador in 1624–5). After ordering the elimination of the court early in 1626, Philip IV of Spain reassigned the salaries paid to its staff to the town's garrison.[95] But local opinion also played a large part in the matter. In the *Dialogues of the Great Things of Brazil* (c.1618) attributed to Ambrosio Fernandes Brandão, a well-to-do sugar planter and trader of Pernambuco and Paraíba, the author's spokesman, Brandônio, criticizes the *relação* on several grounds: its expense, its inaccessibility from distant parts of the settled coast (and the resulting expense of litigation for many parties), its slowness in dealing with business, and lastly its simple superfluousness, since most disputes were resolved privately before reaching the high court level. These were quite specific and practical complaints, doubtless justified in some instances. More generally it is clear that leading colonials, often speaking through the *câmaras*, objected to what they saw as encroaching royal centralism in the presence of the high court. The Albuquerque Coelhos of Pernambuco, for instance, the wealthy descendants of the first donee of that captaincy, still tried to run it as their own domain, and resented the availability of the high court to those who wished to raise objections to their administration. There was here, also, an element of simple regional contention between Brazil's most prosperous area, Pernambuco, and the center of its royal government, Salvador. From influential colonials in Brazil, then, there sounded no voice defending the *relação* when the king decided to remove it in 1626; indeed, persuasive evidence exists that their complaints about the court contributed to Philip IV's decision.[96]

With the *relação* gone, the *ouvidor geral* again became the highest source of justice in Brazil. A separate position of *ouvidor* had already been created for the southern captaincies, and this judge remained in place. The removal of the high court, however, while an economy for the crown, did nothing to make colonials' access to justice simpler or cheaper; quite the opposite, in fact, since the final court of appeal was now in Lisbon, and crossing the Atlantic was dangerous and slow while the war between Spain and the Dutch lasted. And so, reversing its opinion completely, the *câmara* of Salvador began in the early 1640s to argue that the court should be reinstated. In 1652 Lisbon finally heeded the town council's repeated requests. In March of 1653 new judges took their places in Salvador.

And so, once again, weighty colonials had shown the influence they could exert in the government of Brazil. And now, indeed, after the expulsion of the Dutch from Brazil mostly through home-grown effort, colonials found the restored Portuguese crown willing to give them a larger say than before in their own affairs. Among the new judges in 1653 was Simão Alvares da Penha, from Pernambuco. The next year, a second Brazilian, Cristóvão de Burgos, a prosperous and well-connected Bahian, was raised to the bench.[97] These high appointments were a natural culmination of the movement of colonial-born men into the governing bureaucracy's lower strata that had been advancing throughout the century. And while that movement has several possible explanations, its central impetus was simply the growing number of American-born men of influence in Brazil. Especially with the growth of the great extended families, the reality of white Brazilians' local political weight could not be ignored. The colonials'

Table 13.1   Sugar exports, 1627–1670

Year	Amount	
	arrobas	kilograms (million)
1627 or 1628	900,000	13.2
1643	1,200,000	17.6
1650	2,100,000	30.9
1670	2,000,000	29.4

success in driving out the Dutch served simply to sharpen the point. And so, from exercising influence on officials through ties of kinship and business, the colonial elite now advanced to direct action at the highest levels of government. As with the Spanish American creoles after 1600, there was no stopping Brazilian whites from gaining a large say in their own government.

PRODUCTION: SUGAR ABOVE ALL

Underlying the political advance of the colonials in the seventeenth century, in some measure, was certainly the more central economic role in the Portuguese empire that Brazil acquired as a result of the Dutch attacks in Africa and the Orient. Its economic weight continued to lie in sugar. The trend of sugar exports (which differs little from the production trend) seems clearly to have been upward from the beginning of the century until the late 1670s. Annual exports from 1600 to 1620 averaged in the 800,000 *arroba* range (11.75 million kilograms). After this, every available estimate is higher than that average, though the estimates are regrettably few (table 13.1).

Supporting these large exports were steady or rising prices of sugar in European markets until almost 1660. Naturally the upward trend of exports had its interruptions: weather and wars took their toll. Within Brazil an important geographical shift in production occurred. The Dutch occupation of Pernambuco cost that captaincy its lead in output. Some 60 percent of Brazilian sugar was Pernambuco-grown *c.*1600, but only 10 percent fifty years later. Many Pernambucan planters fled with their slaves and money to Bahia during the 1630s, with the result that Bahia then became, and from then remained, Brazil's prime sugar region. By 1660 European prices of sugar were starting to soften, under the influence of the rapidly expanding sugar production of the Caribbean islands. Up to then the possibility of holding back exports had given Brazilian growers some control over the European price.[98] Now other suppliers would step in to fill any gap. And so Brazil, after a century as, in essence, the monopoly supplier of sugar to Europe, found itself in the uncomfortable position of being at the mercy of the external market in which its major product was sold. It is a position that many other producers of primary products have had to endure since then. But Brazil, having had the distinction of being the first large region in the world to produce plentifully on tropical plantations, now also became notable as the first major primary producer to become dependent on external economic conditions on which it had minimal influence. Still, European demand for sugar continued strong, and the Caribbean producers were subject to the same sorts of natural and humanly caused difficulties as affected Brazil. And so, always with fluctuations, Brazilian sugar sales to Europe remained high in the eighteenth century.

Brazil sold other products of the land in the seventeenth century, though none approached sugar in value. The multiplication of cattle in the interior meant that the colony became self-sufficient in leather and meat about 1640. Having previously imported hides and salt meat, it gradually began to export at least leather. In the first decade of the eighteenth century, Brazil sent some 110,000 hides yearly to Lisbon (50,000 from Bahia, 40,000 from Pernambuco, and 20,000 from Rio de Janeiro and other southern places); much leather, though, was worth barely 2 percent of the yearly sugar export of the period.[99] Spices, also, were to be found in the interior forests, especially once Maranhão was settled and became a base for upriver exploration. Types of pepper, clove, and cinnamon grew wild. The main exportable spice, however, was ginger, which was smuggled from Brazil into northern Europe in the early 1600s. Its cultivation in Brazil was encouraged by royal decree in the 1640s. For another forest product, dyewood, European demand continued, and so exports also. The largest export from the land, however – besides sugar – was tobacco. The plant was native to Brazil. The leaf entered Portugal from the colony before 1550, and was considered a medicine, good for toothache, asthma, and indigestion. Its pleasurable qualities were soon also appreciated. In the seventeenth century Brazil became the largest producer, and the first large producer, of tobacco in the world. The growing areas were Bahia and Pernambuco, and then Maranhão, of which it was the sole exportable product of high value. In an effort to take full advantage of this, the Maranhão settlers petitioned in 1637 that foreign tobacco should be excluded from Portugal. Tobacco's profitability was such that in 1639 the town council of Salvador forbade its planting for fear that insufficient land would be available to grow food for the local population. In the second half of the century, tobacco was often the means of payment for slaves in Africa.[100]

SHIPS AND TRADE

Aside from standard craft goods, Brazil produced little in the way of manufactures. The sole important exception was ships. Bahia was the main center for this, with a yard set up in the final years of the sixteenth century. The local supply of wood for hulls and masts was abundant; there were local resins and cotton for caulking; black slave labor was at hand; skilled iron workers could be found on the sugar *engenhos* (though the iron itself was imported from Europe). In 1650 the crown ordered the building of one 700–800-ton galleon a year at Bahia. A vessel of 1,000 tons was laid down in 1659. These were very large ships for their day.[101] Shipyards came to exist also in Pernambuco, and, after 1650, at Rio de Janeiro and on the Paraíba coast in the extreme north-east.

Brazilian-built ships were used in the transatlantic trade. They also carried goods along the South American coast, where for much of the seventeenth century a frequent destination was Buenos Aires. During the union of crowns, Spain gave the Portuguese the advantage of lowered barriers to the markets of the American empire, and Brazilian ports then became lively entrepôts for the transmission of sugar, European goods, and African slaves into southern Spanish America. Silver from the Andean mines paid for these imports. After Portugal departed from the union in 1640, that trade continued as contraband (in which Europeans, notably the Dutch, participated as well as Brazilian merchants). Late in the century Buenos Aires ceased to be the target of Brazilian merchants. The colony's southward expansion had by then advanced so far that in 1682 a Portuguese town could be founded on the north shore of the Río de la Plata, 60 kilometers north-east across the estuary from Buenos Aires. This was Colônia do Sacramento, which as a point of infiltration of alien goods into Spanish America was to be a thorn in the Spanish side for almost a century. Only in 1778, by the Treaty of San Ildefonso that fixed the southern boundaries of Brazil close to their present position, did Portugal finally yield Colônia to Spain.[102]

Like Brazil, Buenos Aires had the advantage (or in the official Spanish view, the drawback) of being on the Atlantic, and was therefore easily accessible to ships and nations trading in that ocean. With few exceptions, such as concessions to the Portuguese after 1580, the Spanish colonial administration, aiming to reserve Spanish America commercially for the home country alone, tried to counteract that natural advantage with exclusionary rules that banned foreign entry into Buenos Aires. (Smugglers, local settlers, and often enough even officials took little notice, it is true.) By contrast, Portuguese policymakers generally accepted that geography was destiny, and in general produced a trading policy far less rigid than the Spaniards'. This is most clearly shown in the absence, in the Portuguese case, of a fleet system designed as the sole carrier of goods to and from Brazil. Despite some attempts at organizing convoys in the sixteenth century for protection of shipping, Portuguese merchants, then and after 1600, preferred to entrust their goods and fortune to large numbers of caravels sailing independently. The loss of one such small ship was not overwhelming. Only in the late 1640s, after drastic losses of ships to the Dutch during the contest for north-eastern Brazil, did the Portuguese crown, partly at the urging of Father Vieira, finally go about providing naval defense by chartering a trading company. This, the General Brazil Trading Company (Companhia Geral do Comércio do Brasil), founded in 1649, was to be the sole supplier to Brazil of four foodstuffs basic to the Portuguese diet: wine, oil, flour, and salt cod. On exports from Brazil it could charge duties. To secure the company's monopoly, in the future only a few ports would be open for transatlantic trade: Lisbon and Oporto in Portugal, and Recife, Salvador, and Rio de Janeiro in the colony. The price to the company of its privileges was the provision, within two years, of 36 warships, each with 20 to 30 cannon and a full complement of sailors and soldiers. These ships were to escort trading convoys across the Atlantic. The company was funded with private investments, mostly from merchants in Lisbon who were "New Christians" (that is, Jews who had converted to Christianity); but, in another example of Portuguese openness, shares were offered in Amsterdam, Paris, and Venice.

The company had mixed success for rather a short time. Its first defended fleet left Lisbon in December 1649. Its warships helped to weaken the Dutch hold in Brazil in the early 1650s. But there were difficulties in raising the intended capital, despite pressure on the New Christian subscribers. Never did all thirty-six ships appear. Complaints came, as was to be expected, from merchants and shipowners in ports excluded from the Brazil trade. And so, as early as 1654, ships were again allowed to sail without convoy, provided they did not leave from Lisbon or carry goods covered by the monopoly. The company soon proved, however, a poor supplier of those monopoly items. Hence, in 1658, the crown abolished its monopoly, and at the same time reduced to ten the number of warships to be provided. In 1664 the governing nine-man council was disbanded; the running of the enterprise passed to the crown. In 1694 the government appropriated the company's funds, compensating shareholders with bonds in the royal tobacco monopoly. In 1720 the General Brazil Trading Company was abolished.[103]

The institution of the company did, however, make the escorted trading fleet a permanent feature of Portuguese transatlantic commerce. But, as the exception granted in 1654 shows, independent sailings still continued. Such ships were probably more numerous than those in the fleets. And smuggling, though impossible to quantify, also persisted, doubtless energized, in fact, by the attempts to regulate the trade more tightly. Many in Brazil, including lower officialdom, stood to gain through contraband. Portuguese smugglers, then, and Englishmen and others arrived with little hindrance in Brazil to sell and buy.[104]

The scant success of the Brazil Company in the long term is a further demonstration of Brazil's easy accessibility to all maritime nations with Atlantic shores. That accessibility may help account for various distinctive features of Brazilian economic life in the seventeenth century. One is the lack, relative to the Spanish colonies, of economic diversification. The directness of Brazil's contact with Europe, and hence its low cost, made the supplying of European manufactures cheap, and therefore weakened incentives to produce them in Brazil itself. Similarly, the sparsity, in comparison with Spanish America, of internal trade and the resulting absence of inland trade networks (apart from cattle drives from around 1700 onwards), reflects the ease with which ships could reach the regions where demand existed. (The nature of Brazilian colonization before the eighteenth century was of course perhaps an even larger influence here. The economic geography of sugar-growing meant that population was densest near the coast.) Third, accessibility may have promoted the robustness that the Brazilian economy seems to show in the seventeenth century. Trade to and from Brazil was largely free of the inefficiencies of the fleet system of the Carrera de Indias, and the associated costs (the high taxes, for example, levied to pay for escort vessels), that burdened Spanish American commerce. That advantage can only have helped stimulate production in Brazil.

One of the most remarkable qualities of seventeenth-century Brazil is pre-cisely its freedom from almost any hint of economic depression – and this in a period when much of Europe suffered at a minimum decades of difficulties, and for which the economic vitality of large parts of Spanish America is at least debatable. Only after about 1670 did Brazil, apparently, feel any economic pinch, after losing its place as sole major supplier of sugar to Europe. Clearly its well-being up to then owed much to the sustained demand for sugar that even the war-torn and plague-ridden Europe of the seventeenth century could offer. And Brazil escaped in good part the problem of the growing shortage and rising cost of labor that the disastrous post-conquest collapse of native population presented to Spanish America. Native Brazilians, of course, also died from the imported diseases, and the numbers of them available for work also fell as they fled inland. But Brazilian natives were never so valuable as workers as the Indians of the main areas of Spanish settlement, lacking as they did most of the skills and also the familiarity with labor organization possessed by the natives of the central Andes and central Mexico. Hence, in crude eco-nomic terms, the loss of native labor was less severe a blow for the Portuguese than it was for the Spaniards. More telling still, though, was that the Portuguese were so easily able to make up the loss with African slaves. Again Brazil's geo-graphical position was an immense help. It was closer to the African sources of slaves than any part of Spanish America. Further, the Portuguese already had long experience as slave buyers in Africa, and had established bases there pre-cisely for that purpose. So powerful were these circumstances that Brazil would most probably have become a land largely of whites and Africans even had its native people not so severely declined.

THE AGE OF GOLD

SHIFTS OF PEOPLE AND POWER

With the discovery of plentiful gold at the end of the century, Brazil regained whatever economic momentum it had lost as a result of increasing Caribbean competition in sugar production. Indeed, the outcomes of the gold strikes were more than merely economic. Most aspects of the colony's life felt gold's influence. The demographic effects appeared almost immediately. As news spread of the finds made in what was to become Minas Gerais, hopeful pros-pectors began to arrive. The first came from the Brazilian coast. Then the lure of gold began to draw men from the Azores, Madeira, and Portugal. Once again little record exists of numbers; but in the 1740s some 1,500 a year may have left Portugal for Brazil.[105] The exodus was large enough to cause worries that a decline in Portugal's population and economy might follow.

Africa also felt the effects of the gold boom. The suddenly louder call for labor increased the already rising import of black slaves into Brazil, and for the more than half-century that the boom lasted, the heavy work of washing for gold consumed much of the increased supply of Africans. Up to 1650 Brazil is thought to have received 250,000 slaves from Africa. Between 1650 and 1820 the enormously larger number of 3,760,000 were landed (80 percent of them from central Africa).[106] Many of the swelling numbers who arrived between 1700 and 1760 quickly found themselves in Minas Gerais or some other mining zone, spending their days peering into gravel and sand for the glint of particles of gold.. By 1715 or so, Minas Gerais had 30,000 black slaves. Despite the rising import of slaves, colonists on the coast were acutely worried about the movement of blacks from coastal plantations into the mining zones. The plantations suffered double damage: loss of hands, and a rise in price of newly imported slaves caused by the miners' avid demand for workers.

Whether black or white, almost all the newcomers to the mining interior were male. Very few miners, and even fewer slaves, were married. Such unions as existed were informal. Not surprisingly, the few female slaves in the region served primarily as "sexual servants for male owners."[107] In addition, slave and free black women engaged in a variety of informal relationships. Since white colonials also consorted eagerly in such arrangements with black and mulata women, the mining towns were places of unusually rapid ethnic mixing. Moreover, because many of the whites who fathered children with black women were bachelors, they often had no other heirs. This may have motivated the common mining-town pattern of white bachelors manumitting and acknowledging as heirs the children born of their female slaves – sometimes while keeping their heirs' mother in servitude. Between 1725 and 1808, almost two-thirds of the bachelor colonists in the town of Sabará named children as heirs; the mothers of these children who were named were all current or former slaves.[108] Over time, this created a distinct slaveholding culture in Minas Gerais. By 1805, two-thirds of free persons were non-white; free persons of color and means often owned slaves themselves.[109]

Inland towns were the most lasting result of the gold boom. In areas where previously barely a hut could be found, substantial towns quickly developed. Minas Gerais had eight before 1718. One of the first was Vila Rica do Ouro Prêto. Today Ouro Prêto (Black Gold) is still very much in place, and has come to stand as the representative symbol of the gold era. In Goiás and Mato Grosso, where mining developed a little later than in Minas and was never so productive, fewer towns were founded.[110] But at least two, Vila Boa de Goiás in Goiás and Cuiabá in Mato Grosso, still stand. In Brazil, as in Spanish America, even infant mining centers were often far more than mere encampments. In both colonial systems these new places were generally set down in remote and previously deserted areas. They necessarily and immediately became centers of government and justice, and as such they quickly took on formal urban traits.

The building of towns and the influx of thousands of newcomers inevitably impinged on the native peoples of the interior. Most Indians had already disappeared from the initial gold area of Minas Gerais around the headwaters of the Velhas river. But prospectors pushing further west ran into native resistance, some of it distinctly fierce. Those traveling from São Paulo to Mato Grosso in the canoes of the eighteenth-century monsoons were likely to be attacked along the rivers by swift and able warriors from various tribes.

The Guaicurú of the Chaco, for example, had mastered the wild horses of their region; intruders could do little against them. Such resistance clearly slowed access to the gold fields that lay deepest in the interior. But it did not block it. On the other hand, attempts to put Indians to mining work were rarely successful for long, although they were destructive while they lasted.[111]

In the strict sense of underground work, there was little mining in Brazil. Only in Jacobina, in inland Bahia, was tunneling into veins the usual form of extraction. In Minas Gerais vein-working was rare. There, and further west, washing of gold-bearing sands and gravels on the surface was what "mining" meant. The dangers of darkness, airlessness, and collapsing roofs and ladders typical of Spanish American silver mining were largely unknown in Brazil. But the work was still hard and bad for the health. Slaves, and the occasional whites to be found physically laboring, shoveled and bent for long hours, sweating in the sun but with legs and feet chilled by the water in which they generally stood. One physician of the time observed that the contrast laid the workers open to "very severe pleurisies, apoplectic and paralytic fits, convulsions, pneumonia, and many other diseases."[112] Washing did not consist simply of digging up stream beds and panning material in wooden bowls. Where possible, dams and channels were used to divert water from streams and rivers so that it flowed over promising strata, washing gold particles (or diamonds) free. This hydraulic work was arduous; and dams were known to break. Slaves were expected to last as useful workers for only seven to twelve years.

The swelling mine populations of the interior took a good deal of feeding, and of supplying in general. Their demand for foods and other goods had a broadly invigorating effect on many types of Brazilian production. The cattle raisers of Maranhão, the north-east, and then of the south, responded readily to the stimulus, sending off great numbers of cattle on the hoof, and quantities of salt beef. Live cattle also carried their hides with them; and leather had multiple uses in gold extraction and in everyday life in the mining towns. Coastal sugar growers were presented with a new internal market for their product, and both artisans and importing traders in the coastal towns found new selling opportunities. Quickly enough, of course, the mining areas began to produce for their own needs. Around the mining centers, and along to routes to them, estates and farms appeared, raising cattle, smaller domestic animals, and foods such as the ubiquitous manioc. But local production never filled local needs. One result for the coast, at least in the early mining years, was inflation, not merely of the price of slaves, but of many goods, foods included. Producers gained, but consumers suffered. The crown's early response was to try banning trade and communication between Bahia and Minas Gerais, and even forbidding the making of roads linking the two regions. But trade could not be stopped. The motive of profit was reinforced, as in similar Spanish American situations, by the fact that what the miners offered in trade – gold – was itself money. Sellers got gold in hand; they needed to make no further exchanges or sales to realize their gains.[113] And so the mining region, particularly Minas Gerais itself, became a powerful force for the economic articulation of a vast area of Brazil, just as the silver mines of the Potosí district had been in the central Andes, a century or more before, 2,300 kilometers away to the west.

Just how much gold Brazil produced is hard to say for sure. The crown charged a royalty of a fifth on production; but collecting that tax in the frontier-like conditions of inland Brazil was no simple matter. Hence tax receipts are a poor guide to output. A substance so compact in value was easily hidden and carried away, no matter what efforts the government might make to seal off the mining zones and control trade. Cattle drovers and other traders who knew the terrain well could spirit gold to the coast with little difficulty. There, in a variety of ships – naval and commercial, Portuguese and foreign – amateur and professional merchants stood ready to bear it away, openly or hidden, for profitable exchange in Europe or west Africa. The scale of smuggling is suggested by the contrast between two sets of figures, one for production in Brazil and the other for arrivals of Brazilian gold in Europe. The first gives total output from 1711 to 1769 as 129,830 kilograms. (Of that amount, Minas Gerais yielded 96,250 kilograms, or 74 percent.) By the second set, 619,000–639,000 kilograms reached Europe between 1711 and 1770.[114] Perhaps historians' research will reveal how Brazil managed to send to Europe almost five times more silver than it produced. For the moment it seems safe to say that the production figures given here certainly understate reality, and that arrivals may have been exaggerated. A large margin of contraband gold remains. A lesser contrast between the two sets of figures is in timing. Arrivals in Europe were at their highest level in the decade 1726–35, while production is shown as peaking from 1735 to 1744. It seems safe to infer that Brazilian gold production was at its height c.1720–45.

If much gold slipped through the tax-collecting net, it was not for lack of effort by the government. Many new officials were appointed to the mining zones, and were charged, among other things, with applying a new mining code written between 1700 and 1703. At least three foundries were set up in major mining towns after 1720, to which miners were to bring their gold to pay the royalty and have the rest cast into ingots bearing the royal arms. These fiscal innovations were only one side of the administrative response to the growth of mining. New judicial districts and local courts appeared. Militia companies were often raised to enforce law in the backlands, patrol for smugglers, and deal with the occasional disorders that arose in towns as, for example, miners protested against taxes. On a larger scale, first the captaincy of Minas Gerais was created in 1720, to be followed by those of Goiás and Mato Grosso (areas that were previously inland sections of the São Paulo captaincy) in 1744 and 1748. In 1752 came the very large innovation of the creation of a second Brazilian *relação*. It was sited at Rio de Janeiro to give people in the mining region, and others in the center and south, relatively quick and economical access to a court of appeal. Finally, eleven years later, arrived the most telling change of all with the raising of Rio, in place of Salvador, to the position of administrative capital of the colony. The official view now was that the success of gold-mining, and the expansion of other production connected to mining, had shifted Brazil's economic and demographic center of gravity from the north-east to the center-south. That was now also where the weight of government must be. Henceforth the colony's chief executive (the post had been upgraded in 1720 from governorship general to viceroyalty) officiated from Rio. And Rio remained the capital of Brazil after independence until 1960, when the new city of Brasília, purpose-built for that role, assumed it.

Rio's rise to pre-eminence actually took place after the decline of gold-mining had begun. The city's elevation did not, however, prove harmful or inappropriate, since the economy of the center and south, after a brief hiatus, again flourished with a resurgence of coastal agriculture. Gold output fell in mid-century, fundamentally because the most accessible placer deposits were by then depleted. To tackle others would have required larger hydraulic efforts (longer diversions of water courses, for instance) than had ever been attempted in Brazil. And for that neither the necessary capital nor entrepreneurial will, or probably skill, seem to have been present.[115]

ECONOMIC RESILIENCE AFTER THE GOLD BOOM

The end of the mining boom in the mid-century left both Brazil and Portugal in the economic doldrums for a time. For Portugal, indeed, that is an under-statement. Over the half-century of Brazilian mining, Portugal had grown to depend on the constant inflow of gold, and of diamonds, to balance its foreign trade. Especially in need of balancing was the trade with Portugal's main commercial partner, Great Britain. Long-standing trading patterns between the two countries had been reinforced in 1703 by the Methuen Treaty, which gave preferential tariff treatment to imports of British wheat, cloth and other manu-factures into Portugal, and to imports of Portuguese wine and olive oil into Britain. The negative effects of this agreement for Portugal, in discouraging industrial development there and in making the country dependent on Britain for manufactured goods, have become a commonplace. Part of the responsi-bility, however, must lie with the products of the Brazilian mines; since, with gold and diamonds to offer in payment, it was simpler for Portugal to import than to produce. Whatever the allocation of blame, if such it be, it is plain that from 1700 to 1750 Portuguese purchases from Britain were enormously larger than sales to Britain: by one estimate, 8,737,000 pounds' worth of imports against 3,209,000 pounds' worth of exports. Brazilian gold and diamonds made up most of the difference. With these in dwindling supply after the mid-century, overseas trade necessarily had to adjust severely; and not only trade, in fact, since a good part of the crown's income came directly or indirectly from gold and diamonds. The solution to these problems was a combination of what in modern terms would be called "import substitution industrialization," applied from the 1760s onwards, together with reinvigoration of Portugal's system of foreign trade. Partly through governmental effort (in, for example, granting loans) and partly through private initiative, Portugal built factories, most of them small, to produce the mainly luxury goods that had previously come in from abroad. Exports of wine and oil continued; to them were added re-exports of Brazilian plantation products, in rapidly growing quantities. And thus the deficit with Britain shrank in the 1770s and 1780s. In the 1790s Portugal actually achieved a surplus in its British trade.[116]

Brazil filled the gap left by the shrinkage of mineral exports by turning back to the land; or more exactly, to the plantation agriculture along the coast that had created such wealth in the century from 1550 to 1650. Sugar remained the most valuable crop and export. But the difference from that earlier period was that plantation owners now found large profits in other tropical crops. This diversification only reinforced Brazil's primary identity as a tropical plantation colony.

The effects of persistent warfare of the late eighteenth century did much to revitalize Brazilian sugar, making it once more the economic backbone of the colony. The Seven Years War (1756–63) brought conflict to the Caribbean. The resulting interruption of sugar supplies from the islands drove up European prices, much to the benefit of Brazilian planters. Prices sank again after 1763, however; and it was not until the War of American Independence (1775–83) that a new rise began. What finally guaranteed a lasting buoyancy in the price was the slave revolt in Saint Domingue in 1791. That French colony had long been the prime producer of sugar in the Caribbean. With the near-disappearance of that source, supply fell sharply below European demand, bringing gain to the remaining producers, the Brazilian planters among them. A rush of *engenho*-building followed. Bahian production began an expansion that continued until the 1840s. Pernambuco, the other old sugar center, thrived too. And in the middle south Rio de Janeiro and São Paulo became major growers and exporters.[117]

Tobacco was another lively export in the late 1700s. It grew widely in the north and north-east, but above all in Bahia, which provided over 90 percent of the commercial crop. Exports possibly doubled from the 1750s to the 1780s, again in response to rising European prices. Italy, Germany, Spain and France received Brazil's better-quality tobacco, mostly via Portugal. The poorer leaf stayed in Brazil, or was sent, as had long been the case, to Africa to be exchanged for slaves.

Four other plantation crops prospered in the economic conditions of the late eighteenth century. Cotton was first exported in the 1760s. Maranhão was the main growing area until 1800, though the crop spread to other parts of the north coast, and also to the north-east. After 1800 the north-east, especially Pernambuco, took the lead in cotton. Simplicity of cultivation, good quality, and strength of price resulting from the growing mechanization of textile-making in Britain and France, underlay cotton's success. Like tobacco, and sugar as well, cotton reached its final European markets mostly as a re-export from Portugal. By 1792 Brazil was the source of 30 percent of the cotton fiber that British mills spun and wove.

Three foodstuffs complete the list of agricultural exports. Rice first left Maranhão for Portugal in the 1760s. By 1781 enough was being shipped to replace the home country's previous imports (mainly from South Carolina). Cacao, almost all from Pará on the north coast, prospered particularly in the decade after 1800, finding profitable markets in Portugal, and via Portugal in

Table 13.2   Growth of coastal towns

Town	Year	Population
Belém	1749	6,574
	1801	12,500
Recife	1750	7,000
	1810	25,000
Salvador	1757	35,922
	1807	51,000
Rio de Janeiro	1760	30,000
	1803	46,944
São Paulo	1765	20,873
	1803	24,311

various European countries. Lastly, there began the rising trend of coffee exports that, in the nineteenth century, was to reach such heights that the crop became almost synonymous with Brazil. Portugal began importing coffee in the 1730s, from Belém in the north. But it was only with the spread of cultivation further southwards – to Pernambuco, Bahia, Rio, Minas Gerais, and São Paulo – between 1760 and 1800 that the plant found its true homes in Brazil. In 1807 the export of coffee reached some 1.5 million kilograms, seven times more than a decade before. By then Brazilian coffee could be drunk throughout western Europe, and from Moscow to north-west Africa.[118]

If rice, cacao, sugar, and coffee lacked the glamour of gold, they were in the long run much more valuable to Brazil. Gold was still being exported early in the nineteenth century. But in 1796 it made up only 17 percent of total exports (to Portugal), and in 1806 a mere 6.6 percent, while at those two dates the four foodstuffs amounted to 51 and 46 percent of all exports. Cotton was the next most valuable product sent to Portugal. Secondary effects of the great shifts in productive lines that Brazil experienced after the 1750s were quick to appear. Naturally enough, as mining subsided, so did the flow of people inland. In fact the flow stopped and may have reversed. The town of Ouro Prêto, for example, had some 20,000 citizens in the 1740s, but only about 7,000 in 1804. Fewer people ate less, so that the farming and stock-raising base that had developed around mining now contracted. At the same time, new labor demand and economic opportunities arose on the coast with the resurgence and diversification of agriculture. Coastal towns grew, as the examples in table 13.2 show.

Demographically, indeed, Brazil reverted considerably to its pre-mining contours in the late 1700s. The head counts of the population that reforming administrations, seeking higher tax income, now finally began to make show that *c.*1800 about 73 percent lived near the coast, most of them in and around the long-standing major ports of Paraíba, Pernambuco, Bahia, and Rio de Janeiro. The most heavily peopled coastal captaincy was Pernambuco, with 19 percent of the total population. It seems at first contradictory, given the near-demise of gold, that Minas Gerais, at that date, led all captaincies in numbers of people, with 19.7 percent of the total. That figure, however, reflects the success of Minas's conversion by the end of the century to plantation agriculture, particularly in sugar and coffee. The total population of Brazil as the nineteenth century began was between 2 and 3 million. It had grown between 2.5 and 4 times over the previous century.[119]

The fundamental reason for Brazil's success as an agricultural exporter in the late 1700s was rising demand for its crops in European countries that were experiencing population growth and early industrialization. But policy also had a part in the colony's agricultural boom. Authorities in Lisbon drafted and applied stimulatory measures. These, it is true, were conceived largely with the benefit of Portugal itself in mind. But thanks to the developing economic reality of which Portugal and Brazil were a part, some of those plans had expansionary effects that spread beyond the mother country.

POMBAL AND REFORM

Serious efforts at economic reform began during the period when Portugal was governed by Sebastião José de Carvalho e Melo, better known as the marquis of Pombal (a title bestowed in 1769). For almost the entire reign of Joseph I of Portugal (1750–77), Pombal was secretary of state and of foreign affairs. The contrast between his own concentrated energy and the indolence of the king left him as an almost autonomous first minister of the realm and the empire, an aristocratic exponent of a despotism that in most of its applications did not stray far from enlightenment.

Pombal had great and comprehensive schemes for the economic restoration of Portugal, an undertaking that became ever more necessary as the inflow of gold from Brazil dwindled. The devastation of Lisbon by a great earthquake in 1755 added urgency to this need. A third of the city collapsed on November 1 of that year, including its administrative and business center; and 15,000 or more died in the falling buildings, or in the subsequent flood and fire.[120] It was as master of the city's rebuilding that Pombal first gained almost limitless power. The outcome was the elegant, open, geometrically regular city that still exists, a monument to enlightened orderliness.

A French visitor to Lisbon shortly before the earthquake noted in his journal "[Portugal] is more of a province than a kingdom. One might say that the King of Portugal is a potentate of the Indies that lodges in a European land."[121] In hindsight the comment seems remarkably prescient, though it is unlikely that its author lived long enough to know of the move to Rio de Janeiro that the Portuguese court was to make in 1807–8. It was also, especially in the economic sense, an accurate assessment of Portugal's position in the empire. Pombal set out to change that position, or at least to modify it to Portugal's advantage.

Broadly seen, Pombal's design for the empire resembled what reform-minded political economists had by then already proposed in Spain: that the colonies' central task was to serve the interests of the metropolis by producing raw materials needed for manufacturing in the home country, and then by providing a market for what was manufactured. To expand manufacture in Portugal Pombal created in 1755 a Junta do Comércio, or Board of Trade, to set up workshops and factories, import foreign craftsmen, provide loans, and oversee production. He was keen that both large factories, and smaller workshops supplying them with partly finished items, should prosper. And indeed they did, producing a wide range of cloth and leather goods, clocks and watches, glassware and hardware, and sundry luxury items, from the 1760s until after 1800. Private effort responded well to governmental encouragement, and thus home-made goods displaced much that had previously been imported into both Portugal itself and the colonies (above all Brazil) from foreign sources (notably Great Britain).[122]

For the profitable and efficient working of the trade link between Portugal and Brazil, the main source of useful raw materials, Pombal also produced a set of reforms. In his view, only large and well-capitalized merchant houses could compete with the British traders who dominated Anglo-Portuguese commerce (and also sent large contraband cargoes to Brazil). He actively suppressed small traders, whom he saw as weak, inefficient, and not least as collaborators with the British in smuggling. The government-created Board of Trade of 1755, indeed, replaced an old corporation of Lisbon merchants, which was abolished. In that same year Pombal's government chartered a company designed to trade with, and develop, Pará and Maranhão in the north of Brazil. Anticipating later Spanish reformers of American silver-mining, who gave social rewards, such as titles of nobility, to successful entrepreneurs, Pombal encouraged investment in this and other companies by offering membership of military orders and chances of ennoblement to prospective shareholders.[123] His aim was to dispel the social disrepute that still tainted commerce. A second Brazilian company was formed in 1759, created to trade with Pernambuco and Paraíba. Like the Maranhão company, one of its tasks was to supply adequate labor, in the form of African slaves, to its appointed region. The companies were, broadly speaking, corporations for development, charged with experimenting with new crops and farming methods, advancing shipbuilding and navigation, and regulating production so as to stabilize the selling price of tropical crops. They were buyers of the products of their regions, and monopoly sellers of imports from Portugal, for which they were to open up markets. Generally speaking, the companies seem to have fulfilled their developmental aims, by, for instance, promoting in their areas trials of new crops which then were exported profitably from Brazil. They operated, of course, in times when demand for such crops was rising, so that the degree to which their efforts truly propelled development is hard to say. The fact that they did not long survive Pombal, being abolished in 1778–9, may suggest that they were not as useful as he had hoped, or perhaps simply that they had done their job by then. In any case, the post-Pombaline government bent to the wishes of merchants in Portugal, and merchants and planters in Brazil, all of whom objected to the companies' control of prices, especially those of slaves.[124] Under the free trade between Portugal and Brazil that then resumed, plantation exports continued their vigorous growth.

Pombal did not stop at economic reform, in either Portugal or the empire, although all his innovating aimed to bring economic gain to Portugal. Like Gálvez and others in Spain, he sought to achieve this through tighter control by colonial government, a gathering up of the reins of power. The number of officials in Brazil was already rising when he came into office, and he added more. In 1767 an improved treasury structure was put in place, after similar reforms in Portugal itself in 1761. In the 1760s also, the colonial militia was upgraded, in part by the importation of English and German officers to train it.[125] Naturally, not all changes were fully effective; but the net result was to narrow colonials' margin of self-determination, and to make the state a more palpably intrusive presence in Brazil.

Some of Pombal's reforms managed to combine enlightened modernity with practical gain. His abolition of slavery in Portugal in 1761 seemed a humanitarian measure; but it left more slaves available for Brazil. In the mid and late 1750s he asserted once again the freedom of Brazilian Indians. He went further than merely ending native slavery, however; he favored removing all distinctions between Indians and whites. The goal seems admirable, if impossibly idealistic; but Pombal had a very practical outcome in mind. He hoped that a decreed social equalizing of American natives and Europeans would promote marriages between them (which he saw as entirely honorable) and hence quicken population growth in Brazil. It seemed to him that the colony was underpeopled, and that Portugal could not control or defend it if it were not more completely settled. Pombal came close, indeed, to the idea famously aphorized by the nineteenth-century Argentine political thinker Juan Bautista Alberdi as "to govern is to populate" (*gobernar es poblar*).[126] But these were the fantasies of a remote theorizer. If Pombal had ever seen in person the size of Brazil, and the social and cultural contrasts between Indians and whites, he would perhaps have concluded that governmental promotion of mixed marriage was unlikely to add much to the population density.

Pombal's Indian policies had, however, a most tangible effect in his administration's relationship with the leading advocates of native Brazilians, the Jesuits. For them, separation of natives from colonials had always been fundamental to the Indians' well-being and survival. Pombal's wish to blend native people into the general population was therefore anathema to them. Without doubt, less noble issues were also at stake. For the Jesuits, control of Indians was a political as well as a humanitarian matter. Politics, and economics also, were very much in Pombal's mind: the Jesuits, with their many mission villages, seemed to have independent control over wide areas of Brazil; and their possession of large, profitable estates was a temptation to him, as it was also to Spanish reformers in the 1760s.

Pombal, however, was possessed of, or rather possessed by, a special animus towards the Jesuits that made his hostility to them more virulent by far than anything that Spanish officials could muster. The sources of this detestation are unclear; but it grew as his power rose in the 1750s. The fact that the Society, a markedly international body, had sent foreign priests to Brazil clearly fed his suspicions. He told the papal nuncio in Lisbon that some, at least, of the Jesuits in Amazonia were in reality disguised European engineers using the slave labor of countless Indians to build fortifications (presumably to exclude Portugal from the region). With perhaps more reason, he believed that Jesuits in the south were collaborating with the British in illegal trade. Quite clearly in the realm of reality was the Society's dominance of education in Brazil, which gave it a unique influence among the white population. To his accusations, imagined or otherwise, about Jesuits' doings in Brazil, Pombal added allegations that they had been involved in political unrest in Portugal itself, including an attempt on the king's life in 1758. The upshot was the government's decree, in September 1759, expelling the Jesuits from Portuguese territories. The number ejected from Brazil was about 670.[127] And so began the assault on the Society that was to continue in the French and Spanish expulsions in 1764 and 1767, and culminate in its suppression by Rome from 1773 to 1814. The royal treasury gained from the sale of some of the Jesuits' lands in Brazil; other estates remained under crown supervision, and indeed passed into the national government's control after independence. Nor were Jesuit estates the only church property to be taken. The seizure of Mercedarian lands in lower Amazonia in the mid 1760s, and the recall of the friars to Portugal, suggest that Pombal was inspired not simply by his private hatred of the Jesuits, but also by the prevailing regalism of the day, reinforced by the secularism of the Enlightenment.

In a limited way he was also a man of the Enlightenment in his attitudes to education. There was, apparently, little notion in him of the intrinsic worth, or pleasure, of gaining knowledge, but he did value new knowledge and ways of thought for their utility in material development and administration. For that reason he created a system of secondary schooling in Portugal, and oversaw a modernization of the University of Coimbra in 1772, adding to it faculties of mathematics and philosophy (which included the natural sciences).[128] Coimbra became the sole Portuguese university; the only other one, at Evora, was a Jesuit institution, and was closed. From Coimbra in the late eighteenth century duly emerged modern-minded men, some rising to the peaks of government, who worked for the material advance of the empire, Brazil included.

In Brazil itself, however, education did not progress under Pombal; the reverse, in fact. The Jesuits had maintained seventeen secondary colleges and seminaries in the colony, and with them had provided almost all the available education. With the expulsion, these schools were without teachers. Colonial Brazil had no university. The contrast with the Spanish colonies, where universities were founded in the sixteenth century, is notable. The Portuguese crown, perhaps because its colonial apparatus was generally smaller and looser than the Spaniards', saw political advantages in making colonials dependent on Coimbra for their higher education. For similar reasons, and again in stark contrast to Spanish America, Brazil had no printing press until 1808. Two attempts to set up presses in the eighteenth century were blocked by the government. Pombal, wishing to center the empire on Portugal, logically upheld the prior line. For him, publishing and higher learning had no place in Brazil.

Brazil, then, felt Pombal's imperious touch in a number of instances, and with it a sense of new subordination to Portugal's interests: more taxes, more officials, new monopoly companies, control of import and export prices, hostility to local manufacture, foreign military instructors, attempts at radical social engineering, and much else. That said, very few in the colony seem finally to have found this increased Portuguese pressure intolerable.[129] Perhaps the reason was in part that the pressure eased after Pombal fell from power in 1777, and Portuguese administration lost the sharp edge that he had put on it. Perhaps also his reforms seemed, on balance, more developmental than extractive. Certainly neither they, nor any measures applied later, had quite the extortionate quality that is evident in Spain's fiscal treatment of the American colonies in the 1790s and later. Again, prosperity may have blunted protest. The same wars that in the 1790s made Spain desperate for American income brought great trading profits to Brazil as well as Portugal. To rising industrialism's demand for raw materials was added that caused by preparations for war in northern Europe. Finally, that unblockable accessibility of Brazil should not be forgotten. Despite any efforts that Portugal could make to stop it, contraband trade persisted on the Brazilian coast. The British, above all others, were constantly there, bypassing Lisbon to exchange their growing abundance of manufactures for Brazil's growing cornucopia of tropical plantation produce. The resulting gains to the upper segment of colonial society can only have served to reduce distress about Portuguese reformism among those best placed to take action against it.

PRODUCTS OF MIND AND SENSIBILITY

Although Brazil lacked universities and presses, it was not, in the eighteenth century at least, without a life of the mind. Such activity is most easily seen in various academies that appeared from the 1720s onwards in the larger towns. The academies were not formal schools, but groups of educated citizens who met to discuss literature, ideas, and Brazil itself. Salvador and Rio de Janeiro were the main places where the groups arose. The names chosen suggest, with the exception of the first, a certain self-confidence or perhaps enlightened optimism. The earliest was the Brazilian Academy of the Forgotten (Academia Brasílica dos Esquecidos, Salvador, 1724–5). Then followed the Academy of the Fortunate (Academia dos Felizes, Rio, 1736–40); the Academy of the Select (Academia dos Selectos, Rio, 1751–2); the Brazilian Academy of the Reborn (Academia Brasílica dos Renascidos, Salvador, 1759–60); the Academia Scientífica (Rio, 1772–9); and finally the Sociedade Literária (Rio, 1786–90, 1794). The transience of these groups possibly indicates that they were the product of the coincidental presence of men of like interests; there was not perhaps the "critical mass" of the intellectually inclined needed to make them permanent. Nonetheless, they left a mark. From the start with the Academy of the Forgotten, for instance, they called attention to Brazil's own qualities – its wealth, beauty, and economic centrality in the empire. One of that group, Caetano de Brito e Figueiredo, proclaimed in his *Dissertação terceira* ("Third Dissertation") that "Golden Brazil is the depository of the most priceless metal, fertile producer of the sweetest sugar canes, and generous cultivator of the most useful plants ... Brazil is the most precious jewel of the Lusitanian scepter, the most valuable stone in the Portuguese crown, which of itself possesses much majesty and beauty."[130] Sebastião da Rocha Pita, another of the "Forgotten," produced in 1730 his *História da América portuguesa*, a renowned history of Brazil that expresses his pride of identity with the colony. Later in the century members of the academies, like parallel figures in Spanish America at the time, made studies of Brazil's animals, plants, agricultural and mineral resources, and geography. Hard fact thus came to reinforce sentiment as a foundation for proto-national feeling, even if that feeling was limited to a very few at the upper end of society.

Many of those who gathered information about Brazil had been educated at Coimbra, and were products of that university's modern reorientation after its reform by Pombal. Their own fascination with the physical reality of Brazil derived from a physiocratic concern with land and agriculture that they absorbed in Portugal. Later they brought Adam Smith to Brazil. The *Wealth of Nations* was among the first works to appear from the newly installed presses after 1808. Two different translations, in fact, appeared from presses in Rio and Salvador, in 1811 and 1812 respectively. Free traders and economic liberals in general then had the classic theoretical statement of their positions close at hand.

The mining town of Ouro Prêto was a third intellectual center of eighteenth-century Brazil. Particularly notable was a group of poets who wrote there late in the century. Generally speaking, however, colonial Brazil's literary production was small in comparison with what emerged from Spanish America. Chronicles, histories, and descriptions from the sixteenth century onwards certainly exist, but not on the scale produced by either of colonial Spanish America's central regions. The same may be said of formal music in colonial Brazil. Such music as is known dates from the second half of the eighteenth century. The first piece with a Portuguese text is a cantata that was sung in Salvador at an early meeting of the Academia dos Renascidos in July of 1759. In Rio de Janeiro and various towns of Minas Gerais a number of mulatto church organists and choirmasters were also active as composers. No trace of Africa appears in their work, however; their inspiration was in European composers of the time, who were the admired models. One of them, José Maurício Nunes Garcia (1767–1830), a leading musical figure in Rio, conducted there in 1819 the first American performance of Mozart's *Requiem*.[131]

Buildings, above all churches, are the richest artistic relic of colonial Brazil. Among them, the most distinctive are those of the second half of the eighteenth century. Sixteenth-century churches had been simple, largely wooden, structures. Greater size and complexity came in the 1600s with the arrival of the Baroque. The churches, though often now splendid, were, however, similar in plan to those of Spanish America: an essentially flat, tri-partite facade (a central section flanked by towers), fronting a rectangular structure containing three aisles. The interiors were at first, also, of a similar simplicity and restraint. But from the 1660s a notion of the "church wholly of gold" (*igreja toda de ouro*) influenced Portugal and Brazil. Interiors decorated with gold leaf laid over carved wood began to appear. An early Brazilian example is the "Gilded Chapel" (1695–1702) of the Franciscan Third Order at Recife.[132]

By that time gold was becoming abundantly available for such purposes, and the previously plain interiors of various large churches in the coastal cities were fitted with dense, even overpowering, gilded and polychromed ornamentation that comprised spiraling columns, masses of carved foliage, gamboling cherubs, and sacred figures peering from niches. In Minas Gerais itself, however, which was the source of the gold used both to gild and pay for these creations, a greater simplicity, at least in decoration, prevailed. Here substantial building in masonry began c.1730. It was after 1750, however, that most of the distinctive churches of the region appeared, churches that now seem to epitomize the architectural style of colonial Brazil. In them, the imposing mass of the Baroque gave way to the daintiness of the rococo. The churches were smaller and lower. In the clearest cases of rococo style, straight lines were replaced by curves. Facades were convex curves; towers were cylindrical; ground plans were rounded, oval, or even double oval in form. Interior decoration was sparer, with delicate and fanciful traceries set rhythmically in open spaces of wall and ceiling. A light, shell-like frame was placed around windows. These churches seem to draw on the rococo style of Bavaria and Austria in the mid eighteenth century – and in reality they may well do so. The suggested linkage is through the marriages of Peter II of Portugal (1667–1706) to a Bavarian princess; of his successor, John V (1707–50) to an Austrian princess; and of Pombal, no less, to another Austrian princess.[133] The Austrian rococo is present in eighteenth-century Portugal, and Portugal is its supposed stepping-stone to Brazil.

Among the designers of the churches of Minas Gerais was a mulatto born in the captaincy's major town, Ouro Prêto, who has been described as "the greatest architect and sculptor Brazil has produced."[134] This was António Francisco Lisboa (c.1738–1814), better known as O Aleijadinho, the little cripple. He is so called because from the age of about 40 a disease, possibly leprosy or syphilis, attacked his hands and feet, and deprived him of movement. Latterly he worked with pen, chisel, or mallet strapped to the remains of his hands. The local soapstone that served for both building and sculpture is, fortunately, soft when newly quarried; it hardens with weathering. Aleijadinho is the architect of the church of São Francisco in Ouro Prêto, among others. He did much decorative stonework, such as portals, altars, and pulpits, for yet other churches. But his most admired creation is one of carved human figures: the ensembles of sixty-six statues in wood, and twelve in stone, at the pilgrim church of Bom Jesus de Matosinhos, overlooking the town of Congonhas do Campo in Minas Gerais. The wooden, polychromed figures are set in six small chapels along the rising approach to the church. They depict scenes from Christ's Passion. The stone statues, representing biblical prophets, stand on plinths built into the walls of a double stairway leading up to the church.

> Placed in strategic positions, the huge figures seem to dance a tremendous ballet as the visitor winds his way back and forth walking up the steps. He is made to

see the statues from all sides and angles. From a distance all twelve prophets, in diverse attitudes, greet him. As one comes nearer, they act in ever-changing groups of different sets of eight, six, four, even two ... Their features are harsh and sharp, their costumes fantastic, with Oriental overtones, their expressions prophetic.[135]

In their scale and severity, these statues seem far from the rococo. Their emotional force and their exoticism perhaps hint at some early infiltration of Romanticism into this remote interior of Brazil; or perhaps they are *sui generis*, simply the late product of Aleijadinho's singular sensibility. Still, it is the rococo that dominates Brazilian architecture in the late eighteenth century, and which can be taken as the closing style of the colonial era. Neoclassicism, in contrast to its prevalence in the late Spanish colonies, barely makes an appearance in Brazil before 1800. The Brazilian reaction to the heavy excesses of Baroque ornament was not the grave austerity of classical imitation, but the lighter, more graceful decorativeness of the rococo. The Spanish crown, whether with inherent political message or not, tried to impose the new solemnity of neoclassicism on its American territories in the late 1700s. The Portuguese did not. The contrast perhaps signals how much lighter the reforming touch of the Portuguese rulers generally was than that of their Spanish counterparts. And that difference was to have a large effect on the manner in which the two colonial structures were soon to gain independence; and, indeed, a bearing on the development of their respective histories through much of the nineteenth century.

ILLUSTRATION 13.1 Indigenous and alien still at odds: Bolivian Indians versus donkey (an animal introduced from Spain in the sixteenth century).

ILLUSTRATION 13.2 Still the all-purpose beast of the Andes (freight, wool, meat, sacrificial victim): young llamas in Bolivia.

ILLUSTRATION 13.3 A modern example of the three-roller mill for crushing sugar cane, in Santa Cruz (eastern Bolivia). This mechanism was used to extract juice from cane in colonial Brazil and Spanish America.

ILLUSTRATION 13.4 *Casta* painting: *De Mulato y Española, Morisco* ("From Mulatto and Spanish Woman, Morisco"), by Francisco Clapera, *c.*1785. In the original meaning, a *morisco* was a Moor who remained in Spain after converting to Christianity. For physical appearance, the term's implication is of skin color darker than the Spanish norm. The painting shows an altercation in which the Spanish wife apparently has the upper hand, perhaps suggesting her higher standing in society's ethnic ranking. Denver Art Museum.

ILLUSTRATION 13.5 *Casta* painting. *De Español e India nace Mestiza* ("From Spaniard and Indian Woman is Born a Mestiza"), by Francisco Clapera, *c*.1785. The commonest and central ethnic and cultural mixture in colonial Spanish America. Denver Art Museum.

ILLUSTRATION 13.6 A Dominican friar with an Indian weaving woman in the central Andes. Here Guaman Poma criticizes abusive friars who fraudulently imprisoned women on grounds of concubinage in order to profit from their labor. From Felipe Guaman Poma de Ayala, *Nueva Coronica y Buen Gobierno*, Paris, 1936.

Part VI

*INDEPENDENCE
AND BEYOND*

FURTHER READING FOR PART VI

The standard account in English of the movements of independence is John Lynch, *The Spanish American Revolutions, 1808–1826.* Two succinct works are Richard Graham, *Independence in Latin America: A Comparative Approach*, and Jay Kinsbruner, *Independence in Spanish America: Civil Wars, Revolutions, and Underdevelopment.* William S. Robertson, *Rise of the Spanish-American Republics as Told in the Lives of their Liberators*, is a traditional but still engaging approach to the subject. John Lynch's *Simón Bolívar: A Life* is an up-to-date study of the great *libertador*. Christon I. Archer (ed.), *The Wars of Independence in Spanish America*, contains both recent research and material from the independence era. For Brazil, see Roderick J. Barman, *Brazil: The Forging of a Nation, 1798–1852.* Volume 3 of Leslie Bethell (ed.), *The Cambridge History of Latin America*, contains essays on the independence of individual regions.

The continuing influence of the colonial centuries on post-independence Latin America is the subject (in a largely economic treatment) of Stanley J. and Barbara H. Stein, *The Colonial Heritage of Latin America: Essays on Economic Dependence in Perspective.* Broader views are in Richard M. Morse, *New World Soundings: Culture and Ideology in the Americas.* Most of the essays in Jeremy Adelman (ed.), *Colonial Legacies: The Problem of Persistence in Latin American History*, mull colonial to postcolonial continuities. Howard J. Wiarda, *The Soul of Latin America: The Cultural and Political Tradition*, offers some more concrete proposals on the topic.

[14] *INDEPENDENCE*

BETWEEN 1810 and 1825 all the Spanish territories on the American mainland gained their independence from Spain. In the Caribbean, by contrast, Cuba and Puerto Rico remained under Spanish rule until 1898; and Hispaniola was occupied and controlled by Haiti from 1822 to 1844, at which point it broke free. Two other large islands once held by Spain had yielded to English attack, Jamaica in 1655 and Trinidad in 1797, and they remained British colonies until 1962.

For obvious enough reasons of national sentiment and historical drama, the fight for independence, and the origins of that fight, have long drawn historians' scrutiny. Their only rival for attention in Latin America's past has been the European conquest itself. The fascination with independence is justified. The story of its achievement is a stirring one; and a tracing of its roots shows them to have been deep and numerous.

Latin American independence came in the midst of an era of sweeping change in the western world. It was indeed part of that change. The Enlightenment, in advertising the potency of human reason, had accustomed those whom it touched to the notion that change was a normal state of being; for what was dangerous, damaging or demeaning in the human condition could be remedied by the proper application of the mind's power. Progress was easily within the human grasp. This message had penetrated Spanish America by the late eighteenth century. Educated creoles (though, it is true, few others) had read and debated the writings of the European Enlightenment. Literary societies of the late eighteenth century, some of them set up by intendants, had often provided a forum for such discussion. Some creoles had also conversed with visiting European savants sent by the Spanish crown to modernize mining or make scientific surveys of the land and its resources. Others, though fewer, had visited Europe, and continued to do so at the opening of the new century. They brought news back with them of all manner of European innovation. But news came from abroad under its own impetus. Colonials were well aware, for instance, of the United States' independence, of the drafting of the new nation's constitution, and of the development of federal government. They were the target of political tracts brought by North American traders, who also gave out copies of the US Declaration of Independence and of the constitution. They were equally informed of the course of revolutionary events in France after 1789. Those events struck some colonials as inspiring and admirable; but, especially as the revolution took an extreme turn in the 1790s, far more found them unnatural and frightening. That view was quickly reinforced by the eruption of the revolution's transatlantic offshoot in the form of the Haitian slave revolt of 1791.

Change, therefore, was in the political air of Spanish America as the eighteenth century ended. Or, better, the possibility of change was in the air. That possibility, rather than any particular set of beliefs, was the political legacy of the Enlightenment to the Spanish colonies. Creoles did not necessarily take up notions of inherent human freedom and equality, nor accept that government should follow the popular will, although some did. But most, perhaps almost all, inevitably absorbed the pervasive questioning of traditional order and stability that the Enlightenment radiated.

In the preliminaries to the independence conflict, and to a considerable degree in its conduct as well, creoles were the prime political actors on the American side. They were the potential political nation in the various colonies. Recent research by historians, however, has revealed for the first time how much smaller-scale disruptive activity took place at the lower levels of colonial society in the years before and during the independence struggle – activity that did not lead to any particular political outcome, but which became part of the unstable political landscape in which that struggle took place. Messianic movements among Indians were sometimes discovered. An example is the failed rising of "el Indio Mariano" (Mariano the Indian) around the western Mexican town of Tepic in the years 1800–2. Mariano was probably an invented character, the creation of Indians who seemed to be planning a large rebellion in the west. He was supposed to be descended from a governor of Tlaxcala, the city-state in central Mexico that had resisted the Mexica Aztecs and then helped the Spanish to conquer them. That linkage lent a great depth of "Mexicanness" and authority to the movement. Mariano was apparently crowned King of the Indies at Tepic in January 1801. The details, even the reality, of this episode were never clear. But the Spanish authorities reacted to it with fearful violence, killing some villagers and arresting hundreds more to be imprisoned and tried in Guadalajara. Such happenings – and there were several – created an uncertainty in New Spain in the first decade of the 1800s that disturbed the Spanish administration.[1]

It is clear, then, that the lower levels of colonial society, the Indians and *castas*, certainly contributed to Spanish nervousness in the American colonies in the years immediately before the wars of independence began. Nonetheless, it is still broadly true that creoles were the people in the colonies who conceived political schemes at the regional or colony-wide level. They were the ones who had the educated awareness needed to do so. For that reason, their growing numbers in the eighteenth century, which made them by far the largest part of the white population in the colonies, had great political meaning. Rising creole consciousness of the different colonies' geographical, economic, and human realities; creole reaction to European, and especially Spanish, disdain of America and its inhabitants; creole resentment at exclusion from office, and, more broadly, from the transatlantic Spanish community; creole acceptance of the pervasive notion that the traditional order was not immutable; and a rising creole sense of how much continued subservience to Spain was costing them: all these gained a political force proportional to the rise in creole numbers. If reasons for changing the old order became potent enough, there were now, as the nineteenth century began, many capable of acting on them.

In the opening years of the century, the causes for creole discontent accumulated. Some were specific to particular colonies, sometimes in fact to particular areas within colonies. Others were more or less generalized. There was certainly a current of "pure" desire for escape from Spanish rule. This was strongest among urban creoles on the east side of South America. They were inhabitants of places that lacked, by the standards of, say, Mexico City, Quito, or Lima, a sense of deep colonial tradition, having grown fast in the eighteenth century from the export of agricultural products to Europe. Some, at least, of their creole citizens tended to radicalism for its own sake. The pre-eminent example is Francisco de Miranda (1750–1816), a merchant's son from Caracas who well before 1800 began to seek foreign support for the ejection of Spain from America. His first inspiration was the United States, which he came to know through living and traveling there in 1784. His second was France. He spent much of the 1790s there, actually commanding French revolutionary troops in the field as a general in 1792, and then being considered by the French as the leader of a projected revolutionizing attack on Spanish America. This came to nothing, as did Miranda's efforts at various times to persuade the United States and British governments to back his liberation schemes with men and materials. In 1806 he raised a volunteer force of 150 men in the United States in the hope of igniting a rebellion in Venezuela, but failed to do so in two attempts. It was only in 1810 that he finally returned to Venezuela, after a declaration against Spain had already been made in Caracas. Briefly in 1812 he was given supreme powers by the rebels. But soon afterwards the Spanish recovered control. Miranda was captured, and died in prison four years later.[2] He has gone down as the greatest of the "precursors" of Spanish American independence. He was not alone. Other expatriate creoles in European capitals imitated him on a smaller scale. One example was Pedro José Caro, possibly a Cuban, but also a property owner in Mexico. Caro visited London in 1797 with letters provided by Miranda introducing him to potentially helpful Englishmen. He asserted that, across Spanish America, 1,400 reputable people were, like him, already working for the cause of independence. Another precursor also in London that same year was a New Granadan, Antonio Nariño. He and Caro may already have sought aid in France for their cause.[3]

A more concrete issue in the exporting regions on the Atlantic coast of South America was free trade. For Buenos Aires, Spain's basic policy of blocking free exchange with lands outside the empire was particularly irksome. The *pampas* hinterland of the city was the apparently limitless source of the leather for which excellent markets existed in the industrializing countries. Mariano Moreno

(1778–1811), a creole lawyer who was one of the chief agitators for change in Buenos Aires, wrote forcefully in 1809 in favor of free trade.[4] Moreno greatly admired Rousseau, and indeed was the editor of a translation of the *Social Contract* published in Buenos Aires. In 1810 he was one of the leading spirits in Buenos Aires's declaration of self-government. For the progressive authors of that action, there was no less burning issue than freedom of trade.

For merchants on the west coast of South America, and in Mexico, by contrast, that question was less urgent. Neither region sensed such potential gain from open participation in the Atlantic trading system as did Caracas with its cacao, and Buenos Aires with its hides. Traders in those older sections of the empire had learned to work within the restrictive limits of Spanish trade policy, though not without frequent complaints. But other discontents with Spanish government were widespread enough by 1800, even in those more traditional, and in most respects more conservative, regions.

There was a sense of the invasiveness of the enlarged bureaucracy that had resulted from the reforms of Charles III's time, an increased awareness of Spanish control (or at least intention to control). Tax rates had risen, and taxes were now more efficiently gathered than before. The state's demands seemed, in fact, to be progressing from taxation to outright seizure, as in the forced liquidation of the *obras pías*. And particularly vexing was the knowledge that these exactions were being made by an enfeebled European state, one that had become in all but name the lackey of France, and that money sucked from the Spanish colonies was in part, at least, ending up in Paris.

Spain's junior position in the association with France founded on the Bourbon link had been clear enough from the beginning of the eighteenth century. It became painfully obvious in the 1790s, when Charles IV had to decide how to treat revolutionary France, a challenge that led to Spain's bouncing between France and England in a seemingly helpless fashion. Faced in 1792 with growing radicalism in the revolution, confirmed by the execution of Louis XVI in January 1793, Spain first formed an alliance with Britain against France.[5] This led to a Spanish invasion of southern France in 1793, a larger retaliatory French movement into northern Spain the next year, and in consequence the Peace of Basle between France and Spain in mid 1795. A year later the two countries allied against Britain. Now disasters rained on Spain thick and fast. Britain was more powerful at sea than France and Spain combined. In February 1797 Admiral Jervis defeated a Spanish fleet off Cape St. Vincent at the southern tip of Portugal, and in America the British took Trinidad. A British blockade of Cadiz and broad assault on Spanish shipping all but cut Spain's links with America, halting the commercial gains that had resulted from the trade reform of 1778, and halting the flow of silver from America at a time of general mining boom. Few were the occasions in the empire's history when American silver was more desperately needed. Then, to meet the colonies' needs for imported foods, manufactures and raw materials, and to allow them to sell their exports, Spain was forced to let them trade with neutral countries. Permission for this was given in late 1797. It was cancelled in April 1799; but trade with neutrals did not then stop, and in reality it was very nearly free trade, since the origins of cargoes could not easily be checked, and ships might enter colonial ports under false papers.[6] Colonials grew used to this open commerce. The United States, a major neutral trader, sent ships to ports throughout Spanish America to sell its goods; and with them also went ashore news of US political successes, news that spread quickly among increasingly receptive creoles.

Hostilities ceased, though only briefly, with the Peace of Amiens in 1802. But even the treaty cost Spain dearly, as Napoleon, First Consul of France since 1799 and soon to be emperor, yielded to Britain Spain's title to Trinidad. Then, when hostilities between France and Britain resumed in May of 1803, he sold Louisiana to the United States to raise money, in spite of an obligation by treaty with Spain never to dispose of that territory. In late 1804 Spain was again pulled into France's combat with the British. An early outcome was Nelson's crushing of the combined allied fleets at Trafalgar in October of 1805 – a defeat that signaled the end of an epic of doughty Spanish seagoing that had begun with the voyages of exploration in the late fifteenth century. For France, the blow was less telling. Although Trafalgar brought Napoleon's naval schemes to a halt, he proved irresistible on land over the following two years, dominating much of Europe through brilliant victories. In October of 1807, by the Treaty of Fontainebleau, he organized with Spain an invasion of Portugal, Britain's continental ally. The Franco-Spanish invasion took place in November 1807, with French troops crossing Spanish territory to participate. Shortly before Lisbon was occupied, British vessels spirited away the Portuguese royal family and court to Rio de Janeiro. France had negotiated the 1807 treaty with Manuel Godoy, Charles IV's first minister, who by its terms was to become prince of the southern tier of Portugal, the Algarve. But in March 1808, Prince Ferdinand, Charles IV's son, led a rising against Godoy, not concerned by the possibility (or perhaps welcoming it) that the king might fall along with his minister. That in effect was the outcome. Charles abdicated in favor of his son, who then became king, as Ferdinand VII. Napoleon, observing the chaos into which Spanish government had descended, and the fall of Godoy, the minister with whom he had dealt in Spain, then resolved to cut through the Spanish tangle with a military occupation of the country and the installation of his brother Joseph as monarch. Napoleon had, in fact, for some years past contemplated placing Spain under his direct control; the confusion of early 1808 provided an easy opening for doing so. On March 23, French troops entered Madrid. Ferdinand believed that they had come to support him. But Napoleon ordered both him and his father to Bayonne, in south-western France. In May Ferdinand was forced to abdicate in favor of Joseph, who became José I of Spain. He was detained in France until Napoleon's own abdication in 1814.[7]

1808–1809

A hundred years had passed since Spain had last been filled with foreign troops, in the War of Succession that had confirmed the Bourbons on the throne. The subordinate linkage to France that had begun with that war and its settlement at Utrecht had now drawn Spain down into the mortification of both occupation and an imposed, alien monarch. But from this humiliation arose a powerful popular reaction, "the first great people's war of modern history."[8] Spaniards, again drawing on a genius for military improvisation that they had shown in the American conquests, began a dogged guerrilla war against the French. Spanish resistance was soon backed by the arrival of British troops, sent by a government which saw the Iberian peninsula as the only European land arena on which Napoleonic France could now be fought. A British force landed in Portugal in August 1808. Its commander was Arthur Wellesley, whose actions over the next five years in what became known in Spanish history as the War of Independence brought him the title of duke of Wellington. The expulsion of the French from Spain in 1813, coupled with the loss of the Grand Army in its retreat from Moscow in the winter of 1812–13, marked the collapse of Napoleon's imperial plans.

The French invasion produced a political as well as a military reaction in Spain. In response to the disappearance of the monarchy, local and regional governing councils, or juntas, sprang up across the country. It was a remarkable practical demonstration of the rooting in Spain of eighteenth-century notions of popular sovereignty, and also, some have argued, of the emergence from long suppression of medieval Spanish notions of participatory government. In September of 1808 a national junta formed, asserting itself as the legitimate source of Spanish and imperial government in defiance of the French regime. This Junta Central met first at Aranjuez, just south of Madrid. French military advance gradually pushed it southwards in 1809. Early in 1810, the Junta yielded to the demands from local councils for a more representative form of national government, and made arrangements for the gathering of a parliament, or *cortes*, with delegates from those parts of Spain still able to send them, and also from the colonies. By mid 1810 almost the only city in Spain secure from French attack was the port of Cadiz, in the far south. The town stands at the tip of a long, narrow promontory, which made for easy defense on land. Spanish and English ships provided protection from seaborne assault, and also brought in supplies. It was here that Spain's first national parliament met in September of 1810, and deliberated over the following three and a half years. This *cortes* of Cadiz was a remarkably liberal body, in part because local people were named as substitutes for delegates from areas of Spain under French occupation, and also for American representatives who were slow to arrive because of the distance they had to travel. Cadiz itself, an outward-looking, middle-class trading community, was markedly liberal in its attitudes. The effect of the substitutions, then, was to emphasize liberalism in the assembly. And this body, in 1812, produced not only Spain's first written constitution, but one that has been called "the banner of liberalism throughout southern Europe and Latin America for decades."[9] On the movement towards independence, the immediate political issue in Spanish America, the effects of the document were certainly telling.

In the colonies the political outcome of the French invasion was as immediate as it was in Spain, and still more profound. Wrenching disputes over how government should proceed produced splits within single administrations. The key issues were those of sovereignty and legitimacy. Clearly the imposed French monarchy possessed neither. The exiled Spanish monarchy had both, but was inaccessible. What was to be made, then, of the Junta Central, once it appeared? Could it be accepted as the current source of Spanish political will and power? To many senior administrators in America, the Junta, and even more the *cortes* after it, seemed not only suspect in claiming to be Spain's supreme governing entities, but also dangerously radical in the manner of their formation. If popular representation were to be admitted as the basis for legitimacy in Spain, might not creoles, on the same principle, insist on participating in American government? Some creoles, in fact, did precisely that. In Mexico, by the late summer of 1808, the viceroy seemed to be entertaining demands from the *cabildo* of Mexico City, which was dominated by creoles, that authority be shared between it and the *audiencia*. The proposal was, in effect, that sovereignty shift from Spain to America. The *audiencia*, whose judges were Spaniards, took conservative alarm at this, and found backing for its opposition among rich, immigrant Spanish merchants and landowners. This alliance was powerful enough to depose the viceroy, in September 1808, and send him back to Spain. A period of authoritarian, indeed repressive, rule by the *audiencia* then ensued, in which private Spanish interests were favored at the expense of the creoles, and wealthy peninsulars set up a semi-private militia, the Volunteers of Ferdinand VII.[10]

Far away to the south a similar fissure in Spanish authority developed a little later in the *audiencia* of Charcas, seated at La Plata in the central Andes. There the president of the court, supported by the archbishop, inclined to accept the authority of the Junta Central in Spain. But the judges of the court saw threatening populism in the Junta's claims to authority, and took the position that the *audiencia* itself must be the supreme governing body in its jurisdiction, which it should rule, according to existing law, in the name of the exiled king. Ambitious creole lawyers in the University of La Plata saw in this division a chance for political power of their own. Feigning alliance with the *audiencia*, and its proposal for self-government for Charcas during the king's forced absence, they plotted to bring about declarations of local self-rule, nominally on behalf of Ferdinand, in various towns in the territory. Only in La Paz did they have success. There, in July 1809, a group of adventurous creoles arrested the Spanish governor and the bishop. A governing *junta tuitiva* (protective council) formed, under the leadership of a *mestizo* named Pedro Domingo Murillo, and briefly took control of La Paz. Dropping any pretense of governing in the king's name, it issued a proclamation stating that "It is now time to overthrow the [Spanish] yoke ... It is now time to organize a new government based on the interests of our fatherland ... It is now time to declare the principle of liberty in these miserable colonies acquired without any title and kept by tyranny and injustice."[11] This was clearly a declaration of outright independence. It was indeed the first such in Spanish America; Bolivians are still proud of that fact, as they are of Murillo himself. Spanish military force was, however, close at hand in Peru, with the result that the insurgency was undone by the end of January 1810.

Other risings took place in 1809: one in Buenos Aires in January, of royalists opposing a viceroy whom they suspected of liberalism; one in Quito in August, of rebellious upper-class creoles who overthrew the *audiencia* and set up a governing junta, ostensibly in Ferdinand's name. This movement collapsed in late October, on the approach of Spanish troops from Guayaquil and the south.[12] Everywhere, in fact, the ground seemed to tremble under Spanish administrators' feet as a result of the French invasion of Spain.

No definitive movement towards independence, however, took place in that year.

1810

The following year was a different matter. As French troops pushed southwards in Spain it seemed, by early 1810, that there would soon be no haven left in the country for any native governing body. Nobody could predict that Cadiz would hold out as it did. As news of the French advance in Andalusia reached America, therefore, it sparked explosions of political action among activist creoles whose radicalism had fed on the instability of the two previous years.

The first outbreak came in Caracas on April 19, 1810. On that day the city council called a *cabildo abierto*. This was a limited sort of town meeting, an "open council" to which, however, only notables had right of attendance. It was a gathering usually called for by the local governor for mainly ceremonial purposes. But on this occasion the captain-general of Venezuela, who was the supreme local authority, was prevented from entering by apparently organized mob action. And the creole-dominated town council, with a few added members, transformed itself into a "junta for the preservation of the rights of Ferdinand VII" that rejected any claim to authority in Venezuela by political entities in Spain. So, in April 1810, Venezuela (or rather Caracas, since the town council could speak only for the capital and its immediate surroundings) declared itself to be self-governing. Its manner of doing this prudently preserved at least the pretense of loyalty to the Spanish monarchy.[13]

A month later Buenos Aires followed suit. Arrival of the news that Seville had fallen to the French provoked implementation of a scheme that creoles in the city council had planned from late 1808. This was, precisely as in Caracas, to summon a *cabildo abierto* and set up a junta to displace the chief local Spanish authority. In Buenos Aires, this was the viceroy of the Río de la Plata, and it was he who was persuaded to call the meeting, apparently expecting to become the leader of the junta. The "open council" convened on May 22, 1810. As in Caracas, organized mobs played a part, excluding men who seemed likely to object to the plan. In this the radicals' control of the local militia also helped. From the meeting emerged a junta that assumed local government in the name of the king. Its leaders were creole, among them the most ardent advocates of free trade. On May 25 this body arrested the viceroy, and in so doing ended Spanish rule in what was to become Argentina.[14] For unlike Caracas, Buenos Aires and its hinterland never came back under Spanish control after that date. Hence, although the *cabildo abierto* had not declared independence, the Río de la Plata can rightly claim to be the first region of Spanish America in which colonial rule ended.

The same movement of ejection of royal governors by juntas of local notables quickly spread to New Granada. It started in Cartagena on June 14, and extended to Cali, Pamplona, Socorro, and finally, on July 20, to Santa Fe de Bogotá itself, where the viceroy was deposed. On September 18 Chile made its move – again the *cabildo abierto* (in Santiago), again the junta of notables taking up the reins of government in the name of Ferdinand VII.[15] Although the people (mostly creoles) who took power in these different South American areas were certainly impelled by their own interests and ambitions, they were also putting into practice the principle of popular sovereignty: when legitimate authority disappeared, or was so weak as to be ineffective, power devolved to the people. The Spanish juntas of 1808 onward provided a model. And although creoles were a minority in Spanish American populations, in the pressing circumstances of 1809–10 they had few qualms about regarding themselves as the people.

By late September of 1810, then, most of Spanish South America outside the central Andean heartland of present Peru and Bolivia had passed into creole control. As it turned out, only in the Río de la Plata was that control permanent; elsewhere Spain struck back before self-government was finally established. But the political shift was already immense. In the space of five months vast and economically vibrant areas of the empire had become autonomous. In general they had proclaimed autonomy within the monarchy. But the monarchy was a conveniently vaporous entity at the time. It was unclear, and still remains so, what the implied assertions of loyalty were worth.

Two days before Santiago de Chile convened its *cabildo abierto* in southern South America, a very different sort of movement had begun in Mexico. Before dawn on September 16, 1810, in the country town of Dolores, the parish priest, Miguel Hidalgo y Costilla, issued the famous *grito*, or "cry," of Dolores. So began a short-lived but spectacular rising, initiated by creoles but soon taken over by unruly popular force. The conservative crackdown precisely two years earlier had driven creole activism underground in New Spain. No possibility of town meetings existed there once the *audiencia* in Mexico City took control in the autumn of 1808. The constitutional route to creole autonomy was blocked. Resistance festered, however, in secret, especially in provincial towns. One of those was Querétaro, 200 kilometers north-west of Mexico City, in the south of the rich farming zone known as the Bajío. There a small group of prosperous creoles, some of them military officers, plotted to ignite a rising against the central *audiencia* and its rigid peninsular backers in October of 1810. Hidalgo joined this group in the summer of that year, Dolores being only 90 kilometers north-west of Querétaro. He was himself a creole, now in his early sixties. Though a priest, he was a man of no great spirituality; most of his career had been spent in teaching rather than in pastoral work, and he seems to have had a greater interest in the writings of the *philosophes* than in those of the Church Fathers. He certainly had absorbed the Enlightenment's message that improvement of the human condition was possible through practical means, and as parish priest of Dolores he spent more time seeking to better the material lives of his flock than in praying for them. To that end he put his own money into small local industries, such as silk-raising, pottery manufacture, tanning, carpentry, and beekeeping. This concern for his parishioners' well-being brought him their affection and loyalty; perhaps especially so in 1810, since the previous two years had been a time of drought, shortage of food, and consequent high prices in central Mexico.

The Querétaro plot was discovered by the authorities, and its leaders in the town were seized on September 13. Hidalgo received word of this setback. In one of the celebrated scenes of Mexican history, he summoned his parishioners, mostly Indian and *mestizo*, with the sound of the church bell, and exhorted them to support him in a rising against Spanish rule. Without planning, therefore, and with no semblance of a trained military force, Hidalgo's rebellion began. He led his people south and west across the Bajío towards Guanajuato, a natural target given the renowned wealth of its silver mines. On the way, they took from the parish church of Atotonilco an image of the Virgin of Guadalupe, which became the movement's symbol. On September 23, Hidalgo led into Guanajuato a much-expanded force, a horde indeed, of 23,000 people. Sacking of the city and killing of the intendant and many other whites followed.

The destruction of Guanajuato revealed the insurrection for what it was quickly becoming: an onslaught on white people, no matter whether Spanish or creole, and on their property, by massed peasants and elements of the urban poor. Here was a mode of popular sovereignty that notables had reason to fear. They probably would not have been comforted had they known, as some perhaps did, that among Hidalgo's followers were poor people who believed that the king, Ferdinand VII, was in New Spain supporting the rebellion against his appointed, but clearly perverted, colonial government.[16] The sentiment of "Viva el rey" was possibly slower to die among commoners than among the elite. Sparks from the conflagration quickly flew far and wide, igniting risings as far away as Zacatecas and San Luis Potosí in the north, and in Guadalajara in the west. By early October Hidalgo's own force numbered 60,000. In mid October he occupied Valladolid (now Morelia) in Michoacan. From there he advanced with 80,000 on Mexico City, and seemed poised to attack it. But in the capital the government had many thousands of trained militiamen, under the command of a most capable Spanish officer, Félix María Calleja, and at Hidalgo's approach almost all creoles in the city forgot their grievances against the Spanish administration and closed ranks with it. Hidalgo prevailed, by force of numbers, in a small fight on October 30. But that was the high point of his campaign. Tens of thousands of his followers deserted after this battle. And from there the rebels' road led downward, to Calleja's definitive victory over them near Guadalajara on January 17, 1811. Hidalgo and his creole lieutenants fled northwards, hoping to reach the United States. But they were captured, and executed in the summer of 1811.

There is irony in Father Hidalgo's ranking as the greatest hero of Mexican independence, because the movement he started almost certainly did more to delay the break from Spain than to advance it. The rising was from the start an ethnic-cum-class war rather than a war of liberation. Given the circumstances of its beginning, it perhaps could hardly have been otherwise. The effect was to alienate from it all but the most extreme of creoles. And, as the story of the movement clearly demonstrated, as long as unity existed between Spaniards and a majority of creoles, independence could not come. It is not even completely clear that independence was, as the movement progressed, Hidalgo's prime aim. He had declared initially that he acted in the king's name; later he called for independence. But, responding to the demands of his followers and to the nature of the movement, he became as much a social as a political reformer. His pronouncements, at least, indicate as much: abolition of the Indian tribute, abolition of the distinctions of *castas*, abolition of slavery, restoration of lands taken from native communities.[17]

Few years in Spanish America's history have been more dramatic than 1810. Between May and September Spain's colonial apparatus suffered a series of hammer blows that seemed to the creoles who inflicted them heavy enough to alter its structure, if not to damage it beyond repair. Precisely how many of the radical creole groups who seized local power in 1810 were at that stage pursuing outright independence is hard to judge. But all were seeking at the very least home rule within a far less demanding colonial system than had emerged from Bourbon reform in the eighteenth century. In the event, only the Río de la Plata achieved that self-governing aim permanently in 1810. Elsewhere, although that year certainly marks a historic break with the past, self-determination still lay some ten to fifteen years in the future. The road to it was to prove long and arduous in most regions.

SPANISH SOUTH AMERICA, 1811–1825

The chronology of independence in the mainland countries of Spanish America is shown in table 14.1. The first colony to achieve self-rule, after the Río de la Plata, was Paraguay. The process here was simplicity itself, and consisted of two military defeats, not of Spaniards but of a force from Buenos Aires. After their coup in May 1810, the creole leaders in Buenos Aires were keen to extend their authority northwards. They had at least three reasons. First, the viceroyalty of the Río de la Plata, created in 1776, had included both Paraguay and Upper Peru (soon to be Bolivia), and Buenos Aires hoped to keep that unit intact and under its control. Second, Upper Peru was still the great silver-producing zone of South America, and for that reason Buenos Aires was particularly anxious to retain it. Third, control of northern territories would provide a deep buffer against possible attacks from the Spanish base of administrative and military power in South America, Peru. To begin the northward push, since a Spanish intendant still governed Paraguay, Buenos Aires dispatched an army to Asunción in late 1810. But the Paraguayans, long conscious of their cultural and political separateness from Buenos Aires, resisted the threat rather than yielding to it and beat the invading force in January and

Table 14.1 Independence in mainland Spanish America

Río de la Plata (later Argentina)	May 1810
Paraguay	May 1811
Chile (battle of Maipú)	February 1818
Colombia (colonial New Granada, battle of Boyacá)	August 1819
Venezuela (battle of Carabobo)	June 1821
Mexico (colonial New Spain)	August 1821
Central America	August 1821
Ecuador (colonial Quito, battle of Pichincha)	May 1822
Peru (battle of Ayacucho)	December 1824
Bolivia (colonial Charcas, then Upper Peru)	January 1825
(Uruguay	October 1828)

The dates are not those of declarations of independence, but of the effective and permanent break from Spanish rule. In some cases, single battles, named here, brought about that separation. They are taken from relevant entries in Tenenbaum (ed.), *Encyclopedia of Latin American History and Culture.*

Clarification is needed in two instances. First, Central America, *c.*1800, consisted of an area now comprising Chiapas and Soconusco (in present southern Mexico), Guatemala, Honduras, Nicaragua, El Salvador, and Costa Rica. Together these regions formed the captaincy-general of Guatemala, which was a unit of the viceroyalty of New Spain. When New Spain gained independence in 1821, Central America did so also, almost without violence. Then, in 1824, the several provinces broke away from Mexico, as the United Provinces of Central America. Late in the 1830s, this attempt at federalism collapsed, and the five present national states emerged as separate units. Panama, which today is the southernmost Central American nation, was at the time a province of Colombia, and so remained until 1903. Second, the territory of present Uruguay was contested in the independence period between Buenos Aires and Brazil. After a period of much uncertainty in the 1820s, during which the region was administered at different times by both, an agreement made between Brazil and the Argentine Federation, at British urging, created the sovereign nation of Uruguay.

March 1811. In May of that year, a junta led by José Gaspar Rodríguez de Francia and others deposed the intendant and declared independence. In 1814 Francia received from a national congress what amounted to dictatorial powers. He remained head of state, authoritarian and isolationist, until his death in 1840.[18]

Buenos Aires had no more success in its efforts to control Upper Peru. Between 1810 and 1817 it sent no fewer than four expeditionary forces up into the mountains of the future Bolivia. But they generally met with indifference or hostility from the local people, who were no more attracted by the prospect of a new source of external control than the Paraguayans had been. The Spanish authorities in Peru proper also sent armies southwards into the highlands to combat the incursions from Buenos Aires. As a result, Upper Peru was much fought over after 1810, with loss of life and damage to property. Adding to disorder and destruction from then until about 1816 were the guerrilla activities of several local leaders, mostly *mestizos*, who emerged in this period, seeking regional power in the mountains and in the east. These men, while being little concerned by the large issue of national independence, probably helped Buenos Aires unwittingly by tying down Spanish forces. With the increase, however, of Spanish strength in South America after the fall of Napoleon and the restoration of Ferdinand VII in 1814, guerrilla activity in the Upper Peruvian highlands was gradually suppressed. And the leaders of the now emerging Argentina decided that an attack on the Spanish base in Peru via Chile would serve their security needs better than further attempts across the central Andean highland.

That story should not be told, however, before events in northern South America from 1810 onwards are related. If Buenos Aires, capital of the Río de la Plata, was one focus of resistance to Spanish rule in South America, Caracas, capital of Venezuela, was the other. And no other single figure was so influential in the struggle for the independence of Venezuela, of northern South America, and indeed of South America as a whole, as that son of Caracas, Simón Bolívar. Although it is obvious that in the insurgents' final success against Spain a multitude of people and circumstances played essential parts, it is also true that Bolívar was a central figure in so much of the independence process that his career illustrates it comprehensively.

Simón Bolívar (1783–1830) was the son of a landed family of Caracas, one that dated from the sixteenth century but had become rich and prominent in the cacao boom of the eighteenth. He was educated privately, and evidently to little academic effect, since when he visited relatives in Madrid in 1799, they were struck by his ignorance.[19] The previous year he had been commissioned as a sub-lieutenant in a militia battalion in Venezuela; but that, and it was very little, was the sum of his military instruction. His great military feats later in life were clearly the fruit of innate ability. His first visit to Europe, mainly to Spain, was from 1799 to 1802. He married in Madrid, in May 1802, the daughter of an ennobled Caracas family, and with her returned to Venezuela. The marriage was terribly brief; his bride died in January 1803. By the end of that year Bolívar was back in Europe, now spending much time in Paris where, by his own account, he read widely, especially in the writings of the Enlightenment. He met Alexander von Humboldt, recently back from his long visits to South and Middle America. He briefly flirted with freemasonry, then a fertile breeding ground for radical political thought. In this second stay in Europe, Bolívar became a convinced republican. He also absorbed, from Machiavelli and other humanists of the Italian Renaissance, the notion that active citizenship in the republic was the source of true virtue.[20] Political activism was indeed soon to become his life's central business. It was in 1805 in Italy, on one of the hills of Rome, that Bolívar was many years later reported to have made a vow that conveys the fire of a young man newly captivated by a political cause: "I swear before the God of my fathers, by my fathers themselves, by my honor and by my country, that my arm shall not rest nor my mind be at peace until I have broken the chains that bind me by the will and power of Spain."[21]

After his return to Venezuela in 1807 he attended to his family estates in a manner of which Voltaire, whose freethinking he already admired, would have approved. But he also associated with other young creoles resentful of Spain's grasp on Venezuela. In 1810 he was one of the activists in Caracas who deposed the captain-general. He then made a brief diplomatic visit to London to solicit British governmental aid for the Venezuelan insurrection. He was unsuccessful, and returned to Caracas in December 1810. Whatever sympathy the British may have had for the rebels in Spanish America, and whatever hopes for free commercial access once the colonies were independent, they could hardly help while allied to Spain against France.

The salient events of Bolívar's career after 1810 provide a rough geographical and chronological map of the independence movement in northern South America.

MINI-CHRONOLOGY

1811 July–August. SB helps to suppress a counter-revolutionary movement in Valencia, 100 kilometers west of Caracas

1812 August 12. SB leaves Venezuela for New Granada after Spanish forces regain control of Venezuela

December 15. In New Granada, SB issues his "Cartagena Manifesto" explaining the failure of the first republic in Venezuela and asking for New Granada's help in a new attempt to free Venezuela

1813 May 7. The president of the New Granadan federation gives SB permission to invade Venezuela

1813 August 6. SB re-enters Caracas. For the next 13 months, the period of the second republic, he rules Venezuela as military dictator

1814 June 15. SB suffers heavy defeat at la Puerta by José Tomás Boves, a Spanish general. Venezuelan patriots abandon Caracas in July

August–December. The patriots retreat from Venezuela, though with much dispute in their ranks. SB again moves to New Granada, where he is given command of troops of the United Provinces of New Granada to force the state of Cundinamarca, in which Bogotá lies, into the New Granadan federation. Cundinamarca is not royalist, but has rejected ties with other now independent regions of New Granada. It surrenders on December 12

1815 May 9. SB leaves New Granada, which will soon be retaken by Spanish forces, for Jamaica

September 6. SB issues his "Jamaica Letter," which summarizes the current state of affairs in Spanish America and urges new attempts at independence

1816 Year spent partly in Haiti, gaining support from its independent government. SB's attempts during the summer to regain a hold in Venezuela fail. But on December 28 he enters the colony east of Caracas, beginning a new effort to liberate northern South America

1817 SB creates a base of operations in the distant east of Venezuela, in the Orinoco plains, at the town of Angostura

1818 January. SB begins westward movement up the Orinoco, and gains the crucial support of José Antonio Páez, leader of the *llaneros* (cattle-herding horsemen of the Orinoco plains, who until 1815 had fought for the Spanish)

Fighting in Venezuela between insurgents and Spanish forces under General Pablo Morillo, who is strong in the Andean west of Venezuela. This continues into the spring of 1819

1819   February 15. The Congress of Angostura is installed, convened to provide a legal basis for an insurgent government in Venezuela

May. SB begins a campaign to liberate New Granada. After crossing the Andes, on August 7 he defeats the royalists at Boyacá, 110 kilometers north-east of Bogotá

December 17. Republic of Colombia (New Granada and Venezuela) formed, at SB's urging

1820   September–October. SB begins to engage Spanish forces in western Venezuela

1821   June 24. SB defeats Spanish forces definitively at Carabobo, south-west of Valencia in Venezuela. He enters Caracas in triumph on June 29

September 7. SB is made first president of Colombia by the constituent Congress of Cúcuta

December. SB goes south from Bogotá to pursue the war of liberation in southern New Granada, a region conservative in both politics and religion

1822   May 24. Insurgents' victory at Pichincha in Quito (Ecuador), under the command of Antonio José de Sucre Alcalá, by now SB's most able lieutenant. This victory ends Spanish rule in the territory of Quito, since Guayaquil, the other major town, has cast off Spanish government, in a rising of October 1820

July 13. SB incorporates Quito into Colombia

July 27. SB meets, at Guayaquil, with José de San Martín, the liberator of Chile, and now Protector of Peru. Apparently as a result of this meeting, which was held in secret, San Martín retires from the campaign for independence in South America, leaving Peru still largely in Spanish hands

1823   March–April. SB sends two large forces south to Peru. He arrives there himself in September, and begins a political struggle with leading creoles in Lima

1824   February 10. A Peruvian congress makes SB dictator, to cut through political infighting

August 6. SB defeats the Spaniards at Junín in the central Peruvian Andes

December 9. Sucre inflicts a final defeat on Spanish forces in Peru (and in South America) at Ayacucho, in the Andes 240 kilometers west of Cuzco. He pursues the remnants of the Spanish army southwards into Upper Peru, where they scatter without further combat

1825   August 6. The Upper Peruvian assembly creates the nation of Bolivia, named in honor of the Liberator, who enters La Paz in triumph on August 18

1826   April 30. SB is re-elected president of Colombia

May 25. SB completes his constitution for Bolivia (a most centralist document providing for a life-long president with powers to name his successor), which he hopes Colombia will also adopt. It does not[22]

Having been the most influential single contributor to the liberation of Venezuela, Colombia, Ecuador, and Peru, and having brought these four new nations together in the federation generally known to historians as Gran Colombia ("Greater Colombia"), Bolívar spent the rest of his days trying to maintain that union. But this was to go against three colonial centuries' worth of separate regional development, 300 years' worth of largely separate local government, in the four components of his new state. His problems were compounded by the extreme regionalism of Colombia itself. In this grand scheme, then, Bolívar failed. He died, of consumption, on December 17, 1830, a grimly disappointed man, and a man abandoned by most, and reviled by many, of those who had once been his friends and allies in the great struggle for independence.

How quickly his role in that struggle grew after 1810 is clear enough in the bare facts of his career just presented. He took part in the unsuccessful fight of the Venezuelan insurgents in 1811–12 against Spanish troops and their loyalist allies in the colony. He, with many other Venezuelan rebels, took refuge in New Granada, many areas of which had already, if temporarily, freed themselves from Spain. There, with the Cartagena Manifesto, he clearly emerged as the leading political voice among the insurgents in northern South America. The rising esteem in which he was held as a military leader is shown by New Granadan support in 1813 for his proposed re-entry into Venezuela. His success in this made him the natural political leader there. As that leader he demonstrated in 1813–14 the penchant for centralizing executive power that was to become an ever more prominent part of his political personality. He by then saw concentrated power as the sole practical counterpoise to the fissile tendencies so obvious to him in the politics of Spanish America.

The restoration of Ferdinand VII to the throne early in 1814, after the Spanish War of Independence had been won, allowed Spain to focus attention and manpower on suppressing rebellion in America. This is visible in Bolívar's defeat by Boves in June 1814, and the subsequent demise of the second republic. Again Bolívar retired to New Granada, where his military eminence led the insurgent authorities to give him an important role in suppressing regional separatism. But New Granada itself succumbed in due course to the Spanish counter-attack, and Bolívar took refuge first in Jamaica and then in Haiti. Only at the end of 1816 did he return to Venezuela to begin his third and finally successful effort at liberation. Now he had a new strategy. From a remote, and, he hoped, secure, base in the eastern Orinoco *llanos* he began, early in 1818, a slow advance to the west; not, however, on Caracas, the Spanish stronghold, but further south, aiming for New Granada. The *llaneros* now added significant strength in cavalry to his army. His decisive defeat of the Spaniards in August 1819 at Boyacá was the death blow to colonial rule in New Granada. At the end of that year, Colombia came into being as a republic comprising New Granada and Venezuela, although the latter was still in Spanish hands. Late in 1820 Bolívar carried the fight back eastward into his homeland, and there inflicted the final defeat on the Spaniards at Carabobo in June of 1821. Now his military and political eminence in northern South America was so great that in September he was the obvious choice as first president of Colombia by the constituent Congress of Cucutá. Since May 1821 that Congress had been drafting a constitution for the new nation – politically a highly centralist document, and therefore in line with Bolívar's own views on governing South America, though it included liberal social measures such as the abolition of Indian tribute and a law freeing slaves' children at birth. Almost immediately after his selection as president, Bolívar decided he must extend his campaign southward towards Peru, the bastion of Spanish power in South America. In the years 1822–4 he and his most capable military lieutenant, Antonio José de Sucre, inflicted a series of defeats on Spain in Ecuador and Peru, culminating in Sucre's victory at Ayacucho at the end of 1824. With that, Spain was effectively ousted from South America. As Ecuador and Peru were liberated, Bolívar, whose political authority was now irresistible, incorporated them into Colombia to form, if only briefly, what was in area the largest Spanish-speaking nation ever to exist in South America.

Below the surface of this bare relation, lies, of course, a multitude of events and stories – complex, tragic, heroic. There were stirring crossings of the Andes in both directions to take the Spaniards by surprise; intricate political maneuverings to bring and hold together feuding insurgent factions, especially in New Granada; constant political planning, with congresses assembling and constitutions a'drafting, to give legal substance to what had been gained by force; ceaseless exercise of charisma to bend others to the Liberator's will and purpose. No writer of that morning of the Romantic age could have invented as protean a hero as Simón Bolívar.

Yet Bolívar died, only five years after reaching the pinnacle of his accomplishments, a despairing and rejected man. In 1826 he had been re-elected president of Colombia. But the centralization of authority that he thought essential to hold that confederation together grated on many political figures in its four constituent states. In 1828 his rule became no less than dictatorial, and in September of that year men who called him "tyrant" tried to kill him in Bogotá. Late in 1829 Venezuela seceded from the federation, and in May 1830 Ecuador did the same. Bolívar had by then resigned from the presidency, and was on his way to retirement, possibly in Europe or the West Indies. But before leaving South America he died – of tuberculosis in December 1830 near Santa Marta on the New Granadan coast. On November 19, 1830, six weeks before his death, Bolívar wrote to Juan José Flores, a Venezuelan who had been one of his generals in the independence wars, and was now president of the recently seceded Ecuador, a letter that contains his most remembered phrase:

> You know that I have been in command for twenty years; and from them I have derived only a few sure conclusions: first, America is ungovernable for us; second, he who serves a revolution plows the sea; third, the only thing that can be done in America is to emigrate; fourth, this country will fall without fail into the hands of an unbridled multitude, to pass later to petty, almost imperceptible, tyrants of all colors and races; fifth, devoured as we are by all crimes and destroyed by ferocity, the Europeans will not deign to conquer us; sixth, if it were possible for a part of the world to return to the primeval chaos, the latter would be the final stage of America ...[23]

But he had not "plowed the sea." For all the political storms that he had suffered, and for all the greater tempests that he rightly predicted would follow, he had been the chief pilot of Spanish South America's departure from the empire. In the broad regions whose affairs he had in varying degree directed, the political present in 1830 was unalterably different from what it had been in 1810. They were now, for better or for worse, politically sovereign nations.

Bolívar's thirteen-year campaign, from the events of April 1810 in Caracas to his arrival in Lima in September 1823, was one arm of a pincer movement that closed on Peru from north and south. The southern arm was built and guided by the other great independence leader in South America, José de San Martín. His story is both shorter and simpler than Bolívar's, but nonetheless one full of inventiveness and exceptional capacity in command.

San Martín (1778–1850) was a creole from Corrientes, in the north of present Argentina, but from early youth he lived and was educated in Spain. At the age of only 11 he became a cadet in the Spanish army, and in the next two decades fought for Spain in a variety of campaigns, rising to the rank of lieutenant colonel. But, late in 1810, the news of the risings in Caracas and Buenos Aires crystallized in him his previously unformed sympathies for the insurgent cause. He left Spanish service, and returned via London to the Río de la Plata.[24] There he soon received command of a cavalry regiment, began to participate in politics, and made a good marriage. In January of 1814 he was made commander of the army of the north, with the task of directing Buenos Aires's third attempt to take Upper Peru, and from there move on to attack the Spanish in Peru itself. But, reflecting on this strategy and its two past failures, he conceived the idea of attacking Peru through Chile rather than through the central Andes. He therefore resigned his command in the north, on grounds of ill health, and obtained the post of governor of Cuyo, a region west of Buenos Aires under the mountains. There, in the provincial capital, Mendoza, from early 1814 to late 1816 he made preparations for an attack on the Spanish regime in Chile, which forces sent from Peru had restored to Spanish rule late in 1814.

In January 1817, San Martín's Army of the Andes crossed the mountains into Chile, using several passes. The army numbered altogether some 5,000, among whom were a substantial minority of Chileans. Chile provided some of the commanders, notably Bernardo O'Higgins, who had been one of the leading lights of the colony's attempted break from Spain between 1810 and 1814. San Martín had intended to surprise the Spanish forces in Chile with a sudden appearance; and indeed he did so. Bringing an army through the mountains, even in midsummer, had been thought so difficult as to verge on impossible. The unexpectedness of his arrival enabled San Martín to occupy large areas north of Santiago with detachments from his main force. But he quickly led the bulk of the army to victory over the Spaniards at Chacabuco, near Santiago, on February 12. Two days later he and O'Higgins entered the capital city in triumph. San Martín differed from Bolívar in having little interest in political leadership; nor did he have any grand scheme for Spanish America that he felt impelled to promote through political activism of his own. For these reasons, and perhaps even more because Chile was for him primarily a stepping stone for the liberation of Peru, he refused the offer, made by the *cabildo* of Santiago, of supreme political power in Chile. That role fell to O'Higgins, whose distinctly dictatorial government lasted until he was driven from the country in January of 1823.

San Martín had not yet, in fact, completed his military business in Chile. The Spanish forces managed to regroup, and in March of 1818 inflicted a defeat on him that brought a new threat to Santiago. But he struck back, and on April 5, at Maipú, near the capital, won the victory that freed the colony from Spanish control once and for all. In accomplishing that, Maipú also secured Chile as a base for San Martín's assault on Peru. It was to that greater purpose that he now turned.[25]

There was no question of a land attack on Peru. The utter dryness of the Atacama desert stood in the way. Therefore ships had to be gathered. The cost of these, and indeed of the whole expedition, fell on Chile and Argentina; and, in the event, rather more heavily on Chile, which became awkwardly indebted to foreign lenders as a result. To command the naval force, Chile engaged Thomas Cochrane, a British naval officer who had risen to eminence in the Napoleonic Wars. Now he joined the many British, North American, and other soldiers of fortune in the force destined for Peru; the numbers of these mercenaries had risen in all insurgent forces in South America as time passed, and some played distinguished senior roles in the wars. Cochrane was one who did so. Though wayward and impulsive, and for those reasons often at loggerheads with San Martín, who was planned caution itself, Cochrane served the attack on Peru well, holding Spanish naval forces on the west coast fully in check. The invading force left Chile in August of 1820. It consisted of 23 ships, manned by 1,600 sailors and carrying some 4,500 troops, largely Chilean and Argentine. Cochrane argued for a frontal attack on Lima; but San Martín chose to land at Pisco, 220 kilometers farther south, in the hope that his presence there would encourage more radical elements in Peru to take action against the Spaniards.

It was at this point that San Martín's grand scheme began to lose momentum. The situation was different from the one he had faced in Chile as he laid plans for that campaign. He had known that in Chile he could count on a large group of influential opponents to Spanish rule; some were indeed already in his army. But in Peru very few such people were to be found. While he had come to Chile, therefore, as an ally, he arrived in Peru as an intervener, almost perhaps an interloper. He seems to have been only too conscious of that. "How could the cause of independence be advanced by my holding Lima, or even the whole country, in military possession?", he asked an interviewer in 1821. "I wish to have all men thinking with me, and do not choose to advance a step beyond the gradual march of public opinion."[26] Bolívar would not have been, and two years later was not, troubled by such scruples.

The loyalty to Spain of the Peruvian creoles was unequalled in Spanish America. Those in Lima were the most faithful of all, and Lima was the unchallenged center of political power in Peru. It was probably the most patrician city of the empire, its leading families proud of their origins in conquerors and early settlers, its lesser creole lights conscious of the city's centuries-long role as viceregal and ecclesiastical capital of Spanish South America. It was more removed from modernizing European influences than even Mexico City. The issue of free trade loomed far less large than in the newly expanded cities of the Atlantic coast of the empire. And it may well be that as rebellion spread in the periphery of Spanish South America from 1810 onwards, creoles in Lima found for themselves a rewarding new role as preservers of colonial rule, in an effort that restored luster to Lima and to themselves. The creation of new vice-royalties in the eighteenth century had reduced the city's political standing, robbing it in 1739 of authority over New Granada and Quito, and in 1776 over Charcas (Upper Peru), Paraguay, and the Río de la Plata. After 1810, however, Lima became the hub of Spanish efforts to reverse the current of insurgency; and with that it partly regained its place as the imperial center of South America. The viceroy in those years, José Fernando de Abascal, had the political wit to capitalize on this revival of the city's status by placing creoles in responsible posts (the presidency of the *audiencia* of Cuzco, for example, and the intendancy of La Paz).[27] For reasons, then, of present politics as well as tradition, many notables in Lima held firm to the Spanish side while mutiny sprouted to the north and south. Finally, those who might still feel the attractive tug of change were likely to be brought up short by the memory of the great rebellion in the Andes of 1780–1. That store of Indian hostility was still there in the interior, ready perhaps to erupt again if the old order were changed. The Haitian rebellion in the early 1790s, and Hidalgo's rising in New Spain much more recently, served only to keep alive fears of the consequences for Spaniards and creoles if imperial control were to lapse.

San Martín therefore faced great inertia in Peru's creole political nation, inertia that he was never able to overcome. Eventually he abandoned his waiting game and advanced on Lima; whereupon the Spanish authorities left the city, and he entered it on July 10, 1821. Faced with this reality, the *cabildo* of creole notables issued a declaration of independence on the 28th of that month. On August 12 San Martín accepted the title of Protector of Peru, appointing as advisers a cabinet drawn from his own followers and from local creoles of apparently liberal inclinations. He, in good liberal fashion, set free the children of slaves born after July 28, 1821; he abolished Indian tribute and all types of forced native labor; he ordered that Indians should in the future be called simply "Peruvians." But all this applied only to the area that he controlled, which was merely Lima and its immediate surroundings. In the mountains the only threat to Spanish dominance was from bands of creole and *mestizo* guerrillas, who were as much bandits seeking to gain from looting as they were freedom fighters. He waited once more for creole support to accrete around him. But rather the reverse happened, as the creoles of Lima grew resentful of the presence of his army and the cost of supporting it, which now fell on them.[28]

And so, when San Martín sailed north to meet Bolívar at Guayaquil in July of 1822, he went in relative weakness. Bolívar's southward sweep from New Granada, through Quito towards Peru was in full flood; San Martín's masterly plan to free Peru, and by doing so to secure the permanence of rebel gains everywhere in South America, had stalled in creole conservatism, fears, and apathy. Little more than speculation exists about what was said in those interviews. San Martín's inclination to believe that monarchy would be the best guarantee of order in Spanish America may well have clashed with Bolívar's adamantine republicanism; for however authoritarian a government Bolívar came to believe Spanish America needed, he always drew the line at kings. Any debate they may have had about how to proceed in Peru (which must surely have been the crux of their discussions) would almost certainly have ended in disagreement. The outcome was that, two months later in Lima, San Martín resigned as Protector of Peru, after warning the Peruvian Congress of the dangers in Spanish America of any "successful soldier" achieving supreme power.[29] He returned via Chile to Mendoza, and in 1823 left Argentina for France, England, Brussels, and ultimately Brunoy, on the outskirts of Paris. He never again set foot in Argentina, Chile, or Peru. He died in 1850 in Boulogne, to which he had moved to escape the dangers of the February Revolution of 1848 in Paris.[30] Twenty-six years before his death, as has already been briefly told, Sucre and Bolívar, unencumbered by San Martín's political or ethical reservations, had done in Peru what they saw must be done, ending 292 years of Spanish imperial rule in South America.

NEW SPAIN, 1811–1821

About a month after San Martín's long-delayed entry into Lima inspired the town council there to declare independence from Spain, New Spain, in August 1821, departed from the empire. That was a coincidence, not a connection – except in the broadest sense that movement towards independence took place in all the mainland colonies during the same years and for the same range of reasons. Quite remarkable, in fact, is the almost complete detachment of the independence process in New Spain and Central America from the parallel unfolding of events in South America. There was next to no contact between the insurgents in the two regions, much less any mutual support with, say, men or money. That lack of connection strongly suggests, in fact, how far Middle America and South America had become separate political and cultural entities even before the empire disappeared.

In Mexico, the defeat of Hidalgo in January of 1811 had not brought insurgency to an end. The torch was taken up by perhaps a greater figure, the *mestizo* priest José María Morelos y Pavón (1765–1815). He was by far a humbler figure than Hidalgo, a carpenter's son, and a man who in his youth may have worked as a mule driver on the road between Mexico City and Acapulco, or as a laborer on an hacienda in the Michoacán lowlands.[31] In either occupation he would have gained a knowledge of that south-western region of Mexico that later stood him in good stead as an insurgent leader. He trained for the priesthood at the college where Hidalgo taught, though no record exists of any particular attachment between the two at the time. After taking orders in 1799 he tended parishes in the western lowlands of Michoacan, an isolated, hot area. He made contact with Hidalgo after the *grito de Dolores* in 1810, and was told to organize a military force on the southern Pacific coast, the area familiar to him, with the aim of taking Acapulco. Morelos persisted in this task after Hidalgo was defeated and executed. What seems to have driven him was not any Enlightenment-inspired belief in human freedom or popular will, but a quite simple, but profound, sense of Christian charity. Against such basic charity, he thought, Bourbon rule in New Spain had offended, by, as one example, oppressing Indians with tribute exactions.[32] It must, therefore, be removed.

By late 1811 Morelos had gathered a force that differed from Hidalgo's in being relatively small, at 9,000, and well equipped, with weapons captured from the Spanish. But it was most notably different in being well disciplined. With this compact but potent army, Morelos gave the Spanish administration of Mexico grave cause for concern for two years. By the late 1812 he controlled much of the south, including the cities of Oaxaca and Orizaba; and in April 1813 he took Acapulco after a long, and probably wasteful, siege. He menaced communication between Mexico City and Veracruz, and the capital certainly lived under the threat of his attack for some time. In the large region under his control he enforced order strictly (in great contrast to Hidalgo, executing soldiers convicted of theft), collecting taxes, and appointing local officials. Finally, however, Morelos fell, like Hidalgo, to the military ability of Calleja, the Spanish commander (who also became viceroy in March of 1813). When in December of that year Morelos moved north to attack Valladolid, in Michoacan, Calleja sent a force to intercept him. Morelos was defeated. One of the key royalist officers in the battle was a creole colonel named Agustín de Iturbide, who seven years later, having changed sides, was to play the central role in Mexico's break from Spain. Morelos was not captured in this engagement, but after it spent almost two years in southern Mexico in slow retreat before an increasingly powerful Spanish opposition.

In September of 1813 a congress of representatives from areas then free of Spanish control had gathered at the small town of Chilpancingo, some 80 kilometers north of Acapulco. Members of this body stayed with Morelos in 1814, and in October of that year issued, at the town of Apatzingán, Mexico's first constitution. It was a liberal document that declared an independent republic. It did not, however, have the desired effect of attracting to Morelos the wide creole support that any successful bid for independence needed. Finally, in November 1815 he was captured. Being found guilty of both heresy and treason, he was defrocked, and then shot on December 22, 1815.[33]

For six years after Morelos's capture late in 1814, guerrilla activities were almost the sole sign in Mexico of hostility to Spanish rule. Even Calleja, viceroy and military chief from March 1813 to September 1816, was unable to eradicate this elusive, fragmented resistance. When his harsh regime was replaced by a more conciliatory administration, the guerrilleros had greater freedom of action. It has long been known that small bands operated from remote mountainous areas; but only more recent research has shown that raiding took place close to cities. The Mexico City to Veracruz road, for instance, which was Mexico's busiest trade route, was under constant threat, and was sometimes cut. The outskirts of Mexico City itself suffered raids in 1816. *Haciendas* around Querétaro were assaulted in 1818. These constant pinpricks, while unlikely in themselves to cause the Spanish to leave, certainly lowered morale among officials, troops, and creole loyalists. The administration's inability to deal with the irritation tended to add to the discontent of those already impatient with

Spanish rule; and that impatience certainly grew with the imposition of taxes to pay the costs of keeping men in the field to chase guerrilleros.[34]

Just as an event in Spain, Napoleon's occupation in 1808, had set in motion the movements towards independence in America, so again in 1820 another occurrence in the peninsula was instrumental in driving those movements towards their conclusion, and especially in Mexico. The event was the quite unexpected rising of an army, that was about to sail from Cadiz to attempt a retaking of the Río de la Plata, against Ferdinand VII.[35] Other army units across Spain quickly joined the revolt, the inspiration of which lay partly in resentment of the large cuts made in the military after 1814, and partly in the hostility of all shades of liberals to the rigid absolutism that Ferdinand had displayed.

The immediate political result of the risings was the restoration of the liberal Cadiz constitution of 1812. Under its terms, Ferdinand suddenly found himself a king subject to the control of a parliament, a constitutional monarch. He did not have to submit to the liberal yoke for long; in 1823 Louis XVIII of France sent an army to free him of it. But by then the damage in America had been done.

Mexican independence in 1821 has long been viewed as a colonial reaction to the liberalism of the revived Spanish parliament (the *cortes*); more specifically as a rejection by influential conservative creoles of, among other unwelcome innovations, anti-church laws deriving from the constitution and passed by that parliament. In that view there is some truth. But the move towards independence in 1820–1 was, not surprisingly, the work of a much wider segment of political opinion among the creoles. Broadly speaking, most of them had few objections to the constitution. The 1812 constitution was in fact preserved in the scheme of Mexican independence that was soon to be proposed. But the conduct and the attitudes of the Cortes towards the colonies did cause a fatal resentment in Mexico. This new parliament, just as in Cadiz eight or so years before, seemed to contradict its own liberalism by showing its determination to keep America subservient to Spain. Many creoles' ideal political arrangement was self-government within a loose imperial framework, a transatlantic Spanish commonwealth. There had never been any likelihood that the monarchy under Ferdinand VII, an intolerant centralist, would contemplate creating any such structure. But the maintenance of a strictly imperialist line by the self-declared and otherwise reformist Cortes of 1820–3 was intolerably galling. When, therefore, under the terms of the 1812 constitution, elections to town councils and provincial assemblies took place in Mexico in mid 1820, and when the viceroy of the day restored the freedom of the press that had been canceled late in 1812, loud protest at restrictive Spanish policy burst out. Urgency was added to the search for a solution by reports of internal conflict among liberals in Spain. Mexicans feared that such disagreements might open the way to restoration of royalist absolutism under Ferdinand, in which case reformers in Mexico could expect renewed repression. So it was that when, in February of 1821, a home-grown proposal appeared for Mexican self-government, it was widely welcomed.

The main author of this proposal, called the Plan of Iguala, was Agustín de Iturbide (1783–1824), the creole who as a royalist officer in 1813 had taken part in the definitive defeat of Morelos. Smarting perhaps under his removal from command in 1816 for supposed misconduct, and possibly also sensing the new wind's gathering force, in late 1820 he changed sides. The following February he and Vicente Guerrero, one of the prominent guerrilla leaders of the years before 1820, published the plan. It was a clever proposal, calculated to appeal to and unite most shades of opinion. By it, Mexico was to become a Catholic monarchy, separate from Spain but ruled by Ferdinand VII as emperor, or by one of his brothers if he declined the throne. Mexico would have a *cortes*. This new government would guarantee independence, the preservation of Catholicism as the sole state religion, and the equality of Spaniards and American Mexicans (which, the belief was, would unite them). These guarantees – of independence, religion, and union – were to be protected by the "Army of the Three Guarantees" consisting of ex-insurgents and former royalist troops who, like Iturbide, had shifted their allegiance. Property also was guaranteed. And all those who held positions in the church, the military, and the government would remain in them if they accepted the plan. Even the viceroy and the judges of *audiencias* would have role in the new regime, in a sovereign junta that would govern while permanent arrangements were developing. Offices in government, though, were to become available to all inhabitants, and caste distinctions were to be abolished.

The Plan of Iguala, replete as it was with carrots for Spaniards, all varieties of creoles, monarchists, seekers of autonomy, churchmen, and even the lower orders of society, was, for long enough, welcomed by all except those on the political extremes. Throughout the first half of 1821 great numbers joined Iturbide. Many royalist troops deserted to him; most of them were, like him, Mexican-born, and they were exhausted by several years of inconclusive fighting against guerrilleros.[36] With such forces he easily overran the colony. Cracks developed, predictably enough, in the Spanish side. Dissatisfied with the viceroy's inability to control Iturbide's revolt, Spanish troops mutinied in Mexico City early in July 1821 and deposed him. In late August Iturbide met the incoming captain-general of Mexico, Juan O'Donojú, at Córdoba, near Veracruz. The two negotiated a treaty there in which O'Donojú, the senior Spanish official in Mexico in the absence of a viceroy, recognized the existence of the independent Mexican empire. He and Iturbide then moved on to Mexico City with the Army of the Three Guarantees. There the remaining Spanish forces, acknowledging O'Donojú's authority, surrendered. Iturbide entered the capital on September 27 as head of the new government. And so Mexico entered its independent existence, with, in that final act of the drama, very little bloodshed, and more in exasperation than in anger.

In contrast to Peru at about the same time, independence did not have to be forced on New Spain, even though its coming was above all a response to external events. The politics that brought self-rule were an internal invention. Mexico's greater willingness to break away, in comparison with Peru, reflects at least its greater absorption over the previous half-century or more of recent

European ideology. It had, by 1820, plenty of moderate liberals. Mexico was also more confident of its wealth and resources than Peru; it had been the rich jewel in the empire's crown throughout the eighteenth century, and still possessed the resources to prosper as an independent economic entity. And although Hidalgo's insurrection had been cause for much alarm among creoles as well as Spaniards, Mexico did not suffer from any internal division comparable to that great cultural hiatus between coast and highlands, Europeans and natives, that had long afflicted Peru (and would continue to do so until the present). Indians, *mestizos*, and whites had long lived in Mexico in greater familiarity than in Peru, if not in perfect harmony. The coastal Peruvian creole's fear of the alien, in the form of highland Indians, had therefore no full counterpart in Mexico. Hence nervousness about Spain's departure was less of a check on movement towards independence there than in Peru. Finally, Mexico left the empire because no good reason remained to stay. Under Charles IV and Ferdinand VII, the monarchy had lost whatever numinous quality it had previously possessed. Parliamentary government by Spain, even with representatives from America sitting in the *cortes*, seemed unlikely to offer any improvement in colonial status. The cost of defending Spain's hold on the colony against challenges from guerrilleros fell on the colony itself; by 1820 the tax burden of that fight – money apparently spent to no effect, as the insurgents took over rural areas – was increasingly resented, and even considered illegal by some.[37] Spanish power was incomparably diminished from what it had been a century, even half a century, before. The stem had withered; and now the branch, Mexico, fell off. That same image of the independence process applies to the other mainland colonies in some measure; but in Mexico's case it is peculiarly fitting.

Cuba, however, did not break from the stem. For this there were two main causes, one external and one internal. The external reason was the Haitian slave rebellion of 1791. If alarming tremors from this earthquake reached distant regions of Spanish America, in Cuba, close to the epicenter, the revolt caused immense consternation. The flight of some 30,000 Frenchmen from Haiti to Cuba between 1709 and 1808, with news of destruction and death, kept this fear alive.[38] To be sure, Cuba benefited economically from the revolt, since it replaced Haiti as the main source of sugar in the Caribbean. But increasing its production required larger imports of African slaves after 1790. The rising proportion of black slaves in the island's population naturally made Spaniards and creoles more fearful still. It is no surprise that the ending of Spain's colonial presence, administrative and military, was too dangerous a prospect for most to contemplate.

Within Cuba, even before the Haitian eruption, creoles had had less cause for discontent with Spanish rule than their counterparts almost anywhere else in the empire. From the end of the Seven Years War, in 1763, Cuba had enjoyed a peculiarly favored position in the Indies. The ease with which Havana had been captured by the British in 1762, and the political and strategic outcome of the war – Spain's being left almost alone to face a consolidated and potentially aggressive British presence in North America – made Madrid acutely aware of the need to build up its military presence in Cuba. The island was, after all, in a key strategic position for the defense of New Spain and other Spanish holdings around the Caribbean. But improvement of Cuba's defenses must be paid for in larger measure than before by the island itself. Spain, therefore, set about modernizing and developing Cuba with remarkable vigor. In 1764 the first intendant appointed to America took office in Havana. The following year free trade was permitted between the Caribbean islands and seven major ports in Spain (the beginning of the expansion of free exchange between Spanish territories that culminated in the trade law of 1778). Restrictions on the import of slaves were eased in practice, if not in law. British and North American slave traders began to sell slaves in Cuba, and in the 1790s foreign merchants were allowed to settle and buy property in the island. From 1790, in fact, Cuba enjoyed greater freedom of commerce, and generally a greater openness to the exterior, than any other part of the empire. In that year it was given permission to trade with allies and neutral countries. Much Cuban sugar went to the USA. All this came about with much consultation between creole planters and merchants and local Spanish government, with the administrators often bending the regulations in the colonials' favor. The Cuban elite, a combination of creole sugar planters and Spanish merchants, in fact achieved by 1800 a considerable amount of say in its own government. It was not the autonomy that more demanding creoles elsewhere would have liked. But, in combination with the need to keep Spain on the scene as a guarantee of security, it was more than enough to deflect creoles away from hankerings for independence.[39] For similar reasons, although its economic improvement did not come until after 1810, Puerto Rico also stayed in the imperial fold after the mainland empire fell.

BRAZIL

In its approach and entry to independence Brazil was, as in its entire history down to the present, more tranquil than Spanish America. The same resentments of the home country's demands and restrictions, the same tensions between colonials and peninsular emigrants to America, and the same sense of a developing separateness were to be found as in Spanish America. But all this was more muted, less urgent. In part the difference lay in a relaxation of pressure for reform in Portugal after the fall of Pombal in 1777. Again, Portugal did not impose on Brazil the weight of fiscal demands that Spain laid on the Indies after 1790. Brazil, rather, in the 1790s enjoyed the gains that accrued to it, as they did to Cuba, from the fading of Haiti as a sugar producer. And in general Brazil's final colonial decades were a time of prosperity as its enlarged range of plantation products found ready markets in Europe. Members of upper colonial society, therefore, had few complaints on material grounds against Portugal. They might have found more cause for discontent in political or intellectual matters. The *câmaras*, or town councils, did lose some of the local authority they had possessed earlier in colonial times. The crown refused to the end to allow the establishment of a university or printing presses in Brazil, so that colonials had to go to Europe (usually to Coimbra) for higher education, and could, in principle, read only such books as the administration allowed to cross the Atlantic. Portugal's efforts to keep Brazil free of alien and disturbing ideas were quite overt. Brazilians who received education in France in the revolutionary years were not allowed to return home.[40] But such open restrictions brought very little reaction in Brazil. One reason for the compliance of potentially active and influential colonials was their general social conservatism. For most of them the French Revolution had the same message as it had for Spanish American creoles: radical political change was fraught with social hazard. The Haitian revolt simply added to their caution. Again, late colonial Brazil was still highly regionalized. Pure distance made collective action by leading colonials in, say, Rio, Salvador, and Recife unlikely. And such feelings as existed of a distinct American identity were generally focused on a person's region of origin, rather than Brazil as a whole. *Pátria* meant one's own captaincy, or some even smaller area.[41]

Only two instances of Brazilian opposition to Portuguese rule stand out in the late colony. The first came just before the French Revolution, in 1788–9, and took place in Minas Gerais; hence its usual name, the Inconfidência Mineira, or "Minas Disloyalty." Its cause was a heavy-handed attempt to raise local taxes and collect debts owed to the crown. Merchants and other socially prominent people of the region stood to lose severely, and some (but fewer than twenty all told) began to conspire to make Minas Gerais into an independent republic. Perhaps, they thought, other captaincies would imitate it. Among the plotters were notable intellectuals of the captaincy, some of them the products of Coimbra. Their inspiration was in the unthreatening precedent of the United States' independence.[42] But the plot was soon uncovered, and its authors arrested. One of the most active was Joaquim José da Silva Xavier, a junior army officer who also on occasion performed as a dentist, and so gained the nickname Tiradentes ("Toothpuller"). The Inconfidência is often referred to as his movement, in part because he was the only conspirator punished by execution.

Ten years later came a very different intrigue, the "Tailors' Plot" in Salvador of 1798. Here the plotters were mainly blacks and mulattos, some slave and some free. Most were city-born, and most were manual workers. Ten of the thirty-two men finally arrested were indeed tailors. Some of the group, at least, had read or heard read French revolutionary writings. The notices that they posted in Salvador in August 1798 called for social and racial equality as well as republican independence (first of the city, and then of the captaincy of Bahia). One of the conspirators declared that it was "necessary for all to become Frenchmen," whereupon "everything being leveled in a popular revolution, all would be rich, released from the misery in which they were living, discrimination between white, black, and mulatto being abolished; because all occupations and jobs would be open and available without distinction to each and every one." Any proposal less likely than this to attract the support of the mass of influential colonials is hard to imagine. Of the conspirators, four of the poorest, doubtless picked as an exemplary warning, were hanged, drawn, and quartered.[43]

It is difficult to see in either the Inconfidência Mineira or the "Tailors' Plot" any serious threat to the political or social status quo of Brazil at the end of the eighteenth century. They were straws stirring in the gentlest of breezes. When, therefore, the Portuguese royal family, carried from Lisbon in British ships along with several thousand courtiers and officials, disembarked in Rio de Janeiro on January 22, 1808, they came to a colony that bore them few grudges. With the arrival of Prince John (regent of Portugal in place of his disturbed mother from 1792 to 1816, and then king as John VI until 1826), an age of monarchy began in Brazil that lasted until 1889.

So much larger was Brazil than Portugal, and Portugal so much dependent on Brazil for its economic well-being, that it could easily be argued that the colony had really become the empire's center of gravity, at least in the material sense. Suggestions that the monarch might move across the Atlantic had in fact been made before, though perhaps not seriously. The Prince Regent, however, took to Brazil, or at least to Rio, with gusto, and finally left in 1821 only under fierce political pressure from Portugal.

During his thirteen years of residence, Brazil gained in political self-esteem. The particular part of it that gained most in that respect was, of course, the capital, Rio de Janeiro, and the area surrounding it. Rio became a far more imposing center of government than it had ever been as a mere viceregal capital. John had brought with him many state papers and much of the Lisbon bureaucracy, since it would clearly be necessary to duplicate in Rio many of the governmental bodies existing in Portugal. Printing presses, initially for government purposes, were set up for the first time, in Rio and then in Salvador. Other innovations, in 1808, were schools of surgery, again in Rio and Salvador, created not so much for the public good as to improve medical services to the military. In the same year, the crown created a Bank of Brazil capable of issuing notes and making loans to the government. Two years later, a Royal Military Academy appeared in Rio, to train officers for the Brazilian section of the Portuguese army (soldiers in the homeland being committed at the time to the fight against the French in the peninsula).[44] These were only some of the accouterments befitting a metropolitan capital that Rio acquired during John's stay. Inevitably, also, its population grew in the same years, rising from $c.50,000$ in 1808 to $c.100,000$ in 1821. Among the citizens were many outsiders. The largest group of these was naturally Portuguese, who came to number (including some who had been there before 1808) around 24,000. But other European nationalities were well represented: 1,500 Spaniards and Spanish Americans; 1,000 Frenchmen; 600 English; 100 Germans; and others, to a total of over 4,200, from assorted European countries and the United States. These numbers refer to men alone, most of whom were professionals and craftsmen.[45] Rio thus became cosmopolitan as well as politically powerful.

Neither the final ejection of the French from Portugal in 1811 nor Napoleon's abdication three years later provided persuasion enough for Prince John to return to Lisbon. He was contentedly settled in Rio, comfortably distant from the importunities of the Portuguese nobility, most of which had not followed him to Brazil.[46] Late in 1815, partly in response to appeals from Portuguese authorities for his return, he officially made Brazil a kingdom, and created the "United Kingdom of Portugal, Brazil, and the Algarves." Brazil was now the constitutional equal of Portugal, and therefore no longer a colony. The monarch was as properly resident there as he was in the traditional homeland.

Although messages of gratitude allegedly poured in on the Prince Regent from around the newly elevated territory, not all in Brazil were happy with the prospect of his remaining indefinitely. The influx of foreigners, especially artisans, to Brazil that had followed the monarchy's arrival had led to some radicalization of political ideas. Republicanism, along North American lines, and denunciation of absolutism, in the French style, gained currency in the port towns, especially among the growing numbers of freemasons now to be found in Brazil. This radicalism joined, in the north, with resentment of the promotion of Rio de Janeiro that had taken place after 1808. The regional rivalry was already old, dating back to the pre-gold age when the north-east was the heart of Brazil. It was in Pernambuco, once the richest of the north-eastern sugar captaincies, that serious trouble broke out in March of 1817. The spark was the attempted arrest, by the governor of the captaincy, of an army officer who belonged to a masonic lodge. The officer, forewarned, instead raised his men in revolt against the local government. Within a day a Republic of Pernambuco was proclaimed and a new government set up. The rebellion spread quickly into the next captaincies northwards, Paraíba and Rio Grande. But almost as quickly it subsided, as loyal troops came into action, and local opposition developed. For many, especially among the more prosperous, the movement was still too extreme in its republicanism, and in its implicit hostility to slavery. Pernambucan autonomy was not worth the possible sacrifice of that age-old economic prop.[47]

However brief the northern rebellion may have been, nevertheless, and however cheering Rio's support of the now King John VI in that crisis, the monarchy suffered in both image and confidence as a result of it. Late in 1817 more troops were brought over from Portugal; in March of the following year, secret societies, including freemasonry, were banned. The crown no longer rested easily in Brazil. At the same time, impatience with royal government was rising in Portugal, where economic conditions remained difficult after the long war against the French. In 1819 discontent in Portugal spread to the army when pay fell several months behind. In August 1820 the garrison of Oporto, in the north of the country, revolted; in September the garrison at Lisbon overthrew the king's regents there and installed a new provisional government. And in November of 1820 the military, imitating the radical model of the Spanish army in the same year, pressured that government into adopting, for interim purposes, the liberal Spanish constitution of 1812.[48] Portugal now became a constitutional monarchy (though with an absent king), directed by liberals.

The course of Brazilian independence, from this point, has certain resemblances to the independence process taking place in Mexico at the same time. Briefly stated, it runs as follows. A parliament was quickly elected in Portugal, and met for the first time in late January 1821. Brazil was allocated 70–75 of the 200 total seats in this assembly; but no Brazilian representatives arrived before August 1821, and from some regions, none ever arrived; hence crucial decisions were taken without Brazilian participation. One of these was that the king should return to Lisbon. John briefly hesitated before acceding to this demand on March 7, 1821; not to return would possibly mean his loss of Portugal. On April 26 he and some 4,000 Portuguese, along with the funds held in the treasury and the Bank of Brazil, departed for Lisbon. As 1821 proceeded, the Portuguese parliament showed ever more clearly its intent to treat Brazil once again as a colony. In September it ordered that all governmental bodies set up in Rio in 1808 should be abolished; in October it named military governors, under direct orders from Lisbon, to all regions of Brazil. Brazilian deputies arriving to take their parliamentary seats were treated with scornful hostility, as inhabitants of a "land of monkeys, of little black men caught on the coast of Africa, and of bananas," in the words of a leading Portuguese liberal.[49] An energetic debate ensued in Brazil about the best course of action to take. No one was prepared to accept anything less than political autonomy. The options ranged from the radicals' preference for independence as a republic to the moderate-liberal and conservative solution of a dual monarchy, with John VI on the throne in Portugal and his son, Peter, on that of Brazil. Peter had not returned to Portugal with his father, who may possibly have advised him to collaborate, if necessary, with Brazilians seeking autonomy. By so doing he would preserve at least the possibility of future reunification of the monarchy. In January 1822 Peter formally announced that he would stay in Brazil. He became the focal point of the attentions of competing political factions. As the story of the final break with Portugal goes, on September 7, 1822 Peter received renewed demands from Lisbon that he return to Portugal and restore Brazil to Portuguese rule; his own orders in Brazil were overridden. He was at that moment on the bank of the river Ipiranga, between Santos and São Paulo. Throwing the papers on the ground, and grinding them under his heel, he reportedly announced "From today on our relations with them are finished. I want nothing more from the Portuguese government, and I proclaim Brazil for ever more separated from Portugal. Long live independence, liberty, and the separation of Brazil." A month later Peter was proclaimed emperor, and in December crowned as Peter (Pedro) I of Brazil in Rio de Janeiro.[50]

That was not quite the end of the story. In the north and the north-east considerable Portuguese army and naval forces remained in place. To dislodge them Peter engaged Thomas Cochrane, who, after winding up his services to the Spanish American independence movements on the west coast in 1822, was now living on an estate he had acquired in Chile. Early in 1823 he put together an improvised Brazilian squadron at Rio, commanded and crewed partly by other British seamen. Although this force was inferior to the considerable Portuguese flotilla that was lying at Salvador, Cochrane's reputation made up the difference in strength, so that when he arrived off Salvador in July of 1823, the Portuguese troops embarked and sailed away under the escort of the warships. Cochrane gave chase as far as the Canaries (and one of his captains, as far as Lisbon), taking or destroying most of the Portuguese vessels. A similar show of naval force along the north coast in late July and August was enough to end the Portuguese presence there. In November of 1823 Cochrane was created marquês de Maranhão in recognition of his part in bringing Brazilian independence to a successful conclusion.[51]

[15] *EPILOGUE*

How widely and how deeply has the post-independence history of Latin America been influenced by the three centuries of colonial experience? To what extent is the Latin America of today the product of that experience? Or – conversely – how far has it shaken off that experience and become the product of its independent self-creation?

The answers to these questions proposed by historians, social scientists, politicians, and various other commentators have been many, varied, and sometimes so debatable as to become the source of fierce controversy. Some answers, however, can be stated easily enough and without much fear of contradiction. The least controversial are those applying to quite specific conditions observable in Latin America in the decades right after independence was gained.

The wars of independence, lasting for a decade or more in some areas, did severe damage to most parts of Spanish America. A basic sort of harm done by the wars was simple loss of life, which was substantial in places. People died not just, or even mostly, in fighting, but also from the diseases for which war provided encouraging conditions. An example is the death from disease of half the Spanish army opposing independence fighters in Venezuela between 1815 and 1817. Although Bolívar's men, being native to the region, did not fall to illness so massively, they, too, died from the dysentery, smallpox, yellow fever, and other diseases that mowed down the Spaniards. War and disease also caused large migrations of people,[1] with disruption of family life, agriculture, and other sorts of production.

Disruption of the normal activities that supported most people's lives was, in fact, universal in the zones that were fought over, and naturally most severe where the fighting was heaviest and most prolonged. Both sides, royalists and rebels, drew on local populations for troops, so that men of working age and ability were taken from producing food and other basic tasks. Both sides seized stored food, grain that had been kept for seed, and animals needed to till the soil and carry its product to market. Along the coasts, shipping might be commandeered and trade thereby disrupted. Maintenance of economically important items was neglected – roads, storage buildings, irrigation systems, underground mine workings, and the refineries essential for producing metals (silver above all).

Thus the new nations emerged from the wars more or less economically crippled. To that problem was added the absence of capital to restore economic infrastructures. Spaniards expelled from the now ex-colonies generally took their silver with them. Money in the Spanish treasury offices had been sent to Spain or had gone to fund opposition to the rebellions; and the rebels had spent whatever they had on arms and armies. Worse still, groups fighting for independence had commonly borrowed from sympathetic foreign countries (notably Great Britain) to finance their efforts. After the wars were done, the loans came due, with interest inflating the principal. With economies so damaged, the new countries found repayment difficult or impossible. The outcome was that they were long unable to borrow more money abroad. The task of restoring economies was therefore arduous. Nothing like a Marshall Plan was offered by any benevolent foreign power. In most cases restoration came about only through gradual healing of the body economic that led eventually to slow growth. In reality, however, hardly any Spanish American countries glimpsed economic prosperity until three or four decades had passed after independence, and demand for the primary products of land and mines began its vigorous late nineteenth-century growth in the industrializing countries of North America and Europe.

Economic recovery was held back also by political disorder. In fact the two problems were tightly intertwined. Lack of political stability added to lenders' reluctance to provide funds; and prevalent poverty encouraged those with any means of asserting themselves to seize political power so that they could use it to get their hands on whatever wealth might remain.

Far too many such people were present in the new countries after independence. In various parts of Spanish America (Mexico, Venezuela, and the central Andes, for example) the wars had thrown up local military leaders who lent their services to either the imperial or the rebel side according to whatever immediate advantage presented itself. Some of these leaders were regional landowners who could call on men from their estates to fight for them; but others arose over time who gained authority, and a following, by demonstrating military (typically guerrilla) ability. The landowners were likely to be white, or light *mestizos*; but the second group included *castas*. When the wars were done, some of these regional military leaders, who can properly be termed "warlords," remained in place, equipped with armed bands and ambition. The combination proved poisonous to the political health of most countries. Some warlords – *caudillo* is a close Spanish equivalent – pursued and gained national power; others lent their services to politicians who, without their military backing, would have been unable to gain and keep office. In either case, the prevalence of *caudillos* after independence undermined most attempts at democratic, elective government for at least half a century. And although rising prosperity from prime exports provided other routes to wealth from the 1860s onwards, the model of the military-based *caudillo* had become entrenched in Spanish American politics, and in part underlay the dictatorships of the twentieth century. If any virtue could be found in the post-independence phenomenon of *caudillos*, it would be that military activity gave some upward social mobility to men from the lower reaches of society. That aspect of the military life has continued in effect.

Militarism was not an inheritance from the colonial centuries (unless the military spirit of the conquistadores can be supposed to have lived on as some hidden virus in the nervous system of colonial society). Martial spirit and activities were rarities during colonial times, with two rather small exceptions: on the frontiers, where *gobernadores* were generally military men, and in the late eighteenth century, when Bourbon reforming included the creation of colonial militias. By contrast, the colonial experience did certainly contribute one damaging *political* flaw to the new Spanish American states. The upper reaches of society, from which political leaders would most obviously emerge, had received very little by way of preparation or practice in government. This, at least, was true once Bourbon reforms began to impinge heavily on the colonies in the 1760s; before this, creoles had played a considerable role in running their own affairs. But that experience had been forgotten by the 1820s; and, of course, the Bourbon purpose had been precisely to exclude colonials from government as far as possible. The outcome was that even the best-intentioned and most honest of post-independence politicians had little practical idea of how to set up and run a national administration. Nor did many of them have any clear political ideology that might underpin government. There were certainly many conservatives, who sought a continuation of the colonial status quo: authoritarian administration, closely tied to the Catholic church, of a hierarchical society. But those who sought a modernizing break from the colonial past had few innately Spanish American ideas that could serve them, and so turned to European liberalism, which, arguably, for many years proved more harmful than helpful to the independent countries. Its intrinsic anti-clericalism, for instance, provoked immense political and even military conflicts in most countries until well past the mid-century, as conservatives united to defend the church. And its advocacy of free markets and economic competition led to the abolition of laws protecting communally held property, with the result that many peasant communities lost their village lands while privately owned estates expanded. In that respect, at least, Indians were better off under Spanish colonial rule than they were under their new national governments.

Weak states and handicapped economies, mutually debilitating, are, then, clear traits of almost all of Spanish America from the achievement of independence until the mid nineteenth century. They are traits whose origins can be found in the colonial era, and mostly in its final decades (including the wars of independence themselves). It is important to note that Brazil was largely free of Spanish America's difficulties, for two main reasons. The first is that it gained independence almost without fighting; it was therefore spared demographic and economic damage, and the rise of warlords. The second is that monarchical government continued in Brazil, with the result that the political and ideological infighting suffered by Spanish America was largely absent in Brazil until after the monarchy ended, in 1889.

The colonial era also bequeathed some clear long-lasting traits to the Spanish American nations. Among these, in fact, are some of the most obvious defining characteristics of Spanish American culture. Perhaps the most profound of those colonial heritages is Catholicism. Despite the fierce efforts of liberals in the nineteenth century, and the inroads made by energetic Protestant evangelism in the late twentieth, Latin America (Brazil belongs to the general pattern here) holds the greatest number of Catholics of any large world region. Iberian missionaries, whatever doubts they may have had about the completeness and orthodoxy of Indians' Christian faith in colonial times, undoubtedly succeeded in rooting their message in the long term. Some 85–90 percent of Latin Americans are Catholics,[2] although far from all of these participate actively in their faith, and many are still far from orthodox in their beliefs. Folk Catholicism, in many variants, is in fact a central feature of the Latin American church; some would argue that it is its most vibrant reality.

Catholicism has impinged deeply on Latin American life during the almost two centuries that have now passed since independence was gained. It has, for example, been a largely conservative influence in politics. With few exceptions (the outstanding one being Liberation Theology in some countries during the last third of the twentieth century) the church has supported conservative, authoritarian governments and has allied itself with social, economic, and political elites. It has generally preferred order to change, especially to revolutionary change. It has defended traditional patterns and features of society, among them the family. Advocacy of family included opposition to contraception, in line with the teachings of Rome. Consequently the church can be held partly responsible for the excessively rapid growth of Latin America's population in much of the twentieth century, a growth that tended to perpetuate poverty.

A second manifest long-term legacy of colonial times is an inclination to centralized authoritarianism in politics. The roots of this tendency are deeper and wider than elites' inexperience in government, and the problem of *caudillos*, in the aftermath of independence. From the beginning of colonial rule, Spain united the three powers of government in single figures at all levels of administration. It was quite natural for it to do so, given governmental practice in Castile at the time, and the urgency of establishing royal authority in the Indies as quickly and powerfully as possible. Union of executive, law-making, and judicial powers remained the norm until colonial times ended. Viceroys, possessors of all three powers, were the supreme, central embodiments of power. It is true, of course, that in practice creoles undermined Spanish authority and gained great influence in government themselves from the early seventeenth century until the mid eighteenth. But the original model remained in place, and in fact received new emphasis from the Bourbons' reforms. And, enlightened as the Bourbon kings of Spain may have been in some respects, separation of powers was not one of the doctrines of the Enlightenment that they brought into Spain. It is true that some creoles did greatly admire the United States' constitution, with its federalism and separated powers; but, in the early political conditions in their new countries, imitations of that constitution quickly proved impractical. One reason for that, also rooted in the colonial era, was that Spanish America possessed almost no practical democratic or representative traditions. Not surprisingly, given the underlying authoritarian nature of government, hardly any trace of elections can be found in Spanish American colonial history. Officials at all levels were appointed by higher powers, not chosen by the people over whom they were to have authority. Some historians have claimed to have caught glimpses of democracy in the selection of town councils (*cabildos*). But, with the exception of a brief, very early period, those glimpses are false. It is worth recording, also, the brief burst of elective activity that took place in 1813–14 for the choosing of colonial delegates to the Congress of Cadiz; but that ceased with the restoration of Ferdinand VII in 1814, and barely disturbed the established Spanish American pattern of top-down authority. The contrast with the British colonies in North America, with their elections of local assemblies, cannot be overemphasized.[3] (Most of what has been said in this paragraph about Spanish America applies also to Brazil, with the usual caveat that Portugal's government of Brazil was generally less stringent than Spain's of its colonies.)

A third long-term outcome for Latin America from its colonial experience – one that immediately strikes any new visitor to most countries – is race mixture. This began, of course, with the physical uniting of genes from people of different ethnic and geographical origins (American natives, Africans, and Europeans, with a minimal Asian contribution); but it produced enduring social and cultural results that define, in good part, what is distinctive about modern Latin America. In no other comparably large region of the world has such wide miscegenation (*mestizaje* in Spanish) taken place in recent centuries. To be sure, the degree of mixing varies from country to country. Probably it is Paraguay that, among the large countries, has the highest proportion of *mestizos* in its population, at between 76 and 94 percent (*c.* 1990). Mexico, at the same date, had 75 percent, and Colombia and Chile both around 70 percent. Lowest in *mestizo* numbers were Argentina and Uruguay (2 and 7.5 percent respectively), where enormous European immigration a century ago swamped other genetic components of the populations. In Brazil, the mixture is now overwhelmingly of white and black. The population divided, *c.* 1990, roughly evenly between whites, on the one hand, and people with a greater or lesser degree of African descent on the other. The remaining native people, almost all deep in the interior, amounted to less than 1 percent of the total.[4]

Mixing, of course, has resulted in far more than people of distinctive appearance in features and skin color. It has contributed to the emergence of distinctive Latin American variants of Spanish, with different nationalities speaking with contrasting accents and using vocabularies that contain many words of local native origin. Brazilian Portuguese differs in the same respects from Iberian Portuguese. Native religions and folklore have fused with Christianity to produce wide varieties of regional and national folk Catholicism. (In Brazil the fusion is very largely of African spirituality and Catholicism.) Memories of, and often pride in, native pasts have blended, sometimes uneasily, with an awareness of Iberian origins to yield a variety of distinctive national histories. Latin American literature, which has had an international readership since the mid twentieth century, in many instances reveals the *mestizo* reality vividly. Perhaps still more people across the world have become aware of Latin America through its popular music, which combines American, African, and European elements (instruments, harmonies, tonalities, and rhythms) in myriad ways to produce the distinctive cha-cha, *son*, *salsa*, and *cumbia* of the Caribbean, the tango of Argentina, the samba and bossa nova of Brazil, the *cueca* of the Andes, and the *corrido* of Mexico, to mention only some of the better-known forms. Far from least is food, almost everywhere combining Old and New World ingredients and methods of preparation. Best known elsewhere in the world is probably Mexican cooking, which blends wheat, meat, and dairy products from Europe with Middle American maize, beans, and chile to produce one of the great cuisines.

Mestizaje has, finally, been the deepest source of Middle and South America's post-colonial identity. Brazil and the former Spanish territories occupy in this respect a middle position in the range of ex-colonies of recent times. To one side of them stand former possessions like the United States, Canada, Australia, and New Zealand, in which colonials, with or without violence, rejected colonial rule and themselves became the masters of their own affairs. The native people of these regions had little or no say in independent government, either at the time of independence or later. On the other side are many other states, mainly in Africa and Asia, from which, again with or without fighting, the colonial powers departed, leaving native people in charge of government. Spanish and Portuguese America occupy an intermediate position, of which Spanish America provides the clearer illustration. After the colonizing power was expelled, those who gained authority were neither simply ex-colonials nor native people. Political power passed after independence in part to creoles, and in part to mixed elements in the population. Creoles certainly shared the values and culture of the departed colonial rulers to a degree; some shared almost all of them, others very few. But nearly all creoles were in some measure also culturally *mestizo*, in that the American homelands with which they identified in a range of affective and material ways were partly defined culturally by their Indianness (with the exception of Argentina and Uruguay). Most creoles, perhaps, were in some measure genetically *mestizo*, though they would have denied it. And then, of course, there were undisputed *mestizos* who after independence exercised great political and military power, mostly as regional *caudillos*, but a few as national presidents: Santa Cruz in Bolivia and Castilla in Peru. The point is, then, that political control in independent Spanish America did not remain in the hands of outsiders nor revert to those of natives but rather became the possession of groups who to differing but significant degrees were the product, the new *mestizo* product, of what had once been the conquering and the conquered elements of the population and culture. (In Brazil much the same has happened, although, as was the pattern in colonial history, somewhat later than in Spanish America. And in Brazil the mixture is not to any significant degree of white and Indian, but of white and black.) This *mestizo* identity has certainly presented challenges to some Latin Americans. Those, mostly in the upper reaches of society, who prefer to emphasize the European origins of their countries, tend to see *mestizaje* as colonial Spaniards did: as a fusion of the negative characteristics of the contributing parties. And those who consider native origins to be the essence of their nations find *mestizos* a dilution, even a perversion, of those origins. Generally, indeed, countries with large *mestizo* components in their populations (Mexico, for example) have tended to question their identity, wondering if they are essentially more native American or more European. In doing so they show that they have not yet accepted being *mestizo* as a valid identity in itself. But that acceptance must come with time, and is doubtless in fact well on the way to becoming prevalent.

Mestizaje had many origins: Iberians "going native" during the early explorations and choosing to live among Indians, the sexual aggression of the conquests, gifts of women to the conquistadores by defeated native groups, conquistadores marrying high-ranking native women, lesser native women voluntarily cohabiting with European men after the conquests for protection and sustenance, royal policies encouraging marriage between Europeans and natives, and the relative lack of European women for several decades after the conquest and occupation of new regions. Beneath many of these processes lay the broad Iberian (most strongly Spanish) aim to incorporate American peoples into Christianity and European civilization. None of this signifies that Spaniards and Portuguese regarded American natives as their equals (except in the short-lived case of high Indian rulers and nobility encountered during the conquests in Spanish America). But, particularly in Spanish America, the entire population came quickly to be conceived of as a single whole, in principle united in Catholicism and in allegiance to the monarchy.

Within that whole, nonetheless, divisions existed – for example the two "republics" of Indians and Europeans. Longer-lasting than that particular separation, however, were the social distinctions that were clearly in place before 1600. In the drawing of those distinctions, a combination of ethnic appearance and color played a large part: a light-complexioned Indian could more easily be taken for a *mestizo* than a dark one; a light-complexioned *mestizo* would more readily pass as a European than one with dark skin. The distinctions became more subtle as time passed and the number of people of mixed descent increased. But distinctions they remained, and passed from colonial to post-independence times. In most countries they persist to the present. In Mexico, as one example, it is a social and economic advantage to be fair (*güero*) in complexion and hair; in Bolivia, as another, it is a handicap to have the thick, straight, black hair typical of Indians. But, just as in the seventeenth century and later colonial times, an individual's appearance and ethnic origins do not completely determine his or her place in society. Gaining even a little wealth may well allow a person to ascend socially. Education can have the same effect (and education tends to lead to income); and with the great expansion of the public education that almost all Latin American countries achieved in the twentieth century, that route to individual social ascent has become increasingly available.

A final indisputable long-term colonial legacy in Latin America is the centrality of family in people's lives. Latin America's distinctiveness here is less a matter of the nuclear family, which is fundamental in many societies across the world, than the prominence of the extended family. The link with sixteenth-century practice seems strikingly tight. Emigrant Spaniards then would rely on cousins and uncles remaining in Spain to attend to their affairs there, exploit the influence of any relatives (perhaps priests or lawyers) who held positions in the church or government, and summon younger brothers and nephews across the Atlantic to help them with their business in the Indies. The extended family in modern Latin America, especially in the middle and upper classes, works in exactly the same ways. Relatives in different cities across a country are the natural people to call on when one has business there. It is a useful family strategy for members to enter different professions – law, medicine, bureaucracy, politics, the church, and so on – so that wide expertise and influence are available to everyone when needed. Godparent relationships (*compadrazgo*) extend these resources and influences beyond blood relatives, and are common at all social levels. Marriages between families can have similar effects.

The outcomes of extended families' strong persistence are, naturally, beneficial and reassuring for the family members. The results for society as a whole are on balance harmful. Especially when family influence comes into play at the higher levels of any organization, whether public or private, the general well-being may suffer through loss of quality of personnel from nepotism. The promotion of able workers to positions in which they could most usefully employ their talents may be slowed or blocked. Money may be wasted through corrupt placing of contracts. In politics, democratic processes may be subverted and public participation discouraged: why bother to vote if the president's, the governor's, or the mayor's brother will be put into office through manipulation of the election? Why pay taxes if that same brother then uses his power to feather his nest from public funds? Latin America is far from unique in tolerating, even encouraging, these sorts of behaviors, of course. They are found in varying measure across the world. But in comparison with most of the Atlantic world, at least, Latin America is generally slow in moving beyond them. That this is so is in part the result of the persistent power of family.

A further aspect of family, both nuclear and extended, is the continued strength of the father's authority. Patriarchy of the traditional sort has weakened because of the extensive education of women in twentieth-century Latin America, among other reasons. But it can still restrict the freedom of action of wives and daughters.

Finally there remain other long-lasting continuations of the colonial experience that are more difficult to define and whose effects are harder to specify – but which may have had a deeper influence on Latin America's independent history than what has already been noted here, and may continue to exert an influence now and in the future.

The first can crudely be termed scientific and technological lag. This is no mere academic matter, since economic growth and technological advance are inseparably intertwined, and technological innovation is often the outcome of scientific discovery. Latin America, in the nineteenth and much of the twentieth centuries, suffered the long-term effects of Hapsburg Spain's divergence from the mainstream of European scientific advance in the seventeenth century.[5] Spain produced no Descartes, no Leibniz, no Galileo, no Newton. It certainly then gave birth to great painters, sculptors, poets, playwrights, theologians, and moralists; but the gains in technological ability that lead to growing national wealth did, and could, not follow from the achievements of such people. In the eighteenth century Spain certainly imported foreign technology, and the study of science grew larger in its intellectual life. The same can be said of Latin America in the nineteenth century, and more decidedly in the twentieth. But the leading edge of scientific and technological invention remained elsewhere; and the greatest rewards go to the leaders. Catching up – advancing to the frontier of knowledge and invention – can be achieved, though with effort and difficulty since the existing leaders are always themselves moving forward. The clearest examples of success in catching up are in Asia (Japan first, then Singapore, Taiwan, South Korea, India, and, latterly, China). A few of the larger and richer Latin American nations are now (but only now) doing the same, at least in some respects: Brazil above all, and Argentina and Mexico also. But elsewhere in Latin America it is mostly a matter of importing North American, or European, or Asian machines, electronics, drugs – or of setting up factories with assembly lines of foreign design and manufacture to make products that are mostly not quite the latest or best thing.

Such gross generalizations as these are obviously open to all sorts of contradiction. There is no desire or intent here to belittle the truly innovative and valuable scientific work that has taken place in Latin America, notably in medicine and biology. But the societies and economies do not yet rest on science and technology to the extent that those of the world's wealthiest countries do. Some might argue that Latin American societies are the richer in human values as a result; others that the more widespread and persisting poverty that results, in part, from Latin America's lag more than offsets that gain.

Lag in technology was in good part the cause of a trading pattern dominant in Latin America for more than a hundred years after independence – the exporting of primary goods (above all the products of the land and of mines) in exchange for the import of finished manufactured goods. This pattern has sometimes been seen as the persistence of a trading model set up in the sixteenth century and becoming so entrenched over the rest of the colonial period that it remained dominant for a century after the colonies disappeared. This sort of exchange, furthermore, has been viewed as a centuries-long stripping of Latin America's assets (starting with silver and gold from the 1500s on) by aggressive and powerful foreign powers – the First World impoverishing the Third World. But it is hard to see, if trade was to take place at all, how it could have been much different. Lacking technology – indeed being dependent on foreign technology – Latin America had few, if any, manufactured products to export that compared in quality and price with what was made in the First World. If it wished to trade, primary products were what it had to offer. That apart, the exchange was at times far from unfavorable. During the great export boom of the late nineteenth and early twentieth centuries, for example, Latin America's terms of trade, as an exporter of primary products to the rapidly expanding industrial powers of the time, were positive. Machinery, for example, such as railroad equipment, was quite cheap in terms of wheat, beef, coffee, bananas, or the ores of tin, copper, or lead – all products that various Latin American countries sold in great volume from the 1860s onward.

As a last instance of persistent colonial legacies with probably potent, but not easily specified or proven, outcomes, the question of hierarchy (raised in chapter 9) must be briefly addressed once more. To the end of colonial times the assumption that society was not only inherently hierarchical, but also *necessarily* hierarchical if it was to function and be governable, remained deeply rooted in Latin America. That notion certainly continued to be influential long after independence. Ethnic variations helped to perpetuate it – whiter was superior, darker was inferior (although the Latin American fluidity so characteristic of those rankings should never be forgotten). So did the arrival of concepts of class distinction and class conflict from Europe in the late nineteenth century. For those then in command of Latin American societies, the proper and naturally assigned place for the urban worker was low on the social scale, just as it always had been for the Indian peasant. The continued, largely conservative, influence of the Catholic church strengthened such suppositions, quite naturally so since one of the sources of the notion of natural social hierarchy was medieval Catholicism. In addition, hierarchy was both sustained by, and itself perpetuated, the patron–client relationships so central to colonial life. From the time when *encomenderos* set up, after the conquests, their big houses peopled with dependants in imitation of noble establishments in Spain, via similar arrangements on *haciendas* lasting into the twentieth century, to the patronage inherent in modern political parties (a good example is the Institutional Revolutionary Party that ran Mexico for much of that century), the social pattern of the rich and influential boss dispensing work, sustenance and other favors to loyal but inherently subservient followers has been central in Latin American life. The conjunction of that pattern with the enduring power of family and patriarchy does not need emphasis.

How much human talent has been prevented from fully expressing itself in Latin America as a result of persistent assumptions of social hierarchy is of course impossible to measure. It is easier to propose that those assumptions have clearly held back progress in the particular case of government by representative democracy. Elections that are open, free, and fair are unlikely to be eagerly promoted by people already in authority who believe that the mass of the electorate is naturally inferior. But here recent history may mark a deep shift. In the closing years of the twentieth century, in an unprecedented number of countries, more honest elections took place than ever before, with universal male and female suffrage. The outcome was that at the opening of the new century all of Latin America, except for Cuba, was governed by legitimately elected regimes. Since then some attempts to back away from these advances have been made by national leaders who have come to believe that they are indispensable, and should therefore not be subject to constitutional limits on re-election (Colombia and, above all, Venezuela come to mind). But internal opposition to these attempts has also arisen, providing some reassurance that representative democracy has taken a stronger hold in Latin America than at any time since independence. If that is so, it seems most likely to reflect, finally, a weakening of the old sense of hierarchy in Latin American society and culture. And that, perhaps, is an indication of a more general fading of colonial legacies.

GLOSSARY

Afro-casta Person of mixed African (or Afro-American) and either white, Indian, or *mestizo* parentage.

aguardiente "Burning water" – i.e. brandy, usually made from wine. In Brazil, *aguardente* was rum, prepared from sugar.

alcalde mayor See *corregidor*.

aldeia Mission village in colonial Brazil, into which Indians were "congregated" by evangelizing priests, mostly Jesuits.

altiplano "High plain." A word applied to the northern Mexican plateau (1,200–2,400 meters), and the plain between the western and eastern Andean chains in Bolivia (*c.*4,000 meters).

arroba Measure of dry weight, in Brazil about 14.75 kilograms, and in Spanish America about 11.5 kilograms.

asiento (de negros) Contract for the supply of African slaves to colonial Spanish America.

audiencia Regional court of appeal, and administrative tribunal, in colonial Spanish America.

Bajío Fertile area of central Mexico, north of Mexico City, and merging northwards into the *altiplano*; excellent land for grain.

bandeirantes "Pathfinders" of the interior of Brazil, typically from São Paulo, pursuing Indian slaves and precious metals, and active mainly in the seventeenth century.

boucanier "Buccaneer." Informal French settler in the Caribbean, particularly in western Hispaniola, in the seventeenth century, generally of a piratical nature. So named from the use of the *boucan*, or grill, to smoke and so preserve meat.

cabildo Town council, in Spanish America.

cabildo abierto "Open council." Town meeting in colonial Spanish America, supposedly open, but in fact usually attended only by local notables.

cacique Indian leader. Colonial Spaniards took the term from the Caribbean and applied it to native leaders of all levels on the mainland.

Carrera de Indias The "Indies run," or shipping of goods to and fro between Spain and America in the officially permitted *flotas* and *galeones*.

castas Generic term for all people in colonial Spanish America who were not whites or Indians; particular people of mixed parentage.

chácara Land for planting, in the Quechua-speaking parts of the Andes.

Charcas Sixteenth- and seventeenth-century name for the area corresponding roughly to modern Bolivia; more commonly known in the eighteenth century as Alto Perú (Upper Peru).

chicha Mildly alcoholic drink of the Andes, consumed from pre-Columbian times to the present, fermented from chewed maize.

chinampa In central Mexico, a cultivated plot on a lake shore, made by piling up mud taken from the lake bed behind a barrier of wood and woven reeds; crops yields from *chinampas* were high.

cimarrón Runaway black (slave or free).

coca *Erythroxylon coca*, or its dried leaves, which from time out of mind native Andeans have chewed to relieve hunger, thirst, and fatigue.

congregación In colonial Spanish America, the gathering of more or less scattered Indians into a single community, existing or new; also known as *reducción*.

Consejo de Indias See Council of the Indies.

consulado In Spain and its colonies, a tribunal overseeing a community of large merchants in a particular place, and trying cases in which they were involved.

corregidor "Co-ruler." In Spain a royally appointed governor of a town. In the colonies, the same, or more commonly a district officer at the lowest level of the bureaucracy, governing one or more native communities. Difficult to distinguish in Spanish America from the *alcalde mayor*.

Council of the Indies Supreme administrative council of state for colonial Spanish America.

creole See *criollo*.

creolization Acquisition of specifically American culture and behaviors by blacks imported as slaves, or their descendants.

criollo Literally a native of a particular region (from Spanish *criar*, "to raise"); a term applicable to any non-native American born in Spanish America, including blacks; but mostly applied to whites born in the colonies.

crioulo Slave born in Brazil, whether of African- or Brazilian-born parents.

curaca Quechua term for a local Indian leader in the Andes.

curacazgo The office held by a *curaca*.

degredado Criminal exiled from Portugal (often to Brazil, in the early sixteenth century).

desembargador Judge in a Portuguese high court (*relação*).

doctrina Rural parish in colonial Spanish America.

ejido In Spain and colonial Spanish America, public lands around a town or village for communal use (mostly grazing of animals).

encomendero Spanish colonist to whom an *encomienda* was granted by the crown or its authorized agent.

encomienda Grant to a Spanish colonist of the tribute (consisting of goods, sometimes cash, and, in the early post-conquest decades, labor) of a number of Indians. In return the colonist was to teach the Indians granted in *encomienda* (trust) to him or to her both Christianity and "civilized" conduct.

engenho Sugar mill and estate in colonial Brazil.

entrada "Entry"; in Brazil, exploratory expedition into the interior, mainly in the seventeenth century; also used in early Spanish America in the same sense.

estancia In Spanish America, a private landholding, usually small, for farming, and particularly for raising livestock. Specifically, in the usage of the Río de la Plata in the eighteenth century, an area of usufruct of pasture and water.

factoría Factory, i.e. premises, in Spanish America for the reception and housing of slaves newly arrived from Africa.

factory Trading post (in, for example, the Portuguese empire), sometimes fortified.

farm   As a verb, to collect the proceeds of a tax or office, having paid a fixed sum to do so to the relevant authority (for example the Spanish treasury); generally profitable.

flota   Literally, "fleet"; specifically the trading fleet intended to sail annually from Spain to New Spain (i.e. Mexico) and back for most of the colonial period.

forastero   Generally, "outsider"; specifically, in the central Andes, an Indian who had moved permanently from his or her native community to another.

Friars Minor   The Franciscans (Order of Friars Minor).

galeones   Literally, "galleons"; specifically, for most of the colonial era, the trading fleet intended to sail annually from Spain to the Caribbean side of the Isthmus of Panama carrying goods for the west coast of South America, and returning goods thence to Spain.

garúa   A thick mist covering parts of the Peruvian coast during the winter.

hacendado   Owner of a *hacienda*.

hacienda   Private, rural estate in Spanish America, often very large in remote and infertile regions, but smaller in areas of good farm land close to population centers; a defining socio-economic unit of Spanish America.

hidalgo   Literally, "child of something"; a person of nobility (in practice, a low level of nobility).

huaca   Native holy site or object in the central Andes; also spelled *waca*.

juro   In Spanish territories, a pension payable from government funds.

kuraka   See *curaca*.

Liberation Theology   A movement in Catholic thought and action, particularly associated with Latin America, and deriving from the Second Vatican Council (1962–5); principally the proposition that the church should take practical action in the world to address the needs of the poor, if necessary through participation in politics, and even in violent action aimed at reform.

mameluco   In Brazil, person of mixed European and native parentage (cf. *mestizo* in Spanish America).

maroon   Runaway black (slave or free) (from Spanish *cimarrón*).

mate   See *yerba mate*.

mestizaje   "Race" mixture.

mestizo   Person of mixed parentage; usually, in Spanish America, of mixed European and Indian descent.

México-Tenochtitlan   Name given to Mexico City for a few decades after the military conquest by the Spanish.

mita   Draft labor requirement imposed on Indians in the Andes, for mining, public works, and other tasks.

mulato   Mulatto, or person of mixed African and European descent.

naboría   Originally, personal dependant of a native leader in the Caribbean; the Spanish took the term to New Spain, where it came to mean an Indian who was the personal servant of a Spaniard; and, more loosely, an Indian who worked for wages.

New Galicia   Name given by the Spanish to a large region of north-western Mexico in colonial times; the capital was Guadalajara.

New Granada   Name used in colonial, and early national, times for the territory covered by present Colombia ("Colombia" came into use in 1863).

New Leon (Nuevo León)   Province of north-eastern Mexico in colonial times, and modern Mexican state in the same area.

New Mexico   Northernmost province of colonial Mexico, beyond the Rio Grande; now a state in the United States.

New Spain   Usual term for Mexico in the colonial period. Strictly speaking, as a viceroyalty "New Spain" embraced not only Mexico, but Central America (as far south as, but not including, Panama), Spanish possessions within the present limits of the United States, the Spanish Caribbean islands, and the Philippines.

obraje   Spinning and weaving workshop, equipped with spinning wheels and mechanical looms.

oidor   Judge in an *audiencia*.

ouvidor geral   Higher crown magistrate in a territorial section, or province, of colonial Brazil.

palenque   Runaway black community, sometimes fortified.

panaka   Inca clan descending from a supreme ruler. (Also spelled as *panaqa* or *panaca*.)

pardo   In Spanish America, person with some degree of African blood; in colonial Brazil, a slave of mixed ancestry.

paulistas   Inhabitants of the town or city of São Paulo in Brazil; particularly famous as *bandeirantes* in the seventeenth century.

peninsular   Spaniard born in the Iberian peninsula.

Peru   In colonial times, name commonly used for the territory corresponding roughly with present Peru. As a viceroyalty, however, "Peru" embraced until 1739 the whole of Spanish South America, and Panama. At that date the viceroyalty of New Granada was created. In 1776 another viceroyalty, that of the Río de la Plata, was added. The Peruvian viceroyalty then consisted only of present Peru and Chile.

peruleros   Merchants from Peru who traveled on the transatlantic Spanish fleets to Seville, to buy goods for sale in South America; regarded as upstart competitors by established exporters in Seville.

peso   Widely used term for a coin or unit of currency. The basic meaning is simply "weight." A peso originally was a certain weighed amount of gold or silver. In colonial Spanish America the largest commonly circulating coin, weighing one ounce, was the *peso de a ocho*, or "piece of eight" – eight referring to the number of *reales* composing the peso. A common unit of account, though not an actual coin, was the *peso ensayado* of 13.25 *reales*.

polity   Organized society/political entity.

polygyny   Marriage of a man with two or more women simultaneously.

principal   Leading person in a native community in Spanish America.

Quito   As a province of colonial Spanish America, the area roughly corresponding to present Ecuador.

Real Hacienda   In colonial times, the Spanish royal treasury.

real oficial   Spanish treasury official in colonial times.

reducción   See *congregación*.

regalism   Principle of the monarch's supremacy over the church.

regular clergy/regulars   Members of religious orders (for example, Franciscans, Dominicans, Jesuits, Augustinians).

relação   High court in Portugal and its colonies, corresponding to the Spanish *audiencia*.

repartimiento   Broadly, "distribution." Used in several senses in colonial Spanish America: as a near-synonym for *encomienda*; as the name for the state's draft assignment of Indians to colonists for labor; and as the term for the forced sale of goods to Indians by local officials of colonial government. In the latter sense also found as *reparto* (*de comercio* or *de efectos*).

resgate   In colonial Brazil, ransoming of Indians taken captive by other Indians, and supposedly in danger of their lives, for the purpose of enslaving them; considered a licit means of obtaining slaves, but much abused.

residencia   In colonial Spanish America, investigation of an official's conduct in office that his successor was legally required to perform.

safra   In Brazil, harvesting of sugar cane.

Sapa Inca "Sole" Inca; i.e. the supreme Inca leader, or emperor.

secular clergy Clergy not belonging to any religious order, but living in the "world" as part of the central church hierarchy of archbishops, bishops, parish priests, etc.

sertão General term for the interior of Brazil; more specifically, the dry and infertile interior of the north-east of Brazil.

situado In colonial Spanish America, subsidy from one treasury office to another, generally to cover military expenses.

Spanish Main See Tierra Firme.

Tierra Firme The Spanish Main[land]; general term for the first shores of the American mainland explored by the Spaniards, from Panama to the Guianas.

tlatoani "He who speaks" (Nahuatl); supreme leader of a polity in pre-conquest Mexico.

trapiche Generally a small mill of some sort, for example for, silver-refining, sugar-processing, or cloth-making.

Upper Peru "Alto Perú"; eighteenth-century term for Charcas (now, roughly speaking, Bolivia).

Valley of Mexico The large valley in which Mexico City, formerly the Aztec capital Tenochtitlan, lies.

vaqueiro Cowherd in colonial Brazil.

vecino Literally "neighbor" in Spanish; in colonial times a householder in a town, usually of some social standing, and therefore usually white (or accepted as white).

viceroy Supreme executive authority in colonial Spanish America, where, before the eighteenth century, two viceroyalties existed: New Spain (1535–) and Peru (1544–). In 1739 New Granada became a viceroyalty, and, in 1776, the Río de la Plata also.

visita In colonial Spanish America, a "visit" or official inspection of some administrator, administrative body, or region by a high-ranking bureaucrat; generally speaking a *visitador* was sent to resolve some particular problem that had arisen.

yanacona/yana In the central Andes, an Indian who, like the *naboría* in the Caribbean, was before the conquest the personal dependant of some powerful figure; after the conquest, an Indian who was the personal servant of a Spaniard.

yerba mate (**or simply** *mate*) *Ilex paraguariensis*: shrub (common in Paraguay, but also found in nearby regions) from whose leaves a bitter tea, or infusion, is prepared.

zambo Person of mixed African and American Indian parentage.

Notes

Chapter 1 Lands and Climates

1 James, *Latin America*, p. 21.
2 Ibid., p. 77.
3 West and Augelli, *Middle America*, pp. 30–1.
4 Ibid., p. 33; Clapperton, "Tectonic history," pp. 12–14.
5 James, *Latin America*, pp. 21–2; Smith, "The Central Andes," p. 256.
6 Clapperton, "Tectonic history," p. 18.
7 *Hammond Comparative World Atlas*, 1989, p. 13.
8 Ibid., pp. 401–3.
9 Ibid., pp. 437–9.
10 Conrad and Demarest, *Religion and Empire*, pp. 161–2.
11 Ibid., p. 162.
12 Dobyns and Doughty, *Peru*, p. 15.
13 Blakemore and Smith, *Latin America*, pp. 256–7.
14 Larson, *Colonialism*, 1988, pp. 28–9.
15 Bennett and Bird, *Andean Culture History*, p. 60.
16 Ibid., pp. 60–2.
17 Ibid., p. 441.
18 Tenenbaum (ed.), *Encyclopedia of Latin American History and Culture*, vol. 2, p. 151.
19 James, *Latin America*, p. 553.

Chapter 2 American Peoples

1 Cortés, *Letters*, p. 108.
2 *Cabildo* of Jauja to Charles V, cited in Hemming, *The Conquest*, p. 120.
3 Conrad and Demarest, *Religion and Empire*, p. 84.
4 An excellent summary of the abundant research on this topic is Meltzer, "Peopling of North America."
5 Moseley, *The Incas* (2001), pp. 83–4.
6 For cassava, Iriarte, "The history of manioc domestication"; for Andean cultivation, Moseley, *The Incas* (2001), pp. 94–7; for Middle America, Coe and Koontz, *Mexico*, pp. 29–34.

7   Fung Pineda, "The late preceramic," esp. p. 94.

8   Moseley, *The Incas* (2001), ch. 6.

9   For Chavín, see ibid., pp. 163–79; also Stone-Miller, *Art of the Andes*, pp. 28–49.

10 Stone-Miller, *Art of the Andes*, pp. 48–9.

11 Coe and Koontz, *Mexico*, pp. 77–8. The preceding account of the Olmec is mainly drawn from this work (pp. 62–91), and also from Pool, *Olmec Archaeology*, *passim*. I am also grateful to Dr. Adam Herring for advice on the Olmec.

12 Stone-Miller, *Art of the Andes*, p. 133.

13 Moseley, *The Incas* (1992), p. 224. The preceding description of Tiwanaku is drawn from this work (pp. 203–8, 224–30), and from the corresponding sections on Tiwanaku in the second edition (2001). Consult also Stone-Miller, *Art of the Andes*, pp. 126–37.

14 See Schreiber, *Wari Imperialism*, p. 97, for a map.

15 Ibid., pp. 266, 274.

16 Moseley, *The Incas* (2001), pp. 231–7.

17 For Moche pottery, see Berrin (ed.), *The Spirit of Ancient Peru*, particularly pp. 41–9; Benson, "Moche art: myth, history and rite."

18 Donnan, *Moche Portraits*, p. 117.

19 Moseley, *The Incas* (2001), p. 196. This brief account of the Moche is mostly condensed from Moseley, pp. 178–96.

20 Coe and Koontz, *Mexico*, p. 119. The account of Teotihuacán given here is a selective summary of pp. 103–20 of this work.

21 Fash and Fash, "Teotihuacán and the Maya," pp. 434–5; for "miniature copy," Coe and Koontz, *Mexico*, p. 119.

22 Fash and Fash, "Teotihuacán and the Maya," p. 458.

23 Thompson, *Rise and Fall*, pp. 187, 239–40.

24 Coe, *Breaking the Maya Code*, pp. 206–7.

25 For Maya line, Herring, *Art and Writing*.

26 See Schele and Freidel, *A Forest of Kings*, p. 375.

27 This account of the Maya is drawn mostly from Coe, *The Maya*, *passim*.

28 Coe, *Mexico*, p. 129.

29 Rostworowski de Diez Canseco, *History of the Inca Realm*, p. 78. The preceding account of the Chimú empire is drawn mostly from Moseley, *The Incas* (2001), pp. 261–75.

30 Davies, *The Aztecs*, p. 8 ff.; Clendinnen, *Aztecs*, pp. 22–3.

31 Smith, *The Aztecs*, pp. 38–41.

32 Conrad and Demarest, *Religion and Empire*, p. 22.

33 Ibid., p. 30.

34 Calnek, "Patterns of empire formation," p. 55.

35 Davies, *The Aztecs*, p. 54.

36 Calnek, "Patterns of empire formation," p. 48.

37 Davies, *The Aztecs*, pp. 41–3.

38 Broda, Carrasco, and Matos Moctezuma, *The Great Temple*, p. 65 ff.

39 Conrad and Demarest, *Religion and Empire*, p. 38.

40 Clendinnen, *Aztecs*, p. 28.

41 S. Cook, "Historical demography of the interior tribes of Colombia," *passim*.

42 Conrad and Demarest, *Religion and Empire*, pp. 173–8; Hassig, *Aztec Warfare*, pp. 263–6.

43 Conrad and Demarest, *Religion and Empire*, p. 38.

44 Clendinnen, *Aztecs*, p. 91.

45 Ibid., p. 97.

46 Ibid., pp. 216–18.

47 Brundage, *A Rain of Darts, passim*.
48 Clendinnen, *Aztecs*, pp. 79–80, 156.
49 Ibid., pp. 48–54.
50 Díaz del Castillo, *The Conquest of New Spain*, p. 214. The "tale" is the famous late medieval Iberian chivalric romance of the knight errant Amadís of Gaul, much in vogue in sixteenth-century Spain.
51 Rojas, *México Tenochtitlan*, ch. 3.
52 Cortés, *Letters*, p. 134. The brief account of Tenochtitlan given here draws from Smith, *The Aztecs*, pp. 196–203, and Coe, *Mexico*, pp. 165–6.
53 Morris, "Progress and prospect," p. 236.
54 Conrad and Demarest, *Religion and Empire*, p. 97.
55 Stern, *Peru's Indian Peoples*, pp. 4–9.
56 Covey, *How the Incas Built their Heartland*, pp. 10–14, 234–5.
57 Ibid., p. 234.
58 Rostworowski de Diez Canseco, *Historia de Tahuantinsuyu*, pp. 59–60.
59 Ramírez, "Historia y memoria."
60 For useful maps of the expansion, Covey, *How the Incas Built their Heartland*, p. 188; also D'Altroy, *The Incas*, p. 66.
61 Hemming, *The Conquest*, p. 132. Mason, *The Ancient Civilizations of Peru*, pp. 208.
62 Conrad and Demarest, *Religion and Empire*, pp. 100–10. Rostworowski de Diez Canseco, *Historia de Tahuantinsuyu*, p. 76.
63 Moseley, *The Incas* (2001), pp. 81–5.
64 Hyslop, *The Inka Road System, passim*.
65 Rostworowski de Diez Canseco, *Historia de Tahuantinsuyu*, pp. 100–3, 132.
66 Ibid., pp. 122, 132–3.
67 Conrad and Demarest, *Religion and Empire*, pp. 124–5.
68 See Covey, *How the Incas Built their Heartland*, pp. 120–1.
69 D'Altroy, *The Incas*, pp. 239, 258–9.
70 Ibid., p. 87.
71 Patterson, *The Inca Empire*, p. 76.
72 Ibid., p. 81. For the variability of Inca provincial control, see D'Altroy, *The Incas*, pp. 249–60. For Inca use of incorporated peoples' *huacas*, and Inca religion generally, Ramírez, *To Feed and Be Fed*, pp. 64–72.
73 Rostworowski de Diez Canseco, *Historia de Tahuantinsuyu*, pp. 122–5.
74 All above from Helms, "The Indians," pp. 37–45.
75 Bruhns, *Ancient South America*, p. 344.
76 Juan de San Martin and Antonio de Lebrija to Charles V, in Parry and Keith, *New Iberian World*, vol. 4, p. 412.
77 Gannon, *The Guarani*, p. 18.
78 Hidalgo, "The Indians of southern South America," p. 106.
79 Ibid., p. 116.
80 Hemming, "The Indians of Brazil," p. 133. This description of Brazilian native people is largely based on Hemming's account.
81 Denevan, *Cultivated Landscapes*, p. 57. See Part II of this book generally for ancient Amazonian cultivation and its effect; also Heckenberger et al., "Amazonia 1492," and Roosevelt, "The maritime, highland, forest dynamic," pp. 325–32.
82 For Caribs, Tainos, and other Arawak speakers in the Caribbean, see Wilson (ed.), *The Indigenous People*, generally. Points here are taken from Highfield, "Some observations" and Allaire, "The Caribs" in that book.
83 Wilson, *Hispaniola*, p. 2.

84 Ibid., pp. 6, 15, 32.
85 "Chichimecs," in Tenenbaum (ed.), *Encyclopedia of Latin American History and Culture*, vol. 2, p. 94.

Chapter 3 Iberia and Africa

1 Morison, *Admiral of the Ocean Sea*, p. 221.
2 McAlister, *Spain and Portugal*, p. 42.
3 Oliveira Marques, *A History of Portugal*, vol. 1, p. 145.
4 Wilford, "Norsemen in America."
5 Parry, *The Age of Reconnaissance*, p. 117.
6 Oliveira Marques, *A History of Portugal*, vol. 1, p. 133.
7 Ibid., p. 148.
8 O'Callaghan, *A History of Medieval Spain*, p. 397.
9 Oliveira Marques, *A History of Portugal*, vol. 1, p. 137.
10 Ibid., p. 130.
11 Diffie and Winius, *Foundations of the Portuguese Empire*, p. 34.
12 Ibid., p. 77; Oliveira Marques, *A History of Portugal*, vol. 1, p. 158.
13 Fernández-Armesto, *Ferdinand and Isabella*, p. 155.
14 Diffie and Winius, *Foundations of the Portuguese Empire*, p. 104.
15 Ibid., p. 306; Oliveira Marques, *A History of Portugal*, vol. 1, p. 154.
16 Oliveira Marques, *A History of Portugal*, vol. 1, p. 154.
17 Ibid., p. 153.
18 Ibid., pp. 240–1.
19 Manning, "African connections," p. 45. The geographical description given here is condensed from this essay, pp. 44–7.
20 Ibid., p. 52, and Thornton, *Africa and Africans*, p. 46.
21 Thornton, *Africa and Africans*, p. 259, and more generally pp. 246–62.
22 Manning, "African connections," pp. 57, 60.
23 See "Map of the Muslim world *c*.A.D. 1500," from W. C. Brice, *An Historical Atlas of Islam* (Leiden, 1981), reproduced online by Barbara R. von Schlegell in "Maps of the Middle East and Islamic history" at ccat.sas.upenn.edu/ bvon/pages/maps. html
24 The preceding is taken from Lovejoy, *Transformations in Slavery*, pp. 15–23.
25 Ibid., pp. 36–40.
26 Respectively, Thornton, *Africa and Africans*, p. 108, and Manning, "African connections," p. 52.
27 Manning, "African connections," pp. 57, 60.
28 Lovejoy, *Transformations in Slavery*, pp. 86–7.
29 Ibid., p. 22.
30 Manning, "African connections," p. 53.
31 For goods exchanged for slaves, see Lovejoy, *Transformations in Slavery*, pp. 106–11, and p. 110 particularly for judgment of the arms-for-slaves question.
32 Fernández-Armesto, *Ferdinand and Isabella*, p. 144.
33 Diffie and Winius, *Foundations of the Portuguese Empire*, pp. 42–4.
34 Fernández-Armesto, *Ferdinand and Isabella*, pp. 144–5; Diffie and Winius, *Foundations of the Portuguese Empire*, p. 59.
35 Diffie and Winius, *Foundations of the Portuguese Empire*, p. 58.
36 Elliott, *Imperial Spain*, ch. 1.
37 Le Flem et al., *La frustración de un imperio*, p. 145.
38 Elliott, *Imperial Spain*, p. 7.

39 Ibid., p. 86.
40 Lunenfeld, *The Council of the Santa Hermandad*, pp. 99–107.
41 Kamen, *Spain, 1469–1714*, p. 21.
42 Pérez, "España moderna," p. 152.
43 Ibid., p. 153.
44 Kamen, *Spain, 1469–1714*, p. 38, and *The Spanish Inquisition*, pp. 36–7; Le Flem et al., *La frustración de un imperio*, pp. 156–7.
45 Kamen, *Spain, 1469–1714*, p. 39.
46 Ibid., p. 41.
47 Pérez, "Isabela la Católica," p. 163, citing Luis Suárez Fernández, *La expulsión de los judíos de España* (MAPFRE, Madrid, 1992), pp. 335–8.
48 Bennassar, *Inquisición española, passim*, esp. pp. 337–41.
49 Le Flem et al., *La frustración de un imperio*, p. 160.
50 Fernández-Armesto, *Ferdinand and Isabella*, p. 92.
51 Kamen, *Spain, 1469–1714*, p. 34; Fernández-Armesto, *Ferdinand and Isabella*, p. 99.
52 Fernández-Armesto, *Ferdinand and Isabella*, p. 89.
53 Kamen, *Spain, 1469–1714*, pp. 35–6.
54 Garrido Aranda, *Moriscos*, p. 51.
55 Kamen, *Spain, 1469–1714*, p. 37.
56 Phelan, *The Millennial Kingdom*, p. 45; also Liss, *Mexico*, pp. 14–15.
57 Diffie and Winius, *Foundations of the Portuguese Empire*, p. 155.
58 Ibid., pp. 159–65.

CHAPTER 4   COLUMBUS AND OTHERS

1 Diffie and Winius, *Foundations of the Portuguese Empire*, pp. 58, 88; Phillips and Phillips, *The Worlds of Christopher Columbus*, p. 98.
2 Phillips and Phillips, *The Worlds of Christopher Columbus*, p. 108; Fernández-Armesto, *Columbus*, p. 30.
3 Morison, *Admiral of the Ocean Sea*, p. 68.
4 Phillips and Phillips, *The Worlds of Christopher Columbus*, p. 130; Fernández-Armesto, *Columbus*, p. 52.
5 Fernández-Armesto, *Columbus*, pp. 45–6.
6 Ibid., p. 70; Phillips and Phillips, *The Worlds of Christopher Columbus*, pp. 133–4.
7 Fernández-Armesto, *Columbus*, p. 26.
8 Ibid., pp. 49–50; Todorov, *The Conquest of America*, p. 26.
9 "Oath sworn regarding Cuba," cited in Todorov, *The Conquest of America*, p. 32; also Morison, *Admiral of the Ocean Sea*, p. 466.
10 Sauer, *The Early Spanish Main*, pp. 72–7.
11 Phillips and Phillips, *The Worlds of Christopher Columbus*, pp. 206–11.
12 Vigneras, *The Discovery of South America*, p. 19.
13 Morales Padrón, *Historia del descubrimiento*, ch. 4.
14 Parry, *The Discovery of the Sea*, p. 222.
15 Ibid., p. 217.
16 Fernández-Armesto, *Amerigo*, pp. 180–8.
17 Morales Padrón, *Historia del descubrimiento*, p. 140.
18 Ibid., p. 151.
19 Ibid., ch. 6.
20 Sauer, *Sixteenth Century North America*, pp. 154–6.
21 Parry and Keith, *New Iberian World*, vol. 3, p. 475.

22 Spate, *The Spanish Lake*, p. 104.
23 Oliveira Marques, *A History of Portugal*, vol. 1, p. 229; Diffie and Winius, *Foundations of the Portuguese Empire*, second map following p. 192.
24 An English translation of the treaty in Parry and Keith, *New Iberian World*, vol. 1, pp. 275–80.

Chapter 5   Experiment in the Caribbean

1   Columbus, *The Life*, p. 85.
2   Sauer, *The Early Spanish Main*, p. 81.
3   Chaunu, *Conquête*, p. 121.
4   Ibid., p. 122; Sauer, *The Early Spanish Main*, pp. 105–6.
5   Rouse, *The Tainos*, p. 155.
6   S. Cook and Borah, *Essays*, vol. 1, p. 410.
7   Ibid, ch. 6; N. D. Cook, "Disease and the depopulation of Hispaniola," pp. 214–20.
8   Sauer, *The Early Spanish Main*, p. 181.
9   López de Gómara, *Cortés*, p. 5.
10 Quoted in Sauer, *The Early Spanish Main*, p. 183.
11 Chaunu, *Conquête*, p. 131.
12 Góngora, *Studies*, pp. 4–5.
13 Tyler, *Two Worlds*, pp. 137–8, citing Las Casas, *Historia de las Indias*, bk. 1, ch. 92.
14 Ibid., p. 213, citing Las Casas, *Historia de las Indias*, bk. 2, ch. 6.
15 Sauer, *The Early Spanish Main*, p. 156. For mining and agriculture under Ovando, see Lamb, *Frey Nicolás*, pp. 167–75.
16 Lamb, *Frey Nicolás*, p. 170.
17 Pagden, *The Fall*, p. 15.
18 Sauer, *The Early Spanish Main*, p. 151; Parry and Keith, *New Iberian World*, vol. 2, p. 256.
19 Sauer, *The Early Spanish Main*, p. 152.
20 Lamb, *Frey Nicolás*, pp. 191–2.
21 Sauer, *The Early Spanish Main*, pp. 199–200.
22 Lamb, *Frey Nicolás*, p. 182–3.
23 Sánchez Bella, *La organización*, p. 12.
24 Ibid., p. 14.
25 Lamb, *Frey Nicolás*, p. 186.
26 Ibid., p. 184.
27 Las Casas, *Historia de las Indias*, bk. 1, chs. 27–30, cited in Parry and Keith, *New Iberian World*, vol. 2, p. 270.
28 Sauer, *The Early Spanish Main*, p. 149; Tyler, *Two Worlds*, pp. 219–24, citing Las Casas, *Historia de las Indias*, bk. 2, ch. 9.
29 Las Casas, *Historia de las Indias*, bk. 2, ch. 8, quoted in Tyler, *Two Worlds*, p. 216.
30 Zavala, *La encomienda indiana*, p. 13.
31 Ibid., p. 15.
32 McAlister, *Spain and Portugal*, p. 157.
33 Lamb, *Frey Nicolás*, p. 213.
34 Floyd, *The Columbus Dynasty*, pp. 144–5.
35 Haring, *The Spanish Empire*, p. 22.
36 Schäfer, *El Consejo Real*, vol. 2, p. 66.
37 Haring, *The Spanish Empire*, p. 84.
38 Lamb, *Frey Nicolás*, p. 212.
39 Haring, *The Spanish Empire*, p. 180.

40 Lamb, *Frey Nicolás*, p. 210; Floyd, *The Columbus Dynasty*, p. 149.
41 Floyd, *The Columbus Dynasty*, pp. 150–1.
42 Ibid., pp. 153–5.
43 Dussel, *Historia general*, vol. 1/1, p. 304, quoting Las Casas, *Historia de las Indias*, bk. 3, ch. 4.
44 Dussel, *Historia general*, vol. 1/1, p. 304.
45 Zavala, *La encomienda indiana*, p. 22.
46 For a translated text of the Laws of Burgos, Parry and Keith, *New Iberian World*, vol. 1, pp. 336–47. See also Simpson, *The Encomienda*, pp. 33–4, and Zavala, *La encomienda indiana*, pp. 22–4.
47 Zavala, *La encomienda indiana*, p. 27.
48 Simpson, *The Encomienda*, p. 53, and ch. 4 *passim*.
49 Zavala, *La encomienda indiana*, pp. 32–7.
50 Chaunu, *Conquête*, p. 132.
51 Sauer, *The Early Spanish Main*, pp. 159–60.
52 S. Cook and Borah, *Essays*, vol. 1, p. 401.
53 Ibid., pp. 409–10; N. D. Cook, "Disease and the depopulation of Hispaniola," pp. 236–9. For smallpox in 1493, N. D. Cook, "Una primera epidemia."
54 Sauer, *The Early Spanish Main*, p. 203.
55 Ibid., p. 203.

CHAPTER 6   MILITARY CONQUEST

1 Díaz del Castillo, *The Conquest of New Spain*, p. 16.
2 Ibid., p. 47.
3 Prescott, *The Conquest of Mexico*, vol. 1, p. 164.
4 Cortés, *Letters*, p. 113.
5 Parry and Keith, *New Iberian World*, vol. 4, pp. 48–50.
6 Vega Carpio [Lope de Vega], *Arauco domado*, Act 1 (p. 117).
7 Hemming, *The Conquest of the Incas*, pp. 154, 201; Espinosa Soriano, *La destrucción del imperio, passim*.
8 Todorov, *The Conquest of America*, p. 74.
9 Kubler, "The behavior of Atahualpa," p. 421. Discussion of the Aztecs here draws from Clendinnen, "'Fierce and unnatural cruelty,'" and *Aztecs*, ch. 11; Díaz del Castillo, *The Conquest of New Spain*; Hassig, *Aztec Warfare*, ch. 16; Todorov, *The Conquest of America*, especially ch. 2; Vaillant, *The Aztecs of Mexico*, ch. 14.
10 Clendinnen, *Aztecs*, p. 269, quoting from Sahagún, *Florentine Codex*, bk. 12.

CHAPTER 7   ADMINISTRATION: THE POWER OF PAPER

1 See Cortés, *Letters, passim*.
2 López de Gómara, *Cortés*, p. 327.
3 Cortés's fourth letter to Charles V, October 15, 1524, in *Letters*, p. 336.
4 Simpson, *The Encomienda*, p. 61.
5 Cortés, *Letters*, pp. 511–12. For the ordinances on Indian treatment, Parry and Keith, *New Iberian World*, vol. 3, pp. 350–2.
6 Gibson, *The Aztecs*, p. 60.
7 Himmerich, *The Encomenderos*, p. 58.
8 López de Gómara, *Cortés*, pp. 340–1.

9   Díaz del Castillo, *Historia verdadera*, vol. 3, p. 138.
10 Simpson, *The Encomienda*, pp. 164–7; also p. 391 n., of his translation of López de Gómara, *Cortés*.
11 Riley, *Fernando Cortés*, pp. 29–30.
12 Elliott, *Imperial Spain*, p. 163.
13 López de Gómara, *Cortés*, p. 408.
14 Schäfer, *El Consejo Real*, vol. 1, p. 16.
15 *Leyes y ordenanzas nuevamente hechas por su Magestad para la gobernación de las Indias y buen tratamiento y conservación de los indios* (complete text, Escuela de Estudios Hispanoamericanos, Seville, 1961); partial translation in Parry and Keith, *New Iberian World*, vol. 1, pp. 348–56.
16 Vargas, *Historia del Ecuador*, pp. 78–9.
17 Lockhart, *Men of Cajamarca*, p. 179.
18 Bataillon, "Les colons du Pérou," p. 492.
19 Garcilaso de la Vega, *Royal Commentaries*, vol. 2, p. 1217.
20 Simmons, *Albuquerque*, pp. 100–2.
21 Mora Mérida, *Historia social de Paraguay*, p. 3.
22 Loveman, *Chile*, p. 70.
23 Parry, *Audiencia of New Galicia*, p. 19.
24 Schäfer, *El Consejo Real*, vol. 2, p. 68.
25 *Leyes y ordenanzas nuevamente hechas*, clauses 10 and 11.
26 Haring, *The Spanish Empire*, p. 131.
27 Elliott, *Imperial Spain*, pp. 71, 166.
28 For Mendoza, see Aiton, *Antonio de Mendoza*.
29 Parry, *Audiencia of New Galicia*, pp. 27–8.
30 Aiton, *Antonio de Mendoza*, p. 87.
31 Góngora, *Studies*, p. 76.
32 *Recopilación*, 3.3.3, 65.
33 Cf. Leonard, *Baroque Times*, ch. 1.
34 For Toledo, see Zimmerman, *Francisco de Toledo*; for amalgamation and mining labor, Bakewell, *Miners*, chs. 1, 3.
35 Lohmann Villena and Sarabia Viejo, *Francisco de Toledo*.
36 Elliott, *Imperial Spain*, p. 161.
37 Burkholder and Johnson, *Colonial Latin America*, p. 74.
38 Elliott, *Imperial Spain*, p. 160.
39 Himmerich, *The Encomenderos*, pp. 58, 92.
40 Lohmann Villena, *El corregidor*; Ramírez, "*El Dueño de Indios*"; Bakewell, "La maduración." For *corregimientos* in New Spain, Ruiz Medrano, *Gobierno*, esp. pp. 69–79 and appendix 1; also Burkholder and Johnson, *Colonial Latin America*, pp. 78–9.
41 For local government, see e.g. Marzahl, *Town in the Empire*.
42 Sánchez-Bella, *La organización financiera*, pp. 97–100.
43 *Recopilación*, 3.8.38.
44 Phelan, *The Kingdom of Quito*, p. 145, and ch. 6 *passim*.
45 Borah, "Representative institutions," *passim*.
46 Dealy, *The Latin Americans*, p. 23.

CHAPTER 8   CHURCH: FRIARS, BISHOPS, AND THE STATE

1   Morison, *Admiral of the Ocean Sea*, p. 397.
2   Barnadas, "The Catholic church," p. 512.

3 For patronage, see ibid., pp. 512–13, and Dussel, *Historia general,* vol. 1/1, p. 241 f. For *Inter caetera* in translation, Parry and Keith, *New Iberian World,* vol. 1, pp. 271–4.

4 Schwaller, *The Church,* p. 68.

5 Schäfer, *El Consejo Real,* vol. 2, p. 192.

6 Barnadas, "The Catholic church," pp. 517–18.

7 Parry and Keith, *New Iberian World,* vol. 1, pp. 385–6.

8 Dussel, *Historia general,* vol. 1/1, pp. 552–8.

9 Ricard, *Spiritual Conquest,* p. 80.

10 Dussel, *Historia general,* vol. 1/1, p. 553.

11 See, in general, Phelan, *The Millennial Kingdom.*

12 Baudot, *Utopía,* p. 96.

13 Clendinnen, *Ambivalent Conquests,* p. 48.

14 Mendieta, *Historia de eclesiástica indiana,* bk. 3, ch. 29; trans. and quoted in Clendinnen, *Ambivalent Conquests,* p. 49.

15 Ricard, *Spiritual Conquest,* p. 219. This account of the Tlatelolco college is drawn from ibid., ch. 14.

16 Dussel, *Historia general,* vol. 1/1, p. 318.

17 Holler, *I, Elena,* p. 14.

18 Lavrin, "Female religious," p. 188.

19 Holler, *Escogidas Plantas,* p. 70.

20 K. Burns, *Colonial Habits.*

21 Premo, *Children of the Father King,* p. 83.

22 Clendinnen, *Ambivalent Conquests,* pp. 74–5.

23 Padden, *The Hummingbird and the Hawk,* p. 259 ff.

24 Gibson, *The Aztecs,* p. 117.

25 Archivo General de Indias (Seville), Indiferente General 2859, vol. 2, ff. 1–18, "El Rey. Despacho que se dio a Don Francisco de Toledo, virrey del Perú," para. 20.

26 Ibid., para. 15.

27 Gibson, *The Aztecs,* pp. 106, 110.

28 Schäfer, *El Consejo Real,* vol. 2, p. 565 ff.

29 Phelan, *Millennial Kingdom,* p. 106.

30 McAlister, *Spain and Portugal,* pp. 427–8; Greenleaf, *The Mexican Inquisition, passim;* for the Inquisition's political role in Spain, Benassar, "Por el Estado," *passim.*

31 Zavala, "La 'Utopía'," and id., "Sir Thomas More," *passim.*

32 Miranda, "El Pátzcuaro de Don Vasco," *passim.*

33 López Lara, "Los hospitales," pp. 119–25.

34 Quoted in Zavala, "Sir Thomas More," p. 105.

35 Zavala, "La 'Utopía'," p. 15.

36 Pagden, *The Fall,* pp. 52–5.

37 Discussion here of natural slavery and Vitoria draws heavily on Pagden, *The Fall,* chs. 3 and 4.

38 Ibid., pp. 94–107.

39 Parry and Keith, *New Iberian World,* vol. 1, p. 387.

40 For Vitoria's reasoning, ibid., pp. 300–6.

41 Góngora, *The Spanish Empire,* p. 56.

42 Baudot, *Utopía,* p. 102.

43 Ricard, *The Spiritual Conquest,* p. 47.

44 Baudot, *Utopía,* p. 175, and chs. 3 and 4, on Olmos generally. Also Wilkerson, "The ethnographic works of Andrés de Olmos."

45 Discussion of Sahagún here draws heavily on Brading, *The First America,* pp. 119–24. See also Edmonson, *Sixteenth-Century Mexico.*

46 León Portilla (ed.), *The Broken Spears*, p. 93. This work is compiled from *Codex Florentino* and other early native accounts of the conquest.

47 Brading, *The First America*, pp. 121–2.

48 Baudot, *Utopía*, pp. 108–12.

49 Cf. Elliott, *Imperial Spain*, pp. 209–17. For the rise of the supposed demonic influence, Cervantes, *The Devil*, p. 8 ff.

50 Wagner, *The Life and Writings of Bartolomé de las Casas*, pp. 5–6.

51 For the quotation, Sanderlin, *Bartolomé de las Casas*, p. 87, from Las Casas, *Historia*, bk. 3, ch. 79; for the colonial hell, Cañizares-Esguerra, *Puritan Conquistadors*, p. 73.

52 Sanderlin, *Bartolomé de las Casas*, p. 16, quoting Antonio de Remesal, *Historia general de las Indias occidentales* (Madrid, 1619), vol. 2, p. 108.

53 Brading, *The First America*, p. 63.

54 Wagner, *The Life and Writings of Bartolomé de las Casas*, p. 135 ff.

55 Ibid., pp. 167–8.

56 Hanke, *The Spanish Struggle*, p. 121.

57 For the text, Parry and Keith, *New Iberian World*, vol. 1, pp. 366–71

58 Wagner, *The Life and Writings of Bartolomé de las Casas*, p. 239.

59 Sanderlin, *Bartolomé de las Casas*, p. 115, citing *Apologética historia*, introductory argument.

60 Ibid., p. 202, quoting *Apologética historia*, ch. 48.

61 For this, more subtly put, Pagden, *The Fall*, ch. 6, particularly pp. 141–3.

62 Brading, *The First America*, pp. 104–10. For Spaniards' many debates and opinions about the possible work of the Devil among native Americans, see Cervantes, *The Devil*, passim.

63 A close analysis in MacCormack, *Religion in the Andes*.

64 Fraser, *The Architecture of Conquest*, pp. 156–9; Kubler, *Mexican Architecture*.

CHAPTER 9   SOCIETY: OLD ORDERS CHANGED

1 Newson, "The demographic impact of colonization," pp. 143, 147, and Newson, "Indian population patterns," p. 41.

2 N. D. Cook, *Demographic Collapse*, p. 111.

3 Denevan, *The Native Population*, pp. xxi–xxiii.

4 For the term, Henige, "Native American population," passim.

5 S. Cook and Borah, *Essays*, vol. 1, p. 376.

6 Ibid., vol. 3, pp. 1, 100. The lower figure for 1548 is a suggested correction by Zambardino, "Mexico's population," p. 14.

7 N. D. Cook, *Demographic Collapse*, p. 253.

8 Sánchez-Albornoz, "The population of colonial Spanish America," p. 7; Wightman, *Indigenous Migration*, pp. 63–73; Saignes, "The colonial condition," pp. 87–94.

9 e.g. S. Cook, "The historical demography of interior tribes of Colombia"; or Newson, "Demographic catastrophe in sixteenth-century Honduras."

10 Review of Brown, *Native Society*, by Karen M. Powers, *Hispanic American Historical Review* 73:4 (Nov. 1993), p. 695.

11 An immense bibliography exists on this topic. Sources used here: N. D. Cook, *Demographic Collapse*; Gibson, *The Aztecs*; Whitmore, *Disease and Death*; Borah, "Epidemics in the Americas"; Henige, "Native American population."

12 Alchon, *Native Society*, pp. 20–5.

13 Newson, "The demographic impact of colonization," pp. 150–1; also Alchon, *A Pest in the Land*, pp. 39–58.

14 MacKenzie, "Columbus blamed."

15   N. D. Cook, *Demographic Collapse*, p. 253.
16   Whitmore, *Disease and Death*, p. 214.
17   Sánchez-Albornoz, "The population of colonial Spanish America," pp. 17–18; the following discussion draws heavily on this essay.
18   Newson, "The demographic impact of colonization," p. 153.
19   Altman, *Emigrants and Society*, p. 253.
20   Stern, *Peru's Indian Peoples*, p. 171.
21   Carrasco, "Indian–Spanish marriage," p. 88.
22   Díaz del Castillo, *Historia verdadera*, ch. 143.
23   Ricard, *Spiritual Conquest*, p. 255.
24   Powers, *Women in the Crucible of Conquest*, pp. 97–8.
25   Lockhart, *Spanish Peru*, pp. 204–5.
26   Burkholder and Johnson, *Colonial Latin America*, p. 105.
27   Konetzke, "La emigración," pp. 13, 24.
28   Garcilaso de la Vega, *Royal Commentaries*, vol. 2, p. 734.
29   Martín, *Daughters of the Conquistadores*, p. 35.
30   Sauer, *The Early Spanish Main*, p. 207.
31   Manning, "African connections," p. 57.
32   Curtin, *The Atlantic Slave Trade*, p. 116; Palmer, *Slaves*, p. 27.
33   Bowser, *The African Slave*, pp. 286–7.
34   Quoted in Mörner, *Estratificación*, p. 13.
35   Morse, "Claims of political tradition," in *New World Soundings*, p. 104.
36   Domínguez Ortiz, *El Antiguo Régimen*, pp. 104–5. Discussion of Spanish society draws on chapter 6 of this work.
37   Ots Capdequí, *El estado español*, p. 25.
38   *Recopilación*, 6.1.27.
39   Borah, *Justice*.
40   Discussion of changes in native society here draws on: Borah, *Justice*, ch. 3; Gibson, *The Aztecs*, ch. 6; Lockhart, *The Nahuas*, ch. 4; Ramírez, "*El Dueño de Indios*," Stern, *Peru's Indian Peoples*, ch. 4.
41   Saignes, "The colonial condition," p. 84.
42   See e.g. Murra, "Aymara lords."
43   Saignes, "The colonial condition," p. 71.
44   Ramírez, "*El Dueño de indios*," p. 609; see also Saignes, "The colonial condition," p. 84.
45   Powers, *Women in the Crucible of Conquest*, pp. 45–6.
46   Kellogg, ""From parallel and equivalent to separate and unequal," p. 134.
47   Spores, "Mixteca *cacicas*," p. 187.
48   Silverblatt, *Moon, Sun, and Witches*, pp. 114–16.
49   Espejo-Hunt and Restall, "Work, marriage, and status," p. 248.
50   MacCormack, *Religion in the Andes*, p. 423.
51   Gruzinski, *The Conquest of Mexico*, p. 64.
52   Powers, *Women in the Crucible of Conquest*, p. 61; Silverblatt, *Moon, Sun, and Witches*, p. 132.
53   Garza Carvajal, *Butterflies Will Burn*, pp. 164–9; Trexler, *Sex and Conquest*, chs. 1 and 2.
54   Harrison, "Theology of concupiscence," p. 145.
55   Lockhart, *The Men of Cajamarca*, p. 32.
56   Ibid., p. 38.
57   Lockhart, *Spanish Peru*, ch. 2.
58   Himmerich, *The Encomenderos*, p. 167.
59   Mörner, *Estratificación*, p. 15.

60   See Lanyon, *The New World of Martín Cortés*, pp. 6–14; Powers, *Women in the Crucible of Conquest*, pp. 78–81.

61   Padden, *The Hummingbird and the Hawk*, p. 230.

62   Figures rounded from those given in S. Cook and Borah, *Essays*, vol. 2, p. 197.

63   Ibid.

64   Burkholder and Johnson, *Colonial Latin America*, p. 105.

65   N. D. Cook, *Demographic Collapse*, p. 151.

66   Palmer, *Slaves*, p. 46.

67   S. Cook and Borah, *Essays*, vol. 2, pp. 197–8.

68   Klein, *African Slavery*, p. 32; Klein and Vinson, *African Slavery*, p. 26; N. D. Cook, *Demographic Collapse*, p. 151; Bowser, *The African Slave*, p. 11.

69   Klein and Vinson, *African Slavery*, pp. 32–3.

70   For Cuzco, see K. Burns, *Colonial Habits*, ch. 1; for Mexico City, see Holler, *Escogidas Plantas*, pp. 118–28.

71   Parry and Keith, *New Iberian World*, vol. 1, p. 418.

72   Saignes and Bouysse-Cassagne, "Dos confundidas identidades," pp. 14–15.

73   Israel, *Race*, p. 66.

74   Lockhart, *Spanish Peru*, p. 182, and ch. 10 generally for Blacks in the sixteenth century.

75   Klein and Vinson, *African Slavery*, pp. 40–1. The term is Matthew Restall's (see ibid., p. 250, for references).

76   For views on this, see Restall (ed.), *Beyond Black and Red*, e.g. ch. 4.

77   Bernand, *Negros esclavos*, pp. 48–9.

78   *Recopilación*, 7.5.15.

79   Hakluyt, *Voyages*, p. 162.

80   Phelan, *The Kingdom of Quito*, p. 7 ff.

81   Israel, *Race*, pp. 69–71.

82   Mota y Escobar, *Descripción*, p. 66.

83   Palmer, *Slaves*, p. 178.

84   Pagden, *The Fall*, p. 18.

85   Morse, "The urban development of Colonial Spanish America," p. 74.

86   Fraser, *The Architecture of Conquest*, p. 155; also p. 36 ff.

87   Ibid., p. 41.

88   Morse, "The urban development of Colonial Spanish America," p. 82.

89   Ibid., p. 90.

90   Konetzke, "La emigración," pp. 2–4, 7.

91   Boyer, *Lives of the Bigamists*, pp. 109–11.

92   Lockhart and Otte, *Letters and People of the Spanish Indies*, p. 141.

93   Ibid., p. 127.

94   Dillard, *Daughters of the Reconquest*, p. 215.

95   Premo, *Children of the Father King*, pp. 13–15 *passim*.

96   Pagden, *The Fall*, p. 53.

97   Martin, *Governance and Society*, p. 158.

98   Seed, *To Love, Honor, and Obey*, p. 31.

99   Lockhart and Otte, *Letters and People of the Spanish Indies*, pp. 66–7.

100 Altman, *Emigrants and Society*, pp. 127–9.

CHAPTER 10   ECONOMY: SHIPS AND SILVER

1   *Recopilación*, 8.8.1.

2   e.g. Parker, *Philip II*, p. 75.

3 Bakewell, *Silver and Entrepreneurship*, p. 188 n. 32.

4 Kamen, *Spain 1469–1714*, p. 166.

5 Lockhart, *The Men of Cajamarca*, p. 13.

6 Muro, "Bartolomé de Medina," p. 209.

7 Garner, "Long-term silver mining trends," p. 902. Other numerical estimates here are from the beginning of the same article.

8 TePaske, "The search for El Dorado," table 1. At Professor TePaske's suggestion, New Granadan production has been increased here by 30 per cent over the amounts shown in that table, to allow for a greater non-registration of gold than he at first estimated.

9 Ibid.

10 Bakewell, "Notes on the Mexican silver mining industry," tables 2(a) and 2(b).

11 Salvucci, *Textiles and Capitalism in Mexico*, p. 48.

12 Bennett and Hoffman, "Ranching," p. 99.

13 Cf. Borah, *Silk Raising*.

14 Viqueira and Urquiola, *Los obrajes*, p. 40.

15 Ibid., pp. 136–9; Bakewell, "Notes on the Mexican silver mining industry," tables 3(a)–3(d).

16 Viqueira and Urquiola, *Los obrajes*, pp. 14, 26.

17 Romero, *Historia económica del Perú*, vol. 1, pp. 207–16.

18 Tyrer, *Historia*, p. 125, and chs. 2 and 3 generally.

19 Watts, *The West Indies*, pp. 104, 112–14.

20 Chevalier, *Land and Society in Colonial Mexico*, p. 78. Discussion of sugar in New Spain here also draws from Barrett, *The Sugar Hacienda*, chs. 1, 2, 6, 10.

21 Romero, *Historia económica del Perú*, vol. 1, p. 182. Discussion here also draws on Borah, *Early Colonial Trade*, pp. 85–6, and McAlister, *Spain*, p. 224.

22 Chevalier, *Land and Society in Colonial Mexico*, pp. 76, 78; for sugar refining, Barrett, *The Sugar Hacienda*, ch. 6, and Cushner, *Lords of the Land*, pp. 67–8.

23 Florescano, "The formation and economic structure of the hacienda," p. 155.

24 Chevalier, *Land and Society in Colonial Mexico*, pp. 73–4.

25 Hamnett, *Politics and Trade in Southern Mexico*, pp. 9–10.

26 Borah, *Early Colonial Trade*, p. 5, and pp. 1–7 generally.

27 Lockhart, *Spanish Peru*, p. 97, and ch. 6 generally.

28 Ibid.

29 Ibid., p. 107.

30 Gruzinski, *The Mestizo Mind*, p. 58

31 Crosby, "Metamorphosis," p. 82.

32 Bakewell, *Silver Mining*, pp. 68–9.

33 Chevalier, *Land and Society in Colonial Mexico*, p. 94.

34 See Melville, *A Plague of Sheep*.

35 Crosby, "Metamorphosis," p. 83.

36 Florescano, "The formation and economic structure of the hacienda," p. 154.

37 McNeill, "American food crops in the Old World," p. 47.

38 McAlister, *Spain*, p. 157.

39 Ots Capdequí, *El estado*, pp. 36–7.

40 Florescano, "The formation and economic structure of the hacienda," pp. 159–64, and Mörner, "Rural economy," pp. 190–2. The following discussion draws heavily on these two essays.

41 Chevalier, *Land and Society in Colonial Mexico*, p. 60.

42 Florescano, "The formation and economic structure of the hacienda," p. 157, citing Simpson, *Exploitation*.

43 Gibson, *The Aztecs*, pp. 225–6.

44 Ibid., p. 231.
45 MacLeod, "Aspects of the internal economy of colonial Spanish America," p. 261.
46 Villamarín and Villamarín, *Indian Labor*, p. 50 ff. Generalizations here about labor on the periphery draw heavily on this work.
47 Bowser, "Africans," p. 366.
48 Sempat Assadourian, *El sistema*, p. 291.
49 Chaunu, *Sevilla y América*, p. 199. This, or its French original, *Séville et l'Amérique, XVIe–XVIIe siècles*, is a convenient part-summary of the immense original by Pierre and Huguette Chaunu, *Séville et l'Atlantique (1504–1650)*, 8 vols (Paris, 1955–9).
50 Chaunu, *Sevilla y América*, p. 203.
51 Ibid., p. 239, and generally, pp. 217–39.
52 Atwell, "International bullion flows," p. 82.
53 Lynch, *The Hispanic World*, pp. 340–2; Elliott, "Spain and America," p. 325.
54 Hoberman, *Mexico's Merchant Elite*, p. 220.
55 Semo, *Historia del capitalismo en México*, p. 172, quoting from Enrique Otte, "La Nueva España en 1529," in *Historia y sociedad en el mundo de habla española* (El Colegio de México, Mexico City, 1970), pp. 103–6.
56 A random selection of items that notarized contracts show arriving in Potosí in 1589.
57 For this and other points raised here, McAlister, *Spain*, pp. 212–13.
58 Ibid., p. 360.
59 Mangan, *Trading Places*, particularly chs. 4 and 5.

CHAPTER 11   THE SEVENTEENTH CENTURY: A SLACKER GRIP

1 Brading, *The First America*, pp. 2, 34; for Philip's defending of Catholicism, and his providential beliefs, Parker, *The Grand Strategy*, pp. 92–3, 99–102, 104–5.
2 Elliott, *Imperial Spain*, p. 283. For losses in the Armada, Martin and Parker, *The Spanish Armada*, pp. 258–60.
3 Lynch, *The Hispanic World*, p. 6.
4 Kamen, *Spain 1469–1714*, pp. 155–7.
5 Lynch, *The Hispanic World*, p. 7.
6 Goslinga, *The Dutch in the Caribbean*, p. 54.
7 Ibid., p. 62. Also Moya Pons, *History of the Caribbean*, pp. 39–43.
8 Lynch, *The Hispanic World*, pp. 261–7; Pérez-Mallaína and Torres Ramírez, *La Armada*, pp. 222–9; and generally for foreign presence on the west coast of South America in the 1600s, Bradley, *The Lure of Peru, passim*.
9 Rich, "The European nations," pp. 702–4.
10 Boxer, *Salvador de Sá*, pp. 171–2.
11 Licenciado Juan Bautista Monzón to the king, Lima, Dec. 17, 1567, in AGI Lima 92.
12 Cf. Israel, *Race*, ch. 3.
13 Baltasar Dorantes de Carranza, *Sumaria relación*, pp. 113–14, quoted in Brading, *The First America*, p. 296.
14 Aguirre Beltrán, *La población negra*, cited in MacLachlan and Rodríguez, *The Forging of the Cosmic Race*, p. 197.
15 Peña, *Oligarquía*, p. 220, and chs. 5 and 6 generally; Israel, *Race*, pp. 80–3.
16 Burkholder, "Bureaucrats," p. 89.

17 Parry, *The Sale of Public Office*, p. 12.
18 Ibid., p. 24.
19 Burkholder, "Bureaucrats," p. 82. The following paragraphs draw heavily on this article.
20 Ibid., p. 84.
21 Ibid., p. 93.
22 Andrien, *Crisis and Decline*, p. 117.
23 Burkholder, "Bureaucrats," p. 86; Andrien, *Crisis and Decline*, p. 119.
24 Burkholder, "Bureaucrats," pp. 87–91.
25 Hoberman, *Mexico's Merchant Elite*, p. 91.
26 Israel, *Race*, p. 158, and ch. 5 generally for this contest.
27 Cf. Andrien, *Crisis and Decline*, pp. 100–1.
28 Muro Romero, "La administración," p. 282, and *passim*.
29 Elliott, *The Count-Duke of Olivares*, pp. 410, 418.
30 Stein and Stein, *Silver, Trade, and War*, p. 55.
31 For trends and commentary, Garner, "Long-term silver mining trends," esp. pp. 900–5; also Bakewell, "Mining."
32 Data on Lima income given here are from Andrien, *Crisis and Decline*, pp. 52–61.
33 Totals, to the nearest thousand, calculated from TePaske, Hernández Palomo, and Hernández Palomo, *La Real Hacienda*, annual summaries for the years shown.
34 Andrien, *Crisis and Decline*, p. 67.
35 Ruiz Rivera, "Remesas," pp. 24–30.
36 Bakewell, *Silver Mining*, p. 232.
37 TePaske and Klein, "The seventeenth-century crisis," p. 133, and *passim*.
38 Morineau, *Incroyables gazettes*, pp. 105 ff., 262.
39 Lynch, *The Hispanic World*, p. 281. Discussion of trade here is largely drawn from ch. 7 of this work, esp. pp. 277–86.
40 Ibid., pp. 278–9; Chaunu, *Sevilla y América*, pp. 242–3.
41 Pérez-Mallaína and Torres Ramírez, *La Armada*, p. 44.
42 Tyrer, *Historia*, pp. 132, 136, 145.
43 Salvucci, *Textiles and Capitalism in Mexico*, pp. 136–44, 150; Super, "The agricultural near north," p. 232; and id., *La vida*, pp. 226–7.
44 Ramírez, *Provincial Patriarchs*, part 2.
45 Davies, *Landowners*, p. 91, and *passim*.
46 Information on commercial agriculture here is partly from Lynch, *The Hispanic World*, pp. 289, 302, 313–14.
47 Ferry, "Encomienda," pp. 611–13; Conniff, "Guayaquil," pp. 390–2.
48 Wortman, *Government and Society in Central America*, p. 15.
49 Morilla Critz, "Crisis y transformación," p. 271.
50 Ibid., p. 264.
51 Vila Vilar, "Las ferias," p. 26.
52 *Recopilación*, 6.1.12 for the 1536 law; for later limitations, ibid., 6.3.18–19 and 6.7.7.
53 Jaramillo, "Migraciones," pp. 270–3, 284–5, 306–8.
54 Swann, "Migration," p. 145.
55 Gibson, *Aztecs*, p. 247.
56 Saignes, "The colonial condition," p. 88; also N. D. Cook, "Migration," p. 56; for Cuzco, Wightman, *Indigenous Migration*, p. 6. The following remarks on *forasteros* are drawn mainly from Wightman.
57 Wightman, *Indigenous Migration*, pp. 112, 146–7.
58 Glave, "The 'Republic of Indians'," p. 506.

59 Ibid., p. 124.
60 Lockhart, *The Nahuas*, pp. 304–18.
61 Ibid., p. 412; for *títulos* generally, ibid., pp. 410–18.
62 Saignes, "The colonial condition," p. 73.
63 Gruzinski, *The Mestizo Mind*, p. 192; for Andean religion, MacCormack, *Religion in the Andes*, pp. 408–10, 417–19, and pp. 406–33 generally for seventeenth-century Andean native cult.
64 MacCormack, *Religion in the Andes*, pp. 420–1.
65 Saignes, "The colonial condition," p. 119.
66 Lockhart, *The Nahuas*, pp. 209, 245.
67 Ibid., pp. 236–7.
68 Cf. Mills, *An Evil Lost to View?*, pp. 74–5.
69 Brading, *The First America*, p. 361. Also Lockhart, *The Nahuas*, p. 248, and, generally for Guadalupe, Taylor, "The Virgin of Guadalupe," and also his *Magistrates of the Sacred*, pp. 279–300.
70 Taylor, "The Virgin of Guadalupe," p. 11; Lockhart, *The Nahuas*, pp. 245, 252.
71 Quotation from Saignes, "The colonial condition," p. 104. See this essay, pp. 103–6 generally, for *cofradías* and also *compadrazgo*.
72 Rausch, *A Tropical Plains Frontier*, pp. 44, 228.
73 McFarlane, *Colombia*, p. 24. This discussion of seventeenth-century New Granada draws heavily on chapter 1 of this work, and also on Villamarín and Villamarín, *Indian Labor*, pp. 80–92.
74 Ferry, "Encomienda," pp. 614, 618–22, 632–5.
75 Gutiérrez, *When Jesus Came*, p. 107, and ch. 3 generally for seventeenth-century New Mexico.
76 Farriss, *Maya Society*, p. 92, and chs. 1, 2, and 3 generally for seventeenth-century Yucatan.
77 Ibid., pp. 64, 427 n. 21.
78 Saeger, "Warfare, reorganization, and readaptation," p. 276.
79 Caraman, *The Lost Paradise*, p. 36, and *passim* for Jesuit missions.
80 Gannon, *The Guaraní*, p. 53.
81 Caraman, *The Lost Paradise*, p. 235.
82 For Paraguay, Lockhart and Schwartz, *Early Latin America*, pp. 260–5; Villamarín and Villamarín, *Indian Labor*, pp. 104–10.
83 For these numbers, and imports, see Bennett, *Africans in Colonial Mexico*, pp. 22–3, and Klein and Vinson, *African Slavery*, p. 42.
84 For the numbers in this paragraph, Klein and Vinson, *African Slavery*, pp. 24–30. For Potosí, Wolff, "Negersklaverei," pp. 160–9.
85 Bernand, *Negros esclavos*, p. 11.
86 Klein and Vinson, *African Slavery*, pp. 123–4.
87 The preceding paragraphs draw directly from Thornton, *Africa and Africans*, ch. 8.
88 Klein and Vinson, *African Slavery*, pp. 156–8. For "syncretic absorption," ibid., p. 162.
89 For discussion of this, see Thornton, *Africa and Africans*, pp. 222–30.
90 For such use of the Inquisition, and of courts generally, Klein and Vinson, *African Slavery*, pp. 169, 172–3; also Villa-Flores, *Dangerous Speech*, pp. 128, 131, 134, 146.
91 Thornton, *Africa and Africans*, p. 292.
92 Remarks here on maroon communities are drawn from Thornton, *Africa and Africans*, pp. 280–94, and Klein and Vinson, *African Slavery*, pp. 175–80.

93   Brockington, *Blacks, Indians and Spaniards*, particularly ch. 5.
94   Zulawski, "Social differentiation," p. 104, and generally for urban work by native women; also Powers, *Women in the Crucible of Conquest*, pp. 152–3.
95   Wightman, *Indigenous Migration*, p. 117.
96   Lockhart, *Spanish Peru*, ch. 9.
97   Charney, *Indian Society*, pp. 82–6.
98   Lavrin, "Women in Spanish American colonial society," p. 331. The following draws widely on this chapter.
99   Gauderman, *Women's Lives in Colonial Quito*, pp. 36–7, 43.
100 Lavrin, "Women in Spanish American colonial society," pp. 327–8.
101 Powers, *Women in the Crucible of Conquest*, pp. 154–5.
102 Socolow, *Women of Colonial Latin America*, pp. 120–1; Few, *Women who Live Evil Lives*, pp. 96–9; Fields, *Pestilence and Head Colds*, ch. 2, p. 51.
103 Socolow, *Women of Colonial Latin America*, p. 117.
104 Cope, *The Limits of Racial Domination*, p. 118.
105 Lavrin, "Women in Spanish American colonial society," p. 333; McCaa, "Marriageways," pp. 24–5.
106 Cervantes, *The Devil*, pp. 88–9.
107 Seed, *To Love, Honor and Obey*, p. 110.
108 Twinam, "Honor, sexuality, and illegitimacy," p. 133 and *passim*.
109 Twinam, "The negotiation of honor," pp. 82–3.
110 Johnson, "Dangerous words," pp. 132–4.
111 Van Deusen, *Between the Sacred and the Worldly*, pp. 21–3.
112 Gutiérrez, *When Jesus Came*, p. 278.
113 Boyer, "Women, *la mala vida*, and the politics of marriage" pp. 258–9.
114 Lavrin, "Lo femenino," pp. 164–5; Stern, *Secret History of Gender*.
115 Alberro, "Beatriz de Padilla."
116 Martín, *Daughters of the Conquistadores*, pp. 172, 177; Lavrin, "Female religious," p. 175.
117 Premo, *Children of the Father King*, pp. 86–8; Mannarelli, *Hechiceras, beatas y expósitas*, pp. 83–4.
118 Lavrin, "Female religious," p. 182.
119 Paz, *Sor Juana*, pp. 64 ff.
120 Brading, *The First America*, p. 372.
121 Translated by Pauline Cook in *The Pathless Grove*, and quoted in Leonard, *Baroque Times*, p. 176.
122 Paz, *Sor Juana*, p. 463. For her ideas, ibid., chs. 11–12, and Leonard, *Baroque Times*, pp. 186–92. For Rodríguez, Trabulse, "Un científico mexicano," p. 150.
123 Brading, *The First America*, p. 338, for this point and others here on Rosa; Martín, *Daughters of the Conquistadores*, pp. 282–94; Graziano, "Rosa de Lima."
124 Leonard's *Baroque Times* is an obvious example.
125 Bayón, "The architecture and art of colonial Spanish America," pp. 724, 744.
126 Stevenson, "The music of colonial Spanish America," p. 785, and pp. 780–7 generally.
127 Bayón, "The architecture and art of colonial Spanish America," p. 742.
128 Kubler and Soria, *Art*, p. 96.
129 Brading, *The First America*, pp. 277, 280–1.
130 Ibid., pp. 362–71; and also for Kircher and Egypt, Paz, *Sor Juana*, pp. 175–8.
131 The phrase is from Schwartz and Salomon, "South American indigenous societies," p. 481. The discussion of seventeenth-century mestizos in these paragraphs is a summary interpretation of pp. 480–92 of that essay.
132 Gibson, "Indian societies," p. 416.

CHAPTER 12   EIGHTEENTH-CENTURY SPANISH
AMERICA: REFORMED OR DEFORMED?

1   For Utrecht and the *asiento*, Walker, *Spanish Politics*, p. 67 ff.; for the war, Lynch, *Bourbon Spain*, pp. 22–45.
2   Lynch, *Bourbon Spain*, pp. 8–10 and *passim*.
3   For New Granada, McFarlane, *Colombia*, pp. 34, 37; for Chile, Carmagnani, "Colonial Latin American demography," *passim*; for Mexico, Garner, *Economic Growth*, p. 15; for the revisionist view of the central Andes, Tandeter, "Población," p. 12.
4   Thornton, *African and Africans*, p. 318.
5   The preceding paragraphs draw directly on Klein and Vinson, *African Slavery*, pp. 76–82.
6   Lockhart and Schwartz, *Early Latin America*, p. 338.
7   Garner, "Long-term silver mining trends," pp. 900–5.
8   For the European valuation of bullion, Tandeter, *Coercion and Market*, pp. 5–10. The same work also analyzes closely the benefits to Potosí of the continued *mita*. For Mexican labor costs, Garner, *Economic Growth*, pp. 128–31. For production at Almadén, Matilla Tascón, *Historia de las minas de Almadén*, vol. 2, pp. 105, 354. For blasting, Bakewell, *Silver and Entrepreneurship*, pp. 76–7.
9   For comments on rising output before the reform era, TePaske, "General tendencies," p. 329, and Coatsworth, "The Mexican mining industry," p. 29.
10 McFarlane, *Colombia*, p. 78; for production and slavery in New Granada, ibid., ch. 3 generally. For gold in Mexico and Chile, Bakewell, "Mining," pp. 143, 149–50.
11 Salvucci, *Textiles and Capitalism in Mexico*, pp. 139–43.
12 Malamud, *La economía colonial*, p. 154.
13 Deans-Smith, *Bureaucrats*, pp. 24, 211.
14 Borah, *Early Colonial Trade*, pp. 124, 158 n. 35.
15 Malamud, *La economía colonial*, p. 150. For Campillo, see also Stein and Stein, *Silver, Trade, and War*, pp. 209–12.
16 Larraín, "Gross National Product," pp. 116–21.
17 Cooney and Whigham, "Paraguayan commerce," pp. 216–20.
18 Weber, *Bárbaros*, pp. 155, 167.
19 Rock, *Argentina*, pp. 42–7, 64.
20 Ferry, "The price of cacao," pp. 317–28.
21 Malamud, *La economía colonial*, pp. 112–13.
22 Parry, Sherlock, and Maingot, *A Short History of the West Indies*, p. 146; for ranking of producers, Malamud, *La economía colonial*, p. 113, citing Moreno Fraginals, *El ingenio*, pp. 40–2; also Watts, *The West Indies*, pp. 298–300.
23 Malamud, *La economía colonial*, pp. 190–2.
24 Ibid., pp. 192–5.
25 For these reforms, ibid., pp. 168–73. For the continuation of fleets, see also Stein and Stein, *Silver, Trade, and War*, p. 186 ff.
26 Walker, *Spanish Politics*, pp. 206–10.
27 Ibid., pp. 217–23; García-Baquero, *Cádiz*, vol. 1, pp. 540–3, vol. 2, figure 7.
28 Fisher, *Commercial Relations*, pp. 87–9.
29 Ibid., pp. 49–53, 88.
30 Kamen, *Philip V*, p. 56.
31 McFarlane, *Colombia*, pp. 187–97.
32 Rock, *Argentina*, pp. 61–2.
33 Lynch, *Bourbon Spain*, p. 350.

34 Gálvez to Areche, in Brading, *The First America*, p. 479.
35 Burkholder, "Bureaucrats," p. 90. For Gálvez, Brading, "Bourbon Spain," p. 404.
36 Van Bath, *Real hacienda*, p. 24.
37 Brading, "Bourbon Spain," p. 408, for conservative estimates; growth rates from Garner, *Economic Growth*, pp. 217–18; for loans and inflation, TePaske, "General tendencies," pp. 323–5.
38 Malamud, *La economía colonial*, p. 157.
39 For various estimates, see Brading, "Bourbon Spain," p. 409; Lynch, *Bourbon Spain*, pp. 349–50; Barbier, "Peninsular finance," p. 23. For New Granada, McFarlane, *Colombia*, p. 223.
40 Burkholder and Johnson, *Colonial Latin America*, p. 238.
41 Jorge de Escobedo, quoted in Barbier, "Peninsular finance," p. 33.
42 Cf. MacLachlan, *Spain's Empire*, p. 123 ff.
43 For regalism, Paquette, *Enlightenment*, ch. 2.
44 Payne, *Spanish Catholicism*, p. 64.
45 Taylor, *Magistrates of the Sacred*, pp. 14–15.
46 Céspedes del Castillo, *América Hispánica*, p. 391. For a succinct account of the Mexican church under Charles III, see Farriss, *Crown and Clergy*, ch. 4.
47 Lynch, *Bourbon Spain*, pp. 261–8 (p. 266 for Charles III).
48 Weber, *Bárbaros*, p. 110.
49 Royal *Instrucción* of 1768, quoted in Dussel, *Historia general*, vol. 1/1, p. 701.
50 Weber, *Bárbaros*, pp. 111–12, citing David Block, *Mission Culture on the Upper Amazon: Native Tradition, Jesuit Enterprise, and Secular Policy in Moxos, 1660–1880* (University of Nebraska Press, Lincoln, 1994), p. 129.
51 Herr, "Disentailment," in Kern and Dodge, *Historical Dictionary*, p. 170.
52 Anna, *The Fall of Royal Government*, p. 11. For New Spain, Hamnett, "The appropriation," *passim*.
53 Lynch, *Bourbon Spain*, p. 106.
54 Brading, *Miners*, pp. 234–5.
55 For Mexico, Archer, *The Army*, pp. 8–38; for Peru, Campbell, "The army," pp. 50–7.
56 Marchena Fernández, "The social world of the military," p. 57; for Humboldt's comment, ibid., p. 59; for Venezuela, Brading, "Bourbon Spain," p. 401.
57 For Buenos Aires, Rock, *Argentina*, p. 44; for comparisons of cities, Sánchez-Albornoz, *La población de América Latina*, p. 121; for summary population figures, Burkholder and Johnson, *Colonial Latin America*, pp. 263–4.
58 For peninsular migration, Sánchez-Albornoz, "The population of colonial Spanish America," pp. 31–2; for Spaniards in Mexico, Burkholder and Johnson, *Colonial Latin America*, p. 264.
59 Katzew, *Casta Painting*, pp. 93, 201–4; also Carrera, *Imagining Identity*, pp. 49–55; and the issue of *Artes de México*, new series, no. 8 (Summer 1990), "La pintura de castas."
60 Cf. Cope, *The Limits of Racial Domination*, pp. 54–7.
61 Hoberman, "Conclusion," p. 316.
62 Cf. Seed, *To Love, Honor and Obey*, pp. 156–7.
63 Ladd, *The Mexican Nobility*, pp. 17, 28; Anna, *The Fall of Royal Government*, p. 22.
64 Socolow, *Women of Colonial Latin America*, p. 75.
65 Arrom, *Women of Mexico City*, p. 158.
66 Socolow, *Women of Colonial Latin America*, p. 123.
67 Quoted ibid., p. 174.
68 Seed, *To Love, Honor and Obey*, pp. 206–7.
69 Shumway, *The Case of the Ugly Suitor*, pp. 76–7.
70 Premo, *Children of the Father King*, p. 137.

71 Ibid., p. 163.
72 Viqueira Albán, *Propriety and Permissiveness*, pp. 20–2.
73 Ibid., pp. 39, 46–51.
74 Cope, *The Limits of Racial Domination*, ch. 7.
75 Gosner, "Religion and rebellion," p. 61 and *passim*.
76 Patch, "Culture, community, and 'rebellion'," pp. 74–5.
77 Florescano, *Precios del maíz*, pp. 159–72.
78 Taylor, *Drinking, Homicide, and Rebellion*, p. 122, and ch. 4 *passim*.
79 O'Phelan, *Rebellions*, p. 87. The discussion here of Andean revolts draws heavily on this book.
80 For messianism in, particularly, the far south of Mexico in the eighteenth century, see Florescano, *Memory*, pp. 146–83. For the Andes, see summary comments in Schwartz and Salomon, "South American indigenous societies," p. 459.
81 Stern, "The age of Andean insurrection," p. 43, and following pages generally for the revolt.
82 Spalding, *Huarochirí*, ch. 9.
83 For Peru, O'Phelan, *Rebellions*, appendix 1; comparison with Mexico in Coatsworth, "Patterns of rural rebellion," p. 32.
84 Juan and Ulloa, *Discourse*, p. 75.
85 O'Phelan, *Rebellions*, pp. 125–6.
86 Ibid., p. 164.
87 For this, and events recounted in this paragraph, Campbell, "Ideology," pp. 124–35.
88 For the term and the figure, Stern, "The age of Andean insurrection," pp. 34–5.
89 Fisher, *Government and Society in Colonial Peru*, p. 92 ff.
90 Campbell, "Ideology," p. 126.
91 McFarlane, "The rebellion of the *barrios*," p. 197 and *passim*.
92 McFarlane, *Colombia*, pp. 51–71, which offers a succinct analysis of the *comunero* affair.
93 Cf. Phelan, *The People and the King*, pp. 87–8.
94 Brading, *The First America*, pp. 428–32, and ch. 19 generally; and, for de Pauw, Gerbi, *The Dispute*, ch. 3.
95 Brading, *The First America*, p. 459, and ch. 20 generally.
96 For these stones see e.g. Carrasco and Matos Moctezuma, *Montezuma's Mexico*; for León y Gama, Brading, *The First America*, pp. 462–4.
97 Lynch, *The Spanish American Revolutions*, p. 34.
98 Discussion on music here draws from Stevenson, "The music of colonial Spanish America," pp. 790–7. For Stampiglia, Grout, *A Short History of Opera*, p. 213.
99 Cf. Alain Pacquier's notes to Gabriel Garrido (director), *De l'Altiplano a l'Amazone: Lima-La Plata, Missions Jésuites*, a recording of compositions by Zipoli, Torrejón y Velasco, and other composers in Spanish America in the seventeenth and eighteenth centuries (joint production by K617 and Association Française d'Action Artistique).
100 Palmer, *Sculpture in the Kingdom of Quito*, chs. 8, 9; Vargas and Crespo Toral, *Arte de Ecuador*, pp. 62–72.
101 Kelemen, *Baroque and Rococo*, vol. 1, p. 81. For Legarda, Palmer, *Sculpture in the Kingdom of Quito*, ch. 8.
102 Fernández, *Mexican Art*, p. 40 and plate 36.
103 Kelemen, *Baroque and Rococo*, vol. 1, p. 38.
104 Mesa and Gisbert, *Bolivia*, pp. 53–5.
105 Bayón, "The architecture and art of colonial Spanish America" p. 717; Burke, "The academy," pp. 487–90.

CHAPTER 13   COLONIAL BRAZIL: SLAVES, SUGAR, AND GOLD

1   For a summary of Vespucci's activities and influence, Parry, *The Discovery of the Sea*, pp. 215–19.
2   Johnson, "The Portuguese settlement," p. 259; the present account of early Brazil draws heavily from this chapter.
3   Metcalf, *Go-Betweens*, p. 62.
4   Ibid., p. 85.
5   Hemming, *Red Gold*, p. 36; for Sousa, also Johnson, "The Portuguese settlement," p. 260, and Cortesão and Calmon, *Brasil*, pp. 345–55.
6   Parry and Keith, *New Iberian World*, vol. 5, pp. 42–4. For the origins of São Paulo, see Morse, *The Bandeirantes*, pp. 7, 10–11.
7   Metcalf, *Go-Betweens*, pp. 81–4.
8   Johnson, "The Portuguese settlement," p. 261.
9   For a sample donation (that of the Pernambuco captaincy to Duarte Coelho in 1534), see Parry and Keith, *New Iberian World*, vol. 5, pp. 44–52. This is analyzed by Johnson in "The Portuguese settlement," pp. 261–2.
10 McAlister, *Spain and Portugal*, pp. 260–4; for the intermarriages, Monteiro, "Crises and transformations," p. 991.
11 Johnson, "The Portuguese settlement," p. 270, and p. 269 ff. in general for the following.
12 Cf. Schwartz, *Sugar Plantations*, pp. 33–7.
13 Hemming, *Red Gold*, pp. 98–9.
14 Ibid., pp. 102–3.
15 Monteiro, "Crises and transformations," pp. 998–9.
16 Johnson, "The Portuguese settlement," p. 272; for Sá and the Tupí, Hemming, *Red Gold*, pp. 83–5.
17 Hemming, *Red Gold*, pp. 85–6.
18 This discussion of disease draws on Hemming, *Red Gold*, pp. 139–45.
19 Sánchez-Albornoz, *La población de América Latina*, p. 83.
20 José de Anchieta, SJ, quoted in Hemming, *Red Gold*, p. 142; percentage dying from Monteiro, "Crises and transformations," p. 1000.
21 Ibid., p. 1004.
22 Oliveira Marques, *A History of Portugal*, vol. 1, p. 311.
23 For the slavery question from the 1566 junta on, Hemming, *Red Gold*, pp. 148–51.
24 Schwartz, *Sugar Plantations*, p. 13. The account given here of the rise of Brazilian sugar draws largely on this work, pp. 15–27.
25 Ibid., pp. 18–19.
26 Mintz, *Sweetness and Power*, p. 96; production and export figures from Schwartz, *Sugar Plantations*, p. 165.
27 The account given here of sugar-making is taken from Schwartz, *Sugar Plantations*, ch. 5, which refers primarily to Bahia.
28 For the *safra* and work, Schwartz, *Sugar Plantations*, pp. 99–106.
29 Ibid., pp. 118, 216.
30 Monteiro, "Crises and transformations," pp. 994–5.
31 For Pernambuco, Schwartz, "Colonial Brazil," p. 437; for Bahia, Schwartz, *Sugar Plantations*, pp. 70–1.
32 Schwartz, *Sugar Plantations*, p. 54.
33 For 1535, Marcílio, "Population of colonial Brazil," p. 53; for 1538, E. B. Burns, *A History of Brazil*, p. 38.

34 Manning, "African connections," p. 57.

35 Schwartz, *Sugar Plantations*, pp. 65, 71, 339 (for the trade); for African sources, Mauro, *Le Portugal*, p. 171 ff., and Manning, "African connections," pp. 55–66.

36 Figures from Johnson, "The Portuguese settlement," p. 279. See also discussion in Marcílio, "Population of colonial Brazil," p. 45.

37 Hemming, *Red Gold*, appendix, pp. 487–501; for Amazonia, Marcílio, "Population of colonial Brazil," p. 39, citing William M. Denevan, "The aboriginal population of Amazonia," in his *Native Population*.

38 McAlister, *Spain and Portugal*, p. 282; Marcílio, "Population of colonial Brazil," pp. 38–41.

39 Schwartz, *Sovereignty and Society*, p. 28. For the legal structure of Portugal and the empire in the sixteenth century, see chs. 2–4 of that work. They are the source for the discussion here.

40 Ibid., p. 38.

41 Ibid., p. 50.

42 Ibid., p. 64, and pp. 62–7 for the structure of the high court.

43 Metcalf, *Go-Betweens*, pp. 243—266.

44 Schwartz, *Sugar Plantations*, pp. 17, 204.

45 Boxer, *The Dutch in Brazil*, p. 20.

46 Vogt, *Portuguese Rule*, p. 145, and, for this discussion, ch. 6 in general.

47 Boxer, *The Portuguese Seaborne Empire*, pp. 110–11, for this and other Dutch attacks on Portuguese holdings; for the same, Oliveira Marques, *A History of Portugal*, vol. 1, ch. 7.

48 For the Dutch attacks, Boxer, *The Dutch in Brazil*, chs. 1, 2.

49 Ibid., pp. 147–8, and ch. 4 generally for the following.

50 Ibid., p. 113, and ch. 4 of that work generally for Johan Maurits.

51 Ibid., p. 119.

52 Ibid., p. 151.

53 Cf. Rodrigues, *Brasil*, p. 76.

54 For this, and the following, E. B. Burns, *A History of Brazil*, pp. 47–8; also Rodrigues, *Brasil*, p. 79, and Cortesão and Calmon, *Brasil*, pp. 459–60.

55 Boxer, *The Dutch in Brazil*, p. 243.

56 Schwartz, *Sugar Plantations*, pp. 125, 183.

57 Oliveira Marques, *A History of Portugal*, vol. 1, p. 305; and Hemming, *Red Gold*, p. 213.

58 Hemming, *Red Gold*, pp. 223–8, and ch. 11 generally for Portuguese exploration of the Amazon in the seventeenth century. For a brief summary, also E. B. Burns, *A History of Brazil*, p. 51 ff.

59 Simonsen, *Historia economica*, vol. 2, p. 138.

60 Cortesão and Calmon, *Brasil*, p. 483.

61 Morse, *The Bandeirantes*, pp. 22–3, citing Cortesão, *Rapôso Tavares*, pp. 70–7.

62 Hemming, *Red Gold*, p. 42.

63 Metcalf, *Go-Betweens*, p. 86.

64 Nazzari, *Disappearance of the Dowry*, p. 10.

65 This account of early São Paulo draws on Morse, *The Bandeirantes*, pp. 10–21.

66 Ellis, "The bandeiras," p. 49. The following discussion of the chronology of *bandeiras* is based on this account.

67 Morse, *The Bandeirantes*, p. 19. For the size of slaving *bandeiras*, Ellis, "The bandeiras," p. 53.

68 Higgins, *"Licentious Liberty,"* p. 36.

69 Russell-Wood, "Colonial Brazil," pp. 547–8, 560–1.

70 Buarque de Holanda, "The Monsoons," p. 155, for this and other points on these expeditions.

71 E. B. Burns, *A History of Brazil*, pp. 64–5. Discussion of cattle here draws generally on this work, pp. 64–8.

72 Hemming, *Red Gold*, p. 352, and ch. 16 generally for cattle in the seventeenth century.

73 Ibid., pp. 352, 371.

74 Ibid., ch. 16 *passim*.

75 Population figures here from Marcílio, "Population of colonial Brazil," pp. 47, 54; McAlister, *Spain and Portugal*, p. 351; Schwartz, *Sugar Plantations*, pp. 86, 349–50; Schwartz, *Sovereignty and Society*, pp. 105–6, 242.

76 Cf. Schwartz, *Sugar Plantations*, pp. 69, 249–50, 322; also his "Colonial Brazil," pp. 491–2.

77 Schwartz, *Sugar Plantations*, p. 391. For a summary of slave demography, ibid., p. 350; and chs. 13 and 14 *passim* for family, marriage, mortality, and other life events among Bahian slaves. For a shorter and simpler account, see Conniff and Davis, *Africans in the Americas*, ch. 5.

78 Thornton, *Africa and Africans*, p. 320.

79 Souza, *The Devil and the Land of the Holy Cross*, pp. 125–9.

80 Schwartz, "The Mocambo," p. 328.

81 Davis, "Afro-Brazilian Women," p. 254.

82 Conniff and Davis, *Africans in the Americas*, pp. 97–8; Hemming, *Red Gold*, p. 393; generally on seventeenth-century slave resistance, Schwartz, *Sugar Plantations*, pp. 468–72. For suicide etc., ibid. pp. 370–1. For fraternities, Schwartz, "Colonial Brazil," p. 493.

83 Schwartz, *Sugar Plantations*, pp. 330–2; Conniff and Davis, *Africans in the Americas*, p. 97.

84 Hemming, *Red Gold*, pp. 317–18. This account of the Jesuits' efforts in the north of Brazil, and of Vieira's part in them, draws heavily from ch. 15 of that book.

85 E. B. Burns, *A Documentary History*, p. 83.

86 Hemming, *Red Gold*, p. 319.

87 Ibid., p. 337.

88 Wright et al., "Destruction, resistance, and transformation," p. 364. This paragraph is drawn from pp. 345–73 of this chapter.

89 Schwartz, "Colonial Brazil," p. 498.

90 Schwartz, *Sovereignty and Society*, pp. 346–7, 352, 382 ff.

91 Ibid., p. 340, and ch. 13 (on which this discussion draws) generally for links between officials and colonials.

92 Ibid., p. 342.

93 Nazzari, *Disappearance of the Dowry*, p. 5.

94 Schwartz, *Sovereignty and Society*, pp. 328–9, and generally for this discussion of marriage and illicit activities, ibid., pp. 162–3, 324–56.

95 Ibid., pp. 220–1.

96 Ibid., pp. 229–30, and ch. 10 generally for explanations of the suppression; for Brandônio's points and Fernandes Brandão, the latter's *Dialogues*, pp. 9, 42–4.

97 Schwartz, *Sovereignty and Society*, p. 353; for the restoration of the court, ibid., pp. 234–42.

98 Schwartz, *Sugar Plantations*, p. 184; for Pernambuco and Bahia, ibid., p. 178. For exports and prices, Mauro, *Le Portugal*, pp. 278–80, 600–1.

99 Mauro, *Le Portugal*, p. 426.

100 Ibid., pp. 433–4, and pp. 426–32 for other products of the land.

101 Ibid., pp. 47–54 for this and other information here about shipbuilding.

102 For seventeenth-century trade in the Río de la Plata, see Moutoukias, "Power," *passim* (here, p. 772). For the San Ildefonso treaty, and the defining of Brazil's limits generally, Mansuy-Diniz Silva, "Portugal and Brazil," pp. 472–5.

103 Cf. Simonsen, *Historia económica*, vol. 2, pp. 184–7; Boxer, *Portuguese Seaborne Empire*, pp. 223–5; Schwartz, *Sugar Plantations*, pp. 181–2.

104 McAlister, *Spain and Portugal*, p. 386.

105 Russell-Wood, "Colonial Brazil," p. 554. The following discussion draws heavily on this essay.

106 Manning, "African connections," pp. 57–60.

107 Higgins, *"Licentious Liberty,"* p. 38.

108 Ibid., p. 45.

109 Ibid., pp. 39–40.

110 Russell-Wood, "Colonial Brazil," p. 560.

111 Hemming, "Indians and the frontier," pp. 536–8.

112 Luís Gomez Ferreira, quoted in Boxer, *The Golden Age*, p. 184. See pp. 38–9, 182–5, 216–17 of this for practices of gold and diamond extraction in eighteenth-century Brazil.

113 Russell-Wood, "Colonial Brazil," pp. 553, and pp. 577–8 for local production.

114 Ibid., p. 594, for production, drawing on Virgílio Noya Pinto, *O ouro brasileiro e o comércio anglo-português* (São Paulo, 1979), p. 144; arrivals from Morineau, *Incroyables gazettes*, p. 139.

115 Cf. Prado, *The Colonial Background*, pp. 196–7; Russell-Wood, "Colonial Brazil," p. 582; Boxer, *The Golden Age*, p. 312.

116 For Portuguese trade and manufacture, Mauro, "Portugal and Brazil," pp. 460–8; Mansuy-Diniz Silva, "Portugal and Brazil," pp. 502–7.

117 Schwartz, *Sugar Plantations*, pp. 422–34; Alden, "Late colonial Brazil," pp. 627–31.

118 Alden, "Late colonial Brazil," p. 646; and for agricultural production and exports generally, ibid., pp. 626–53.

119 Ibid., p. 609. For the population figures cited here, and eighteenth-century demography in general, pp. 602–23, and for agriculture, trade, and economic change, pp. 627–53.

120 Maxwell, *Pombal*, pp. 21–4.

121 The Chevalier des Courtils, quoted in Maxwell, *Pombal*, p. 48.

122 Mansuy-Diniz Silva, "Portugal," pp. 491–2, and ibid., pp. 479–94, generally for the following.

123 Maxwell, *Pombal*, pp. 76–7.

124 Mansuy-Diniz Silva, "Portugal and Brazil," p. 495.

125 Ibid., pp. 484–5.

126 Cf. Maxwell, *Pombal*, pp. 52–4.

127 Alden, "Late colonial Brazil," p. 616, and pp. 612–19 generally; Maxwell, *Pombal*, pp. 72–3, 84.

128 Ibid., pp. 96–108.

129 Cf. Barman, *Brazil*, ch. 1 *passim*.

130 E. B. Burns, "The intellectuals," p. 231, and pp. 217–19, 229–42 generally for this description of the academies.

131 Stevenson, "A note on the music of colonial Brazil," p. 802, and pp. 799–803 generally. For a listing of works of colonial literature, Bethell, "A note," *passim*.

132 Kubler and Soria, *Art*, p. 190.

133 Kelemen, *Baroque and Rococo*, vol. 1, p. 253, and pp. 239–55 generally for Brazilian Baroque and Rococo.

134 Kubler and Soria, *Art*, p. 194, and pp. 118–19, 194–5 generally for Aleijadinho.

135 Ibid., p. 195.

CHAPTER 14   INDEPENDENCE

1   Archer, Introduction to *The Wars of Independence*, pp. 23–4. For "el indio Mariano," Van Young, *The Other Rebellion*, pp. 455–6.
2   For a succinct account of Miranda, Robertson, *Rise of the Spanish-American Republics*, ch. 2.
3   Rydjord, *Foreign Interest*, p. 155.
4   Robertson, *Rise of the Spanish-American Republics*, p. 145, and ch. 5 generally for Moreno; also on free trade in Buenos Aires, Puiggrós, *Historia económica*, ch. 7, and Rock, *Argentina*, pp. 73–6.
5   For this and the following, Lynch, *Bourbon Spain*, pp. 388–95.
6   Whitaker, *The United States*, p. 6 ff., and for trade with neutrals, Lynch, *Bourbon Spain*, pp. 367–8.
7   For France and Spain in these years, Lynch, *Bourbon Spain*, pp. 403–7, 419–21.
8   Payne, *A History of Spain and Portugal*, vol. 2, p. 423.
9   Kern and Dodge, *Historical Dictionary*, p. 164. For Spanish resistance, juntas, and the cortes, see also Payne, *A History of Spain and Portugal*, vol. 2, pp. 422–6, and Carr, *Spain*, pp. 81–105.
10   Lynch, *The Spanish American Revolutions*, pp. 304–6.
11   Arnade, *The Emergence of the Republic of Bolivia*, p. 28.
12   Lynch, *The Spanish American Revolutions*, p. 237; for Buenos Aires, Socolow, *The Merchants*, p. 132.
13   Lombardi, *Venezuela*, p. 124.
14   Rock, *Argentina*, pp. 73–6.
15   For New Granada, Lynch, *The Spanish American Revolutions*, pp. 239–40; for Chile, Loveman, *Chile*, pp. 110–11.
16   Van Young, *The Other Rebellion*, pp. 453, 464–6.
17   For Hidalgo, Hamill, *The Hidalgo Revolt*, *passim*; succinct accounts in Anna, "The independence of Mexico and Central America," pp. 61–5; Bazant, *A Concise History*, pp. 10–21; Villoro, "La revolución," pp. 325–31.
18   Cf. Lynch, *The Spanish American Revolutions*, pp. 105–18.
19   Johnson, *Simón Bolívar*, p. 37. This is a sound summary of Bolívar's life and beliefs, with selections of his writings. For a full narrative biography, Masur, *Simón Bolívar*; for a succinct account of Bolívar's career and political ideas, see Brading, *The First America*, ch. 27.
20   Brading, *The First America*, p. 609.
21   Quoted in Trend, *Bolívar*, p. 41.
22   Chronology condensed from Bushnell (ed.), *The Liberator*, pp. xxii–xxxiv.
23   Quoted ibid., p. 86.
24   Rojas, *El santo*, p. 46.
25   For the liberation of Chile, Robertson, *Rise of the Spanish-American Republics*, pp. 183–91; Lynch, *The Spanish American Revolutions*, pp. 139–41.
26   Quoted in Lynch, *The Spanish American Revolutions*, p. 177.
27   Domínguez, *Insurrection or Loyalty*, pp. 261–2.
28   Cf. Lynch, *The Spanish American Revolutions*, pp. 175–84.
29   Bushnell, *Simón Bolívar*, p. 135.
30   Rojas, *El santo*, p. 503.
31   Taylor, *Magistrates of the Sacred*, p. 464.
32   Ibid., p. 469. For a summary of Morelos's political and religious thought, ibid., pp. 463–72.
33   For Morelos, Timmons, *Morelos*.

34 Archer, "'La causa buena'," pp. 27–9.
35 The following draws heavily on Anna, "The independence of Mexico and Central America," pp. 82–9.
36 Archer, "Introduction," p. 34.
37 Ibid., pp. 33–4.
38 Domínguez, *Insurrection or Loyalty*, p. 161.
39 For Cuban affairs and loyalty, ibid., pp. 101–6, 140, 161; also Thomas, "Cuba," pp. 281–6.
40 Barman, *Brazil*, p. 34, and pp. 18–41 generally for the late colonial years.
41 Ibid., p. 27.
42 Bethell, "The independence of Brazil," p. 165.
43 Entry for "Inconfidência dos alfaiates" in Tenenbaum (ed.), *Encyclopedia of Latin American History and Culture*, vol. 3, p. 259; the quotation, in Barman, *Brazil*, p. 36.
44 Cf. Barman, *Brazil*, pp. 46–7, and ch. 2 generally for changes in Brazil in John's time.
45 Bethell, "The independence of Brazil," p. 174.
46 Barman, *Brazil*, p. 49.
47 Ibid., pp. 56–61.
48 Ibid., pp. 55, 61–4.
49 Bethell, "The independence of Brazil," p. 183, and pp. 179–87 for the final phase of Brazilian independence.
50 Ibid., p. 187.
51 Ibid., pp. 188–90.

Chapter 15 Epilogue

1 Sánchez-Albornoz, *La población de América Latina*, pp. 114–16. For disease in Venezuela, Earle, "'A grave for Europeans'?," pp. 286–8.
2 Tenenbaum (ed.), *Encyclopedia of Latin American History and Culture*, vol. 2, p. 37.
3 Elliott, *Empires*, pp. 134, 386–7.
4 These percentages are from Tenenbaum (ed.), *The Cambridge Encyclopedia of Latin America and the Caribbean*, p. 161.
5 For a spirited defense of Spanish science, particularly in the sixteenth century, see Cañizares-Esguerra, *Nature, Empire, and Nation*.

BIBLIOGRAPHY

A Brief General Orientation

Almost all the topics touched on in this book, and many that are not, are discussed in one or more volumes of Leslie Bethell (ed.), *The Cambridge History of Latin America*, 11 vols. (Cambridge: Cambridge University Press, 1984–95). Volume 11 of that work, published in 1995, consists of a set of bibliographical essays that provide a comprehensive guide to what has been written on Latin American history. An older, but still useful, work is Charles C. Griffin (ed.), *Latin America: A Guide to the Historical Literature* (University of Texas Press, Austin, 1971). A continuing guide to new writing is the *Handbook of Latin American Studies* (annually from the Hispanic Division, Library of Congress, Washington, DC), now available online via the Library of Congress website.

For quick reference, the five volumes of Barbara A. Tenenbaum (ed.), *Encyclopedia of Latin American History and Culture* (New York: Simon & Schuster/Macmillan, 1995), are invaluable. Also most useful, and well illustrated, is Simon Collier, Thomas E. Skidmore, and Harold Blakemore (eds), *The Cambridge Encyclopedia of Latin America and the Caribbean* (2nd edn, Cambridge: Cambridge University Press, 1992).

Abbreviations

CEHLA   Victor Bulmer-Thomas, John H. Coatsworth, and Roberto Cortés Conde (eds), *The Cambridge Economic History of Latin America*, vol. 1: *The Colonial Era and the Short Nineteenth Century*, Cambridge, Cambridge University Press, 2006.

CHLA   Leslie Bethell (ed.), *The Cambridge History of Latin America*, 11 vols., Cambridge University Press, Cambridge, 1984–95.

CHNPA   Frank Salomon and Stuart B. Schwartz (eds), *The Cambridge History of the Native Peoples of the Americas*, Cambridge University Press, Cambridge, 1999.

ELAH   Barbara A. Tenenbaum (ed.), *Encyclopedia of Latin American History and Culture*, 5 vols., Simon & Schuster/Macmillan, New York, 1995.

HAHR   *Hispanic American Historical Review*

Works Cited

Adams, Richard E. W., and MacLeod, Murdo, *The Cambridge History of the Native Peoples of the Americas*, vol. 2: *Mesoamerica*, Cambridge University Press, Cambridge, 2000.

Adelman, Jeremy (ed.), *Colonial Legacies: The Problem of Persistence in Latin American History*, Routledge, New York, 1999.

Ades, Dawn, *Art in Latin America*, Yale University Press, New Haven, 1989.

Aguirre Beltrán, Gonzalo, *La población negra de México*, Fondo de Cultura Económica, Mexico City, 1972.

Ahlfeld, Federico E., *Geografía física de Bolivia*, Los Amigos del Libro, La Paz–Cochabamba, Bolivia, 1969.

Aiton, Arthur S., *Antonio de Mendoza: First Viceroy of New Spain*, Duke University Press, Durham, NC, 1927.

Alberro, Solange, "Beatriz de Padilla: mistress and mother," in Gary Nash and David Sweet (eds), *Struggle and Survival in Colonial America*, University of California Press, Berkeley, 1981, pp. 247–56.

Alchon, Suzanne A., *Native Society and Disease in Colonial Ecuador*, Cambridge University Press, Cambridge, 1991.

Alchon, Suzanne A., *A Pest in the Land: New World Epidemics in Global Perspective*, University of New Mexico Press, Albuquerque, 2003.

Alden, Dauril, "Late colonial Brazil, 1750–1808," in *CHLA*, vol. 2, pp. 601–60.

Allaire, Louis, "The Caribs of the Lesser Antilles," ch. 18 in Wilson (ed.), *The Indigenous People of the Caribbean*.

Altman, Ida, *Emigrants and Society: Extremadura and America in the Sixteenth Century*, University of California Press, Berkeley and Los Angeles, 1989.

Altman, Ida, and Lockhart, James, *Provinces of Early Mexico: Variants of Spanish American Regional Evolution*, UCLA Latin American Center Publications, Los Angeles, 1976.

Andrien, Kenneth J., *Crisis and Decline: The Viceroyalty of Peru in the Seventeenth Century*, University of New Mexico Press, Albuquerque, 1985.

Andrien, Kenneth J. (ed.), *The Human Tradition in Colonial Latin America*, Scholarly Resources, Wilmington, DE, 2002.

Andrien, Kenneth J., *The Kingdom of Quito, 1690–1830: The State and Regional Development*, Cambridge University Press, Cambridge, 1995.

Andrien, Kenneth, and Johnson, Lyman L. (eds), *The Political Economy of Spanish America in the Age of Revolution, 1750–1850*, University of New Mexico Press, Albuquerque, 1994.

Anna, Timothy E., *The Fall of Royal Government in Peru*, University of Nebraska Press, Lincoln, 1979.

Anna, Timothy E., "The independence of Mexico and Central America," in *CHLA*, vol. 3, pp. 51–94.

Archer, Christon I., *The Army in Bourbon Mexico, 1760–1810*, University of New Mexico Press, Albuquerque, 1977.

Archer, Christon I., "'La causa buena': the counterinsurgency army of New Spain and the Ten Years' War," in Rodríguez (ed.), *Rank and Privilege*, pp.

Archer, Christon I. (ed.), *The Wars of Independence in Spanish America*, Scholarly Resources, Wilmington, DE, 2000.

Arnade, Charles W., *The Emergence of the Republic of Bolivia*, University of Florida Press, Gainesville, 1957.

Arrom, Silvia, *The Women of Mexico City, 1790–1857*, Stanford University Press, Stanford, 1985.

Artes de México (Mexico City), new series, no. 8 (Summer 1990), "La pintura de castas."

Atwell, William S., "International bullion flows and the Chinese Economy *circa* 1530–1650," *Past & Present* 95 (May 1982), pp. 68–90.

Bailey, Gauvin A., *Art of Colonial Latin America*, Phaidon, London, 2005.

Bakewell, Peter, "La maduración del gobierno del Perú en la década de 1560," *Historia Mexicana* 39:1 (July–Sept. 1989), pp. 41–70.

Bakewell, Peter, *Miners of the Red Mountain: Indian Labor in Potosí, 1545–1650*, University of New Mexico Press, Albuquerque, 1984.

Bakewell, Peter, "Mining in Colonial Spanish America," in *CHLA*, vol. 2, pp. 110–51.

Bakewell, Peter, "Notes on the Mexican silver mining industry in the 1590s," *Humanitas* (Universidad de Nuevo León, Monterrey) 19 (1978), pp. 383–409.

Bakewell, Peter, *Silver and Entrepreneurship in Seventeenth-Century Potosí: The Life and Times of Antonio López de Quiroga*, University of New Mexico Press, 1988 (repr. Southern Methodist University Press, Dallas, 1994).

Bakewell, Peter, *Silver Mining and Society in Colonial Mexico: Zacatecas, 1546–1700*, Cambridge University Press, Cambridge, 1971.

Balmori, Diana, Voss, Stuart F., and Wortman, Miles, *Notable Family Networks in Latin America*, University of Chicago Press, Chicago, 1984.

Barbier, Jacques A., "Peninsular finance and colonial trade: the dilemma of Charles IV's Spain," *Journal of Latin American Studies* 12:1 (May 1980), pp. 21–37.

Barman, Roderick J., *Brazil: The Forging of a Nation, 1798–1852*, Stanford University Press, Stanford, 1988.

Barnadas, Josep M., "The Catholic Church in colonial Spanish America," in *CHLA*, vol. 1, pp. 511–40.

Barrett, Ward, *The Sugar Hacienda of the Marqueses del Valle*, University of Minnesota Press, Minneapolis, 1970.

Bataillon, Marcel, "Les colons du Pérou contre Charles Quint: analyse du mouvement pizarriste (1544–1548)," *Annales ESC* 22:3 (May–June 1967), pp. 479–94.

Baudot, Georges, *Utopía e historia en México: los primeros cronistas de la civilización mexicana (1520–1569)*, Espasa-Calpe, Madrid 1983 (tr. of *Utopie et histoire au Mexique*, Édouard Privat, Toulouse, 1977).

Bauer, Arnold, *Chilean Rural Society from the Spanish Conquest to 1930*, Cambridge University Press, Cambridge, 1975.

Bauer, Arnold, "Rural Spanish America, 1870–1930," in *CHLA*, vol. 4, pp. 151–86.

Bayón, Damián, "The architecture and art of colonial Spanish America," in *CHLA*, vol. 2, pp. 709–45.

Bazant, Jan, *A Concise History of Mexico, from Hidalgo to Cárdenas, 1805–1940*, Cambridge University Press, Cambridge, 1977.

Bennassar, Bartolomé, "Por el Estado, contra el Estado," in his *Inquisición española*, pp. 321–36.

Bennassar, Bartolomé (ed.), *Inquisición española: poder político y control social*, Editorial Crítica, Barcelona, 1981.

Bennett, Deb, and Hoffmann, Robert S., "Ranching in the New World," in Viola and Margolis (eds), *Seeds of Change*, pp. 90–111.

Bennett, Herman L., *Africans in Colonial Mexico: Absolutism, Christianity, and Afro-Creole Consciousness, 1570–1640*, Indiana University Press, Bloomington, 2003.

Bennett, Wendell C., and Bird, Junius B., *Andean Culture History: The Archaeology of the Central Andes from Early Man to the Incas*, 2nd edn, American Museum of Natural History, The Natural History Press, Garden City, NY, 1964.

Benson, Elizabeth, "Moche art: myth, history, and rite," in *The Spirit of Ancient Peru: Treasures from the Museo Arqueológico Rafael Larco Hoyle*, Thames & Hudson, London and New York, 1997, 41–50.

Bernand, Carmen, *Negros esclavos y libres en las ciudades hispanoamericanas*, Fundación Histórica Tavera, Madrid, 2001.

Berrin, Kathleen (ed.), *The Spirit of Ancient Peru: Treasures from the Museo Arqueológico Rafael Larco Herrera*, Thames & Hudson/Fine Arts Museums of San Francisco, London and San Francisco, 1997.

Bethell, Leslie (ed.), *The Cambridge History of Latin America*, 11 vols., Cambridge University Press, Cambridge, 1984–95.

Bethell, Leslie, "The independence of Brazil," in *CHLA*, vol. 3, pp. 157–96.

Bethell, Leslie, "A note on literature and intellectual life in colonial Brazil," in *CHLA*, vol. 2, pp. 705–7.

Blakemore, Harold, and Smith, Clifford T. (eds), *Latin America: Geographical Perspectives*, 2nd edn, Methuen, London, 1983.

Borah, Woodrow W., *Early Colonial Trade and Navigation between Mexico and Peru*, Ibero-Americana 38, University of California Press, Berkeley and Los Angeles, 1954.

Borah, Woodrow W., "Epidemics in the Americas: major issues and future research," *Latin American Population History Bulletin* 19 (Spring 1991), pp. 2–13.

Borah, Woodrow W., *Justice by Insurance: The General Indian Court of Colonial Mexico and the Legal Aides of the Half-Real*, University of California Press, Berkeley and Los Angeles, 1983.

Borah, Woodrow W., "Representative institutions in the Spanish empire in the sixteenth century," *The Americas* 12:3 (Jan. 1956), pp. 246–57.

Borah, Woodrow W., *Silk Raising in Colonial Mexico*, Ibero-Americana 20, University of California Press, Berkeley and Los Angeles, 1943.

Boruchoff, David A. (ed.), *Isabel la Católica, Queen of Castile: Critical Essays*, Palgrave Macmillan, New York, 2003.

Bowser, Frederick P., *The African Slave in Colonial Peru, 1524–1650*, Stanford University Press, Stanford, 1974.

Bowser, Frederick P., "Africans in Spanish American colonial society," in *CHLA*, vol. 2, pp. 357–79.

Boxer, C. R., *The Dutch in Brazil, 1624–1654*, Clarendon Press, Oxford, 1957.

Boxer, C. R., *The Golden Age of Brazil, 1695–1750*, University of California Press, Berkeley and Los Angeles, 1962.

Boxer, C. R., *The Portuguese Seaborne Empire, 1415–1825*, Hutchinson, London, 1969.

Boxer, C. R., *Salvador de Sá and the Struggle for Brazil and Angola, 1602–1686*, Athlone Press, University of London, London, 1952.

Boyer, Richard, *Lives of the Bigamists: Marriage, Family, and Community in Colonial Mexico*, University of New Mexico Press (Diálogos), Albuquerque, 2001.

Boyer, Richard, "Women, *la mala vida*, and the politics of marriage," in Lavrin (ed.), *Sexuality and Marriage*, pp. 252–86.

Brading, D. A., "Bourbon Spain and its American empire," in *CHLA*, vol. 1, pp. 389–439.

Brading, D. A., *The First America: The Spanish Monarchy, Creole Patriots, and the Liberal State, 1492–1867*, Cambridge University Press, Cambridge, 1991.

Brading, D. A., *Miners and Merchants in Bourbon Mexico, 1763–1810*, Cambridge University Press, Cambridge, 1971.

Bradley, Peter T., *The Lure of Peru: Maritime Intrusion into the South Sea, 1598–1701*, Macmillan, Basingstoke, 1989.

Brockington, Lolita Gutiérrez, *Blacks, Indians and Spaniards in the Eastern Andes: Reclaiming the Forgotten in Colonial Mizque, 1550–1782*, University of Nebraska Press, Lincoln, 2006.

Broda, Johanna, Carrasco, David, and Matos Moctezuma, Eduardo, *The Great Temple of Tenochtitlan: Center and Periphery in the Aztec World*, University of California Press, Berkeley and Los Angeles, 1987.

Bruhns, Karen Olsen, *Ancient South America*, Cambridge University Press, Cambridge, 1994.

Brundage, Burr Cartwright, *A Rain of Darts: The Mexica Aztecs*, University of Texas Press, Austin, 1972.

Brundage, Burr Cartwright, *Two Earths, Two Heavens: An Essay Contrasting the Aztecs and the Incas*, University of New Mexico Press, Albuquerque, 1975.

Buarque de Holanda, Sérgio, "The monsoons," in Morse (ed.), *The Bandeirantes*, pp. 152–66.

Bulmer-Thomas, Victor, Coatsworth, John H., and Cortés Conde, Roberto (eds), *The Cambridge Economic History of Latin America*, vol. 1: *The Colonial Era and the Short Nineteenth Century*, Cambridge, Cambridge University Press, 2006.

Burke, Marcus, "The academy, neoclassicism, and independence," in O'Neill (ed.), *Mexico*, pp. 487–96.

Burkholder, Mark A., "Bureaucrats," ch. 4 in Hoberman and Socolow (eds), *Cities and Society in Colonial Latin America*.

Burkholder, Mark A., and Johnson, Lyman L., *Colonial Latin America*, Oxford University Press, New York, 1990.

Burns, E. Bradford (ed.), *A Documentary History of Brazil*, Alfred A. Knopf, New York, 1966.

Burns, E. Bradford, *A History of Brazil*, Columbia University Press, New York, 1970.

Burns, E. Bradford, "The intellectuals as agents of change and the independence of Brazil, 1724–1822," in Russell-Wood (ed.), *From Colony to Nation*, pp. 211–46.

Burns, E. Bradford, *Latin America: A Concise Interpretive History*, 6th edn, Prentice Hall/ Simon & Schuster, Englewood Cliffs, NJ, 1994.

Burns, E. Bradford, *Race Relations in the Portuguese Colonial Empire, 1415–1825*, Clarendon Press, Oxford, 1963.

Burns, Kathryn, *Colonial Habits: Convents and the Spiritual Economy of Cuzco, Peru*, Duke University Press, Durham, NC, 1999.

Bushnell, David (ed.), *The Liberator, Simón Bolívar: Man and Image*, Alfred A. Knopf, New York, 1970.

Bushnell, David, *Simón Bolívar: Liberation and Disappointment*, Pearson Longman, New York, 2004.

Calnek, Edward E., "Patterns of empire formation in the valley of Mexico, late post-classic period, 1200–1521," in Collier, Rosaldo, and Wirth (eds), *The Inca and Aztec States*, pp. 43–62.

Campbell, Leon G., "The army of Peru and the Túpac Amaru revolt, 1780–1783," *HAHR* 56:1 (Feb. 1976), pp. 31–57.

Campbell, Leon G., "Ideology and factionalism during the great rebellion, 1780–1782," in Stern (ed.), *Resistance, Rebellion, and Consciousness in the Andean Peasant World*, pp. 110–39.

Cañizares-Esguerra, Jorge, *Nature, Empire, and Nation: Explorations of the History of Science in the Iberian World*, Stanford University Press, Stanford, 2006.

Cañizares-Esguerra, Jorge, *Puritan Conquistadors: Iberianizing the Atlantic, 1550–1700*, Stanford University Press, Stanford, 2006.

Caraman, Philip, *The Lost Paradise: The Jesuit Republic in South America*, Seabury Press, New York, 1976.

Carmagnani, Marcello, "Colonial Latin American demography: growth of Chilean population, 1700–1830," *Journal of Social History* 1:2 (Winter 1967), pp. 179–91.

Carr, Raymond, *Spain, 1808–1975*, 2nd edn, Clarendon Press, Oxford, 1982.

Carrasco, David, *Quetzalcóatl and the Irony of Empire: Myths and Prophecies in the Aztec Tradition*, University of Chicago Press, Chicago, 1984.

Carrasco, David, and Matos Moctezuma, Eduardo, *Moctezuma's Mexico: Visions of the Aztec World*, University Press of Colorado, Niwot, CO, 1992.

Carrasco, David, Jones, Lindsay, and Sessions, Scott (eds), *Mesoamerica's Classic Heritage: From Teotihuacán to the Aztecs*, University Press of Colorado, Boulder, 2000.

Carrasco, Pedro, "Indian–Spanish marriage in the first century of the colony," in Schroeder, Wood, and Haskett (eds), *Indian Women of Early Mexico*, pp. 87–103.

Carrasco, Pedro, "The political economy of the Aztec and Inca states," in Collier, Rosaldo, and Wirth (eds), *The Inca and Aztec States*, pp. 23–40.

Carrera, Magali M., *Imagining Identity in New Spain: Race, Lineage, and the Colonial Body in Portraiture and Casta Paintings*, University of Texas Press, Austin, 2003.

Carroll, Patrick, "Africans in mainland Spanish America," in Conniff and Davis (eds), *Africans in the Americas*, pp. 107–21.

Cervantes, Fernando, *The Devil in the New World: The Impact of Diabolism in New Spain*, Yale University Press, New Haven, 1994.

Céspedes del Castillo, Guillermo, *América Hispánica, 1492–1898*, vol. 6 of Manuel Tuñón de Lara (ed.), *Historia de España*, Editorial Labor, Madrid, 1983.

Cevallos-Candau, Francisco Javier, et al. (eds), *Coded Encounters: Writing, Gender, and Ethnicity in Colonial Latin America*, University of Massachusetts Press, Amherst, 1994.

Chambers, Sarah C., *From Subjects to Citizens: Honor, Gender, and Politics in Arequipa, Peru, 1780–1854*, Pennsylvania State University Press, University Park, 1999.

Charney, Paul, *Indian Society in the Valley of Lima, Peru, 1532–1824*, University Press of America, Lanham, MD, 2001.

Chaunu, Pierre, *Conquête et exploitation des nouveaux mondes (XVIe siècle)*, Nouvelle Clio, Presses Universitaires de France, Paris, 1969.

Chaunu, Pierre, *L'Expansion européenne, du XIIIe au Xve siècle*, 2nd edn, Nouvelle Clio, Presses Universitaires de France, Paris, 1989.

Chaunu, Pierre, *Sevilla y América, siglos XVI y XVII*, University of Seville, Seville, 1983.

Chevalier, François, *Land and Society in Colonial Mexico: The Great Hacienda*, University of California Press, Berkeley and Los Angeles, 1966.

Chowning, Margaret, *Rebellious Nuns: The Troubled History of a Mexican Convent, 1752–1863*, Oxford University Press, Oxford, 2006.

Clancy, Flora S., and Peter D. Harrison (eds), *Vision and Revision in Maya Studies*, University of New Mexico Press, Albuquerque, 1990.

Clapperton, Chalmers, "Tectonic history and structure," in Collier, Skidmore, and Blakemore (eds), *The Cambridge Encyclopedia of Latin America and the Caribbean*, pp. 12–18.

Clendinnen, Inga, *Ambivalent Conquests: Maya and Spaniard in Yucatan, 1517–1570*, Cambridge University Press, Cambridge, 1987.

Clendinnen, Inga, *Aztecs: An Interpretation*, Cambridge University Press, Cambridge, 1991.

Clendinnen, Inga, "'Fierce and unnatural cruelty': Cortés and the conquest of Mexico," *Representations* 33 (Winter 1991), pp. 65–100.

Coatsworth, John H., "The Mexican mining industry in the eighteenth century," in Jacobsen and Puhle (eds), *The Economies of Mexico and Peru*, pp. 26–45.

Coatsworth, John H., "Patterns of rural rebellion in Latin America: Mexico in colonial perspective," in Katz (ed.), *Riot, Rebellion, and Revolution*, pp. 21–62.

Coe, Michael D., *Breaking the Maya Code*, Thames & Hudson, New York, 1992.

Coe, Michael D., *The Maya*, 7th edn, Thames & Hudson, New York, 2005.

Coe, Michael D., *Mexico: From the Olmecs to the Aztecs*, 4th edn, Thames & Hudson, New York, 1994.

Coe, Michael D., and Koontz, Rex, *Mexico: From the Olmecs to the Aztecs*, 5th edn, Thames & Hudson, London, 2002.

Collier, George A., Rosaldo, Renato I., and Wirth, John D. (eds), *The Inca and Aztec States, 1400–1800: Anthropology and History*, Academic Press, New York, 1982.

Collier, Simon, Skidmore, Thomas E., and Blakemore, Harold (eds), *The Cambridge Encyclopedia of Latin America and the Caribbean*, 2nd edn, Cambridge University Press, Cambridge, 1992.

Columbus, Ferdinand [Fernando Colón], *The Life of the Admiral Christopher Columbus by his Son, Ferdinand*, tr. and annotated by Benjamin Keen, Rutgers University Press, New Brunswick, NJ, *c*.1959.

Conniff, Michael L., "Guayaquil through independence: urban development in a colonial system," *The Americas* 33:3 (Jan. 1977), pp. 385–410.

Conniff, Michael L., and Davis, Thomas J., *Africans in the Americas: A History of the Black Diaspora*, St. Martin's Press, New York, 1994.

Conrad, Geoffrey W., and Demarest, Arthur A., *Religion and Empire: The Dynamics of Aztec and Inca Expansionism*, Cambridge University Press, Cambridge, 1984.

Cook, Noble David, *Demographic Collapse: Indian Peru, 1520–1620*, Cambridge University Press, Cambridge, 1981.

Cook, Noble David, "Disease and the depopulation of Hispaniola, 1492–1518," *Colonial Latin American Review* 2:1–2 (1993), pp. 211–45.

Cook, Noble David, "Migration in colonial Peru: an overview," ch. 3 in Robinson (ed.), *Migration in Colonial Spanish America*.

Cook, Noble David., "¿Una primera epidemia americana de viruela en 1493?," *Revista de Indias* 227 (Jan.–Apr. 2003), pp. 49–64.

Cook, Noble David, and Lovell, W. George (eds), *"Secret Judgments of God": Old World Disease in Colonial Spanish America*, University of Oklahoma Press, Norman, 1992.

Cook, Pauline, *The Pathless Grove*, Decher Press, Prairie City, IL, 1951.

Cook, Sherburne F., "The historical demography of the interior tribes of Colombia in the studies of Juan Friede and Germán Colmenares," in Cook and Borah, *Essays in Population History*, vol. 1, pp. 411–29.

Cook, Sherburne F., and Borah, Woodrow, *Essays in Population History*, 3 vols, University of California Press, Berkeley and Los Angeles, 1971–9.

Cooney, Jerry W. and Whigham, Thomas L., "Paraguayan commerce with the outside world," ch. 10 in Andrien and Johnson (eds), *The Political Economy of Spanish America*.

Cope, R. Douglas, *The Limits of Racial Domination: Plebeian Society in Colonial Mexico City*, University of Wisconsin Press, Madison, 1994.

Cortés, Hernán, *Letters from Mexico*, tr. and ed. A. R. Pagden, Orion Press, New York, 1971.

Cortesão, Jaime, *Rapôso Tavares e a formação territorial do Brasil*, Rio de Janeiro, 1958.

Cortesão, Jaime, and Calmon, Pedro, *Brasil*, vol. 26 of A. Ballesteros (ed.), *Historia de América*, Salvat Editores, Barcelona, 1956.

Covey, R. Alan, *How the Incas Built their Heartland: State Formation and the Innovation of Imperial Strategies in the Sacred Valley, Peru*, University of Michigan Press, Ann Arbor, 2006.

Crosby, Alfred W., "Metamorphosis of the Americas," in Viola and Margolis (eds), *Seeds of Change*, pp. 70–89.

Curtin, Philip D., *The Atlantic Slave Trade: A Census*, University of Wisconsin Press, Madison, 1969.

Cushner, Nicholas P., *Lords of the Land: Sugar, Wine, and Jesuit Estates of Coastal Peru, 1600–1767*, State University of New York Press, Albany, 1980.

D'Altroy, Terence N., *The Incas*, Blackwell, Oxford, 2002.

Davies, Keith A., *Landowners in Colonial Peru*, University of Texas Press, Austin, 1984.

Davies, Nigel, *The Aztecs: A History*, University of Oklahoma Press, Norman, 1980.

Davis, Darien, "Afro-Brazilian women, civil rights, and political participation," in Darien, *Slavery and Beyond: The African Impact on Latin America and the Caribbean*, Rowman & Littlefield, Lanham, MD, 1995, pp. 253–64.

Dealy, Glen C., *The Latin Americans: Spirit and Ethos*, Westview Press, Boulder, CO, 1992.

Deans-Smith, Susan, *Bureaucrats, Planters, and Workers: The Making of the Tobacco Monopoly in Bourbon Mexico*, University of Texas Press, Austin, 1992.

Denevan, William M., *Cultivated Landscapes of Native Amazonia and the Andes*, Oxford University Press, Oxford, 2001.

Denevan, William M. (ed.), *The Native Population of the Americas in 1492*, 2nd edn, University of Wisconsin Press, Madison, 1992.

Díaz del Castillo, Bernal, *The Conquest of New Spain*, tr. J. M. Cohen, Penguin Books, Harmondsworth, 1963.

Díaz del Castillo, Bernal, *Historia verdadera de la conquista de la Nueva España*, 3 vols, Espasa-Calpe Mexicana, SA, Mexico City, 1950.

Diffie, Bailey W., and Winius, George D., *Foundations of the Portuguese Empire, 1415–1580*, University of Minnesota Press, Minneapolis, 1977.

Dillard, Heath, *Daughters of the Reconquest: Women in Castilian Town Society, 1100–1300*, Cambridge University Press, Cambridge, 1994.

Dobyns, Henry F., and Doughty, Paul L., *Peru: A Cultural History*, Oxford University Press, New York, 1976.

Domínguez, Jorge I., *Insurrection or Loyalty: The Breakdown of the Spanish American Empire*, Harvard University Press, Cambridge, MA, 1980.

Domínguez Ortiz, Antonio, *El Antiguo Régimen: los reyes católicos y los Austrias*, Alianza Editorial, Madrid, 1973.

Donahue-Wallace, Kelly, *Art and Architecture of Viceregal Latin America, 1521–1821*, University of New Mexico Press, Albuquerque, 2008.

Donnan, Christopher B., *Moche Portraits from Ancient Peru*, University of Texas Press, Austin, 2004.

Dorantes de Carranza (ed.), *Sumaria relación de las cosas de la Nueva España*, José María de Agreda y Sánchez, Mexico City, 1970.

Dussel, Enrique D., *Historia general de la Iglesia en América Latina*, vol. 1/1: *Introducción general a la historia de la Iglesia en América Latina*, Salamanca, Ediciones Sígueme, 1983.

Earle, Rebecca, "'A grave for Europeans'? Disease, death, and the Spanish-American revolutions," ch. 12 in Archer (ed.), *The Wars of Independence in Spanish America*.

Edmonson, Munro S. (ed.), *Sixteenth-Century Mexico: The Work of Sahagún*, School of American Research and University of New Mexico Press, Albuquerque, 1974.

Elliott, J. H., *The Count-Duke of Olivares: The Statesman in an Age of Decline*, Yale University Press, New Haven, 1986.

Elliott, J. H., *Empires of the Atlantic World: Britain and Spain in America 1492–1830*, Yale University Press, New Haven, 2006.

Elliott, J. H., *Imperial Spain, 1469–1716*, Edward Arnold, London, 1963.

Elliott, J. H., "Spain and America in the sixteenth and seventeenth centuries," in *CHLA*, vol. 1, pp. 287–334.

Elliott, J. H., "The Spanish conquest and settlement of America," in *CHLA*, vol. 1, pp. 149–206.

Ellis, Myriam, "The bandeiras in the geographical expansion of Brazil," in Morse (ed.), *The Bandeirantes*, pp. 48–63.

Espejo-Hunt, Martha, and Restall, Matthew, "Work, marriage, and status: Maya women of colonial Yucatan," in Schroeder, Wood, and Haskett (eds.), *Indian Women of Early Mexico* 231–54.

Espinoza Soriano, Waldemar, *La destrucción del imperio de los incas: la rivalidad política y señorial de los curacazgos andinos*, Ediciones Retablo de Papel, Lima, 1973.

Esteva Fábregat, Claudio, *El mestizaje en Iberoamérica*, Alhambra, Madrid, 1988.

Farriss, N[ancy] M., *Crown and Clergy in Colonial Mexico, 1759–1821*, Athlone Press, University of London, 1968.

Farriss, N[ancy] M., *Maya Society under Colonial Rule: The Collective Enterprise of Survival*, Princeton University Press, Princeton, 1984.

Fash, William L. and Fash, Barbara W., "Teotihuacán and the Maya. a classic heritage," in Carrasco, Jones, and Sessions (eds), *Mesoamerica's Classic Heritage*, pp. 433–63.

Fernandes Brandão, Ambrósio (attrib.), *Dialogues of the Great Things of Brazil*, tr. Frederick A. H. Hall, William F. Harrison, and Dorothy W. Welker, University of New Mexico Press, Albuquerque, 1987.

Fernández, Justino, *Mexican Art*, Spring Books, London, 1965.

Fernández-Armesto, Felipe, *Amerigo: The Man who Gave his Name to America*, Random House, New York, 2007.

Fernández-Armesto, Felipe, *Columbus*, Oxford University Press, Oxford, 1991.

Fernández-Armesto, Felipe, *Columbus and the Conquest of the Impossible*, Phoenix, London, 2000.

Fernández-Armesto, Felipe, *Ferdinand and Isabella*, Dorset Press, New York, 1991.

Ferry, Robert J., "Encomienda, African slavery, and agriculture in seventeenth-century Caracas," *HAHR* 61:4 (Nov. 1981), pp. 609–35.

Ferry, Robert J., "The price of cacao, its export, and rebellion in eighteenth-century Caracas: boom, bust, and the Basque monopoly," ch. 10 in Johnson and Tandeter (eds), *Essays on the Price History of Eighteenth-Century Latin America*.

Few, Martha, *Women who Live Evil Lives: Gender, Religion, and the Politics of Power in Colonial Guatemala*, University of Texas Press, Austin, 2002.

Fields, Sherry, *Pestilence and Head Colds: Encountering Illness in Colonial Mexico*, Columbia University Press, Gutenberg-e, New York, 2007, http://www.gutenberg-e.org/fields/.

Fisher, J. R., *Commercial Relations between Spain and Spanish America in the Era of Free Trade, 1778–1796*, Centre for Latin American Studies, University of Liverpool, Liverpool, 1985.

Fisher, J. R., *Government and Society in Colonial Peru: The Intendant System, 1784–1814*, Athlone Press, University of London, 1970.

Fisher, J. R., Kuethe, Alan J. and McFarlane, Anthony (eds), *Reform and Insurrection in Bourbon New Granada and Peru*, Louisiana State University Press, Baton Rouge, 1990.

Florescano, Enrique, "The formation and economic structure of the hacienda in New Spain," in *CHLA*, vol. 2, pp. 153–88.

Florescano, Enrique, *Memory, Myth, and Time in Mexico, from the Aztecs to Independence*, University of Texas Press, Austin, 1994.

Florescano, Enrique, *Precios del maíz y crisis agrícolas en México (1708–1810)*, El Colegio de México, Mexico City, 1969.

Florescano, Enrique, et al., *Atlas histórico de México*, 2nd edn, Siglo Veintiuno Editores, Mexico City, 1984.

Floyd, Troy S., *The Columbus Dynasty in the Caribbean, 1492–1526*, University of New Mexico Press, Albuquerque, 1973.

Fraser, Valerie, *The Architecture of Conquest: Building in the Viceroyalty of Peru, 1535–1635*, Cambridge University Press, Cambridge, 1990.

Fung Pineda, Rosa, "The late preceramic and initial period," in Keatinge (ed.), *Peruvian Prehistory*, pp. 67–96.

Galloway, J. H., "Brazil," in Blakemore and Smith (eds), *Latin America: Geographical Perspectives*, pp. 325–82.

Gannon, Barbara, *The Guaraní under Spanish Rule in the Río de la Plata*, Stanford University Press, Stanford, 2003.

García-Baquero González, Antonio, *Cádiz y el Atlántico, 1717–1778 (El comercio colonial español bajo el monopolio gaditano)*, 2 vols, Escuela de Estudios Americanos, Seville, 1976.

Garcilaso de la Vega, El Inca, *Royal Commentaries of the Incas and General History of Peru*, tr. Harold V. Livermore, 2 vols, University of Texas Press, Austin, 1966.

Garner, Richard L., *Economic Growth and Change in Bourbon Mexico*, University Press of Florida, Gainesville, 1993.

Garner, Richard L., "Long-term silver mining trends in Spanish America: a comparative analysis of Peru and Mexico," *American Historical Review* 93:4 (1988), pp. 898–935.

Garrido, Gabriel (director), *De l'Altiplano à l'Amazone: Lima–La Plata, missions jesuites*, CD K617 and Association Française d'Action Artistique [no place], 1992.

Garrido Aranda, Antonio, *Moriscos e indios: precedentes hispánicos de la evangelización de México*, Universidad Nacional Autónoma de México, Mexico City, 1980.

Garza Carvajal, Federico, *Butterflies Will Burn: Prosecuting Sodomites in Early Modern Spain and Mexico*, University of Texas Press, Austin, 2003.

Gauderman, Kimberly, *Women's Lives in Colonial Quito: Gender, Law, and Economy in Spanish America*, University of Texas, Austin, 2003.

Gerbi, Antonello, *The Dispute of the New World: The History of a Polemic, 1750–1900*, University of Pittsburgh Press, Pittsburgh, 1973.

Gerhard, Peter, *A Guide to the Historical Geography of New Spain*, Cambridge University Press, Cambridge, 1972.

Gibson, Charles, *The Aztecs under Spanish Rule: A History of the Indians of the Valley of Mexico, 1519–1810*, Stanford University Press, Stanford, 1964.

Gibson, Charles, "Indian societies under Spanish rule," in *CHLA*, vol. 2, pp. 381–419.

Glave, Luis Miguel, "The 'Republic of Indians' in revolt (*c*.1680–1790)," ch. 22 in *CHNPA*, vol. 3: *South America*, part 2.

Góngora, Mario, *Studies in the Colonial History of Spanish America*, Cambridge University Press, Cambridge, 1975.

Goslinga, Cornelis, *The Dutch in the Caribbean and on the Wild Coast, 1580–1680*, University of Florida Press, Gainesville, 1971.

Gosner, Kevin. "Religion and rebellion in colonial Chiapas," in Schroeder (ed.), *Native Resistance and the Pax Colonial in New Spain*, pp. 47–66.

Graham, Richard, *Independence in Latin America: A Comparative Approach*, 2nd edn, McGraw-Hill, New York, 1994.

Graziano, Frank, "Rosa de Lima and the tropes of sanctity," *Public* 8, Public Access, Toronto, 1993, pp. 49–55.

Greenleaf, Richard E., *The Mexican Inquisition of the Sixteenth Century*, University of New Mexico Press, Albuquerque, 1969.

Griffiths, Nicholas, *The Cross and the Serpent: Religious Repression and Resurgence in Colonial Peru*, University of Oklahoma Press, Norman, 1996.

Grout, Donald J., *A Short History of Opera*, 3rd edn, Columbia University Press, New York, 1988.

Gruzinski, Serge, *The Conquest of Mexico: The Incorporation of Indian Societies into the Western World, 16th–18th Centuries*, tr. Eileen Corrigan, Polity Press, Cambridge, 1993.

Gruzinski, Serge, *The Mestizo Mind: The Intellectual Dynamics of Colonization and Globalization*, tr. Deke Dusinberre, Routledge, New York, 2002.

Gutiérrez, Ramón A., *When Jesus Came, the Corn Mothers Went Away: Marriage, Sexuality, and Power in New Mexico, 1500–1846*, Stanford University Press, Stanford, 1991.

Hakluyt, Richard, *Voyages to the New World: A Selection*, ed. David F. Hawke, Bobbs-Merrill, Indianapolis, 1972.

Hamill, Hugh M., Jr., *The Hidalgo Revolt: Prelude to Mexican Independence*, University of Florida Press, Gainesville, 1966.

Hammond Comparative World Atlas, Hammond Inc., Maplewood, NJ, 1989.

Hamnett, Brian R., "The appropriation of Mexican church wealth by the Spanish Bourbon government: the 'consolidación de vales reales,' 1805–1809," *Journal of Latin American Studies* 1:2 (Nov. 1969), pp. 85–113.

Hamnett, Brian R., *Politics and Trade in Southern Mexico, 1750–1821*, Cambridge University Press, Cambridge, 1971.

Hanke, Lewis, *The Spanish Struggle for Justice in the Conquest of America*, American Historical Association/Little, Brown, Boston, 1965 (repr. Southern Methodist University Press, Dallas, 2002).

Haring, Clarence H., *The Spanish Empire in America*, Oxford University Press, New York, 1947.

Harrison, Regina, "The theology of concupiscence: Spanish-Quechua confessional manuals in the Andes," in Cevallos-Candau et al. (eds), *Coded Encounters*, pp. 135–50.

Hassig, Ross, *Aztec Warfare: Imperial Expansion and Political Control*, University of Oklahoma Press, Norman, 1988.

Heckenberger, Michael J., et al., "Amazonia 1492: pristine forest or cultural parkland?," *Science* 301/5640 (Sept. 19, 2003), pp. 1710–14.

Helms, Mary W., "The Indians of the Caribbean and circum-Caribbean at the end of the fifteenth century," in *CHLA*, vol. 1, pp. 37–57.

Hemming, John, *The Conquest of the Incas*, Harcourt, Brace, Jovanovich, San Diego, 1973.

Hemming, John, "The Indians of Brazil in 1500," in *CHLA*, vol. 1, pp. 119–43.

Hemming, John, "The Indians and the frontier in colonial Brazil," in *CHLA*, vol. 2, pp. 501–45.

Hemming, John, *Red Gold: The Conquest of the Brazilian Indians, 1500–1760*, Harvard University Press, Cambridge, MA, 1978.

Henige, David, "Native American population at contact: standards of proof and styles of discourse in the debate," *Latin American Population History Bulletin* 22 (Fall 1992), pp. 2–23.

Henshall, Janet D., and Momsen, R. P., *A Geography of Brazilian Development*, Bell, London, 1974.

Herr, Richard, "Disentailment," in Kern and Dodge, *Historical Dictionary of Modern Spain*, pp. 168–73.

Herring, Adam, *Art and Writing in the Maya Cities, A.D. 600–800: The Poetics of Line*, Cambridge University Press, Cambridge 2005.

Hidalgo, Jorge, "The Indians of southern South America in the middle of the sixteenth century," in *CHLA*, vol. 1, pp. 37–57.

Higgins, Kathleen J., *"Licentious Liberty" in a Brazilian Gold-Mining Region: Slavery, Gender, and Social Control in Eighteenth-Century Sabará, Minas Gerais*, Pennsylvania State University Press, University Park, 1999.

Highfield, Arnold R., "Some observations on the Taino language," ch. 16 in Wilson (ed.), *The Indigenous People of the Caribbean*.

Himmerich, Robert T., *The Encomenderos of New Spain, 1521–1555*, Ph.D. dissertation, University of California, Los Angeles, 1984.

Historia General de México, comp. Daniel Cosío Villegas, 4 vols, El Colegio de México, Mexico City, 1977.

Hoberman, Louisa Schell, "Conclusion," in Hoberman and Socolow (eds), *Cities and Society in Colonial Latin America*.

Hoberman, Louisa Schell, *Mexico's Merchant Elite, 1590–1660: Silver, State, and Society*, Duke University Press, Durham, NC, 1991.

Hoberman, Louisa Schell, and Socolow, Susan M. (eds), *Cities and Society in Colonial Latin America*, University of New Mexico Press, Albuquerque, 1986.

Holler, Jacqueline, *Escogidas Plantas: Nuns and Beatas in Mexico City, 1531–1601*, Columbia University Press, New York, 2005 (2003).

Holler, Jacqueline, *I, Elena de la Cruz: Heresy, Gender, and Crisis in Mexico City, 1568*, MA thesis, Simon Fraser University, Vancouver, 1992.

Hulme, Peter, *Colonial Encounters: Europe and the Native Caribbean, 1492–1797*, Methuen, London, 1986.

Hyslop, John, *The Inka Road System*, Academic Press, New York, 1984.

Iriarte, José, "The history of manioc domestication," website of Department of Archaeology, School of Geography, Archaeology and Earth Resources, University of Exeter, Apr. 28, 2007.

Isbell, William H., "City and state in middle horizon Huari," in Keatinge (ed.), *Peruvian Prehistory*, pp. 164–89.

Israel, J. I., *Race, Class and Politics in Colonial Mexico, 1610–1670*, Oxford University Press, Oxford, 1975.

Jacobsen, Nils, and Puhle, Hans-Jürgen, *The Economies of Mexico and Peru during the Late Colonial Period, 1760–1810*, Colloquium, Berlin, 1986.

Jaffary, Nora E. (ed.), *Gender, Race, and Religion in the Colonization of the Americas*, Ashgate, Aldershot, 2007.

James, Preston E., *Latin America*, 4th edn, Bobbs-Merrill, Indianapolis, 1975.

Jaramillo, Miguel, "Migraciones y formación de mercados laborales: la fuerza de trabajo indígena de Lima a comienzos del siglo XVII," *Economía* 29–30 (June–Dec. 1992), pp. 265–320.

Johnson, H. B., "The Portuguese settlement of Brazil, 1500–1580," in *CHLA*, vol. 1, pp. 249–86.

Johnson, John J., *Simón Bolívar and Spanish American Independence, 1783–1830*, D. Van Nostrand, Princeton, NJ, 1968.

Johnson, Lyman, "Dangerous words, provocative gestures, and violent acts: the disputed hierarchies of plebeian life in colonial Buenos Aires," in Johnson and Lipsett-Rivera (eds), *The Faces of Honor*, pp. 127–51.

Johnson, Lyman, and Lipsett-Rivera, Sonya (eds), *The Faces of Honor: Sex, Shame, and Violence in Colonial Latin America*, University of New Mexico Press (Diálogos), Albuquerque, 1998.

Johnson, Lyman L., and Tandeter, Enrique, *Essays on the Price History of Eighteenth-Century Latin America*, University of New Mexico Press, Albuquerque, 1990.

Josephy, Alvin M., Jr., *America in 1492: The World of the Indian Peoples before the Arrival of Columbus*, Alfred A. Knopf, New York, 1992.

Juan y Santacilia, Jorge, and Ulloa, Antonio de, *Discourse and Political Reflections on the Kingdoms of Peru*, tr. John J. TePaske and Besse E. Clement, University of Oklahoma Press, Norman, 1978.

Kamen, Henry, *Philip V of Spain: The King who Reigned Twice*, Yale University Press, New Haven, 2001.

Kamen, Henry, *Spain, 1469–1714: A Society of Conflict*, Longman, London, 1983.

Kamen, Henry, *The Spanish Inquisition*, Meridian Books, New American Library, New York, 1965.

Katz, Friedrich, *Riot, Rebellion, and Revolution: Rural Social Conflict in Mexico*, Princeton University Press, Princeton, NJ, c.1988.

Katzew, Ilona, *Casta Painting: Images of Race in Eighteenth-Century Mexico*, Yale University Press, New Haven, 2004.

Keatinge, Richard W. (ed.), *Peruvian Prehistory: An Overview of Pre-Inca and Inca Society*, Cambridge University Press, Cambridge, 1988.

Kelemen, Pál, *Baroque and Rococo in Latin America*, 2 vols, Dover Publications, New York, 1967.

Kellogg, Susan, "From parallel and equivalent to separate and unequal: Tenochca Mexica women, 1500–1700," in Schroeder, Wood, and Haskett (eds), *Indian Women of Early Mexico*, pp. 123–44.

Kent, Robert B., *Latin America: Regions and People*, Guildford Press, New York, 2006.

Kern, Robert W., and Dodge, Meredith D., *Historical Dictionary of Modern Spain, 1700–1988*, Greenwood Press, Westport, CT, 1990.

Kicza, John E. (ed.), *The Indian in Latin American History: Resistance, Resilience, and Acculturation*, Scholarly Resources Books, Wilmington, DE, 1993.

Kinsbruner, Jay, *Independence in Spanish America: Civil Wars, Revolutions, and Underdevelopment*, University of New Mexico Press, Albuquerque, 1994.

Kirk, Stephanie, *Convent Life in Colonial Mexico: A Tale of Two Communities*, University Press of Florida, Tampa, 2007.

Klarén, Peter F., "Peruvian Aprista party," in *ELAH*, vol. 4, pp. 379–80.

Klein, Herbert S., *African Slavery in Latin America and the Caribbean*, Oxford University Press, New York, 1986.

Klein, Herbert S., *Bolivia: The Evolution of a Multi-Ethnic Society*, 2nd edn, Oxford University Press, Oxford, 1992.

Klein, Herbert S., *Haciendas and "Ayllus": Rural Society in the Bolivian Andes in the Eighteenth and Nineteenth Centuries*, Stanford University Press, Stanford, 1993.

Klein, Herbert S., and Vinson, Ben, *African Slavery in Latin America and the Caribbean*, 2nd edn, Oxford University Press, New York, 2007.

Konetzke, Richard, "La emigración de mujeres españolas a América durante la época colonial," in *Revista Internacional de Sociología*, vol. 3, Madrid, 1945, pp. 123–50 (repr. in *Lateinamerika: Gesammelte Aufsätze*, Böhlau, Cologne, 1983, pp. 1–28).

Kubler, George, "The behavior of Atahualpa, 1531–1533," *HAHR*, 25:4 (Nov. 1945), pp. 413–27.

Kubler, George, *Mexican Architecture of the Sixteenth Century*, 2 vols, Yale Historical Publications, New Haven, 1948.

Kubler, George, and Soria, Martín, *Art and Architecture in Spain and Portugal and their American Dominions, 1500–1800*, Penguin Books, Baltimore, 1969.

Ladd, Doris M., *The Mexican Nobility at Independence, 1780–1826*, Institute of Latin American Studies, University of Texas, Austin, 1976.

Lafaye, Jacques, "Literature and intellectual life in colonial Spanish America," in *CHLA*, vol. 2, pp. 663–704.

Lamb, Ursula, *Frey Nicolás de Ovando, gobernador de las Indias (1501–1509)*, Consejo Superior de Investigaciones Científicas, Madrid, 1956.

Landers, Jane G., and Robinson, Barry M. (eds), *Slaves, Subjects, and Subversives: Blacks in Colonial Latin America*, University of New Mexico Press, Albuquerque, 2006.

Lane, Kris, *Quito 1599: City and Colony in Transition*, University of New Mexico Press, Albuquerque, 2002.

Lanning, Edward P., *Peru before the Incas*, Prentice-Hall, Englewood Cliffs, NJ, 1967.

Lanyon, Anna, *The New World of Martín Cortés*, Da Capo Press, Cambridge, MA, 2003.

Larraín, José, "Gross National Product and prices: the Chilean case in the seventeenth and eighteenth centuries," ch. 5 in Johnson and Tandeter (eds), *Essays on the Price History of Eighteenth-Century Latin America*.

Larson, Brooke, *Colonialism and Agrarian Transformation in Bolivia. Cochabamba, 1550–1900*, Princeton University Press, Princeton, 1988.

Lavrin, Asunción, "Female religious," in Hoberman and Socolow (eds), *Cities and Society in Colonial Latin America*, pp. 165–95.

Lavrin, Asunción, "Lo femenino: women in colonial historical sources," in Cevallos-Candau et al. (eds), *Coded Encounters*, pp. 153–76.

Lavrin, Asunción (ed.), *Sexuality and Marriage in Colonial Latin America*, University of Nebraska Press, Lincoln, 1989.

Lavrin, Asunción, "Women in Spanish American colonial society," in *CHLA*, vol. 2, pp. 321–55.

Le Flem, Jean-Paul, et al. (eds), *La frustración de un imperio (1476–1714)*, vol. 5 of Manuel Tuñón de Lara (ed.), *Historia de España*, Editorial Labor, Barcelona, 1984.

León Portilla, Miguel (ed.), *The Broken Spears: The Aztec Account of the Conquest of Mexico*, Beacon Press, Boston, 1966.

Leonard, Irving A., *Baroque Times in Old Mexico: Seventeenth-Century Persons, Places, and Practices*, University of Michigan Press, Ann Arbor, 1959.

Levine, Robert M., and Crocitti, John J. (eds), *The Brazil Reader: History, Culture, Politics*, Duke University Press, Durham, NC, 1999.

Lewis, Laura, *Hall of Mirrors: Power, Witchcraft, and Caste in Colonial Mexico*, Duke University Press, Durham, NC, 2003.

Leyes y ordenanzas nuevamente hechas por su Magestad para la gobernación de las Indias y buen tratamiento y conservación de los indios: que se han de guardar en el Consejo y Audiencias Reales que en ellas residen: y por todos los otros gobernadores, jueces y personas particulares de ellas, ed. Antonio Muro Orejón, Escuela de Estudios Hispanoamericanos, Seville, 1961.

Liss, Peggy K., "Isabel, myth and history," ch. 3 in Boruchoff (ed.), *Isabel la Católica*.

Liss, Peggy K., *Isabel the Queen: Life and Times*, Oxford University Press, New York, 1992.

Liss, Peggy K., *Mexico under Spain, 1521–1556*, University of Chicago Press, Chicago, 1975.

Lockhart, James, *The Men of Cajamarca: A Social and Biographical Study of the First Conquerors of Peru*, Institute of Latin American Studies, University of Texas, Austin, 1972.

Lockhart, James, *The Nahuas after the Conquest: A Social and Cultural History of the Indians of Central Mexico, Sixteenth through Eighteenth Centuries*, Stanford University Press, Stanford, 1992.

Lockhart, James, *Spanish Peru, 1532–1560: A Colonial Society*, University of Wisconsin Press, Madison, 1968.

Lockhart, James, and Otte, Enrique (ed. and tr.), *Letters and People of the Spanish Indies, Sixteenth Century*, Cambridge University Press, Cambridge, 1975.

Lockhart, James, and Schwartz, Stuart B., *Early Latin America: A History of Colonial Spanish America and Brazil*, Cambridge University Press, Cambridge, 1983.

Lohmann Villena, Guillermo, *El corregidor de indios en el Perú bajo los Austrias*, Ediciones Cultura Hispánica, Madrid, 1957.

Lohmann Villena, Guillermo, and Sarabia Viejo, María Justina, *Francisco de Toledo: disposiciones gubernativas para el Virreinato del Perú*, 2 vols, Escuela de Estudios Hispanoamericanos, Seville, 1986–9.

Lombardi, John V., *Venezuela: The Search for Order, the Dream of Progress*, Oxford University Press, New York, 1982.

Lombardi, John V., and Lombardi, Cathryn L., *Latin American History: A Teaching Atlas*, University of Wisconsin Press, Madison, 1983.

López de Gómara, Francisco, *Cortés: The Life of the Conqueror by his Secretary*, tr. and ed. Lesley B. Simpson, University of California Press, Berkeley and Los Angeles, 1966.

López Lara, Ramón, "Los hospitales de la Concepción," in *Vasco de Quiroga: educador de adultos*, El Colegio de Michoacán and CREFAL, Pátzcuaro, 1984, pp. 113–28.

Lovejoy, Paul E., *Transformations in Slavery: A History of Slavery in Africa*, 2nd edn, Cambridge University Press, Cambridge, 2000.

Loveman, Brian, *Chile: The Legacy of Hispanic Capitalism*, 2nd edn, Oxford University Press, New York, 1988.

Lunenfeld, Marvin, *The Council of the Santa Hermandad: A Study of the Pacification Forces of Ferdinand and Isabella*, University of Miami Press, Coral Gables, 1970.

Lynch, John, *Bourbon Spain, 1700–1808*, Basil Blackwell, Oxford, 1989.

Lynch, John, *The Hispanic World in Crisis and Change, 1598–1700*, Basil Blackwell, Oxford, 1992.

Lynch, John, *Simón Bolívar: A Life*, Yale University Press, New Haven, 2006.

Lynch, John, *The Spanish American Revolutions, 1808–1826*, 2nd edn, W. W. Norton, New York, 1986.

McAlister, Lyle N., *Spain and Portugal in the New World, 1492–1700*, University of Minnesota Press, Minneapolis, 1984.

McCaa, Robert, "Marriageways in Mexico and Spain, 1500–1900," *Continuity and Change* 9:1 (1994), pp. 11–43.

MacCormack, Sabine, *Religion in the Andes: Vision and Imagination in Early Colonial Peru*, Princeton University Press, Princeton, 1991.

McFarlane, Anthony, *Colombia before Independence: Economy, Society, and Politics under Bourbon Rule*, Cambridge University Press, Cambridge, 1993.

McFarlane, Anthony, "The rebellion of the *Barrios*: urban insurrection in Bourbon Quito," in Fisher, Kuethe, and McFarlane (eds), *Reform and Insurrection in Bourbon New Granada and Peru*, pp. 197–254.

MacKenzie, Debora, "Columbus blamed for the spread of syphilis," NewScientist.com news service, 15 Jan. 2008.

MacLachlan, Colin M., *Spain's Empire in the New World: The Role of Ideas in Institutional and Social Change*, University of California Press, Berkeley and Los Angeles, 1988.

MacLachlan, Colin M. and Rodríguez, Jaime O., *The Forging of the Cosmic Race: A Reinterpretation of Colonial Mexico*, University of California Press, Berkeley and Los Angeles, 1980.

MacLeod, Murdo J., "Aspects of the internal economy of colonial Spanish America: labour; taxation; distribution and exchange," in *CHLA*, vol. 2, pp. 219–64.

McNeill, William H., "American food crops in the Old World," in Viola and Margolis (eds), *Seeds of Change*, pp. 43–59.

Malamud Rikles, Carlos D., *La economía colonial americana en el siglo XVIII*, in José María Jover Zamora (ed.), *La época de la ilustración: Las Indias en el siglo XVIII*, vol. 31, pt 2 of *Historia de España Menéndez Pidal*, Espasa-Calpe, Madrid, 1988.

Mangan, Jane E., *Trading Places: Gender, Ethnicity, and the Urban Economy in Colonial Potosí*, Duke University Press, Durham, NC, 2005.

Mannarelli, María Emma, *Hechiceras, beatas y expósitas: mujeres y poder inquisitorial en Lima*, Ediciones del Congreso del Perú, Lima, 1998.

Manning, Patrick, "African connections with American colonization," ch. 2 in *CEHLA*, vol. 1.

Mansuy-Diniz Silva, Andrée, "Portugal and Brazil. imperial re-organization, 1750–1808," in *CHLA*, vol. 1, pp. 469–508.

Marchena Fernández, Juan, "The social world of the military in Peru and New Granada: the colonial oligarchies in conflict, 1750–1810," in Fisher, Kuethe, and McFarlane (eds), *Reform and Insurrection in Bourbon New Granada and Peru*, pp. 54–95.

Marcílio, Maria Luiza, "The population of colonial Brazil," in *CHLA*, vol. 2, pp. 37–63.

Marett, Robert, *Peru*, Praeger, New York, 1969.

Martin, Cheryl English, *Governance and Society in Colonial Mexico: Chihuahua in the Eighteenth Century*, Stanford University Press, Stanford, 1996.

Martin, Colin, and Parker, Geoffrey, *The Spanish Armada*, Penguin Books, Harmondsworth, 1989.

Martín, Luis, *Daughters of the Conquistadores: Women of the Viceroyalty of Peru*, Southern Methodist University Press, Dallas, 1983.

Martin, Simon, "In line of the founder: a view of dynastic politics at Tikal," ch. 1 in Jeremy A. Sabloff (ed.), *Tikal: Dynasties, Foreigners, and Affairs of State*, School of American Research, Santa Fe, NM, 2003.

Marzahl, Peter, *Town in the Empire: Government, Politics, and Society in Seventeenth-Century Popayán*, Institute of Latin American Studies, University of Texas, Austin, 1978.

Mason, J. Alden, *The Ancient Civilizations of Peru*, Penguin Books, Harmondsworth, 1957.

Masur, Gerhard, *Simón Bolívar*, University of New Mexico Press, Albuquerque, 1969.

Matilla Tascón, Antonio, *Historia de las minas de Almadén*. vol. 2: *Desde 1646 a 1799*, Minas de Almadén y Arrayanes, SA/Instituto de Estudios Fiscales, Madrid, 1987.

Mauro, Frédéric, "Portugal and Brazil: political and economic structures of empire, 1580–1750," in *CHLA*, vol. 1, pp. 441–68.

Mauro, Frédéric, *Le Portugal, le Brésil et l'Atlantique au XVIIe siècle (1570–1670): Étude économique*, Fondation Calouste Gulbenkian, Centre Culturel Portugais, Paris, 1983.

Maxwell, Kenneth R., *Conflicts and Conspiracies: Brazil and Portugal, 1750–1808*, Cambridge University Press, Cambridge, 1973.

Maxwell, Kenneth R., *Pombal: Paradox of the Enlightenment*, Cambridge University Press, Cambridge, 1995.

Meltzer, David J., "Peopling of North America," *Development in Quaternary Science* 1 (2003), pp. 539–63.

Melville, Elinor G. K., *A Plague of Sheep: Environmental Consequences of the Conquest of Mexico*, Cambridge University Press, Cambridge, 1994.

Mendieta, Gerónimo de, *Historia eclesiástica indiana*, Porrúa, Mexico City, 1971.

Mesa, José de, and Gisbert, Teresa, *Bolivia: monumentos históricos y arqueológicos*, Instituto Panamericano de Geografía e Historia, Mexico City, 1970.

Metcalf, Alida C., *Go-Betweens and the Colonization of Brazil, 1500–1600*, University of Texas Press, Austin, 2005.

Mills, Kenneth R., *An Evil Lost to View? An Investigation of Post-Evangelisation Andean Religion in Mid-Colonial Peru*, monograph series no. 18, Institute of Latin American Studies, University of Liverpool, Liverpool, 1994.

Mills, Kenneth R., *Idolatry and its Enemies: Colonial Andean Religion and Extirpation 1640–1750*, Princeton University Press, Princeton, 1997.

Mintz, Sidney W., *Sweetness and Power: The Place of Sugar in Modern History*, Penguin Books, Harmondsworth, 1986.

Miranda, Francisco, "El Pátzcuaro de Don Vasco: un modelo de integración étnica y cultural," in *Vasco de Quiroga: Educador de adultos*, El Colegio de Michoacán and CREFAL, Pátzcuaro, 1984, pp. 78–96.

Monteiro, John, "The crises and transformations of invaded societies: coastal Brazil in the sixteenth century," ch. 13 in *CHNPA*, vol. 3: *South America*, part 1.

Mora Mérida, José Luis, *Historia social de Paraguay, 1600–1650*, Escuela de Estudios Hispanoamericanos, Seville, 1973.

Morales Padrón, Francisco, *Historia del descubrimiento y conquista de América*, Editora Nacional, Madrid, 1963.

Moreno Fraginals, Manuel, *El ingenio: complejo económico-social cubano del azúcar*, 3 vols, Havana, 1978.

Morilla Critz, Jos, "Crisis y transformación de la economía de Nueva España en el siglo XVII: un ensayo crítico," *Anuario de Estudios Americanos* 45 (1988), pp. 241–72.

Morineau, Michel, *Incroyables gazettes et fabuleux métaux: Les retours des trésors américains d'après les gazettes hollandaises (XVIe–XVIIIe siècles)*, Maison des Sciences de l'Homme, Paris/Cambridge University Press, Cambridge, 1985.

Morison, Samuel E., *Admiral of the Ocean Sea: A Life of Christopher Columbus*, Little, Brown, Boston, 1942.

Mörner, Magnus, *Estratificación social hispanoamericana durante el período colonial*, research paper series no. 28, Institute of Latin American Studies, Stockholm, 1980.

Mörner, Magnus, "The rural economy and society of colonial Spanish South America," in *CHLA*, vol. 2, pp. 189–217.

Morris, Craig, "Progress and prospect in the archaeology of the Inca," in Keatinge (ed.), *Peruvian Prehistory*, pp. 233–56.

Morse, Richard M. (ed.), *The Bandeirantes: The Historical Role of the Brazilian Pathfinders*, Alfred A. Knopf, New York, 1965.

Morse, Richard M., *New World Soundings: Culture and Ideology in the Americas*, Johns Hopkins University Press, Baltimore, 1989.

Morse, Richard M., "The urban development of colonial Spanish America," in *CHLA*, vol. 2, pp. 67–104.

Moseley, Michael E., *The Incas and their Ancestors: The Archaeology of Peru*, Thames & Hudson, London, 1992 (rev. edn, 2001).

Mota y Escobar, Alonso de la, *Descripción geográfica de los Reynos de Nueva Galicia, Nueva Vizcaya y Nuevo León* [1605], Instituto Jalisciense de Antropología e Historia, Guadalajara, 1966.

Moutoukias, Zacarías, "Power, corruption, and commerce: the making of the local administrative structure in seventeenth-century Buenos Aires," *HAHR* 68:4 (Nov. 1988), pp. 771–801.

Moya Pons, Frank, *History of the Caribbean: Plantations, Trade, and War in the Atlantic World*, Marcus Wiener Publications, Princeton, 2007.

Muro, Luis, "Bartolomé de Medina, introductor del beneficio de patio en Nueva España," in Trabulse (ed.), *Historia de la ciencia*, pp. 203–17.

Muro Romero, Fernando, "La administración de Indias. De la unidad imperial a la diversidad americana: el tránsito del siglo XVII," in *Unité et diversité de l'Amérique Latine*, vol. 1, Maison des Pays Ibériques, Université de Bordeaux III, 15–18 Sept. 1982, pp. 275–99.

Murra, John V., "Aymara lords and their European agents at Potosí," *Nova Americana* 1 (Turin, 1978), pp. 231–43.

Nazzari, Muriel, *Disappearance of the Dowry: Women, Families, and Social Change in São Paulo, Brazil, 1600–1900*, Stanford University Press, Stanford, 1991.

Newson, Linda A., "Demographic catastrophe in sixteenth-century Honduras," in David J. Robinson (ed.), *Studies in Spanish-American Population History*, Westview Press, Boulder, CO, 1981, pp. 217–41.

Newson, Linda A., "The demographic impact of colonization," ch. 5 in *CEHLA*, vol. 1.

Newson, Linda A., "Indian population patterns in colonial Spanish America," *Latin American Research Review* 20:3 (1985), pp. 41–74.

O'Callaghan, Joseph F., *A History of Medieval Spain*, Cornell University Press, Ithaca, NY, 1975.

Oliveira Marques, A. H. de, *History of Portugal*, 2nd edn, 2 vols. bound in 1, Columbia University Press, New York, 1976.

O'Neill, John P. (ed.), *Mexico: Splendors of Thirty Centuries*, Metropolitan Museum of Art/Little, Brown, New York and Boston, 1990.

O'Phelan Godoy, Scarlett, *Rebellions and Revolts in Eighteenth Century Peru and Upper Peru*, Böhlau, Cologne, 1985.

Ots Capdequí, J. M., *El estado espanol en las Indias*, Fondo de Cultura Económica, Mexico City, 1965.

Padden, R. C., "Cultural adaptation and militant autonomy among the Araucanians of Chile," in Kicza (ed.), *The Indian in Latin American History*, pp. 69–88 (1st pub. in *Southwestern Journal of Anthropology* 13:1 (Spring 1957), pp. 103–21).

Padden, R. C., *The Hummingbird and the Hawk: Conquest and Sovereignty in the Valley of Mexico, 1503–1541*, Harper & Rowe, New York, 1970.

Pagden, Anthony, *The Fall of Natural Man: The American Indian and the Origins of Comparative Ethnology*, Cambridge University Press, Cambridge, 1986.

Palmer, Colin A., *Slaves of the White God: Blacks in Mexico, 1570–1650*, Harvard University Press, Cambridge, MA, 1976.

Palmer, Gabrielle G., *Sculpture in the Kingdom of Quito*, University of New Mexico Press, Albuquerque, 1987.

Paquette, Gabriel P., *Enlightenment, Governance, and Reform in Spain and its Empire, 1759–1808*, Palgrave Macmillan, Basingstoke, 2008.

Parker, Geoffrey, *The Grand Strategy of Philip II*, Yale University Press, New Haven, 1998.

Parker, Geoffrey, *Philip II*, Little, Brown, Boston, 1978.

Parkes, Henry B., *A History of Mexico*, Eyre & Spottiswoode, London, 1962.

Parry, John H., *The Age of Reconnaissance*, New American Library, New York, 1964.

Parry, John H., *The Audiencia of New Galicia in the Sixteenth Century: A Study in Spanish Colonial Government*, Cambridge University Press, Cambridge, 1948.

Parry, John H., *The Discovery of the Sea*, University of California Press, Berkeley and Los Angeles, 1981.

Parry, John H., *The Sale of Public Office in the Spanish Indies under the Hapsburgs*, Ibero-Americana 37, University of California Press, Berkeley and Los Angeles, 1953.

Parry, John H., and Keith, Robert G. (eds), *New Iberian World: A Documentary History of the Discovery and Settlement of Latin America to the Early Seventeenth Century*, 5 vols, Times Books/Hector & Rose, New York, 1984.

Parry, John H., Sherlock, Philip, and Maingot, Anthony, *A Short History of the West Indies*, 4th edn, St. Martin's Press, New York, 1987.

Patch, Robert W., "Culture, community, and 'rebellion' in the Yucatec Maya uprising of 1761," in Schroeder (ed.), *Native Resistance and the Pax Colonial in New Spain*, pp. 67–83.

Patterson, Thomas C., *The Inca Empire: The Formation and Disintegration of a Pre-Capitalist State*, Berg, Oxford, 1991.

Payne, Stanley G., *A History of Spain and Portugal*, 2 vols., University of Wisconsin Press, Madison, 1973.

Payne, Stanley G., *Spanish Catholicism: An Historical Overview*, University of Wisconsin Press, Madison, 1984.

Paz, Octavio, *Sor Juana: Or, the Traps of the Faith*, Harvard University Press, Cambridge, MA, 1988.

Peña, José de la, *Oligarquía y propiedad en Nueva España, 1550–1624*, Fondo de Cultura Económica, Mexico City, 1983.

Pendergast, David M., "Up from the dust: the central lowlands postclassic as seen from Lamanai and Marco González, Belize," in Clancy and Harrison (eds), *Vision and Revision in Maya Studies*, pp. 169–77.

Pérez, Joseph, "Isabel la Católica and the Jews," ch. 8 in Boruchoff (ed.), *Isabel la Católica*.

Pérez, Joseph, "España moderna (1474–1700), aspectos políticos y sociales," in Le Flem et al. (eds), *La frustración de un imperio*, pp. 137–259

Pérez-Mallaina, Pablo E., and Torres Ramírez, Bibiano, *La Armada del Mar del Sur*, Escuela de Estudios Hispanoamericanos, Seville, 1987.

Phelan, John L., *The Kingdom of Quito in the Seventeenth Century: Bureaucratic Politics in the Spanish Empire*, University of Wisconsin Press, Madison, 1967.

Phelan, John L., *The Millennial Kingdom of the Franciscans in the New World*, 2nd edn, University of California Press, Berkeley and Los Angeles, 1970.

Phelan, John L., *The People and the King: The Comunero Revolution in Colombia, 1781*, University of Wisconsin Press, Madison, 1978.

Phillips, William D., and Phillips, Carla Rahn, *The Worlds of Christopher Columbus*, Cambridge University Press, Cambridge, 1992.

Pike, Fredrick B., *The Modern History of Peru*, Frederick A. Praeger, New York, 1967.

Pool, Christopher A., *Olmec Archaeology and Early Mesoamerica*, Cambridge University Press, Cambridge, 2007.

Powers, Karen Vieira, *Women in the Crucible of Conquest: The Gendered Genesis of Spanish American Society, 1500–1600*, University of New Mexico Press, Albuquerque, 2005.

Prado, Caio, Jr., *The Colonial Background of Modern Brazil*, tr. Suzette Macedo, University of California Press, Berkeley and Los Angeles, 1969.

Premo, Bianca, *Children of the Father King: Youth, Authority, and Legal Minority in Colonial Lima*, University of North Carolina Press, Chapel Hill, 2005.

Prescott, William H., *The Conquest of Mexico*, 2 vols, Dent, London, 1962.

Puiggrós, Rodolfo, *Historia económica del Río de la Plata*, Ediciones Siglo Veinte, Buenos Aires, 1948.

Radding, Cynthia, *Wandering Peoples: Colonialism, Ethnic Spaces, and Ecological Frontiers in Northwestern Mexico, 1700–1850*, Duke University Press, Durham, NC, 1997.

Ramírez, Susan E., *"El Dueño de Indios*: thoughts on the consequences of the shifting bases of power of the *Curaca de los viejos antiguos* under the Spanish in sixteenth-century Peru," *HAHR* 67:4 (Nov. 1987), pp. 575–610.

Ramírez, Susan E., "Historia y memoria: la construcción de las tradiciones dinásticas andinas," *Revista de Indias* 236 (2006), pp. 13–56.

Ramírez, Susan E., *Provincial Patriarchs: Land Tenure and the Economics of Power in Colonial Peru*, University of New Mexico Press, Albuquerque, 1986.

Ramírez, Susan E., *To Feed and Be Fed: The Cosmological Bases of Authority and Identity in the Andes*, Stanford University Press, Stanford, 2005.

Rausch, Jane M., *A Tropical Plains Frontier: The Llanos of Colombia, 1531–1831*, University of New Mexico Press, Albuquerque, 1984.

Recopilación de Leyes de los Reinos de las Indias, mandadas imprimir, y publicar, por la Magestad Católica del Rey Don Carlos II, 4 vols, Madrid, 1681 (facsimile edn, Ediciones Cultura Hispánica, Madrid, 1973).

Restall, Matthew (ed.), *Beyond Black and Red: African–Native Relations in Colonial Latin America*, University of New Mexico Press, Albuquerque, 2005.

Ricard, Robert, *The Spiritual Conquest of Mexico: An Essay on the Apostolate and the Evangelizing Methods of the Mendicant Orders in New Spain, 1523–1572* (Paris, 1933), tr. Lesley B. Simpson, University of California Press, Berkeley and Los Angeles, 1966.

Rich, E. E., "The European nations and the Atlantic," in J. P. Cooper (ed.), *The New Cambridge Modern History*, vol. 4: *The Decline of Spain and the Thirty Years War, 1609–48/59*, Cambridge University Press, Cambridge, 1970, pp. 672–706.

Riley, G. Micheal, *Fernando Cortés and the Marquesado in Morelos, 1522–1547: A Case Study in the Socioeconomic Development of Sixteenth-Century Mexico*, University of New Mexico Press, Albuquerque, 1973.

Robertson, William S., *Rise of the Spanish-American Republics as Told in the Lives of their Liberators*, Collier Books, New York, 1961.

Robinson, David J. (ed.), *Migration in Colonial Spanish America*, Cambridge University Press, Cambridge, 1990.

Rock, David, *Argentina, 1516–1987: From Spanish Colonization to Alfonsín*, University of California Press, Berkeley and Los Angeles, 1987.

Rodrigues, José Honório, *Brasil: Período colonial*, Instituto Panamericano de Geografía e Historia, Comisión de Historia, Mexico City, 1953.

Rodríguez, Linda A. (ed.), *Rank and Privilege: The Military and Society in Latin America*, Scholarly Resources Books, Wilmington, DE, 1994.

Rojas, José Luis de, *México Tenochtitlan: economía y sociedad en el siglo XVI*, El Colegio de Michoacán/Fondo de Cultura Económica, Zamora and Mexico City, 1986.

Rojas, Ricardo, *El santo de la espada: vida de San Martín*, Editorial Losada, Buenos Aires, 1940.

Romano, Ruggiero, *Coyunturas opuestas: La crisis del siglo XVII en Europa e Hispanoamérica*, El Colegio de México/Fondo de Cultura Económica, Mexico City, 1993.

Romero, Emilio, *Historia económica del Perú*, 2nd edn, vol. 1, Editorial Universo, Lima [no date].

Roosevelt, Anna C., "The maritime, highland, forest dynamic and the origins of complex culture," ch. 4 in *CHNPA*, vol. 3: *South America*, part 1.

Rostworowski de Diez Canseco, María, *Historia del Tahuantinsuyu*, Instituto de Estudios Peruanos, Lima, 1988.

Rostworowski de Diez Conseco, María, *History of the Inca Realm*, tr. Harry B. Iceland, Cambridge University Press, Cambridge, 1999.

Rouse, Irving, *The Tainos: Rise and Decline of the People who Greeted Columbus*, Yale University Press, New Haven, 1992.

Ruiz Medrano, Ethelia, *Gobierno y sociedad en Nueva España: Segunda Audiencia y Antonio de Mendoza*, El Colegio de Michoacán, Zamora, 1991.

Ruiz Rivera, Julián, "Remesas de caudales del Nuevo Reino de Granada en el XVII," *Anuario de Estudios Americanos* 34 (1977), pp. 241–71.

Russell-Wood, A. J. R., "Colonial Brazil: the gold cycle, c.1690–1750," in *CHLA*, vol. 2, pp. 547–600.

Russell-Wood, A. J. R., *Fidalgos and Philanthropists: The Santa Casa da Misericórdia of Bahia, 1550–1755*, Macmillan, London, 1968.

Russell-Wood, A. J. R. (ed.), *From Colony to Nation: Essays on the Independence of Brazil*, Johns Hopkins University Press, Baltimore, 1975.

Russell-Wood, A. J. R., *The Portuguese Empire: A World on the Move*, Johns Hopkins University Press, Baltimore, 1998.

Rydjord, John, *Foreign Interest in the Independence of New Spain: An Introduction to the War fro Independence*, Octagon Books, New York, 1972 (1st pub. Duke University Press, Durham, NC, 1935).

Saeger, James S., "Warfare, reorganization, and readaptation at the margins of Spanish rule: the Chaco and Paraguay (1573–1882)," ch. 18 in *CHNPA*, vol. 3: *South America*, part 2.

Safford, Frank, "Politics, ideology and society in post-independence Spanish America," in *CHLA*, vol. 3, pp. 347–421.

Sahagún, Bernardino de, *The Florentine Codex: General History of the Things of New Spain*, 12 books in 13 vols, tr. Arthur J. O. Anderson and Charles Dibble, School of American Research, Santa Fe, NM, 1950–82.

Saignes, Thierry, "The colonial condition in the Quechua-Ayamara heartland (1570–1780)," ch. 15 in *CHNPA*, vol. 3: *South America*, part 2.

Saignes, Thierry, and Bouysse-Cassagne, Thérèse, "Dos confundidas identidades: mestizos y criollos del siglo XVII," in Tomoeda and Millones (eds), *500 años de mestizaje en los Andes*, pp. 14–26.

Salomon, Frank. and Schwartz, Stuart B. (eds), *The Cambridge History of the Native Peoples of the Americas*, vol. 3, parts 1 and 2: *South America*, Cambridge University Press, Cambridge, 1999.

Salvucci, Richard J., *Textiles and Capitalism in Mexico: An Economic History of the Obrajes, 1539–1840*, Princeton University Press, Princeton, 1987.

Sánchez-Albornoz, Nicolás, *La población de América Latina: desde los tiempos pre-colombinos hasta el año 2000*, Alianza Editorial, Madrid, 1973 (2nd edn, Madrid, 1994).

Sánchez-Albornoz, Nicolás, "The population of Colonial Spanish America," in *CHLA*, vol. 2, pp. 3–35.

Sánchez Bella, Ismael, *La organización financiera de las Indias: siglo XVI*, Escuela de Estudios Hispanoamericanos, Seville, 1968.

Sanderlin, George (tr. and ed.), *Bartolomé de las Casas: A Selection of his Writings*, Alfred A. Knopf, New York, 1971.

Sauer, Carl O., *The Early Spanish Main*, University of California Press, Berkeley and Los Angeles, 1966.

Sauer, Carl O., *Sixteenth Century North America: The Land and the People as seen by the Europeans*, University of California Press, Berkeley and Los Angeles, 1971.

Schäfer, Ernst, *El Consejo Real y Supremo de las Indias: su historia, organización y labor administrativa hasta la terminación de la Casa de Austria*, 2 vols, Escuela de Estudios Hispanoamericanos, Seville, 1935–47.

Schele, Linda, and Freidel, David, *A Forest of Kings: The Untold Story of the Ancient Maya*, William Morrow, New York, 1990.

Schreiber, Katharina J., *Wari Imperialism in Middle Horizon Peru*, Museum of Anthropology, University of Michigan, Ann Arbor, 1992.

Schroeder, Susan (ed.), *Native Resistance and the Pax Colonial in New Spain*, University of Nebraska Press, Lincoln, 1998.

Schroeder, Susan, Wood, Stephanie, and Haskett, Robert (eds), *Indian Women of Early Mexico*, University of Oklahoma Press, Norman, 1997.

Schwaller, John F., *The Church and Clergy in Sixteenth-Century Mexico*, University of New Mexico Press, Albuquerque, 1987.

Schwartz, Stuart B., "Colonial Brazil, *c.*1580–*c.*1750: plantations and peripheries," in *CHLA*, vol. 2, pp. 423–99.

Schwartz, Stuart B., "The Mocambo: slave resistance in Colonial Bahia," in Richard Price (ed.), *Maroon Societies: Rebel Slave Communities in the Americas*, Anchor Press, Garden City, NY, 1973.

Schwartz, Stuart B., "Rethinking Palmares: slave resistance in colonial Brazil," ch. 4 in Schwartz, *Slaves, Peasants, and Rebels*.

Schwartz, Stuart B., *Slaves, Peasants, and Rebels: Reconsidering Brazilian Slavery*, University of Illinois Press, Urbana and Chicago, 1992.

Schwartz, Stuart B., *Sovereignty and Society in Colonial Brazil: The High Court of Bahia and its Judges, 1609–1751*, University of California Press, Berkeley and Los Angeles, 1973.

Schwartz, Stuart B., *Sugar Plantations in the Formation of Brazilian Society: Bahia, 1550–1835*, Cambridge University Press, Cambridge, 1985.

Schwartz, Stuart B., and Salomon, Frank, "South American indigenous societies (colonial era)," ch. 21 in *CHNPA*, vol. 3: *South America*, part 2.

Scobie, James R., *Argentina: A City and a Nation*, Oxford University Press, New York, 1964.

Scobie, James R, "The growth of Latin American cities," in *CHLA*, vol. 4, pp. 233–65.

Seed, Patricia, *To Love, Honor and Obey in Colonial Mexico: Conflicts over Marriage Choice, 1574–1821*, Stanford University Press, Stanford, 1988.

Semo, Enrique, *Historia del capitalismo en México*, Lecturas Mexicanas, Secretaría de Educación Pública, Mexico City, 1987; tr. Lidia Lozano as *The History of Capitalism in Mexico: Its Origins, 1521–1763*, University of Texas Press, Austin, 1993.

Sempat Assadourian, Carlos, *El sistema de la economía colonial: mercado interno, regiones, y espacio económico*, Instituto de Estudios Peruanos, Lima, 1982.

Shumway, Jeffrey M., *The Case of the Ugly Suitor and Other Histories of Love, Gender, and Nation in Buenos Aires, 1776–1870*, University of Nebraska Press, Lincoln, 2005.

Sigal, Pete (ed.), *Infamous Desire: Male Homosexuality in Colonial Latin America*, University of Chicago Press, Chicago, 2003.

Silverblatt, Irene, *Moon, Sun, and Witches: Gender Ideologies and Class in Inca and Colonial Peru*, Princeton University Press, Princeton, 1987.

Simmons, Marc, *Albuquerque: A Narrative History*, University of New Mexico Press, Albuquerque, 1984.

Simonsen, Roberto S., *Historia economica do Brasil, 1500–1820*, Companhia Editora Nacional, São Paulo, 1937.

Simpson, Lesley B., *The Encomienda in New Spain: The Beginning of Spanish Mexico*, University of California Press, Berkeley and Los Angeles, 1966.

Simpson, Lesley B., *Exploitation of Land in Central Mexico in the Sixteenth Century*, Ibero-Americana 13, University of California Press, Berkeley and Los Angeles, 1952.

Skidmore, Thomas E., *Brazil: Five Centuries of Change*, Oxford University Press, New York, 1999.

Smith, Clifford T., "The Central Andes," in Blakemore and Smith (eds), *Latin America: Geographical Perspectives*, pp. 253–324

Smith, Michael E., *The Aztecs*, Basil Blackwell, Oxford, 1996.

Socolow, Susan M., "Acceptable partners: marriage choice in colonial Argentina, 1778–1810," in Lavrin (ed.), *Sexuality and Marriage*, pp. 209–51.

Socolow, Susan M., *The Merchants of Buenos Aires, 1778–1810: Family and Commerce*, Cambridge University Press, Cambridge, 1978.

Socolow, Susan M., *The Women of Colonial Latin America*, Cambridge University Press, Cambridge, 2000.

Souza, Laura de Mello e, *The Devil and the Land of the Holy Cross: Witchcraft, Slavery, and Popular Religion in Colonial Brazil*, University of Texas Press, Austin, 2003.

Spalding, Karen, *Huarochirí: An Andean Society under Inca and Spanish Rule*, Stanford University Press, Stanford, 1984.

Spate, O. H. K., *The Spanish Lake*, vol. 1 of *The Pacific since Magellan*, University of Minnesota Press, Minneapolis, 1979.

Spores, Ronald, "Mixteca *cacicas*: status, wealth, and the political accommodation of native elite women in early colonial Oaxaca," in Schroeder, Wood, and Haskett (eds), *Indian Women of Early Mexico*, pp. 185–97.

Stein, Stanley J., and Stein, Barbara H., *The Colonial Heritage of Latin America: Essays on Economic Dependence in Perspective*, Oxford University Press, Oxford, 1970.

Stein, Stanley J., and Stein, Barbara H., *Silver, Trade, and War: Spain and America in the Making of Early Modern Europe*, Johns Hopkins University Press, Baltimore, 2000.

Stern, Steve J., "The age of Andean insurrection, 1742–1782: a reappraisal," in Stern (ed.), *Resistance, Rebellion, and Consciousness*, pp. 34–93.

Stern, Steve J., *Peru's Indian Peoples and the Challenge of Spanish Conquest: Huamanga to 1640*, University of Wisconsin Press, Madison, 1982.

Stern, Steve J. (ed.), *Resistance, Rebellion, and Consciousness in the Andean Peasant World, 18th to 20th Centuries*, University of Wisconsin Press, Madison, 1987.

Stern, Steve, *The Secret History of Gender: Women, Men, and Power in Late Colonial Mexico*, University of North Carolina Press, Chapel Hill, 1995.

Stevenson, Robert, "The music of colonial Spanish America," in *CHLA*, vol. 2, pp. 771–98.

Stevenson, Robert, "A note on the music of colonial Brazil," in *CHLA*, vol. 2, pp. 799–803.

Stone-Miller, Rebecca, *Art of the Andes from Chavín to Inca*, Thames & Hudson, London, 1995.

Super, John C., "The agricultural near north: Querétaro in the seventeenth century," ch. 9 in Altman and Lockhart (eds), *Provinces of Early Mexico*.

Super, John C., *La vida en Querétaro durante la colonia, 1531–1810*, Fondo de Cultura Económica, Mexico City, 1983.

Swann, Michael M., "Migration, mobility, and the mining towns of colonial northern Mexico," ch. 8 in Robinson (ed.), *Migration in Colonial Spanish America*.

Tandeter, Enrique, *Coercion and Market: Silver Mining in Colonial Potosí, 1692–1826*, University of New Mexico Press, Albuquerque, 1993.

Tandeter, Enrique, "Población y economía en los Andes (siglo XVIII)," *Revista Andina* (Cuzco) 13:1 (July 1995), pp. 7–42.

Taylor, William B., *Drinking, Homicide, and Rebellion in Colonial Mexican Villages*, Stanford University Press, Stanford, 1979.

Taylor, William B., *Landlord and Peasant in Colonial Oaxaca*, Stanford University Press, Stanford, 1972.

Taylor, William B., *Magistrates of the Sacred: Priests and Parishioners in Eighteenth-Century Mexico*, Stanford University Press, Stanford, 1996.

Taylor, William B., "The Virgin of Guadalupe in New Spain: an inquiry into the social history of Marian devotion," *American Ethnologist* 14 (Feb. 1987), pp. 9–33.

Tenenbaum, Barbara A. (ed.), *Encyclopedia of Latin American History and Culture*, 5 vols, Simon & Schuster Macmillan, New York, 1995.

TePaske, John J., "General tendencies and secular trends in the economies of Mexico and Peru, 1750–1810: the view from the *cajas* of Mexico and Lima," in Jacobsen and Puhle (eds), *The Economies of Mexico and Peru*, pp. 316–39.

TePaske, John J., "The search for El Dorado: gold production in New Granada, New Spain, and Peru, 1521–1810," unpublished paper.

TePaske, John J., Hernández Palomo, José, and Hernández Palomo, Mariluz, *La Real Hacienda de Nueva España: La Real Caja de México (1576–1816)*, Instituto Nacional de Antropología e Historia, Mexico City, 1976.

TePaske, John J., and Klein, Herbert S., "The seventeenth-century crisis in New Spain: myth or reality?," *Past and Present* 90 (Feb. 1981), pp. 116–35.

Thomas, Hugh, *Conquest: Montezuma, Cortés, and the Fall of Old Mexico*, Simon & Schuster, New York, 1995.

Thomas, Hugh, "Cuba from the middle of the eighteenth century to *c*.1870," in *CHLA*, vol. 3, pp. 277–96.

Thompson, J. Eric. S., *The Rise and Fall of Maya Civilization*, 2nd edn, University of Oklahoma Press, Norman, 1966.

Thornton, John, *Africa and Africans in the Making of the Atlantic World, 1400–1800*, Cambridge University Press, Cambridge, 1998.

Timmons, Wilbert H., *Morelos: Priest, Soldier, Statesman of Mexico*, Texas Western College Press, El Paso, 1963.

Todorov, Tzvetan, *The Conquest of America: The Question of the Other*, Harper & Row, New York, 1985.

Tomoeda, Hiroyasu, and Millones, Luis (eds), *500 años de mestizaje en los Andes*, Senri Ethnological Studies no. 33, National Museum of Ethnology, Osaka, 1992.

Trabulse, Elías (ed.), *Historia de la ciencia y la tecnología*, El Colegio de México, Mexico City, 1991.

Trabulse, Elías, "Un científico mexicano del siglo XVII: Fray Diego Rodríguez y su obra," in Trabulse (ed.), *Historia de la ciencia*, pp. 146–79.

Trend, J. B., *Bolívar and the Independence of Spanish America*, Bolivarian Society of Venezuela/Macmillan, New York, 1951.

Trexler, Richard, *Sex and Conquest: Gendered Violence, Political Order, and the European Conquest of the Americas*, Cornell University Press, Ithaca, NY, 1999.

Tutino, John, *From Insurrection to Revolution in Mexico: Social Bases of Agrarian Violence, 1750–1940*, Princeton University Press, Princeton, 1986.

Twinam, Ann, "Honor, sexuality, and illegitimacy in colonial Spanish America," in Lavrin (ed.), *Sexuality and Marriage*, pp. 118–55.

Twinam, Ann, "The negotiation of honor: elites, sexuality, and illegitimacy in eighteenth-century Spanish America," in Johnson and Lipsett-Rivera (eds), *Faces of Honor*, pp. 68–102.

Tyler, S. Lyman, *Two Worlds: The Indian Encounter with the European, 1492–1509*, University of Utah Press, Salt Lake City, 1988.

Tyrer, Robson B., *Historia demográfica y económica de la Audiencia de Quito: población indígena e industria textil, 1600–1800*, Banco Central de Ecuador, Quito, 1988.

Vaillant, George C., *The Aztecs of Mexico*, Penguin Books, Harmondsworth, 1961.

Van Bath, B. H. Slicher, *Real hacienda y economía en Hispanoamérica, 1541–1820*, Centrum voor Studie en Documentatie van Latijns Amerika, Amsterdam, 1989.

Van Deusen, Nancy, *Between the Sacred and the Worldly: The Institutional and Cultural Practice of "Recogimiento" in Colonial Lima*, Stanford University Press, Stanford, 2001.

Van Young, Eric, *The Other Rebellion: Popular Violence, Ideology, and the Mexican Struggle for Independence, 1810–1821*, Stanford, Stanford University Press, 2001.

Vargas, José María, *Historia del Ecuador: Siglo XVI*, Universidad Católica, Quito, 1977.

Vargas, José María, and Crespo Toral, Hernán, *Arte de Ecuador (siglos XVIII–XIX)*, Salvat Editores Ecuatoriana SA, Quito, 1977.

Vázquez, Josefina Z., "Los primeros tropiezos," in *Historia General de México*, vol. 3, pp. 1–84.

Vega Carpio, Félix Lope de, *Arauco domado*, Editorial Zig-Zag, Santiago de Chile, 1954.

Verlinden, Charles, *The Beginnings of Modern Colonization. Eleven Essays with an Introduction* Cornell University Press, Ithaca, NY, 1970.

Vigneras, Louis-André, *The Discovery of South America and the Andalusian Voyages*, Newberry Library/University of Chicago Press, Chicago, 1976.

Vila Vilar, Enriqueta, "Las ferias de Portobelo: apariencia y realidad del comercio con Indias," *Anuario de Estudios Hispanoamericanos* 39 (1982), pp. 275–340.

Villa-Flores, Javier, *Dangerous Speech: A Social History of Blasphemy in Colonial Mexico*, University of Arizona Press, Tucson, 2006.

Villamarín, Juan A., and Villamarín, Judith E., *Indian Labor in Mainland Colonial Spanish America*, Latin American Studies Program, University of Delaware, Newark, 1975.

Villoro, Luis, "La revolución de independencia," in *Historia General de México*, vol. 2, pp. 303–56.

Viola, Herman J., and Margolis, Carolyn (eds), *Seeds of Change: A Quincentennial Commemoration*, Smithsonian Institution Press, Washington, DC, 1992.

Viqueira, Carmen, and José Ignacio Urquiola, *Los obrajes en la Nueva España: 1530–1630*, Consejo Nacional para la Cultura y las Artes, Mexico City, 1990.

Viqueira Albán, Juan Pedro, *Propriety and Permissiveness in Bourbon Mexico*, tr. Sonya Lipsett-Rivera and Sergio Rivera Ayala, Scholarly Resources Books, Wilmington, DE, 1999.

Vogt, John, *Portuguese Rule on the Gold Coast, 1469–1682*, University of Georgia Press, Athens, GA, 1979.

Wagner, Henry Raup, *The Life and Writings of Bartolomé de las Casas*, University of New Mexico Press, Albuquerque, 1967.

Walker, Geoffrey J., *Spanish Politics and Imperial Trade, 1700–1789*, Indiana University Press, Bloomington, 1979.

Ward, Peter M., "Cities and urbanization," in *ELAH*, vol. 2, pp. 164–9.

Watts, David, *The West Indies: Patterns of Development, Culture and Environmental Change since 1492*, Cambridge University Press, Cambridge, 1987.

Weber, David J., *Bárbaros: The Spaniards and their Savages in the Age of Enlightenment*, Yale University Press, New Haven, 2005.

West, Robert C., and Augelli, John P., *Middle America: Its Lands and Peoples*, Prentice-Hall, Englewood Cliffs, NJ, 1966.

Whitaker, Arthur P., *The United States and the Independence of Latin America, 1800–1830*, W. W. Norton, New York, 1964.

Whitmore, Thomas M., *Disease and Death in Early Colonial Mexico: Simulating Amerindian Depopulation*, Westview Press, Boulder, CO, 1992.

Wiarda, Howard J., *The Soul of Latin America: The Cultural and Political Tradition*, Yale University Press, New Haven, 2001.

Wightman, Ann M., *Indigenous Migration and Social Change: The Forasteros of Cuzco, 1520–1720*, Duke University Press, Durham, NC, 1990.

Wilford, John Noble, "Norsemen in America flourished, then faded," *New York Times*, "Science Times," July 7, 1992.

Wilkerson, Jeffrey K., "The ethnographic works of Andrés de Olmos, precursor and contemporary of Sahagún," ch. 3 in Edmonson (ed.), *Sixteenth-Century Mexico*.

Wilson, Samuel M., *Hispaniola: Caribbean Chiefdoms in the Age of Columbus*, University of Alabama Press, Tuscaloosa, 1990.

Wilson, Samuel M. (ed.), *The Indigenous People of the Caribbean*, University Press of Florida, Gainesville, 1997.

Wolff, Inge, "Negersklaverei und Negerhandel in Hochperu, 1545–1650," *Jahrbuch für Geschichte von Staat, Wirtschaft und Gesellschaft Lateinamerikas* 1 (1964), pp. 157–86.

Wortman, Miles L., *Government and Society in Central America, 1680–1840*, Columbia University Press, New York, 1982.

Wright, Robin M., Carneiro da Cunha, Manuela, and Núcleo de História Indígena e do Indigenismo, "Destruction, resistance, and transformation: southern, coastal, and northern Brazil (1580–1890)," ch. 19 in *CHNPA*, vol. 3: *South America*, part 2.

Zambardino, Rudolph A., "Mexico's population in the sixteenth century: demographic anomaly or mathematical illusion?," *Journal of Interdisciplinary History* 11:1 (Summer 1980), pp. 1–27.

Zamora, Margarita, *Reading Columbus*, University of California Press, Berkeley and Los Angeles, 1993.

Zavala, Silvio, *La encomienda indiana*, 2nd edn, Editorial Porrúa, Mexico City, 1973.

Zavala, Silvio, "Ideario de Vasco de Quiroga," in *Recuerdo de Vasco de Quiroga*, Editorial Porrúa, Mexico City, 1965, pp. 45–74.

Zavala, Silvio, "La 'Utopía' de Tomás Moro en la Nueva España," in *Recuerdo de Vasco de Quiroga*, Editorial Porrúa, Mexico City, 1965, pp. 11–40.

Zavala, Silvio, "Sir Thomas More in New Spain: a utopian adventure of the Renaissance," in *Recuerdo de Vasco de Quiroga*, Editorial Porrúa, Mexico City, 1965, pp. 101–16.

Zepeda, Tomás, *La República Mexicana: geografía y atlas*, Editorial Progreso, Mexico City, 1962.

Zimmerman, Arthur F., *Francisco de Toledo, Fifth Viceroy of Peru, 1569–1581*, Caxton Printers, Caldwell, ID, 1938 (repr. Greenwood Press, New York, 1968).

Zulawski, Ann, "Social differentiation, gender, and ethnicity: urban Indian women in colonial Bolivia, 1640–1725," *Latin American Research Review* 25:2 (1990), pp. 93–113.

INDEX

Abascal, José Fernando de, 484
academies: 18th-century Brazil, 455
Acapulco, 253, 486
adelantado, 113
administration (colonial Brazil), 404–6,
 415–19, 436–40, 447–8, 451–5
administration (colonial Spanish America),
 166–70; Bourbon reforms, 364–9;
 character, 168–70, 498–9; by Colombus,
 100; crisis of 1808, 470; of early Caribbean,
 113–19; as negotiation, 296; *see also*
 audiencias; bureaucracy; Council of the
 Indies; viceroys
Africa, 75–80; Castilian interest in, 81–2; early
 Christianizing, 77; early explorations of,
 68–9; Islam in, 78; Portuguese incursions
 into, 72–3, 78, 404, 420; religions, 77;
 slave-taking, 75–80; sub-Saharan savanna,
 75–6; wars in, 79
Africans (in Brazil), 413–15, 423, 431–3, 442,
 444–5, 453; skills from Africa, 76–7
Africans (in Spanish America), 213–18;
 cultural transfers to America, 324–8; freeing
 of, 218–19; musical influence, 344–5;
 numbers, 213, 322–4; resistance by,
 217–18; skills from Africa, 76–7; social
 perceptions of, 215–16; *see also* slaves and
 slaving
agriculture: in Amazonia, 65: area suited to,
 20; colonial Spanish, 238–44, 303–5,
 357–60; in early Spanish Hispaniola, 115;
 export-oriented, 358–60; origins in Latin
 America, 27–8; productivity of labor in,
 303–4, 357–8; techniques and tools, 243–4;
 at Tiwanaku, 36; *see also*
 specific crops
Alcáçovas, Treaty of, 82, 90

alcalde mayor, 163, 293; and *reparto de*
 comercio, 382
alcalde ordinario, 293
aldeias, 408–9, 414, 425, 434–5
Aleijadinho, O (António Francisco Lisboa),
 457–8
Alexander VI (Pope), 172
Almadén, 232, 298, 354
Almagro, Diego de, 150
altiplano: Bolivian, 7; Mexican, 5, 67, 131,
 195, 227, 240, 303–4
Alvarado, Pedro de, 129–30
Alvares, Diogo, 403
Alvares Cabral, Pedro, 103, 410
Alvares da Penha Deusdará, Simão, 437, 439
amalgamation, 228–30, 255
Amazon (Amazonia): basin, 9; Portuguese
 exploration and settlement, 424–5, 436;
 pre-colonial populations, 64–5;
 slaving in, 434
Amiens, Peace of, 469
Andes: microclimates, 16; structure, 7–8
Angostura, Congress of, 479
Apatzingán, Constitution of, 486
Aquinas, St Thomas, 203
Araucanian Indians, *see* Mapuche
Arawak-speaking Indians, 64–6
Archaic period (of early Indian cultures),
 27–30
architecture, 343, 394; Indian and *mestizo*
 influence on, 345; pre-Conquest, chapter 2
 passim; *see also* Baroque
Areche, José Antonio de, 383
Arequipa, 304
Aristotle, 185–6, 191, 203
Armada (1588), 286
Army of the Three Guarantees, 488

asiento de negros, 349, 361
Asunción (Paraguay), 321
Atacama desert, 18
Atahualpa, 61, 132, 136
Atlantic: exploration of, 68–71, 80–2; islands settled, 73–5
audiencias: creation of, in America, 154–7; creoles in, 294–6, 366; functions and purposes, 154–5, 167, 418; in Hispaniola, 119; in Mexico, 149, 471–2; as origins of modern nations, 158; in Peru, 151–2, 384; sale of office in, 294; in Spain, 84
Augustinians (in mainland Spanish America), 174
Austria (Rococo influence in Brazil), 457
authoritarianism (post-Independence), 498
Ayacucho (battle), 273, 479, 481
ayllu, 55
Azores: discovered, 73; settled, 74
Aztecs: "Calendar" Stone, 392; conquest of, 127–31; creole views of, 346, 392–3; political weaknesses, 129, 135–7; pre-conquest culture, 48–54

Bahamas, 124
Bahia, 405–6, 408, 411, 415, 430, 440, 449–50; academies, 455; Dutch attacks, 421; *relação*, 417–18, 437–8; shipbuilding, 441; Tailors' Plot, 491; tobacco, 449
Bajío, 241, 249
Balboa, *see* Núñez de Balboa
ball game (pre-colonial), 34, 66
bandeirantes, 321, 425–7
Barbados, 423
Baroque, 271, 338, 343–4, 393–4, 456–7
Basle, Peace of, 468
Basques, 223
beatas (and *beaterios*), 177, 263; Indian, 209
Belém, 424, 450
Belize, 289
Benavente, Toribio de, 193
bishoprics (in Spanish America), 173, 180–1
Black Legend, 198–9
blacks, *see* Africans
Bobadilla, Francisco de, 102, 114
Bogotá (Santa Fe de), 62, 134, 317; *audiencia*, 156
Bolívar, Simón, 273, 477–80; centralist, 480, 485
Bolivia: conquest of, 133; independence, 273, 471, 476–7; landforms, 7; revolts (18th century), 380–4
bonds (governmental), 372
Bourbons: and church, 369–73; and militarism, 373–4; reformism in Spanish America, 357, 362, 364–9, 395–6;

regulation of marriage and society, 377–8; in Spain, 350–1; and titles (noble), 377
Boves, José Tomás, 478
Brazil: academies, 455; architecture, 456–7; cacao, 450; captaincies, 405–6, 447; cattle, 429–30, 441; climate, 10; coffee, 450; colonial, compared to Spanish America, 444, 455, 458; colonial government, 403–6, 415–19, 436–40, 446–8, 451–5; colonials in government, 436–9; cotton, 449; diamonds, 428; under Dutch rule, 419–24; dyewood, 402, 441; education, 454, 490–1; families, 438; flora and fauna, 422; gold, 428, 444–7, 450, 456–7; hides, 441; independence, 490–4; inward expansion, 424–8, 444–5, 450; landforms, 9, 10; monarchy and empire, 492, 497; national awareness and cohesion, 423, 455–6; native peoples, 63–5, 403, 406–10, 413–15, 433–6, 445–6, 453; Pombal's reforms, 451–5; population, 406, 409, 415, 430, 443, 450, 492; Portuguese discovery, 103, 401; Portuguese settlement, 403–6; rice, 450; shipbuilding, 441–2; slaves and slavery (African), 77, 413–15, 430–3; slaves and slavery (Indian), 406–7, 409–10, 433–6; society, 430–3; spices, 441; sugar, 410–11, 410–14, 421, 440–1, 449, 490; tobacco, 419, 434, 441, 449; town councils, 437, 490; trade, 441–4, 446–7, 452, 455
Britain, *see* England
Brito e Figueiredo, Caetano de, 455–6
Buenos Aires: Africans imported, 232; contraband, 290, 302, 442; junta of 1810, 472; leather exports, 358; population, 375; trade, 442
bullion, *see* gold; mining; silver
bureaucracy, 468; in colonial Brazil, 416–17, 439; in early Spanish Caribbean, 102, 113; jurisdictional conflict, 166–7; origins in Spain, 85; post-conquest, 145, 153–70; professionalization, 168–9, 366–7; *see also* administration; *audiencias*; viceroys

cabildo, 164–5, 221; creoles in, 293; 499
cabildo abierto, 472–3
cacao, 28, 304, 318, 359, 343, 449
caciques, 66, 206–7, 208, 242
Cadiz: Constitution of 1812, 470, 487, 493; Cortes, 470
Cajamarca, 132
Calleja, Félix María, 474, 486
câmaras, 437, 490
Campillo y Cossío, José del, 357, 362
Canary Islands: Castilians in, 81; explored, 69–70; slaving in, 73
Cão, Diogo, 90
Cape Verde islands, 74–5

capital, *see* investment
Capitulations of Santa Fe, 99, 102
Carabobo (battle), 479, 480
Caracas: foundation, 134; Company, 359;
  declaration of 1810, 472
Caramurú, *see* Alvares, Diogo
caravel, 69
Carib Indians, 65, 86
Caribbean: churchmen, 119–20, 171–2;
  foreign interlopers, 287–91; landforms, 7;
  native population, 65–6; 124–5; Spanish
  exploration, 101–4; Spanish farming, 239;
  Spanish settlement, 109–12, 124–5; *see also*
  individual islands and countries
Carrera de Indias, 250–1, 302–3, 306, 361–2
carting, 244
Casa de Contratación, 116, 251, 361
castas, 212–15, 375–6; *see also* miscegenation
Catalonia: trade with America, 363;
  exploratory voyages, 68–9; revolt (1640),
  422
Catholic Monarchs, 82–9; and Columbus,
  98–9; *see also* Isabella
cattle, 239, 244, 249, 429–30, 441, 446; in
  Africa, 76
caudillos, 496, 498
Cavalcanti de Albuquerque (family), 438
Central America: early explorations, 106;
  independence, 476; shipbuilding, 237
Chacabuco (battle), 482
Chan Chan, *see* Chimú
Chanca, 56, 58
Charcas: Bourbon reform, 365; conquest of,
  133; independence, 471, 476–7; landforms,
  7; revolts (18th century), 380–4
Charles III (of Spain), 365–6
Charles IV (of Spain), 395, 468–9
Charles V (Holy Roman Emperor), 134, 187;
  and clergy, 174; and *encomienda*, 123
Chavín de Huantar, 31–2
Chiapas, 190
Chibcha culture, 61–2, 134
Chichen Itza, 44–5
Chichimeca culture, 67, 240
Chichimecatecuhtli, Don Carlos, 179
Chile: Almagro's expedition to, 150; *audiencia*,
  156; climate, 18, 20; *encomienda*, 247–8;
  government, 154; independence, 473,
  482–3; Indian slavery, 248; landforms, 7,
  10; native peoples, 62–3, 153–4; population,
  351, 353; Spanish settlement, 133; wheat,
  241, 358
Chilpancingo, Congress of, 486
Chimú (kingdom of Chimor), 46–7, 57
chinampas, 53
church (Catholic): in Africa, 77; *beaterios*, 177;
  and conservatism, 498, 504; councils, 370;

in Hispaniola, 119–20; and Indian beliefs,
  312–16; missions, 123, 174–7, 318–22;
  music, 344–5; nunneries, 178, 335–6;
  property disentailed, 372,; source of credit,
  255, 336; in Spain, 89, 369–70; and state,
  119–20, 171–3, 369–73; wealth, 369–70,
  371–2; *see also* bishoprics; clergy; patronage;
  and particular regions
Cieza de León, Pedro de, 193
cimarrones, 326–7
Classic period (of Indian cultures), 35–44
Clavijero, Francisco Javier de, 391
clergy (regular): conflict with secular
  government, 180–1, 370–2; conflicts within,
  179; as missionaries, 174–7, 318–21;
  observing Indians, 183–93; wealth, 179–80;
  see also church *and specific orders*
clergy (secular), 182; *see also* church
climate: effect on agriculture, 20; *see also*
  specific regions
Coatlicue, 392
cochineal, 236–7
Cochrane, Thomas, 483, 494
Codex Florentino, 188
coffee, 450
Coimbra (University), 454, 456
Colombia, *see* New Granada
Colônia do Sacramento, 365, 442
Columbus, Bartolomé, 114
Columbus, Christopher: history and
  personality, 97–100, 110, 113; originality,
  68; voyages, 101–3
Columbus, Diego, 118–19
compadrio, 438
compass, 69
comunero revolt (New Granada), 385–6
Conceptionist order, 178
concubinage, 200
Congonhas do Campo, 457
congregación, 220, 244; in Caribbean, 121–3;
  in Peru, 161, 309
conquests: explanations of, 135–9; of
  peripheries, 133–5; Renaissance aspects
  of, 138; *see also specific regions*
conservatism, 497–8
contraband, 288, 304–5, 359, 360–1, 364,
  441, 443, 455; of gold (Brazil), 447
conversos, *see* Jews
copper, 62, 67
Córdoba, Treaty of, 488
Coricancha, 57
corregidor, 164; and *reparto de comercio*, 382
corregimientos, 163; sale of, 294
Cortés, Hernán, 104, 112, 155, 200, 221, 235,
  237, 269; conquest of Aztecs, 54, 126–31;
  death, 149; governor and captain-general
  of Mexico, 145–9; journey to Honduras,

147; marriage, 149; possessions and title, 148–9; in Spain, 149–50
Cortés, Martín, 212
cotton, 28, 31, 62, 449
Council of the Indies: founding and function, 162–3; reformed, 364
Council of Trent, 180, 182–3
crafts, 29, 237–8, 357
creoles: drawn to Europe, 392–3, 465; in government and politics, 292–7, 366, 386, 391–2, 484, 500; growing numbers, 375, 466–7; and independence movements, 466–71, 472–4, 484; in military, 373–4; nativism and self-awareness, 345–6, 391–2; scorned by Gálvez, 366
creolization (of Africans), 324–8
criollos, see creoles; as term describing Africans, 324
Cuauhtemoc, 147
Cuba, 489–90; Spanish conquest, 112; sugar, 359–60, 490
Cucutá, Congress of, 479, 480
curacas, 59–60, 206–8, 310
Cuzco, 22, 153, 178, 261, 263, 309, 329, 383–4; audiencia created, 384; climate, 16; pre-conquest growth, 55–7; school (of painting), 345

Darién, 112, 217
defense (Spanish America), 362, 368, 373–4; cost, 300–1
degredados, 403–4, 406
democracy, 164, 496, 498–9, 502, 504
dependence (economic), 440–1
desembargador, 417, 437–8
desert: Mexican, 19; west coast of South America, 17–18, 236
Dialogues of the Great Things of Brazil, 439
Dias, Bartolomeu, 91
Díaz del Castillo, Bernal, 53, 127, 200
disease: in Brazil, 409, 415, 436; in Caribbean, 124–5; in mainland Spanish America, 130, 197–9; in Spain, 287
Dolores (Grito de), 474
Dominicans: in Hispaniola, 120–1, 172; in mainland Spanish America, 174, 187
dowry, 330
Drake, Sir Francis, 217, 288
Dutch: into Africa, 420; into Asia, 420; in Brazil, 419–23; in Caribbean, 288–9; in North America (New Amsterdam), 423; trade in Brazil, 419; trade in Spanish America, 288–9, 304–5, 442; war with Spain, 286; West India Company, 289, 421
dyes and dyewood, 236–7, 402, 421

Eckhout, Albert, 422
Ecuador, see Quito
El Dorado, 134
El Niño, 18, 47
encomienda, 163, 179, 190–1, 198–9, 204, 206, 210–11, 242–3, 245, 327; capital accumulation in, 254; in Hispaniola, 118, 122–3; in Mexico, 123, 146–7, 148, 158–9, 200; in New Mexico, 319; in Peru, 151–2; 17th-century persistence, 317–18; in Spain, 118; survival on peripheries, 247–8, 317–18, 319, 321
engenhos (sugar), 410–13
England: in Brazil and Brazilian trade, 424, 455; in Caribbean, 289–90; hostile to Spain, 286, 468–9; and Portugal, 448; in Spanish American trade, 361; textiles, 356
Enlightenment, 337, 367, 369, 391–2, 465
Escorial, San Lorenzo del, 220–1
estates: rural, 243, 429–30, 446; social, 203–4, 431; see also engenhos; haciendas
ethnic mixing, see miscegenation
exploration, see specific regions
exports: agricultural in 18th century, 358–60; see also trade and specific countries and commodities

factories, see industrialization
families, 199–202, 293–4, 377–8, 426, 438, 498, 501–2; in social organization, 221–4
farming, see agriculture
farms, 243
Federmann, Nikolaus, 134
feline/were-feline deities, 31, 33
Ferdinand VII (of Spain), 469, 480, 487, 487–8
fleets (trading), 250–2, 361–2
Florida, 104, 269
Fontainebleau, Treaty of, 469
forasteros, 196, 309
Formative period (of early Indian cultures), 30–5
France, 349–50, 358–9; "Antarctic," 419; in Brazil, 402, 424; and independence movements, 466–7, 491; revolution, 392, 466, 467, 491; in Spanish American trade, 358–9
Franciscans: in Hispaniola, 120, 172; and Indian languages, 187; in mainland Spanish America, 175–7, 271, 318–19; in Mexico, 172–3, 174–7, 269; millenarianism, 175; in Spain, 89
frontiers, see periphery
Fuggers, 228

galleons, 250; Manila, 252
Gálvez, José de, 366, 373, 382

Gama, Vasco da, 91
Gante, Pedro de, 176, 184
garúa, 18
Gê-speaking Indians, 64
Gelves, marquis of (viceroy of Mexico), 296
General Brazil Trading Company, 442–3
General History of the Things of New Spain, 188
Genoa: colonizing model, 73; exploratory
  voyages, 68–9
Germany, 228
goats, 240
Godoy, Manuel, 469
godparents, 438
Goiás, 445
gold: African, 70–1, 72; amounts produced ,
  231, 354–5; Andean, 227; in Brazil,
  428–9, 444–7, 450, 457; in Chile, 354–5;
  in Cuba, 112; in Hispaniola, 112, 114;
  in Mexico, 126, 226, 354–5; in New
  Granada , 62, 134, 226, 227, 231,
  317, 352; in Peru, 226–7; slave labor, 249
government, *see* administration
governorships/governor (*gobernador*), 163
Gran Colombia, 273, 479–80
Granada, 85, 87–9, 99
Great Britain, *see* England
Greater Colombia, *see* Gran Colombia
Guadalajara, 159
Guanajuato, 227, 299, 373, 474
Guaraní Indians, 62–3, 320–2
Guayaquil, 237, 304; meeting of Bolívar and
  San Martín, 484–5
guayras, 227, 230
Guerrero, Vicente, 488
Guiana Highlands, 9
Guianas, 288, 290
Guinea, 75
Guitarrero cave, 27
guns, 135; exchanged for African slaves, 80
Guzmán, Beltrán Nuño de, 155

haciendas (*de campo*), 243; in Mexico, 304,
  309; *see also* estates
Haiti, 478; origins, 288; *see also* Saint
  Domingue
Henry, Prince (the "Navigator"), 72, 74
Heyn, Piet, 289, 421
Hidalgo y Costilla, Miguel, 473–5, 485–6
hierarchy: social, 202–4, 504
Hispaniola: church in, 119–20; first towns,
  115; French incursions, 289; under
  Ovando, 114–18; population, 65–6, 110,
  116, 124; Spanish base in Caribbean,
  111–12; Spanish settlement, 101–2,
  110; *see also* Haiti; Saint Domingue
Historia de la Indias (by Las Casas), 190, 192
Hojeda, Alonso de, 111–12

Holguín, Melchor Pérez de, 250
Honduras, 147–8; English in, 290
honor, 333–4
horses, 115, 239; in conquests, 135;
  exchanged for African slaves, 80
hospital, 184–5
Huancavelica, 232, 298, 354
Huarochirí, 381
Huayna Capac, 57–9, 61
Huilliche (Indians), 62
Huitzilopochtli, 50–2, 54
Humboldt, Alexander von, 374, 477

identity (post-colonial), 500
idolatry, 313–14, 319
Iguala, Plan of, 488
illegitimacy, 332–3
Incas: administration and colonization by, 17,
  56–60; agriculture, 263; empire, 22, 54–61;
  Spanish conquest of, 131–3
Inconfidência Mineira, 491
independence movements: aftereffects of wars,
  495–7; chronology of (Spanish South
  America), 476; impetus for, 465–72;
  see also specific regions
Indians: adoption of Christianity, 312–16;
  affected by European animals, 240;
  agriculture rising, 27–8; Asian origins, 26;
  Brazilian, 63–5, 403–4, 406–10, 415,
  433–6, 444, 445–6, 453; creole view of,
  345–6; disadvantages in conquests, 135–7;
  early crafts, 29; early priesthood, 28–9;
  early society, 28–9; eating meat, 239;
  enslavement of, 124, 248, 407, 433–5;
  freedom of, 123; labor of, 161, 244–8,
  307–8, 309–10, 354, 407, 409–10, 433–5;
  legal status of, 204–5; mental world, 312;
  migrations, 307–11; music, 344; as "natural
  slaves," 185–6; 191; observed by friars,
  183–94; on peripheries, 316–22;
  population decline, 188, 195–9, 242, 415;
  population recovery, 351; religion
  persisting, 313–15; revolts, 379–85;
  sedentism, 28–9; seen as barbarians, 184,
  185, 186; 17th-century adaptations,
  307–16; social transformations, 160–2;
  Spanish administration of, 382; Spanish
  view of in Laws of Burgos, 122; women,
  200, 328–9
indigo, 236
industrialization: European, 360; pre-colonial,
  40; Spanish American, 357
Inquisition: in Spain, 86–7, 89; in Spanish
  America, 182–3, 326, 338
intendants, 367, 382, 465, 490
Inter caetera (papal bull), 171
Inti, 57, 59

investment: in colonial Brazil, 413, 419; postcolonial, 496; in Spanish colonies, 254–6, 306, 336

iron (Africa), 77

irrigation, 36–7, 47, 57, 262–3

Isabela (town), 101, 110

Isabella (of Castile), 82–3; *see also* Catholic Monarchs

Italy: source of music, 393

Iturbide, Agustín de, 486, 488

Jamaica, 111, 289, 478

Jeronymites, 123

Jesuits: in Brazil, 406–10, 433–6, 453–4; expulsion from Spanish lands, 371; in mainland Spanish America, 174; in Paraguay, 319–21, 427; and Pombal, 453–4; writing on Spanish America, 391

Jews: in Brazil, 423; expulsion from Spain, 85–6

Jiménez de Cisneros, Francisco, (archbishop, cardinal, regent of Spain), 89, 122, 174

Jiménez de Quesada, Gonzalo, 134

John VI (of Portugal), 492–5

Junín (battle), 273, 479

juntas, 472–3; Junta Central (Spain), 470

Kongo, 75; Christianizing of, 77

kuraka see curacas

labor: in colonial Brazil, 406–10, 431–3, 444; in colonial Mexico, 146, 319; in colonial Peru, 151; in colonial Spanish America generally, 244–9, 308–11; in early Spanish Caribbean, 114–15, 117–18, 83–4, 121–4, 125; Inca forms, 59–60; *see also* encomienda; *mita*; *repartimiento*; slaves and slavery

la Cosa, Juan de, 102–3, 112

la Cruz, Sor Juana Inés de, 336–7, 345

la Gasca, Pedro de, 152–3

La Paz, 384

La Venta, 34–5

Lake Titicaca, 16, 384

land: grants, 242, 359; tenure, 241–2, 357–8; *see also* estates; *haciendas*

landform: effect on agriculture, 18; *see also individual countries*

Las Casas, Bartolomé de, 112, 122–3, 189–93; writings, 190–2

lateen sail, 69

Laws of Burgos, 121–2, 146

Legazpi, Miguel López de, 106–7

liberals and liberalism: in Portugal, 493; post-Independence, 497; in Spain, 470, 487

Lima, 213, 308, 483–4; Africans in, 323; nunneries, 335; San Francisco, 271; Santa Rosa de, 337–8

Lisbon, 98, 451

llaneros, 478

Llanos de Mojos, 64

loans, *see* investment

Lohmann, Gaspar, 228

Lopes Carvalho, João, 403

Louisiana, 365, 469

Lucayos, 124

Lupaqa, 61

Machu Picchu, 261

Madeira, 73–4, 410–11

Magellan, Ferdinand (Fernão Magalhes), 104–5

Maipú (battle), 483

maize, 27, 53, 55, 63, 241, 244, 263

Malinche, La, *see* Marina

mamelucos, 425–6, 431

Mapuche, 62–3, 153–4

Maranhão, 424, 430, 446; Company, 452; cotton, 449; Indian slavery, 433–5; rice, 449

Marcgraf, Georg, 422

Marina, Doña (Malinaltzin), 127, 200, 212

maroons, 217–18, 327

marriage: 199–202, 209, 215, 332, 334, 377; in Brazil, 432, 437–8, 453; favored by Spanish policy, 116, 222; linking families, 222–3, 292; Pragmatic Sanction (1778), 377–8

Matanzas (Cape and battle), 289, 421

Mato Grosso, 445

Maya culture, 40–4, 88, 209; Tikal, 267

Mayapan, 45

Medina, Bartolomé de, 228

Mendicants, *see* clergy (regular) and *specific orders*

Mendieta, Gerónimo de, 182, 187

Mendoza, Don Antonio de, 158–60, 184, 233, 239–40

Mercedarians, 454; in mainland Spanish America, 174

merchants, 306; Mexican, 252–4; of Seville, 251–2; sources of capital, 254; *see also* trade

mercury, 231–2, 298, 354

messianism, 380–1, 384

mestizos and *mestizaje*, *see* miscegenation

Methuen Treaty, 448

Mexica, *see* Aztecs

Mexico: Africans in, 213, 218, 323; *audiencia*, 155–6, 471; central highlands, 6, 15; church and churchmen in, 172–3, 184–5; climate, 15, 19; creoles' descriptions, 391–2; defense costs, 300; dyes, 236–7; farming, 239–42;

gold-mining, 355; grains, 241;
independence, 471, 473–5, 485–9;
landforms, 6–7; *mestizos* in, 212, 375–6,
489; population, 196, 351–2, 374–5;
rebellions, 378–9; remittances to Spain,
300–1; revenues from, 368; silver-mining,
160, 226–30, 298–9, 352–4; Spanish
exploration of, 104, 106, 126; sugar, 235,
304; textiles, 233–4, 303; tobacco, 356–7;
viceroys, 158–60, 471
Mexico City: cathedral, 339, 344; convents,
335; riots (colonial), 296, 379
Michoacán, 66, 84
microclimates, 15–16, 263
midwives, 331
militarism and military: rise (18th century),
372–3; sources, 154, 496–7; *see also* defense;
Mexico
millenarianism, 175
Minas Gerais, 428, 444, 444–6, 450, 457, 491
mining (gold): in Brazil, 428–9, 444–7, 450,
457; Spanish American production, 231,
354–5; *see also* gold
mining (mercury), 231–2
mining (silver): in Andes, 227–32, 353–4;
Bourbon revival, 354; capital, 255; German
influences, 228; labor in, 229, 246, 308,
354; in Mexico, 160, 226–31, 232, 353–4;
production, 225, 298–9, 354–5; technology,
227–30, 354; *see also specific mining sites*
mints, 255, 317
Miranda, Francisco de, 467
miscegenation, 116, 199–200, 211–15, 376,
499–501; in Brazil, 403, 425–6, 431, 445,
499–500; "cultural," 212, 311, 329, 325–6,
346–8, 376, 499–500; in Mexico, 212,
375–6, 489, 499; numbers, 212–13, 351; in
Paraguay, 321–2, 499; schools for *mestizas*,
178; suspicion of *mestizos*, 214–15, 347
mita/mit'a, 161, 245–6, 307–10; pre-conquest,
59; in silver-mining, 229, 354
mitimas/mitmaqkuna, 60
Mixtec culture, 45–6, 208
Mixton War, 159
Mizque, 327–8
mocambos, 432
Moche/Mochica culture, 37–8
Moctezuma: II, 90, 91, 92; Doña Isabel, 200
monarchism, 485–6
monções, 429
montaña, 261
Monte Albán, 45
Monte Verde, 26–7
Montesinos, Antonio de, 82–3, 84, 183
Montezuma, *see* Moctezuma II
More, Sir Thomas, 184
Morelos y Pavón, José María, 485–6

Moreno, Mariano, 467–8
Mosquito Coast, 290
Motolinía, *see* Benavente, Toribio de
Mozart, Wolfgang Amadeus, 456
Muisca, *see* Chibcha
mulatos, 202, 213, 328
Murillo, Pedro Domingo, 471
music, 500; colonial Brazilian, 456; colonial
Spanish American, 238, 344–5, 393

naborías, 307
Nahuatl, 187, 311
Napo (river), 424
Napoleon Bonaparte, 395, 469, 492
Narváez, Pánfilo de, 112
Nassau-Siegen, Johan Maurits van, 421–2
Navidad (settlement), 101
neoclassicism, 394, 458
nepotism, 502
New Galicia, 155, 159; *audiencia*, 115
New Granada: climate, 15, 18; *comunero*
revolt, 385–6; emeralds, 61, 62; *encomienda*,
317; gold, 62, 134, 226–7, 231, 317, 355;
independence, 473, 479–80; Indian labor,
247, 317–18; native cultures, 61–2, 134,
316; population, 351–3; regionalization,
316; remittances to Spain, 300, 368;
Spanish settlement, 112, 134; viceroyalty of
New Granada created, 364
*New Laws and Ordinances for the Government of
the Indies* (1542), 151–2, 158–9, 190, 199
New Mexico, 13, 319
Ngola, 75
Nicaragua, 237
Nóbrega, Manoel de, 407–8
Núñez de Balboa, Vasco, 105, 112
Núñez Vela, Blasco, 151–2
nuns and nunneries, 177–8, 335–6

obrajes, 233–4, 355–6
obras pías, 372, 465
O'Higgins, Bernardo, 482
Olid, Cristóbal de, 147
oligarchies (17th-century Spain) 297
Olivares, Conde-Duque de, 296, 221–2
Olmec culture, 32–5
Olmos, Andrés de, 187
Omnimoda (papal bull), 174
opera (in Spanish America), 393
Oporto, 493
Orinoco, 102, 480; basin, 10
Oruro, 308; silver-mining, 298, 354; rising
(1739), 380
Ouro Prêto, 445, 450, 456, 457
ouvidor geral, 416, 439
Ovando, Nicolás de, 110; administration of
Hispaniola, 114–20, 124–5

Pachacutec, 56, 261
Páez, José Antonio, 478
painters, 343, 345; Indian, 345
Palacios Rubios, Juan López de, 185
palenque, 326–7
Palmares, 433
pampas, 10, 19, 63, 358
panaka, 59, 208
Panama: Africans in, 214, 217; *audiencia*, 156; early settlement, 105–6, 112; Isthmian trade, 251
Paraguay: agricultural exports, 358; first Spanish settlement, 321–2; independence, 475–6; Indian labor, 247–8; Jesuit *reducciones*, 320–1, 371, 427; miscegenation, 321–2, 499; native peoples, 62, 321
Paris, Peace of, 365
patron–client bonds, 504
patronage (royal, of church), 120, 160, 171–2, 370; Concordat of 1753, 370; Ordinance of, 181
paulistas, 425
Perestrelo family, 97–8
periphery (of colonies); *encomienda* on, 316–18; militarism on, 154, 496–7; missions on, 318–22
Pernambuco, 403, 405, 310, 449; Company, 452; cotton, 449; rising (1817), 493; sugar, 411, 440, 449
Peru: Africans in, 213, 323; conquest of, 131–3; creoles' descriptions, 392; desert, 18, 184–5; first viceroy named, 151; independence, 481, 483–5; population, 196, 351, 375; post-conquest civil wars, 150–2; rebellions (18th century), 380–5; regular clergy in, 180–1; 17th-century economy, 304; sugar, 236; textiles, 234; under Viceroy Toledo, 161; wine, 304
peruleros, 306
Philip II (of Spain), 162, 188, 221, 225, 416–17; policies in Europe, 281, 286–7; and regular clergy, 180–1
Philip III (of Spain), 174, 434
Philip V (of Spain), 349
Philippines, 301; *audiencia*, 156; controlled by Spain, 108; linked to Mexico, 106–7; trade, 281
Pichincha (battle), 273, 479
Picunche Indians, 63
pigs, 135, 239
pirates: in Atlantic, 402; in Caribbean, 252, 288, 289; in Pacific, 290
Piratininga, 404, 426
Pisac, 263
Pizarro, Francisco, 212, 223; assassinated, 150; conqueror of Incas, 131–3, 136; explorer, 105–6; and family, 222

Pizarro, Gonzalo, 152
poderosos, 297
poets, 336–7, 456
Pombal, marquis of (Sebastio José de Carvalho e Melo), 451–4, 457
Ponce de León, Juan, 104, 111
Ponce de León, Luis, 148
population (Latin American): areas of concentration, 20; creole, 291–2, 375, 466; decline (Indian), 188, 195–9, 242, 415; 18th-century growth, 351–2; pre-conquest, 51, 195–6; Spanish (in America), 199–200, 201; *see also specific regions*
Portugal and Portuguese: and Brazilian gold, 448; colonial administration by, 74, 403–6, 415–18, 451–4; colonial trade policy, 442–3, 451–2; economic policies (18th century), 448–9, 451–3; expansion into Africa, 72–3, 404, 420; expansion into Asia, 107–8, 404, 420; exploring Atlantic, 70–1; and Great Britain, 448, 468; invaded by France and Spain, 469, 492; Junta do Comércio, 452; migration to Brazil, 444; Moorish occupation of, 71; revolt (1820), 493; rounding south of Africa, 90–1; slaves freed, 453; trading companies, 452; under Spanish control, 322, 416–17, 419–20, 422
Post, Frans, 422
Post-Classic (period of Indian cultures), 44–61
potatoes, 27, 242
Potiguar culture, 63
Potosí, 227, 230–2, 246, 255, 365; Africans in, 232; Casa de Moneda, 394; San Lorenzo (church), 345; silver production, 225, 229, 231, 298–9, 353–4
Pre-Classic, *see* Formative
production: regionalization of, 249–50; *see also particular goods and regions*
Puebla (de los Angeles), 233–4, 303; Spanish–Indian marriages, 200; style (architecture), 345
Pueblo Revolt, 319, 379
Puerto Rico, 490; Spanish conquest, 111
Purépecha, *see* Tarascan

Querétaro, 303, 356, 473
Quetzalcóatl, 39, 46, 105
quilombo, 432
Quiroga, Vasco de, 184–5
Quito, 424; Africans in, 217; *audiencia*, 1156 climate, 14–15; conquest of, 133; independence, 479, 481; revolt (1765), 385; sculpture, 393; textiles, 234, 303, 356

race mixture, *see* miscegenation

Ramalho, João, 404, 426

rebellions: late colonial, 378–86

Recife, 423, 450

Reconquest, the, 71, 87–8, 128

reducción, see congregación

register ships, 362

relação, 417–18, 437–9; Rio de Janeiro, 447

repartimiento (of labor), 245–8, 307–9; in Caribbean, 125; in Hispaniola, 118–19; in Yucatan, 319

reparto de comercio, 382, 384

repúblicas (in society), 204

resgate, 410, 413, 435

residencia, 167

revenues, *see* treasury

Revolution, French, 392, 466, 467, 491

Reyes Católicos, *see* Catholic Monarchs

rice, 449; in Africa, 76

Rio de Janeiro, 419, 448, 450; academies, 455; music, 456; as royal capital, 492–3; sugar, 449

Río de la Plata: basin, 10; exports, 358–9; independence, 472; Spanish discovery, 103–4; viceroyalty, 365

Rocha Pita, Sebastião de, 456

Rococo, 393–4, 457

Rousseau, Jean-Jacques, 468

Sá, Mem de, 408–10, 411, 419

sacrifice (human), 52

Sacsahuaman, 25

Sahagún, Bernardino de, 188

Saint Domingue, 289, 291; slave revolt, 359, 449, 392; sugar, 359, 342; *see also* Haiti

sale of office, 294–5, 366

Salvador, *see* Bahia

San Lorenzo (Olmec site), 32–4

San Luis Potosí, 227, 355

San Martín, José de, 482–5

Sandoval, Tello de, 159

Santa Hermandad, 84

Santa Rosa de Lima, 337–8

Santiago (Chile), 156, 394

Santo Domingo, 110, 115; *audiencia*, 154

Santo Tomás, Domingo de, 193

Santos Atahualpa, Juan, 381

São Francisco river, 428, 429

São Jorge da Mina, 90, 420

São José de Rio Negro, 425

São Luis, 319, 424, 435

São Paulo, 404, 425–6, 450; sugar, 449

São Tomé, 410

São Vicente, 405, 406, 415; sugar, 411

schools, 177, 335–6

Sebastião (king of Portugal), 410, 416

Sechín Alto, 30–1

Secretary of the Indies and Marine, 268

Segura de la Frontera, 269

Sepúlveda, Juan Ginés de, 148

sertão, 429

settlement, *see specific places*

Seville, 251–2

sexual behavior, 38, 200, 209–10, 332–3

sheep, 234, 240, 244, 249

shipbuilding, 237, 356; in Brazil, 441

shipping: technology of, 69

Sigüenza y Góngora, Don Carlos, 337, 346

silk, 233

silver (Spanish American): production, 225, 229–31, 298–9, 302, 353–4; remitted to Spain, 301–2; smuggled, 302; and trade, 252, 255; value in Orient, 252–3

situados, 300–01

slaves and slaving: in Africa, 78–80; *asiento de negros*, 349–50, 361; in Atlantic islands, 74; in Brazil, 407, 410, 413–15, 426–7, 431–3, 432–5, 436, 445; in Chile, 248; in Cuba, 489–90; manumission, 218–19, 433; numbers exported from Africa, 77–9, 432, 445; religions and spirituality, 324–6; runaway communities, 217–18, 326–7, 432; skills useful to Europeans, 76; sources in Africa, 75–7; in Spanish America, 201–2, 213–14, 215–19, 248, 322–8; taken by Columbus, 102; in Venezuela, 318; *see also* Africans *and specific regions*

smallpox: in Brazil, 305; in conquest of Aztecs, 92–3

smelting (of silver), 176–7, 179, 222

Smith, Adam, 456

smuggling, *see* contraband

society (Spanish America): corporate components, 160; order in, 378; structure, 157–60, 287, 501; trends of change, 160–3; *see also* Africans; creoles; Indians; miscegenation

Sousa, Martim Afonso de, 404, 429

Sousa, Tomé de, 406

South America: conquest of, 95; exploration of, 64–5, 67

South Sea Company, 358, 361

Spain: American explorations by, 101–7; Atlantic explorations by, 70–1, 80–2; bankruptcies, 286; Constitution of 1812, 470, 487; Cortes, 470, 487; juntas, 470; liberalism, 470, 487; Moorish occupation of, 71; nobles, 84–5, 287; overextension (fiscal and political), 281, 286–7, 287, 422; revived trade with colonies, 362–3; strengthening of monarchy, 83–9; subordinate to France, 350, 468–70;

unification of, 83; War of Independence, 470; War of Succession, 349–50

Spice Islands, 420

Sublimis Deus (papal bull), 186

Sucre Alcalá, Antonio José de, 273, 479

sugar: in Atlantic islands, 73–4, 235; in Brazil, 407, 410–15, 418, 421, 438, 440–1, 442, 449; in Caribbean islands, 359–60, 423, 440; foreign investment, 419; in Hispaniola, 115, 235; in Mexico, 235–6, 304; in Peru, 236, 304; refining, 236, 410–13; slave labor, 248, 413–15

Tabatinga, 424

Tahuantinsuyu, 22, 59

"Tailors' Plot," 491

Taino Indians, 65

Tairona, 61–2

Tarascan culture, 66, 131, 227; mining and metalwork, 67

Taxco, 175

taxes, 295, 296–7, 299, 362, 367, 382–3, 385, 395, 468; on gold production (Brazil), 447; on silver production, 230–1, 354; in Spain, 286; *see also* tribute

tectonic plates, 8

Teixeira, Pedro, 424–5

Tenochtitlan, 22, 49, 53, 128–31

Teotihuacán, 39–40, 265, 267

Tepaneca, 49

Tepeaca, 269

terrorism (in conquests), 198

Texcoco, 49, 176, 234

textiles: colonial, 232–4, 303, 355–6; imports from Europe, 356; in Mexico, 232–4, 303, 356; pre-colonial, 29

Tezcatlipoca, 50, 52

Tikal, 267

Tiradentes (Joaquim José da Silva Xavier), 491

tithes, 303–4

Titicaca (lake), 36, 56

titles (noble), 377

títulos, 311–12

Tiwanaku, 35–7

Tlaloc, 50

Tlatelolco college, 176–7

Tlaxcala, 129–30, 234

tobacco, 305, 356; Brazilian, 419, 434, 441, 449

Toledo, Don Francisco de, 161, 180–1; and Indian labor, 245; and silver-mining, 229

Tolsá, Manuel, 394

Toltecs, 44, 46, 49

Tordesillas, Treaty of, 108, 401, 425

Torquemada, Juan de, 346

Toscanelli, Paolo dal Pozzo, 98

towns: administration, 164–5; design, 220; in Hispaniola, 115; in Spanish America, 219–21, 238–9; wage labor in, 308–9; *see also* cabildo; *câmaras*

trade: fleets, 250–1, 361–2; foreign, in colonial Caribbean, 288–9, 304–5, 361; free, 467–8, 469, 490; "free", under Bourbons, 362–3; intra-colonial, 249–50, 306–7; local, by Indian women, 329; with neutrals, 468; oceanic, 250–4, 302, 360–3, 468; post-colonial, 503; in single ships, 361–2; from Tiwanaku, 36; transpacific, 252–3; *see also* contraband; exports *and specific regions*

Trafalgar, battle of, 469

treasury (colonial Spanish America), 113, 165; in early colonial Mexico, 147; revenues, 225, 298–301, 367–8, 396; sale of office in, 294

Tres Zapotes, 35

tribute: Aztec, 51, 52; Inca, 59; in Spanish colonies, 203–4, 226, 307–8; in Yucatan, 319

Trinidad, 102, 469

Triple Alliance (Aztec), 49, 52

Tula, 46

Túpac Amaru II (José Gabriel Condorcanqui), 383–5

Túpac Katari, 384

Túpac (*or* Topa) Yupanqui. 56–7

Tupí culture, 63–4, 407

Union of Crowns (Spain and Portugal), 417, 424, 442

United States of America: and independence of Latin America, 466, 467; trade with Latin America, 469

Upper Peru, *see* Charcas

Urdaneta, Andrés de, 106–7

Urubamba (river), 261, 263

Uruguay, 476

Utrecht, Peace of, 349–50

Vaca de Castro, Cristóbal, 151

vales reales, 372

Valladolid (debate at), 191

Velasco, Don Luis (the elder), viceroy of Mexico, 239–40

Velázquez, Diego, 112, 126, 128, 145, 147

Venezuela: cacao, 304–5, 359; *encomienda* in, 318; independence, 467, 472, 479, 476, 477–80; settlement, 134

Veracruz, 219, 252; founded, 128

Verapaz, 190

Vespucci, Amerigo, 103, 401–2

viceroys/viceroyalties, 113, 151–2, 168, 471; 18th-century additions, 364–5; functions and powers, 160–1

Vieira, António, 433–6

Villalpando, Cristóbal de, 343
Viracocha, 55
Virgin of Guadalupe, 314–15, 474
Virgin Mary, 54, 271, 314–15, 338
visita, 167
Vitoria, Francisco de, 142, 185–6
volcanoes, 6, 7, 8, 15

wage labor; Indian (in Brazil), 414; Indian
  (in Spanish colonies), 246–7, 308–9
Waldseemüller, Martin, 103
war: absence of (colonial Spanish America),
  154; of American (USA) independence,
  363, 449; of Austrian Succession, 362;
  Aztec, 52; Inca, 58; of Jenkins' Ear, 359,
  362; Mixton, 118, 159; Seven Years, 360,
  365, 449, 489; of [Spanish] Independence,
  470; of Spanish Succession, 349–50, 361
Wari, 37, 56
Wellesley, Arthur (duke of Wellington), 470
Welsers, 134, 228
wheat, 240–1, 358

wine, 249, 304
women: black, 201–2, 334–5; economic
  activities, 331, 377; elite, 333;
  freedoms, 330; Guaraní, 321–2;
  and illegitimacy, 332–3; immigrant Spanish,
  199–202; Indian, 200, 208–10, 328–9;
  inheritance, 330; in marriage,
  330, 377; as midwives and nurses, 331; and
  patriarchy, 334

yanaconas, 307, 328
Yanga's rebellion, 218
yerba mate, 306, 320, 358
Yucatan, 6–7, 20; Franciscans in, 319; indigo,
  236; native people, 40–4, 45
Yupanqui, 55, 56; *see also* Pachacutec

Zacatecas, 160, 218, 227, 239, 299, 308;
  cathedral, 394
Zapotec, 46
Zaragoza, Treaty of, 108
Zumárraga, Juan de, 155, 173, 176, 177